T0369071

Glorious Qur'an in Poetic Stance

Part IV
With Scientific Elucidations

Rashid Seyal

iUniverse, Inc.
New York Bloomington

Glorious Qur'an in Poetic Stance, Part IV
With Scientific Elucidations

iUniverse books may be ordered through booksellers or by contacting:

iUniverse
1663 Liberty Drive
Bloomington, IN 47403
www.iuniverse.com
1-800-Authors (1-800-288-4677)

ISBN: 978-1-4401-6113-1 (pbk)
ISBN: 978-1-4401-6115-5 (cloth)
ISBN: 978-1-4401-6114-8 (ebk)

Printed in the United States of America

iUniverse rev. date: 11/2/2009

About the Glorious Qur'an in Poetic Stance Part-IV

The Holy Scripture of the Qur'an is most enticing and enchanting, captivating and concerning. It provides unfeigned direction for the virtuous. It gives a detailed enunciation of the faith. It teaches men to adhere to a common belief and conviction that is deeper than human consciousness. In Glorious Qur'an in Poetic Stance, Part IV author Rashid Seyal answers questions about this ancient text that has appealed to a broad audience over a long period of time.

Seyal's work on the Qur'anic poetry and the philosophical interpretation in light of modern day science has given a new direction to understanding the Holy Scripture. In this, the last edition of a four-part series, Glorious Qur'an in Poetic Stance, Part IV elucidates on the:

- Divine perception of time
- Purpose of creation
- Seas which do not mix up
- Super symmetry
- Wan Najmi i Izza Hawwa

The cadence and course of Dr. Seyal's writing on the poetic stance of the Holy Scripture besides its Philosophical and scientific discernment looks very imposing and inspiring within the folds of the true message of the text.

However one thing is conspicuous and convincing, that Lord Almighty has given him the essential essence of this noble job to achieve. He seems to be motivated in the perpetuation of this most prudent and prodigious work for the drill and direction of people living in the developed world, who can affirm and embrace any ideology based on logic and intellect.

Written in three languages—English poetry, Arabic, and Urdu translations—Glorious Qur'an in Poetic Stance, Part IV strives to make sense of a text that needs quite a bit of scientific knowledge in its all district and domains to interpret the Holy Scripture.

The poetic stance in Glorious Qur'an owes a strong debt to Qur'an-i-Hakim Urdu translation by Syed Shabir Ahmad
(By Qur'an Asan Tehreek- Lahore Pakistan).
I am extremely indebted to:
Justice Rt. Dr. S. Fida Muhammad Madani,
(Supreme Courts of Pakistan)
who is also president of Qur'an Asan Tehreek, **allowing me to use this text.**

CONTENTS

Divine Perception of Time

Wormhole Theory
Elucidating Prophet's Journey of Mee'ráj

Early people presumably first realized time passed when they saw that they lived in a world of constant change. We have come to place a premium on measuring the flow of time as if by measuring it, we could begin to understand it.

Devising accurate calendars and clocks, however, proved to be one of the man's most elusive and protracted intellectual pursuits. The long struggle to affix numbers to the passage of time parallels our organizing ourselves in a complex, modern world.

But in The Holy Qur'an there is a use of numbers in the chapter *"The cave"*, where God says:

18:25
And it's said they're there *(cave) in sleep*
For over years three hundreds *in sweep*
And add nine to the count in keep
(300 solar years = 309 lunar years)

This verse miraculously communicates that 300 solar years are exactly the same as 309 lunar years!
In the light of the recent careful astronomical measurements and exact estimates, it became evident that:
The average duration of the lunar month is ---------------29.550329 days
Days in lunar year: ----29.550329x12= 354.60394
Days in 309 lunar years------------: 354.60394 x 309= **109572.66 days**
One solar year equals -----------------365.2422 days
Days in 300 solar years: ------------- - 365.2422 x 300= **109572.66 days**

After having all this information, envision the Qur'anic Script, affirming 1400 years before, the ratio of Solar and Lunar years *i.e.* months and days and for that matter their relative motion in their orbits that has been affirmed scientifically during the early last Century.
Similarly the repetitions of certain words pertaining to the time domain further assert that we must pursue the philosophy of the Holy Scripture before turning to any subject, if we can really comprehend the core of the text.

Day (Yawm) is repeated 365 times in singular form.
While its pleural and dual forms "Days (ayyam and yawmayn)" together are 30 times.
The number of repetitions of the word "month" (Shahar) is 12.
Seeking guidance from the Holy Scripture was and is expedient in most of the situations like the time.

It began in the great civilizations that awakened five millennia ago along the life giving rivers of the Middle East: in summer between the Tigris and Euphrates and in Egypt along the Nile. Drawn like most ancient people to the movements of the heavens and the changing seasons, the Babylonians developed a year of 360 days and then divided it into 12 lunar months of 30 days each. This was not a simple feat, since the sun and moon do not dance in step, the moon's cycles occurring approximately every 29½ days and the earth's every 365¼ days.

The Philosophy of Time

When **Lord Almighty** asserts that the matters of the world reach **Him in a Day** of your count that equals one thousand years (Al Sajdah: 32), as we will later calculate in this chapter, these matters of concern are nothing but the speed of light. So we conclude that the basic unit of speed with **Almighty** is the speed of light and all other notions referring to the speed are the multiples of that. As His Almighty asserts that **angels and spirits reach Him in a Day of fifty** thousand years of count (Al Maarij: 1-4), *not of your count*. It clearly elucidates the speed of angels and spirits is 1000x 50,000 = 50,000,000 i.e. fifty millions. The details of the subject will be discussed later in this chapter.
Time is defined as the measure of motion in regard to 'before' and 'after': Aristotle.
The way old concept of time is described so far is nothing but a real confusion.
I'll endeavor to have philosophical look of the Time before trying to have scientific discernment of the subject in the light of Qur'an.

Time has frequently struck philosophers as mysterious. Some have even felt that it was incapable of rational discursive treatment and that it could be grasped only by intuition. This bafflement in attitude probably arises from the fact that time always seems to be mysteriously slipping away from us; no sooner do we grasp a bit of it in our consciousness then it slips away into the past. As very rightly affirmed in The Holy Qur'an:

By the vision of time
Man stays in dissipation well in decline
But for those determining Faith in prime
Who asperse and anoint virtuosity in sublime
Pursue and persevere probity in pray
And firm in endurance *stay to obey*
(Al Qur'an: Al Asar 103)

We shall see, that this notion of time as something, which continually slips past us, is based not on commotion and confusion, mystification and perplexity, daze and distraction but in factuality gives us lesson to value its each bit and piece to cherish the bliss not only hither in vale but also Hereafter in trail.

What's time?

This looks like a request for a definition, and yet no definition is forthcoming.
However, most interesting concepts cannot be elucidated by explicit definitions. Thus, to explain the meaning of the word length, we cannot give an explicit definition, but we can do things that explain how to tell that one thing is longer than another and how to measure length. In the same way we can give an account of our use of the word time even though we cannot do so by giving an explicit definition. In short, this puzzle is not of a sort that arises peculiarly in the case of time. Beyond pointing this out, therefore, it is not appropriate here to go further into the matter.

Augustine was also puzzled by how we could measure time. He seems to have been impressed by the lack of analogy between spatial and temporal measurement. For example, you can put a ruler alongside a table-top, and the ruler and the table top are all there at once. On the other hand, if you measure a temporal process, you do it by comparing it with some other process, such as the movement of the hand of a watch. At any moment of the comparison, part of the process to be measured has passed away, and part of it is yet to be.

Creation: Substance, Attributes and Time:

Once upon a timeless, when there was no discernment of time or creation and when there was not even whippersnapper in existence and not even the inspiration of proposition except for the Bounty of my Lord. At that twinkling and trice when His Almighty deliberated to bring the World into existence, He looked on the whim of surmise with a look of excellence. For there was nothing in actuality not the sign and simile of initiation that is the source of all existence; can bear the perfect manifestation of Almighty Allah. Perhaps it was only Nature that belonged to the basic framework of all the material and the Precept and Principle of the Providence that governed those basic ingredients of the material, and the Decree and Deliberation of Nature that directed the whole cosmic order.

That was the moment when the cadence of time with all its attributes essentially came into substantiality. Before creation its attributes were pertaining to nihility' with no discernment of present, past or future along the Interminable arrow of Time as discussed in Fate of the Universe. Nothing is known before this earliest instant- that scientists use the term big bang:

Instantaneous to Eternal:

The units of time range from the infinitesimally brief to the interminably long. The descriptions given here attempt to convey a sense of this vast chronological span.
Whenever we are trying to enunciate the process of creation, we shall have to look at it in a most meticulous and unbiased way of defined discernment of vision: The universe and the Human being. While contemplating both in one setting we find the entire universe as a dense material that explodes in one go of "Be" the Big Bang *(plank time)* - the 'Fa Ya Koon' as addressed in Qur'an, and starts its passage towards its indeterminate Journey of Cosmic order that we have not yet been able to perceive even today with our quite all highly

evolved body of knowledge and then, when and how long it would exist to host the living being could be any body's guess. In Qur'an, it is clearly and repeatedly enunciated that all this pretentious and pompous paraphernalia was brought into being in six phases or eons and will meet its destiny as discussed in Fate of the Universe.

Speed is one way to jump ahead in time, gravity is another:

In general theory of relativity, Einstein predicted that gravity slows time. Clocks run a bit faster in the attic than in the basement, which is closer to the center of Earth and therefore deeper down in a gravitational field. Similarly, clocks run faster in space than on the ground. Once again the effect is minuscule, but it has been directly measured using accurate clocks. Indeed, these time-warping effects have to be taken into account in the Global Positioning System. If they were not, sailors, taxi drivers and cruise missile could find themselves many kilometers off the track.

At the surface of a neutron star, gravity is so strong that time is slowed by about 30 percent relative to Earth time. Viewed from such a star, events here would resemble a fast-forwarded video.

A black hole represents the ultimate time warp, at the surface of the black hole, as the time stands still relative to Earth. This means that if you fell into a black hole from nearby, in the brief interval it took you to reach the surface, all of eternity would pass by in the wider universe. The region within the black hole is therefore beyond the end of time, as far as the outside universe is concerned.

If an astronaut could zoom very close to a black hole and return unscathed admittedly a fanciful, not to mention foolhardy, prospect he could leap thousands of years into the future or could be back into the past in similar scale.

So far I have discussed traveling forward in time. What about going backward? This is much more problematic. In 1948 **Kurt Godel** of the Institute for Advanced Study in Princeton, NJ, produced a solution of Einstein's gravitational field equations that described a rotating universe. In this universe, an astronaut could travel through space so as to reach his own past. This comes about because of the way gravity affects light. **The rotation of the universe would drag light around with it, enabling a material object to travel in a closed loop in space that is also a closed loop in time, without at any stage exceeding the speed of light in the immediate neighborhood of the particle.** Godel's solution was shrugged aside as a mathematical curiosity after all, observations show no sign that the universe as a whole is spinning. His result served nonetheless to demonstrate that going back in time is not forbidden by the theory of relativity. Indeed, Einstein confessed that he was troubled by the thought that his theory might permit travel into the past under some circumstances.

Other scenarios have been found to permit travel into the past. For example, in 1974 Frank **J. Tipler** of Tulane University calculated that a massive, **infinitely long cylinder spinning on its axis at near the speed of light could let astronauts visit their own past, again by dragging light around the cylinder into a loop**. In 1991 **J. Richard Gott** of Princeton University predicted that cosmic strings structures that cosmologists think were created in the early stages of the big bang could produce similar results. But in mid 1980s the most realistic scenario for a time machine emerged, based on the concept of a wormhole.

In science fiction, wormholes are sometimes called star-gates; they offer a shortcut between two widely separated points in space. Jump through a hypothetical wormhole, and you might come out moments later on the other side of the galaxy. Wormholes naturally fit into the general theory of relativity, (Lord Almighty while explaining the three types of passages in the sky: '*Tareeq*' for the routine flight the other '*Maarij*' the escalator type for rapid fights and the third '*Hubbuk*' the spinning passages like moving wormholes wrapping time and space, asserts that He was not oblivious of the sophistication of creation as later discussed in this chapter) whereby gravity warps not only time but also space. The theory allows the analogue of alternative road and tunnel routes connecting two points in space. Mathematicians refer to such a space as multiply connected. Just as a tunnel passing under a hill can be shorter than the surface street, a wormhole may be shorter than the usual route through ordinary space.

Prophet's journey of Mee'raaj has baffled quite a few and nobody could affirm, as to how it could have happened. I'm giving scientific details in the light of Qur'anic affirmations.

Al- Maarij: 70:4
The angels and Spirit ascent unto Him in a day
The sort whereof is fifty thousand years a day

Al- Sajdah: 32:4-5

It's Allah Who,
Created the earth and heavenly *mall*
That's in eons six *in all*
And all between the infinite *sway in pace*
And settled on Throne *adorned in place*
You've none to keep or interpose *in glance*
Other than Lord hither *in stance*
Wouldn't you then caution *in trance*
He Commands all *the term in sway*
Of the heavens and earth *set in array*
All affairs at conclusion trend *in pace*
To The Lord Almighty *in Grace*
In a Day of tally *in trace*
Years thousand of your count *in place*

For "what's time":

How did Prophet Muhammad PBUH travel all the way in person with Angel Gabriel, as it was not an illusion or fantasy or only a spiritual perception for otherwise there would not have been any need of appropriating this incident in The Holy Scripture. The whole incident took place in few moments of time when we refer to the psychological time.

The understanding of wormhole theory gives a clear concept of such like occurrences to be easily perceived today. Scientific fictions and facts are coming close to our discernment and deliberation of the Universe as ordained in the Holy Scripture. How could one perceive the travel in time domain without even a fraction of moment passing on this earth? Perhaps this doggerel mentioned in "Brief History of Time" by Stephen Hawking depicts most befittingly.

There was a young lady of White
Who traveled much faster than light?
She departed one day,
In relative way
And arrived on the previous night

Let us cite another example that would probably make the things much easier to understand.
Say "A" is traveling in a train with seven compartments. The compartment closer to the engine is Sunday, the next one Monday and the last is Saturday. "A" leaves the train from "Friday" compartment with much faster than the speed of the light in the opposite direction and the reaches the train from in front of it (like a moving wormhole) "A" is likely to catch the first "Sunday" compartment much earlier than the "Friday" compartment. Consider of all such moves in the whole cosmic sway where every pin to comet is in the move with a relative speed to one another and close to the brim of black hole the time is static. So traveling in the time domain is not foreign to our understanding if we take all these variables into account.

Scientists believe that large wormholes might exist naturally in deep space, a relic of the big bang. Otherwise it is conceivable that the next generation of particle accelerators will be able to create subatomic wormholes. (Scientific American September 2002)
As detailed in the text Qur'an affirms the existence of these wormholes. If we can somehow prove that Prophet Muhammad [PBUH] traveled much faster than the speed of light *(30 Billion times the speed of Light)* through Wormholes like passages (23:17 and 70:3) through different strata of skies and coming back through moving Wormholes (51:7), we can scientifically prove the Cosmic Journey of "Mee'raaj"

Alpha Centauri is 20 million millions miles away from the Earth. Thus one imagines or creates a Wormhole that would lead from the vicinity of the solar system, and static as compared to the earth, to Alpha Centauri. The distance through the Wormhole might be only a few million miles. This would allow the news of the happenings on earth well before time in such case one would have to travel back to earth from Alpha Centauri, through another moving Wormhole.

Ordinary matter gives space-time a positive curvature, like the surface of the sphere. To allow travel into the past, space- time must have a negative curvature like the surface of the saddle. So the Wormholes between two regions of space-time would make it possible to travel faster than light into the past or future.

Another way of discernment could possibly be explained in this pretence as described earlier is through *spirituality*. For all that we concern in this context and perceive that Time is not one for all domains. There was a time before the creation of the Universe that we 'Term' the state of Timelessness or Nihility, we may name it Time 'F' i.e. pertaining to Nihility or "Fanaa" or staying in the 'Interminable Arrow' of time and when the sprawl of creation took its stride the time also started its journey, we may term it time 'B' we may also call, Servility, *because it was subsequent to creation* or "Baqaa Time".

The discernment of these two i.e. time pertaining to Nihility and in subsequence Servility, is imperceptible but only when the earthy pot of the body melts into the soul and loses all its identity into Nihility or 'Interminable Arrow' and that's when you concentrate on heart and slowly ruminate the Holy Name "Allah". Soon you'll feel your body melting into soul and soul becoming a part of the Whole. That's the state of mind when the blood supply to the left parietal lobe is gone. Some scientists affirm that it's only the Divine Source of nourishment during those moments of deep meditation. In such moments you sway in the cosmic array like the wind whispering in play. This flitting and fleeting illumination or edification is gone when we totter and stumble back to our run-of-the-mill frame of mind with our brains obsessed with the conventional earthy seductive possessions. And when this earthy pot once again accomplishes its identity, the turn of time takes its course in tine of term Baqaa or Servility for it's conditional to creation. That's what we are concerned to account in our day-to-day life without encumbrance of duality in mind.

This time (Baqaa or Servility) has three notions of interpretation:

The **Thermodynamic** arrow of time is to follow a definite path ever since the creation of time and universe whereas the **Cosmological** arrow of time will be reversed if ever the universe starts contracting. But at the moment we are really concerned with the **Psychological** arrow of time in our day to day life for what we apprise notion of past, present and future or we may call yesterday today and tomorrow. Now we trend towards Qur'anic assertions in this regard. After creating the skies, Lord created passages between the skies, where angels are abiding the Dictum in Dictate of Lord Almighty, as stated by Hazarat Ali, prophet's first cousin, in his first address in '*Nehj ul Balagha*'. Indeed he was referring the Wormholes. Now let us bear in mind certain Qur'anic assertions that affirm the speed of light besides other cosmic affairs and also the speed of the angels traveling through **'Different Passages'** like 'Wormholes' in the different strata of the Multiverses.

- And We,
  Created over you seven ways *in cosmic sway*
  We're not oblivious of 'Our' creation *in array* (23:17)
  (These are probably seven routine passages for the angels to move towards the skies or seven different kinds of wormholes i.e. static; escalator; spinning; jumping straight from past to future; future to past; past to present and future to present)

- A discipline of Lord *in prime*
  The Lord of all tracts in trail *to climb*
  The angels and Spirits ascent unto Him in a day
  The sort whereof is fifty thousand years a day (70:3-4)
  (These elevator type passages are for the rapid drive of angels towards the heavens)

- Vow be to the passages *(in skies)* swinging *in trail* (51:07)
  (The word used for such passages is changing in position and how nicely it affirms 'The spinning and moving Wormholes' through different strata of the Multiverses)

If you carefully concentrate on the text of the verse (70:3-4) it clearly indicates the speed of the angels climbing through the passages in the skies (details given in the text).

Speed of Light and Lunar Orbital Motion:

Fourteen centuries ago, the Qur'an was directed from Lord Almighty to all the humanity through Prophet Muhammad PBUH, who lived in the Arabian Peninsula. The Arab people *(even now)* use the lunar calendar in their calculation of time.
The Qur'an addressed them in the only language they could understand without defying their seemliness. Lord Almighty asserts in the Qur'an:

(10:5)
He created sun grandeur *in glow*
And the moon He set to gleam *in flow*
And held a determined term *in stride*
That you may discern the years *in count*
Lord had all this source, a truth *in adore*
He details trivia in trends *for some in lore*
For what they'd concern in score

The lunar year is twelve months: the month is defined recently as the time of one revolution of the moon in its orbit around the earth and Lord Almighty hints at such orbit in the Qur'an:

(21:33).
He's The Lord!
Who created night and the day *in call*
Besides, gleam of moon and glitter of sol
They bob and drift in each ellipse *in mall*

Here an essential scientific fact is clearly stated, namely, the existence of the earth's sun and moon's orbit' besides, a reference is made to the traveling of these celestial bodies in space with their own motion! A new concept had therefore been established in the Qur'an, hundreds of years before it were discovered by modern science. Today the concept of the lunar year is widely spread and, as we know, the moon is our nearest neighbor in space, and a companion to our planet. It is often said that the earth and moon form a twin-planet.

As the moon orbits around the earth, the change in the relative positions of the moon, earth and sun cause the moon to show its phases. *The time between consecutive new moons is 29.53 days and is called the syndic month.* During this time, however, the earth and consequently the moon's orbit have traveled some way around the sun, so the position of the moon against the background of stars is different. *The time for the moon to return to the same position in the sky as viewed from earth is called the sidereal month (27.32 days)*, which represents the actual real net time of one revolution in the moon's orbit. This orbit is almost circular having an average radius r=384264 km.

Referring to the Qur'anic verse (10:5), we observe that it discriminates between the apparent *syndic* period for knowing the number of years and the real sidereal period for reckoning in scientific calculations. These two systems of measuring time are now given in the text books of Astronomy as indicated in table.

Table Lunar month and terrestrial day

Period	Sidereal	Syndic
Lunar Month = T	27.321661 days = 655.71986 hours	.53059 days
Terrestrial day =t	23 h, 56 min 4.0906 sec 86164.0906 sec	24 hours = 86400 sec

The purpose of the proposition is to determine the value of the greatest speed mentioned in the following relativistic Qur'anic verses. In these verses the sidereal system should be used for both the lunar month and the terrestrial day as accurate measured period *(with respect to a distant apparently fixed star).*

A new Relation in the Earth-Moon System:

The length of the moon's orbit 'L' and the time t of one terrestrial day are correlated in a marvelous Qur'anic verse which describes a universal constant velocity of a certain cosmic affair as follows:

***A day is equal to years thousand in stance**
32:5 *(Al Sajdah)*
He Commands all *the term in sway*
Of the heavens and earth *set in array*
All at conclusion affairs trend *in pace*
To The Lord Almighty *in Grace*
In a Day of tally *in trace*
Years thousand of your count *in place*
In a Day of your count years thousand in stance

The Qur'anic expression "of your reckoning" leaves no doubt as to our understanding of the year as the lunar year. The verse begins with a reference to a certain "cosmic affair" which Lord Almighty creates and commands. This affair travels, permanently through the whole Multiverses between different strata of the heavens and the Earth, so speedily that it crosses in one day a maximum distance in space equivalent to that which the moon passes during one thousand lunar years (i.e. during 12000 Sidereal months). The question, which now poses is:

What could this cosmic affair be?

And what is its greatest velocity as expressed in this Qur'anic equation? To answer this question we trend to Qur'anic verse that has been understood in terms of the following equation:

Distance crossed in vacuum by the universal cosmic affair in One sidereal day = length of 12000 revolutions of the moon around the earth.
Ct = 12000 L...................... (1)
Where:
'C' is the velocity of the cosmic affair,

'T' is the time interval of one terrestrial sidereal day defined as the time of one rotation of the earth about its axis (relative to the stars i.e. 23 hr, 56 min, 4.0906 sec = 86164.0906 sec.)
'L' is the inertial distance, which the moon covers in revolution around the earth during one sidereal month.

'L' is the net length of the moon's orbit due to its own geocentric motion, without the interference of its spiral motion caused by the earth's revolution around the sun (i.e. the lunar orbit length excluding the effect of the solar gravitational field on the measured value).
Let 'V' the measured average orbital velocity of the moon deduced from the average radius R of the lunar geocentric orbit, measured from an orbiting earth during its heliocentric motion)

V= 2 Pi R/T .... (2)
Substituting:
R = 384264 km and T = 655.71986 hr (the sidereal lunar month)
$V = (2 \times 3.1416 \times 384264) / 655.71986 = 3682.07$ km/hr
This value is given in all the textbook of astronomy and is accepted by NASA.
Let θ be the angle traveled by the earth moon system around the sun during one sidereal month of period 27.321661 days. We can calculate θ if we take into consideration the period (365.25636 days) of one heliocentric revolution (1 year) of the earth - moon system.
$\theta = 27.321661 * 360/365.25636 = 26, 92848$
Thus θ is a characteristic constant of this system depending on uniform periods of the month and the year. Since the presence of the sun changes the geometrical properties of space and time, we must screen out its gravitational effect on the earth-moon system. According to the validity condition of the second postulate of spatial relativity, i.e. we must only consider the lunar geocentric motion without the heliocentric motion of the earth-moon system.
Thus a velocity component $V_0 = V \cos \theta$ representing the net orbital velocity of the moon is introduced for calculating the net length L of the lunar orbit assuming a stationary earth.

$L = V \cos(\theta) T$ ...... (3)
From equation (1) and (3) we get a new Qur'anic relation for the earth moon system:
$Ct = 12000 V \cos(\theta) T$ ... (4)
$C = 12000 V \cos(\theta) T/t$ (5)

Substituting the sidereal values of the periods t and T from table (2), the NASA value of the measured orbital lunar velocity V = 3682.07 Km/hr., and the calculated value of $\cos \theta = \cos 26.92848 = 0.89157$, we get the velocity of the cosmic affair from equation 5, as expressed in the Holy Qur'an.

$C = 12000 \times 3682.07 \times 0.89157 \times 655.71986/86164.0906$
C= 299792.5 km/s

Referring to the international value of C = 299792.458 km/s we find an extremely marvelous agreement. Thus we conclude that the cosmic affair, mentioned in the previous

Qur'anic verse, is identical to Light and all similar cosmic affairs traveling in vacuum with this maximum speed such as: all types of electro magnetic waves propagating between the heavens and the earth, the expected Gravitational waves spreading all over the universe, and all particles traveling in this cosmic greatest speed such as neutrinos. It is very interesting to mention here the second Qur'anic verse that hints at the same relativistic Qur'anic equation in the earth- moon system: Lord Almighty asserts:

"A day in the sight of Thy Lord is like a thousand years of your reckoning" (22:47)
The interpretation of the above verses in the light of scientific discernment, determines a fascinating order to comprehend the speed of the angels in the cosmic glide.

Speed of the ordinary angels:

*A day is equal to years thousand in stance
32:5 *(Al Sajda)*
He Commands all *the term in sway*
Of the heavens and earth *set in array*
All at conclusion affairs trend *in pace*
To The Lord Almighty *in Grace*
In a Day of tally *in trace*
Years thousand of your count *in place*
In a Day of your count years thousand in stance
*An angels ascends to Lord Almighty in a day of fifty thousand years
70:4 *(Al Maarij)*
The angels and Spirit ascent unto Him in a day
The sort whereof is fifty thousand years a day

Just concern the order of the day in 32:5 is mentioned years thousand of your count and in 70:4 asserts years fifty thousands in count. Could it be a day equals to (1000 x 50,000) i.e. 50,000,000 times the speed of light as we have discussed in the text.

Speed of special angels of Lord:

All Acclaim in Adulation for Lord *in adore*
Who contrived *out of Nihility in score*
The heavens and the earth *in place*
Who made the angels *courier in space*

With fin to fly *thither in glide*
Wings in two or three or four pairs *to slide*
He appends to contrive to spread *in array*

As He intends to trend *in display*
For Lord has power over all *in sway* 35:1 *(Al Fatr)*

His Almighty asserts that if an angel or a spirit has to reach 'Me' from earth it would take day of 50,000 years of count *(not of your count)* where the day, *as affirmed earlier, is* a day of 1000-years of your count. This clearly shows that there are messengers of Lord, whose speed is (1000 x 50,000) i.e. 50,000,000 times the speed of light. Then there are verses, clearly indicating that angles having two, three or four pairs of wings, quite likely referring to their relation with the speed *(of the messengers of Lord)* 50,000,000 times the speed of light. Now consider all the way of communication of Lord Almighty through certain passages like Wormhole, with a speed two three and four times, the 50,000,000 times the speed of light i.e. 100,000,000; 150,000,000 or 200,000,000 times the speed of light, i.e. 50- 200 million times the speed of light.

The speed of the cosmic sprawl is 186000 miles per second of our count for the Multiverses. For how long it would continue, cannot be perceived by a man like of today?
With the foregoing discussion I would like to sum up the details once again to clearly understand the wrapping up of the time and space.

Speed of Archangel Gabriel:

This affirms the distances in the cosmic sway are far beyond our comprehension and to reach such places, to establish the dictum of Lord Almighty, definitely needs a speed and passages also far beyond our discernment. It is affirmed in *Hadidh* that number of wings of Angel Gabriel are 600 i.e. his speed 600 times the speed of an ordinary angel or 600 x 50,000,000: i.e. 30,000,000,000 i.e. 30 billion times the speed of light and through the escalator type passages *(Maarij)*. And so it affirms prophet's journey of Mee'raaj, as he was escorted by Archangel Gabriel, was far beyond our discernment to comprehend- when he returns the latch was still swinging.

In Surah *Al Maarij* verse 3 the passages mentioned as '**Maarij**' are actually the escalator type of passages. Consider the actual speed of travel through these passages when the speed of Archangel Gabriel is 30 billion times the speed of light and if the speed of the escalators is also something like of that, you can deduce from the above narration, how Prophet Muhammad PBUH had traveled with a speed 30 billion times the speed of light with Arch Angel Gabriel through the passages (70:3-4) in the different strata of the Multiverses and the skies and the coming back through special passages '**Hubbuk'** moving like whirl wind (moving wormholes), wrapping time and space and getting the holy Prophet back in time (well actually in his past) that coincided his time of departure from the place. When Lord Almighty describes these passages, He soon affirms that Your Lord was not quite oblivious of the **Nature of His Creation, what** He intended for the organization of the Whole Cosmic Sway and particularly for the administration of the Cosmic Order. Because we actually cannot compromise as to how after spending that much of time Prophet could be back in a blink of an eye that is actually one hundredth of a second. But I presume he was a bit early so he was driven slowly while back in time when he could perceive the Caravan moving towards Makkah and he predicted that they'll reach on a particular time here in the city. And he was back through **Hubbuk** (moving worm holes) like passages (51:07) when the latch was still swinging.

In The Holy Qur'an Lord Almighty has described the passages of three types with three different names: *"Tareeq" (Al Muminun: 17)* the seven routine passages for the scheduled assignments for the angels probably with the basic speed of 50 million times the speed of light and **Lord Almighty asserts in this Surah that He was not oblivious of the plan of creation.**; There are special passages escalator type *"Maarij" (Al Maarij: 3,4)* for the angels having a speed of 100 to 200 times the speed of light and while passing through such passages the speed of the angels could be far beyond our discernment. And finally the passages "*Hubbuk" (Al Zariat:7*) for the return journey that are changing their position (Whirl wind like moving passages spinning at their axis far beyond the speed of light and wrapping the *time and space* and getting back the person/ angels/ spirits back in time). The void between the clusters of galaxies of four different types in the cosmic order might be providing an infinitely long cylinder spinning passages on its axis would let the person travel through such passages visit his own past by dragging light and squeezing space and time into the loop.

Similarly if we look at the journey of Prophet Muhammad PBUH, **it was actually a journey back in time. After leading the prayers of all the prophets and going to the indeterminate cosmic sway and visiting all that, what Lord Almighty wished him to observe and then coming through the moving wormholes that virtually squeezed and wrapped the time and space, and what actually coincided exactly the time he had left the place, he was abiding before leaving for the sacred journey of Mee'raaj.**

In scientific fiction wormholes are often called the star-gates: that offer a shortcut between two widely separated points in space, **jump through** a wormhole as mentioned in *Al Maarij (70:1-4)* and coming out moments later on the other side of Galaxy. Wormholes naturally fit into the general theory of relativity, whereby gravity also wraps not only the time but also the space. I have tried to learn the philosophy of gravitational force in this journey that could possibly be yet another way to squeeze the time and space, but perhaps we have to work more on the Holy Scripture to comprehend its wisdom.

People often cannot reconcile with the speed **Prophet Muhammad** PBUH traveled in the Comic Sway during Mee'raaj but have you ever thought of your travel in the **Cosmic Order while abiding on Earth:**

We on Earth are spinning around at its axis with a speed of 1670 kilometer per hour then with it, around its orbit (around sun) at the speed of 108,000 kilometer per hour; and so with it as a part of solar system around Milky Way Galaxy at the speed of 720,000 kilometer per hour and again with the Milky Way Galaxy swaying with a speed of 950,000 kilometer per hour in its (Milky Way) universe and the universe spinning in the Multiverses with a speed of --?-- kilometers per hour and the Multiverses swaying with a speed of ---?-- kilometers per hour in the strata of parallel Universes. The parallel Universes spinning around with a speed of---?-- kilometer per hour in the Cosmic Order and then all speeding away with a speed of 300,000 kilometers per second from the core of Big Bang or **Kun:**
Fa Ya Koon and we don't even feel dizzy traveling with such a stupendous speed in the **Cosmic Order.**

Today's scientific trends affirm that perhaps in quite near future man shall be able to create **Atomic Wormholes** between different strata of the universe and also acquire a speed far greater times than the speed of light and would probably be able to travel towards the far afar galactic order. But there is a catch in this man-managed journey by the future scientists, because after a definite limits in the space the **cosmic rays will be so intense that the space shuttle would need 600 tons of water to elude the affects of cosmic rays** *(as it is not even possible for the astronaut to land on Mars, for there is no such shield to elude the torment of cosmic rays)* and for the space craft, it is not possible to carry that huge amount of water. This is an interesting subject to. I'll make it convenient to explain this sometime later in an appropriate place.

For decades, time travel lay beyond the edge of creditable science. In recent years, however, the topic has become something of a very common subject among theoretical physicists. The encouragement has been partly holiday distraction, time travel that's fun to think about. But this research has a serious side too. Comprehension to the relation between cause and effect is a key part of attempts to construct a unified theory of physics. If unrestricted time travel were possible, even in principle, the nature of such a unified theory could be drastically affected. So the man shall be able to accomplish such marvels, i.e. to travel to the far distant universe and come back in a wink of instance.

I am confident with the foregoing discussion reader will be able to understand the cosmic journey of Prophet Muhammad PBUH that's indeed a travel back in time.

To summarize once again:

While traveling towards heavens Prophet Muhammad PBUH was traveling in his future as we do in our routine but this travel was with the speed that's far beyond our cognition *(30 billion times the speed of light)* through the escalator *(Al Maarij)* type of passages that might have doubled the ultimate speed. But when he was coming back, it was basically a travel back in time i.e. in his own past through the spinning *(beyond the speed of light and also changing their position like whirlwind)* passages *(Al Hubbuk)* that could wind up the time and space. I would like to add a word for my readers that speed of light is one way to wind up the space and time and gravitation is another. I've just affirmed the travel of Prophet Muhammad PBUH in the light of wormhole theory.

The gravitational element will be around as long as the prophet's journey was through the **cosmic order** sweep with billions and trillions of cosmic bodies in the stellar sprawl around, but once he was beyond the cosmic order the gravitational element was no longer there, as there is void beyond the limits of cosmic order, that's limited by the lower skies. There is a point of concern in this pretext that spinning wormholes with speed greater than of light could possibly also evade the implement of gravitational force in the cosmic order as long as stellar bodies are around.

A word about the gravitational element as to how it influences the time: If we have a watch in the basement and another in the attic, the one in the attic runs faster than the one in basement as the element of gravitation of earth is more when it is closer to the core of earth.
Can you comprehend the distance he traveled?
Indeed, you cannot!

Our universe was billions to trillions kilometers apart in first few moments of big bang and then it's expanding at the speed of around 300,000 kilometers per second ever since 15 billion light years; and mind you, each light year is 6 trillion miles *(if our Grand Universe expanded just one meter it would be twice its size and if it expanded six trillion miles a second how much its size will be)*. And the limit of its expanse is the lowest sky and how far afar it would take to reach that limit of cosmic order. The cosmic sway is beyond lowest skies, where there are other six other skies each most probably with the same distance of Nihility of big bang to the first or the lower skies, when the expanding universe will experience big smash resulting in series of big crunch eventuating in singularity, forming a seedling for the new creation. *(Details in Fate of the Universe)*

Scientists affirm the existence of wormhole passages as relic of big bang, and Qur'an confirms the existence of such passages (23:17; 51:07; 70:3-4). Scientists also contend that in future we shall be able to produce atomic wormholes in different strata of the Universe.

Speed is one way to wrap up the time and space, and gravitation is another. The spinning moving wormholes (Al Hubbuk) probably with the speed of light could also elude the gravitational influence of the stellar sprawl.

His Almighty asserts that if an angel or a spirit has to reach 'Me' from earth, it would take a day of 50,000 years of count *(not of your count)* where the day, *as affirmed earlier*, a day of 1000-years of your count. This clearly shows that there are messengers of Lord, whose speed is (1000 x 50,000) i.e. 50,000,000 times the speed of light. Then there are verses, clearly indicating that angles having two, three or four pairs of wings, quite likely referring to their relation with the speed *(of the messengers of Lord)* 50,000,000 times the speed of light. Now consider all the way of communication of Lord Almighty through certain passages like Wormhole, with a speed two, three and four times, the 50,000,000 times the speed of light i.e. 1,000,000,000; 1,500,000,000 or 2,000,000,000 times the speed of light, i.e. 50- 200 million times the speed of light. The speed of Archangel Gabriel is 30 billion times the speed of light as already affirmed. Prophet Muhammad [PBUH] traveled towards heavens with speed of 30 billion times the speed of light through Al Maarij and came back in his own past through 'Hubbuk' the spinning passages wrapping up the time and space

{In Hadidh it is affirmed that Archangel Gabriel has 600 wings i.e. having a speed 30 billion times the speed of light And Prophet [PBUH] accompanied Archangel Gabriel through Al Maarij-like passages while going and coming back in his past through spirally swinging passages Al Hubbuk and reaching just at the time of his departure}

Diagrammatic appearance of the Prophet's [PBUH] Journey is illustrated on the next page.

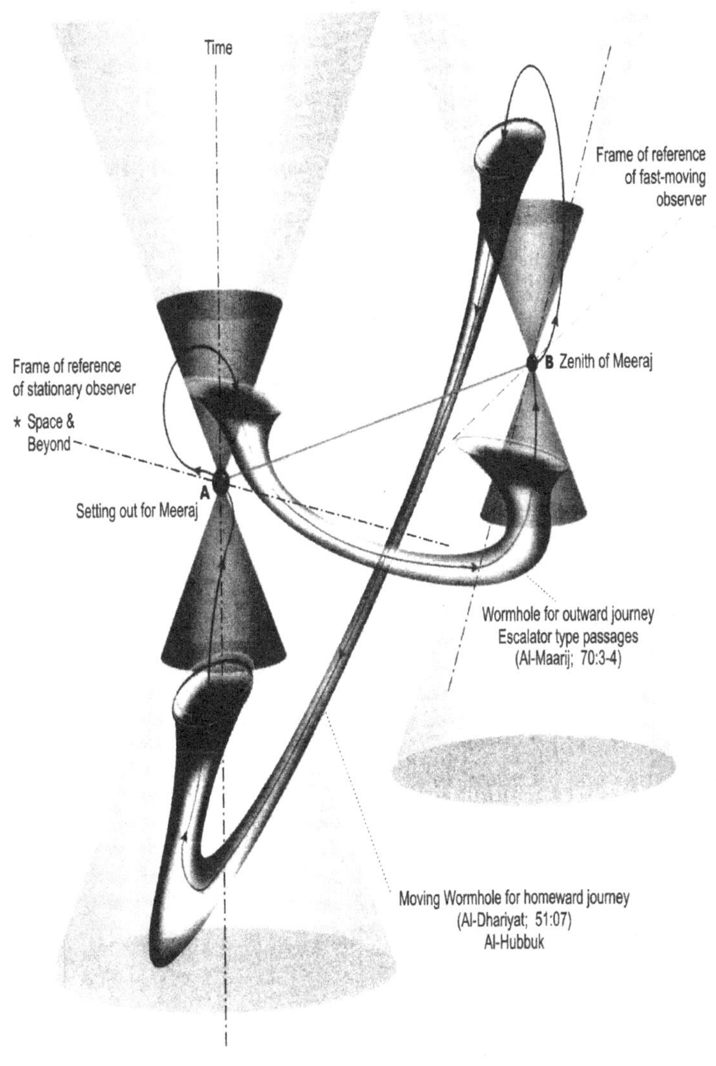

*** Space & Beyond:**

Space or Cosmic Order {Our domain of expansion of the universe is the lowest skies (Al-Saffat 37:6)}
Beyond in Cosmic Sway with six skies (With no gravitational element)

Modified from Brief History of Time by Stephen Hawking

And We,
Created over you **seven ways** *in cosmic sway*
We're not oblivious of 'Our' creation *in array* (**Al Muminun**, 23:17)

- A discipline of Lord *in prime*
The Lord of all tracts in trail *to climb*
The angels and Spirits ascent unto Him in a day
The sort whereof is **fifty thousand years a day** (**Al Maarij**, 70:3-4)

- Vow be to the passages *(in skies)* **swinging** *in trail* (**Al Zariat,** the Winnowing Winds 51:07)

(The word used for such passages is changing in position and how nicely it affirms 'the spinning and moving Wormholes' through different strata of the Multiverses and beyond for a rapid swing into the future or instant retreat into the past - A travel back in time)

32:5 ***(Al Sajda)***
He Commands all *the term in sway*
Of the heavens and earth *set in array*
All at conclusion affairs trend *in pace*
To The Lord Almighty *in Grace*
In a Day of tally *in trace*
Years thousand of your count *in place*
In a Day of your count years thousand in stance

70:4 ***(Al Maarij)***
The angels and Spirit ascent unto Him in a day
The sort whereof is fifty thousand years a day

35:1 (***Al Malaika*** *or Al Fatir)*
All Acclaim in Adulation for Lord *in adore*
Who contrived *out of Nihility in score*
The heavens and earth *in place*
Who made the angels *courier in space*
With fin to fly *thither in glide*
Wings in two, or three, or four pairs *to slide*
He appends to contrive to create *in array*
As He intends to trend *in display*
For Lord has power over all *in sway*

<u>Wan Najm i Izza Hawwa:</u> وَالنَّجمِ إذَاهَوٰى

In the very first verse of 53 Surah Al Najm Lord Almighty avows a star:
In almost all the translations of The Holy Qur'an,
The translation of the above text is mentioned as:

"*Vow to the star that's <u>setting</u> in stride*"
And later in verse 49 Lord Almighty asserts:
He's Lord of Sirius, a star, so immense in qualities

Al Najm (The Star) 53:1-14
Vow to the star that's shifting in stance
Your friend isn't dissuaded or lost in trance
Nor does he deem to invoke on desire
Nothing but sent down to him for Vision to inspire

He's taught by one Mighty with Astral in Demand
Gifted with force of Sapience in Elegant Command

While he was in best cuff and glib of limit to diverge
Then he trends intimately next and nigh to converge

He's at a Ted of but two bows span in sway
So did Lord inspired His Savant to convey

The Prophet's heart lied not in sway
Will you dispute him, what he saw to convey

For indeed he saw him at a second dip and slide
Aside 'Astral O Esteemed Sidra none can pass in aside
Nigh to an Elegant Blissful Garden to abide

When! Supper O Supreme Sidra awning a mystical shawl
His ken and view shared or skewed not, or getting to slant
For indeed he saw Great Symbols of His Peerless Lord
(Sidra: Lote Tree)

"By the star when it sets down: (*changes its original position or shifting in stance*)"

But I didn't feel comfortable with this translation. I requested quite a few scholars for the other meaning of the text, because the following Verses of the Holy Scripture clearly elucidate that this star is not an ordinary star in the Cosmic Order, but has very special property assigned with special duty like that Prophet Muhammad PBUH affirmed hither in vale.
Could it be? *"Shifting its original stance or position"*
I felt comfortable when I was told of this meaning of the text given in the stance and stanza of the Holy Scripture, for in the following verse His Almighty asserts that your friend is not off his mind or dissuaded from the true path of the discipline. He had been amongst you for quite sometime enjoying a most dignified status and you found him the "Truthful" and the

"Trustworthy". As to why he has, all of a sudden turned towards some teachings that had never ever been asserted or affirmed before that stance. As to why he's defying your *Laat, Munaat and Uzzaa* and proclaiming a new discipline.
He was there in the glorious ascent of Mee'raaj and alluring the Bliss of Almighty; at another moment people were throwing trash on him, in the streets of Makkah and in Taif people were pelting stones on him.

"He is not irresponsible or gone crazy *i.e. letting him change his original most dignified status*".
In the next few Verses His Almighty refers to His special messenger angel Gabriel assigned to pass the word of Qur'an to Prophet Muhammad [PBUH].

The messenger a very special of all the angels, who falls from his original exalted status down to Earth to pass The Word of Lord Almighty to His savant.

In this pretext consider the qualities of such a star that **Lord Almighty** is referring in this script.
Edwin Hubble set the stage for today's studies of galaxy formation when he discovered that the Milky Way was not alone. In the predawn hours of October 6, 1923 at the Mount Wilson Observatory in California, he photographed a fuzzy, spiral shaped clump of stars known as M31, or Andromeda, which most astronomers assumed as part of the Milky Way. He soon realized that within the clump he had found a tiny jewel; a star known as a '*Cepheid*' variable, whereas Lord Almighty attributes a name '*Sirius' in the same Surah verse 49,* to this star of immense qualities. This type of a star has a wonderful property. Its brightness waxes and wanes like lock-work, and the longer it takes to vary, the greater is the star's intrinsic brightness. That means the star can be used to measure cosmic distances.

This special star mentioned in verse '49' this Surah, '*Cepheid* or *Sirius*' assigned as gem and jewel of the cosmic order:
It stays bright for quite sometime and then dwindles down from its original status of brightness to dimness, it stays in that order for quite sometime and then returns to its original status. This order of change in position or falling from the original status helps the cosmologists find the distances between different stars and galaxies. This notion helps to solve many riddles in the cosmic sway.

So as this star is asserted as Gem and Jewel of the Cosmic Order, Prophet Muhammad [PBUH] is Gem and Jewel of the Humanity and Archangel Gabriel as Gem and jewel of the Angels. Before closing the discussion I would like to pen a few words in this context. Lord Almighty enumerates innumerable qualities of *'Cepheid* or *Sirius'*. *There is word for the future cosmologist to look into the other qualities of this star that could possibly prove a mile-stone in cosmic research.*

Purpose of Creation

What's your concern hither *in term*
That 'We',
Created you without any plan *in concern*
And
That you're not destined to 'Me' *in return*
(23:115-116)

I've no vision to discern, but have some inkling to pen a few words in concern.
Allah Almighty loves his living beings far more than a mother.
Sure?
Of course, indeed!
O K! Then, when a contorted and crippled baby is born, how tormenting and painful it is for the mother?
Sure enough, there's no doubt about it.
Don't you think Lord Almighty will also be concerned about this disturbing situation?
It's quite likely.

Just trend towards the soil and the cultivation:

We sow a seed of cotton or some grain but what really comes out?
Besides cotton or grain there are so many undesired herbal plants.

We treat the soil with so many approaches to get rid of the undesirable rubbish plants, and only then we yield the crop of our choice, even though we're not quite appeased of its ultimate outcome that it would've yielded without those unwanted plants. But what actually we don't know of the cause, for what it was expedient for the superfluous yield to be there before the germination of the desired product. So these are exterminated only when these are visible or come out of the soil.

So is the genetic swing in sway for what the detrimental genes are there for the purpose of the Whole, and so these are taken care of sooner or later by the Nature.
Am I clear?
Indeed! It's like that.

If we trend towards the creation of the cosmic order and also the living beings as a whole, in the "Proscenium of Creation", couldn't there be some unwelcome products in produce in the genetic array and cosmic sway for the discipline of the whole in cosmic array?

Because:
For the order of the whole there has to be good and bad.

For the preference in competence in the genetic swing and sway is in reality the perfection with precision of the Order of Nature.

Could it all be with a stroke of chance? How could one discern his order of Discipline, until one looks into the details of each effect and equipage with unbiased eye?
Why don't you ask yourself: **'Who' has arranged all these fascinating effects and equipage for us?**
Maybe I'm absolutely wide of the mark, but could it be?

Lord Almighty wanted to settle many scores before the creation of **His Real Perfect Design** that's the life to cherish the bliss of everlasting world in the **Hereafter**. Maybe we are unwittingly performing certain definite assignments without ever realizing the eventual purpose of their formation or impression. **And what's the source of knowledge**? Even persons like Einstein affirmed that it's all intuitive perception that opens new vistas of concern and I myself stand a witness to that.

For all the diversity of life on this planet, ranging from tiny bacteria to majestic blue whales, from sunshine-harvesting plants to mineral-digesting endoliths, miles underground, only one kind of "life as we know it" exists. All these organisms are based on nucleic acids- DNA and RNA- and proteins, working together more or less described by the so-called central dogma of molecular biology: DNA stores information that is transcribed into RNA, which then serves as template for producing a protein. The proteins, in turn, serve as important structural elements in tissues and, as enzymes, are the cells workhorses. Yet the scientists dream of synthesizing life that is utterly alien to this world- both to better understand the minimum component required for life (as part of the quest to uncover the essence of life originated on earth) and, frankly, to see if they can do it. That is they hope to put together a novel combination of molecules that can self organize, metabolize (make use of energy source), grow, reproduce and evolve. A synthetic molecule discovered in 1995, called peptide nucleic acid (PNA) combines the information-storage properties of DNA with chemical stability of a protein-like backbone.

The ultimate nature of assignment endowed to the man is at least not very clear to us, but in Qur'an Lord Almighty asserts that I've not created you (i.e. men of all caste, creed and culture) without any definite design in plan (24:115). It very clearly affirms that the creation of all the mankind and not of The Muslim Community alone is planned with a definite reason.
What could be that?
Could it be something like that?

A handful of genes that control the body's defenses during hard times can also dramatically improve health and prolong life in diverse organisms. Understanding how they work may reveal the keys **to extending human life span while banishing diseases of old age i.e. delaying dotage and relishing the boons of life span experiences with senescence, f**or in the Hereafter there is a life in prime with no dotage in decline. But how could that be possible?

- Genes that control an organism's ability to withstand adversity, cause changes throughout the body that renders it temporarily supercharged for survival.
- Activated over the long term, this stress response prolongs life span and forestalls disease in a wide range of organisms.

- **Sirtuins** are a family of genes that may be master regulators of the survival mechanisms.
- Understanding how they produce their health and longevity enhancing effects could lead to disease treatments and ultimately longer, disease free human life spans, for that's the life in the Hereafter with ever youth in profuse with no dotage in refuse.
- Another concern is stem cell transplant creating almost new organ instead of the damaged one.

The real purpose of life is a food for thought for all, who read the Holy Scriptures intently between the lines. Similarly when we trend to the numeral and numerical system in the Holy Scripture, we are fascinated to find a logical connection in the order of discernment, what I call the **faith healing** as discussed in *Kun: Fa Ya Koon.*

Before understanding the philosophy of creation of man, we shall have to understand the basic integral unit of human body that not only forms the brick work of the human body as an earthy pot but also forms the basis of vivacity that holds the life or Efflux or soul to perform in our very simple to most complex task while playing on the most delicate orchestra of the human genetic proscenium- the life at the cellular 'DNA' level.

Each one of us is composed of genetic array and there are about three and a half billion codes or letters written on the Genome the nucleic acids- DNA and RNA- and proteins, working together more or less as described by the central dogma of molecular biology: DNA stores information that is transcribed into RNA, which then serves as a template for producing a protein. The proteins, in turn, serve as important structural elements in tissues and, as enzymes, are the cell's workhorses.

If we could read 10 letters or codes a second it would take 11 years to read the whole text and even if we had 11 years at our discretion to read the whole text we still cannot make out as how it received the vivacity to perform most intricate functioning in our life. We are all the same for 99.9% of the genetic code. It is only 0.1% we are different from each other. Our creation or initiation was not an ordinary job. Lord Almighty created the Genetic Array of the human being in a perfect order with His own hands (38:75) and did not leave it at its own for procreation. There has been a proper order and discipline in this procreation but for the order of whole there has to be definite transmutation in the genetic make up. For the order of the whole there has to be good and bad for otherwise this life would not have been a place to live.

More than one fifth of the proteins (and hence genes) in each human being exist in a form that differs only 0.1 % in the majority of the population. This remarkable genetic variability, or polymorphism, among "normal" people accounts for much of the normal variation in body traits such as height, intelligence, and blood pressure. These genetic differences also determine the ability of each individual to meet environmental challenges, including those, which produce disease. All human diseases can be considered to result from an interaction between an individual's unique genetic makeup and the environment. In certain diseases the genetic component is so overwhelming that it expresses itself in a predictable manner without a requirement for extraordinary environmental challenges. Such diseases are termed genetic disorders.

Geneticists have discovered thousands of mutations responsible for the disease in humans, but founder mutations stand apart. The victims of many genetic diseases die before reproducing, stopping the mutant genes from reaching future generations. But founder mutations often spare their carriers and therefore can spread from the original founder to his or her descendants. And some of the disorders resulting from the mutations are common, such as the hereditary hemochromatosis, sickle cell anemia and cystic fibrosis.

Mutations arise from the random changes in our DNA. Most of the damage gets repaired or eliminated at birth and thus does not get passed down to the subsequent generations. But some mutations, called the germ-line mutations, are passed down, often with serious medical consequences to the offspring, who inherit them- more than 1,000 different diseases arise from the mutations in different human genes and what protection they give the humanity at large is yet to be explored as in some of the cases we are given indication of protection from certain problems to the carriers of mutant genes.

Striking fact is how common these mutations can be hundreds or even thousands of times more frequent than typical mutations that cause disease. Most disease mutations exist at a frequency of one in a few thousand to one in a few million. But founder mutations can occur in as much as a few percent of the population.

This anomaly-shouldn't evolution is to get rid of the harmful genes rather than select for them offers an important clue as to why founder mutations have persisted so far and spread. The answer perhaps not surprisingly, is that under some circumstances founder mutations prove beneficial. Most founder mutations are recessive; only a person with two copies of the affected gene, one from each parent, will suffer from the disease. The much larger percentage of people with only one copy, are called carriers. They can pass on the gene to their children and have no symptoms of disease themselves, and the single copy of the founder mutation gives the carrier an advantage in the struggle for survival.

For example, carriers of the hereditary hemochromatosis mutation are thought to be protected from iron-deficiency anemia (a life-threatening condition in the past), because the protein encoded by that mutated gene makes the person absorb iron more effectively than can those who carry two normal copies of the gene. Carriers thus had an edge when dietary iron was scarce.

Perhaps the best-known example of a double-edged genetic mutation is the one responsible for sickle cell disease. The sickle cell mutation apparently arose repeatedly in regions riddled with malaria in Africa and the Middle East. A single copy of a sickle cell gene helps the carrier survive malarial infection. But two copies doom the bearer to pain and a shortened life span. The sickle cell mutation today can be found in five different regions, leading to the conclusion that the mutation appeared independently five times in five different founders. (Al-though sickle cell disease usually results from a founder mutation, some cases do arise from other mutations.)

Two competing forces govern the frequency of a founder mutation in the population. Someone who has two copies will probably die before reproducing, but those who have only one copy will survive preferentially over those with no copies. This produces so-called balancing selection, in which the beneficial effects drive the frequency of the mutant gene up while the harmful effects damp down the frequency. Evolution gives and evolution takes away, so that over time the gene maintains a relatively steady level in the population.

For example, a recent discovery may explain the persistence of factor V Leiden, a mutation in the factor V gene, which is responsible for other carriers of this mutation are resistant to the lethal effects of bacterial infections in the bloodstream, a huge threat to survival in the pre-antibiotics past and still a cause of death today.

Noteworthy Founder Mutations

Affected gene	Condition	Mutation origin	Migration	Possible advantage of one copy
HF	Iron overload	Far Northwestern Europe	South and East across Europe	Protection from anemia
CFTR	Cystic Fibrosis	Southeast Europe/ Middle East	West and North across Europe	Protection from diarrhea
Hb $_S$	Sickle cell disease	Africa/Middle East	To New World	Protection from malaria
FV Leiden	Blood clots	Western Europe	Worldwide	Protection from sepsis
ALDH2	Alcohol toxicity	Far East Asia	North and West across Asia	Protection from alcoholism, possibly hepatitis B
LCT	Lactose tolerance	Asia	West and North Across Eurasia	Allows consumption of milk from domesticated animals
GJB2	Deafness	Middle East	West and North Across Europe	Unknown

It is not conceivable to imagine that all men and clan cherish equanimity in poise for their conduct in course, propensity and proficiency in intelligence and competence. So is the point and plan of comprehension with sapience in sagacity besides health and wealth that must vary from person to person. So there had to be certain mutations with innovations in the genetic proscenium for otherwise this World would not have been a place to endure life.

Seas, which do not Mix Up

Al- Rahman: 55: 19-20
He's let free two sinuous seas in obtrude
But a fence *(mid them)* doesn't let to intrude

An Naml 27:61
Isn't He the best, Who made earth an abide
And let the streams swing and surge in stride
And put the hills and gills there in slide
And put the bar mid two seas in surge
Is there a god other than Lord in verge
But nay!
Quite a few don't discern in urge

In the verse stated above, it is indicated that two bodies of water meet each other yet do not mix together since there is a barrier preventing it. How could a man of fourteen centuries back think of all that intricate ocean currents shown today by the most advanced research?

Modern research has in recent times encountered that in the places where two contrasted seas meet with divergent properties there is a barrier between them. This barrier divides the two seas so that the stream of water flowing in the sea has its own temperature, salinity and density.

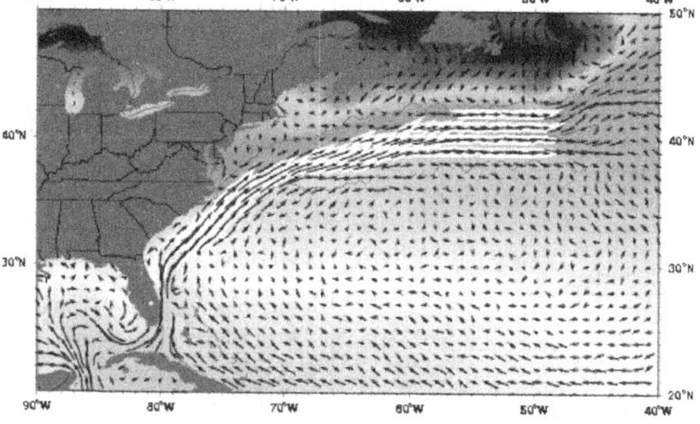

The **Gulf Stream** as represented by the Mariano Global Surface Velocity Analysis *(MGSVA)*. The Gulf Stream is the western boundary current of the N. Atlantic subtropical gyre. The Gulf Stream transports significant amount of warm water *(heat)* towards North Pole. The averaging of velocity data from a meandering current produces a wide mean picture of the flow. The core of the Gulf Stream current is about 90 km wide and has peak velocities of greater than 2 m/s *(5 knots)*.

Beginning in the Caribbean and ending in the northern North Atlantic, the Gulf Stream System is one of the world's most intensely studied current systems. This extensive western

boundary current plays an important role in the pole-ward transfer of heat and salt and serves to warm the European subcontinent. The Gulf Stream begins upstream of Cape Hatters, where the Florida Current ceases to follow the continental shelf. The position of the Stream, as it leaves the coast, changes throughout the year. In the fall, it shifts north, while in the winter and early spring it shifts south (Auer 1987; Kelly and Gille 1990; Frankignoul et al. 2001). Compared with the width of the current (about 100-200 km), the range of this variation (30-40 km) is relatively small (Hogg and Johns 1995). However, recent studies by Mariano et al. (2002) suggest: that the meridional range of the annual variation in stream path may be closer to 100 km. Other characteristics of the current are more variable. Significant changes in its transport, meandering, and structure can be observed through many time scales as it travels northeast.
Similarly another example: the water of **Mediterranean Sea** is warm, saline and less dense as compared to water of Atlantic Ocean. When Mediterranean Sea enters the Atlantic over the Gibraltar Sill, it moves several hundred Kilo- meters into the Atlantic at a depth of about 1,000 meters with its own warm, saline and less dense characteristics. Although, there are colossal ocean sprays, forcible tidal flow and rise and fall of ocean currents in these seas, they do not mix or transgress this barrier.

The human eye cannot see the difference between the two seas that meet. Rather they appear to us as one homogeneous sea. This information has been discovered only recently using advanced equipment to measure temperatures, salinity, density, oxygen, etc., whereas the Holy Qur'an clearly mentioned this more than fourteen centuries ago.

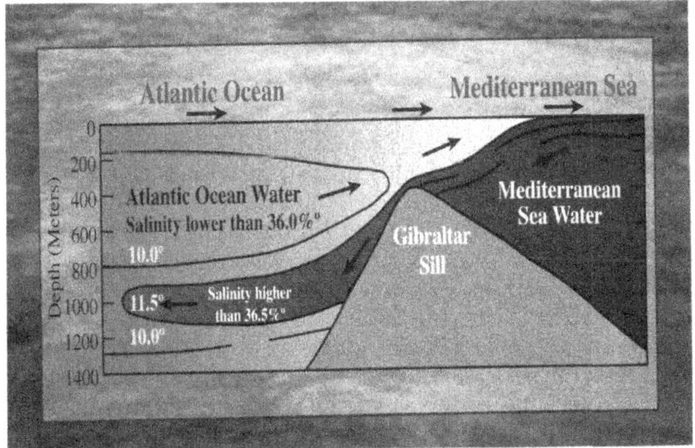

While mentioning of the sea in Holy Qur'an it is elucidated that there are two waters, which flow together but there is a barrier that carry through between these two indeterminately. How could Prophet have known this fact and conveyed, except with the knowledge endowed by His Almighty Allah? Besides mentioning the details of these two Waters His Almighty's bestowals of the sea world have been enunciated. The pearls is just a citation of the variety of the beautiful gem stones that we can gather from the depth of sea

and also cherish the splendor and beauty of the coral reefs with the picturesque elegance in and around the depth of the sea world.
How could one imagine the awe-inspiring dazzle and display, elegance and enchantments, allure and attraction, splendor and seductiveness besides the pulchritude of coral islands in the depth of blues fourteen hundreds years before?

Generally, when two oceans meet one another, their water overrun and the ratio of their salt and temperature reach at equilibrium. Yet, this is not the case with the Mediterranean Sea and the Atlantic Ocean, and Red Sea and Indian Ocean. Although the said oceans visually mix with each other, their water does not mingle due to a barrier in between them. This barrier is the force known as the "surface tension."

Fresh Water Currents in the Sea:

And Lord endowed a sway to aside
Two of the seas that stem in slide

One is delectable, delicious in taste
Other one salted and astringent in waste

But there's shawl mid them in slide
A deterrent defying their mix in glide 25:53

Nor two frame of flowing water stay in alike
One delectable, delicious and agile to imbibe

And other saline and salty, briny and bitter to savor
But in waters is meat crisp and tender in flavor *36:12*

Southern hemisphere SST anomalies mapped every 6 months for a period of 4 years. This sequence is derived from observations made from 1982 to 1995 through empirical orthogonal function (EOF) analysis.

A newly discovered feature of the ocean circulation around Antarctica is the Antarctic Circumpolar *Wave (ACW)*. This wave travels westward *against* the massive circumpolar current, in which it is embedded. The result is that the ACW travels eastward around Antarctica, but more slowly than the current, circling the globe each 8 - 9 years. The ACW has a *wave number* of two, i.e. there are two large regions of relatively warm water, each 3 to 6 thousand kilometers across, separated by two equally huge patches of cold water. The amplitude of the ACW is highest between 50-60. It is not clear how these waves are triggered and maintained, the likely factors are the strong westerly winds in the region, the bottom topography, and the meridional temperature gradient in the upper ocean. There may be a connection with the El Niño Southern Oscillation, but it appears weak at best.
The ACW clearly affects the overlying atmosphere, in particular the temperature and winds over the southern seas, but also the weather of the three southern continents bordering these seas. A warm region implies higher surface pressures and a tendency for long-wave ridging in the upper troposphere, resulting in drier-than-normal wetter, especially just east of the ridge. In 1998 a cold region passed south of Tasmania. A warm pool should be to the south of Tasmania in 2000. A cold region implies a stronger meridional temperature

gradient, and therefore a stronger jet stream and more frontal activity. This implies more winter rain along the southern fringes of Australia.

The structure of the AWC suggests a 4 to 5-year cycle of rainfall. In coastal regions of the Australia Bight, and as far as the Australian Alps, there is some evidence of a 4 year cycle in the annual rainfall, and ACW cold phases correspond with above-normal precipitation. In Southwest Australia droughts recur every 3-12 years; the spectral variation shows a weak peak at a period of around 4 years. The ACW alternation may be more important than El Niño's in governing rainfall on the southern fringes of Australia. In New Zealand also temperatures and precipitation amounts in autumn and winter have a weak 4-6 year periodicity in sync with the ACW.

Thus precipitation onto Australia is affected by a changing combination of the ACW to the south, **El Niño events** to the east, and also the **'Indian Ocean Dipole'** (IOD) to the west. There are other variations in the North Atlantic and North Pacific, but they are too remote to have any effect.

The IOD is related to the **northwest cloud bands**, i.e. rain-producing disturbances that stretch across Australia from northwest to southeast. They are the chief cause of rain in the center of the country. The phenomenon involves warm water around Indonesia and New Guinea (especially in La Niña years); with colder water in the middle of the Indian Ocean, west of Australia.

Schematic display of the surface currents (solid curves) and deep currents (dashed curves) of the North Atlantic:

The grey scale of the curves depicts their approximate temperatures.

Credit: Jack Cook, Woods Hole Oceanographic Institution

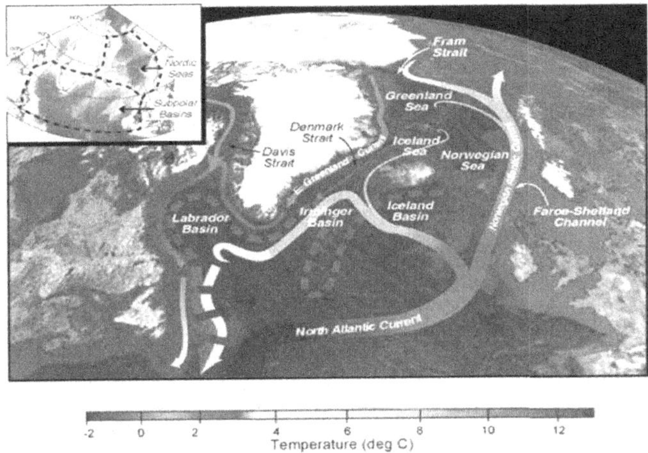

Super-Symmetry:

UNCOVERING "Al Meezan" Discipline of true Divine measure or SUPERSYMMETRY: "Order of measure"

Raised the heavens and set its confines
That you may not transgress its defines
Have *order of measure** as in the cosmic role
The earth He designated for the living soul (*Al Rahman*)
**Al Meezan or the order of discipline*

The natural world around us abounds with *order of measure* or symmetry "*Al Meezan*", order of Measure i.e. regularity and harmony, uniformity and balance, equilibrium and proportion approximates symmetries. The bilateral symmetry of most animals, the rotational symmetry of the sun, the five fold symmetry of many starfish, and the manifold symmetries of fruit and flowers. Symmetry or order of measure becomes so commonplace, it takes something as extraordinary, as a snowflake to awaken our awe.

The early Verses of Surah Rahman refer to the creation of mankind, the galactic adoration with sun, moon and stars besides different cosmic orders. His Almighty refers to the strict discipline ordained in the creation of the universe and its various disciplines as just elucidated forewarn the man to appropriate such subjection in their conventional life as He has adduced from the tiniest particle like atom to the incomprehensible cosmic order. This does not mean that the subjugation should only be left to the routine measure of the commodities but a discipline of performance and rapprochement, disposition and demeanor, endowment and approximation should be venerated in all spheres of life. Every one should observe a rightful injunction of discipline in communication and negotiation to redeem the legitimate command of discipline of His Almighty as in the Creation of the Universe and the life The pictures referring to the creation of the Universe and very early stages of creation of human fetus in the mother's womb ordain an undistorted discipline of measure and order of rule governing the 'Whole'. Before concluding this I would like to give details of one of the most fascinating order of discipline and veracity of measure in the Divine Order for the living being in ecosystem.

Particle physics is replete with symmetries: in particular, the fundamental forces are dictated by symmetries called gauge symmetries. Specify the gauge group and the interaction strength, and essentially all the behavior of the force is determined. For instance, electromagnetism involves a gauge symmetry group called U (1), which is the symmetry of rotations of a circle in a plane.

Much of fundamental physics, it turns out, amounts to uncovering other kinds of "Al Meezan" that characterize the universe. Einstein's theory of special relativity, for example, is a theory of the symmetries of empty space and time, which are governed by the **Poincare group.** (Groups are the mathematical structures that describe symmetries). Effects such as length contraction and time dilation, which flatten fast moving clocks and make them run slow, are operations of the symmetry group, similar to rotating your point of view in space, but with time as part of the rotation you encounter similar situation.
Conservation of electric charge is a consequence of the U (1) symmetry. As proved by mathematician **Emmy Noether** in 1915, whenever the symmetry appears in mechanics,

there is also a conservation law. The theorem works for both classical and quantum mechanics and tells us, for instance, that the law of conservation of energy follows from symmetry with respect to translations in time. That is, energy is conserved because the equations of motion yesterday are the same as those today. Conservation of momentum (symmetry under translation in space) and angular momentum (symmetry under rotations) are similar.

Finally, take the very definition of a particle in quantum field theory this direct linkage of symmetry to the most basic structure of matter and forces is what requires electrons and other particles to have an intrinsic quantity of angular momentum known as spin. A particle's mass is also a symmetry-related label.
Compared to the symmetries that govern the universe, snowflakes start to seem quite terrestrial.

A Definite Order of Measures is a remarkable symmetry. In elementary particle physics, it interchanges particles of completely dissimilar types the kind called fermions, such as electrons, protons and neutrons, which make up the material world and those called bosons (such as photons), which generate the forces of nature. Fermions are inherently the individualists and loners of the quantum particle world; no two fermions ever occupy the same quantum state. Their aversion to close company is strong enough to hold up a neutron star against collapse even when the crushing weight of gravity has overcome every other force of nature. Bosons, in contrast, are convivial copycats and readily gather in identical states. Every boson in a particular state encourages more of its species to emulate it. Under the right conditions, bosons form regimented armies of clones, such as the photons in a laser beam or the atoms in super-fluid helium 4.

Yet somehow in the mirror of super-symmetry, standoffish fermions look magically like sociable bosons, and vice versa.

At least that is the theory. Elementary particle theorists have studied that holds the key to the next major advance in our understanding of the fundamental particles and forces.
In the 1980s nuclear theorists proposed that super-violent collisions were not necessarily the only way to see super-symmetry; they predicted that a different form of super-symmetry could exist in certain atomic nuclei. Here, too, the symmetry relates what in physics are quite dissimilar objects: nuclei with even numbers of protons and neutrons and those with odd numbers.

Symmetries play major roles throughout physics the basic of our understanding the whole cosmic order. All ordinary symmetries respect the distinction between bosons and fermions. Super-symmetry theories incorporate powerful mathematical properties that interchange bosons and fermions. Such theories may be crucial for deeply understanding particle physics, but experimenters have not yet detected super-symmetry of elementary particles.
In atomic nuclei, protons and neutrons each form pairs that behave like composite bosons. Nuclei thereby form four distinct classes (even – even, even-odd, odd-even and odd-odd) depending on whether the protons and neutrons can each completely pair off. Physicists predicted that a variant of super-symmetry should relate a magic square of four nuclei of these types. Experimenters have now confirmed that prediction.

SUPERSYMMETRY (Strict order of measure) **IN PARTICAL PHYSICS**:

Symmetries form the foundation of the Standard Model. Electrons and electron neutrinos, for example, are related by symmetry, which also relates 'up quarks' to 'down quarks'. A different manifestation of the same symmetry associates Z and W particles. Gluons are all related by a color symmetry, which also relates different colors of quarks. All these symmetries relate fermions to fermions and bosons to bosons.

This elementary particle super-symmetry is also intimately related to the symmetries of space-time that underlies Einstein's theory of special relativity. That is the super symmetry extends those symmetries. The super symmetry of nuclei is fundamentally different because it does not have that connection to space-time. The common ground between these two applications of super symmetry in physics is that they both rely on super algebra.

Order of Discipline in Atmosphere:

Every drop of water in the top 100 meters of the ocean contains thousands of free-floating, microscopic floras called phytoplankton. These single celled organisms including diatoms and other algae inhabit three quarters of the earth's surface, and yet they account for less than 1 percent of the 600 billion metric tons of carbon contained within its phytosynthetic biomass. But being small does not stop this virtually invisible forest from making a bold mark on the planet's most critical natural cycles.

Arguably one of the most consequential activities of marine phytoplankton is their influence on climate. Until recently, however, few researchers appreciated the degree to which these diminutive ocean dwellers can draw the greenhouse gas carbon dioxide (CO_2) out of the atmosphere and store it in the deep sea. New satellite observations and extensive oceanographic research projects are finally revealing how sensitive these organisms are to changes in global temperatures, ocean circulation and nutrient availability.

Exploring how human activities can alter phytoplankton's impact on the planet's carbon cycle is crucial for predicting the long-term ecological balancing effects of such actions.

Climate: Regulators:

Evincing ecological balance and the discipline of measure

Rapid life cycles of marine phytoplankton transfer heat-trapping carbon dioxide (CO_2) from the atmosphere and **Upper Ocean** to the deep sea, where the gas remains sequestered until currents return it to the surface hundreds of years later.
If all of the world's marine phytoplankton were to die today, the concentration of CO_2 in the atmosphere would rise by 200 parts per million or 35 percent in a matter of centuries.
Adding certain nutrients to the ocean surface can dramatically enhance the growth of phytoplankton and thus their uptake of CO_2 via phytosynthesis.

The creation of sun and moon are cited as very special favors with special citation of all their celestial movements in a perfect order. *(Al Rahman)*

The stars and the trees all set to adore
He has lifted the sky that looks so azure

Nicely ordained their magnitude in place
That you may not transgress in pace
But observe each of your living subjugation
Lawfully to the discipline of its perpetuation
Thoroughly, as you perceive in cosmic array
Strictly measure observed by the nature to obey

Stars and Trees Beseech His Adulation,
Who could have known this fact except His Almighty?

Today the modern research shows that Plants can communicate with each other. Ilya Raskin, a botanist at Rutgers University, shows how he and his colleagues demonstrated this in an experiment. Dozens of tobacco plants, picked because of their potent chemical response to a particular virus, were placed in two airtight chambers. Tubes carried air between the chambers. The scientists injected the plants in one chamber with the virus. Within two days those infected emitted a volatile chemical into the air, stimulating the plants in the second chamber to produce chemicals in their leaves that protected them against the virus. This experiment followed the model that guides most scientific research today: Develop hypotheses, run tests, and produce data that other researchers can confirm or challenge by conducting similar experiments. Until recently botanists did not understand chemicals like those produced by the tobacco plants. But now it is known that plants produce a design of chemicals that defend them against disease and also help them propagate. Knowledge about such chemicals could lead to the elaboration of inured plants and to changes in our basic understanding of how they function. "But there is still a huge amount going on in plants that we do not understand," Ruskin tells. Such vast gaps in our knowledge exist in virtually all branches of science.

Likewise, Kathy Sawyer shows in "New Light on the Universe" that most of the mass that fills the universe has yet to be located. Now an expanding universe and the big bang theory are cornerstones of cosmology, the pat of astronomy that studies the origins of the universe and its time space relationships. Advances in genetics and astronomy are driven by the number crunching capabilities of faster computers and by improved imaging techniques that make microscopes and telescopes more powerful. Such tools enable scientists to see things they had never seen before or even considered possible. Genetic researchers can examine objects that are only a millionth of an inch in diameter, while astronomers can see galaxies perhaps 11 billion light years away. It is easy to forget how revolutionary modern science really is. Just a few hundred years ago, in the 16th and 17th centuries, most Europeans thought that the sun revolved around the Earth and the four elements: air, fire, water, and earth created and defined all life. Scholars mostly parroted what they had learned from classical writers like Aristotle, who believed, among other things, that the Earth was enclosed by celestial spheres where nothing ever changed and everything was always perfect. Then pioneers such as Galileo Galilee and Isaac Newton demonstrated that experimentation and analysis could best understand the nature of the world. Why did not the scientific revolution (a phrase that did not come into popular usage until the mid-20th century) take place much earlier? Ancient Greek mathematicians and astronomers had calculated the circumference of the Earth, charted the stars, and figured the distance to the moon. By AD 1100 Chinese scholars had developed a seismograph, a magnetic compass, and the concept of infinite empty space. Why did not the scientific revolution occur in either of those places? Among the best guesses so far: Only in 16th century European scientists began to embrace quantification, the use of mathematics to measure the results of experiments.

One of the most significant effects of the scientific revolution has been population growth. Until modern science brought sewer systems and immunization in the 19th century, about half of all children died before age five. By the end of the 19th century childhood death rates had fallen, and human population began to surge. With advances in medicine, population continues growing and further challenging our ability to live in to ordain discipline, harmony "order of measure" with the nature.

Will scientific progress continue? Or will science reach some limit like the Pillars of Hercules, the classical and medieval symbol for what lies at the edge of the known? On these gates, according to legend, was written:

"Ne plus ultra – No further" The Pillars of Hercules for modern science may become moral and spiritual. Scientists and society will have to decide how much to change the genetic structures of plants and animals, and whether to fiddle with the very genes that make us human. In the meantime the achievements and challenges of modern science propel us further into the unknown. But Qur'an clearly enunciates at many places and invites attention of the men of wisdom to scrutinize the details of the cosmic order and our living planet this blue pearl of the universe and it will open new perspective of exploration, study and scrutiny to affirm more ratiocinative assertion, before the modern scientific evolution.

Raised the cosmos and fixed *to sustain*
That you may not transgress *its domain***:** Al Rahman: 7

The Universal space contains all the laws of Universe, (Inertia, gravity, quantum mechanics, biogenetics, electromagnetic emission, the atomic laws, evolution and what not). Every cubic centimeter of Space from one end of the universe to the other is filled with a definite law that makes the Universe and everything in it to work. *These natural laws in turn created space and determined the size of the Universe. Where the laws end, the Universe ends – but it still continues to grow at the speed of light.*

If the laws only extended outward, in all directions, just one meter, this would be the size of the Universe. There would be no space beyond this sphere of influence. It could not extend one bit further. The Laws of Universal Space precisely determine and control all actions and interactions of matter and energy, within the Universe, from the tiniest space between the subatomic particles to the vast expanse of the Universe. The laws of Almighty created Universal Space, without its laws, the Universe would not exist.

Energy is nothing without matter to push around. Matter has no mass without energy. Together, under the absolute rule of the Laws of Space, they create this complex, dynamic Universe we live in. Even if there were no matter or energy in Universal Space, it would still exist as long as Divine laws existed, although it would be rather pointless.

I cannot bring myself to believe that all these exquisite, impeccable, tangled and all pervading laws of nature just happened to come into being without some Infinitely Wise and All Powerful Reality creating them. I am talking about natural laws of the Universe, and there is the 'All Powerful Reality' His Almighty Allah behind all these philosophies of mankind, other living beings and the cosmic order.

The Universe is finite with regard to size and time. Where the influence of the Law of Universal Space does not hold the Universe also ends. Beyond the Laws of 'Universal Space' either matter or energy cannot remain and besides also the smallest fraction of measurement. Is there an ultimate barrier, the boundary of the Universe? *Lower sky is the limit.* Because His Almighty proclaims "I am the Owner of the entire sweep and span of the Vistas" to which there is no end. The Universe began when His Almighty created its laws, perhaps as long as a trillion light years ago.

The law of space governs everything within the Universe. They do not go on forever nor do they gradually weaken and dissipate. They are either completely in force or they do not exist at all. Where the laws do not apply, neither the energy nor matter can exist, therefore there is no space. The boundary of the Universe is not a wall; it is simply where the laws of the Universe end (details: Fate of the Universe)

The Universe is shaped like a hollow sphere with nature's laws, governing and unifying everything within the sphere. The laws of nature create space, as we know it. Outside the sphere, beyond the boundary of the Universe, nothing can exist. It is completely devoid of all energy and matter. Beyond the boundary the Laws of Universal Space do not exist, therefore nothing can exist, not even the space itself can exist.

The stars and planets could not form since there would be no mass or gravity to hold them together. A light ray could not travel in this region because there are no laws to guide it. There would be no possible way to determine if this region ended just beyond our reach or extended out to infinity.

In the text His Almighty soon after elucidating His discipline of Cosmic Order that 'He' has organized so ubiquitously in a fascinating discipline of measure advises the man to observe the same in his daily routine and not to dissuade the veracity of true Order of measure.

EXTREMOPHILES:

It had long been remembered ad nauseam for my mind to comprehend as to how one would endure the extreme temperatures of the Hell. Recent studies reveal very fascinating discoveries in this direction.

They Thrive on Boiling Heat, Freezing Cold, Radiation and Toxic Chemicals and they have triggered A Revolution in Biology.

This is the abyss, which the convicts had defied
In feral simmering water, they linger to abide Al Rahman: 43, 44

It's hard to conceive a more unfavorable place on earth than the hydrothermal outlets that pep up the ocean floor. These rifts and slits in the sea undersurface disgorge water superheated by rising magma to as high as 400° and adulterated with toxic materials such as hydrogen sulfide, cadmium, arsenic and lead. Yet notwithstanding these virulent surroundings, life not only perseveres but also prospers in the form of communities of microbes that nurture on poison and multiply in temperatures that could hard-boil an egg.

The frozen continent of Antarctica is almost equivalently pestilent, but at the other end of the temperature scale. Penetrate into the ice cap a kilometer, then another and you reach, senselessness, a body of water known as Lake Vostok that emulates Lake Ontario in size. While scientists haven't yet worked with a drill into the lake itself, they have plucked up samples of frozen lake water clinging to the bottom of the ice cap that accommodate unambiguous indication of microbial DNA. Although it floats near the freezing point, cut off from light and outside nutrients, Lake Vostok is abounding with microorganisms. "Nobody," marvels John Priscu, a Montana State University microbiologist, who has studied the samples, "thought there could be any life down there."

Unprecedented as these conclusions might once have seemed; they have become almost commonplace. In the past few months alone, researchers have extracted colonies of microbes that thrive at 58° C in an underground hot spring in Idaho and found others eating into volcanic rock 366 m beneath the sea floor. Over the past few years, in fact, scientists have been finding life in all sorts of places where biology textbooks say it should not exist. Microorganisms are thriving in thermal springs in Yellowstone National Park and in pristine veins of water 3 km underground in South Africa. They are living in solid rock at the bottom of deep mines. They are growing in brine pools, five times saltier than the ocean, in tiny pockets of liquid embedded in sea ice and in places with toxic levels of heavy metals, acids and even radiation.

Taken one at a time, these creatures formally known as Extremophiles or lovers of extreme environments are fascinating curiosities. Collectively, they have triggered a scientific revolution, forcing researchers to rethink biology's most basic assumptions about how life began.

Extremophiles also represent a biotech bonanza, pumping out unique substances that could be invaluable in all sorts of industrial and medical applications. Polymerase chain reaction (PCR), for example, the DNA-augmenting methods used most prestigiously in the O.J. Simpson assassination litigation, takes advantage of an enzyme manufactured by a Yellowstone 'Extremophiles'.

But the consequence of these microbes goes much to a greater consequence. While some Extremophiles are bacteria, some are so different from any other single celled organism that scientists have created a new biological kingdom, called Archaea (from archaic), to accommodate them. As the name suggests, Archaea may be similar to the very first organism that populated the earth billions of years ago. The implication: life on our planet may first have arisen, not in a warm tidal pool as Darwin and others theorized but under conditions of sulfurous, searing heat.

Finally, there is a cosmic dimension to these bugs. So called exobiologists and astrobiologists, who speculate about life beyond Earth, have long assumed that liquid water is a minimum requirement for existence. But if that water can range from frigid to boiling, and if burial underground is not a problem, then it's not crazy to think that life exists in the permafrost beneath the surface of Mars, or in the ice capped ocean that may encircle Jupiter's moon Europa, or in the seas that may exist on Saturn's moon Titan. Indeed, NASA considers Extremophiles so relevant to its search for life in the universe that in 1997 it created the Astrobiology Institute at its Ames Research Center near San Francisco, devoted in part to the study of these peculiar organisms.

And indeed, life began to turn up just about everywhere scientists looked. Geologists had been arguing since 1920s, in fact, that chemical contaminants found in crude oil suggested that some sort of life was thriving underground. They were not taken seriously until the 1980s, though, when Department of Energy scientists realized that if subsurface microbes really did exist, they might play a key role in regulating the purity of groundwater. So they began digging boreholes at DOE sites in South Carolina and Washington State.

Sure enough, they found bugs living more than 460 m down cut off, like their ocean vent cousins, from any conceivable contact with the surface. No one knows how deep the biosphere extends, but Tullis Onstott, a geologist at Princeton, has followed the trail 3 km straight down: he began exploring South African gold mines in 1998, and so far he and his international colleagues have pulled out scores of heat tolerant, hydrogen eating bugs from subsurface water.

'It's also clear that there are plenty of surprises left'. Says Priscu: "In the '70s, when I first got interested in this field, many colleagues called claims of life in extreme environments 'hand waving.' Since then, he and the other extremologists have found life inside glaciers, at the bottom of mines, in searing heat, freezing cold, crushing pressure and lethal toxicity. And that is after exploring only a tiny fraction of the planet. What they have discovered so far has transformed biology. What they will find next, is anybody's guess.

What the bugs can do for us:

The discovery that life can thrive under horrific conditions is a major scientific advance. But it could also turn out to be hugely profitable. Extremophiles survive by manufacturing all sorts of novel molecules. Some digest harsh chemicals; some protect DNA against destruction by radiation; some stave off searing heat or freezing cold. Entrepreneurs are racing to turn these molecules into products, just as was done in the 1980s with Thermus aquaticus, the Yellowstone bug exploited in the PCR technique widely used today to analyze DNA.

San Diego based Diversa Corp. is one of the most active prospectors. The company has searched for useful microbes at geothermal and hydrothermal vents, in acidic soils and alkaline springs, in marine sediments at industrial sites and all over Antarctica, among other places. Eventually, says Diversa CEO Jay Short, we want to sample every portion of the globe. Any profits will be shared with the country of origin.

The company already has several Extremophiles derived products on the market and plans to launch five more this year. One is an enzyme from a deep ocean vent bacterium that improves the synthesis of high fructose corn syrup (used as a sweetener in soft drinks). Another will be used in genetic research. Yet another will make animal feed more nutritious.

Diversa has 14 more products in the pipeline that it hopes could be used for everything from manufacturing pulp and paper to processing food, generating biofuel and synthesizing drugs. While most of the activity thus far has been focused on the enzymes the microbes churn out, the bugs themselves are also being eyed for commercial exploitation.

And this is just one company. Extremophiles have already rewritten biology textbooks; they may soon be rewriting profit statements as well.

His Almighty adored the sky with innumerable Multiverses with galaxies and each galaxy is studded with billions of stars and the earth abounds with filum and granum, fauna and flora with fascinating floral wreathe and filigree of trees of diverse set, sort and species.

Just consider the supreme unifying force and the systemically organized way of the Universe with a definite law governing the lot whole of the cosmic order.

It is important to keep in mind, however, that the exquisite diversity in our mitochondrial code that allows us to trace these events is a classic exception that proves the rule. In most of the rest of our genes, 99.9 percent of them every human being alive is exactly the same. Moreover, most of the variations in the remaining one tenth of a percent do not bunch up into geographic regions or racial groups but instead are spread around the globe. Put another way, the snips and snippets of code that taken together make one person unique, are scattered about in other unique genomes all over the world, binding all of us in a splendid tangle of interrelationship.

Genomically speaking, even bacteria are our cousins in code. The last and most powerful secret revealed by our genes, in fact, is the indisputable unity of everything alive.

The message we conclude from this parable is that those deplorable determined to abide in the most unfortunate place shall not only be able to thrive on the most toxic foods in the extreme temperatures of the Hell but also be able to communicate and be able to perform certain errands as well.

For those who fear facing His Almighty Lord

How would you cherish the beauty of the Whole until you strive to reach the subliminal image of the Whole, and that is only possible when you scarify the part of your whole i.e. sleep, to adore the Bounty of Lord, The His Almighty's Resplendent Excellence and Elegance, Illustriousness and Ingeniousness. The quintessence of sacramental rites is the Divine Speech for which we behold the Beauty. The Divine Names revealed imply a Divine Presence, which becomes operative to the extent that the Name takes possession of the mind, which supplicates it. Man cannot concentrate or focus on the 'Infinite' itself.

When the distinctive favored Name is recited, where the form of the Name has assimilated very intellective prominence, the Divine Essence of Name evinces fortuitously, for this revered form escorts to nothing outside itself. It has no assertive and assured consanguinity but with its Essence and in conclusion its confines are glowing in that Nature. Thus melding with Divine Name compliments Union with His Almighty. Since His Almighty has made us in His own image, we should be able to discern Him in the depth of our minds instead of staring in the void or starting with metaphysical abstractions or other verbal distinctions. The moment we listen to the phrase: 'His Almighty is Light, Sublime, Inspiring, Imposing, Majestic, Exalted, Virtuous and A Truth', we are vanquished in the beauty of it.

When a man who always has made a routine the utterance of His Almighty's blessed name "Allah,' Whose' company is he keeping? The Proximity is that of Allah but at times the fleshy stipulations of body supervene and one gets inadvertently indulged in misappropriation, but in determination to strive for His vindication. He seeks His Almighty's forgiveness with regret and remorse, compunction and contrition, submissiveness and subservience because no body can avoid the fleshy demands of the body like sensual regalements and glutinous flavor. Exoneration is His favored gesture, if we sincerely beg His favor at each moment of our sustenance. And when you especially aspire to sustain and succor the company with benison, blessing and benefaction of His Almighty, then late hours of the night is the best time to converse with Him directly without any encumbrance and transitional reference. Sit comfortably on the prayer rug after ablution or on any immaculate place. Look towards your heart and start reciting the most venerated Name 'Allah' as you exhale. After a few moments you will experience an echo from the core of your heart that will couple you in your beatified monologue. After a few minutes of true meditation the vistas of the whole will start opening up and you will feel an enchantment, elation and exaltation, calmness and composure, appeasement and affiliation never experienced before in life. At that moment have a sincere desire in the niche and kernel of your inaccessible self without interrupting the dazzling utterance? Be convinced that you will be blessed with your cherished aspiration if it is in your finest consequence, because His Almighty has created us a part of the whole and not as an unconstrained being. And to appropriate in the whole, one has to be comfortable as part of the whole. Figuratively speaking if every body enters upon demanding to thaw the highest point, how could that be possible, but to aspire for, wish and want for something before His Almighty is not proscribed.

When we actually discern the ecstasy through Vision while recounting the Holy Name, we instinctively feel that His Almighty Allah can bestow us the significance and consequence, eminence and prominence of our lives. This evanescent and fleeting illumination or edification is gone when we totter and stumble back to our run-of-the-mill frame of mind with our brains obsessed with the conventional earthy seductive femme fatale and possessions. Try as we might the same pacification, peacefulness the moment of inarticulate and reticent aspiration can not be accomplished.

Yes! The Bliss of Solitude, the Inner Murmur of Fortitude and the Vision of Gratitude could only be cherished and perceived with persistence, patience and perseverance in obeisance with His Almighty.

All things, which participate in anything, which is common to them all, move towards that which is of the same kind with them-selves. Everything which is earthy turns towards the earth, everything which is liquid flows together, and everything which is of an aerial kind does the same, so that they require something to keep them in bits and pieces, and the utilization of energy.

Correspondingly, then everything, which partakes in the common reasonable nature moves in like manner towards that which is of the same kind with itself. The ultimate objective of all reasoned doctrine is to live conformably to Nature, both a man's own nature and the nature of the universe. Prophet Mohammed [PBUH] ordained living according to Nature in the light, track and trail of true faith. If we look at the history, we find what the Greek philosophers meant when they spoke in a style and guise of eloquence, not imprecise or inconclusive, but distinct unbiased and undistorted.

The mankind has a mortal or earthy, brainy and virtuous disposition appropriate for determined application, and on the whole man accomplishes these uses during his stay before he leaves this vale. So community carries through to luxuriate. The social state is evidently the Natural State of man, the state for which his Nature implements him; and community surrounded by incalculable aberrations still survives. And conceivably we may say that the narrative of the former and our current enlightenment gives us a rational confidence that its disorderliness will dwindle, and that sequence, of its executive regulation, may be aggrandized and resolutely instituted.

We cannot envision how the command of the cosmos is continued. We cannot even visualize how our own vivacity from day to day is held up, nor how we accomplish the unsophisticated conduct of the body, nor how we develop and conceive and course, although we understand many of the basic factors. The fundamental incandescence assumes to gleam and entrance the mortal perception when he beholds on every side the Divine Endowments from speck to the vast expanse of the Universe, and instinctively one proclaims the benevolence and beneficence, magnanimity and munificence of His Almighty:

Which of the favors, you may deny of your Most
Exalted O Elevated Lord?
Blessed Be Thy Name O Great Grand O Glorious Lord

آياتها ٣٧ سورة الجاثية مكية (٤٥) (٦٥) ركوعاتها ٤

بِسْمِ اللّٰهِ الرَّحْمٰنِ الرَّحِيْمِ

شروع اللہ کے نام سے جو بڑا مہربان نہایت رحم والا ہے

حٰمٓ ①	حا۔میم ①
تَنْزِيْلُ الْكِتٰبِ مِنَ اللّٰهِ	نازل کی جارہی ہے یہ کتاب اللہ کی طرف سے
الْعَزِيْزِ الْحَكِيْمِ ②	جو زبردست اور بڑی حکمت والا ہے ②
اِنَّ فِي السَّمٰوٰتِ وَ الْاَرْضِ	حقیقت یہ ہے کہ آسمانوں اور زمین میں
لَاٰيٰتٍ لِّلْمُؤْمِنِيْنَ ③	بے شمار نشانیاں ہیں اہلِ ایمان کے لیے ③
وَ فِيْ خَلْقِكُمْ وَمَا يَبُثُّ	اور تمہاری اپنی پیدائش میں بھی اور یہ جو پھیلا رہا ہے وہ
مِنْ دَآبَّةٍ اٰيٰتٌ	جاندار (اس میں بھی) بہت سی نشانیاں ہیں
لِّقَوْمٍ يُّوْقِنُوْنَ ④	ان لوگوں کے لیے جو یقین رکھتے ہیں ④
وَاخْتِلَافِ الَّيْلِ وَ النَّهَارِ	اور رات اور دن کے ایک دوسرے کے پیچھے آنے جانے میں
وَمَآ اَنْزَلَ اللّٰهُ	اور یہ جو نازل فرماتا ہے اللہ
مِنَ السَّمَآءِ مِنْ رِّزْقٍ فَاَحْيَا	آسمان سے رزق (بارش) پھر زندہ کرتا ہے
بِهِ الْاَرْضَ بَعْدَ مَوْتِهَا	اس کے ذریعہ سے زمین کو، اس کے مردہ ہو جانے کے بعد
وَتَصْرِيْفِ الرِّيٰحِ اٰيٰتٌ	اور ہواؤں کی گردش میں بھی بہت سی نشانیاں ہیں
لِّقَوْمٍ يَّعْقِلُوْنَ ⑤	ان لوگوں کے لیے جو عقل سے کام لیتے ہیں ⑤
تِلْكَ اٰيٰتُ اللّٰهِ نَتْلُوْهَا	یہ اللہ کی آیات ہیں جن کی تلاوت کر رہے ہیں ہم

منزل ٦

045-AL JATHIYAH

In the name of Lord, the Most Beneficent, Most Merciful

001 Ha Mim.

002 Divination of Qur'an in stance
That's from Lord to glance
Exalted in Might
With Sense of Sapience so Bright

003 Indeed!
For the men and clan of faith in premise
In heavens and earth, are Signs so precise

004 And in your birth (so adoring in trail)
And for the cattle dispersed in vale
There're Signs to brace
For the men of Faith in pace

005 Swapping of night and the day in stride
And indeed Lord convey a word to aside

Provisions from the sky held in abide
That rouse and revive seared soil in dried

And the shift and drift of winds in gale
These are signs, men of sapience to avail

006 Such are Signs of Lord held in stance
We repeat to thee the in verity in just

عَلَيْكَ بِالْحَقِّ ۚ فَبِاَيِّ حَدِيْثٍۭ	تمہارے سامنے بالکل ٹھیک ٹھیک ۔ پھر آخر کس بات پر
بَعْدَ اللّٰهِ وَ اٰيٰتِهٖ يُؤْمِنُوْنَ ۝٦	اللہ اور اس کی آیات کو چھوڑ کر ایمان لائیں گے یہ لوگ ۝٦
وَيْلٌ لِّكُلِّ اَفَّاكٍ اَثِيْمٍ ۝٧	تباہی ہے ہر جھوٹے بداعمال شخص کے لیے ۝٧
يَّسْمَعُ اٰيٰتِ اللّٰهِ تُتْلٰى عَلَيْهِ	جو سنتا ہے اللہ کی آیات جو پڑھی جاتی ہیں اس کے سامنے
ثُمَّ يُصِرُّ مُسْتَكْبِرًا	پھر بھی اڑا رہتا ہے (اپنے کفر پر) تکبر کے ساتھ
كَاَنْ لَّمْ يَسْمَعْهَا ۚ	گویا کہ اس نے سنی ہی نہیں اللہ کی آیات
فَبَشِّرْهُ بِعَذَابٍ اَلِيْمٍ ۝٨	سو خوشخبری دے دو اسے دردناک عذاب کی ۝٨
وَاِذَا عَلِمَ مِنْ اٰيٰتِنَا	اور جب اس کے علم میں آتی ہے ہماری آیات میں سے
شَيْـًٔا اتَّخَذَهَا هُزُوًا ۭ	کوئی آیت تو اڑاتا ہے وہ اس کا مذاق ۔
اُولٰٓئِكَ لَهُمْ عَذَابٌ مُّهِيْنٌ ۝٩ ۭ	یہ وہ لوگ ہیں جن کے لیے ہے رسوا کن عذاب ۝٩
مِنْ وَّرَآئِهِمْ جَهَنَّمُ ۚ وَلَا يُغْنِيْ	ان کے آگے جہنم ہے اور نہ کام آئے گی
عَنْهُمْ مَّا كَسَبُوْا	ان کے کوئی چیز اس میں سے جو انہوں نے کمایا
شَيْـًٔا وَّلَا مَا اتَّخَذُوْا	ذرا بھی اور نہ وہ جنہیں بنا رکھا ہے انہوں نے
مِنْ دُوْنِ اللّٰهِ اَوْلِيَآءَ ۚ	اللہ کے سوا (اپنا) سرپرست (کام آئیں گے)
وَلَهُمْ عَذَابٌ عَظِيْمٌ ۝١٠ ۭ	اور ان کے لیے ہے عذاب عظیم ۝١٠
هٰذَا هُدًى ۚ وَالَّذِيْنَ	یہ (قرآن) سراسر ہدایت ہے اور وہ لوگ جنہوں نے
كَفَرُوْا بِاٰيٰتِ رَبِّهِمْ	انکار کر دیا ماننے سے اپنے رب کی آیات کو
لَهُمْ عَذَابٌ مِّنْ رِّجْزٍ اَلِيْمٌ ۝١١ ع	ان کے لیے ہے عذاب سخت دردناک ۝١١
اَللّٰهُ الَّذِيْ سَخَّرَ لَكُمُ	وہ اللہ ہی ہے جس نے مسخر کیا تمہارے لیے

Then, how'd they get to trust
After defying the Signs of Lord in gust

007 Woe be to each vile vendor of fib in stride

008 He heeds to the Signs of Lord in recite
Yet is callous and brazenly excited in slight

As if had not heard or perceived in plight
Reveal him a flagrant sentence in blight

009 And when he learns of Our Signs so seer
To that he takes a jest in jeer
For them,
There'll be scandalous Sentence in teer

010 Them to aside Hell pyre in tear
And of no gain in good to them in leer
Nor they adore a guard in smear

If ever they held other than Lord in peer
For them is a terrific torture in fear

011 That's the unfailing,
Counseling for them in concern
And those who defy,
The Signs Lord to discern
For them is atrocious aversion in term

012 O Man!
Bestowal of sea from Lord in urge
With endowment of sail in surge

الْبَحْرَ لِتَجْرِيَ الْفُلْكُ فِيهِ بِأَمْرِهِ
سمندر کو تاکہ چلیں کشتیاں اس میں اس کے حکم سے

وَلِتَبْتَغُوا مِنْ فَضْلِهِ
اور تاکہ تم تلاش کرو اس کا فضل

وَلَعَلَّكُمْ تَشْكُرُونَ ﴿١٢﴾
اور تاکہ تم شکر گزار بنو ﴿١٢﴾

وَسَخَّرَ لَكُمْ مَا فِي السَّمَاوَاتِ
اور مسخر کر دی ہیں اس نے تمہارے لیے وہ چیزیں جو آسمانوں میں ہیں

وَمَا فِي الْأَرْضِ جَمِيعًا مِنْهُ
اور جو زمین میں ہیں سب کی سب اپنی طرف سے۔

إِنَّ فِي ذَٰلِكَ لَآيَاتٍ
بلا شبہ ان باتوں میں بے شمار نشانیاں ہیں

لِقَوْمٍ يَتَفَكَّرُونَ ﴿١٣﴾
ان لوگوں کے لیے جو غور و فکر کرتے ہیں ﴿١٣﴾

قُلْ لِلَّذِينَ آمَنُوا يَغْفِرُوا
اے نبی کہہ دیجیے ان سے جو ایمان لا چکے ہیں کہ درگزر سے کام لیں

لِلَّذِينَ لَا يَرْجُونَ
ان لوگوں کے بارے میں جو کوئی اندیشہ نہیں رکھتے

أَيَّامَ اللَّهِ لِيَجْزِيَ
اللہ کی طرف سے برے دن آنے کا ۔ تاکہ خود بدلہ دے اللہ

قَوْمًا بِمَا كَانُوا يَكْسِبُونَ ﴿١٤﴾
ان لوگوں کو ان اعمال کا جو وہ کماتے رہے ﴿١٤﴾

مَنْ عَمِلَ صَالِحًا فَلِنَفْسِهِ
جو شخص کرتا ہے نیک عمل سو وہ اپنے ہی لیے کرتا ہے

وَمَنْ أَسَاءَ فَعَلَيْهَا
اور جو برے کام کرتا ہے اس کا نقصان اسی کو پہنچتا ہے۔

ثُمَّ إِلَىٰ رَبِّكُمْ تُرْجَعُونَ ﴿١٥﴾
پھر اپنے رب کی طرف لوٹائے جاؤ گے تم ﴿١٥﴾

وَلَقَدْ آتَيْنَا بَنِي إِسْرَائِيلَ
اور واقعہ یہ ہے کہ عطا کی تھی ہم نے بنی اسرائیل کو

الْكِتَابَ وَالْحُكْمَ وَالنُّبُوَّةَ
کتاب اور حکم اور نبوت

وَرَزَقْنَاهُمْ مِنَ الطَّيِّبَاتِ
اور نوازا تھا ہم نے انہیں پاکیزہ چیزوں سے

وَفَضَّلْنَاهُمْ عَلَى الْعَالَمِينَ ﴿١٦﴾
اور فضیلت دی تھی ہم نے انہیں دنیا بھر کے لوگوں پر ﴿١٦﴾

وَآتَيْنَاهُمْ بَيِّنَاتٍ مِنَ الْأَمْرِ
اور دی تھیں ہم نے انہیں واضح ہدایات دین کے معاملہ میں۔

That you may trend His Bounty to brace
And be appreciative of His Boons in place

013 All in heavens and hither in vale
Subjected to your trends in trail
Behold!
There're Signs from Lord in Grace
All who trend to Mercy to brace

014 Tell the men,
Who give credence to faith in abide
To condone the men in beside

Who don't concern in faith
The days so dire from Lord in place

It's for Lord to amend in stance
Good and evil hither in trance
For what they accomplished in glance

015 If one trends to truth in pace
It asserts to serve his soul in grace
If he trends to evil in place

It's for his soul,
To bear the burnt in stance
Finally,
You'll return to Lord in glance

016 We gifted the Book hither in fore
To the progeny of Israel in lore
With might in command
And Prophet-hood in stance

We endowed provisions in score
With things precious and pure to secure
We preferred over other clan in adore

017 And We gifted them lucid Signs in drill
It's only after the sapience of lore in thrill

فَمَا اخْتَلَفُوْٓا اِلَّا مِنْۢ بَعْدِ	سو نہیں اختلاف کیا انہوں نے باہم مگر اس کے بعد
مَا جَآءَهُمُ الْعِلْمُ ۙ بَغْيًۢا بَيْنَهُمْ ۭ	کہ آگیا تھا ان کے پاس علم ایک دوسرے کی ضد میں ۔
اِنَّ رَبَّكَ يَقْضِيْ بَيْنَهُمْ	بلا شبہ تیرا رب فیصلہ فرمائے گا ان کے درمیان
يَوْمَ الْقِيٰمَةِ فِيْمَا	قیامت کے دن ان معاملات کا
كَانُوْا فِيْهِ يَخْتَلِفُوْنَ ﴿١٧﴾	جن میں وہ اختلاف کرتے رہے ﴿١٧﴾
ثُمَّ جَعَلْنٰكَ عَلٰي شَرِيْعَةٍ	اس کے بعد اے نبیؐ قائم کیا ہے ہم نے تمہیں ایک کھلے راستے پر
مِّنَ الْاَمْرِ فَاتَّبِعْهَا وَلَا تَتَّبِعْ	دین کے معاملہ میں ۔ سو تم اسی پر چلو اور نہ اتباع کرو
اَهْوَاۗءَ الَّذِيْنَ لَا يَعْلَمُوْنَ ﴿١٨﴾	ان لوگوں کی خواہشات کا جو علم نہیں رکھتے ﴿١٨﴾
اِنَّهُمْ لَنْ يُّغْنُوْا عَنْكَ مِنَ اللّٰهِ	یقیناً یہ لوگ کچھ کام نہیں آسکتے تمہارے اللہ کے مقابلہ میں
شَيْـــًٔا ۭ وَاِنَّ الظّٰلِمِيْنَ	ذرا بھی ۔ اور بے شک ظالم لوگ
بَعْضُهُمْ اَوْلِيَاۗءُ بَعْضٍ ۚ وَاللّٰهُ	باہم ایک دوسرے کے ساتھی ہیں اور اللہ
وَلِيُّ الْمُتَّقِيْنَ ﴿١٩﴾	حامی و مددگار ہے متقیوں کا ﴿١٩﴾
هٰذَا بَصَاۗىِٕرُ لِلنَّاسِ	یہ بصیرت کی روشنیاں ہیں سب انسانوں کے لیے
وَهُدًى وَّرَحْمَةٌ لِّقَوْمٍ يُّوْقِنُوْنَ ﴿٢٠﴾	اور ہدایت و رحمت ہے ان لوگوں کے لیے جو یقین رکھتے ہیں ﴿٢٠﴾
اَمْ حَسِبَ الَّذِيْنَ اجْتَرَحُوا	کیا سمجھے بیٹھے ہیں وہ لوگ جنہوں نے ارتکاب کیا ہے
السَّيِّاٰتِ اَنْ نَّجْعَلَهُمْ كَالَّذِيْنَ	برائیوں کا کہ ہم کر دیں گے انہیں مانند ان لوگوں کے جو
اٰمَنُوْا وَعَمِلُوا الصّٰلِحٰتِ ۙ	ایمان لائے اور کیے جنہوں نے نیک عمل
سَوَاۗءً مَّحْيَاهُمْ وَمَمَاتُهُمْ ۭ	کہ یکساں ہو جائے ان دونوں گروہوں کی زندگی اور موت؟
سَاۗءَ مَا يَحْكُمُوْنَ ﴿٢١﴾ ع	بہت برا ہے وہ حکم جو یہ لگاتے ہیں ﴿٢١﴾

They diced to split in place
With impertinent spite mid them in slight
Lord to decide on Day of Sagacity in sight
The concerns of divergence* held in stride
*a cause of divide mid them

018 Then We put you,
On a determined course in conduct
So follow the dictum of faith in instruct

But don't trend to the way in adore
The men,
Who don't have a bit of know in lore

019 For you,
They wouldn't be of any worth in call
Keeping view of Lord
It's only the base in instruct
Who poise to protect each in select
But Lord is Guardian of devout in fact

020 That's the clear signs for the men to brace
And trend in Escort and His Mercy in pace
For the men and clan of faith in place

021 What!
Those who chase and chance evil in trends
Deem to discern in concern
That!
We'll be like of those in amends

Who trust in faith and have the discipline in right
Equal will be their life and death in plight
Poor is the whim, they decide in slight

وَخَلَقَ اللّٰهُ السَّمٰوٰتِ وَالْاَرْضَ	اور پیدا فرمایا ہے اللہ نے آسمانوں کو اور زمین کو
بِالْحَقِّ وَلِتُجْزٰى كُلُّ نَفْسٍ	برحق اور اس لیے کہ بدلہ دیا جائے ہر متنفس کو
بِمَا كَسَبَتْ وَهُمْ لَا يُظْلَمُوْنَ ﴿۲۲﴾	اس کی کمائی کا اور لوگوں پر ہرگز ظلم نہ کیا جائے گا ﴿۲۲﴾
اَفَرَءَيْتَ مَنِ اتَّخَذَ	کیا پھر غور کیا ہے تم نے اس شخص کے حال پر جس نے بنالیا ہے
اِلٰهَهٗ هَوٰىهُ وَاَضَلَّهُ	اپنا معبود اپنی خواہش نفس کو اور گمراہ کر دیا ہے اسے
اللّٰهُ عَلٰى عِلْمٍ وَّخَتَمَ عَلٰى سَمْعِهٖ	اللہ نے علم کے باوجود اور مہر لگا دی ہے اس کے کانوں پر
وَقَلْبِهٖ وَجَعَلَ عَلٰى بَصَرِهٖ غِشٰوَةً ؕ	اور دل پر اور ڈال دیا ہے اس کی آنکھوں پر پردہ ؟
فَمَنْ يَّهْدِيْهِ مِنْ بَعْدِ اللّٰهِ ؕ	سو کون ہے جو ہدایت دے اسے اللہ کے (گمراہ کر دینے کے) بعد؟
اَفَلَا تَذَكَّرُوْنَ ﴿۲۳﴾	کیا تم لوگ کوئی سبق نہیں لیتے ؟ ﴿۲۳﴾
وَقَالُوْا مَا هِيَ اِلَّا	اور کہتے ہیں یہ لوگ کہ نہیں ہے زندگی مگر
حَيَاتُنَا الدُّنْيَا نَمُوْتُ وَنَحْيَا	یہی ہماری دنیاوی زندگی یہیں، مرتے ہیں ہم اور زندہ رہتے ہیں
وَمَا يُهْلِكُنَاۤ اِلَّا الدَّهْرُ ۚ	اور نہیں ہلاک کرتی ہمیں مگر گردش ایام۔
وَمَا لَهُمْ بِذٰلِكَ مِنْ عِلْمٍ ۚ	حالانکہ نہیں ہے انہیں اس بات کا ذرا بھی علم۔
اِنْ هُمْ اِلَّا يَظُنُّوْنَ ﴿۲۴﴾	یہ محض گمان سے کام لیتے ہیں ﴿۲۴﴾
وَاِذَا تُتْلٰى عَلَيْهِمْ اٰيٰتُنَا بَيِّنٰتٍ	اور جب پڑھ کر سنائی جاتی ہیں انہیں ہماری واضح آیات
مَّا كَانَ حُجَّتَهُمْ اِلَّاۤ اَنْ	تو نہیں ہوتی ہے ان کی حجت مگر یہ کہ
قَالُوا ائْتُوْا بِاٰبَآئِنَاۤ	کہتے ہیں کہ اٹھا لاؤ ہمارے باپ دادا کو،
اِنْ كُنْتُمْ صٰدِقِيْنَ ﴿۲۵﴾	اگر ہو تم سچے ﴿۲۵﴾
قُلِ اللّٰهُ يُحْيِيْكُمْ	ان سے کہیے اللہ ہی زندگی بخشتا ہے تمہیں

022 Lord!
Created heavens and earth in elegant design
So one may find amends in (logical) consign

What he deserved in pace
And none be persecuted in trace
Beyond his done and doings in pace

023 Did you concern a man in vale
Who cherishes his lust as god in trail

Lord discerns him quite well in trace
And let him drift in futile surge in pace

Secured his hearing and core to discern
And sheathed his sight to concern

Who's then to escort (him) in daze
When Lord deserted him to stray in haze
Wouldn't you abide admonition in phase

024 And they trend to utter and relate
What?
A term in vale, the only affirmed in state

For that's the only determined term in trail
We'll die in doom and live in bloom
Nothing but only the time to consume
Our doom of destiny in boom

But of all they've no sight and spot in lore
They simply trend to presume in core

025 And when Our Clear signs are set to relate
They've nothing to assert but trend to debate

Get back our fathers* once more to aside
If you're really true to your word in stride

- they say if you're really true to your word then bring back our forefathers back to life

026 Say:
It's Lord to give life and death in doom
And to Him we beg and beseech in pray

ثُمَّ يُمِيتُكُمْ ثُمَّ يَجْمَعُكُمْ — پھر وہی تمہیں موت دیتا ہے پھر وہی جمع کرے گا تمہیں

إِلَىٰ يَوْمِ الْقِيَامَةِ لَا رَيْبَ فِيهِ — قیامت کے دن، کہ نہیں ہے کوئی شک اس کے آنے میں

وَلَٰكِنَّ أَكْثَرَ النَّاسِ لَا يَعْلَمُونَ ﴿٢٦﴾ — مگر اکثر انسان نہیں جانتے ﴿٢٦﴾

وَلِلَّهِ مُلْكُ السَّمَاوَاتِ وَالْأَرْضِ — اور اللہ ہی کے لیے ہے بادشاہی آسمانوں کی اور زمین کی۔

وَيَوْمَ تَقُومُ السَّاعَةُ يَوْمَئِذٍ — اور جس دن آ کھڑی ہو گی گھڑی قیامت کی اس دن

يَخْسَرُ الْمُبْطِلُونَ ﴿٢٧﴾ — خسارے میں پڑ جائیں گے باطل پرست لوگ ﴿٢٧﴾

وَتَرَىٰ كُلَّ أُمَّةٍ جَاثِيَةً — اور دیکھو گے تم ہر گروہ کو گھٹنوں کے بل گرا ہوا۔

كُلُّ أُمَّةٍ تُدْعَىٰ إِلَىٰ كِتَابِهَا — ہر گروہ کو پکارا جائے گا کہ آئے اور اپنا اعمال نامہ دیکھے۔

الْيَوْمَ تُجْزَوْنَ مَا كُنْتُمْ تَعْمَلُونَ ﴿٢٨﴾ — آج بدلہ دیا جائے گا تمہیں ان اعمال کا جو تم کرتے رہے ﴿٢٨﴾

هَٰذَا كِتَابُنَا يَنْطِقُ عَلَيْكُمْ — یہ ہے ہماری تحریر جو گواہی دے رہی ہے تمہارے اوپر

بِالْحَقِّ ۚ إِنَّا كُنَّا نَسْتَنْسِخُ — بالکل ٹھیک ٹھیک۔ یقیناً ہم لکھواتے جا رہے تھے

مَا كُنْتُمْ تَعْمَلُونَ ﴿٢٩﴾ — وہ تمام اعمال جو تم کیا کرتے تھے ﴿٢٩﴾

فَأَمَّا الَّذِينَ آمَنُوا وَعَمِلُوا الصَّالِحَاتِ — پھر وہ لوگ جو ایمان لائے اور کیے انہوں نے نیک عمل

فَيُدْخِلُهُمْ رَبُّهُمْ فِي رَحْمَتِهِ ۚ — سو داخل کرے گا انہیں تو ان کا رب اپنی رحمت میں۔

ذَٰلِكَ هُوَ الْفَوْزُ الْمُبِينُ ﴿٣٠﴾ — یہی ہے کھلی کامیابی ﴿٣٠﴾

وَأَمَّا الَّذِينَ كَفَرُوا — رہے وہ لوگ جنہوں نے کفر کیا۔ (ان سے کہا جائے گا):

أَفَلَمْ تَكُنْ آيَاتِي تُتْلَىٰ عَلَيْكُمْ — کیا یہ حقیقت نہیں ہے کہ میری آیات پڑھی جاتی تھیں تمہارے سامنے

فَاسْتَكْبَرْتُمْ وَكُنْتُمْ قَوْمًا مُجْرِمِينَ ﴿٣١﴾ — اور تم تکبر کیا کرتے تھے۔ اور بن کر رہے تم لوگ مجرم ﴿٣١﴾

وَإِذَا قِيلَ إِنَّ وَعْدَ اللَّهِ حَقٌّ — اور جب کہا جاتا تھا کہ اللہ کا وعدہ سچا ہے

He'll assemble you on the Day of Demand
Of which there's no scruple in stance
But quite a few don't discern in trance

027 To Him belongs heavens and earth in pace
And Day of Dictum of Dictate in place

That Day sellers of fiction in soul
Will doom in gloom and perish in whole

028 And you'll then concern in sight
All the sects of the clans in blight
Down to knee in plight

Then all the sects will be called to trend
To their done and doings in spend

The Day you'll be compensated in pace
For all your done and doings in trace

029 For you!
Our Record tells of verity in decision
For We held your trends in precision

030 Then those who held faith in grace
And sustained truthful deeds in pace
To them!
Lord will concede His Bounty in proceeds
That's the pre-eminence for all to perceive

031 But who defied dictum of Lord in trends
They'll be affirmed in amends

If Our Signs weren't drilled in stance
But O conceit, you never cared in trance

And you're of the sinful men in span
Responsible of your evils in plan

032 And when it was asserted to place
That pledge of Lord true to brace

وَّ السَّاعَةُ لَا رَيْبَ فِيْهَا	اور قیامت، نہیں ہے کچھ شک اس کے آنے میں۔
قُلْتُمْ مَّا نَدْرِيْ مَا السَّاعَةُ	تو تم کہتے تھے ہم نہیں جانتے کہ قیامت کیا ہے؟
اِنْ نَّظُنُّ اِلَّا ظَنًّا	ہمیں تو بس ایک گمان سا گزرتا تھا
وَّمَا نَحْنُ بِمُسْتَيْقِنِيْنَ ﴿٣٢﴾	اور ہم کوئی بات یقین سے نہیں کہہ سکتے تھے ﴿٣٢﴾
وَبَدَا لَهُمْ سَيِّاٰتُ مَا عَمِلُوْا وَحَاقَ	اور کھل جائیں گی ان پر برائیاں ان کے اعمال کی اور مسلط ہو جائے گی
بِهِمْ مَّا كَانُوْا بِهٖ يَسْتَهْزِءُوْنَ ﴿٣٣﴾	ان پر وہی چیز جس کا وہ مذاق اڑایا کرتے تھے ﴿٣٣﴾
وَقِيْلَ الْيَوْمَ نَنْسٰىكُمْ كَمَا	اور کہا جائے گا آج بھلائے دیتے ہیں ہم تمہیں اسی طرح
نَسِيْتُمْ لِقَآءَ يَوْمِكُمْ هٰذَا وَمَاْوٰىكُمُ	جیسے تم بھول گئے تھے اپنے اس دن کی پیشی کو اور تمہارا ٹھکانا
النَّارُ وَمَا لَكُمْ مِّنْ نّٰصِرِيْنَ ﴿٣٤﴾	جہنم ہے اور نہیں ہوگا تمہارا کوئی مددگار ﴿٣٤﴾
ذٰلِكُمْ بِاَنَّكُمُ اتَّخَذْتُمْ	تمہارا یہ انجام اس بنا پر ہے کہ بنا لیا تھا تم نے
اٰيٰتِ اللّٰهِ هُزُوًا وَّغَرَّتْكُمُ	اللہ کی آیات کو مذاق اور دھوکے میں ڈال دیا تھا تم کو
الْحَيٰوةُ الدُّنْيَا ۚ فَالْيَوْمَ لَا يُخْرَجُوْنَ	دنیاوی زندگی نے سو اس دن نہ نکالے جائیں گے وہ
مِنْهَا وَلَا هُمْ يُسْتَعْتَبُوْنَ ﴿٣٥﴾	جہنم میں سے اور نہ ان کی توبہ قبول کی جائے گی ﴿٣٥﴾
فَلِلّٰهِ الْحَمْدُ	سو اللہ ہی کے لیے ہے تمام حمد و شکر
رَبِّ السَّمٰوٰتِ وَرَبِّ الْاَرْضِ	جو مالک ہے آسمانوں کا اور رب ہے زمین کا،
رَبِّ الْعٰلَمِيْنَ ﴿٣٦﴾	وہی پروردگار ہے سارے جہان والوں کا ﴿٣٦﴾
وَلَهُ الْكِبْرِيَآءُ	اسی کو سزاوار ہے بڑائی
فِي السَّمٰوٰتِ وَالْاَرْضِ	آسمانوں میں اور زمین میں
وَهُوَ الْعَزِيْزُ الْحَكِيْمُ ﴿٣٧﴾	اور وہ ہے زبردست اور بڑی حکمت والا ﴿٣٧﴾

And Hour,
With no scruple and suspense in lore
You used to assert in place
We don't discern in pace

What's the Hour of Concern in trace
We hold it as a glimpse of notion in stance
But we don't have a bit of assertion in glance

033 They'll discern to concern in trail
Their doings of evil, hither in vale

And they'll be fully girdled in pace
For what they jeered in place

034 That Day they'll be told in plight
This Day,
We'll forget (you) in slight
As you slighted The Day, in Blight

And your abide is Hell Pyre to reside
There's none to aid and abet in stride

035 It's for your dubious trends in trip
For you jeered Signs of Lord in slip
And the lust of vale seduced (you) in dip

So they,
Wouldn't be relieved of the Fire in grasp
Nor they'll be favored a bit in clasp

036 All acclaim and Adulation for The Lord in sway
Who's The lord of heavens and earth in array
Lord, Who sustains all the Worlds in display

037 To Him is the Pomp and Praise in adore
Of all the heavens and earth in score
And He's Exalted in Might
Full of Sapience in lore

سُوْرَةُ الْاَحْقَافِ مَكِّيَّةٌ (۴۶) (۶۶)

اٰيَاتُهَا ۳۵ — رُكُوْعَاتُهَا ۴

بِسْمِ اللّٰهِ الرَّحْمٰنِ الرَّحِيْمِ

شروع اللہ کے نام سے جو بڑا مہربان نہایت رحم والا ہے

حٰمٓ ۞ ۱	حا۔میم ۱
تَنْزِيْلُ الْكِتٰبِ مِنَ اللّٰهِ	نازل کی جا رہی ہے یہ کتاب اللہ کی طرف سے
الْعَزِيْزِ الْحَكِيْمِ ۲	جو ہے زبردست اور بڑی حکمت والا ۲
مَا خَلَقْنَا السَّمٰوٰتِ وَالْاَرْضَ	نہیں پیدا فرمایا ہم نے آسمانوں کو اور زمین کو
وَمَا بَيْنَهُمَا اِلَّا بِالْحَقِّ	اور ان چیزوں کو جو ان دونوں کے درمیان ہیں مگر برحق،
وَاَجَلٍ مُّسَمًّى ط وَالَّذِيْنَ	اور ایک وقتِ مقرر کے لیے لیکن وہ لوگ جنہوں نے
كَفَرُوْا عَمَّآ	انکار کر دیا ہے ماننے سے اس (حقیقت) کے جس سے
اُنْذِرُوْا مُعْرِضُوْنَ ۳	انہیں ڈرایا جا رہا ہے وہ منہ موڑے ہوئے ہیں ۳
قُلْ اَرَءَيْتُمْ مَّا تَدْعُوْنَ	(اے نبیؐ) ان سے کہو! کبھی تم نے سوچا کہ یہ جنہیں تم پکارتے ہو
مِنْ دُوْنِ اللّٰهِ اَرُوْنِيْ مَاذَا خَلَقُوْا	اللہ کے سوا مجھے دکھاؤ کیا پیدا کیا ہے انہوں نے
مِنَ الْاَرْضِ اَمْ لَهُمْ شِرْكٌ	زمین میں یا ہے ان کی کوئی شرکت
فِي السَّمٰوٰتِ ط اِيْتُوْنِيْ	آسمانوں (کی تخلیق و تدبیر) میں؟ لاؤ میرے پاس
بِكِتٰبٍ مِّنْ قَبْلِ هٰذَآ	کوئی کتاب جو آئی ہو اس سے پہلے
اَوْ اَثٰرَةٍ مِّنْ عِلْمٍ اِنْ كُنْتُمْ صٰدِقِيْنَ ۴	یا کوئی علمی روایت (بطورِ ثبوت) اگر ہو تم سچے ۴
وَمَنْ اَضَلُّ مِمَّنْ يَّدْعُوْا	اور کون زیادہ گمراہ ہے اس شخص سے جو پکارے

046-AL AHQAF

In the name of Lord, the Most Beneficent, Most Merciful

001 Ha Mim.

002 Qur'an a divination of Lord in pace
Astral in Might with Sapience in grace

003 We created heavens and earth in sway
And also between the cosmic array

But for the just and resolute term in trace
But there are some, who reject in faith
And elude augury and admonition in pace

This Verse clearly elucidates the time determined for the Universes: See page-1264

004 O Muhammad!
Do you see,
What's that they created in land
Or had a share of heavens in plan

Bring me a Book divulged hither in fore
Or a bit of lore you held in score
If you're true to your word in adore

005 Who's more adrift in stray
Who begs to obey

مِنْ دُوْنِ اللّٰهِ مَنْ لَّا يَسْتَجِيْبُ لَهٗٓ	اللہ کے سوا انہیں جو نہیں جواب دے سکتے اسے
اِلٰى يَوْمِ الْقِيٰمَةِ وَهُمْ	قیامت تک بلکہ وہ تو
عَنْ دُعَآئِهِمْ غٰفِلُوْنَ ۵	ان کی پکار سے بھی بے خبر ہیں ۵
وَاِذَا حُشِرَ النَّاسُ كَانُوْا لَهُمْ اَعْدَآءً	اور جب اکٹھے کیے جائیں گے سب انسان تو ہوں گے یہ (معبود) ان کے دشمن
وَّكَانُوْا بِعِبَادَتِهِمْ كٰفِرِيْنَ ۶	اور ہو جائیں گے ان کی عبادت سے منکر ۶
وَاِذَا تُتْلٰى عَلَيْهِمْ اٰيٰتُنَا	اور جب سنائی جاتی ہیں ان کو ہماری آیات
بَيِّنٰتٍ قَالَ الَّذِيْنَ كَفَرُوْا	جو صاف اور واضح ہیں تو کہتے ہیں یہ لوگ جنہوں نے کفر کیا ہے
لِلْحَقِّ لَمَّا جَآءَهُمْ ۙ	حق کے بارے میں، جب بھی وہ ان کے سامنے آتا ہے
هٰذَا سِحْرٌ مُّبِيْنٌ ۷	کہ یہ کھلا جادو ہے ۷
اَمْ يَقُوْلُوْنَ افْتَرٰىهُ ۭ	کیا یہ کہتے ہیں کہ خود گھڑ لیا ہے اس رسول نے یہ قرآن؟
قُلْ اِنِ افْتَرَيْتُهٗ	ان سے کہیے اگر خود گھڑ لیا ہے میں نے اسے
فَلَا تَمْلِكُوْنَ لِيْ مِنَ اللّٰهِ شَيْـًٔا ۭ	تو نہیں بچا سکو گے تم مجھے اللہ کی پکڑ سے ذرا بھی۔
هُوَ اَعْلَمُ بِمَا تُفِيْضُوْنَ فِيْهِ ۭ	وہ بہتر جانتا ہے ان باتوں کو جو تم بنا رہے ہو اس کے بارے میں۔
كَفٰى بِهٖ شَهِيْدًۢا بَيْنِيْ وَبَيْنَكُمْ ۭ	کافی ہے اللہ کی گواہی میرے اور تمہارے درمیان۔
وَهُوَ الْغَفُوْرُ الرَّحِيْمُ ۸	اور وہی ہے معاف فرمانے والا اور ہر حال میں رحم کرنے والا ۸
قُلْ مَا كُنْتُ بِدْعًا مِّنَ الرُّسُلِ	ان سے کہیے نہیں ہوں میں کوئی نرالا رسول
وَمَآ اَدْرِيْ مَا يُفْعَلُ بِيْ	اور مجھے نہیں معلوم کہ کیا کیا جائے گا میرے ساتھ
وَلَا بِكُمْ ۭ اِنْ اَتَّبِعُ	اور نہ (وہ جو کیا جائے گا) تمہارے ساتھ؛ نہیں پیروی کرتا میں
اِلَّا مَا يُوْحٰٓى اِلَيَّ وَمَآ اَنَا	مگر اس وحی کو جو بھیجی جاتی ہے میری طرف اور نہیں ہوں میں

Other than Lord in pray
Who wouldn't return his call in entreat
Till The Day of Culmination in treat
Indeed!
They'll be insentient of their cry in beseech

006 And when all the men and clan
Will get to assemble in plan
On the Day of Revival affirmed in span

They'll be quite resentful (of them) in place
And refuse their worship altogether in pace

007 When Our,
Obvious Signs are voiced (to them) in preach
The Infidels then speak and repeat

Of the truth that's for them to concern
They say:
That's but a conjuring in term

008 Or do they repeat to speak:
He's milled and tamped in treat
Say:
Had I trodden at my own in accord
Then you cannot secure a favor in assort
From the Discipline of My Lord in part

For He senses to the best in stride
For what you talk close and beside
Lord is enough mid us to decide

And He is Most Clement in sway
And Most Compassionate in array

009 Say:
I'm not a new of the messengers in pace
Nor do I know in place
Karma or kismet of me or you in trace

إِلَّا نَذِيرٌ مُّبِينٌ ۝٩	مگر صاف صاف خبردار کرنے والا ۝٩
قُلْ أَرَءَيْتُمْ إِن كَانَ مِنْ عِندِ ٱللَّهِ	ان سے کہیے کبھی تم نے سوچا کہ اگر ہو یہ اللہ کی طرف سے
وَكَفَرْتُم بِهِۦ	اور انکار کر دیا تم نے اس کا (تو تمہارا انجام کیا ہوگا؟)
وَشَهِدَ شَاهِدٌ مِّنۢ بَنِىٓ إِسْرَٰٓءِيلَ	جبکہ گواہی دے چکا ہے ایک گواہ بنی اسرائیل میں سے
عَلَىٰ مِثْلِهِۦ فَـَٔامَنَ وَٱسْتَكْبَرْتُمْ	اسی جیسے کلام پر چنانچہ وہ ایمان لے آیا مگر تم اپنے گھمنڈ میں پڑے رہے
إِنَّ ٱللَّهَ لَا يَهْدِى ٱلْقَوْمَ ٱلظَّٰلِمِينَ ۝١٠ ع	بلاشبہ اللہ نہیں راہ دکھاتا ظالم لوگوں کو ۝١٠
وَقَالَ ٱلَّذِينَ كَفَرُوا۟	اور کہتے ہیں یہ لوگ جنہوں نے ماننے سے انکار کر دیا ہے
لِلَّذِينَ ءَامَنُوا۟ لَوْ كَانَ خَيْرًا	ان لوگوں سے جو ایمان لے آئے ہیں کہ اگر ہوتا یہ کوئی اچھا کام
مَّا سَبَقُونَآ إِلَيْهِ ۚ وَإِذْ لَمْ يَهْتَدُوا۟	تو نہ سبقت لے جاتے یہ لوگ ہم پر اب چونکہ یہ نہ ہدایت پا سکے
بِهِۦ فَسَيَقُولُونَ هَٰذَآ إِفْكٌ قَدِيمٌ ۝١١	اس سے تو ضرور کہیں گے یہ تو پرانی من گھڑت باتیں ہیں ۝١١
وَمِن قَبْلِهِۦ كِتَٰبُ مُوسَىٰٓ إِمَامًا	حالانکہ اس سے پہلے (آ چکی ہے) موسیٰ کی کتاب رہنما
وَرَحْمَةً ۚ وَهَٰذَا كِتَٰبٌ مُّصَدِّقٌ	اور رحمت بن کر اور یہ کتاب تصدیق کر رہی ہے (اس کی)
لِّسَانًا عَرَبِيًّا لِّيُنذِرَ ٱلَّذِينَ	(اور نازل کی گئی ہے) زبانِ عربی میں تاکہ متنبہ کرے ان لوگوں کو جو
ظَلَمُوا۟ وَبُشْرَىٰ لِلْمُحْسِنِينَ ۝١٢	ظلم کر رہے ہیں اور بشارت دے اچھا اور معیاری کام کرنے والوں کو ۝١٢
إِنَّ ٱلَّذِينَ قَالُوا۟ رَبُّنَا ٱللَّهُ	یقیناً وہ لوگ جنہوں نے کہا ہمارا رب تو اللہ ہے
ثُمَّ ٱسْتَقَٰمُوا۟ فَلَا خَوْفٌ	پھر جم گئے (اس پر) تو نہیں ہے کوئی خوف
عَلَيْهِمْ وَلَا هُمْ يَحْزَنُونَ ۝١٣	ان کے لیے اور نہ وہ غمگین ہوں گے ۝١٣
أُو۟لَٰٓئِكَ أَصْحَٰبُ ٱلْجَنَّةِ خَٰلِدِينَ فِيهَا	ایسے لوگ جنتی ہیں جو ہمیشہ رہیں گے اس میں۔
جَزَآءًۢ بِمَا كَانُوا۟ يَعْمَلُونَ ۝١٤	بدلے میں ان اعمال کے جو وہ کرتے رہے ۝١٤

I conform that's divulged to me in glow
I'm but to apprise lucid drill in endow

010 Say:
Don't you concern word in preach
If it's really from Lord in treat
That you trend to defy in conceit
What's going to be your plight in deceit
When one from progeny of Israel in abide
Has affirmed like of this in stride
And he's consistent to aside
Whereas in vanity you defy to deplore
Indeed!
Lord escorts not the unjust in lore

011 Dissenters then voice:
To the men of faith, who affirm to conclude
If this Missive was good in prelude
We would be the first to affirm to include
Perceiving!
They've nothing to steer in conduct
They'll say:
That's but a style and stigma in instruct
And an old fib in construct

012 Hither in fore,
There's Book of Moses, an escort in conduct
A compassion in lore:
And this Book settles Arabic in dialect
To caution the prejudiced in core
And tidings in good, who're just in instruct

013 Verily!
Who assert and affirm in grace
Our Lord is Allah, and stay firm in pace
For them there's no fear in trace
Nor to grieve in place

014 Such will be fellows of Gardens in Grace
Abiding therein amends
For dutiful conduct in pace

وَوَصَّيْنَا الْإِنْسَانَ بِوَالِدَيْهِ	اور ہدایت کی ہے ہم نے انسان کو اپنے والدین کے ساتھ
إِحْسَانًا ۖ حَمَلَتْهُ	اچھے سلوک کی۔ اٹھائے رکھا اسے (اپنے پیٹ میں)
أُمُّهُ كُرْهًا وَوَضَعَتْهُ كُرْهًا ۖ	اس کی ماں نے مشقت اٹھا کر اور جنا بھی اسے مشقت اٹھا کر۔
وَحَمْلُهُ وَفِصَالُهُ ثَلَاثُونَ شَهْرًا ۚ	اور اس کے حمل اور دودھ چھڑانے میں لگ گئے تیس مہینے۔
حَتَّىٰ إِذَا بَلَغَ أَشُدَّهُ وَبَلَغَ	یہاں تک کہ جب پہنچ گیا وہ اپنی پوری طاقت کو اور ہو گیا
أَرْبَعِينَ سَنَةً ۙ قَالَ رَبِّ	چالیس سال کا تو دعا کی اس نے: اے میرے رب!
أَوْزِعْنِي أَنْ أَشْكُرَ نِعْمَتَكَ الَّتِي	تو مجھے توفیق دے کہ میں شکر ادا کرتا رہوں تیری ان نعمتوں کا جو
أَنْعَمْتَ عَلَيَّ وَعَلَىٰ وَالِدَيَّ	تو نے عطا فرمائی ہیں مجھے اور میرے والدین کو
وَأَنْ أَعْمَلَ صَالِحًا تَرْضَاهُ	اور (توفیق دے) کہ کروں میں نیک عمل جن سے تو راضی ہو
وَأَصْلِحْ لِي فِي ذُرِّيَّتِي ۖ	اور صالح بنا دے میری خاطر میری اولاد کو۔
إِنِّي تُبْتُ إِلَيْكَ	میں توبہ کرتا ہوں تیرے حضور
وَإِنِّي مِنَ الْمُسْلِمِينَ ﴿١٥﴾	اور بلاشبہ میں ہوں فرمانبرداروں میں سے ﴿١٥﴾
أُولَٰئِكَ الَّذِينَ نَتَقَبَّلُ عَنْهُمْ	یہ وہ لوگ ہیں کہ قبول فرما لیتے ہیں ہم ان کے
أَحْسَنَ مَا عَمِلُوا وَنَتَجَاوَزُ	وہ اچھے اعمال جو انہوں نے کیے اور درگزر کرتے ہیں
عَنْ سَيِّئَاتِهِمْ فِي أَصْحَابِ الْجَنَّةِ ۖ	ان کی برائیوں سے، شامل ہوں گے یہ اہل جنت میں۔
وَعْدَ الصِّدْقِ الَّذِي كَانُوا يُوعَدُونَ ﴿١٦﴾	یہ سچا وعدہ ہے جو ان سے کیا جا رہا ہے ﴿١٦﴾
وَالَّذِي قَالَ لِوَالِدَيْهِ أُفٍّ لَكُمَا	اور وہ شخص جو کہتا ہے اپنے والدین سے کہ میں بیزار ہوں تم سے
أَتَعِدَانِنِي أَنْ	کیا تم مجھے خوف دلاتے ہو اس بات سے کہ
أُخْرَجَ وَقَدْ خَلَتِ	میں نکالا جاؤں گا (قبر سے مرنے کے بعد حالانکہ گزر چکی ہیں

015 We decreed for the men and clan
Preference for parents in plan

In anguish his mother did bear in pace
And in distress she gave birth in place

From hauling in womb to weaning in adore
It's months thirty in score

Eventually when he trends in grace
The prime in power age forty to brace

He trends to implore, Lord in entreat
O my Lord! He relates and repeats

Gift me ease and appease,
That I be grateful for Thy Bestowal in treat

And also for both of my parents to allure
I beg Thee O Lord in implore
A term of piety of grace in adore

As You commend to affirm
Be amiable to me for my scion in term

Truly I trend to Thee earnest in pace
And indeed! I incline to Islam in grace

016 Such are the men and clan in surround
We'll embrace best of (their) deeds in abound

And ignore (their) evil done and doings in slight
Them to abide in Gardens of Bliss in delight
A pledge of precision for them in plight

017 But there's a man in stay
Who voice to his parents in dismay
Indignity in stray!

Do you bear the pledge in stride
That I'll be raised up from the pit to aside

الْقُرُوْنُ مِنْ قَبْلِيْ ۚ	بہت سی نسلیں مجھ سے پہلے (ان میں سے کوئی نہیں اٹھا)۔
وَهُمَا يَسْتَغِيْثٰنِ اللّٰهَ وَيْلَكَ	اور ماں باپ اللہ کی دہائی دے کر کہتے ہیں، ارے بدنصیب!
اٰمِنْ ۖ اِنَّ وَعْدَ اللّٰهِ حَقٌّ ۚ	ایمان لے آ۔ اور جان لے کہ اللہ کا وعدہ سچا ہے
فَيَقُوْلُ مَا هٰذَآ اِلَّآ اَسَاطِيْرُ الْاَوَّلِيْنَ ﴿١٧﴾	مگر وہ کہتا ہے کہ نہیں ہیں یہ باتیں مگر کہانیاں اگلے وقتوں کی ﴿١٧﴾
اُولٰٓئِكَ الَّذِيْنَ حَقَّ عَلَيْهِمُ الْقَوْلُ	یہ وہ لوگ ہیں کہ چسپاں ہو چکا ہے جن پر فیصلہ عذاب کا
فِيْٓ اُمَمٍ قَدْ خَلَتْ	اور شامل ہو گئے ہیں ان امتوں میں جو گزر چکی ہیں
مِنْ قَبْلِهِمْ مِّنَ الْجِنِّ وَالْاِنْسِ ۭ	ان سے پہلے، جنوں اور انسانوں کی۔
اِنَّهُمْ كَانُوْا خٰسِرِيْنَ ﴿١٨﴾	یقیناً وہ تھے ہی گھاٹا اٹھانے والے ﴿١٨﴾
وَلِكُلٍّ دَرَجٰتٌ	اور ہر ایک کے لیے ہیں درجے
مِّمَّا عَمِلُوْا ۚ وَلِيُوَفِّيَهُمْ	ان کے اعمال کے مطابق اور ضرور پورا پورا بدلہ دیا جائے گا
اَعْمَالَهُمْ وَهُمْ لَا يُظْلَمُوْنَ ﴿١٩﴾	ان کے اعمال کا اور ان پر ہرگز ظلم نہ کیا جائے گا ﴿١٩﴾
وَيَوْمَ يُعْرَضُ الَّذِيْنَ كَفَرُوْا	اور جس دن لا کھڑے کیے جائیں گے وہ لوگ جنہوں نے کفر کیا
عَلَى النَّارِ ۭ اَذْهَبْتُمْ	آگ پر۔ تو ان سے کہا جائے گا ختم کر دی تم نے
طَيِّبٰتِكُمْ فِيْ حَيَاتِكُمُ الدُّنْيَا	اپنے حصے کی نعمتیں اپنی دنیا کی زندگی میں ہی
وَاسْتَمْتَعْتُمْ بِهَا ۚ فَالْيَوْمَ	اور خوب لطف اٹھایا ان سے لہٰذا آج
تُجْزَوْنَ عَذَابَ الْهُوْنِ	بدلے میں دیا جائے گا تمہیں ذلت کا عذاب
بِمَا كُنْتُمْ تَسْتَكْبِرُوْنَ	اس بنا پر کہ تم بڑے بن بیٹھے تھے
فِي الْاَرْضِ بِغَيْرِ الْحَقِّ وَبِمَا	زمین میں بغیر کسی حق کے اور اس وجہ سے کہ
كُنْتُمْ تَفْسُقُوْنَ ﴿٢٠﴾ ع ٢	تم نافرمانیاں کیا کرتے تھے ﴿٢٠﴾

Even though many a men and clan
Have gone in span
Never to return once more in plan

The two (parents) trend to Lord in entreat
O Lord aid and abet with an ease in appease
Reproach and scold their son in treat

Despair for you in stance
Abide you the faith in glance

For the pledge of Lord is true to aside
But he asserted once more in deride
That's but a fable of age-old in stride

018 Such are the men destined in decree
As of the men hither fore in plea

May be of the Jinni and men in plight
Who doomed and died in slight
They'll be definitely doomed in blight

019 And to all are assigned class in scale
In concurrence with deeds in prevail
A reward for course of conduct in trail

As Dictum of Lord affirmed to aside
With no bias of favor for them in stride

020 The Day!
Cynics will face The Fire in flame
They'll be there for ever to remain
And they'll be then told to sustain

You'd cherished the delights in vale
And relished the lure of lust in dale
But today you trend to disgrace in trail

For your scorn and snub in the land
Without any just conduct in plan
For you ignored the instruct in span

وَاذْكُرْ أَخَا عَادٍ ؕ	اور سناؤ انہیں قصہ عاد کے بھائی (ہودؑ) کا ۔
إِذْ أَنذَرَ قَوْمَهُ بِالْأَحْقَافِ	جب متنبہ کیا اس نے اپنی قوم کو سرزمینِ احقاف میں
وَقَدْ خَلَتِ النُّذُرُ مِنْ بَيْنِ يَدَيْهِ	جبکہ گزر چکے تھے متنبہ کرنے والے ان سے پہلے بھی
وَمِنْ خَلْفِهِ أَلَّا تَعْبُدُوا	اور (آتے رہے) اس کے بعد بھی ـــ کہ نہ عبادت کرو تم کسی کی
إِلَّا اللَّهَ ؕ إِنِّي أَخَافُ	سوائے اللہ کے ۔ مجھے اندیشہ ہے
عَلَيْكُمْ عَذَابَ يَوْمٍ عَظِيمٍ ﴿۲۱﴾	تمہارے بارے میں ایک ہولناک دن کے عذاب کا (۲۱)
قَالُوا أَجِئْتَنَا لِتَأْفِكَنَا	انہوں نے کہا کیا تم آئے ہو اس لیے کہ برگشتہ کردو ہمیں بہکا کر
عَنْ آلِهَتِنَا فَأْتِنَا	ہمارے معبودوں سے ۔ اچھا تو اب لے آؤ ہم پر
بِمَا تَعِدُنَا إِنْ كُنْتَ مِنَ الصَّادِقِينَ ﴿۲۲﴾	وہ (عذاب) جس سے تم ڈراتے ہو ہمیں اگر ہو تم سچے (۲۲)
قَالَ إِنَّمَا الْعِلْمُ عِنْدَ اللَّهِ ۫	انہوں نے جواب دیا کہ بس اس کا علم تو اللہ ہی کو ہے
وَأُبَلِّغُكُمْ مَا أُرْسِلْتُ بِهِ	اور میں پہنچا رہا ہوں تم کو وہ پیغام جو بھیجا گیا ہے مجھے دے کر
وَلَٰكِنِّي أَرَاكُمْ قَوْمًا تَجْهَلُونَ ﴿۲۳﴾	لیکن میں دیکھتا ہوں تمہیں کہ تم لوگ جہالت برت رہے ہو (۲۳)
فَلَمَّا رَأَوْهُ عَارِضًا مُسْتَقْبِلَ	پھر جب دیکھا انہوں نے اس (عذاب) کو بادل کی شکل میں آتے ہوئے
أَوْدِيَتِهِمْ ۙ قَالُوا هَٰذَا عَارِضٌ	اپنی وادیوں کی طرف تو کہنے لگے: یہ تو بادل ہے جو
مُمْطِرُنَا ؕ بَلْ هُوَ مَا	ہمیں سیراب کردے گا نہیں بلکہ یہ وہ چیز ہے
اسْتَعْجَلْتُمْ بِهِ ؕ رِيحٌ	کہ جلدی مچا رہے تھے تم جس کی ۔ یہ ہوا کا طوفان ہے
فِيهَا عَذَابٌ أَلِيمٌ ﴿۲۴﴾	جس میں ہے دردناک عذاب (۲۴)
تُدَمِّرُ كُلَّ شَيْءٍ بِأَمْرِ رَبِّهَا	تباہ کر ڈالے گا یہ ہر چیز کو اپنے رب کے حکم سے
فَأَصْبَحُوا لَا يُرَىٰ إِلَّا مَسَاكِنُهُمْ ؕ	آخر کار وہ ہوگئے ایسے کہ نہ نظر آتی تھیں مگر ان کے رہنے کی جگہیں۔

021 Cite in stance of Hud in stride
A close of kin, Ad's in abide

He admonished his men in surround
Regard!
O my men and clan hither in around

Beware of the sinuous twist in trends
Of the sandy strip in strides
But there were the men to warn in before
And even there after in adore

Pray none, but only your Lord in Grace
Indeed!
I dread a discipline for you to brace
On The Day of Might affirmed in pace

022 They Voiced in trance
Do you intend us to spin in stance
From the axiom of our gods in glance

Then bring us torture and trial in run
If you're affirming the truth in turn

023 He said:
The vision of lore is with Lord in score
I expound to you the Calling in lore

For what I'm destined to discern
For I find you ignorant in concern

024 Then they perceived a cloud in sky
Like an immense gale in fly
Trending towards their lands in twinkle
They said:
The cloud is to get us rain in sprinkle
Nay!
You're calling anguish to dash in rush
A gust is flagrant feud in push and gush

025 It's to demolish in dash and slash
By the Dictum of Lord in abash

كَذٰلِكَ نَجْزِى الْقَوْمَ الْمُجْرِمِيْنَ ﴿۲۵﴾	اسی طرح ہم سزا دیتے ہیں مجرم لوگوں کو ﴿۲۵﴾
وَلَقَدْ مَكَّنّٰهُمْ فِيْمَا	اور یقیناً ہم نے دیا تھا ان کو قدرت و اختیار ان چیزوں پر
اِنْ مَّكَّنّٰكُمْ فِيْهِ وَجَعَلْنَا	کہ نہیں دیا ہے ہم نے تم کو قدرت و اختیار ان میں اور دیے تھے ہم نے
لَهُمْ سَمْعًا وَّاَبْصَارًا وَّاَفْـِٕدَةً	انہیں کان اور آنکھیں اور مرکزِ حواس (دل و دماغ)۔
فَمَآ اَغْنٰى عَنْهُمْ سَمْعُهُمْ وَلَآ اَبْصَارُهُمْ	لیکن کسی کام نہ آئے ان کے کان اور نہ ان کی آنکھیں
وَلَآ اَفْـِٕدَتُهُمْ مِّنْ شَىْءٍ اِذْ	اور نہ ان کے دل و دماغ ذرا بھی اس وجہ سے کہ
كَانُوْا يَجْحَدُوْنَ بِاٰيٰتِ اللّٰهِ وَحَاقَ بِهِمْ	وہ انکار کرتے تھے اللہ کی آیات کا اور آگھیرا ان کو
مَّا كَانُوْا بِهٖ يَسْتَهْزِءُوْنَ ﴿۲۶﴾	اس چیز نے جس کا وہ مذاق اڑایا کرتے تھے ﴿۲۶﴾
وَلَقَدْ اَهْلَكْنَا مَا حَوْلَكُمْ	اور بے شک ہم ہلاک کر چکے ہیں ان کو جو تمہارے ارد گرد ہیں
مِّنَ الْقُرٰى وَصَرَّفْنَا الْاٰيٰتِ	کئی بستیاں اور بار بار طرح طرح سے بھیج کر اپنی آیات (ان کو سمجھایا)
لَعَلَّهُمْ يَرْجِعُوْنَ ﴿۲۷﴾	شاید کہ وہ باز آجائیں ﴿۲۷﴾
فَلَوْلَا نَصَرَهُمُ الَّذِيْنَ	پھر کیوں نہ مدد کی ان کی انہوں نے جن کو
اتَّخَذُوْا مِنْ دُوْنِ اللّٰهِ قُرْبَانًا	بنا رکھا تھا ان لوگوں نے اللہ سے تقرب کا ذریعہ،
اٰلِهَةً ۭ بَلْ ضَلُّوْا عَنْهُمْ ۚ	معبود مان کر، واقعہ یہ ہے کہ وہ کھوئے گئے ان سے۔
وَذٰلِكَ اِفْكُهُمْ	اور یہ تھا انجام ان کے جھوٹ کا
وَمَا كَانُوْا يَفْتَرُوْنَ ﴿۲۸﴾	اور ان معبودوں کا جو انہوں نے گھڑ رکھے تھے ﴿۲۸﴾
وَاِذْ صَرَفْنَآ اِلَيْكَ	اور وہ واقعہ جب متوجہ کیا تھا ہم نے تمہاری طرف
نَفَرًا مِّنَ الْجِنِّ يَسْتَمِعُوْنَ الْقُرْاٰنَ ۚ	جنوں کے ایک گروہ کو تا کہ وہ سنیں قرآن۔
فَلَمَّا حَضَرُوْهُ	پھر جب وہ حاضر ہوئے تھے اس جگہ (جہاں تم قرآن پڑھ رہے تھے)

By morn there's not, but debris in stash
Such is the return for the evil and vile in abash

026 We got them profusion of might in plan
O Quraysh!
For what We didn't get you a bit in span

We endowed them heed to hear in concern
Look in trends to discern

Bestowal of core to care in term
And the sense of intellect in faith to affirm

But once they defied and denied in core
The Signs and Symbols of Lord in adore

They're trapped all in around
For what they sneered in abound

027 We ravished the men and clan hither in fore
All in around and surround in score

We conveyed Our Verses here in place
That they may trend to faith in pace

028 Why wasn't the aid and abet held to stay
Of the lords and gods they held to obey

Other than (Mighty) Lord in adore
As means and manners for Lord to secure
Nay!
They* deserted them in bent and bias
For that's indeed their find, a fib in class

*Idols

029 Regard!
We trended towards you to aside
A troupe of Jinni thither in stride

Heeding to Qur'an, calm and sublime
When they stood quite close in time

قَالُوْٓا اَنْصِتُوْا ۚ
تو انہوں نے کہا ایک دوسرے سے خاموش ہو جاؤ ۔

فَلَمَّا قُضِيَ وَلَّوْا
پھر جب تلاوت ختم ہو گئی تو پلٹے وہ

اِلٰى قَوْمِهِمْ مُّنْذِرِيْنَ ﴿۲۹﴾
اپنی قوم کی طرف خبردار کرنے کے لیے ﴿۲۹﴾

قَالُوْا يٰقَوْمَنَآ اِنَّا
انہوں نے کہا اے ہماری قوم کے لوگو! صورتِ حال یہ ہے کہ ہم نے

سَمِعْنَا كِتٰبًا اُنْزِلَ مِنْۢ بَعْدِ مُوْسٰى
سنی ہے ایک کتاب جو نازل کی گئی ہے موسیٰ کے بعد

مُصَدِّقًا لِّمَا بَيْنَ يَدَيْهِ
جو تصدیق کرنے والی ہے ان کتابوں کی جو اس سے پہلے آچکی ہیں

يَهْدِيْٓ اِلَى الْحَقِّ
اور جو رہنمائی کرتی ہے حق کی طرف

وَاِلٰى طَرِيْقٍ مُّسْتَقِيْمٍ ﴿۳۰﴾
اور راہِ راست کی طرف ﴿۳۰﴾

يٰقَوْمَنَآ اَجِيْبُوْا
اے ہماری قوم کے لوگو! قبول کر لو دعوت

دَاعِيَ اللّٰهِ وَاٰمِنُوْا بِهٖ
اللہ کی طرف بلانے والے کی اور لے آؤ ایمان اس پر

يَغْفِرْ لَكُمْ مِّنْ ذُنُوْبِكُمْ
معاف فرما دے گا اللہ تمہارے گناہ

وَيُجِرْكُمْ مِّنْ عَذَابٍ اَلِيْمٍ ﴿۳۱﴾
اور بچائے گا تم کو دردناک عذاب سے ﴿۳۱﴾

وَمَنْ لَّا يُجِبْ دَاعِيَ اللّٰهِ
اور جو نہیں قبول کرے گا دعوت اللہ کی طرف بلانے والے کی

فَلَيْسَ بِمُعْجِزٍ فِي الْاَرْضِ
تو وہ (اللہ کو) عاجز نہیں کر سکے گا زمین میں

وَلَيْسَ لَهٗ مِنْ دُوْنِهٖٓ
اور نہ ہوں گے اس کے لیے اللہ کے سوا

اَوْلِيَآءُ ۚ اُولٰٓئِكَ
کوئی حامی و سرپرست ۔ ایسے لوگ

فِيْ ضَلٰلٍ مُّبِيْنٍ ﴿۳۲﴾
پڑے ہوئے ہیں کھلی گمراہی میں ﴿۳۲﴾

اَوَلَمْ يَرَوْا اَنَّ اللّٰهَ
کیا نہیں غور کیا انہوں نے کہ وہ اللہ ہی ہے

الَّذِيْ خَلَقَ السَّمٰوٰتِ وَالْاَرْضَ
جس نے پیدا فرمائے ہیں آسمان اور زمین

They said: Listen to it so sober and sublime
When recitation was done and over in time

For what they trended and listened in hush
They returned to their clan to warn in rush

030 They said:
O our clan in surround
We perceived a Book unveiled in abound
After Moses, a missive of Lord in around

Assenting of all hither in fore
A guide to escort a truth in lore
An actuality of faith a word in adore

031 O our clan hither and aside
Listen to Lord's messenger in stride

And trust Him for all in trends
He'll absolve your flaw and frailty in bends
And cede you of a dreadful doom in amends

032 If some doesn't attend to one in grace
Who calls to the Dictum of Lord to brace

He cannot baffle Dictum of Lord in trail
And none to defend other than Lord in pace

Such are the men and clan in place
Drifting in distinct stagger in base

033 Don't they discern and concern in array
Who created the heavens and earth in sway
And was never tired of creation in display

وَلَمْ يَعْيَ بِخَلْقِهِنَّ	اور جو نہیں تھکا ان کے پیدا فرمانے سے،
بِقٰدِرٍ عَلٰٓى اَنْ يُّحْيِ‍ۦَ	وہ ضرور قادر ہے اس بات پر کہ زندہ کرے
الْمَوْتٰى ؕ بَلٰٓى اِنَّهٗ	مردوں کو، کیوں نہیں یقیناً وہ
عَلٰى كُلِّ شَیْءٍ قَدِیْرٌ ۳۳	ہر چیز پر پوری قدرت رکھتا ہے ۳۳
وَيَوْمَ يُعْرَضُ	اور جس دن پیش کیے جائیں گے
الَّذِيْنَ كَفَرُوْا عَلَى النَّارِ ؕ	یہ کافر لوگ آگ پر۔
اَلَيْسَ هٰذَا بِالْحَقِّ ؕ	(اور پوچھا جائے گا) کیا نہیں ہے یہ حقیقت؟
قَالُوْا بَلٰى وَرَبِّنَا ؕ	وہ کہیں گے ہاں! قسم ہمارے رب کی (یہ حقیقت ہے)۔
قَالَ فَذُوْقُوا الْعَذَابَ	کہا جائے گا سو چکھو اب مزہ عذاب کا
بِمَا كُنْتُمْ تَكْفُرُوْنَ ۳۴	اس انکار کے نتیجہ میں جو تم کرتے رہے ۳۴
فَاصْبِرْ كَمَا	پس (اے نبیؐ) صبر کرو جس طرح
صَبَرَ اُولُوا الْعَزْمِ مِنَ الرُّسُلِ	صبر کرتے رہے ہیں بڑی ہمت و حوصلہ والے رسول
وَلَا تَسْتَعْجِلْ لَّهُمْ ؕ	اور نہ جلدی کرو ان کے معاملہ میں۔
كَاَنَّهُمْ يَوْمَ	انہیں یوں معلوم ہوگا اس دن
يَرَوْنَ مَا يُوْعَدُوْنَ ۙ	جب وہ دیکھیں گے عذاب، جس سے انہیں ڈرایا جا رہا ہے
لَمْ يَلْبَثُوْٓا	کہ نہیں رہے تھے یہ (دنیا میں)
اِلَّا سَاعَةً مِّنْ نَّهَارٍ ؕ	مگر دن کی ایک گھڑی۔
بَلٰغٌ ۚ فَهَلْ يُهْلَكُ	بات پہنچا دی گئی سو نہیں ہلاک ہوں گے
اِلَّا الْقَوْمُ الْفٰسِقُوْنَ ۳۵	مگر وہ لوگ جو نافرمان اور بدکار ہیں ۳۵

He's adept to endow life to the dead in doom
Indeed!
He's the power over all (the sway) in bloom

034 On The Day,
The cynics will face Hell in ablaze
They'll be asked to concern in place

Isn't it the truth affirmed in pace
They'll affirm in proceed
Yes, sure indeed!
By Lord they'll mimic in maze

Now savor and flavor the torment in hurt
For what you denied the truth in curt

035 So diligently endure in pace
As did all the messengers in grace
For highly cherished chore in place

Don't hurry for the cynics, a dread in doom
On The Day they'll affirm in gloom

When they'll trend to aside
Retribution pledged in stride

Then they'll care to concern in trace
As if they'd lived hither in place

Not more than an hour of a day in stance
But they'd a Word affirmed to glance

Now only the sinner to stray
Determined a destined doom to secure

(۴۷) سُوْرَةُ مُحَمَّدٍ مَّدَنِيَّةٌ (۹۵)
اٰيَاتُهَا ۳۸ — رُكُوْعَاتُهَا ۴

بِسْمِ اللّٰهِ الرَّحْمٰنِ الرَّحِيْمِ

شروع اللہ کے نام سے جو بڑا مہربان نہایت رحم والا ہے

اَلَّذِيْنَ كَفَرُوْا وَصَدُّوْا عَنْ سَبِيْلِ اللّٰهِ	جن لوگوں نے کفر کیا اور روکا اللہ کی راہ سے،
اَضَلَّ اَعْمَالَهُمْ ①	رائیگاں کر دیا اللہ نے ان کے اعمال کو ①
وَالَّذِيْنَ اٰمَنُوْا وَعَمِلُوا الصّٰلِحٰتِ	اور وہ لوگ جو ایمان لائے اور کیے انہوں نے نیک اعمال
وَاٰمَنُوْا بِمَا نُزِّلَ عَلٰى مُحَمَّدٍ	اور ایمان لے آئے اس پر جو نازل ہوا ہے محمدؐ پر
وَّهُوَ الْحَقُّ مِنْ رَّبِّهِمْ	اور ہے وہ سراسر حق ان کے رب کی طرف سے۔
كَفَّرَ عَنْهُمْ سَيِّاٰتِهِمْ	دور کر دیں اللہ نے ان سے ان کی برائیاں
وَاَصْلَحَ بَالَهُمْ ②	اور درست کر دیے ان کے احوال ②
ذٰلِكَ بِاَنَّ الَّذِيْنَ كَفَرُوا	یہ اس لیے ہے کہ وہ لوگ جنہوں نے کفر کیا،
اتَّبَعُوا الْبَاطِلَ وَاَنَّ الَّذِيْنَ اٰمَنُوا	پیروی کی ہے انہوں نے باطل کی اور وہ لوگ جو ایمان لائے
اتَّبَعُوا الْحَقَّ مِنْ رَّبِّهِمْ	پیروی کی ہے انہوں نے اس حق کی جو ان کے رب کی طرف سے (آیا ہے)
كَذٰلِكَ يَضْرِبُ اللّٰهُ	اس طرح بتلائے دیتا ہے اللہ
لِلنَّاسِ اَمْثَالَهُمْ ③	انسانوں کو ان کی ٹھیک ٹھیک حیثیت ③
فَاِذَا لَقِيْتُمُ الَّذِيْنَ كَفَرُوْا	پھر جب مقابلہ ہو تمہارا ان لوگوں سے جو کافر ہیں
فَضَرْبَ الرِّقَابِ حَتّٰٓى اِذَآ	تو ان کی گردنیں اڑاؤ۔ یہاں تک کہ جب
اَثْخَنْتُمُوْهُمْ فَشُدُّوا الْوَثَاقَ	کچل دو تم انہیں تو مضبوط باندھو (قیدیوں کو)

047-MUHAMMAD

In the name of Lord, the Most Beneficent, Most Merciful

001 Who deny and defy faith of Lord in pace
And restrict conduct in course of Lord to brace
Lord will render their deeds in waste

002 But who affirm and conform faith in proceeds
And trend verity in all their doings in deeds

And trust in,
Divulgence to Muhammad in acclaim
For it's a word of trust from Lord to sustain

Lord to eliminate their ills in plight
And refine their conduct of course in delight

003 That's because,
Those revoking Lord in trance
And following conceited plan in stance

Whereas,
Who trust and follow the truth in pace
Lord affirms the likeness in place
For the men and clan to comply in trace

004 When you meet Infidels in combat
Smite their neck in reach and contact

And eventually in instruct,
When you overcome in fray
Then force a bond in contract
Then henceforth in stay,

فَاِمَّا مَنًّا بَعْدُ وَ اِمَّا فِدَآءً	پھر اس کے بعد یا تو بطور احسان یا فدیہ لے کر (چھوڑ دو)
حَتّٰى تَضَعَ الْحَرْبُ اَوْزَارَهَا ۚ	یہاں تک کہ جنگ ختم ہو جائے۔
ذٰلِكَ ۛ وَلَوْ يَشَآءُ اللّٰهُ	یہ ہے صحیح طریقہ اور اگر چاہتا اللہ
لَانْتَصَرَ مِنْهُمْ وَلٰكِنْ لِّيَبْلُوَا	تو خود ہی نبٹ لیتا ان سے لیکن (اس نے چاہا) کہ آزمائے
بَعْضَكُمْ بِبَعْضٍ ۗ	تم کو ایک دوسرے کے ذریعے سے۔
وَ الَّذِيْنَ قُتِلُوْا فِيْ سَبِيْلِ اللّٰهِ	اور وہ لوگ جو قتل کیے گئے اللہ کی راہ میں
فَلَنْ يُّضِلَّ اَعْمَالَهُمْ ۴	سو ہرگز نہیں ضائع کرے گا اللہ ان کے اعمال ۴
سَيَهْدِيْهِمْ	وہ ضرور انہیں دکھائے گا سیدھی راہ
وَيُصْلِحُ بَالَهُمْ ۵	اور درست کر دے گا ان کے احوال ۵
وَ يُدْخِلُهُمُ الْجَنَّةَ	اور داخل کرے گا انہیں اس جنت میں
عَرَّفَهَا لَهُمْ ۶	جس سے وہ واقف کرا چکا ہے انہیں ۶
يٰۤاَيُّهَا الَّذِيْنَ اٰمَنُوْۤا اِنْ تَنْصُرُوا	اے وہ لوگو جو ایمان لائے ہو اگر مدد کرو گے تم
اللّٰهَ يَنْصُرْكُمْ	اللہ کی تو وہ بھی تمہاری مدد کرے گا
وَيُثَبِّتْ اَقْدَامَكُمْ ۷	اور جما دے گا مضبوطی سے تمہارے قدم ۷
وَ الَّذِيْنَ كَفَرُوْا فَتَعْسًا لَّهُمْ	اور وہ لوگ جنہوں نے کفر کیا سو ہلاکت ہے ان کے لیے
وَ اَضَلَّ اَعْمَالَهُمْ ۸	اور ضائع کر دیا ہے اللہ نے ان کے اعمال کو ۸
ذٰلِكَ بِاَنَّهُمْ كَرِهُوْا مَاۤ اَنْزَلَ	یہ اس لیے ہے کہ انہوں نے ناپسند کیا اس کو جسے نازل فرمایا ہے
اللّٰهُ فَاَحْبَطَ اَعْمَالَهُمْ ۹	اللہ نے، لہٰذا غارت کر دیے اللہ نے ان کے اعمال ۹
اَفَلَمْ يَسِيْرُوْا فِي الْاَرْضِ	کیا نہیں چلے پھرے ہیں یہ زمین میں

For munificence or deliverance in strain
Until war allays its annoyance in remain

If Lord had desired in award
He'd precisely recompense in accord

He ordains a term in combat
As test of trial in instruct

Once dead in means and manners in pace
For The Bounty of Lord in Grace

He wouldn't let their doings in waste
(Even so these are quite trivial in trace)

005 He sign and steer them in stance
To mend their temper in glance

006 Permit them to the Gardens in pace
For they're pledged in place

007 O you the men and clan in faith
If you strive in stance,
For the cause of Lord to brace
He'll make you firm in grace
And assist and abet, you all in glance

008 But who renounce,
Dignity of Lord to brace
For them is ruination in pace
And Lord !
Lets their deeds to drift in waste

009 That's so,
For they despise Divulgence of Lord to brace
Lord trends their course and conduct in waste

010 Don't they trek and travel in land
And see not the fate of those in plan
Who've passed hither fore in span

فَيَنْظُرُوا كَيْفَ كَانَ عَاقِبَةُ الَّذِينَ	تا کہ دیکھتے کیا ہوا انجام ان لوگوں کا جو
مِنْ قَبْلِهِمْ ۖ دَمَّرَ اللّٰهُ عَلَيْهِمْ ۖ	ان سے پہلے گزر چکے ہیں؟ تباہ و برباد کر دیا اللہ نے انہیں۔
وَلِلْكٰفِرِينَ أَمْثَالُهَا (۱۰)	اور کافروں کے لیے ہیں ایسے ہی نتائج (۱۰)
ذٰلِكَ بِأَنَّ اللّٰهَ مَوْلَى الَّذِينَ	یہ اس لیے کہ یقیناً اللہ حامی و ناصر ہے ان لوگوں کا جو
اٰمَنُوا وَأَنَّ الْكٰفِرِينَ	ایمان لائے اور حقیقت یہ ہے کہ کافر،
لَا مَوْلٰى لَهُمْ (۱۱) ع	نہیں ہے کوئی حامی و ناصر ان کا (۱۱)
إِنَّ اللّٰهَ يُدْخِلُ الَّذِينَ اٰمَنُوا	بلا شبہ اللہ داخل کرے گا ان لوگوں کو جو ایمان لائے
وَعَمِلُوا الصّٰلِحٰتِ جَنّٰتٍ	اور کیے انہوں نے نیک اعمال ایسی جنتوں میں
تَجْرِي مِنْ تَحْتِهَا الْأَنْهٰرُ ۖ	کہ بہہ رہی ہوں گی ان کے نیچے نہریں۔
وَالَّذِينَ كَفَرُوا يَتَمَتَّعُونَ	اور وہ لوگ جو کافر ہیں مزے لوٹ رہے ہیں
وَيَأْكُلُونَ كَمَا تَأْكُلُ	اور کھا پی رہے ہیں (چند روزہ زندگی میں) جیسے کھاتے ہیں
الْأَنْعٰمُ وَالنَّارُ مَثْوًى لَهُمْ (۱۲)	جانور اور جہنم آخری ٹھکانہ ہے ان کا (۱۲)
وَكَأَيِّنْ مِنْ قَرْيَةٍ هِيَ أَشَدُّ قُوَّةً	اور کتنی ہی بستیاں — جو بہت زیادہ زور آور تھیں
مِنْ قَرْيَتِكَ الَّتِي أَخْرَجَتْكَ	تمہاری اس بستی سے جس نے تمہیں نکالا ہے —
أَهْلَكْنٰهُمْ فَلَا نَاصِرَ لَهُمْ (۱۳)	ہلاک کر دیا ہم نے ان کو سو نہ ہوا کوئی مددگار ان کا (۱۳)
أَفَمَنْ كَانَ عَلٰى بَيِّنَةٍ	سو بھلا وہ شخص جو ہو صاف اور صریح ہدایت پر
مِنْ رَبِّهِ كَمَنْ	اپنے رب کی، ان کی طرح ہو سکتا ہے
زُيِّنَ لَهُ سُوءُ عَمَلِهِ	جن کے لیے خوشنما بنا دیے گئے ہوں ان کے برے عمل
وَاتَّبَعُوا أَهْوَاءَهُمْ (۱٤)	اور پیرو بن گئے ہوں وہ اپنی خواہشات کے؟ (۱٤)

They're damned by Lord in trail
And such is the term for them to avail
Those, who defy Dictum of Lord in vale

011 That's so,
For Lord is to guard, who trust and believe
And those defying the term in belief
Don't have the protector around to relief

012 Indeed!
Who trust in faith and abide verity in pace
Lord will get them to Gardens in place

Where streams ebb and flow, aside and below
Those who deny Dictum of Lord in endow
Them to cherish worldly lust in glow

They devour and gobble as cattle in graze
And finally savor burn of Pyre in blaze

013 And how many mighty counties and locale
Than of the city in trail

That have pushed you out in place
We smashed and shattered in pace
And there's none to aid and abet in trace

014 Who's to surpass in order of escort
The one affirmed clear way in resort

And one whose evil conduct tempt in lore
They pursue their lust of evils in core

مَثَلُ الْجَنَّةِ الَّتِىْ وُعِدَ الْمُتَّقُوْنَ	احوال اس جنت کا جس کا وعدہ کیا گیا ہے متقیوں سے
فِيْهَآ اَنْهٰرٌ مِّنْ مَّآءٍ غَيْرِ اٰسِنٍ	یہ ہے کہ، ہوں گی اس میں نہریں صاف ستھرے پانی کی
وَاَنْهٰرٌ مِّنْ لَّبَنٍ لَّمْ يَتَغَيَّرْ طَعْمُهٗ	اور نہریں دودھ کی کہ نہ فرق آیا ہو گا اس کے ذائقے میں
وَاَنْهٰرٌ مِّنْ خَمْرٍ لَّذَّةٍ لِّلشّٰرِبِيْنَ	اور نہریں شراب کی جو لذیذ ہوں گی پینے والوں کے لیے۔
وَاَنْهٰرٌ مِّنْ عَسَلٍ مُّصَفًّى	اور نہریں صاف شفاف شہد کی۔
وَلَهُمْ فِيْهَا مِنْ كُلِّ الثَّمَرٰتِ	اور ان کے لیے جنت میں ہوں گے ہر طرح کے پھل
وَمَغْفِرَةٌ مِّنْ رَّبِّهِمْ	اور بخشش ہوگی ان کے رب کی طرف سے۔
كَمَنْ هُوَ خَالِدٌ	(کیا یہ لوگ) ان کی مانند ہو سکتے ہیں جو ہمیشہ رہیں گے
فِى النَّارِ وَسُقُوْا مَآءً حَمِيْمًا	جہنم میں اور پلایا جائے گا انہیں کھولتا ہوا پانی
فَقَطَّعَ اَمْعَآءَهُمْ ۱۵	جو ٹکڑے ٹکڑے کر ڈالے گا ان کی آنتوں کو ۱۵
وَمِنْهُمْ مَّنْ	اور (اے نبیؐ) ان میں سے کچھ لوگ ایسے ہیں جو
يَّسْتَمِعُ اِلَيْكَ حَتّٰٓى اِذَا	کان لگا کر سنتے ہیں تمہاری باتیں، یہاں تک کہ جب
خَرَجُوْا مِنْ عِنْدِكَ قَالُوْا	نکل کر جاتے ہیں تمہارے پاس سے تو پوچھتے ہیں
لِلَّذِيْنَ اُوْتُوا الْعِلْمَ مَاذَا قَالَ	ان لوگوں سے جنہیں دیا گیا ہے علم کہ کیا کہا تھا رسولؐ نے
اٰنِفًا اُولٰٓئِكَ الَّذِيْنَ طَبَعَ اللّٰهُ	ابھی ابھی؟ یہ وہ لوگ ہیں کہ مہر کر دی ہے اللہ نے
عَلٰى قُلُوْبِهِمْ وَاتَّبَعُوْٓا اَهْوَآءَهُمْ ۱۶	ان کے دلوں پر اور پیرو بنے ہوئے ہیں اپنی خواہشات کے ۱۶
وَالَّذِيْنَ اهْتَدَوْا زَادَهُمْ	اور وہ لوگ جنہوں نے ہدایت پائی مزید عطا کرتا ہے اللہ ان کو
هُدًى وَّاٰتٰهُمْ تَقْوٰىهُمْ ۱۷	ہدایت اور عطا فرماتا ہے انہیں ان کے حصہ کا تقوٰی ۱۷
فَهَلْ يَنْظُرُوْنَ اِلَّا السَّاعَةَ	سو نہیں انتظار کر رہے یہ (منکرین) مگر قیامت کی گھڑی کا

015 There's a fable of the garden to narrate
The reverent are avowed to stay in state

With rills of pure elegant water in glow*
With streams of milk sinuous in flow

So exquisite in flavor not to change in taste
Rivers of wine, the drinks in state

Drifts of tide of sheer honey so clear
Therein variety of fruit like pear

Them to cherish Bounty of Lord in pace
(How they can be equal with the men in waste)

The men of the Fire in grip
Them to savor fuming water in sip
Cutting their bowels in sidle and dip

*to drink

016 And there are men mid them in abide
Who listen to your word in advice

But as they drift in away
Then ask men of sapience in fray
What did he say,
Just then as we're there in stay

They're in lechery and lust in derision
And Lord!
Sealed their core in abrasion and attrition

017 But who secure sincere term in escort
Lord greatens his gleam in escort

He endows them piety in pace
And confines evil trends in base

018 Do they tarry and trail in rapport
Waiting for the Hour to trend in abrupt

اَنْ تَاْتِيَهُمْ بَغْتَةً ۚ فَقَدْ جَآءَ	کہ آجائے وہ ان پر اچانک سو یقیناً آچکی ہیں
اَشْرَاطُهَا ۚ فَاَنّٰى لَهُمْ	اس کی علامات ۔ پھر کونسا موقع ہوگا ان کے لیے —
اِذَا جَآءَتْهُمْ ذِكْرٰىهُمْ ﴿۱۸﴾	جب آہی جائے گی ان پر وہ گھڑی — نصیحت قبول کرنے کا ﴿۱۸﴾
فَاعْلَمْ اَنَّهٗ لَآ اِلٰهَ اِلَّا اللّٰهُ	پس (اے نبیؐ) خوب جان لو کہ نہیں ہے کوئی معبود سوائے اللہ کے
وَاسْتَغْفِرْ لِذَنْۢبِكَ وَلِلْمُؤْمِنِيْنَ	اور معافی مانگو اپنے قصور کی اور (معافی مانگو) مومن مردوں کے لیے
وَالْمُؤْمِنٰتِ ۗ وَاللّٰهُ يَعْلَمُ	اور مومن عورتوں کے لیے ۔ اور اللہ واقف ہے
مُتَقَلَّبَكُمْ وَمَثْوٰىكُمْ ﴿۱۹﴾ ع ۲	تمہاری سرگرمیوں سے بھی اور تمہارے ٹھکانے سے بھی ﴿۱۹﴾
وَيَقُوْلُ الَّذِيْنَ اٰمَنُوْا لَوْلَا نُزِّلَتْ	اور کہتے تھے وہ لوگ جو ایمان لائے کیوں نہیں نازل کی جاتی
سُوْرَةٌ ۚ فَاِذَآ اُنْزِلَتْ	کوئی سورت (جس میں جنگ کا حکم ہو) مگر جب نازل کی گئی
سُوْرَةٌ مُّحْكَمَةٌ وَّذُكِرَ فِيْهَا	ایک سورت واضح احکام والی اور ذکر کیا گیا اس میں
الْقِتَالُ ۙ رَاَيْتَ الَّذِيْنَ فِيْ قُلُوْبِهِمْ	جنگ کا تو دیکھا تم نے ان لوگوں کو جن کے دلوں میں
مَّرَضٌ يَّنْظُرُوْنَ اِلَيْكَ نَظَرَ	بیماری تھی کہ وہ دیکھتے ہیں تمہاری طرف ایسے جیسے دیکھتا ہے
الْمَغْشِيِّ عَلَيْهِ مِنَ الْمَوْتِ ۭ	وہ شخص جس پر بے ہوشی طاری ہوگئی ہو موت کی ۔
فَاَوْلٰى لَهُمْ ﴿۲۰﴾	سو افسوس ہے ان کے حال پر ﴿۲۰﴾
طَاعَةٌ وَّقَوْلٌ مَّعْرُوْفٌ ۣ	(زبان پر تو ان کے ہے) اطاعت کا اقرار اور اچھی اچھی باتیں ۔
فَاِذَا عَزَمَ الْاَمْرُ ۣ	لیکن جب (جنگ کا) قطعی حکم دے دیا گیا،
فَلَوْ صَدَقُوا اللّٰهَ	تو اس وقت اگر سچے نکلتے یہ اللہ سے (کیے ہوئے اپنے عہد میں)
لَكَانَ خَيْرًا لَّهُمْ ﴿۲۱﴾	تو ہوتا یہ بہتر ان کے لیے ﴿۲۱﴾
فَهَلْ عَسَيْتُمْ	تو اے منافقو! تم سے (اس کے سوا) اور کیا توقع کی جا سکتی ہے

But there were quite a few Signs in place
And when it's to take a toll of them in pace
How'd they avail admonition to brace

019 (O Muhammad!)
Discern and Concern hither in lore
There's no god but Only Lord in adore
Beg and beseech His admonition to allure

And also beg His reprieve in plan
For the faithful men and dame in span

For Lord discerns your moves in pace
And as you dwell your resides in place

020 Those who assert in faith trend to affirm
Why isn't a Surah sent for us in concern
(For a turn in combat hither in term)

But when a Surah, a key in concern
Revealed for them to discern

And combat is cited in fray
You'll see some with ill in stay

Looking you agape in amaze
As if the death is looming in haze
Sorry for their trends in daze

021 Indeed!
They vocalize in term
And assert to support and talk to affirm
But for the categorical war in term,
When the dictum is for them to concern

They rather jeer and sneer in maze
Wasn't it better to abide in phase
If they're true to Lord in praise

022 What could be expected of you* in pace
If you revert to your trends in place

*Hypocrites

إِنْ تَوَلَّيْتُمْ أَنْ تُفْسِدُوا فِي الْأَرْضِ	کہ اگر تم الٹے منہ پھر گئے تو فساد مچاؤ گے زمین میں
وَتُقَطِّعُوا أَرْحَامَكُمْ ﴿٢٢﴾	اور آپس میں قطع رحمی کرو گے؟ ﴿٢٢﴾
أُولَٰئِكَ الَّذِينَ لَعَنَهُمُ	یہی ہیں وہ لوگ کہ دور کر دیا ہے انہیں اپنی رحمت سے
اللَّهُ فَأَصَمَّهُمْ	اللہ نے اور بہرا کر دیا ہے انہیں
وَأَعْمَىٰ أَبْصَارَهُمْ ﴿٢٣﴾	اور اندھی کر دی ہیں ان کی آنکھیں ﴿٢٣﴾
أَفَلَا يَتَدَبَّرُونَ الْقُرْآنَ	سو کیا نہیں غور کرتے یہ قرآن پر
أَمْ عَلَىٰ قُلُوبٍ أَقْفَالُهَا ﴿٢٤﴾	کیا ان کے دلوں پر قفل چڑھے ہوئے ہیں؟ ﴿٢٤﴾
إِنَّ الَّذِينَ ارْتَدُّوا عَلَىٰ أَدْبَارِهِمْ	بلاشبہ وہ لوگ جو الٹے پھر گئے ہیں
مِنْ بَعْدِ مَا تَبَيَّنَ لَهُمُ الْهُدَى	اس کے بعد کہ کھل کر آ گئی تھی ان کے سامنے ہدایت،
الشَّيْطَانُ سَوَّلَ لَهُمْ	شیطان نے آسان بنا دیا ہے ان کے لیے (یہ کام)۔
وَأَمْلَىٰ لَهُمْ ﴿٢٥﴾	اور دراز کر رکھا ہے جھوٹی توقعات کا سلسلہ ان کے لیے ﴿٢٥﴾
ذَٰلِكَ بِأَنَّهُمْ قَالُوا لِلَّذِينَ	یہ اس لیے ہوا کہ انہوں نے کہا تھا ان لوگوں سے جو
كَرِهُوا مَا نَزَّلَ اللَّهُ	ناپسند کرتے تھے اس چیز کو جو نازل کی ہے اللہ نے
سَنُطِيعُكُمْ فِي بَعْضِ الْأَمْرِ	کہ ہم ضرور مانیں گے تمہاری باتیں بعض معاملات میں۔
وَاللَّهُ يَعْلَمُ إِسْرَارَهُمْ ﴿٢٦﴾	اور اللہ خوب جانتا ہے ان کی خفیہ باتیں ﴿٢٦﴾
فَكَيْفَ إِذَا تَوَفَّتْهُمُ	پھر کیا حال ہوگا اس وقت جب روحیں قبض کریں گے ان کی
الْمَلَائِكَةُ يَضْرِبُونَ	فرشتے مارتے ہوئے
وُجُوهَهُمْ وَأَدْبَارَهُمْ ﴿٢٧﴾	ان کے چہروں پر اور ان کی پیٹھوں پہ ﴿٢٧﴾
ذَٰلِكَ بِأَنَّهُمُ اتَّبَعُوا مَا	یہ اس لیے ہوگا کہ انہوں نے پیروی کی ہے اس (طریقہ) کی جو

You would trend to evil in trace
Hither in the land
And crack and cleft ties of kith and kin in plan

023 Such are the accursed by the Lord in term
For He's turned them deaf to discern
And blind to concern

024 Don't they trend soberly to seek
The Sense and Sagacity of Qur'an in speech

Or if their core is secured in lore
To perceive verity of Word in core

025 Indeed!
Those of the men, who inverse and desert
After having clear direction in concert
Devil hazed and raised false hopes as expert

026 They called on the men and clan
Who defy revelations of Lord in plan

We'll comply you in sort partial and part
But secret,
Of the core are known to The Lord

027 But how would it be a term in precise
When angels seize their souls in demise
And slash their faces and rear in dice

028 That's because,
They endured fury of Lord in fray

اَسْخَطَ اللّٰهَ وَكَرِهُوْا
ناراض کرنے والا ہے اللہ کو اور ناپسند کیا ہے انہوں نے

رِضْوَانَهٗ فَاَحْبَطَ اَعْمَالَهُمْ ﴿۲۸﴾ ع ۹
اس کی رضا کا راستہ سو ضائع کر دیے اللہ نے ان کے سب اعمال ﴿۲۸﴾

اَمْ حَسِبَ الَّذِيْنَ فِيْ قُلُوْبِهِمْ مَّرَضٌ
کیا سمجھے بیٹھے ہیں وہ لوگ جن کے دلوں میں بیماری ہے

اَنْ لَّنْ يُّخْرِجَ اللّٰهُ اَضْغَانَهُمْ ﴿۲۹﴾
کہ نہیں ظاہر کرے گا اللہ ان کے دلوں کے کھوٹ؟ ﴿۲۹﴾

وَلَوْ نَشَآءُ لَاَرَيْنٰكَهُمْ فَلَعَرَفْتَهُمْ
اور اگر ہم چاہیں تو ضرور دکھا دیں ہم تمہیں پھر پہچان لو تم ان کو

بِسِيْمٰهُمْ ؕ وَلَتَعْرِفَنَّهُمْ
ان کے چہروں سے اور ضرور جان لیتے ہو تم ان کو

فِيْ لَحْنِ الْقَوْلِ ؕ وَاللّٰهُ يَعْلَمُ
(ان کے) اندازِ گفتگو سے اور اللہ خوب جانتا ہے

اَعْمَالَكُمْ ﴿۳۰﴾
تم سب کے اعمال کو ﴿۳۰﴾

وَلَنَبْلُوَنَّكُمْ حَتّٰى نَعْلَمَ
اور ہم ضرور آزمائش میں ڈالیں گے تم کو تاکہ دیکھ لیں ہم

الْمُجٰهِدِيْنَ مِنْكُمْ وَالصّٰبِرِيْنَ ۙ
ان کو جو جہاد کرنے والے ہیں تم میں سے اور ثابت قدم رہنے والے ہیں

وَنَبْلُوَا اَخْبَارَكُمْ ﴿۳۱﴾
اور جانچ لیں تمہارے حالات کو ﴿۳۱﴾

اِنَّ الَّذِيْنَ كَفَرُوْا وَصَدُّوْا
یقیناً وہ لوگ جنہوں نے کفر کیا اور روکا

عَنْ سَبِيْلِ اللّٰهِ وَشَآقُّوا الرَّسُوْلَ مِنْۢ بَعْدِ
اللہ کی راہ سے اور مخالفت کی رسول کی اس کے بعد بھی

مَا تَبَيَّنَ لَهُمُ الْهُدٰى ۙ
کہ واضح ہو چکی تھی ان کے لیے راہِ راست

لَنْ يَّضُرُّوا اللّٰهَ شَيْـًٔا ؕ
ہرگز نہیں نقصان پہنچا سکیں گے وہ اللہ کو ذرا بھی ۔

وَسَيُحْبِطُ اَعْمَالَهُمْ ﴿۳۲﴾
اور اللہ غارت کر دے گا ان کے اعمال کو ﴿۳۲﴾

يٰۤاَيُّهَا الَّذِيْنَ اٰمَنُوْۤا اَطِيْعُوا اللّٰهَ
اے لوگو جو ایمان لائے ہو اطاعت کرو اللہ کی

وَاَطِيْعُوا الرَّسُوْلَ
اور اطاعت کرو رسول کی

وَلَا تُبْطِلُوْۤا اَعْمَالَكُمْ ﴿۳۳﴾
اور مت برباد کرو اپنے اعمال ﴿۳۳﴾

They defied favor of Lord to obey
So He made their deeds dwindle in stray

029 Or do they assume in stance
Whose veer of core is evil in trance

That Lord wouldn't let to divulge
Their trends in spite them to converge

030 Had We intended a term in treat
You could've shown (them) in screech
By their special signs in impeach

But indeed!
You'll discern them by tone in speech
And Lord,
Care and concern your doings in deeds

031 We'll put you to trial in place
Until in tribulation We assert in pace

Who strive to keep on endurance in grace
And We'll distill your temper in trace

032 Those who defy Lord hither in trail
And Hold back from His trends in vale

And defy the Messenger in trance
After a term of guidance in glance

They cannot the least harm The Lord in hurt
But he'll make their deeds waste in curt

033 O you the men and clan in faith
Trend to Lord and His Messenger to pace
And don't get your doings gone in waste

إِنَّ الَّذِينَ كَفَرُوا وَصَدُّوا	یقیناً وہ لوگ جنہوں نے کفر کیا اور روکا
عَنْ سَبِيلِ اللَّهِ ثُمَّ مَاتُوا وَهُمْ كُفَّارٌ	اللہ کی راہ سے پھر مر گئے اس حالت میں کہ وہ کافر تھے
فَلَنْ يَغْفِرَ اللَّهُ لَهُمْ ﴿٣٤﴾	سو ہرگز نہیں معاف کرے گا اللہ انہیں ﴿٣٤﴾
فَلَا تَهِنُوا وَتَدْعُوا إِلَى السَّلْمِ	لہٰذا نہ ہمت ہارو تم اور (نہ) درخواست کرو صلح کی ۔
وَأَنْتُمُ الْأَعْلَوْنَ وَاللَّهُ مَعَكُمْ	اور تم ہی غالب رہنے والے ہو اور اللہ تمہارے ساتھ ہے
وَلَنْ يَتِرَكُمْ أَعْمَالَكُمْ ﴿٣٥﴾	اور ہرگز نہیں ضائع کرے گا وہ تمہارے اعمال کو ﴿٣٥﴾
إِنَّمَا الْحَيَاةُ الدُّنْيَا لَعِبٌ	بے شک یہ دنیاوی زندگی ہے محض کھیل
وَلَهْوٌ وَإِنْ تُؤْمِنُوا	اور تماشا ۔ اور اگر تم مومن رہے
وَتَتَّقُوا يُؤْتِكُمْ	اور تقویٰ کی روش اختیار کی تم نے تو دے گا وہ تمہیں
أُجُورَكُمْ وَلَا يَسْأَلْكُمْ أَمْوَالَكُمْ ﴿٣٦﴾	تمہارے اجر اور نہ مانگے گا تم سے تمہارے مال ﴿٣٦﴾
إِنْ يَسْأَلْكُمُوهَا	اور اگر کہیں مانگ لے تم سے تمہارے مال
فَيُحْفِكُمْ تَبْخَلُوا	اور طلب کرلے تم سے سب کے سب تو تم بخل کرو گے
وَيُخْرِجْ أَضْغَانَكُمْ ﴿٣٧﴾	اور ظاہر کر دے گا اللہ تمہارے دلوں کے کھوٹ ﴿٣٧﴾
هَا أَنْتُمْ هَٰؤُلَاءِ تُدْعَوْنَ لِتُنْفِقُوا	دیکھو! یہ تم ہی ہو جنہیں دعوت دی جا رہی ہے کہ خرچ کرو
فِي سَبِيلِ اللَّهِ فَمِنْكُمْ مَنْ يَبْخَلُ	اللہ کی راہ میں ۔ سو تم میں سے کچھ تو وہ ہیں جو بخل کرتے ہیں ۔
وَمَنْ يَبْخَلْ فَإِنَّمَا يَبْخَلُ عَنْ نَفْسِهِ	اور جو بخل کرتا ہے تو بس بخل کرتا ہے وہ اپنے آپ ہی سے ۔
وَاللَّهُ الْغَنِيُّ وَأَنْتُمُ الْفُقَرَاءُ	اور اللہ تو غنی ہے اور تم ہی محتاج ہو ۔
وَإِنْ تَتَوَلَّوْا يَسْتَبْدِلْ قَوْمًا غَيْرَكُمْ	اور اگر تم منہ موڑو گے تو وہ لے آئے گا اور لوگوں کو تمہاری جگہ
ثُمَّ لَا يَكُونُوا أَمْثَالَكُمْ ﴿٣٨﴾	پھر نہ ہوں گے وہ تم جیسے ﴿٣٨﴾

034 Those, who renounce Lord in trail
And foil His dictum for the men to avail
Then doom to death, defying in haste
Lord isn't to absolve their ills in waste

035 Be not irksome and irresolute, wailing in sort
And begging for term of amity in accord

When Lord is with you, in conquer and reward
And wouldn't deprive you of adorable awards
For all your goodly deeds and doings in assort

036 This vale is but a mirth and play
If you assume in faith to obey
And guard to protect from evil in display

He'll gift and grant you amends in awards
And wouldn't hold you,
From your belongings in regards

037 If He was to ask you for all in effects
You'd be greedy to hold in precept
He'll show up your ills in respect
That's of your defied whims in concepts

038 Regard,
It's you, who're advised to expend* in pace
Abiding the dictum of Lord in grace
But of you,
There're some measly and miserly in place
But if some is so miserly in trace
That's for his own souls to secure

But Lord is free of all these alms in wants
And it's you, who strive for amends in slants
If you defy,
He'll replace you for other men and clan
Then they wouldn't be like you in span

*dole out alms for the cause of Allah to His men devoted for faith

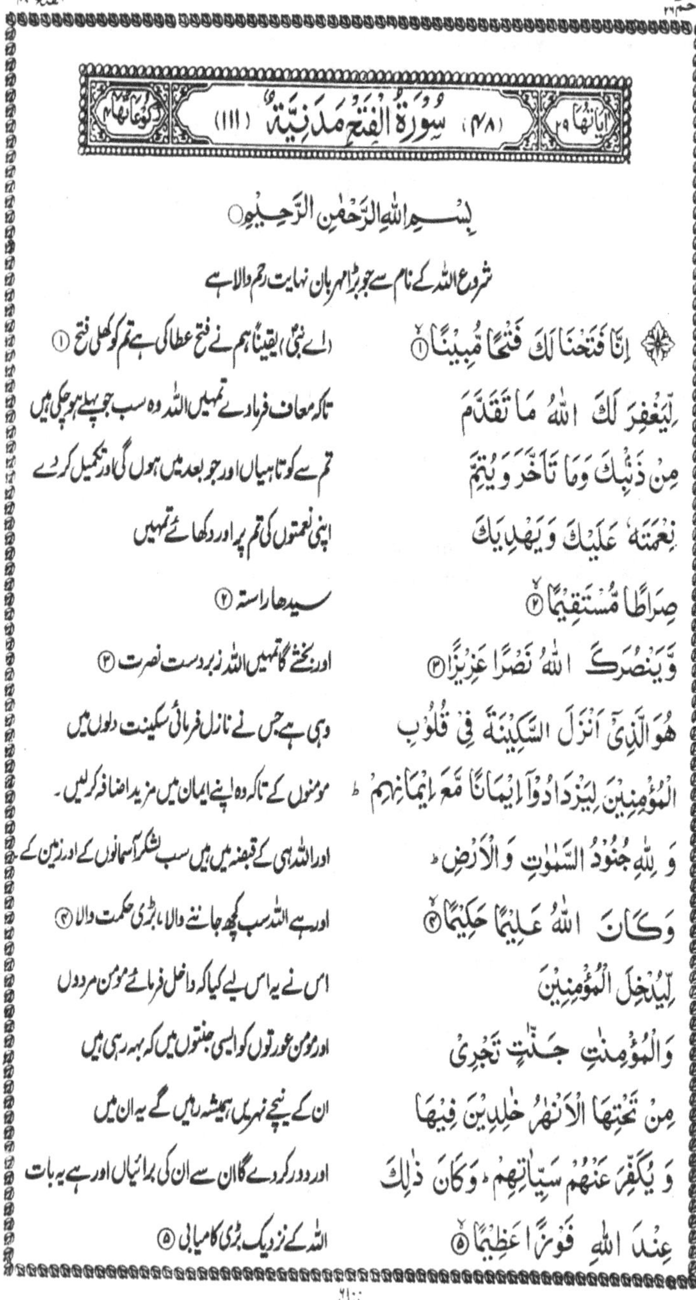

آیاتها ٢٩ (٤٨) سُورَةُ الْفَتْحِ مَدَنِيَّة (١١١) رکوعاتها ٤

بِسْمِ اللَّهِ الرَّحْمَٰنِ الرَّحِيمِ

شروع اللہ کے نام سے جو بڑا مہربان نہایت رحم والا ہے

إِنَّا فَتَحْنَا لَكَ فَتْحًا مُّبِينًا ۝١	(اے نبیؐ) یقیناً ہم نے فتح عطا کی ہے تم کو کھلی فتح ١
لِّيَغْفِرَ لَكَ اللَّهُ مَا تَقَدَّمَ	تاکہ معاف فرمادے تمہیں اللہ وہ سب جو پہلے ہو چکی ہیں
مِن ذَنبِكَ وَمَا تَأَخَّرَ وَيُتِمَّ	تم سے کوتاہیاں اور جو بعد میں ہوں گی اور تکمیل کردے
نِعْمَتَهُ عَلَيْكَ وَيَهْدِيَكَ	اپنی نعمتوں کی تم پر اور دکھائے تمہیں
صِرَاطًا مُّسْتَقِيمًا ۝٢	سیدھا راستہ ٢
وَيَنصُرَكَ اللَّهُ نَصْرًا عَزِيزًا ۝٣	اور بخشے گا تمہیں اللہ زبردست نصرت ٣
هُوَ الَّذِي أَنزَلَ السَّكِينَةَ فِي قُلُوبِ	وہی ہے جس نے نازل فرمائی سکینت دلوں میں
الْمُؤْمِنِينَ لِيَزْدَادُوا إِيمَانًا مَّعَ إِيمَانِهِمْ ۗ	مومنوں کے تاکہ وہ اپنے ایمان میں مزید اضافہ کرلیں۔
وَلِلَّهِ جُنُودُ السَّمَاوَاتِ وَالْأَرْضِ ۚ	اور اللہ ہی کے قبضہ میں ہیں سب لشکر آسمانوں کے اور زمین کے
وَكَانَ اللَّهُ عَلِيمًا حَكِيمًا ۝٤	اور ہے اللہ سب کچھ جاننے والا، بڑی حکمت والا ٤
لِّيُدْخِلَ الْمُؤْمِنِينَ	اس نے یہ اس لیے کیا کہ داخل فرمائے مومن مردوں
وَالْمُؤْمِنَاتِ جَنَّاتٍ تَجْرِي	اور مومن عورتوں کو ایسی جنتوں میں کہ بہہ رہی ہیں
مِن تَحْتِهَا الْأَنْهَارُ خَالِدِينَ فِيهَا	ان کے نیچے نہریں ہمیشہ رہیں گے یہ ان میں
وَيُكَفِّرَ عَنْهُمْ سَيِّئَاتِهِمْ ۚ وَكَانَ ذَٰلِكَ	اور دور کردے گا ان سے ان کی برائیاں اور ہے یہ بات
عِندَ اللَّهِ فَوْزًا عَظِيمًا ۝٥	اللہ کے نزدیک بڑی کامیابی ٥

048-AL FATH

In the name of Lord, the Most Beneficent, Most Merciful

001 Indeed!
We got you a clear triumph in pace
002 That Lord may absolve in grace
The err and slips of your past in trace

And accomplish you, His ease and appease
To steer you in compliant trail to please

003 Lord may aid and assuage in grace
With sane and sound surety to brace

004 Lord blessed the men in lore
His serenity of tranquil in core

So them to affirm and conform in faith
All might in smite,
Of the heavens and earth in array
Belongs to The Bounty of Lord in sway

For Lord is full of Sapience in lore
And Intelligence at core

005 That He may endow in appease
Believing Men and dame to please
And let to the Gardens in ease

Where streams surge, swift in flow
Slip in slide, aside and below
Them to dwell therein endow
And remove their ills of wills in blow

Before Lord!
That's the cherished award in glow
For the men of faith in bestow

وَيُعَذِّبَ الْمُنٰفِقِيْنَ وَالْمُنٰفِقٰتِ	اور (تاکہ) سزا دے منافق مردوں اور منافق عورتوں کو
وَالْمُشْرِكِيْنَ وَالْمُشْرِكٰتِ الظَّآنِّيْنَ	اور مشرک مردوں اور مشرک عورتوں کو جو گمان رکھتے ہیں
بِاللّٰهِ ظَنَّ السَّوْءِ ؕ	اللہ کے بارے میں برے برے گمان۔
عَلَيْهِمْ دَآئِرَةُ السَّوْءِ ۚ وَغَضِبَ اللّٰهُ	وہ خود ہی آگئے برائی کے پھیر میں اور اللہ کا غضب ہوا
عَلَيْهِمْ وَلَعَنَهُمْ	ان پر اور دور کر دیا انہیں اس نے اپنی رحمت سے
وَاَعَدَّ لَهُمْ جَهَنَّمَ ؕ وَسَآءَتْ مَصِيْرًا ﴿۶﴾	اور مہیا کر دی ان کے لیے جہنم جو ہے بہت برا ٹھکانہ ﴿۶﴾
وَلِلّٰهِ جُنُوْدُ السَّمٰوٰتِ وَالْاَرْضِ ؕ	اور اللہ ہی کے قبضہ میں ہیں سب لشکر آسمانوں کے اور زمین کے۔
وَكَانَ اللّٰهُ عَزِيْزًا حَكِيْمًا ﴿۷﴾	اور ہے اللہ زبردست اور بڑی حکمت والا ﴿۷﴾
اِنَّآ اَرْسَلْنٰكَ شَاهِدًا	بے شک ہم نے ہی بھیجا ہے تمہیں شہادت دینے والا،
وَّمُبَشِّرًا وَّنَذِيْرًا ﴿۸﴾	اور بشارت دینے والا اور متنبہ کرنے والا (بنا کر) ﴿۸﴾
لِّتُؤْمِنُوْا بِاللّٰهِ وَرَسُوْلِهٖ	تاکہ ایمان لاؤ تم (اے لوگو!) اللہ پر اور اس کے رسول پر
وَتُعَزِّرُوْهُ وَتُوَقِّرُوْهُ ؕ وَتُسَبِّحُوْهُ	اور تعظیم و توقیر کرو رسول کی اور تسبیح کرو اللہ کی
بُكْرَةً وَّاَصِيْلًا ﴿۹﴾	صبح و شام ﴿۹﴾
اِنَّ الَّذِيْنَ يُبَايِعُوْنَكَ اِنَّمَا	یقیناً جو لوگ بیعت کر رہے تھے تمہاری، درحقیقت
يُبَايِعُوْنَ اللّٰهَ ؕ يَدُ اللّٰهِ	وہ بیعت کر رہے تھے اللہ کی۔ اللہ کا ہاتھ تھا
فَوْقَ اَيْدِيْهِمْ ۚ فَمَنْ نَّكَثَ	ان کے ہاتھوں کے اوپر۔ اب جو شخص عہد شکنی کرے گا
فَاِنَّمَا يَنْكُثُ عَلٰى نَفْسِهٖ ۚ	تو بہرحال اس کی عہد شکنی کا وبال اسی کی ذات پر ہوگا
وَمَنْ اَوْفٰى بِمَا عٰهَدَ	اور جو پورا کرے گا اس بات کو، عہد کیا ہے اس نے
ع عَلَيْهُ اللّٰهَ فَسَيُؤْتِيْهِ اَجْرًا عَظِيْمًا ﴿۱۰﴾	جس پر اللہ سے تو ضرور عطا فرمائے گا اسے اللہ بڑا اجر ﴿۱۰﴾

006 And He may,
Castigate Hypocrites of the men and the dame
And of polytheists men and dame
Who affirm in the same

Appropriate vile in whim
For The Lord in prim

They abide rundle of evil in accord
With fury of Lord in assort

They're accursed of Lord in pace
As Hell is readied for them in place
That's the malicious reside in base

007 To Him belongs all the Might in smite
Of the heavens and the earth in plight

Lord is Exalted in Might
Full of Sapience in Bright

008 Indeed!
We've assigned you as an observer to prevail
As he gets you a good word in trail
And to admonish the men in detail

009 So O you the men and clan in span
Trust in Lord and His Messenger in plan

That you may assist and acclaim in lore
And Glorify Lord in adore
And His tributes morn and eve in score

010 Indeed!
Who pledged in allegiance to you in stance
It's same of allegiance with Lord in glance

Hand of Lord was over their hand to grasp
Then one who tamper His vow to clasp
Does hurt his soul in place

And who conforms his pledge in pace
With Lord,
He's to endow glorious boons in place

سَيَقُوْلُ لَكَ الْمُخَلَّفُوْنَ	ضرور کہیں گے تم سے وہ لوگ جو پیچھے رہ گئے تھے
مِنَ الْاَعْرَابِ شَغَلَتْنَآ اَمْوَالُنَا	بدوی عربوں میں سے کہ مشغول کر رکھا تھا ہمیں ہمارے مالوں
وَاَهْلُوْنَا فَاسْتَغْفِرْ لَنَا ۚ	اور گھر والوں (کی فکر) نے سو مغفرت کی دعا کریں آپ ہمارے لیے۔
يَقُوْلُوْنَ بِاَلْسِنَتِهِمْ مَّا لَيْسَ	وہ کہتے ہیں اپنی زبانوں سے وہ باتیں جو نہیں ہیں
فِيْ قُلُوْبِهِمْ ۭ قُلْ فَمَنْ يَّمْلِكُ	ان کے دلوں میں۔ ان سے کہیے اچھا تو کس میں یہ طاقت ہے
لَكُمْ مِّنَ اللّٰهِ شَيْـًٔا اِنْ اَرَادَ	کہ روک دے تم سے اللہ کو ذرا بھی اگر وہ چاہے
بِكُمْ ضَرًّا اَوْ اَرَادَ بِكُمْ نَفْعًا ۭ	تمہیں نقصان پہنچانا یا چاہے تمہیں نفع پہنچانا۔
بَلْ كَانَ اللّٰهُ بِمَا	حقیقت یہ ہے کہ ہے اللہ ان باتوں سے جو
تَعْمَلُوْنَ خَبِيْرًا (۱۱)	تم کر رہے ہو پوری طرح باخبر (۱۱)
بَلْ ظَنَنْتُمْ اَنْ لَّنْ يَّنْقَلِبَ الرَّسُوْلُ	دراصل تم نے یہ سمجھ رکھا تھا کہ ہرگز نہیں لوٹیں گے رسولؐ
وَالْمُؤْمِنُوْنَ اِلٰٓى اَهْلِيْهِمْ اَبَدًا	اور مومن اپنے گھروں کی طرف کبھی
وَّزُيِّنَ ذٰلِكَ فِيْ قُلُوْبِكُمْ	اور بہت اچھی لگی تھی یہ بات تمہارے دلوں کو
وَظَنَنْتُمْ ظَنَّ السَّوْءِ ښ	اور اسی وجہ سے کرنے لگے تھے تم برے برے گمان
وَكُنْتُمْ قَوْمًۢا بُوْرًا (۱۲)	حالانکہ ہو تم وہ لوگ جنہیں بہرحال ہلاک ہونا ہے (۱۲)
وَمَنْ لَّمْ يُؤْمِنْ بِاللّٰهِ وَرَسُوْلِهٖ	اور جو نہیں ایمان رکھتے اللہ پر اور اس کے رسول پر
فَاِنَّآ اَعْتَدْنَا	تو بےشک تیار کر رکھا ہے ہم نے
لِلْكٰفِرِيْنَ سَعِيْرًا (۱۳)	ایسے کافروں کے لیے بھڑکتی ہوئی آگ کا الاؤ (۱۳)
وَلِلّٰهِ مُلْكُ السَّمٰوٰتِ وَالْاَرْضِ ۭ	اور اللہ ہی کے لیے ہے بادشاہی آسمانوں کی اور زمین کی۔
يَغْفِرُ لِمَنْ يَّشَاۗءُ وَيُعَذِّبُ مَنْ يَّشَاۗءُ ۭ	معاف کردے جسے چاہے اور سزا دے جسے چاہے۔

011 Those of the Arabs, abiding in deserts
Who tarried in trail, in concerts

Come to you to affirm
We're to care flocks and herds in term

And with our close of kin in place
Do you beg for clemency in pace
They assert with idiom in trace

But within their core, they trend to deny
(O Muhammad!)
You assert to affirm in reply

Who's the authority to intercede in stride
Other than Lord to concern in abide

If He's to harm and hurt in place
Or to cherish gain and good in pace
But Lord is in know of your doings in trace

012 Absolutely not!
You had rather a whim in stride
Messenger and devotee wouldn't return to resides

You're comforted in your veer of core
And you'd a picture of wicked whim in lore

For you're the clan of evil stance in concern
(Anyhow you've to die in term)

013 And if some dare and defy Lord in grace
And His Messenger in pace

We've prepared an awful doom in gloom
For who renounce The Lord in Bloom
Him to savor
A burn of Fire, in flavor

014 To Him belongs the rule and edit
Of the heavens and earth in summit
He may absolve to some in decides

وَكَانَ اللّٰهُ غَفُوْرًا رَّحِيْمًا ﴿۱۴﴾	اور ہے اللہ بہت بخشنے والا، ہر حال میں رحم کرنے والا ﴿۱۴﴾
سَيَقُوْلُ الْمُخَلَّفُوْنَ	ضرور کہیں گے یہ پیچھے رہ جانے والے
اِذَا انْطَلَقْتُمْ اِلٰى مَغَانِمَ لِتَاْخُذُوْهَا	کہ جب جانے لگو تم مالِ غنیمت حاصل کرنے کے لیے
ذَرُوْنَا نَتَّبِعْكُمْ ۚ	تو ہمیں بھی اجازت دو کہ تمہارے ساتھ چلیں۔
يُرِيْدُوْنَ اَنْ يُّبَدِّلُوْا كَلٰمَ اللّٰهِ	یہ چاہتے ہیں کہ بدل دیں اللہ کے فرمان کو۔
قُلْ لَّنْ تَتَّبِعُوْنَا	کہہ دیجیے تم ہرگز نہیں چل سکتے ہمارے ساتھ
كَذٰلِكُمْ قَالَ اللّٰهُ مِنْ قَبْلُ ۚ	یہ بات تمہارے حق میں فرما چکا ہے اللہ پہلے ہی۔
فَسَيَقُوْلُوْنَ بَلْ تَحْسُدُوْنَنَا ۚ	سو یہ ضرور کہیں گے، نہیں بلکہ تم ہم سے حسد کرتے ہو۔
بَلْ كَانُوْا لَا يَفْقَهُوْنَ اِلَّا قَلِيْلًا ﴿۱۵﴾	اصل بات یہ ہے کہ یہ لوگ صحیح بات کو کم ہی سمجھتے ہیں ﴿۱۵﴾
قُلْ لِّلْمُخَلَّفِيْنَ مِنَ الْاَعْرَابِ	کہہ دیجیے ان پیچھے رہ جانے والے بدوؤں سے
سَتُدْعَوْنَ اِلٰى قَوْمٍ	کہ عنقریب تمہیں دعوت دی جائے گی (مقابلہ کی) ایسے لوگوں سے جو
اُولِىْ بَاْسٍ شَدِيْدٍ تُقَاتِلُوْنَهُمْ	بڑے زور آور ہیں۔ تم کو ان سے جنگ کرنی ہوگی
اَوْ يُسْلِمُوْنَ ۚ فَاِنْ تُطِيْعُوْا	یا وہ مطیع فرمان ہو جائیں گے۔ پھر اگر تم نے اطاعت کی (ہمارے حکم کی)
يُؤْتِكُمُ اللّٰهُ اَجْرًا حَسَنًا ۚ وَاِنْ	تو دے گا تم کو اللہ اچھا اجر۔ اور اگر
تَتَوَلَّوْا كَمَا تَوَلَّيْتُمْ مِّنْ قَبْلُ	تم منہ موڑو گے جیسے منہ موڑتے رہے ہو اس سے پہلے
يُعَذِّبْكُمْ عَذَابًا اَلِيْمًا ﴿۱۶﴾	تو دے گا تم کو اللہ دردناک عذاب ﴿۱۶﴾
لَيْسَ عَلَى الْاَعْمٰى حَرَجٌ وَّلَا عَلَى الْاَعْرَجِ	نہیں ہے اندھے پر کوئی حرج اور نہ لنگڑے پر
حَرَجٌ وَّلَا عَلَى الْمَرِيْضِ حَرَجٌ ۗ	کوئی حرج اور نہ مریض پر کوئی حرج (کہ نہ شریک ہوں جنگ میں)
وَمَنْ يُّطِعِ اللّٰهَ وَرَسُوْلَهٗ	اور جو شخص اطاعت کرے گا اللہ کی اور اس کے رسول کی،

To some He trends to trounce in strides
But Lord is Compassionate and Tender to aside
015 Those who tarried in trail
And didn't get to combat in scale

They'll trend to assert and say:
When you're free to take boodle in fray
Favor us to follow (you) to comply in sway

They cherish to change in trance
The dictum of Lord in stance

Tell them in words so refined
You cannot chase (us) in this design
Lord has avowed earlier in prime

Then they'll assert to sustain:
You're invidious of us in claim
Indeed not!
But they cannot sustain the truth to remain
016 Say:
To the Arabs abiding in deserts
Who tarried in trail to desert

You'll be called to combat
Against men of power hither in instruct
Then you would've to confront in fray

Or they'll accede to the word in faith
So if you conform in compliance
Our dictum of faith
Lord is to award grants in reliance

But if you deny and drift in thrift
As you did before in swift
Lord is to castigate even more in rift

017 There's no blame on the blind in place
Nor for lame and the ailing in pace

For them to combat in fray
But, who accedes to obey
Lord and His Messenger in stay

يُّدْخِلْهُ جَنّٰتٍ تَجْرِيْ	داخل کرے گا اسے اللہ ایسی جنتوں میں کہ بہہ رہی ہیں
مِنْ تَحْتِهَا الْاَنْهٰرُ ۚ وَمَنْ يَّتَوَلَّ	جن کے نیچے نہریں اور جو منہ پھیرے گا
يُعَذِّبْهُ عَذَابًا اَلِيْمًا ﴿۱۷﴾	دے گا اسے اللہ دردناک عذاب ﴿۱۷﴾
لَقَدْ رَضِيَ اللّٰهُ عَنِ الْمُؤْمِنِيْنَ	بلاشبہ راضی ہو گیا اللہ مومنوں سے
اِذْ يُبَايِعُوْنَكَ تَحْتَ الشَّجَرَةِ	جب وہ بیعت کر رہے تھے تم سے درخت کے نیچے
فَعَلِمَ مَا فِيْ قُلُوْبِهِمْ	سو وہ جانتا تھا ان کے دلوں کی کیفیت
فَاَنْزَلَ السَّكِيْنَةَ عَلَيْهِمْ	سو نازل فرمائی اللہ نے سکینت ان پر
وَاَثَابَهُمْ فَتْحًا قَرِيْبًا ﴿۱۸﴾	اور انعام میں عطا فرمائی انہیں قریبی فتح ﴿۱۸﴾
وَّمَغَانِمَ كَثِيْرَةً يَّاْخُذُوْنَهَا ۭ	اور مالِ غنیمت، بہت سا جو (عنقریب) حاصل کریں گے وہ۔
وَكَانَ اللّٰهُ عَزِيْزًا حَكِيْمًا ﴿۱۹﴾	اور ہے اللہ زبردست اور بڑی حکمت والا ﴿۱۹﴾
وَعَدَكُمُ اللّٰهُ مَغَانِمَ كَثِيْرَةً	وعدہ فرمایا تھا تم سے اللہ نے ڈھیروں مالِ غنیمت کا
تَاْخُذُوْنَهَا فَعَجَّلَ	جو تم حاصل کرو گے سو اس نے فوری طور پر عطا کر دی
لَكُمْ هٰذِهٖ وَكَفَّ اَيْدِيَ النَّاسِ عَنْكُمْ ۚ	تمہیں یہ فتح اور روک دیے لوگوں کے ہاتھ تم سے۔
وَلِتَكُوْنَ اٰيَةً لِّلْمُؤْمِنِيْنَ	تاکہ بن جائے یہ بات ایک نشانی مومنوں کے لیے
وَيَهْدِيَكُمْ صِرَاطًا مُّسْتَقِيْمًا ﴿۲۰﴾	اور رہنمائی کرے اللہ تمہاری سیدھے راستے کی طرف ﴿۲۰﴾
وَّاُخْرٰى	اور (وعدہ کرتا ہے وہ تم سے اس کے علاوہ) دوسری غنیمتوں کا کہ
لَمْ تَقْدِرُوْا عَلَيْهَا قَدْ اَحَاطَ	نہیں قادر ہوئے تم ان پر ابھی گھیر رکھا ہے
اللّٰهُ بِهَا ۭ وَكَانَ اللّٰهُ	اللہ نے انہیں بھی (تمہارے لیے)۔ اور ہے اللہ
عَلٰي كُلِّ شَيْءٍ قَدِيْرًا ﴿۲۱﴾	ہر چیز پر پوری طرح قادر ﴿۲۱﴾

Lord will endow in grants
The Gardens of bliss to reside
Where streams surge in stride

If some recant to show his back
Lord is to smite invidious in aback

018 Lord was appeased of the faithful in stance
When they professed below the tree in glance

He knew their veer of core in concern
And conferred serenity in term
He awarded a swift subjugation in trance

019 Them to cherish many a reward in plight
For,
Lord is Exalted in Might
Full of Sapience in Bright

020 Lord has affirmed many a gifts in glance
For you to cherish in trance
He's endowed you quite a few in stance

And He restricted the men (you) to grasp
That's a Sign for the Devote to clasp

So Him to escort (you) in a way
That's the way in truth to stay

021 And there are awards to procure
Beyond your concept in score

But Lord has scope beyond scale and span
And He's command over all (things) in plan

وَلَوْ قٰتَلَكُمُ الَّذِيْنَ كَفَرُوْا	اور اگر جنگ کرتے تم سے (اس وقت) کافر
لَوَلَّوُا الْاَدْبَارَ ثُمَّ لَا يَجِدُوْنَ	تو ضرور پیٹھ پھیر جاتے اور نہ پاتے وہ (اپنے لیے)
وَلِيًّا وَّلَا نَصِيْرًا ﴿٢٢﴾	کوئی حامی اور نہ مددگار ﴿٢٢﴾
سُنَّةَ اللّٰهِ الَّتِيْ قَدْ خَلَتْ	یہ اللہ کی سنت ہے جو چلی آ رہی ہے
مِنْ قَبْلُ ۚ وَلَنْ تَجِدَ لِسُنَّةِ اللّٰهِ تَبْدِيْلًا ﴿٢٣﴾	پہلے سے۔ اور نہ پاؤ گے تم اللہ کی سنت میں کوئی تبدیلی ﴿٢٣﴾
وَهُوَ الَّذِيْ كَفَّ اَيْدِيَهُمْ عَنْكُمْ	یہ اللہ ہی ہے جس نے روک دیے ان کے ہاتھ تم سے
وَاَيْدِيَكُمْ عَنْهُمْ بِبَطْنِ مَكَّةَ	اور تمہارے ہاتھ ان سے وادیٔ مکہ میں
مِنْ بَعْدِ اَنْ اَظْفَرَكُمْ عَلَيْهِمْ ۭ	اس کے بعد کہ غلبہ عطا کر چکا تھا وہ تمہیں ان پر۔
وَكَانَ اللّٰهُ بِمَا تَعْمَلُوْنَ بَصِيْرًا ﴿٢٤﴾	اور اللہ دیکھ رہا تھا اسے جو تم کر رہے تھے ﴿٢٤﴾
هُمُ الَّذِيْنَ كَفَرُوْا وَصَدُّوْكُمْ	یہ وہ لوگ تھے جنہوں نے انکار کیا (رسالت کا) اور روک دیا تھا تمہیں
عَنِ الْمَسْجِدِ الْحَرَامِ وَالْهَدْيَ مَعْكُوْفًا	مسجدِ حرام سے اور قربانی کے جانوروں کو روکا تھا
اَنْ يَّبْلُغَ مَحِلَّهٗ ۭ وَلَوْلَا رِجَالٌ مُّؤْمِنُوْنَ	کہ وہ پہنچیں اپنی قربانی کی جگہ تک اور اگر نہ ہوتے (مکہ میں) کچھ ایسے مومن مرد
وَنِسَاۗءٌ مُّؤْمِنٰتٌ لَّمْ تَعْلَمُوْهُمْ	اور مومن عورتیں جنہیں تم نہیں جانتے،
اَنْ تَطَـُٔوْهُمْ فَتُصِيْبَكُمْ مِّنْهُمْ	اندیشہ تھا کہ تم انہیں پامال کر دو گے اور آئے گا ان کی وجہ سے تم پر
مَّعَرَّةٌۢ بِغَيْرِ عِلْمٍ ۚ	الزام (حالانکہ ہوتا یہ حادثہ) نادانستگی میں (تو جنگ نہ روکی جاتی)۔
لِيُدْخِلَ اللّٰهُ	(جنگ اس لیے روکی گئی) تاکہ داخل کرے اللہ
فِيْ رَحْمَتِهٖ مَنْ يَّشَاۗءُ ۚ	اپنی رحمت میں جسے چاہے۔
لَوْ تَزَيَّلُوْا لَعَذَّبْنَا	اور اگر الگ ہو گئے ہوتے (یہ مومن مرد اور عورتیں) تو سزا دیتے ہم
الَّذِيْنَ كَفَرُوْا مِنْهُمْ عَذَابًا اَلِيْمًا ﴿٢٥﴾	ان کو جنہوں نے کفر کیا ہے اہلِ مکہ میں سے دردناک سزا ﴿٢٥﴾

022 If cynics incline to combat in fray
Indeed!
They'll retreat in stray
Then they wouldn't have a guard as ally

023 Lord Has a definite discipline in lore
For what He asserted hither in fore
There's no change in His Discipline in stay

024 Lord for you!
Restricted their grasp mid Makkah in place
Then He endowed (you) subjugation in pace
Lord discerns your deeds and doings in trace

025 These are the men and clan in trail
Who disputed Divine Inspiration in vale

And didn't let you,
Enter Sacred Mosque in adore
And offering of the cattle in score

And held you to reach in pace
Site of immolation in place

Had it not been men and dame in faith*
Whom you couldn't distinguish in haste

And you'd have squashed in innocence
That an incursion would've added in nescience
(Allah would've settled you to coerce in way,
But he held you back in fray)

That Lord!
May concede to Clemency in grace
Whom He cherishes to adore in brace

If they'd have stayed asunder in abide
We'd have trounced the cynics in glide
With a heinous sentence in stride

*whoever staying in Makkah and was fearing being killed in case of war

اِذْ جَعَلَ الَّذِيْنَ كَفَرُوْا	چنانچہ جب پیدا کر لیا کافروں نے
فِيْ قُلُوْبِهِمُ الْحَمِيَّةَ	اپنے دلوں میں تعصب ۔
حَمِيَّةَ الْجَاهِلِيَّةِ فَاَنْزَلَ اللّٰهُ	یعنی جاہلانہ تعصب کو تو نازل فرمائی اللہ نے
سَكِيْنَتَهٗ عَلٰى رَسُوْلِهٖ وَعَلَى الْمُؤْمِنِيْنَ	اپنی سکینت اپنے رسولؐ پر اور مومنوں پر
وَاَلْزَمَهُمْ كَلِمَةَ التَّقْوٰى وَكَانُوْٓا	اور پابند رکھا انہیں تقویٰ کی بات کا اور تھے یہی لوگ
اَحَقَّ بِهَا وَاَهْلَهَا ۭ	زیادہ حقدار تقویٰ کے اور اس کے اہل بھی ۔
وَكَانَ اللّٰهُ بِكُلِّ شَيْءٍ عَلِيْمًا ۲۶	اور ہے اللہ ہر چیز کو پوری طرح جاننے والا ۲۶
لَقَدْ صَدَقَ اللّٰهُ رَسُوْلَهُ	فی الواقع سچا دکھایا تھا اللہ نے اپنے رسول کو
الرُّءْيَا بِالْحَقِّ ۚ لَتَدْخُلُنَّ	خواب جو حق کے مطابق تھا کہ ضرور داخل ہوگے تم
الْمَسْجِدَ الْحَرَامَ اِنْ شَاۗءَ اللّٰهُ اٰمِنِيْنَ ۙ	مسجدِ حرام میں اللہ کے اذن سے پورے اطمینان کے ساتھ
مُحَلِّقِيْنَ رُءُوْسَكُمْ وَمُقَصِّرِيْنَ ۙ	منڈھواؤ گے اپنے سر اور ترشواؤ گے اپنے بال
لَا تَخَافُوْنَ ۭ فَعَلِمَ مَا	اور تمہیں کوئی خوف نہ ہوگا۔ پس وہ جانتا تھا وہ بات جو
لَمْ تَعْلَمُوْا فَجَعَلَ	تم نہیں جانتے۔ اس لیے اس نے عطا فرمائی
مِنْ دُوْنِ ذٰلِكَ فَتْحًا قَرِيْبًا ۲۷	اس خواب کے پورا ہونے سے پہلے یہ قریبی فتح ۲۷
هُوَ الَّذِيْٓ اَرْسَلَ	وہی ہے وہ ذات جس نے بھیجا
رَسُوْلَهٗ بِالْهُدٰى وَدِيْنِ الْحَقِّ	اپنا رسولؐ ہدایت اور دینِ حق کے ساتھ
لِيُظْهِرَهٗ عَلَى الدِّيْنِ كُلِّهٖ ۭ	تاکہ غالب کر دے اسے تمام ادیان پر ۔
وَكَفٰى بِاللّٰهِ شَهِيْدًا ۲۸	اور کافی ہے اللہ گواہی کے لیے (اس حقیقت پر) ۲۸
مُحَمَّدٌ رَّسُوْلُ اللّٰهِ ۭ	محمدؐ اللہ کے رسول ہیں۔

026 While Cynics got disgusted in core
That's revulsion of ignorance in lore

Then Lord endowed His ease in appease
To His Messenger and men in belief

To affirm in grace fortitude to brace
They really merited in stance
And were worthy in glance
And Lord is knowledgeable of all in pace

027 Indeed!
Lord affirmed the vision in trance
For His Messenger thither in glance

That's asserted by Lord to stay
That you to enter Sacred Mosque to pray

Minds assured, heads shiny, hair nip in low
With no awe and dread thither in blow

For He discerned to concern all in pace
That you didn't know a bit in trace

And He endowed you besides this term
A prompt triumph (for you) to affirm

028 It's He, Who apprised in pace
His Messenger, with escort in precision
And the faith of Truth in grace
To expound over all faiths in decision
And Lord is sufficient to affirm in pace

029 Muhammad!
The Messenger of Lord in abide
Those of his men around and aside

وَ الَّذِيْنَ مَعَهٗٓ — اور وہ لوگ جو ان کے ساتھ ہیں،

اَشِدَّآءُ عَلَى الْكُفَّارِ — زور آور ہیں کافروں پر

رُحَمَآءُ بَيْنَهُمْ — (اور) مہربان ہیں آپس میں،

تَرٰىهُمْ رُكَّعًا — پاؤ گے تم انہیں مشغول رکوع میں،

سُجَّدًا يَّبْتَغُوْنَ — سجدے میں تلاش کرتے ہیں (ان کاموں سے)

فَضْلًا مِّنَ اللّٰهِ وَرِضْوَانًا ز — اللہ کا فضل اور اس کی خوشنودی۔

سِيْمَاهُمْ فِيْ وُجُوْهِهِمْ — ان کی پہچان یہ ہے کہ ان کے چہروں پر

مِّنْ اَثَرِ السُّجُوْدِ ؕ ذٰلِكَ — سجود کے اثرات نمایاں ہیں۔ یہ ہیں

مَثَلُهُمْ فِي التَّوْرٰىةِ ۛ — ان کے اوصاف تورات میں،

وَ مَثَلُهُمْ فِي الْاِنْجِيْلِ ۛ — اور ان کی مثال انجیل میں۔

كَزَرْعٍ اَخْرَجَ — (اس طرح ہے) کہ گویا ایک کھیتی ہے جس نے نکالی

شَطْـَٔهٗ فَاٰزَرَهٗ — اپنی کونپل پھر اس کو تقویت دی

فَاسْتَغْلَظَ فَاسْتَوٰى — پھر وہ گدرائی پھر وہ سیدھی کھڑی ہوگئی

عَلٰى سُوْقِهٖ يُعْجِبُ — اپنے تنے پر جو خوش کرتی ہے

الزُّرَّاعَ لِيَغِيْظَ — کاشتکار کو تاکہ جلیں

بِهِمُ الْكُفَّارَ ؕ وَعَدَ — انہیں دیکھ کر کافر۔ وعدہ کیا ہے

اللّٰهُ الَّذِيْنَ اٰمَنُوْا — اللہ نے ان لوگوں سے جو ایمان لائے ہیں

وَ عَمِلُوا الصّٰلِحٰتِ مِنْهُمْ — اور کیے انہوں نے نیک عمل اس گروہ میں سے

مَّغْفِرَةً وَّاَجْرًا عَظِيْمًا (۲۹) — مغفرت کا اور اجرِ عظیم کا (۲۹)

Stay strong to strike the cynic in place
Calm and clement with each in grace
You see them to submit and surrender in pray
Seeking His Elegance and Delight to Brace
On their fore are signs of salaam
That's their semblance in psalm
Like that of Torah and Gospel in pace
It's like a grain with its petioles to sprout
Then prompt to sinewy structure in stout
It becomes thick and stands so firm in grout
The tiller marvel thrilling in entrance
It trends infidels with fury in glance
Lord has pledged hither in stance
With the men of Faith in trail
Who trend to the noble deeds in vale
For them,
Clemency in Mercy a grand gift to avail

"The brief history of 21st century shows that neither side has mastered these lessons. If we are to avoid catastrophe, the Muslims and the Western Worlds must learn not merely to tolerate but to appreciate one another. A good place to start with is with the personality of Prophet Muhammad a most sophisticated and complex figure in the history of humanity, who resists facile ideologically driven categorization, who sometime did things that were difficult or impossible to accept, but he had profound genius and lead a faith a cultural tradition that was not based on sword but whose name is 'Islam' that signifies peace and reconciliation."

Karen Armstrong "Muhammad Prophet of Today"

اٰیاتہا ۱۸ سورۃ الحجرات مدنیۃ (۴۹) (۱۰۶) رکوعاتہا ۲

بِسْمِ اللّٰهِ الرَّحْمٰنِ الرَّحِيْمِ

شروع اللہ کے نام سے جو بڑا مہربان نہایت رحم والا ہے

يٰۤاَيُّهَا الَّذِيْنَ اٰمَنُوْا لَا تُقَدِّمُوْا
اے لوگو جو ایمان لائے ہو نہ پیش قدمی کرو

بَيْنَ يَدَيِ اللّٰهِ وَرَسُوْلِهٖ وَاتَّقُوا اللّٰهَ ؕ
آگے اللہ اور اس کے رسول کے اور ڈرو اللہ سے

اِنَّ اللّٰهَ سَمِيْعٌ عَلِيْمٌ ۝١
بے شک اللہ ہے سب کچھ سننے والا اور سب کچھ جاننے والا ۝١

يٰۤاَيُّهَا الَّذِيْنَ اٰمَنُوْا لَا تَرْفَعُوْۤا اَصْوَاتَكُمْ
اے لوگو جو ایمان لائے ہو نہ بلند کرو اپنی آوازیں

فَوْقَ صَوْتِ النَّبِيِّ وَلَا تَجْهَرُوْا
اوپر نبی کی آواز کے اور نہ اونچی کرو اپنی آواز

لَهٗ بِالْقَوْلِ كَجَهْرِ
اس کے سامنے بات کرتے وقت جیسے اونچی آواز میں بولتے ہو تم

بَعْضِكُمْ لِبَعْضٍ اَنْ تَحْبَطَ
ایک دوسرے سے کہیں ایسا نہ ہو کہ غارت ہو جائیں

اَعْمَالُكُمْ وَاَنْتُمْ لَا تَشْعُرُوْنَ ۝٢
تمہارے اعمال اور تمہیں خبر بھی نہ ہو ۝٢

اِنَّ الَّذِيْنَ يَغُضُّوْنَ اَصْوَاتَهُمْ
بلاشبہ وہ لوگ جو پست رکھتے ہیں اپنی آواز

عِنْدَ رَسُوْلِ اللّٰهِ اُولٰٓئِكَ الَّذِيْنَ
رسول اللہ کے حضور، یہی لوگ ہیں

امْتَحَنَ اللّٰهُ قُلُوْبَهُمْ لِلتَّقْوٰى ؕ
جن کے دلوں کو جانچ لیا ہے اللہ نے تقویٰ کے لیے۔

لَهُمْ مَّغْفِرَةٌ وَّاَجْرٌ عَظِيْمٌ ۝٣
ان کے لیے ہے مغفرت اور اجرِ عظیم ۝٣

اِنَّ الَّذِيْنَ يُنَادُوْنَكَ مِنْ وَّرَآءِ الْحُجُرٰتِ
درحقیقت وہ لوگ جو پکارتے ہیں تمہیں حجروں کے باہر سے

اَكْثَرُهُمْ لَا يَعْقِلُوْنَ ۝٤
ان میں سے اکثر بے عقل ہیں ۝٤

وَلَوْ اَنَّهُمْ صَبَرُوْا حَتّٰى تَخْرُجَ
اور اگر وہ صبر کرتے یہاں تک کہ تم نکل کر آجاتے

049-AL HUJURAT

In the name of Lord, the Most Beneficent, Most Merciful

001 O you the men and clan in faith
Don't cherish in adore your choice in score
Before that of Lord and His Messenger in lore

But awe and dread Lord in all term in trail
For He heeds in concerns your doings in vale

002 O you the men and clan in faith
Don't raise your voice in response
To the voice of Prophet in glance
And don't talk aloud to him in stance

As you converse to each in giggle
Lest your deeds get lost in snigger
And you sense it not in (your) trance

003 Who converse in low voice and tone
Before the Prophet in decency
Lord has affirmed their core in clemency

Their core stay in grace of Lord in alone
For them is Reprieve of Reward in adorn

004 In fact,
When some call you from out of the room
That don't have a bit of intellect in bloom

005 They could've endurance in plight
Until you're there (before them) in sight

إِلَيْهِمْ لَكَانَ خَيْرًا لَّهُمْ ۚ
ان کے پاس تو ہوتا یہ کہیں بہتر ان کے لیے۔

وَاللَّهُ غَفُورٌ رَّحِيمٌ ﴿٥﴾
اور اللہ ہے بہت درگزر فرمانے والا اور ہر حالت میں رحم کرنے والا ﴿٥﴾

يَا أَيُّهَا الَّذِينَ آمَنُوا إِن جَاءَكُمْ
اے لوگو جو ایمان لائے ہو اگر لے کر آئے تمہارے پاس

فَاسِقٌ بِنَبَإٍ فَتَبَيَّنُوا أَن
کوئی فاسق کوئی خبر تو تحقیق کر لیا کرو کہیں ایسا نہ ہو کہ

تُصِيبُوا قَوْمًا بِجَهَالَةٍ فَتُصْبِحُوا
تم نقصان پہنچا بیٹھو کسی گروہ کو نادانستہ اور ہونا پڑے تمہیں

عَلَىٰ مَا فَعَلْتُمْ نَادِمِينَ ﴿٦﴾
اپنے کیے پر نادم ﴿٦﴾

وَاعْلَمُوا أَنَّ فِيكُمْ رَسُولَ اللَّهِ ۚ
اور خوب جان رکھو کہ بے شک تم میں موجود ہے اللہ کا رسول۔

لَوْ يُطِيعُكُمْ فِي كَثِيرٍ مِّنَ الْأَمْرِ
اگر مان لیا کرے وہ تمہاری بات بہت سے معاملات میں

لَعَنِتُّمْ وَلَٰكِنَّ اللَّهَ حَبَّبَ
تو تم مشکلات میں مبتلا ہو جاؤ لیکن اللہ نے محبت عطا کر دی ہے

إِلَيْكُمُ الْإِيمَانَ وَزَيَّنَهُ
تم کو ایمان کی اور پسندیدہ بنا دیا ہے اسے

فِي قُلُوبِكُمْ وَكَرَّهَ إِلَيْكُمُ الْكُفْرَ وَالْفُسُوقَ
تمہارے دلوں کے لیے اور نفرت دلا دی ہے تمہیں کفر سے اور فسق سے

وَالْعِصْيَانَ ۚ أُولَٰئِكَ هُمُ الرَّاشِدُونَ ﴿٧﴾
اور نافرمانی سے۔ ایسے ہی لوگ ہدایت یافتہ ہیں ﴿٧﴾

فَضْلًا مِّنَ اللَّهِ وَنِعْمَةً ۚ
اللہ کے فضل سے اور اس کے احسان سے۔

وَاللَّهُ عَلِيمٌ حَكِيمٌ ﴿٨﴾
اور اللہ ہے سب کچھ جاننے والا اور بڑی حکمت والا ﴿٨﴾

وَإِن طَائِفَتَانِ مِنَ الْمُؤْمِنِينَ اقْتَتَلُوا
اور اگر دو گروہ اہلِ ایمان میں سے آپس میں لڑ پڑیں

فَأَصْلِحُوا بَيْنَهُمَا ۖ فَإِن بَغَتْ
تو صلح کرا دو ان دونوں کے درمیان، پھر اگر زیادتی کرے

إِحْدَاهُمَا عَلَى الْأُخْرَىٰ فَقَاتِلُوا
ان میں سے ایک دوسرے گروہ پر تو جنگ کرو

الَّتِي تَبْغِي حَتَّىٰ تَفِيءَ
اس سے جس نے زیادتی کی ہے یہاں تک کہ وہ پلٹ آئے

إِلَىٰ أَمْرِ اللَّهِ ۚ فَإِن فَاءَتْ
اللہ کے حکم کی طرف۔ پھر اگر وہ پلٹ آئے

That would've been better for them in place
But Lord is Bounteous and Beneficent in pace

006 O you the men and clan in faith!
If an evil man is before you to aside
A word to reveal fore you in stride

Establish verity of word in propose
Lest you hurt the men in close
And then you regret in stance
For your doings in trance

007 And know!
There's Messenger of Lord mid you
If he'd to follow your advice in true
In many of the matters you tend to eschew

You're sure to stumble in blow
But Lord adored you the faith in glow
And determined it so dazzling in (your) core

He made denial of faith odious in sedition
Indeed! These are the men abiding in lore
Who tread in stride so pious in rendition

He made your hearts so loving in faith that the denial in faith is quit awful for you.

008 A boon and benefaction from Lord in Grace
Lord is Knowing and Sagacious in pace
Ebullient in Enlightenment, Him to brace

009 If two groups of allegiants get to brawl
Trend to amity mid them in stroll
But if one is to err or break a term in accord
Then fight against the one betraying in accord

Till it submits to assert Dictum of Lord to aside
But once it submits and affirms in stride
Then trend to amity and equity in abide
And be just in trust

فَاَصْلِحُوْا بَيْنَهُمَا بِالْعَدْلِ	توصلح کرا دو ان دونوں گروہوں کے درمیان عدل کے مطابق
وَ اَقْسِطُوْا ۭ اِنَّ اللّٰهَ يُحِبُّ الْمُقْسِطِيْنَ ۝٩	اور انصاف کرو۔ بلاشبہ اللہ پسند کرتا ہے انصاف کرنے والوں کو ۝٩
اِنَّمَا الْمُؤْمِنُوْنَ اِخْوَةٌ فَاَصْلِحُوْا	دراصل مومن تو آپس میں بھائی بھائی ہیں لہٰذا صلح کرا دیا کرو
بَيْنَ اَخَوَيْكُمْ وَاتَّقُوا اللّٰهَ	اپنے بھائیوں کے درمیان اور ڈرو اللہ سے
لَعَلَّكُمْ تُرْحَمُوْنَ ۝١٠	امید ہے کہ تم پر رحم کیا جائے گا ۝١٠
يٰٓاَيُّهَا الَّذِيْنَ اٰمَنُوْا لَا يَسْخَرْ قَوْمٌ	اے لوگو جو ایمان لائے ہو نہ مذاق اڑائیں مرد
مِّنْ قَوْمٍ عَسٰٓى اَنْ يَّكُوْنُوْا	مردوں کا ہو سکتا ہے کہ ہوں وہ (جن کا مذاق اڑایا جا رہا ہے)
خَيْرًا مِّنْهُمْ وَلَا نِسَاۗءٌ	بہتر مذاق اڑانے والوں سے اور نہ (مذاق اڑائیں) عورتیں
مِّنْ نِّسَاۗءٍ عَسٰٓى اَنْ يَّكُنَّ	عورتوں کا، ہو سکتا ہے کہ ہوں وہ (جن کا مذاق اڑایا جا رہا ہے)
خَيْرًا مِّنْهُنَّ ۚ وَلَا تَلْمِزُوْٓا	بہتر مذاق اڑانے والیوں سے۔ اور نہ عیب لگاؤ
اَنْفُسَكُمْ وَلَا تَنَابَزُوْا	ایک دوسرے پر اور نہ یاد کرو ایک دوسرے کو
بِالْاَلْقَابِ ۭ بِئْسَ الِاسْمُ الْفُسُوْقُ	برے القاب سے۔ بہت برا ہے نام پیدا کرنا فسق میں
بَعْدَ الْاِيْمَانِ ۚ وَمَنْ لَّمْ يَتُبْ	ایمان کے بعد اور جو نہ باز آئیں گے (اس روش سے)
فَاُولٰۗىِٕكَ هُمُ الظّٰلِمُوْنَ ۝١١	سو یہی لوگ ہیں ظالم ۝١١
يٰٓاَيُّهَا الَّذِيْنَ اٰمَنُوا اجْتَنِبُوْا	اے لوگو جو ایمان لائے ہو بچتے رہو
كَثِيْرًا مِّنَ الظَّنِّ ۡ اِنَّ بَعْضَ الظَّنِّ	بہت گمان کرنے سے، بلاشبہ بعض گمان
اِثْمٌ وَّلَا تَجَسَّسُوْا وَلَا يَغْتَبْ	گناہ ہوتے ہیں اور نہ تجسس کرو اور نہ غیبت کرے
بَّعْضُكُمْ بَعْضًا ۭ اَيُحِبُّ اَحَدُكُمْ	کوئی کسی کی۔ کیا پسند کرے گا تم میں سے کوئی شخص
اَنْ يَّاْكُلَ لَحْمَ اَخِيْهِ مَيْتًا	کہ وہ کھائے گوشت اپنے مردہ بھائی کا؟

For Lord!
Loves in score only the trust in just

010 Allegiants are but a kin-ship in clear
So make amity in accord (mid them) so dear

And awe and dread Lord for you to steer
So you to secure His Clemency in fear

011 O you the men and clan in Faith!
Don't giggle and grin at others in trance
It may be so for a while in glance
The next* be better than the first** in stance

Don't tend to slander or be sardonic in gush
O dames! Don't call some with names in norm
It's like to be hypocrisy in form
Nor call to one in idiotic diminutive in rush

After affirming the faith in pace
It may be, for while in sort
The next be better than the first in part
Bad is the term of profanity in trace

And if one is not going to regret
He's of the evil doer in quest

*Men, who are giggled at by others**

012 O you the men and clan in Faith!
Elude streak in surmise, likely in pace
For guess and gossip is a sin to brace

And spy not to spot other in conduct
Nor speak ill of the other in construct

How'd you like to nibble in state
Flesh of a dead kin in relate

فَكَرِهْتُمُوْهُ ؕ وَاتَّقُوا اللّٰهَ ؕ	ظاہر ہے کہ گھن آئے گی تمہیں اس سے ۔ پس ڈرو اللہ سے ۔
اِنَّ اللّٰهَ تَوَّابٌ رَّحِيْمٌ ﴿۱۲﴾	یقیناً اللہ ہے بڑا توبہ قبول کرنے والا اور مہربان ﴿۱۲﴾
يٰۤاَيُّهَا النَّاسُ اِنَّا خَلَقْنٰكُمْ	اے انسانو! حقیقت یہ ہے کہ پیدا کیا ہے ہم نے تم کو
مِّنْ ذَكَرٍ وَّ اُنْثٰى	ایک مرد اور ایک عورت سے
وَجَعَلْنٰكُمْ شُعُوْبًا	پھر بنا دیا ہے ہم نے تم کو قومیں
وَّ قَبَآئِلَ لِتَعَارَفُوْا ؕ	اور قبیلے تاکہ تم ایک دوسرے سے پہچانے جاؤ ۔
اِنَّ اَكْرَمَكُمْ	بلاشبہ تم میں زیادہ عزت والا
عِنْدَ اللّٰهِ اَتْقٰكُمْ ؕ	اللہ کے نزدیک وہ ہے جو تم میں زیادہ پرہیزگار ہے ۔
اِنَّ اللّٰهَ عَلِيْمٌ خَبِيْرٌ ﴿۱۳﴾	بے شک اللہ ہے ہر بات جاننے والا اور پوری طرح باخبر ﴿۱۳﴾
قَالَتِ الْاَعْرَابُ اٰمَنَّا ؕ	کہتے ہیں یہ بدوی لوگ کہ ایمان لے آئے ہم ۔
قُلْ لَّمْ تُؤْمِنُوْا وَلٰكِنْ	ان سے کہیے! نہیں ایمان لائے تم بلکہ
قُوْلُوْۤا اَسْلَمْنَا	یوں کہو کہ "مسلمان" ہو گئے ہیں ہم
وَلَمَّا يَدْخُلِ الْاِيْمَانُ	اور ہرگز نہیں داخل ہوا ہے ابھی ایمان
فِيْ قُلُوْبِكُمْ ؕ وَاِنْ	تمہارے دلوں میں ۔ اور اگر
تُطِيْعُوا اللّٰهَ	تم فرمانبرداری اختیار کرو گے اللہ
وَرَسُوْلَهٗ لَا يَلِتْكُمْ	اور اس کے رسول کی تو نہ کمی کرے گا وہ
مِّنْ اَعْمَالِكُمْ شَيْئًا ؕ	تمہارے اعمال میں کچھ بھی ۔
اِنَّ اللّٰهَ غَفُوْرٌ رَّحِيْمٌ ﴿۱۴﴾	بے شک اللہ ہے بہت درگزر کرنے والا اور ہر حالت میں رحم کرنے والا ﴿۱۴﴾
اِنَّمَا الْمُؤْمِنُوْنَ	حقیقت میں مومن تو

Nay, Indeed!
You'd rather repulse in disgust
But awe and dread Lord in trust
For Lord is Rewarding and Kind in instruct

013 O the men and clan in place!
We created you of a couple in pace
And (held you) in the realm and race

Varied names in elect and decide
That you may know each in abide
And not to trend, scorn each in deride

Before Lord!
Most pious of you is the virtuous in trail
Indeed!
Lord discerns and concerns all trivial in scale

014 Those of the Arabs abiding in desert
They trend to assert:
We affirm to believe and trust

Say!
You really don't trend to faith in slight
But instead you enjoin relief in plight

We proffer our wills and ways in accord
To the Bounty of Lord for all in assort

But if you obey Lord and messenger in stay
He wouldn't let your deeds, go in stray
For!
Lord is Forbearing, Forgiving in pray

015 Only those men and clan stay in trust
Who trust in Lord and Messenger in just

And have never determined in distrust
But have toiled with their self and effects

الَّذِينَ آمَنُوا بِاللَّهِ	وہ لوگ ہیں جو ایمان لے آئے اللہ پر
وَرَسُولِهِ ثُمَّ لَمْ يَرْتَابُوا	اور اس کے رسول پر پھر کوئی شک نہ کیا انہوں نے
وَجَاهَدُوا بِأَمْوَالِهِمْ	اور جہاد کیا اپنے مالوں
وَأَنفُسِهِمْ فِي سَبِيلِ اللَّهِ ط	اور جانوں سے اللہ کی راہ میں۔
أُولَٰئِكَ هُمُ الصَّادِقُونَ ﴿١٥﴾	یہی لوگ ہیں سچے ﴿۱۵﴾
قُلْ أَتُعَلِّمُونَ	اے نبیؐ ان سے کہیے: کیا جتلاتے ہو تم
اللَّهَ بِدِينِكُمْ ط وَاللَّهُ	اللہ کو اپنی دین داری؟ حالانکہ وہ اللہ
يَعْلَمُ مَا فِي السَّمَاوَاتِ	جانتا ہے ہر وہ بات جو آسمانوں میں ہے
وَمَا فِي الْأَرْضِ ط وَاللَّهُ	اور وہ جو زمین میں ہے۔ اور اللہ تو
بِكُلِّ شَيْءٍ عَلِيمٌ ﴿١٦﴾	ہر چیز کا پورا علم رکھتا ہے ﴿۱۶﴾
يَمُنُّونَ عَلَيْكَ	احسان جتاتے ہیں یہ لوگ تم پر
أَنْ أَسْلَمُوا ط قُلْ	کہ انہوں نے اسلام قبول کر لیا۔ کہیے
لَا تَمُنُّوا عَلَيَّ إِسْلَامَكُمْ ج	نہ احسان جتاؤ تم مجھ پر اپنے اسلام کا۔
بَلِ اللَّهُ يَمُنُّ عَلَيْكُمْ	بلکہ اللہ احسان رکھتا ہے تم پر
أَنْ هَدَاكُمْ لِلْإِيمَانِ	کہ اس نے ہدایت دی تمہیں ایمان کی،
إِن كُنتُمْ صَادِقِينَ ﴿١٧﴾	اگر ہو تم (اپنے دعوے میں) سچے ﴿۱۷﴾
إِنَّ اللَّهَ يَعْلَمُ	یقیناً اللہ جانتا ہے
غَيْبَ السَّمَاوَاتِ وَالْأَرْضِ ط	ہر پوشیدہ چیز آسمانوں کی اور زمین کی۔
وَاللَّهُ بَصِيرٌ بِمَا تَعْمَلُونَ ﴿١٨﴾ ع ٢	اور اللہ دیکھ رہا ہے اسے جو تم کرتے ہو ﴿۱۸﴾

In the reason of Lord hither in abide
They're the sincere for all in stride

016 What!
Will you direct Lord in stance
For your creed and concept to glance
But Lord concerns a bit in plan

That's in the heavens and earth in array
He's Knowing of all in sway

017 They impress you for a favor in pace
For Faith in Islam, they inclined to brace
You trend to assert and affirm:
Your term in faith isn't for me in place

Indeed not!
It's favor of Lord, (for you) in endow
That He favored you to faith in glow
If you're really just in trust to grow

018 Indeed!
Lord sees and sustains in girth
Enigma of heavens and that of the earth
Lord concerns your deeds and doings in mirth

ایاتہا ۴۵ — (۵۰) سُوْرَۃُ قٓ مَکِّیَّۃٌ (۳۴) — رکوعاتہا ۳

بِسْمِ اللّٰهِ الرَّحْمٰنِ الرَّحِيْمِ

شروع اللہ کے نام سے جو بڑا مہربان نہایت رحم والا ہے

قٓ ۚ وَالْقُرْاٰنِ الْمَجِيْدِ ۱	ق ۔ قسم ہے قرآن مجید کی ۱
بَلْ عَجِبُوْٓا اَنْ جَآءَهُمْ	بلکہ تعجب ہے ان لوگوں کو اس بات پر کہ آگیا ان کے پاس
مُنْذِرٌ مِّنْهُمْ فَقَالَ	ایک متنبہ کرنے والا جوان ہی میں سے ہے پھر کہنے لگے
الْكٰفِرُوْنَ هٰذَا شَيْءٌ عَجِيْبٌ ۲	منکر یہ تو بڑی عجیب بات ہے ۲
ءَاِذَا مِتْنَا وَكُنَّا	کیا جب مر جائیں گے ہم اور ہو جائیں گے
تُرَابًا ۚ ذٰلِكَ	مٹی (تو دوبارہ اٹھائے جائیں گے) ۔ یہ
رَجْعٌۢ بَعِيْدٌ ۳	دوبارہ اٹھایا جانا بعید ہے (عقل سے) ۳
قَدْ عَلِمْنَا مَا تَنْقُصُ الْاَرْضُ مِنْهُمْ ۚ	حالانکہ ہمارے علم میں ہے جو کچھ کم کرتی ہے زمین ان کے جسم میں سے
وَعِنْدَنَا كِتٰبٌ حَفِيْظٌ ۴	اور ہمارے پاس ہے ایک کتاب جس میں سب کچھ محفوظ ہے ۴
بَلْ كَذَّبُوْا بِالْحَقِّ لَمَّا جَآءَهُمْ	بلکہ انہوں نے تو جھٹلا دیا حق کو جب وہ ان کے پاس آیا
فَهُمْ فِيْٓ اَمْرٍ مَّرِيْجٍ ۵	سو یہ اب (اسی وجہ سے) الجھن میں پڑے ہوئے ہیں ۵
اَفَلَمْ يَنْظُرُوْٓا اِلَى السَّمَآءِ	اچھا تو کیا نہیں دیکھا انہوں نے کبھی آسمان کو
فَوْقَهُمْ كَيْفَ بَنَيْنٰهَا وَزَيَّنّٰهَا	اپنے اوپر! کس طرح ہم نے بنایا اس کو اور آراستہ کیا؟
وَمَا لَهَا مِنْ فُرُوْجٍ ۶	اور نہیں ہے اس میں کوئی رخنہ ۶
وَالْاَرْضَ مَدَدْنٰهَا وَاَلْقَيْنَا	اور زمین کو بچھایا ہم نے اور ڈال دیے

050-QAF

In the name of Lord, the Most Beneficent, Most Merciful

001 Qaf:
Vow be to The Glorious Qur'an in Concern
You're Messenger of Lord in term

002 They acclaim in daze and amaze
How come a Messenger assigned in daze
Mid them, out as glimmer in haze

So the Cynics assert to affirm
That's but queer and bizarre to discern

003 What!
When we're dead and dirt in pit
We'll brought back to life
That's quite mysterious in looks

004 We discern to concern all in impel
How much of them is for the soil to dispel
It's with Us, in teeming trivialities to spell

005 They renounce the verity to discern
When it's there, for them to concern
They're dazed and amazed in term

006 Don't they look at the heavens awning atop
How We created and arrayed in assort
And there's no cleft and crack or fault in craft

007 And the earth in sway
With firm mountains (held) in array

فِيْهَا رَوَاسِيَ وَاَنْۢبَتْنَا فِيْهَا	اس میں (پہاڑوں کے) لنگر اور اگائیں اس میں
مِنْ كُلِّ زَوْجٍۢ بَهِيْجٍ ۝٧	ہر طرح کی خوش منظر نباتات ۝٧
تَبْصِرَةً وَّذِكْرٰى لِكُلِّ عَبْدٍ	آنکھیں کھولنے کے لیے اور یاد دہانی کی خاطر ہر اس بندے کو
مُّنِيْبٍ ۝٨	جو (حق کی طرف) رجوع کرنے والا ہے ۝٨
وَنَزَّلْنَا مِنَ السَّمَآءِ مَآءً مُّبٰرَكًا	اور برسایا ہم نے آسمان سے برکت والا پانی
فَاَنْۢبَتْنَا بِهٖ جَنّٰتٍ وَّحَبَّ الْحَصِيْدِ ۝٩	پھر اگائے اس سے باغات اور کھیتی کے اناج ۝٩
وَالنَّخْلَ بٰسِقٰتٍ	اور (پیدا کیے) کھجور کے درخت لمبے لمبے
لَّهَا طَلْعٌ نَّضِيْدٌ ۝١٠	لگتے ہیں جس میں خوشے تہ بہ تہ ۝١٠
رِّزْقًا لِّلْعِبَادِ ۙ وَاَحْيَيْنَا	یہ انتظام ہے رزق کا بندوں کے لیے اور زندگی عطا کرتے ہیں ہم
بِهٖ بَلْدَةً مَّيْتًا ۭ	اس پانی کے ذریعہ سے مردہ زمین کو۔
كَذٰلِكَ الْخُرُوْجُ ۝١١	اسی طرح ہوگا (مرے ہوئے انسانوں کا زمین سے) نکلنا ۝١١
كَذَّبَتْ قَبْلَهُمْ قَوْمُ نُوْحٍ	جھٹلایا تھا ان سے پہلے قوم نوحؑ نے
وَّاَصْحٰبُ الرَّسِّ وَثَمُوْدُ ۝١٢	اور اصحاب الرس نے اور ثمود نے ۝١٢
وَعَادٌ وَّفِرْعَوْنُ وَاِخْوَانُ لُوْطٍ ۝١٣	اور عاد نے اور فرعون نے اور لوطؑ کے بھائیوں نے ۝١٣
وَّاَصْحٰبُ الْاَيْكَةِ وَقَوْمُ تُبَّعٍ ۭ كُلٌّ كَذَّبَ	اور ایکہ والوں نے اور قوم تبعؑ نے، ہر ایک نے جھٹلایا
الرُّسُلَ فَحَقَّ وَعِيْدِ ۝١٤	رسولوں کو، بالآخر چسپاں ہوگئی (ان پر) میری وعید ۝١٤
اَفَعَيِيْنَا بِالْخَلْقِ الْاَوَّلِ ۭ	کیا تھک گئے تھے ہم پہلی بار کی تخلیق سے؟ (کہ دوبارہ نہ پیدا کرسکتے)
بَلْ هُمْ فِيْ لَبْسٍ	حقیقت یہ ہے کہ یہ لوگ شک میں پڑے ہوئے ہیں
مِّنْ خَلْقٍ جَدِيْدٍ ۝١٥ ع ۱۵	دوبارہ پیدا کیے جانے کے بارے میں ۝١٥

There We caused stunning produce in pace
All with the pair in place

008 That's spot in sight by all in array
By all the men of faith (of Lord) in sway

009 And We endow sprinkle in spray
From the sky, a bliss in array

Thus We create gardens in sweep
And endow you the cereals to reap

010 There are,
Superb palm (trees) high in stance
With fruit and stalks in glance
Piled in shoots with twigs in trance

011 Means to sustain men of faith in place
And We endow the life to the land
With sprinkle in spray in desolate span
So will be your revival in plan
After your death in demise

012 Hither in fore men and clan of Noah in stay
Had denied the life of Hereafter to obey
So were the men of Rass and Thamud in stray

013 And Ad, Pharaoh, lut in doleful slit and slot

014 Followers of Wood and Tubba, a nauseous of lot
Each one defied the Messengers of Lord
And My ,
Doom in gloom was affirmed in accord

015 If We're tired and spent in initiation
During its first term of creation
That they're dazed in stance
For Our new concept of Creation

وَلَقَدْ خَلَقْنَا الْاِنْسَانَ	اور یہ حقیقت ہے کہ ہم ہی نے پیدا کیا ہے انسان کو
وَنَعْلَمُ مَا تُوَسْوِسُ بِهٖ نَفْسُهٗ ۚۖ	اور ہم جانتے ہیں کہ کیا کیا وسوسے پیدا ہوتے ہیں اس کے دل میں۔
وَنَحْنُ اَقْرَبُ اِلَيْهِ مِنْ حَبْلِ الْوَرِيْدِ ﴿۱۶﴾	اور ہم زیادہ قریب ہیں اس کے اس کی رگِ جان سے بھی ﴿۱۶﴾
اِذْ يَتَلَقَّى الْمُتَلَقِّيٰنِ	اس وقت بھی جب لکھ رہے ہوتے ہیں دو کاتب
عَنِ الْيَمِيْنِ وَعَنِ الشِّمَالِ قَعِيْدٌ ﴿۱۷﴾	اس کے دائیں طرف اور بائیں طرف بیٹھے ہوئے ﴿۱۷﴾
مَا يَلْفِظُ مِنْ قَوْلٍ اِلَّا لَدَيْهِ	نہیں نکالتا وہ زبان سے کوئی بات مگر اس کے قریب ہی
رَقِيْبٌ عَتِيْدٌ ﴿۱۸﴾	ایک نگران تیار رہتا ہے (لکھنے کو) ﴿۱۸﴾
وَجَآءَتْ سَكْرَةُ الْمَوْتِ بِالْحَقِّ ؕ	اور طاری ہو گئی موت کی بے ہوشی سب حقیقت کھولنے کے لیے۔
ذٰلِكَ مَا كُنْتَ مِنْهُ تَحِيْدُ ﴿۱۹﴾	یہ ہے وہ چیز کہ تم اس سے بھاگتے تھے ﴿۱۹﴾
وَنُفِخَ فِي الصُّوْرِ ؕ ذٰلِكَ	اور پھونکا گیا صور، یہ ہے
يَوْمُ الْوَعِيْدِ ﴿۲۰﴾	وہ دن جس سے خوف دلایا جاتا تھا (تجھے) ﴿۲۰﴾
وَجَآءَتْ كُلُّ نَفْسٍ مَّعَهَا	اور آ گیا ہر شخص اس حال میں کہ اس کے ساتھ ہے
سَآئِقٌ وَّشَهِيْدٌ ﴿۲۱﴾	ایک ہانک کر لانے والا اور ایک گواہی دینے والا ﴿۲۱﴾
لَقَدْ كُنْتَ فِيْ غَفْلَةٍ مِّنْ هٰذَا	درحقیقت تھا تو پڑا ہوا غفلت میں اس سے
فَكَشَفْنَا عَنْكَ غِطَآءَكَ	سو ہٹا دیا ہے ہم نے تیرے سامنے سے پڑا ہوا پردہ
فَبَصَرُكَ الْيَوْمَ حَدِيْدٌ ﴿۲۲﴾	سو تیری نگاہ آج کے دن خوب تیز ہے ﴿۲۲﴾
وَقَالَ قَرِيْنُهٗ هٰذَا	اور کہے گا اس کا ساتھی یہ ہے
مَا لَدَيَّ عَتِيْدٌ ﴿۲۳﴾ ؕ	وہ جو میری تحویل میں تھا حاضر ﴿۲۳﴾
اَلْقِيَا فِيْ جَهَنَّمَ كُلَّ كَفَّارٍ عَنِيْدٍ ﴿۲۴﴾ ۙ	(حکم دیا جائے گا) پھینک دو جہنم میں ہر ناشکرے سرکش کو ﴿۲۴﴾

016 We created the man in stance
We discern the evil of his soul in trance

For We're nearer to him in pace
Than of his jugular vein in place

017 Regard!
There're angels two assigned in term
For his deeds and doings in concern
One on the right,
And other on the left in sight

018 Each of his word and phrase
That he pronounce in narrate
That's put to record by sentinel in place

019 And trance of death in daze
That to affirm truth in phase
That's what you eluded in haze

020 And bugle then puffed shrill and sharp
That's the Day of Caution in clasp

021 With each soul in stride,
There'll be an angel to drive
And other to bear witness in beside

022 (It will be said)
You're heedless of this term in span
Now We've shed your veil in stance
So piercing is perception of the Day in Glance

023 And his angel in escort will affirm
That's all in my tally to concern

024 (Then dictum of dictate will trend in haze)
Toss and cast into the Hell in blaze
For all these perverse in daze
For they refused The Word to brace

مَّنَّاعٍ لِّلْخَيْرِ مُعْتَدٍ	جو روکنے والا تھا خیر کے کاموں سے، حد سے تجاوز کرنے والا
مُّرِيبٍ ﴿٢٥﴾	اور شک میں پڑا ہوا ﴿٢٥﴾
الَّذِي جَعَلَ مَعَ اللَّهِ إِلَٰهًا آخَرَ	جس نے بنا رکھے تھے اللہ کے ساتھ دوسرے معبود
فَأَلْقِيَاهُ فِي الْعَذَابِ الشَّدِيدِ ﴿٢٦﴾	سو ڈال دو اسے سخت ترین عذاب میں ﴿٢٦﴾
قَالَ قَرِينُهُ رَبَّنَا	عرض کرے گا اس کا ساتھی اے ہمارے مالک!
مَا أَطْغَيْتُهُ وَلَٰكِن	نہیں بنایا تھا میں نے اس کو سرکش بلکہ
كَانَ فِي ضَلَالٍ بَعِيدٍ ﴿٢٧﴾	یہ خود ہی پرلے درجے کی گمراہی میں مبتلا تھا ﴿٢٧﴾
قَالَ لَا تَخْتَصِمُوا لَدَيَّ وَقَدْ	ارشاد ہوگا نہ جھگڑا کرو میرے حضور جبکہ
قَدَّمْتُ إِلَيْكُم بِالْوَعِيدِ ﴿٢٨﴾	ہم پہلے ہی خبردار کر چکے ہیں تم کو انجامِ بد سے ﴿٢٨﴾
مَا يُبَدَّلُ الْقَوْلُ لَدَيَّ وَمَا أَنَا	نہیں بدلا کرتی بات ہمارے ہاں اور نہیں ہیں ہم
بِظَلَّامٍ لِّلْعَبِيدِ ﴿٢٩﴾	ظلم کرنے والے اپنے بندوں پر ﴿٢٩﴾
يَوْمَ نَقُولُ لِجَهَنَّمَ هَلِ امْتَلَأْتِ	جس دن پوچھیں گے ہم جہنم سے کیا تو بھر گئی؟
وَتَقُولُ هَلْ مِن مَّزِيدٍ ﴿٣٠﴾	اور وہ کہے گی کیا کچھ اور بھی ہے؟ ﴿٣٠﴾
وَأُزْلِفَتِ الْجَنَّةُ	اور قریب لائی جائے گی جنت،
لِلْمُتَّقِينَ غَيْرَ بَعِيدٍ ﴿٣١﴾	متقیوں کے لیے، کچھ دور نہ ہوگی ﴿٣١﴾
هَٰذَا مَا تُوعَدُونَ	یہ ہے وہ چیز جس کا تم سے وعدہ کیا جاتا تھا،
لِكُلِّ أَوَّابٍ حَفِيظٍ ﴿٣٢﴾	ہر اس شخص کے لیے جو تھا رجوع کرنے والا اور یاد رکھنے والا ﴿٣٢﴾
مَنْ خَشِيَ الرَّحْمَٰنَ بِالْغَيْبِ	جو ڈرتا رہا رحمٰن سے بن دیکھے
وَجَاءَ بِقَلْبٍ مُّنِيبٍ ﴿٣٣﴾	اور آیا ہے لیے ہوئے دلِ گرویدہ ﴿٣٣﴾

025 Who barred what was good in stance
Betrayed all the bounds of virtue in glance
Cast scruples and suspense in trance

026 Who held duo other than Lord in pace
Toss him to agonizing sentence in blaze

027 His friends and fellow will assert in swift
Our Lord!
I didn't wrong him in a way to drift
But he himself was defiant in thrift

028 Lord will assert to affirm in stance
Bicker and brawl not before me in trance
There's admonition from Me in advance
For a discipline so furious in span

029 Mine pledge is affirmed in plan
And I don't wrong to My men and clan

030 One day,
We'll question the Hell to relate
Are you filled to the brim in state

It'll assert to affirm in pace
If there more to come in place

031 And Gardens will be so close in glance
To the men of virtue in stance
It wouldn't be far and afar in span

032 (A phonation will utter and declare)
That's what was sworn for you so fair
For who sincerely turned to Lord in regret
And was caring to concern Faith in select
(In earnest attrition wouldn't be left to defect)

033 Who awe in reverence in pace
Amiable veiled Notation in grace
And trended his core, fidelity to brace

ادْخُلُوهَا بِسَلٰمٍ	داخل ہو جاؤ جنت میں سلامتی کے ساتھ۔
ذٰلِكَ يَوْمُ الْخُلُودِ ﴿٣٤﴾	یہ دن ہے ہمیشہ رہنے کا ﴿٣٤﴾
لَهُمْ مَّا يَشَآءُونَ فِيهَا	ان کے لیے ہوگی وہاں ہر وہ چیز جو وہ چاہیں گے
وَلَدَيْنَا مَزِيدٌ ﴿٣٥﴾	اور ہمارے پاس ہے اس سے بھی زیادہ ﴿٣٥﴾
وَكَمْ أَهْلَكْنَا	اور کتنی ہی ہلاک کر چکے ہیں ہم
قَبْلَهُمْ مِّنْ قَرْنٍ هُمْ	ان سے پہلے قومیں جو تھیں
أَشَدُّ مِنْهُمْ بَطْشًا	بہت زیادہ ان سے طاقتور
فَنَقَّبُوا فِي الْبِلَادِ	اور چھان مارا انہوں نے دنیا کے ملکوں کو۔
هَلْ مِنْ مَّحِيصٍ ﴿٣٦﴾	پھر کیا ملی انہیں کوئی جائے پناہ ﴿٣٦﴾
إِنَّ فِي ذٰلِكَ لَذِكْرٰى	بلاشبہ اس میں ہے ایک سامانِ عبرت
لِمَنْ كَانَ لَهُ قَلْبٌ	ہر اس شخص کے لیے جو دلِ آگاہ رکھتا ہے
أَوْ أَلْقَى السَّمْعَ وَهُوَ شَهِيدٌ ﴿٣٧﴾	اور کان دھرتا ہے دل سے متوجہ ہو کر ﴿٣٧﴾
وَلَقَدْ خَلَقْنَا	بلاشبہ پیدا فرمایا ہم نے
السَّمٰوٰتِ وَالْأَرْضَ	آسمانوں اور زمین کو
وَمَا بَيْنَهُمَا	اور ان سب چیزوں کو جو ان کے درمیان ہیں
فِي سِتَّةِ أَيَّامٍ ۖ وَّمَا مَسَّنَا	چھ دنوں میں۔ اور نہیں لاحق ہوئی ہمیں
مِنْ لُّغُوبٍ ﴿٣٨﴾	کسی قسم کی تھکان ﴿٣٨﴾
فَاصْبِرْ عَلٰى مَا	پس اے نبیؐ صبر کرو ان باتوں پر جو
يَقُولُونَ وَسَبِّحْ	یہ کہتے ہیں اور تسبیح کرو

034 Enter you there in amity and accord
That's the Day of perpetuity in assort

035 They'll adore in score,
What they cherished to allure

And more in score,
With Our Presence in adore

036 How many a clan in score
We ravished hither in fore

They're stronger in Might
Than of them, all ways in plight

Then they ambled the land in surround
There's no site of refuge to elude in around

037 Indeed!
There's a Missive for some to allure
Who trends to discern in core
Or has a whim to concern in lore

And who lends ear to the word in adore
An then affirms the verity in sure

038 We created the heavens and the earth
And all between the Cosmic sweep in search

That's in Eons Six in pace
For Us!
There wasn't a bit of exhaustion in trace

039 O Prophet!
Abide in endurance to survive
For what they trend to contrive

بِحَمْدِ رَبِّكَ	اپنے رب کی حمد کے ساتھ
قَبْلَ طُلُوْعِ الشَّمْسِ	سورج طلوع ہونے سے پہلے
وَقَبْلَ الْغُرُوْبِ ﴿٣٩﴾	اور اس کے غروب سے پہلے ﴿٣٩﴾
وَمِنَ الَّيْلِ فَسَبِّحْهُ	اور رات کو بھی پھر اس کی تسبیح کرو
وَاَدْبَارَ السُّجُوْدِ ﴿٤٠﴾	اور سجدوں کے بعد بھی ﴿٤٠﴾
وَاسْتَمِعْ يَوْمَ يُنَادِ	اور سنو جس دن پکارے گا
الْمُنَادِ مِنْ مَّكَانٍ قَرِيْبٍ ﴿٤١﴾	ایک منادی کرنے والا قریب ہی سے ﴿٤١﴾
يَّوْمَ يَسْمَعُوْنَ	جس دن سن رہے ہوں گے لوگ
الصَّيْحَةَ بِالْحَقِّ	صور پھونکے جانے کی آواز بالکل ٹھیک،
ذٰلِكَ يَوْمُ الْخُرُوْجِ ﴿٤٢﴾	یہ دن ہوگا مردوں کے زمین سے نکلنے کا ﴿٤٢﴾
اِنَّا نَحْنُ نُحْيٖ وَنُمِيْتُ	یقیناً ہم ہی زندگی بخشتے ہیں اور موت دیتے ہیں
وَاِلَيْنَا الْمَصِيْرُ ﴿٤٣﴾	اور ہماری ہی طرف سب کو پلٹنا ہے ﴿٤٣﴾
يَوْمَ تَشَقَّقُ الْاَرْضُ عَنْهُمْ	یہ وہ دن ہوگا جب پھٹ جائے گی زمین لوگوں کے لیے
سِرَاعًا	(اور وہ اس میں سے نکل کر تیز تیز بھاگے جا رہے ہوں گے۔
ذٰلِكَ حَشْرٌ عَلَيْنَا يَسِيْرٌ ﴿٤٤﴾	یہ حشر برپا کرنا ہمارے لیے بہت آسان ہے ﴿٤٤﴾
نَحْنُ اَعْلَمُ بِمَا يَقُوْلُوْنَ	ہم خوب جانتے ہیں جو باتیں یہ بنا رہے ہیں
وَمَا اَنْتَ عَلَيْهِمْ بِجَبَّارٍ	اور نہیں ہو تم ان سے جبراً بات منوانے والے۔
فَذَكِّرْ بِالْقُرْاٰنِ مَنْ	سو تم نصیحت کرتے رہو قرآن سے ہر اس شخص کو جو
يَّخَافُ وَعِيْدِ ﴿٤٥﴾	ڈرتا ہو میری (عذاب کی) وعید سے ﴿٤٥﴾

And celebrate praises of Lord ever in entreat
Before dawn and awning of dusk in reach

040 And part of the night pray in adore
Also venerate His Acclaim in core
Also prone in prostration in pray

041 And heed for the Day,
When Caller will call quite close in stay

042 The Day they in reality will heed
A Bang of Blare in proceed
Day of Revival and rebirth of creed

043 Indeed!
It's We, Who endow life in demise
To Us is Ultimate Return in premise

044 The Day,
Earth is ripped to shreds in waste
And people are held dashing in haste

That will be the cramming in sorts
That's so easy for Us in escort

045 We better know in treat
For what they utter and repeat

You cannot cow and crawl in pace
Them by force to entreat

So caution with the word of Qur'an in place
For one, who dread My admonition in trace

اٰيَاتُهَا ۶۰ (۵۱) سُوْرَةُ الذّٰرِيٰتِ مَكِّيَّةٌ (۶۷) رُكُوْعَاتُهَا ۳

بِسْمِ اللّٰهِ الرَّحْمٰنِ الرَّحِيْمِ

شروع اللہ کے نام سے جو بڑا مہربان نہایت رحم والا ہے

وَالذّٰرِيٰتِ ذَرْوًا ﴿۱﴾	قسم ہے ان ہواؤں کی جو بکھیرتی ہیں اڑا کر ﴿۱﴾
فَالْحٰمِلٰتِ وِقْرًا ﴿۲﴾	پھر (ان کی جو) اٹھانے والی ہیں (پانی سے) لدے ہوئے بادل ﴿۲﴾
فَالْجٰرِيٰتِ يُسْرًا ﴿۳﴾	پھر (ان کی جو) چلنے والی ہیں سبک رفتاری سے ﴿۳﴾
فَالْمُقَسِّمٰتِ اَمْرًا ﴿۴﴾	پھر (ان کی جو) تقسیم کرنے والی ہیں ایک بڑے کام (بارش) کو ﴿۴﴾
اِنَّمَا تُوْعَدُوْنَ لَصَادِقٌ ﴿۵﴾	حق یہ ہے کہ جس چیز سے تمہیں ڈرایا جا رہا ہے، وہ سچی ہے ﴿۵﴾
وَّاِنَّ الدِّيْنَ لَوَاقِعٌ ﴿۶﴾	اور بلا شبہ اعمال کا بدلہ ضرور مل کر رہنے والا ہے ﴿۶﴾
وَالسَّمَآءِ ذَاتِ الْحُبُكِ ﴿۷﴾	اور قسم ہے آسمان کی جس میں راستے ہیں ﴿۷﴾
اِنَّكُمْ لَفِيْ قَوْلٍ	یقیناً تم پڑے ہوئے ہو ایسی باتوں میں
مُّخْتَلِفٍ ﴿۸﴾	جو ایک دوسرے سے مختلف ہیں ﴿۸﴾
يُّؤْفَكُ عَنْهُ مَنْ اُفِكَ ﴿۹﴾	روگردانی کرتا ہے اس سے وہ شخص جو حق سے پھرا ہوا ہو ﴿۹﴾
قُتِلَ الْخَرّٰصُوْنَ ﴿۱۰﴾	مارے گئے قیاس و گمان سے حکم لگانے والے ﴿۱۰﴾
الَّذِيْنَ هُمْ فِيْ غَمْرَةٍ سَاهُوْنَ ﴿۱۱﴾	وہ جو (جہالت میں) غرق اور غفلت میں مدہوش ہیں ﴿۱۱﴾
يَسْـَٔلُوْنَ اَيَّانَ يَوْمُ الدِّيْنِ ﴿۱۲﴾	پوچھتے ہیں آخر کب آئے گا روزِ جزا؟ ﴿۱۲﴾
يَوْمَ هُمْ عَلَى النَّارِ يُفْتَنُوْنَ ﴿۱۳﴾	یہ وہ دن ہو گا جب یہ آگ پر تپائے جائیں گے ﴿۱۳﴾
ذُوْقُوْا فِتْنَتَكُمْ	(اور کہا جائے گا) چکھو مزا اپنے فتنے کا،

051-AL DHARIYAT

In the name of Lord, the Most Beneficent, Most Merciful

001/ Vow be to winds that sunder in soot
004 And those lift and bear hefty clouds in scoop

And those blow with agile pace in swoop
Then scatter and assign by dictum in loop

005 Indeed!
/ That's professed (with you) is just in proceed
006 Indeed!
007 Judgment and Justice is destined in decreed
008
009

Vow be to the swinging ways* in the sky in trance
Indeed! You're differing in your claims in stance

He evades the one in pace
Who's deluded of verity in trace

*Moving wormhole (Page : 1908)

010 Anguish in agony for the fibbers in bias
011 Who dither reckless in a torrent of chaos
012

They say: in daze and amaze
When is the Day, us to gaze
Of Rule and edit we've to face

013 This will be the day
/ When they'll be,
014 Tried and tossed in blaze

هٰذَا الَّذِيْ كُنْتُمْ بِهٖ تَسْتَعْجِلُوْنَ ﴿۱۴﴾	یہ ہے وہ جس کے لیے تم جلدی مچا رہے تھے ﴿۱۴﴾
اِنَّ الْمُتَّقِيْنَ	البتہ متقی لوگ (اس روز)
فِيْ جَنّٰتٍ وَّعُيُوْنٍ ﴿۱۵﴾	ہوں گے باغوں میں اور چشموں میں ﴿۱۵﴾
اٰخِذِيْنَ مَآ اٰتٰىهُمْ	لے رہے ہوں گے جو عطا فرمایا ہوگا انہیں
رَبُّهُمْ ۭ اِنَّهُمْ	ان کے رب نے۔ بلاشبہ یہ لوگ
كَانُوْا قَبْلَ ذٰلِكَ مُحْسِنِيْنَ ﴿۱۶﴾	تھے اس سے پہلے بہت اچھا اور معیاری کام کرنے والے ﴿۱۶﴾
كَانُوْا قَلِيْلًا	تھے یہ لوگ ایسے کہ کم ہی
مِّنَ الَّيْلِ مَا يَهْجَعُوْنَ ﴿۱۷﴾	راتوں کو سویا کرتے تھے ﴿۱۷﴾
وَبِالْاَسْحَارِ هُمْ	اور رات کے پچھلے پہروں میں یہ
يَسْتَغْفِرُوْنَ ﴿۱۸﴾	استغفار کیا کرتے تھے ﴿۱۸﴾
وَفِيْٓ اَمْوَالِهِمْ حَقٌّ	اور تھا ان کے مالوں میں حق
لِّلسَّاۗىِٕلِ وَالْمَحْرُوْمِ ﴿۱۹﴾	مانگنے والوں اور حاجت مندوں کا ﴿۱۹﴾
وَفِي الْاَرْضِ اٰيٰتٌ	اور زمین میں بہت سی نشانیاں ہیں
لِّلْمُوْقِنِيْنَ ﴿۲۰﴾	یقین لانے والوں کے لیے ﴿۲۰﴾
وَفِيْٓ اَنْفُسِكُمْ ۭ اَفَلَا تُبْصِرُوْنَ ﴿۲۱﴾	اور تمہارے اپنے وجود میں بھی۔ کیا پھر تم کو سوجھتا نہیں؟ ﴿۲۱﴾
وَفِي السَّمَاۗءِ رِزْقُكُمْ	اور آسمان میں ہے تمہارا رزق
وَمَا تُوْعَدُوْنَ ﴿۲۲﴾	اور وہ چیز بھی جس کا تم سے وعدہ کیا جا رہا ہے ﴿۲۲﴾
فَوَرَبِّ السَّمَاۗءِ وَالْاَرْضِ	سو قسم ہے آسمان و زمین کے مالک کی
اِنَّهٗ لَحَقٌّ	بلاشبہ یہ بات ایک حقیقت ہے

Flavor you the anguish and agony in chase
For what you prompt to pursue in daze

015 For Virtuous,!
They'll abide Gardens with springs in slide

016 Enjoying for what Lord blessed to aside
For they adored a discipline (of life) in abide

017 They did sleep, but for a while at night
018 And got to pray all through the night
In early hours of dawn in plight

(That's the late hours of the night)
They beg clemency of Lord in slight

019/ And they disbursed to needy in deprive
020 Of their riches and effects to thrive
021

There're some, who begged in adjure
But quite a few didn't extend in implore

In the land and surround
There're Signs (for the men of faith) in abound

And there are signs (within you) to allure
Wouldn't you trend to concern in lore

022 From Heavens in endow
There's provision in glow
That's affirmed hither in bestow

مِّثْلَ مَآ اَنَّكُمْ تَنْطِقُوْنَ ﴿۲۳﴾	ایسی ہی جیسا کہ تمہارا باتیں کرنا ﴿۲۳﴾
هَلْ اَتٰىكَ	(اے نبیؐ) کیا پہنچی ہے تمہیں
حَدِيْثُ ضَيْفِ اِبْرٰهِيْمَ	حکایت ابراہیمؑ کے مہمانوں کی
الْمُكْرَمِيْنَ ﴿۲۴﴾	جو بہت معزز تھے؟ ﴿۲۴﴾
اِذْ دَخَلُوْا عَلَيْهِ فَقَالُوْا	جب وہ آئے ابراہیمؑ کے پاس اور انہوں نے کہا:
سَلٰمًا ۭ قَالَ سَلٰمٌ ۚ	سلام ہو تو انہوں نے جواب دیا: تم پر بھی سلام ہو۔
قَوْمٌ مُّنْكَرُوْنَ ﴿۲۵﴾	"یہ لوگ اجنبی معلوم ہوتے ہیں۔" ﴿۲۵﴾
فَرَاغَ اِلٰٓى اَهْلِهٖ	پھر وہ چپکے سے چلے گئے اپنے گھر والوں کے پاس
فَجَآءَ بِعِجْلٍ سَمِيْنٍ ﴿۲۶﴾	اور لائے ایک (بھنا ہوا) بچھڑا موٹا تازہ ﴿۲۶﴾
فَقَرَّبَهٗٓ اِلَيْهِمْ	اور اسے پیش کیا ان کے آگے
قَالَ اَلَا تَاْكُلُوْنَ ﴿۲۷﴾	کہا: آپ کھاتے کیوں نہیں؟ ﴿۲۷﴾
فَاَوْجَسَ مِنْهُمْ خِيْفَةً ۭ	(جب انہوں نے نہ کھایا) تو محسوس کیا ابراہیمؑ نے اپنے دل میں ان سے ڈر۔
قَالُوْا لَا تَخَفْ ۭ	انہوں نے کہا، ڈریے نہیں۔
وَبَشَّرُوْهُ بِغُلٰمٍ عَلِيْمٍ ﴿۲۸﴾	اور خوشخبری دی انہیں ایک ذی علم لڑکے کی ﴿۲۸﴾
فَاَقْبَلَتِ امْرَاَتُهٗ	یہ سن کر آگے بڑھی ان کی بیوی
فِيْ صَرَّةٍ فَصَكَّتْ وَجْهَهَا	چیختی بڑبڑاتی ہوئی اور پیٹ لیا اس نے اپنا ماتھا
وَقَالَتْ عَجُوْزٌ عَقِيْمٌ ﴿۲۹﴾	اور کہا: بوڑھی اور بانجھ (بچہ جنے گی)! ﴿۲۹﴾
قَالُوْا كَذٰلِكِ ۙ قَالَ رَبُّكِ ۭ	مہمانوں نے کہا، ایسا ہی ہوگا فرمایا ہے تیرے رب نے۔
اِنَّهٗ هُوَ الْحَكِيْمُ الْعَلِيْمُ ﴿۳۰﴾	بلاشبہ وہی ہے بڑی حکمت والا اور سب کچھ جاننے والا ﴿۳۰﴾

023 Indeed, by Lord!
He's Lord of,
The Heavens and earth in spread
That's indeed a truth in dread

It's as true to affirm in concern
As you speak wisely to each in term

024 (O Muhammad!)
Have you got the fable of feast
Abraham had the honor in treat
A few of the revered guests in reach

025 When they conveyed him the greetings in peace
He returned greetings to them in appease
But they looked quite queer in pace

026 Then he prompted to his kin in place
And got fatted calf for the feast in treat

027 And put it before them to eat
He said:
Aren't you inclined to eat a bit O please
(When they didn't eat a bit in spread)

028 Of them* he perceived a dismay in dread
They said*: Don't you panic in plan
We're to give cheery news of a son in span
Endowed with knowledge of faith to spread

*Angels

029 But his wife,
Came tittering aloud in jeer
She smote her fore and said in sneer
An arid old dame so flouted in age
030 They said:
Even so thy Lord proclaim to manage
He's full of Sapience and Lore in sage

قَالَ فَمَا خَطْبُكُمْ	ابراہیمؑ نے پوچھا، اچھا تو کیا مہم درپیش ہے تمہیں
أَيُّهَا الْمُرْسَلُونَ ۝۳۱	اے اللہ کے فرشتو؟ ۝۳۱
قَالُوا إِنَّا أُرْسِلْنَا	انہوں نے کہا، ہمیں بھیجا گیا ہے
إِلَىٰ قَوْمٍ مُجْرِمِينَ ۝۳۲	ایک مجرم قوم کی طرف ۝۳۲
لِنُرْسِلَ عَلَيْهِمْ حِجَارَةً مِنْ طِينٍ ۝۳۳	تاکہ برسائیں ہم ان پر پتھر، (پکی ہوئی) مٹی کے ۝۳۳
مُسَوَّمَةً عِنْدَ رَبِّكَ	جو نشان زدہ ہوں تیرے رب کی طرف سے،
لِلْمُسْرِفِينَ ۝۳۴	حد سے گزر جانے والوں کے لیے ۝۳۴
فَأَخْرَجْنَا مَنْ كَانَ فِيهَا مِنَ الْمُؤْمِنِينَ ۝۳۵	سو نکال لیا ہم نے ان کو جو تھے اس میں اہل ایمان ۝۳۵
فَمَا وَجَدْنَا فِيهَا	لیکن نہ پایا ہم نے وہاں
غَيْرَ بَيْتٍ مِنَ الْمُسْلِمِينَ ۝۳۶	سوائے ایک گھر کے کوئی مسلمان گھرانہ ۝۳۶
وَتَرَكْنَا فِيهَا آيَةً لِلَّذِينَ	اور باقی رہنے دی وہاں ایک نشانی ان لوگوں کے لیے جو
يَخَافُونَ الْعَذَابَ الْأَلِيمَ ۝۳۷	ڈرتے ہیں دردناک عذاب سے ۝۳۷
وَفِي مُوسَىٰ إِذْ	اور (تمہارے لیے عبرت ہے) موسیٰؑ کے قصے میں جب
أَرْسَلْنَاهُ إِلَىٰ فِرْعَوْنَ بِسُلْطَانٍ مُبِينٍ ۝۳۸	بھیجا تھا ہم نے اسے فرعون کی طرف ایک واضح سند کے ساتھ ۝۳۸
فَتَوَلَّىٰ بِرُكْنِهِ وَقَالَ	تو وہ اکڑ گیا اپنے بل بوتے پر اور کہنے لگا
سَاحِرٌ أَوْ مَجْنُونٌ ۝۳۹	(کہ یہ) یا تو جادوگر ہے یا کوئی دیوانہ ۝۳۹
فَأَخَذْنَاهُ وَجُنُودَهُ	سو پکڑا ہم نے اسے اور اس کے لشکروں کو
فَنَبَذْنَاهُمْ فِي الْيَمِّ	اور پھینک دیا ہم نے ان سب کو سمندر میں
وَهُوَ مُلِيمٌ ۝۴۰	اس طرح کہ وہ ملامت زدہ ہو کر رہ گیا ۝۴۰

031 (Abraham) said:
And what's charge in command
O Messengers of Lord hither in stance

032 They said,
We're here for men and clan
Who're put to a sin in plan

033 And get to strike (them) in stray
Shower of stones baked in clay

034 Marked from your Lord in pace
For men and clan, who flout in faith

035 Then,
We isolated, men of the faith in pace

036 We hardly,
Found a man of faith in place
But for an abode of reside in trace

037 There We'd a Sign for such to aside
Who awe the odious sentence in abide

038 And there's a Sign for you* to receive
The fable of Moses to conceive
For if you're sure in sapience to perceive
Regard!
We sent him to Pharaoh in glow
With Our Power in show

*Prophet

039 Pharaoh with his chiefs dissented in stance
A scary wizard* obsessed for a play in trance

*They called Moses a scary wizard

040 So We took him with forces in confute
Into the sea in surge
And he's then thrown in rebuke,
For his heinous trends in urge

وَفِيْ عَادٍ اِذْ
اور تمہارے لیے عبرت ہے، قوم عاد کے واقعہ میں جب

اَرْسَلْنَا عَلَيْهِمُ الرِّيْحَ الْعَقِيْمَ ﴿٤١﴾
بھیجی ہم نے ان پر تباہ و برباد کر دینے والی ہوا ﴿٤١﴾

مَا تَذَرُ مِنْ شَيْءٍ اَتَتْ عَلَيْهِ
نہیں چھوڑتی تھی وہ کوئی چیز جس پر سے وہ گزر جاتی تھی

اِلَّا جَعَلَتْهُ كَالرَّمِيْمِ ﴿٤٢﴾
مگر کر ڈالتی تھی وہ اسے ریزہ ریزہ ﴿٤٢﴾

وَفِيْ ثَمُوْدَ اِذْ قِيْلَ
اور تمہارے لیے عبرت ہے، قوم ثمود کے واقعہ میں جب کہا گیا تھا

لَهُمْ تَمَتَّعُوْا حَتّٰى حِيْنٍ ﴿٤٣﴾
ان سے کہ مزے لوٹ لو ایک خاص وقت تک ﴿٤٣﴾

فَعَتَوْا عَنْ اَمْرِ رَبِّهِمْ
مگر وہ سرکش ہو گئے اور نہ مانا اپنے رب کا حکم

فَاَخَذَتْهُمُ الصّٰعِقَةُ
تو آ لیا ان کو ایک اچانک ٹوٹ پڑنے والے عذاب نے

وَهُمْ يَنْظُرُوْنَ ﴿٤٤﴾
ان کے دیکھتے دیکھتے ﴿٤٤﴾

فَمَا اسْتَطَاعُوْا مِنْ قِيَامٍ
پس نہ تو سکت تھی ان میں اٹھنے کی

وَّمَا كَانُوْا مُنْتَصِرِيْنَ ﴿٤٥﴾
اور نہ تھے وہ اپنا بچاؤ کرنے کے قابل ﴿٤٥﴾

وَقَوْمَ نُوْحٍ
اور تمہارے لیے عبرت ہے، قوم نوح کے واقعہ میں

ع ٢ مِّنْ قَبْلُ ۭ اِنَّهُمْ كَانُوْا قَوْمًا فٰسِقِيْنَ ﴿٤٦﴾
جو ان سے پہلے گزر چکی ہے یقیناً تھے ہی یہ لوگ نافرمان و بدکار ﴿٤٦﴾

وَالسَّمَاۗءَ بَنَيْنٰهَا بِاَيْىدٍ
اور آسمان کو بنایا ہے ہم نے اپنی قدرت سے

وَّاِنَّا لَمُوْسِعُوْنَ ﴿٤٧﴾
اور بلاشبہ ہم اس سے بھی زیادہ وسعت رکھتے ہیں ﴿٤٧﴾

وَالْاَرْضَ فَرَشْنٰهَا فَنِعْمَ الْمٰهِدُوْنَ ﴿٤٨﴾
اور زمین کو بچھایا ہے ہم نے اور کیا ہی اچھے ہموار کرنے والے ہیں ہم ﴿٤٨﴾

وَمِنْ كُلِّ شَيْءٍ خَلَقْنَا زَوْجَيْنِ
اور ہر چیز کے بنائے ہیں ہم نے جوڑے

لَعَلَّكُمْ تَذَكَّرُوْنَ ﴿٤٩﴾
تاکہ تم سبق لو ﴿٤٩﴾

فَفِرُّوْٓا اِلَى اللّٰهِ ۭ اِنِّىْ لَكُمْ
پس دوڑو اللہ کی طرف، یقیناً میں ہوں تمہارے لیے

041 And as for 'Aad:
We assigned them to sustain
A turbulent gust a twister in strain

042 It reduced them to jiffy in fray
To ruinous rotten tick in stray
Withered as husk, spread in array

043 And for Thamud!
They're told to relish in delight
There in abide for a while in plight

044 They insolently defied in pray
The Word of Lord to obey
So to them!
A stunning rumble seized in stray
It's so swift and sudden in array

045 They couldn't stand,
Nor could escape in confusion

046 So did men of Noah,
Violating in delusion

047 With power and skill in pace
We rear and raise sky in place
It's We, Who create vistas in Space

048 And We spread and tether in phase
The earth how exquisitely in place

049 Of all the things in run
We created of all the pairs in term
That you may be guided to discern

050 Hasten you to the Dictum of Lord in faith
I'm but to admonish in place
His command clear and sincere in pace

مِّنْهُ نَذِيْرٌ مُّبِيْنٌ ٥٠	اس کی طرف سے واضح طور پر متنبہ کرنے والا ٥٠
وَلَا تَجْعَلُوْا مَعَ اللّٰهِ اِلٰهًا اٰخَرَ ۭ اِنِّىْ	اور نہ بناؤ اللہ کے ساتھ معبود کسی دوسرے کو۔ یقیناً میں ہوں
لَكُمْ مِّنْهُ نَذِيْرٌ مُّبِيْنٌ ٥١	تمہارے لیے اس کی طرف سے واضح طور پر خبردار کرنے والا ٥١
كَذٰلِكَ مَآ اَتَى الَّذِيْنَ مِنْ قَبْلِهِمْ	اسی طرح نہیں آیا ان لوگوں کے پاس بھی جو ان سے پہلے گزر چکے ہیں
مِّنْ رَّسُوْلٍ اِلَّا قَالُوْا سَاحِرٌ اَوْ مَجْنُوْنٌ ٥٢	کوئی رسول مگر کہا انہوں نے کہ جادوگر ہے یا دیوانہ ہے ٥٢
اَتَوَاصَوْا بِهٖ ۚ	کیا ان لوگوں نے آپس میں کوئی سمجھوتہ کرلیا تھا اس بات پر؟
بَلْ هُمْ قَوْمٌ طَاغُوْنَ ٥٣	نہیں بلکہ یہ سب سرکش لوگ ہیں ٥٣
فَتَوَلَّ عَنْهُمْ فَمَآ اَنْتَ بِمَلُوْمٍ ٥٤	سو موڑ لو تم اپنا رخ ان سے کہ نہیں ہے تم پر کچھ ملامت ٥٤
وَّذَكِّرْ فَاِنَّ الذِّكْرٰى تَنْفَعُ الْمُؤْمِنِيْنَ ٥٥	اور نصیحت کرتے رہو اس لیے کہ نصیحت فائدہ پہنچاتی ہے اہل ایمان کو ٥٥
وَمَا خَلَقْتُ الْجِنَّ وَالْاِنْسَ	اور نہیں پیدا کیا ہے میں نے جن و انس کو
اِلَّا لِيَعْبُدُوْنِ ٥٦	مگر محض اس غرض سے کہ میری عبادت کریں ٥٦
مَآ اُرِيْدُ مِنْهُمْ مِّنْ رِّزْقٍ	نہیں چاہتا ہوں میں ان سے کوئی رزق
وَّمَآ اُرِيْدُ اَنْ يُّطْعِمُوْنِ ٥٧	اور نہیں چاہتا ہوں میں کہ وہ مجھے کھلائیں ٥٧
اِنَّ اللّٰهَ هُوَ الرَّزَّاقُ ذُو الْقُوَّةِ الْمَتِيْنُ ٥٨	یقیناً اللہ تو خود ہی رزاق ہے اور زبردست قوت کا مالک ہے ٥٨
فَاِنَّ لِلَّذِيْنَ ظَلَمُوْا	اور بلاشبہ ان لوگوں کے لیے جنہوں نے ظلم کیا ہے
ذَنُوْبًا مِّثْلَ ذَنُوْبِ اَصْحٰبِهِمْ	ویسا ہی عذاب تیار ہے جیسا عذاب ان کے ساتھیوں کو مل چکا ہے
فَلَا يَسْتَعْجِلُوْنِ ٥٩	سو انہیں مجھ سے جلدی نہ مچانی چاہیے ٥٩
فَوَيْلٌ لِّلَّذِيْنَ كَفَرُوْا	اس لیے کہ تباہی ہے ان لوگوں کے لیے جو کفر کرتے ہیں
ع مِنْ يَّوْمِهِمُ الَّذِيْ يُوْعَدُوْنَ ٦٠	اس دن (کے عذاب) سے جس سے انہیں ڈرایا جا رہا ہے ٦٠

051 Don't you treat to duo in pray
Other than Lord in adore
I'm but to admonish in lore
His Dictum so clear and sincere to obey

052 Similarly,
To all the Messengers hither in fore
People in place affirmed in lore
(In a similar conduct)
They addressed the messenger in score
Hexed in stance or obsessed in core

053 Are they united this missive to convey
Nay,
But they're defying past all the confines in stay

054 So get to a side in time
And don't trend to them in incline
You're not to blame, their drift in define

055 But guide them the way in entreat
For instruct helps only the faithful in preach

056 I've created Jinni and men in plan
That they may trend to entreat in span

057 I don't stay in need of feed in sway
Nor do I need sustenance in array

058 For Lord is well possessed in Command
He's Exalted in Might, Resolute in stance

059 For the arrogant in part
Their bit and part is like dole and dot
As of others hither in fore defied in plot
To Me!
They shouldn't press to hasten in slot

060 Woe be to the depraved in assort
For the Day pledged (of misery) in retort
For what they're dreaded in slot

آیاتہا ۴۹ (۵۲) سُوْرَةُ الطُّوْرِ مَكِّيَّةٌ (۷۶) رکوعاتہا ۲

بِسْمِ اللّٰهِ الرَّحْمٰنِ الرَّحِيْمِ ○

شروع اللہ کے نام سے جو بڑا مہربان نہایت رحم والا ہے۔

وَالطُّوْرِ ①	قسم ہے طور کی ①
وَكِتٰبٍ مَّسْطُوْرٍ ②	اور قسم ہے کتاب کی جو لکھی ہوئی ہے ②
فِيْ رَقٍّ مَّنْشُوْرٍ ③	کھلے اوراق میں ③
وَّالْبَيْتِ الْمَعْمُوْرِ ④	اور قسم ہے آباد گھر کی ④
وَالسَّقْفِ الْمَرْفُوْعِ ⑤	اور قسم ہے اونچی چھت کی ⑤
وَالْبَحْرِ الْمَسْجُوْرِ ⑥	اور قسم ہے موجزن سمندر کی ⑥
اِنَّ عَذَابَ رَبِّكَ لَوَاقِعٌ ⑦	بے شک تیرے رب کا عذاب ضرور واقع ہونے والا ہے ⑦
مَّا لَهٗ مِنْ دَافِعٍ ⑧	نہیں ہے اسے کوئی دفع کرنے والا ⑧
يَّوْمَ تَمُوْرُ السَّمَآءُ	(یہ واقع ہوگا) اس دن جب ڈگمگائے گا آسمان
مَوْرًا ⑨	بڑی شدت سے ⑨
وَّتَسِيْرُ الْجِبَالُ سَيْرًا ⑩	اور چل پڑیں گے پہاڑ ایک خاص انداز سے ⑩
فَوَيْلٌ يَّوْمَئِذٍ لِّلْمُكَذِّبِيْنَ ⑪	سو تباہی ہے اس دن جھٹلانے والوں کے لیے ⑪
الَّذِيْنَ هُمْ فِيْ خَوْضٍ يَّلْعَبُوْنَ ⑫ وقف لازم	وہ جو آج اپنی حجت بازیوں کے کھیل میں مشغول ہیں ⑫
يَوْمَ يُدَعُّوْنَ	جس دن دھکیلا جائے گا انہیں
اِلٰى نَارِ جَهَنَّمَ دَعًّا ⑬	جہنم کی آگ کی طرف، دھکے مار مار کر ⑬

052-AL TUR

In the name of Lord, the Most Beneficent, Most Merciful

001 Vow be to the Mount* of Deliverance in pace
002 Vow be to the Book inscribed in grace
003 That's in the open scroll in trace

*Tur

004/ Vow be to the House visited often in locale
006 Vow be to the awning high* in prevail
And vow be to the Sea surging in sail

*sky

007/ Indeed!
008 Doom of Lord is sure to converge
There's none to divert or diverge

009/ The Day all will be in factual stir and blur
010 And mountains soar in stir
Around and surround in spur

011 Woe be to the men and clan in aside
Defying the verity of Day in deride

012 They frolic in spank so silly in stride

013 They'll be pushed there in glide
That's Hell beguiling in slide

هٰذِهِ النَّارُ الَّتِيْ	(کہا جائے گا) یہ ہے وہ آگ
كُنْتُمْ بِهَا تُكَذِّبُوْنَ ۝١٤	جسے تم جھٹلایا کرتے تھے ۝١٤
اَفَسِحْرٌ هٰذَآ اَمْ اَنْتُمْ لَا تُبْصِرُوْنَ ۝١٥	کیا جادو ہے یہ؟ یا تمہیں کچھ سوجھ نہیں رہا؟ ۝١٥
اِصْلَوْهَا فَاصْبِرُوْٓا اَوْ لَا تَصْبِرُوْا ۚ	جاؤ جھلسو اس میں پھر خواہ صبر کرو یا نہ کرو،
سَوَآءٌ عَلَيْكُمْ ۭ اِنَّمَا تُجْزَوْنَ	یکساں ہے تمہارے لیے۔ بس بدلہ دیا جا رہا ہے تمہیں
مَا كُنْتُمْ تَعْمَلُوْنَ ۝١٦	ویسا ہی جیسے عمل تم کرتے رہے ۝١٦
اِنَّ الْمُتَّقِيْنَ فِيْ جَنّٰتٍ وَّنَعِيْمٍ ۝١٧	یقیناً متقی باغوں میں اور نعمتوں میں ہوں گے ۝١٧
فٰكِهِيْنَ بِمَآ اٰتٰىهُمْ	لطف لے رہے ہوں گے ان چیزوں کا جو عطا فرمائی ہیں انہیں
رَبُّهُمْ ۚ وَوَقٰىهُمْ رَبُّهُمْ عَذَابَ الْجَحِيْمِ ۝١٨	ان کے رب نے۔ اور بچائے گا انہیں ان کا رب عذابِ جہنم سے ۝١٨
كُلُوْا وَاشْرَبُوْا هَنِيْۗـــًٔا	(ان سے کہا جائے گا) کھاؤ اور پیو مزے سے
بِمَا كُنْتُمْ تَعْمَلُوْنَ ۝١٩	صلے میں ان اعمال کے جو تم کرتے رہے ۝١٩
مُتَّكِـــِٕيْنَ عَلٰي سُرُرٍ مَّصْفُوْفَةٍ ۚ	وہ تکیے لگائے بیٹھے ہوں گے مسندوں پر قطار اندر قطار
وَزَوَّجْنٰهُمْ بِحُوْرٍ عِيْنٍ ۝٢٠	اور بیاہ دیں گے ہم انہیں خوبصورت آنکھوں والی حوروں سے ۝٢٠
وَالَّذِيْنَ اٰمَنُوْا وَاتَّبَعَتْهُمْ	اور وہ لوگ جو ایمان لائے اور چلی ان کے نقشِ قدم پر
ذُرِّيَّتُهُمْ بِاِيْمَانٍ اَلْحَقْنَا	ان کی اولاد کسی درجۂ ایمان میں، ملا دیں گے ہم
بِهِمْ ذُرِّيَّتَهُمْ وَمَآ اَلَتْنٰهُمْ	ان کے ساتھ ان کی اس اولاد کو اور نہ گھٹائیں گے ہم
مِّنْ عَمَلِهِمْ مِّنْ شَيْءٍ ۭ كُلُّ امْرِی ٔ	ان کے عمل میں سے کچھ بھی۔ ہر انسان
بِمَا كَسَبَ رَهِيْنٌ ۝٢١	اپنے کمائے ہوئے اعمال کے بدلہ میں رہن ہے ۝٢١
وَاَمْدَدْنٰهُمْ بِفَاكِهَةٍ وَّلَحْمٍ	اور دیے چلے جائیں گے ہم انہیں لذیذ پھل اور گوشت

014 That's the Hell you defied in doom

015 Then they'll affirm in gloom
Is it a term of deception in boom
Or you don't trend to see in bloom

016 Burn you there, for you defied in deceit
It's the same in treat
Even if you endure with calm in pace
Even so you don't have the patience in place

But that's the decision in deeds
That you conveyed in proceeds

017 For virtuous in abide
They'll cherish in delight
Gardens of Bliss there to reside

018 Enjoying bliss of Lord endowed in glee
Lord cede them of Fire, a favor in spree

019/ They'll be told:
020 Dine and nibble to enjoy in pace
For your virtuous deeds in place

Recline to repose on Thrones in glitter
Set in ranks, so puny and piddle
Join* those friends and fellows in snicker
With luxuriant and lustrous eyes in giggle

*marry

021 And those of the men and clan in faith
Whose kin follow trust in grace
To them We'll join their kin in trail

Nor We'll deprive them a term in award
For their goodly deeds proceeds in rewards
For what they're promised hither in regard

022 We'll endow (them) in gift and grants
Fruit and meat or else (they plea) in stance

مِّمَّا يَشْتَهُوْنَ ﴿٢٢﴾	ہر قسم کے جو وہ چاہیں گے ﴿٢٢﴾
يَتَنَازَعُوْنَ فِيْهَا كَاْسًا	جھپٹ جھپٹ کر لے رہے ہوں گے وہ وہاں ایسے جامِ شراب
لَّا لَغْوٌ فِيْهَا وَلَا تَاْثِيْمٌ ﴿٢٣﴾	جس کے اثر سے نہ بیہودہ باتیں کریں گے اور نہ گناہ کے کام ﴿٢٣﴾
وَيَطُوْفُ عَلَيْهِمْ غِلْمَانٌ	اور دوڑتے پھریں گے ان کی خدمت کے لیے ایسے لڑکے جو
لَّهُمْ كَاَنَّهُمْ لُؤْلُؤٌ مَّكْنُوْنٌ ﴿٢٤﴾	ان ہی کے لیے مخصوص ہوں گے گویا کہ وہ چھپا کر رکھے ہوئے موتی ہیں ﴿٢٤﴾
وَاَقْبَلَ بَعْضُهُمْ عَلٰى بَعْضٍ	اور مخاطب ہوں گے اہل جنت ایک دوسرے سے
يَّتَسَآءَلُوْنَ ﴿٢٥﴾	حال احوال پوچھنے کے لیے ﴿٢٥﴾
قَالُوْٓا اِنَّا كُنَّا قَبْلُ	کہیں گے ہم ایسے لوگ تھے جو اس سے پہلے
فِيْٓ اَهْلِنَا مُشْفِقِيْنَ ﴿٢٦﴾	رہتے تھے اپنے گھر والوں میں اللہ سے ڈرتے ہوئے ﴿٢٦﴾
فَمَنَّ اللّٰهُ عَلَيْنَا	آخر کار احسان کیا اللہ نے ہم پر
وَوَقٰىنَا عَذَابَ السَّمُوْمِ ﴿٢٧﴾	اور بچا لیا ہمیں جھلسا دینے والی ہوا کے عذاب سے ﴿٢٧﴾
اِنَّا كُنَّا مِنْ قَبْلُ نَدْعُوْهُ ؕ	یقیناً ہم پہلے (پچھلی زندگی میں) اس سے دعائیں مانگا کرتے تھے۔
اِنَّهٗ هُوَ الْبَرُّ الرَّحِيْمُ ﴿٢٨﴾ ع	واقعی وہ بڑا ہی محسن اور نہایت رحم کرنے والا ہے ﴿٢٨﴾
فَذَكِّرْ فَمَآ اَنْتَ	پس اے نبیؐ تم نصیحت کیے جاؤ کہ نہیں ہو تم
بِنِعْمَتِ رَبِّكَ بِكَاهِنٍ وَّلَا مَجْنُوْنٍ ﴿٢٩﴾	اپنے رب کے فضل سے کاہن اور نہ مجنون ﴿٢٩﴾
اَمْ يَقُوْلُوْنَ شَاعِرٌ نَّتَرَبَّصُ	کیا یہ لوگ کہتے ہیں کہ یہ شخص شاعر ہے اور انتظار کر رہے ہیں ہم
بِهٖ رَيْبَ الْمَنُوْنِ ﴿٣٠﴾	اس کے حق میں گردشِ ایام کا؟ ﴿٣٠﴾
قُلْ تَرَبَّصُوْا فَاِنِّيْ مَعَكُمْ	ان سے کہو انتظار کرو اور میں بھی ہوں تمہارے ساتھ
مِّنَ الْمُتَرَبِّصِيْنَ ﴿٣١﴾	انتظار کرنے والوں میں سے ﴿٣١﴾

023 They in thrill exchange goblets in glee
One with each else in spree

Drinks in desire, what they aspire
With no daze of defile ills in tire

024 There'll be lads (at their bet and call) in surround
Youths as jewel, cautious and devout in abound

025 They'll trend to each in state
Engaging in mutual query in state

026 They'll assert to affirm in pace
We're sentient of our kin in place
And feared for an evil destiny in chase

027 But Lord was so kind to us in grace
And then He eluded us to face
The burn of blustery gust in blaze

028 Certainly!
We begged Him thither in vale
Yes indeed!
He's Most Compassionate and Kind in trail

029 So O Prophet,
Ardor in adore with Esteem Lord in Praise
By the Bounty of Lord in Grace

You aren't soothsayer in pace
Nor you're hexed or vexed in place

030 Or do they say and speak
That he's a poet in meet
We watch (for him) a term in screech

031 You tell them for once in stance
You tarry in trail hither in trance
And I too wait for a term to glance

أَمْ تَأْمُرُهُمْ أَحْلَامُهُم بِهَٰذَا
کیا حکم دیتی ہیں ان کو ان کی عقلیں ایسی ہی باتوں کا

أَمْ هُمْ قَوْمٌ طَاغُونَ ﴿۳۲﴾
یا پھر وہ سب سرکش لوگ ہیں ؟ ﴿۳۲﴾

أَمْ يَقُولُونَ تَقَوَّلَهُ ۚ
کیا یہ کہتے ہیں کہ گھڑ لیا ہے اس قرآن کو اس نے خود ہی؟

بَل لَّا يُؤْمِنُونَ ﴿۳۳﴾
نہیں اصل بات یہ ہے کہ یہ ایمان نہیں رکھتے ﴿۳۳﴾

فَلْيَأْتُوا بِحَدِيثٍ مِّثْلِهِ
اچھا تو انہیں چاہیے کہ یہ بنا لائیں کوئی کلام اسی شان کا

إِن كَانُوا صَادِقِينَ ﴿۳۴﴾
اگر ہیں یہ سچے ﴿۳۴﴾

أَمْ خُلِقُوا مِنْ غَيْرِ شَيْءٍ
کیا یہ پیدا ہو گئے ہیں بغیر کسی خالق کے

أَمْ هُمُ الْخَالِقُونَ ﴿۳۵﴾
یا یہ خود ہی اپنے خالق ہیں ؟ ﴿۳۵﴾

أَمْ خَلَقُوا السَّمَاوَاتِ وَالْأَرْضَ ۚ
یا پیدا کیا ہے انہوں نے خود ہی آسمانوں کو اور زمین کو۔

بَل لَّا يُوقِنُونَ ﴿۳۶﴾
اصل بات یہ ہے کہ یہ یقین نہیں رکھتے ﴿۳۶﴾

أَمْ عِندَهُمْ خَزَائِنُ رَبِّكَ
کیا ان کے قبضے میں ہیں تیرے رب کے خزانے

أَمْ هُمُ الْمُصَيْطِرُونَ ﴿۳۷﴾
یا انہی کا حکم چلتا ہے (ان پر)؟ ﴿۳۷﴾

أَمْ لَهُمْ سُلَّمٌ يَسْتَمِعُونَ
کیا ان کے پاس ہے کوئی سیڑھی کہ سن گن لیتے ہیں یہ

فِيهِ ۖ فَلْيَأْتِ
اس پر چڑھ کر (عالم بالا کی)؟ اچھا تو لائے

مُسْتَمِعُهُم بِسُلْطَانٍ مُّبِينٍ ﴿۳۸﴾
وہ شخص جس نے کچھ سنا ہے ان میں سے کوئی کھلی دلیل ﴿۳۸﴾

أَمْ لَهُ الْبَنَاتُ وَلَكُمُ الْبَنُونَ ﴿۳۹﴾
کیا اللہ کے لیے تو ہیں بیٹیاں اور تمہارے لیے ہیں بیٹے؟ ﴿۳۹﴾

أَمْ تَسْأَلُهُمْ أَجْرًا فَهُم
کیا مانگتے ہو تم ان سے کوئی اجر جس کی وجہ سے وہ

مِّن مَّغْرَمٍ مُّثْقَلُونَ ﴿۴۰﴾
اس زبردستی پڑی چٹی کے بوجھ تلے دب گئے ہیں؟ ﴿۴۰﴾

أَمْ عِندَهُمُ الْغَيْبُ
کیا ان کے پاس ہے غیب کے حقائق کا علم

032 Is it the turn of their push and spur in lore
That itch and impel in chore
Or if they slip to slide limits in adore

033 Or do they iterate and relate
He contrived,
The Missive by him in dictate
Nay, in reality in pace
They don't abide the faith in state

034 Let them bring recital like in stance
If they're true to their word in trance

035 Were they created of nihility in stay
Without any creator in sway
Or they're the Creator of them in array

036 Did they create the heavens and the earth
Indeed!
They don't have a bit of notion in worth

037 Have they Riches and Fortunes of Lord in hold
Or do they've their dint and Demand in control

038 Or do they've a ladder to sky
By which to scale heavens so high
And heed to privities of heavenly mall

Then let him get to a proof in pace
For what they listened in place

039 Has He only daughters to aside
Whereas you've sons in beside

040 Or have you asked,
For any pittance and prize
So they're impelled,
With a stack of debt in guise

041 Or they've the know of veiled in grip
That they're putting down to pen in slip

فَهُمْ يَكْتُبُوْنَ ﴿٤١﴾	جسے وہ لکھ رہے ہیں؟ ﴿٤١﴾
اَمْ يُرِيْدُوْنَ كَيْدًا ؕ فَالَّذِيْنَ	کیا یہ چاہتے ہیں کوئی چال چلنا؟ تو وہ لوگ جنہوں نے
كَفَرُوْا هُمُ الْمَكِيْدُوْنَ ﴿٤٢﴾	کفر کیا ہے ان کی چال انہی پر پڑے گی ﴿٤٢﴾
اَمْ لَهُمْ اِلٰهٌ غَيْرُ اللّٰهِ ؕ	کیا ان کا ہے کوئی معبود اللہ کے سوا؟
سُبْحٰنَ اللّٰهِ عَمَّا يُشْرِكُوْنَ ﴿٤٣﴾	پاک ہے اللہ اس شرک سے جو یہ کرتے ہیں ﴿٤٣﴾
وَاِنْ يَّرَوْا كِسْفًا مِّنَ السَّمَآءِ	اور اگر دیکھ لیں یہ لوگ کوئی ٹکڑا آسمان کا
سَاقِطًا يَّقُوْلُوْا سَحَابٌ مَّرْكُوْمٌ ﴿٤٤﴾	گرتا ہوا تو کہیں گے بادل ہیں جو امڈے چلے آرہے ہیں ﴿٤٤﴾
فَذَرْهُمْ حَتّٰى	سو اے نبیؐ چھوڑ دیجیے انہیں (ان کے حال پر) یہاں تک کہ
يُلٰقُوْا يَوْمَهُمُ الَّذِيْ فِيْهِ يُصْعَقُوْنَ ﴿٤٥﴾	پہنچ جائیں اپنے اس دن کو جس میں یہ مار گرائے جائیں گے ﴿٤٥﴾
يَوْمَ لَا يُغْنِيْ عَنْهُمْ كَيْدُهُمْ شَيْـًٔا	جس دن نہ کام آئے گی ان کے ان کی کوئی چال ذرا بھی
وَّلَا هُمْ يُنْصَرُوْنَ ﴿٤٦﴾	اور نہ ان کو کوئی مدد ہی پہنچے گی ﴿٤٦﴾
وَاِنَّ لِلَّذِيْنَ ظَلَمُوْا	اور یقیناً ان لوگوں کے لیے جو ظلم کر رہے ہیں
عَذَابًا دُوْنَ ذٰلِكَ	ایک عذاب ہے پہلے بھی اس عذاب سے۔
وَلٰكِنَّ اَكْثَرَهُمْ لَا يَعْلَمُوْنَ ﴿٤٧﴾	لیکن ان میں سے بہت سے جانتے نہیں ﴿٤٧﴾
وَاصْبِرْ لِحُكْمِ رَبِّكَ	پس اے نبیؐ صبر کرو اپنے رب کا فیصلہ آنے تک
فَاِنَّكَ بِاَعْيُنِنَا وَسَبِّحْ	اس لیے کہ بلاشبہ تم ہماری نگاہ میں ہو اور تسبیح کرو
بِحَمْدِ رَبِّكَ حِيْنَ تَقُوْمُ ﴿٤٨﴾	اپنے رب کی حمد کے ساتھ جب تم اٹھو ﴿٤٨﴾
وَمِنَ الَّيْلِ فَسَبِّحْهُ	اور رات کو بھی پھر اس کی تسبیح کرو
وَاِدْبَارَ النُّجُوْمِ ﴿٤٩﴾	اور اس وقت بھی جب پلٹتے ہیں ستارے ﴿٤٩﴾

042 Or do they intend to construe a plot
But those of the cynics hither in slot
Themselves to hold the burnt in blot

043 Or Do they've a god,
Other than Bounty of Lord
But He's Illustrious of all in assort
For what they trend to refer in sort

044 Did they see heavenly piece in strike
Falling (on them) in a turn of blight
Then they'd trend to assert in slight
It's but the pile of cloud in flight

045 So let them tarry alone in alarm
Until they face Day's hit in Swarm
For they'll be forced to languish in alarm

046 The Day, that's destined to affirm
When their plot wouldn't avail in term
And they wouldn't be eased in concern

047 And indeed!
For those of the men and clan in deprave
There's one more sentence in stave
But quite a few discern it not to behave

048 Now tarry in trail for a while to endure
When Dictum of Lord affirms in score
For indeed!
You're before our eyes in place
So Admire and Applaud Lord in grace
When you're up to affirm in pace

Pray your Lord for the part of night*
049 Also ardor and adore His Bounty in plight
When stars get to dwindle in light

That's early hours of the dawn in stance
And the night is winding its shawl in glance

*Bliss of night vigil

اٰیاتھا ۶۲ (۵۳) سُوْرَةُ النَّجْمِ مَكِّيَّةٌ (۲۳) رکوعاتھا ۳

بِسْمِ اللّٰهِ الرَّحْمٰنِ الرَّحِيْمِ

شروع اللہ کے نام سے جو بڑا مہربان نہایت رحم والا ہے

وَالنَّجْمِ إِذَا هَوٰى ۞ (۱)	قسم ہے تارے کی جب وہ غروب ہونے لگے (۱)
مَا ضَلَّ صَاحِبُكُمْ وَمَا غَوٰى (۲)	نہ بھٹکا ہے تمہارا رفیق اور نہ بہکا (۲)
وَمَا يَنْطِقُ عَنِ الْهَوٰى (۳)	اور نہیں بولتا ہے وہ اپنی خواہش نفس سے (۳)
إِنْ هُوَ إِلَّا وَحْيٌ يُّوْحٰى (۴)	نہیں ہے یہ کلام مگر ایک وحی، جو نازل کی جارہی ہے (۴)
عَلَّمَهٗ شَدِيْدُ الْقُوٰى (۵)	تعلیم دی ہے اسے زبردست قوت والے نے (۵)
ذُوْ مِرَّةٍ فَاسْتَوٰى (۶)	جو بڑا صاحب حکمت ہے۔ پھر سامنے آکھڑا ہوا (۶)
وَهُوَ بِالْأُفُقِ الْأَعْلٰى (۷)	جبکہ وہ بالائی اُفق پر تھا (۷)
ثُمَّ دَنَا فَتَدَلّٰى (۸)	پھر قریب آیا اور آہستہ آہستہ آگے بڑھا (۸)
فَكَانَ قَابَ قَوْسَيْنِ	یہاں تک کہ ہوگیا برابر دو کمانوں کے
أَوْ أَدْنٰى (۹)	یا اس سے بھی کم فاصلہ رہ گیا (۹)
فَأَوْحٰى إِلٰى عَبْدِهٖ	تب وحی پہنچائی اس نے اللہ کے بندے کو
مَا أَوْحٰى (۱۰)	جو وحی پہنچائی تھی (۱۰)
مَا كَذَبَ الْفُؤَادُ مَا رَأٰى (۱۱)	نہ جھوٹ جانا رسولؐ کے دل نے اسے جو دیکھا اس نے (۱۱)
أَفَتُمٰرُوْنَهٗ	کیا تم اس سے جھگڑتے ہو
عَلٰى مَا يَرٰى (۱۲)	اس چیز پر جو وہ (آنکھوں سے) دیکھتا ہے (۱۲)

053-AL NAJM

In the name of Lord, the Most Beneficent, Most Merciful

001 Vow be to the star that dwindles* in sway

*Star changing it stance moment to moment that behavior of the star has lead the cosmologist to measure distances in the cosmic order, and this star is "Cepheid' in our Milky way Galaxy. This Star is called gem and jewel of the cosmic order as Prophet Muhammad is Gem and Jewel of humanity (Page : 1925)

002 Your Friend isn't drifted or led in astray
003 Nor does he asserts of his selfg in desire

004 It's conveyed (to him) a Vision in inspire
005 He's taught by One Mighty in Prime

006 Gifted of Sense and Sapience in Sublime
007 He's Astral O Astute in stance
While he's in best cuff and glib in glance

008 Then he got so close and advanced in trance

009 Till he was at a pace of two bow-span in aside
Or even a bit closer in stride

010 So Lord inspired His Savant in pace
A discipline of course and conduct to aside

What He resolved in place
To bear and deliver in grace

011 The Prophet is not a bit in astray
For word he's affirmed to convey
(It was all the truth in stay)

012 How'd you dispute in sway
For what he observed* to convey

*with his own eyes

وَلَقَدْ رَاٰهُ نَزْلَةً اُخْرٰى ﴿۱۳﴾	اور بلاشبہ وہ اسے دیکھ چکا ہے اترتے ہوئے ایک بار اور بھی ﴿۱۳﴾
عِنْدَ سِدْرَةِ الْمُنْتَهٰى ﴿۱۴﴾	"سدرۃ المنتہیٰ" کے قریب ﴿۱۴﴾
عِنْدَهَا جَنَّةُ الْمَاْوٰى ﴿۱۵﴾	اس کے آس پاس ہے "جنت الماویٰ" ﴿۱۵﴾
اِذْ يَغْشَى السِّدْرَةَ مَا يَغْشٰى ﴿۱۶﴾	جب چھا رہا تھا سدرہ پر جو کچھ چھا رہا تھا ﴿۱۶﴾
مَا زَاغَ الْبَصَرُ وَمَا طَغٰى ﴿۱۷﴾	نہ چندھیائی نگاہ اور نہ حد سے بڑھی ﴿۱۷﴾
لَقَدْ رَاٰى مِنْ اٰيٰتِ رَبِّهِ الْكُبْرٰى ﴿۱۸﴾	بلاشبہ اس نے دیکھیں اپنے رب کی بڑی بڑی نشانیاں ﴿۱۸﴾
اَفَرَءَيْتُمُ اللّٰتَ وَالْعُزّٰى ﴿۱۹﴾	بھلا دیکھا ہے تم نے لات کو اور عزیٰ کو؟ ﴿۱۹﴾
وَمَنٰوةَ الثَّالِثَةَ الْاُخْرٰى ﴿۲۰﴾	اور تیسری ایک اور (دیوی) مناۃ کو ﴿۲۰﴾
اَلَكُمُ الذَّكَرُ وَلَهُ الْاُنْثٰى ﴿۲۱﴾	کیا تمہارے لیے تو ہیں بیٹے اور اللہ کے لیے ہیں بیٹیاں؟ ﴿۲۱﴾
تِلْكَ اِذًا قِسْمَةٌ ضِيْزٰى ﴿۲۲﴾	یہ تو پھر ہے بڑی دھاندلی کی تقسیم! ﴿۲۲﴾
اِنْ هِيَ اِلَّآ اَسْمَآءٌ سَمَّيْتُمُوْهَآ اَنْتُمْ	نہیں ہیں یہ مگر چند نام جو رکھ لیے ہیں تم نے
وَاٰبَآؤُكُمْ مَّآ اَنْزَلَ	اور تمہارے آباؤ اجداد نے، نہیں نازل فرمائی ہے
اللّٰهُ بِهَا مِنْ سُلْطٰنٍ	اللہ نے ان کے بارے میں کوئی سند،
اِنْ يَّتَّبِعُوْنَ اِلَّا الظَّنَّ	نہیں پیروی کر رہے ہیں یہ لوگ مگر وہم و گمان کی
وَمَا تَهْوَى الْاَنْفُسُ ۚ وَلَقَدْ جَآءَهُمْ	اور خواہشاتِ نفس کی۔ حالانکہ آچکی ہے ان کے پاس
مِّنْ رَّبِّهِمُ الْهُدٰى ﴿۲۳﴾	ان کے رب کی طرف سے ہدایت ﴿۲۳﴾
اَمْ لِلْاِنْسَانِ	کیا یہ انسان کا حق ہے کہ اسے مل جائے
مَا تَمَنّٰى ﴿۲۴﴾	ہر وہ چیز جس کی وہ تمنا کرے؟ (ظاہر ہے کہ نہیں) ﴿۲۴﴾
فَلِلّٰهِ الْاٰخِرَةُ وَالْاُوْلٰى ﴿۲۵﴾	تو پھر اللہ ہی مالک ہے آخرت کا بھی اور دنیا کا بھی ﴿۲۵﴾

013 For indeed!
He saw him at a second dip and slide
(Even so once before and beside)
014 Aside,
Astral O Esteemed Sidra none can pass in place

015 Also near and beside,
There's an Blissful Garden in Grace

016/ Look!
018 Super O Supreme Sidra Awning a Mystical shawl
His view didn't shared or skewed nor got to scrawl
For surely he saw, the symbols of Peerless Lord

019/ Have you seen Lat, and Uzza as gods in abide
020 And then of the Third Manat, goddess in aside

021/ What!
For you the sex of male in abide
And for Him dame to aside
022 Regard, indeed!
Such rank and file, quite despotic in stride

023 That's nothing but the names in assign
Created by you and your fathers in design
For what Lord held no term in dictate
They concoct at their own in relate

Even so they held in escort
Dictum of Lord in accord
But they tended to their lust in score
Even so they'd discipline of Lord in before

024/ Nay!
025 If the man is just to secure
What he covet and crave to allure
(Indeed not)
But it's all for The Lord to command in scale
Even so hither in vale
Or the Hereafter in trail

وَكَمْ مِّنْ مَّلَكٍ فِي السَّمٰوٰتِ	اور کتنے ہی فرشتے ہیں آسمانوں میں،
لَا تُغْنِيْ شَفَاعَتُهُمْ شَيْـًٔا	نہیں کام آسکتی جن کی شفاعت ذرا بھی
اِلَّا مِنْ بَعْدِ اَنْ يَّاْذَنَ اللّٰهُ	مگر اس کے بعد کہ اجازت دے اللہ (شفاعت کی)
لِمَنْ يَّشَآءُ وَيَرْضٰى ٢٦	جسے چاہے اور (جن کے لیے) پسند کرے ٢٦
اِنَّ الَّذِيْنَ لَا يُؤْمِنُوْنَ بِالْاٰخِرَةِ	بلاشبہ جو لوگ نہیں ایمان رکھتے آخرت پر
لَيُسَمُّوْنَ الْمَلٰٓئِكَةَ تَسْمِيَةَ الْاُنْثٰى ٢٧	وہ نام رکھتے ہیں فرشتوں کے عورتوں کے سے ٢٧
وَمَا لَهُمْ بِهٖ مِنْ عِلْمٍ	حالانکہ نہیں ہے انہیں اس کے بارے میں کچھ بھی علم
اِنْ يَّتَّبِعُوْنَ اِلَّا الظَّنَّ وَاِنَّ الظَّنَّ	نہیں پیروی کرتے وہ مگر گمان کی۔ اور بلاشبہ گمان
لَا يُغْنِيْ مِنَ الْحَقِّ شَيْـًٔا ٢٨	کام نہیں دے سکتا حق کی جگہ ذرا بھی ٢٨
فَاَعْرِضْ عَنْ مَّنْ تَوَلّٰى ۙ	سو اے نبیؐ منہ پھیر لو اس شخص سے جو منہ موڑتا ہے
عَنْ ذِكْرِنَا وَلَمْ يُرِدْ اِلَّا الْحَيٰوةَ الدُّنْيَا ٢٩	ہمارے ذکر سے اور جو نہیں طالب مگر دنیاوی زندگی کا ٢٩
ذٰلِكَ مَبْلَغُهُمْ مِّنَ الْعِلْمِ	یہی ہے انتہا ان لوگوں کے علم کی۔
اِنَّ رَبَّكَ هُوَ اَعْلَمُ	بے شک تیرا رب ہی ہے جو خوب جانتا ہے
بِمَنْ ضَلَّ عَنْ سَبِيْلِهٖ	اسے جو بھٹک گیا اس کے راستے سے
وَهُوَ اَعْلَمُ بِمَنِ اهْتَدٰى ٣٠	اور وہی خوب جانتا ہے اسے بھی جو سیدھے راستے پہ ہے ٣٠
وَلِلّٰهِ مَا فِي السَّمٰوٰتِ	اور اللہ ہی مالک ہے ہر اس چیز کا جو آسمانوں میں ہے
وَمَا فِي الْاَرْضِ ۙ لِيَجْزِيَ الَّذِيْنَ	اور جو زمین میں ہے تاکہ بدلہ دے ان لوگوں کو جنہوں نے
اَسَآءُوْا بِمَا عَمِلُوْا وَيَجْزِيَ	برے کام کیے ان کے اعمال کا اور دے
الَّذِيْنَ اَحْسَنُوْا بِالْحُسْنٰى ٣١	ان لوگوں کو جنہوں نے اچھے کام کیے، اچھا بدلہ ٣١

الربع

026 Even if all angels,
Of the heavens esteem in score
And beg His mediation in implore

But it's for Lord to accede in request
To whom he pleases to apprise in best

027/ Those who don't trust Hereafter to pace
028 They name the angels as dame in place

They don't have a know in precise
They follow not but guess in surmise
Against truth,
Speculation is not to avail in premise

029 So O Prophet;
Elude and evade who desist to avail
The Missive of Lord in trail
And covet and crave for lust in dale

030 That's for,
The knowing of such men in conduct
Indeed Lord,
Discerns, who dither in instruct
And knows,
Who follows the best in conduct

031 All that's in the heavens and earth in sway
Conforms to missive of The Lord in array

So He returns the evil in pace
Conforming their deeds and doings in place

And endow in grants to the best in award
Who accomplishes noble doings in regard

اَلَّذِيْنَ يَجْتَنِبُوْنَ كَبٰٓئِرَ الْاِثْمِ	یہ وہ لوگ ہیں جو بچتے ہیں بڑے بڑے گناہوں سے
وَالْفَوَاحِشَ اِلَّا اللَّمَمَ	اور بے حیائی کے کاموں سے اِلّا یہ کہ کچھ قصور ان سے سرزد ہو جائے۔
اِنَّ رَبَّكَ وَاسِعُ الْمَغْفِرَةِ	بلاشبہ تیرا رب ہے وسیع مغفرت والا۔
هُوَ اَعْلَمُ بِكُمْ اِذْ	وہ خوب جانتا ہے تمہیں اس وقت سے جب
اَنْشَاَكُمْ مِّنَ الْاَرْضِ وَاِذْ اَنْتُمْ اَجِنَّةٌ	پیدا کیا اس نے تم کو زمین سے اور جب تم جنین کی شکل میں تھے
فِيْ بُطُوْنِ اُمَّهٰتِكُمْ فَلَا تُزَكُّوْٓا اَنْفُسَكُمْ	اپنی ماؤں کے پیٹوں میں۔ سو اپنی پاکیزگی کے دعوے نہ کرو
هُوَ اَعْلَمُ بِمَنِ اتَّقٰى ﴿۳۲﴾	وہی بہتر جانتا ہے کہ متقی کون ہے؟ ﴿۳۲﴾
اَفَرَءَيْتَ الَّذِيْ تَوَلّٰى ﴿۳۳﴾	پھر کیا دیکھا ہے تم نے اے نبیؐ اس شخص کو جو پھر گیا راہِ حق سے ﴿۳۳﴾
وَاَعْطٰى قَلِيْلًا وَّاَكْدٰى ﴿۳۴﴾	اور دیا اس نے تھوڑا سا اور پھر ہاتھ روک لیا؟ ﴿۳۴﴾
اَعِنْدَهٗ عِلْمُ الْغَيْبِ فَهُوَ يَرٰى ﴿۳۵﴾	کیا اس کے پاس علمِ غیب ہے کہ وہ دیکھ رہا ہے؟ ﴿۳۵﴾
اَمْ لَمْ يُنَبَّاْ بِمَا فِيْ صُحُفِ مُوْسٰى ﴿۳۶﴾	کیا نہیں خبر دی گئی اسے ان باتوں کی جو درج ہیں صحیفوں میں موسیٰؑ کے ﴿۳۶﴾
وَاِبْرٰهِيْمَ الَّذِيْ وَفّٰٓى ﴿۳۷﴾	اور (صحیفوں میں) ابراہیمؑ کے جس نے وفا کا حق ادا کر دیا؟ ﴿۳۷﴾
اَلَّا تَزِرُ وَازِرَةٌ وِّزْرَ اُخْرٰى ﴿۳۸﴾	یہ کہ نہیں اٹھاتا کوئی بوجھ اٹھانے والا بوجھ دوسرے کا ﴿۳۸﴾
وَاَنْ لَّيْسَ لِلْاِنْسَانِ اِلَّا مَا سَعٰى ﴿۳۹﴾	اور یہ کہ نہیں ملتا انسان کو مگر وہی کچھ جس کی وہ کوشش کرتا ہے ﴿۳۹﴾
وَاَنَّ سَعْيَهٗ سَوْفَ يُرٰى ﴿۴۰﴾	اور یہ کہ اس کی کمائی عنقریب اسے دکھائی جائے گی ﴿۴۰﴾
ثُمَّ يُجْزٰىهُ الْجَزَآءَ الْاَوْفٰى ﴿۴۱﴾	پھر جزا دی جائے گی اسے پوری پوری جزا ﴿۴۱﴾
وَاَنَّ اِلٰى رَبِّكَ الْمُنْتَهٰى ﴿۴۲﴾	اور یہ کہ تیرے رب ہی کے پاس پہنچنا ہے آخرکار (سب کو) ﴿۴۲﴾
وَاَنَّهٗ هُوَ اَضْحَكَ وَاَبْكٰى ﴿۴۳﴾	اور یہ کہ وہی ہنساتا ہے اور رلاتا ہے ﴿۴۳﴾
وَاَنَّهٗ هُوَ اَمَاتَ وَاَحْيَا ﴿۴۴﴾	اور یہ کہ وہی موت دیتا ہے اور زندہ کرتا ہے ﴿۴۴﴾

032 Who elude and evade low and lewd in dale
With only a bit of dip in slip in trail
Truly Lord is copious to condone in dip

He discerns the instance first in place
When you're created in grades
From the dust* in place

The you're veiled in your mother's womb in stay
So claim not your piety in stay

He discerns and concerns in pace
Who's the virtuous a bit in trace

*Arz

033/ O Prophet! Lord discerns in chore
034 Did you concern, who reverse in lore

He doles out alms a bit in stance
Then reverts his terrific play in trance
Not doling out a bit in glance

035/ What!
036 Does he hold know of veiled in stance
So that he can affirm in glance
Nay!
Wasn't he apprised to discern
What's revealed to Moses in concern

037/ And of Abraham!
038 Who concluded his allegiance in term
No carrier of load can bear in pace
The saddle in yoke of another in pace

039/ Man cannot secure unless he attempts in score
040 The award of toil is clear in adore

041/ Then he'll be pleased best in award
042 With Lord is decisive end in regard

043/ He confers and conveys smile and tears
044 And gift and grants life and death in fears

وَاَنَّهٗ خَلَقَ الزَّوْجَيْنِ الذَّكَرَ وَالْاُنْثٰى ﴿٤٥﴾ — اور یہ کہ وہی پیدا فرماتا ہے جوڑے نر اور مادہ ﴿۴۵﴾

مِنْ نُّطْفَةٍ اِذَا تُمْنٰى ﴿٤٦﴾ — ایک بوند سے جب وہ ٹپکائی جاتی ہے ﴿۴۶﴾

وَاَنَّ عَلَيْهِ النَّشْاَةَ الْاُخْرٰى ﴿٤٧﴾ — اور یہ کہ اسی کے ذمہ ہے زندگی بخشنا دوسری بار ﴿۴۷﴾

وَاَنَّهٗ هُوَ اَغْنٰى وَاَقْنٰى ﴿٤٨﴾ — اور یہ کہ وہی غنی کرتا ہے اور نپا تلا دیتا ہے ﴿۴۸﴾

وَاَنَّهٗ هُوَ رَبُّ الشِّعْرٰى ﴿٤٩﴾ — اور یہ کہ وہی رب ہے شعریٰ (ستارہ) کا ﴿۴۹﴾

وَاَنَّهٗۤ اَهْلَكَ عَادَا ۨالْاُوْلٰى ﴿٥٠﴾ — اور یہ کہ اسی نے ہلاک کیا عادِ اولیٰ کو ﴿۵۰﴾

وَثَمُوْدَا۟ فَمَاۤ اَبْقٰى ﴿٥١﴾ — اور ثمود کو پھر کچھ باقی نہ چھوڑا ﴿۵۱﴾

وَقَوْمَ نُوْحٍ مِّنْ قَبْلُ ؕ — اور (ہلاک کیا) قومِ نوحؑ کو اس سے پہلے۔

اِنَّهُمْ كَانُوْا هُمْ اَظْلَمَ وَاَطْغٰى ﴿٥٢﴾ — یقیناً وہ تھے ہی سخت ظالم اور سرکش ﴿۵۲﴾

وَالْمُؤْتَفِكَةَ اَهْوٰى ﴿٥٣﴾ — اور اوندھی گرنے والی بستیوں کو اٹھا پھینکا ﴿۵۳﴾

فَغَشّٰىهَا مَا غَشّٰى ﴿٥٤﴾ — پھر چھا گیا ان پر جو کچھ کہ چھایا ﴿۵۴﴾

فَبِاَىِّ اٰلَاۤءِ رَبِّكَ تَتَمَارٰى ﴿٥٥﴾ — پس (اے انسان!) اپنے رب کی کن کن نعمتوں میں تو شک کرے گا ﴿۵۵﴾

هٰذَا نَذِيْرٌ مِّنَ النُّذُرِ الْاُوْلٰى ﴿٥٦﴾ — یہ محمدؐ بھی متنبہ کرنے والے ہیں پہلے متنبہ کرنے والوں کی طرح ﴿۵۶﴾

اَزِفَتِ الْاٰزِفَةُ ﴿٥٧﴾ — قریب آ لگی ہے آنے والی گھڑی (قیامت کی) ﴿۵۷﴾

لَيْسَ لَهَا مِنْ دُوْنِ اللّٰهِ كَاشِفَةٌ ﴿٥٨﴾ — نہیں ہے اسے اللہ کے سوا کوئی ٹالنے والا ﴿۵۸﴾

اَفَمِنْ هٰذَا الْحَدِيْثِ تَعْجَبُوْنَ ﴿٥٩﴾ — کیا یہی باتیں ہیں جن پر تم تعجب کرتے ہو؟ ﴿۵۹﴾

وَتَضْحَكُوْنَ وَلَا تَبْكُوْنَ ﴿٦٠﴾ — اور ہنستے ہو اور روتے نہیں ہو؟ ﴿۶۰﴾

وَاَنْتُمْ سٰمِدُوْنَ ﴿٦١﴾ — اور تم گا بجا کر ٹالتے ہو؟ ﴿۶۱﴾

فَاسْجُدُوْا لِلّٰهِ وَاعْبُدُوْا ۩ ﴿٦٢﴾ — پس جھک جاؤ اللہ کے آگے اور اسی کی بندگی بجا لاؤ ﴿۶۲﴾

045/ He caused and conceived in pair, male and dame
046 From a drop in drip lodged in the womb to remain

047/ It is for Him,
048 Endow you a life after a term in demise
It's He,
Who endows riches in lot or measure in precise
049/ He's Lord of <u>Sirius*</u>
050 *(probably Cepheid as discussed in Verse 1)
A star of immense qualities in claim
And The Lord is He,
Who ravished mighty old 'Aad to remain
051 And Thamud were smashed all in blame

052 Before them,
The clan of Noah were ruined in pace
They're insolent and insulting in place
Besides being flimsy and felon in base

053/ And He wrecked and smashed cities in locale
054 Ruins are covered to bear wink in trail

055/ For which of His grants you'll deny in reply
(Muhammad;)
056 Like an admonisher is like the old* in stance

*prophets of olden times

057/ The Term of Demand is looming in glance
058 There's none to defer in plan
Other than Lord in span

059/ Do you daze in amaze
060 When you listen to such in narrate

And you snigger in stance
And don't sob in glance

061/ You stay in spoiling your time in leisure
Singing and dancing in stagger
062
So the O men in stay
Beg and beseech your Lord humble in pray

آیاتها ۵۵ — سُوْرَةُ الْقَمَرِ مَكِّيَّةٌ (۵۴) (۳۷) — رکوعاتها ۳

بِسْمِ اللّٰهِ الرَّحْمٰنِ الرَّحِيْمِ

شروع اللہ کے نام سے جو بڑا مہربان نہایت رحم والا ہے

اِقْتَرَبَتِ السَّاعَةُ وَانْشَقَّ الْقَمَرُ ۱	قریب آگئی گھڑی قیامت کی اور پھٹ گیا چاند ۱
وَاِنْ يَّرَوْا اٰيَةً يُّعْرِضُوْا	اور ان کا حال یہ ہے کہ اگر دیکھتے ہیں کوئی نشانی تو منہ موڑ جاتے ہیں
وَيَقُوْلُوْا سِحْرٌ مُّسْتَمِرٌّ ۲	اور کہتے ہیں کہ یہ تو جادو ہے جو پہلے سے چلا آرہا ہے ۲
وَكَذَّبُوْا وَاتَّبَعُوْٓا	چنانچہ جھٹلایا انہوں نے (اس کو بھی) اور پیچھے لگ گئے
اَهْوَآءَهُمْ وَكُلُّ اَمْرٍ	اپنی خواہشات کے۔ حالانکہ ہر معاملہ کو
مُّسْتَقِرٌّ ۳	ایک انجام تک پہنچ کر رہنا ہے ۳
وَلَقَدْ جَآءَهُمْ مِّنَ الْاَنْۢبَآءِ	اور یقیناً آچکی ہیں ان کے پاس (پچھلی قوموں کی) ایسی خبریں
مَا فِيْهِ مُزْدَجَرٌ ۴	جن میں ہے کافی سامانِ عبرت ۴
حِكْمَةٌۢ بَالِغَةٌ	ایسی حکمت جو نصیحت کے مقصد کو پورا کرتی ہے،
فَمَا تُغْنِ النُّذُرُ ۵	مگر کچھ فائدہ نہ دیا ان تنبیہات نے ۵
فَتَوَلَّ عَنْهُمْ ۘ يَوْمَ يَدْعُ الدَّاعِ	پس رخ پھیر لو ان سے۔ جس دن پکارے گا ایک پکارنے والا
اِلٰى شَيْءٍ نُّكُرٍ ۶	ایک سخت ناگوار چیز کی طرف ۶
خُشَّعًا اَبْصَارُهُمْ يَخْرُجُوْنَ	(اس وقت) سہمی ہوئی ہوں گی آنکھیں ان کی نکلیں گے وہ
مِنَ الْاَجْدَاثِ كَاَنَّهُمْ	اپنی قبروں سے اس طرح جیسے کہ وہ ہوں
جَرَادٌ مُّنْتَشِرٌ ۷	منتشر ٹڈیاں ۷

وقف لازم

054-AL QAMAR

In the name of Lord, the Most Beneficent, Most Merciful

001 The Hour, destined is to loom in soon
When moon will shred to split in boom

002 But if they see a Symbol to concern
They rather defy to affirm
And say:
That's but a spell in term

003 They deny to defy,
And trend in trail of their lust to comply
All mean and theme has a term in deploy

004 They've had already a word in lore
There's enough to restraint in chore

005 Perfected prudence a word in preach
But Warner profit them not in treat

006 So O Prophet!
Get to aside of them in stride
The Day, when the Caller call to aside
A Doom in Gloom for them to aside

007 They'll discern the destiny in doom
Their eyes atoning in gloom

From their pit and vault
When they'll be out in pace
Like the locusts spread in place

مُّهْطِعِينَ إِلَى الدَّاعِ ۖ	دوڑے جا رہے ہوں گے وہ سب پکارنے والے کی طرف۔
يَقُولُ الْكَافِرُونَ هَٰذَا يَوْمٌ عَسِرٌ ⑧	کہیں گے کافر یہ دن تو بڑا کٹھن ہے ⑧
كَذَّبَتْ قَبْلَهُمْ قَوْمُ نُوحٍ	جھٹلا چکی ہے ان سے پہلے قومِ نوحؑ
فَكَذَّبُوا عَبْدَنَا وَقَالُوا	سو جھٹلایا انہوں نے ہمارے بندے کو اور کہا:
مَجْنُونٌ وَازْدُجِرَ ⑨	یہ تو دیوانہ ہے۔ اور اسے جھڑک دیا گیا ⑨
فَدَعَا رَبَّهُ أَنِّي	آخرکار اس نے پکارا اپنے رب کو کہ میں
مَغْلُوبٌ فَانتَصِرْ ⑩	مغلوب ہو چکا ہوں سو اب تو انتقام لے (ان سے) ⑩
فَفَتَحْنَا أَبْوَابَ السَّمَاءِ	سو کھول دیے ہم نے آسمان کے دہانے
بِمَاءٍ مُّنْهَمِرٍ ⑪	موسلا دھار بارش کے لیے ⑪
وَفَجَّرْنَا الْأَرْضَ عُيُونًا فَالْتَقَى الْمَاءُ	اور جاری کر دیے زمین سے چشمے سو آملا پانی (ہر طرف سے)
عَلَىٰ أَمْرٍ قَدْ قُدِرَ ⑫	پورا کرنے کے لیے اس کام کو جو مقدر ہو چکا تھا ⑫
وَحَمَلْنَاهُ عَلَىٰ ذَاتِ	اور سوار کرا دیا ہم نے نوحؑ کو اس (کشتی) پر جو
أَلْوَاحٍ وَدُسُرٍ ⑬	تختوں اور کیلوں والی تھی ⑬
تَجْرِي بِأَعْيُنِنَا جَزَاءً	جو چل رہی تھی ہماری نگرانی میں۔ یہ بدلہ تھا
لِّمَن كَانَ كُفِرَ ⑭	اس شخص کی خاطر جس کی ناقدری کی گئی تھی ⑭
وَلَقَد تَّرَكْنَاهَا آيَةً	اور بے شک رہنے دیا ہے ہم نے اس کشتی کو بطورِ نشانی
فَهَلْ مِن مُّدَّكِرٍ ⑮	تو کیا ہے کوئی نصیحت قبول کرنے والا؟ ⑮
فَكَيْفَ كَانَ عَذَابِي وَنُذُرِ ⑯	سو دیکھ لو کیسا تھا میرا عذاب اور کیسی تھیں (میری تنبیہات؟) ⑯
وَلَقَدْ يَسَّرْنَا الْقُرْآنَ لِلذِّكْرِ	اور بلاشبہ آسان بنا دیا ہے ہم نے اس قرآن کو نصیحت کے لیے

008 Hurrying and scurrying in command
With riveted eyes, looming in stance

Tough is the Day, resolute in trance
The Cynics will say: wearing in glance

009 Before this term in place
Clan of Noah defied in pace

Flouted our savant, hexed in abide
And he was then evicted in stride

010 Then he beseeched His Lord in accord
I'm stunned and subdued in assort
O Lord!
Put them to torment in sort

011 We opened the gates of sky in main
There with swash and splash in rain

012 And Springs surged and spew in gush
As earth turned to springs in rush
Waters surged to swill in spike
To a level ordained in height

013 We took him,
On the ark of wide lumber in wood
Padded with palm-fiber fixed in a hood

014 Ark then floated under Our care for term
Retribution of one, who defied to discern

015 We've a Sign left, for all time to concern
If there's some to have caution to discern

016 But how awful was My discipline and advice
Indeed!
We've had Qur'an in an elegant premise

017

Facile to conceive and discern in precise
Who's to listen caution and council in advise

فَهَلْ مِنْ مُّدَّكِرٍ ﴿١٧﴾ — سو کیا ہے کوئی نصیحت قبول کرنے والا؟ ﴿١٧﴾

كَذَّبَتْ عَادٌ فَكَيْفَ كَانَ — جھٹلایا تھا عاد نے سو (دیکھ لو) کیسا تھا

عَذَابِيْ وَنُذُرِ ﴿١٨﴾ — میرا عذاب اور (کیسی تھیں) میری تنبیہات؟ ﴿١٨﴾

إِنَّآ أَرْسَلْنَا عَلَيْهِمْ رِيْحًا صَرْصَرًا — بلاشبہ ہم نے بھیج دی ان پر سخت طوفانی ہوا

فِيْ يَوْمِ نَحْسٍ مُّسْتَمِرٍّ ﴿١٩﴾ — ایک ایسے منحوس دن میں جس کی نحوست نہ ختم ہونے والی تھی ﴿١٩﴾

تَنْزِعُ النَّاسَ كَأَنَّهُمْ — جو اٹھا اٹھا کر پھینک رہی تھی لوگوں کو اس طرح گویا کہ وہ

أَعْجَازُ نَخْلٍ مُّنْقَعِرٍ ﴿٢٠﴾ — کھجور کے تنے ہیں جڑ سے اکھڑے ہوئے ﴿٢٠﴾

فَكَيْفَ كَانَ عَذَابِيْ وَنُذُرِ ﴿٢١﴾ — سو دیکھ لو کیسا تھا میرا عذاب اور (کیسی تھیں) میری تنبیہات؟ ﴿٢١﴾

وَلَقَدْ يَسَّرْنَا الْقُرْاٰنَ لِلذِّكْرِ — اور بلاشبہ آسان بنا دیا ہے ہم نے قرآن کو نصیحت کے لیے

فَهَلْ مِنْ مُّدَّكِرٍ ﴿٢٢﴾ ع — سو کیا ہے کوئی نصیحت قبول کرنے والا؟ ﴿٢٢﴾

كَذَّبَتْ ثَمُوْدُ بِالنُّذُرِ ﴿٢٣﴾ — جھٹلایا تھا ثمود نے تنبیہات کو ﴿٢٣﴾

فَقَالُوْٓا أَبَشَرًا مِّنَّا وَاحِدًا — سو کہا تھا انہوں نے کیا ایک آدمی جو ہم ہی میں سے ایک ہے

نَّتَّبِعُهٗٓ إِنَّآ إِذًا — اس کی پیروی کریں ہم؟ تو یقیناً اس کے معنی یہ ہوں گے کہ ہم

لَّفِيْ ضَلٰلٍ وَّسُعُرٍ ﴿٢٤﴾ — بہک گئے ہیں اور ہماری مت ماری گئی ہے ﴿٢٤﴾

ءَأُلْقِيَ الذِّكْرُ عَلَيْهِ مِنْۢ بَيْنِنَا — کیا نازل کی گئی ہے صرف اسی پر وحی ہم میں سے،

بَلْ هُوَ كَذَّابٌ أَشِرٌ ﴿٢٥﴾ — نہیں بلکہ وہ ہے پرلے درجے کا جھوٹا اور شیخی باز ﴿٢٥﴾

سَيَعْلَمُوْنَ غَدًا مَّنِ — عنقریب معلوم ہو جائے گا انہیں کل کہ کون ہے

الْكَذَّابُ الْأَشِرُ ﴿٢٦﴾ — پرلے درجے کا جھوٹا اور شیخی باز ﴿٢٦﴾

إِنَّا مُرْسِلُوا النَّاقَةِ فِتْنَةً لَّهُمْ — بلاشبہ ہم بھیج رہے ہیں اونٹنی کو آزمائش بنا کر ان کے لیے

018 The Aad also rejected My Word in concern
Disgusting was then My castigation in term
Besides My warnings (them) to discern

019 We held frenzied gust, furious in curse
That's a day of horrific disaster in burst

020 Tearing men as teensy roots in array
Like the palm trees slashing in stray

021 But how,
Awful was My punch in strike
And My Care and Caution in advice

022 We've Qur'an in an elegant premise
Facile to conceive and discern in precise
Then who's there to hold caution in device

023 The Thamud,
Defied their Warner in advice

024 For they asserted to affirm in stride
A man from us asking for a faith to aside
Shall we follow such a man in abide

Perhaps, indeed!
Then we'll be erring to sense in stance
And then we'll be raving in trance

025 Of all the men and clan mid us in stay
He's to receive the Missive to convey
Not exactly!
He's but a cheeky chisel in astray

026 Agony and remorse for them in concern
Soon they'll discern to affirm
Who's the fibber or arrogant in term

027 For We'll,
Send she-camel (for a term) in trial
So you observe sober serenity in moil

فَارْتَقِبْهُمْ وَاصْطَبِرْ ﴿۲۷﴾	سو انتظار کرو اور صبر کرو ﴿۲۷﴾
وَنَبِّئْهُمْ اَنَّ الْمَآءَ قِسْمَةٌ بَيْنَهُمْ ۚ	اور خبردار کردو انہیں کہ پانی کی تقسیم ہوگی ان کے اور اونٹنی کے درمیان
كُلُّ شِرْبٍ مُّحْتَضَرٌ ﴿۲۸﴾	ہر ایک کو اپنی باری پر حاضر ہونا ہوگا ﴿۲۸﴾
فَنَادَوْا صَاحِبَهُمْ	آخرکار انہوں نے پکارا اپنے ساتھی کو
فَتَعَاطٰى فَعَقَرَ ﴿۲۹﴾	اور اس نے اس کام کا بیڑا اٹھایا اور اس کی کونچیں کاٹ دیں ﴿۲۹﴾
فَكَيْفَ كَانَ عَذَابِىْ وَنُذُرِ ﴿۳۰﴾	سو دیکھ لو کیسا تھا میرا عذاب اور کیسی تھیں میری تنبیہات؟ ﴿۳۰﴾
اِنَّآ اَرْسَلْنَا عَلَيْهِمْ صَيْحَةً وَّاحِدَةً	ہم نے بھیجا ان پر ایک زبردست دھماکا
فَكَانُوْا كَهَشِيْمِ الْمُحْتَظِرِ ﴿۳۱﴾	سو ہو کر رہ گئے وہ کچلی ہوئی باڑھ کے چورے کی مانند ﴿۳۱﴾
وَلَقَدْ يَسَّرْنَا الْقُرْاٰنَ لِلذِّكْرِ	اور بلاشبہ آسان بنا دیا ہے ہم نے قرآن کو نصیحت کے لیے
فَهَلْ مِنْ مُّدَّكِرٍ ﴿۳۲﴾	تو کیا ہے کوئی نصیحت قبول کرنے والا؟ ﴿۳۲﴾
كَذَّبَتْ قَوْمُ لُوْطٍ بِالنُّذُرِ ﴿۳۳﴾	جھٹلایا قوم لوطؑ نے تنبیہات کو ﴿۳۳﴾
اِنَّآ اَرْسَلْنَا عَلَيْهِمْ حَاصِبًا	ہم نے بھیج دی ان پر پتھراؤ کرنے والی ہوا
اِلَّآ اٰلَ لُوْطٍ ۚ نَجَّيْنٰهُمْ بِسَحَرٍ ﴿۳۴﴾	سوائے آلِ لوطؑ کے۔ نجات دی ہم نے انہیں رات کے پچھلے پہر ﴿۳۴﴾
نِّعْمَةً مِّنْ عِنْدِنَا ۚ كَذٰلِكَ نَجْزِىْ	اپنے فضلِ خاص سے۔ اسی طرح جزا دیتے ہیں ہم
مَنْ شَكَرَ ﴿۳۵﴾	ہر اس شخص کو جو شکرگزاری کا رویہ اختیار کرتا ہے ﴿۳۵﴾
وَلَقَدْ اَنْذَرَهُمْ بَطْشَتَنَا	اور یقیناً ڈرایا تھا انہیں لوطؑ نے ہماری پکڑ سے
فَتَمَارَوْا بِالنُّذُرِ ﴿۳۶﴾	لیکن انہوں نے شک کیا ہماری تنبیہات میں ﴿۳۶﴾
وَلَقَدْ رَاوَدُوْهُ	اور بلاشبہ انہوں نے روکنے کی کوشش کی لوطؑ کو
عَنْ ضَيْفِهٖ فَطَمَسْنَآ اَعْيُنَهُمْ	اپنے مہمانوں کی حفاظت سے تو ہم نے ان کو اندھا کر دیا

028 And tell them
Portion drinking of water (mid them) in pace
To have their drinks, (definite term) in place
So drink as desired site and spot in space

029 But they called to a man in corrupt
With sword he crippled her* abrupt

*she camel

030 But how,
Awful was My discipline in premise

031 For We sent a single strong gust to slice
They're like arid stubble in dice
Scatters in pens of cattle in strife

032 We've Qur'an in an elegant premise
Facile to conceive and discern in precise

So if there's some in surround
To have a word of caution in abound

033 Men of Lut deserted his caution in alarm

034 We sent a twister fierce in throng
Throwing stones thither in swarm

Killing all but the kin (of Lut) in stance
As We saved them in the early of dawn

035 From Us,
There's a gift and grant in adoration
Those, who ardor and adore in adulation

036 And Lut did warn his men and clan
Period in Punish from Us in span
But they defied Our caution in plan

037/ They even sought his guests to snatch
039 But We blinded (them) of eyes in catch

فَذُوقُوا عَذَابِي وَنُذُرِ ﴿٣٧﴾	سو چکھو مزہ میرے عذاب کا اور میری تنبیہات کا ﴿٣٧﴾
وَلَقَدْ صَبَّحَهُم بُكْرَةً	اور یقیناً آیا ان کو صبح تڑکے ہی
عَذَابٌ مُّسْتَقِرٌّ ﴿٣٨﴾	ایک ایسے عذاب نے جو نہ ٹلنے والا تھا ﴿٣٨﴾
فَذُوقُوا عَذَابِي وَنُذُرِ ﴿٣٩﴾	سو چکھو مزہ میرے عذاب کا اور میری تنبیہات کا ﴿٣٩﴾
وَلَقَدْ يَسَّرْنَا الْقُرْآنَ لِلذِّكْرِ	اور یقیناً آسان بنا دیا ہے ہم نے قرآن کو نصیحت کے لیے
فَهَلْ مِن مُّدَّكِرٍ ﴿٤٠﴾	تو کیا ہے کوئی نصیحت قبول کرنے والا؟ ﴿٤٠﴾
وَلَقَدْ جَاءَ آلَ فِرْعَوْنَ النُّذُرُ ﴿٤١﴾	اور بے شک آئی تھیں آلِ فرعون کے پاس بھی بہت سی تنبیہات ﴿٤١﴾
كَذَّبُوا بِآيَاتِنَا كُلِّهَا	جھٹلا دیا انہوں نے ہماری ساری نشانیوں کو
فَأَخَذْنَاهُمْ أَخْذَ عَزِيزٍ مُّقْتَدِرٍ ﴿٤٢﴾	سو پکڑ لیا ہم نے انہیں جیسے پکڑتا ہے کوئی زبردست قوت والا ﴿٤٢﴾
أَكُفَّارُكُمْ خَيْرٌ مِّنْ أُولَٰئِكُمْ	کیا تم میں جو کافر ہیں وہ بہتر ہیں ان سے جن کا ذکر کیا گیا ہے
أَمْ لَكُم بَرَاءَةٌ فِي الزُّبُرِ ﴿٤٣﴾	یا تمہارے لیے معافی لکھی ہوئی ہے آسمانی کتابوں میں؟ ﴿٤٣﴾
أَمْ يَقُولُونَ نَحْنُ	یا یہ کہتے ہیں کہ ہم
جَمِيعٌ مُّنتَصِرٌ ﴿٤٤﴾	ایک مضبوط جتھا ہیں خود اپنا بچاؤ کر لیں گے؟ ﴿٤٤﴾
سَيُهْزَمُ الْجَمْعُ	عنقریب شکست دے دی جائے گی جتھے کو
وَيُوَلُّونَ الدُّبُرَ ﴿٤٥﴾	اور بھاگ جائیں گے وہ پھیر کر پیٹھ ﴿٤٥﴾
بَلِ السَّاعَةُ	بلکہ قیامت کی گھڑی ہی
مَوْعِدُهُمْ وَالسَّاعَةُ	ان سے نمٹنے کا اصل وقت مقرر ہے اور وہ گھڑی ہو گی
أَدْهَىٰ وَأَمَرُّ ﴿٤٦﴾	بڑی آفت اور تلخ تر ﴿٤٦﴾
إِنَّ الْمُجْرِمِينَ	یقیناً یہ مجرم لوگ

Now taste My omen and augury in receipt
Early in the morn they're held in conceit
So savor you,
My Fury in annoy and caution in receipt

040 We've Qur'an in an elegant premise
Facile to conceive and discern in precise

So if there's some in surround
To have a word of caution in abound

041 People of Pharaoh had Warner in concern
But discarded Our notation to discern

042 Men in around, defied Our Signs in abound
We got them to such a sentence to surround

That's a mighty throw in blow
As determined,
By One Exalted of Might in throw
Who's to carry His Resolve in glow

043 O Infidels!
Are you preferred over them in instruct
Have you a privilege in The Books in conduct

044 Or do they say:
We've an iron grip in accord
And can protect ourselves in assort

045 Soon their throng will flee in swarm
And turn their backs in alarm

046 Nay,
Hour thus pledged will be held in stance
Them to cherish awards in trends
The Hour will be grave and bitter in trance

047 Indeed!
The sinful drifted in array
Out of their wits, nutty in stray
Don't have the sense to conclude in stay

وقف لازم

فِيْ ضَلٰلٍ وَّ سُعُرٍ ﴿٤٧﴾	بھٹک گئے ہیں اور ان کی مت ماری گئی ہے ﴿٤٧﴾
يَوْمَ يُسْحَبُوْنَ	جس دن یہ گھسیٹے جائیں گے
فِي النَّارِ عَلٰى وُجُوْهِهِمْ ۭ	آگ میں اپنے منہ کے بل
ذُوْقُوْا مَسَّ سَقَرَ ﴿٤٨﴾	(اور ان سے کہا جائے گا) چکھو مزہ جہنم کی لپیٹ کا ﴿٤٨﴾
اِنَّا كُلَّ شَيْءٍ خَلَقْنٰهُ	بے شک ہم نے ہر چیز پیدا کی ہے
بِقَدَرٍ ﴿٤٩﴾	ایک تقدیر کے مطابق ﴿٤٩﴾
وَمَآ اَمْرُنَآ اِلَّا وَاحِدَةٌ	اور نہیں ہوتا ہے ہمارا حکم مگر یکدم
كَلَمْحٍۢ بِالْبَصَرِ ﴿٥٠﴾	جیسے پلک جھپکتی ہے ﴿٥٠﴾
وَلَقَدْ اَهْلَكْنَآ	اور بلاشبہ ہم ہلاک کر چکے ہیں
اَشْيَاعَكُمْ	تم جیسے بہت سے گروہوں کو،
فَهَلْ مِنْ مُّدَّكِرٍ ﴿٥١﴾	سو کیا ہے کوئی نصیحت قبول کرنے والا؟ ﴿٥١﴾
وَكُلُّ شَيْءٍ فَعَلُوْهُ	اور ہر عمل جو انہوں نے کیا تھا
فِي الزُّبُرِ ﴿٥٢﴾	درج ہے اعمال ناموں میں ﴿٥٢﴾
وَكُلُّ صَغِيْرٍ	اور ہر چھوٹی بات
وَّكَبِيْرٍ مُّسْتَطَرٌ ﴿٥٣﴾	اور بڑی چیز لکھی ہوئی ہے ﴿٥٣﴾
اِنَّ الْمُتَّقِيْنَ	یقیناً متقی لوگ
فِيْ جَنّٰتٍ وَّ نَهَرٍ ﴿٥٤﴾	ہوں گے باغوں میں اور نہروں میں ﴿٥٤﴾
فِيْ مَقْعَدِ صِدْقٍ عِنْدَ مَلِيْكٍ	سچی عزت کی جگہ قریب بادشاہ کے
مُّقْتَدِرٍ ﴿٥٥﴾ ع	جو بڑا صاحب اقتدار ہے ﴿٥٥﴾

048 The Day,
They'll be towed on faces in fire
They'll taste a touch of (Hell in) pyre

049/ Surely!
050 We created all in a definite measure
And Our,
Sway to grasp, like a wink to treasure

051 Hither in fore,
We smashed many a clan
Like you in span
Then who's there to endure caution in lore

052/ All that they do and discern,
053 That's affirmed in the Book of concern

All matters in pace
Whether trifling and immense in term
That's put to record in trace

054/ Virtuous to aside Gardens in array
055 Where Streams,
Gush in rush and surge in sway

So Majestic and prime is the place
In the proximity of Lord in grace

Regnant O Ruling in glow
Supreme O Prime in endow

آیاتها ۷۸ (۵۵) سُوْرَةُ الرَّحْمٰنِ مَدَنِيَّةٌ (۹۷) رکوعاتها ۳

بِسْمِ اللّٰهِ الرَّحْمٰنِ الرَّحِيْمِ

شروع اللہ کے نام سے جو بڑا مہربان نہایت رحم والا ہے

اَلرَّحْمٰنُ ۝ (۱)	اللہ نے جو رحمٰن ہے (۱)
عَلَّمَ الْقُرْاٰنَ ۝ (۲)	سکھایا اسی نے قرآن (۲)
خَلَقَ الْاِنْسَانَ ۝ (۳)	پیدا فرمایا اسی نے انسان کو (۳)
عَلَّمَهُ الْبَيَانَ ۝ (۴)	اور سکھایا اسے بولنا (۴)
اَلشَّمْسُ وَالْقَمَرُ بِحُسْبَانٍ ۝ (۵)	سورج اور چاند پابند ہیں ایک حساب کے (۵)
وَّالنَّجْمُ وَالشَّجَرُ يَسْجُدٰنِ ۝ (۶)	اور جھاڑیاں اور درخت اسی کو سجدہ کررہے ہیں (۶)
وَالسَّمَآءَ رَفَعَهَا وَوَضَعَ الْمِيْزَانَ ۝ (۷)	اور آسمان کو بلند کیا اللہ نے اور قائم کردیا نظامِ توازن (۷)
اَلَّا تَطْغَوْا فِي الْمِيْزَانِ ۝ (۸)	تاکہ نہ خلل ڈالو تم بھی عدل و توازن میں (۸)
وَاَقِيْمُوا الْوَزْنَ بِالْقِسْطِ	اور ٹھیک ٹھیک تولو انصاف کے ساتھ
وَلَا تُخْسِرُوا الْمِيْزَانَ ۝ (۹)	اور نہ گھاٹا دو تولتے وقت (۹)
وَالْاَرْضَ وَضَعَهَا لِلْاَنَامِ ۝ (۱۰)	اور زمین کو بنایا ہے اس نے مخلوقات کے لیے (۱۰)
فِيْهَا فَاكِهَةٌ وَّالنَّخْلُ	اس میں لذیذ پھل ہیں اور کھجور کے درخت ہیں
ذَاتُ الْاَكْمَامِ ۝ (۱۱)	جن کے پھل غلافوں میں لپٹے ہوئے ہیں (۱۱)
وَالْحَبُّ ذُو الْعَصْفِ وَالرَّيْحَانُ ۝ (۱۲)	اور طرح طرح کے غلے جن میں بھوسا بھی ہوتا ہے اور دانہ بھی (۱۲)
فَبِاَيِّ اٰلَآءِ رَبِّكُمَا تُكَذِّبٰنِ ۝ (۱۳)	پس اپنے رب کی کن کن نعمتوں کو جھٹلاؤ گے تم (اے جن وانس)؟ (۱۳)

055-AL RAHMAN

In the name of Lord, the Most Beneficent, Most Merciful

001/ The, Gracious and the most abounding
002 Taught us Qur'an the most astounding

003/ He made the man and taught him to speak
004 (And adored him with assertion to beseech)

005/ The sun and the moon are made in adoration
006 The stars and the trees beseech His adulation

007 Raised the Heavens and set its brink*
008 That you may not transgress its brim

*Lower sky the boundary limits of the expansion of the Multiverses

009/ Have order of measure (as designed in role)
010 And earth,
He determined for the living of soul

011 Wherein fruit and sheathed palm-trees
(Erected by Super and Sagacious God, in vale)

012 Husked grain and scented spice (adore Bounty of
Superb O Sovereign Lord, in trail)

013 Which of the favors, you may deny of your Most
Compliant, Complacent O Compassionate Lord in array

خَلَقَ الْإِنْسَانَ
پیدا فرمایا اس نے انسان کو

مِنْ صَلْصَالٍ كَالْفَخَّارِ ۝۱۴
ٹھیکری جیسے سوکھے سڑے گارے سے ۱۴

وَخَلَقَ الْجَانَّ مِنْ مَارِجٍ مِنْ نَارٍ ۝۱۵
اور پیدا کیا اس نے جنوں کو آگ کے شعلے سے ۱۵

فَبِأَيِّ آلَاءِ رَبِّكُمَا تُكَذِّبَانِ ۝۱۶
پس اپنے رب کے کن کن عجائبِ قدرت کو جھٹلاؤ گے تم (اے جن و انس)؟ ۱۶

رَبُّ الْمَشْرِقَيْنِ وَرَبُّ الْمَغْرِبَيْنِ ۝۱۷
جو رب ہے دونوں مشرقوں کا اور رب ہے دونوں مغربوں کا ۱۷

فَبِأَيِّ آلَاءِ رَبِّكُمَا تُكَذِّبَانِ ۝۱۸
سو اپنے رب کی کن کن قدرتوں کو جھٹلاؤ گے تم (اے جن وانس)؟ ۱۸

مَرَجَ الْبَحْرَيْنِ يَلْتَقِيَانِ ۝۱۹
رواں کیے اس نے دو دریا آپس میں ٹکراتے ہوئے ۱۹

بَيْنَهُمَا بَرْزَخٌ لَا يَبْغِيَانِ ۝۲۰
حائل ہے ان کے درمیان ایک پردہ کہ وہ تجاوز نہیں کرتے اپنی حد سے ۲۰

فَبِأَيِّ آلَاءِ رَبِّكُمَا تُكَذِّبَانِ ۝۲۱
پس اپنے رب کے کن کن کرشموں کو جھٹلاؤ گے تم (اے جن وانس)؟ ۲۱

يَخْرُجُ مِنْهُمَا اللُّؤْلُؤُ وَالْمَرْجَانُ ۝۲۲
نکلتے ہیں ان دونوں میں سے موتی اور مونگے ۲۲

فَبِأَيِّ آلَاءِ رَبِّكُمَا تُكَذِّبَانِ ۝۲۳
پس اپنے رب کی قدرت کے کن کن کمالات کو جھٹلاؤ گے تم (اے جن وانس)؟ ۲۳

وَلَهُ الْجَوَارِ الْمُنْشَآتُ
اور اسی کے ہیں یہ جہاز جو اونچے اٹھے ہوئے ہیں

فِي الْبَحْرِ كَالْأَعْلَامِ ۝۲۴
سمندر میں پہاڑوں کی مانند ۲۴

فَبِأَيِّ آلَاءِ رَبِّكُمَا تُكَذِّبَانِ ۝۲۵
پس اپنے رب کے کن کن احسانات کو جھٹلاؤ گے تم (اے جن وانس)؟ ۲۵

كُلُّ مَنْ عَلَيْهَا فَانٍ ۝۲۶
ہر چیز جو زمین پر ہے فنا ہو جانے والی ہے ۲۶

وَيَبْقَىٰ وَجْهُ رَبِّكَ
اور باقی رہے گی ذات تیرے رب کی

ذُو الْجَلَالِ وَالْإِكْرَامِ ۝۲۷
جو عظمت و انعام والا ہے ۲۷

فَبِأَيِّ آلَاءِ رَبِّكُمَا تُكَذِّبَانِ ۝۲۸
پس اپنے رب کے کن کن کمالات کو جھٹلاؤ گے تم (اے جن وانس)؟ ۲۸

يَسْأَلُهُ مَنْ فِي السَّمَاوَاتِ
مانگ رہے ہیں اسی سے (اپنی حاجتیں) وہ جو ہیں آسمانوں میں

014/ Created the man that of potter in clay*
016 And jinni He created of smokeless in blaze
Which of the favors, you may deny
Proximal O Perceptive Lord in sway

*Creation of human race

017 These Easts and Wests,
018 Endure Almighty God in Grace
Which of the favors, you may deny
Beatific O Blissful Lord to brace

019/ He's let free two sinuous seas in obtrude
021 But a fence (mid them) doesn't let to intrude
Which of the favors, you may deny
Chaste O Chivalrous Lord, to conclude

022/ From both you treasure pearls (in brief)
023 And you cherish alluring beauty (coral) in reef
Which of the favors, you may deny in belief
Assertive O Abiding Lord, in sweep

024/ Lofty ships displayed on blue
025 Elevated so high (mast in flew)
Which of the favors, you may deny to eschew
Mighty O Momentous Lord, in Blue

026/ All in hither shall have to depart
028 But glory of Lord will endure to impart
Which of the favors, you may deny in sort
Surviving O Sagacious Lord, in accord

وَالْأَرْضِ ۚ كُلَّ يَوْمٍ هُوَ فِي شَأْنٍ ﴿٢٩﴾ اور زمین میں۔ ہر آن ہے وہ نئی شان میں ﴿٢٩﴾

فَبِأَيِّ آلَاءِ رَبِّكُمَا پس اپنے رب کی کن کن صفاتِ حمیدہ کو

تُكَذِّبَانِ ﴿٣٠﴾ جھٹلاؤ گے تم (اے جن وانس)؟ ﴿٣٠﴾

سَنَفْرُغُ لَكُمْ عنقریب فارغ ہوئے جاتے ہیں ہم تمہارے احتساب کے لیے

أَيُّهَ الثَّقَلَانِ ﴿٣١﴾ اے زمین کے دو بوجھو (گروہِ جن وانس) ﴿٣١﴾

فَبِأَيِّ آلَاءِ رَبِّكُمَا پس اپنے رب کے کن کن احسانات کو

تُكَذِّبَانِ ﴿٣٢﴾ جھٹلاؤ گے تم (اے جن وانس)؟ ﴿٣٢﴾

يَا مَعْشَرَ الْجِنِّ وَالْإِنْسِ إِنِ اسْتَطَعْتُمْ اے گروہِ جن وانس اگر تم کر سکتے ہو

أَنْ تَنْفُذُوا مِنْ أَقْطَارِ السَّمَاوَاتِ وَالْأَرْضِ کہ نکل بھاگو آسمانوں اور زمین کی سرحدوں سے

فَانْفُذُوا ۚ لَا تَنْفُذُونَ تو بھاگ دیکھو۔ نہیں بھاگ سکتے تم

إِلَّا بِسُلْطَانٍ ﴿٣٣﴾ اس کے لیے بڑا زور چاہیے ﴿٣٣﴾

فَبِأَيِّ آلَاءِ رَبِّكُمَا سو اپنے رب کی کن کن قدرتوں کو

تُكَذِّبَانِ ﴿٣٤﴾ جھٹلاؤ گے تم اے جن وانس؟ ﴿٣٤﴾

يُرْسَلُ عَلَيْكُمَا شُوَاظٌ مِنْ نَارٍ چھوڑا جائے گا تم پر شعلہ آگ کا

وَنُحَاسٌ فَلَا تَنْتَصِرَانِ ﴿٣٥﴾ اور دھواں پھر تم اس کا مقابلہ نہ کرسکو گے ﴿٣٥﴾

فَبِأَيِّ آلَاءِ رَبِّكُمَا سو اپنے رب کی کن کن قدرتوں کا

تُكَذِّبَانِ ﴿٣٦﴾ انکار کرو گے تم اے جن وانس؟ ﴿٣٦﴾

فَإِذَا انْشَقَّتِ السَّمَاءُ فَكَانَتْ پھر جب پھٹ جائے گا آسمان تو ہو جائے گا وہ

وَرْدَةً كَالدِّهَانِ ﴿٣٧﴾ سرخ لال چمڑے کی طرح ﴿٣٧﴾

029/ To Him beseech all in heavens and this vale
030 His Dazzling Grandeur Glimmer in scale
Which of the favors, you may deny in dale
Astral O Amazing Lord, in trail

031 You both (men and jinni) of living domains
032 We'll design, defied of your dirty remains
Which of the favors, you may deny in claim
August and Astute Lord, to sustain

033 O you company of jinni and men
Have you an inkling ever to discern
The trivia of earth and vistas of Whole
Shove permeate earth and the Cosmic adore
You'll never penetrate but for dictum in score
Virtuous O Valorous God, in Lore

034 Which of the favors, you may deny
Decent O Distinguished Lord, in score

035/ How'd you escape to elope,
036 Burn of blaze and choke in smoke
Besides the flash of brass in stroke
Sent in wake of insinuating probe
Which of the favors, you may deny in scope
Insinuating O Inspiring Lord, in abode

037/ And when heaven rifts and tears in part
038 And becomes red hot like emollient assort

فَبِاَيِّ اٰلَاۤءِ رَبِّكُمَا	سو اپنے رب کی کن کن قدرتوں کو
تُكَذِّبٰنِ ٣٨	جھٹلاؤ گے تم اے جن وانس؟ ٣٨
فَيَوْمَىِٕذٍ لَّا يُسْـَٔلُ	پھر اس دن نہیں پوچھا جائے گا
عَنْ ذَنْۢبِهٖٓ اِنْسٌ وَّلَا جَاۤنٌّ ٣٩	اس کے اپنے گناہوں کے بارے میں کسی جن وانس سے ٣٩
فَبِاَيِّ اٰلَاۤءِ رَبِّكُمَا	سو اپنے رب کے کن کن احسانات کو
تُكَذِّبٰنِ ٤٠	جھٹلاؤ گے تم اے جن وانس؟ ٤٠
يُعْرَفُ الْمُجْرِمُوْنَ بِسِيْمٰهُمْ	پہچان لیے جائیں گے مجرم اپنے چہروں سے
فَيُؤْخَذُ بِالنَّوَاصِيْ	اور پکڑ کر گھسیٹا جائے گا انہیں پیشانی کے بالوں سے
وَالْاَقْدَامِ ٤١	اور پاؤں سے ٤١
فَبِاَيِّ اٰلَاۤءِ رَبِّكُمَا	سو اپنے رب کی کن کن قدرتوں کو
تُكَذِّبٰنِ ٤٢	جھٹلاؤ گے تم اے جن وانس؟ ٤٢
هٰذِهٖ جَهَنَّمُ الَّتِيْ	(اس وقت کہا جائے گا) یہ ہے وہ جہنم،
يُكَذِّبُ بِهَا الْمُجْرِمُوْنَ ٤٣	جھٹلایا کرتے تھے جسے مجرم ٤٣
يَطُوْفُوْنَ بَيْنَهَا وَبَيْنَ حَمِيْمٍ اٰنٍ ٤٤	چکر لگاتے رہیں گے وہ آگ اور کھولتے پانی کے درمیان ٤٤
فَبِاَيِّ اٰلَاۤءِ رَبِّكُمَا تُكَذِّبٰنِ ٤٥	سو اپنے رب کی کن کن قدرتوں کو جھٹلاؤ گے تم اے جن وانس؟ ٤٥
وَلِمَنْ خَافَ	اس کے برعکس اس شخص کے لیے جو ڈرتا رہا
مَقَامَ رَبِّهٖ جَنَّتٰنِ ٤٦	اپنے رب کے حضور پیش ہونے سے، دو دو جنتیں ہیں ٤٦
فَبِاَيِّ اٰلَاۤءِ رَبِّكُمَا تُكَذِّبٰنِ ٤٧	سو اپنے رب کے کن کن انعامات کو جھٹلاؤ گے تم اے جن وانس؟ ٤٧
ذَوَاتَآ اَفْنَانٍ ٤٨	بھرپور ہری بھری ڈالیوں والی ٤٨

وقف لازم

ع

Which of the favors, you may deny in sort
Astounding O Abounding Lord in accord

039/ The day neither man nor jinni in bin
040 Will be (inquired or) asked of their trends in sin
(Didn't Lord admonish you thither in prim?)*
Which of the favors, you may deny for Him
Receptive O Reverent Lord, in prim

041 Convicts will be known in specific marks
Snared and seized by feet in (fore) locks
(Didn't Lord illuminate you thither in sort?)*

042 Which of the favors, you may deny in part
Radiant O Refulgent Lord, in accord

043/ That's the abyss, convicts defied in deride
044 In feral simmering water they stray in slide
(Weren't you apprised by Lord thither in abide)*

045 Which of the favors, you may deny in stride
Splendid O Stupendous Lord, to aside

046 For who awe and dread facing Lord in acclaim
Therein two Gardens, they abide to remain

047 Which of the favors, you may deny in claim
Flowering O Festooned Lord, to sustain

048 Full with all kinds of delectations (and gains)

فَبِاَیِّ اٰلَآءِ رَبِّكُمَا تُكَذِّبٰنِ ﴿۴۹﴾ — سو اپنے رب کی کن کن نعمتوں کو جھٹلاؤ گے تم اے جن و انس؟ ﴿۴۹﴾

فِیْهِمَا عَیْنٰنِ تَجْرِیٰنِ ﴿۵۰﴾ — ان دونوں جنتوں میں دو دو چشمے رواں ہیں ﴿۵۰﴾

فَبِاَیِّ اٰلَآءِ رَبِّكُمَا تُكَذِّبٰنِ ﴿۵۱﴾ — سو اپنے رب کی کن کن نعمتوں کو جھٹلاؤ گے تم اے جن و انس؟ ﴿۵۱﴾

فِیْهِمَا مِنْ كُلِّ فَاكِهَةٍ زَوْجٰنِ ﴿۵۲﴾ — ہیں دونوں جنتوں میں ہر قسم کے لذیذ پھلوں کی دو دو قسمیں ﴿۵۲﴾

فَبِاَیِّ اٰلَآءِ رَبِّكُمَا تُكَذِّبٰنِ ﴿۵۳﴾ — سو اپنے رب کی کن کن نعمتوں کو جھٹلاؤ گے تم اے جن و انس؟ ﴿۵۳﴾

مُتَّكِـِٕیْنَ عَلٰى فُرُشٍۭ بَطَآىِٕنُهَا — بیٹھے ہوں گے تکیے لگا کر ایسے فرشوں پر جن کے استر

مِنْ اِسْتَبْرَقٍ ؕ وَ جَنَا — دبیز ریشم کے ہوں گے اور پھل

الْجَنَّتَیْنِ دَانٍ ﴿۵۴﴾ — دونوں جنتوں کے جھکے پڑ رہے ہوں گے ﴿۵۴﴾

فَبِاَیِّ اٰلَآءِ رَبِّكُمَا تُكَذِّبٰنِ ﴿۵۵﴾ — سو اپنے رب کی کن کن نعمتوں کو جھٹلاؤ گے تم اے جن و انس؟ ﴿۵۵﴾

فِیْهِنَّ قٰصِرٰتُ الطَّرْفِ ۙ — ہوں گی ان نعمتوں کے درمیان شرمیلی نگاہوں والیاں

لَمْ یَطْمِثْهُنَّ اِنْسٌ قَبْلَهُمْ — کہ نہ چھوا ہوگا انہیں کسی انسان نے ان سے پہلے

وَ لَا جَآنٌّ ﴿۵۶﴾ — اور نہ کسی جن نے ﴿۵۶﴾

فَبِاَیِّ اٰلَآءِ رَبِّكُمَا تُكَذِّبٰنِ ﴿۵۷﴾ — سو اپنے رب کے کن کن انعامات کو جھٹلاؤ گے تم اے جن و انس؟ ﴿۵۷﴾

كَاَنَّهُنَّ الْیَاقُوْتُ وَ الْمَرْجَانُ ﴿۵۸﴾ — خوبصورت ایسی گویا کہ وہ یاقوت اور مرجان ہیں ﴿۵۸﴾

فَبِاَیِّ اٰلَآءِ رَبِّكُمَا تُكَذِّبٰنِ ﴿۵۹﴾ — سو اپنے رب کی کن کن نعمتوں کو جھٹلاؤ گے تم اے جن و انس؟ ﴿۵۹﴾

هَلْ جَزَآءُ الْاِحْسَانِ اِلَّا الْاِحْسَانُ ﴿۶۰﴾ — نہیں ہے اعلیٰ درجہ کی نیکی کا بدلہ مگر اعلیٰ درجے کی جزا ﴿۶۰﴾

فَبِاَیِّ اٰلَآءِ رَبِّكُمَا تُكَذِّبٰنِ ﴿۶۱﴾ — سو اپنے رب کی کن کن نعمتوں کو جھٹلاؤ گے تم اے جن و انس؟ ﴿۶۱﴾

وَ مِنْ دُوْنِهِمَا جَنَّتٰنِ ﴿۶۲﴾ — اور ان دو جنتوں کے علاوہ دو جنتیں اور ہیں ﴿۶۲﴾

فَبِاَیِّ اٰلَآءِ رَبِّكُمَا تُكَذِّبٰنِ ﴿۶۳﴾ — سو اپنے رب کی کن کن نعمتوں کو جھٹلاؤ گے تم اے جن و انس؟ ﴿۶۳﴾

049 Which of the favors, you may deny to sustain
Dazzling O Devoted Lord of Domains

050 Wherein two fountains flowing
(Sinuous in sort)

051 Which of the favors, you may deny in resort
Appealing O Adorned Lord, in assort

052/ Where all kind of fruit is in pair,
053 But let in apart
Which of the favors, you may deny in part
Domineering O Demagogue Lord in accord

054/ Reclining on couches bedecked in lace
055 Fruit of both gardens so close to brace
Which of the favors, you may deny in pace
Exquisite O Excellent Lord, in Grace

056/ Therein those of modest bashful vision
057 Neither men nor jinni touched in illusion
Which of the favors, you may deny in delusion
Elegant O Embellished Lord, in Precision

058/ Like beauty of rubies and coral in grand
059 Which of the favors, you may deny in span
Arty O Crafty Lord, in plan

060/ What's preferred of compassion in glance
061 Other than bounteous term in stance
Which of the favors, you may deny in trance
Punctilious O Prudent Lord in span

062/ Inveigle of two gardens (in lure to adore)
063 Which of the favors, you may deny in core
Resplendent O Resolute Lord, in score

مُدْهَآمَّتٰنِ ﴿۶۴﴾	گھنی سرسبز و شاداب جنتیں ﴿۶۴﴾
فَبِاَیِّ اٰلَآءِ رَبِّکُمَا تُکَذِّبٰنِ ﴿۶۵﴾	سو اپنے رب کی کن کن نعمتوں کو جھٹلاؤ گے تم اے جن و انس؟ ﴿۶۵﴾
فِیْهِمَا عَیْنٰنِ نَضَّاخَتٰنِ ﴿۶۶﴾	ان دونوں میں بھی چشمے ہوں گے ابلتے ہوئے ﴿۶۶﴾
فَبِاَیِّ اٰلَآءِ رَبِّکُمَا تُکَذِّبٰنِ ﴿۶۷﴾	سو اپنے رب کی کن کن نعمتوں کو جھٹلاؤ گے تم اے جن و انس؟ ﴿۶۷﴾
فِیْهِمَا فَاکِهَةٌ	ان جنتوں میں ہوں گے لذیذ پھل
وَّنَخْلٌ وَّرُمَّانٌ ﴿۶۸﴾	اور کھجوریں اور انار ﴿۶۸﴾
فَبِاَیِّ اٰلَآءِ رَبِّکُمَا تُکَذِّبٰنِ ﴿۶۹﴾	سو اپنے رب کی کن کن نعمتوں کو جھٹلاؤ گے تم اے جن و انس؟ ﴿۶۹﴾
فِیْهِنَّ خَیْرٰتٌ حِسَانٌ ﴿۷۰﴾	ان نعمتوں کے درمیان ہوں گی خوب سیرت اور خوبصورت عورتیں ﴿۷۰﴾
فَبِاَیِّ اٰلَآءِ رَبِّکُمَا تُکَذِّبٰنِ ﴿۷۱﴾	سو اپنے رب کی کن کن نعمتوں کو جھٹلاؤ گے تم اے جن و انس؟ ﴿۷۱﴾
حُوْرٌ مَّقْصُوْرٰتٌ فِی الْخِیَامِ ﴿۷۲﴾	حوریں ٹھہرائی ہوئی خیموں میں ﴿۷۲﴾
فَبِاَیِّ اٰلَآءِ رَبِّکُمَا تُکَذِّبٰنِ ﴿۷۳﴾	سو اپنے رب کی کن کن نعمتوں کو جھٹلاؤ گے تم اے جن و انس؟ ﴿۷۳﴾
لَمْ یَطْمِثْهُنَّ اِنْسٌ قَبْلَهُمْ	نہیں چھوا ہوگا انہیں کسی انسان نے ان سے پہلے
وَلَا جَآنٌّ ﴿۷۴﴾	اور نہ کسی جن نے ﴿۷۴﴾
فَبِاَیِّ اٰلَآءِ رَبِّکُمَا تُکَذِّبٰنِ ﴿۷۵﴾	سو اپنے رب کی کن کن نعمتوں کو جھٹلاؤ گے تم اے جن و انس؟ ﴿۷۵﴾
مُتَّکِـِٕیْنَ عَلٰی رَفْرَفٍ خُضْرٍ	تکیہ لگائے بیٹھے ہوں گے سبز قالینوں پر
وَّعَبْقَرِیٍّ حِسَانٍ ﴿۷۶﴾	جو نادر اور خوبصورت ہوں گے ﴿۷۶﴾
فَبِاَیِّ اٰلَآءِ رَبِّکُمَا تُکَذِّبٰنِ ﴿۷۷﴾	سو اپنے رب کی کن کن نعمتوں کو جھٹلاؤ گے تم اے جن و انس؟ ﴿۷۷﴾
تَبٰرَکَ اسْمُ رَبِّکَ	بہت برکت والا ہے نام تیرے رب کا
ذِی الْجَلٰلِ وَالْاِکْرَامِ ﴿۷۸﴾	جو عظمت اور انعام والا ہے ﴿۷۸﴾

064/ Studded with dark green leaves in flow
065 Which of the favors, you may deny in endow
Gorgeous O Gleaming Lord, in glow

066/ There're two,
067 Ebullient and effervescent springs in around
Which of the favors, you may deny in surround
Imposing O Illustrious Lord in abound

068/ Wherein fruit like,
069 Date palm and pomegranates swing in surround
Which of the favors, you may deny in around
Elated O Exalted Lord in abound

070/ There you to adore comely in charm
071 Which of the favors, you may deny in norm
Stunning O Sumptuous Lord in swarm

072/ In pavilions balmy blooming in calm
073 Which of the favors, you may deny in norm
Absolute O Assured Lord, in swarm

074/ Men or jinni never fondled in before
075 Which of the favors, you may deny in lore
Cherished O Charming Lord, in core

076/ On green cushions,
077 And charming rugs they repose in allure
078 Which of the favors, you may deny in core
Dainty O Discerning Lord in adore
Blessed be Thy Name,
O Great, Grand Glorious Lord in Score

آیاتها ٩٦ — سُورَةُ الْوَاقِعَةِ مَكِّيَّةٌ (٥٦) (٤٦) — رکوعاتها ٣

بِسْمِ اللّٰهِ الرَّحْمٰنِ الرَّحِيْمِ

شروع اللہ کے نام سے جو بڑا مہربان نہایت رحم والا ہے

إِذَا وَقَعَتِ الْوَاقِعَةُ ①	جب پیش آ جائے گا وہ ہونے والا واقعہ ①
لَيْسَ لِوَقْعَتِهَا كَاذِبَةٌ ②	تو نہ ہوگا اس کے وقوع کو کوئی جھٹلانے والا ②
خَافِضَةٌ رَّافِعَةٌ ③	(ہوگا یہ) تہہ و بالا کر دینے والا ③
إِذَا رُجَّتِ الْأَرْضُ رَجًّا ④	جب ہلا ڈالی جائے گی زمین یکبارگی ④
وَّبُسَّتِ الْجِبَالُ بَسًّا ⑤	اور ریزہ ریزہ کر دیئے جائیں گے پہاڑ پوری طرح ⑤
فَكَانَتْ هَبَاءً مُّنْبَثًّا ⑥	تو ہو جائیں گے وہ مانندِ غبار بکھرے ہوئے ⑥
وَّكُنْتُمْ أَزْوَاجًا ثَلٰثَةً ⑦	اور ہو گے تم گروہ تین قسم کے ⑦
فَأَصْحٰبُ الْمَيْمَنَةِ ۵	سو دائیں بازو والے،
مَا أَصْحٰبُ الْمَيْمَنَةِ ⑧	کیا کہنا دائیں بازو والوں (کی خوش نصیبی) کا! ⑧
وَأَصْحٰبُ الْمَشْئَمَةِ ۵	اور بائیں بازو والے
مَا أَصْحٰبُ الْمَشْئَمَةِ ⑨	کیا ٹھکانہ بائیں بازو والوں (کی بدنصیبی) کا! ⑨
وَالسّٰبِقُوْنَ السّٰبِقُوْنَ ⑩	اور سبقت لے جانے والے تو ہیں ہی سبقت لے جانے والے ⑩
أُولٰٓئِكَ الْمُقَرَّبُوْنَ ⑪	یہ تو ہیں ہی مقرّب لوگ ⑪
فِيْ جَنّٰتِ النَّعِيْمِ ⑫	جو رہیں گے نعمت بھری جنتوں میں ⑫
ثُلَّةٌ مِّنَ الْأَوَّلِيْنَ ⑬	بہت ہوں گے پہلوں میں سے ⑬

056-AL WAQIAH

In the name of Lord, the Most Beneficent, Most Merciful

001 When decisive doom is destined to pass

002 There'll none to defy regarding its cross

003 All will toss and stir low in blow
Others so high in turbulent throw

004 Earth next jiggled and jarred in gust
To the nadir of parts and sorts in burst

005 And the mountains crumble in burst
Dot and whit

006 Swindling in blow
Like
The dust strewn in throw

007 You'll be styled in sort
Three in ranks and grades in part

008 Then friend and fellow,
Of the Right Hand beaming in glow
How'd you determine friend and fellow,
There cherishing in endow

009 And Associates,
Of The Split Paw (left hand) gone and split
What will be their friends in doom and pit

010 And firm in Faith,
They'll be high in lead and bit

011 They'll be close to Lord in blush

012 In Gardens of Bliss, delighted in hush

013 A number of men and clan
Of the old earlier in span

وَقَلِيْلٌ مِّنَ الْاٰخِرِيْنَ ﴿۱۴﴾	اور کم ہوں گے پچھلوں میں سے ﴿۱۴﴾
عَلٰى سُرُرٍ مَّوْضُوْنَةٍ ﴿۱۵﴾	(یہ سب) آراستہ پیراستہ مسندوں پہ ﴿۱۵﴾
مُّتَّكِـِٕيْنَ عَلَيْهَا مُتَقٰبِلِيْنَ ﴿۱۶﴾	تکیے لگائے بیٹھے ہوں گے آمنے سامنے ﴿۱۶﴾
يَطُوْفُ عَلَيْهِمْ وِلْدَانٌ مُّخَلَّدُوْنَ ﴿۱۷﴾	لیے پھریں گے ان کے اردگرد ایسے لڑکے جو ہمیشہ لڑکے ہی رہیں گے ﴿۱۷﴾
بِاَكْوَابٍ وَّاَبَارِيْقَ ۙ وَكَاْسٍ	ساغر، صراحی اور جام
مِّنْ مَّعِيْنٍ ﴿۱۸﴾	نتھری ہوئی شراب کے ﴿۱۸﴾
لَّا يُصَدَّعُوْنَ عَنْهَا	ایسی کہ نہ سر چکرائے اسے پی کر
وَلَا يُنْزِفُوْنَ ﴿۱۹﴾	اور نہ عقل میں فتور آئے ﴿۱۹﴾
وَفَاكِهَةٍ	اور (پیش کریں گے) لذیذ پھل
مِّمَّا يَتَخَيَّرُوْنَ ﴿۲۰﴾	تاکہ اس میں سے جسے چاہیں پسند کرلیں ﴿۲۰﴾
وَلَحْمِ طَيْرٍ	اور (پیش کریں گے) گوشت پرندوں کا
مِّمَّا يَشْتَهُوْنَ ﴿۲۱﴾	تاکہ لے لیں اپنی رغبت کے مطابق ﴿۲۱﴾
وَحُوْرٌ عِيْنٌ ﴿۲۲﴾	اور حوریں ہوں گی خوبصورت آنکھوں والی ﴿۲۲﴾
كَاَمْثَالِ اللُّؤْلُؤِ الْمَكْنُوْنِ ﴿۲۳﴾	ایسی حسین جیسے موتی جنہیں چھپا کر رکھا گیا ہو ﴿۲۳﴾
جَزَآءًۢ	(یہ سب کچھ ملے گا انہیں) اجر کے طور پہ
بِمَا كَانُوْا يَعْمَلُوْنَ ﴿۲۴﴾	ان اعمال کی جو وہ کرتے رہے ﴿۲۴﴾
لَا يَسْمَعُوْنَ فِيْهَا لَغْوًا	نہیں سنیں گے وہ وہاں کوئی بے ہودہ کلام
وَّلَا تَاْثِيْمًا ﴿۲۵﴾	اور نہ گناہ کی بات ﴿۲۵﴾
اِلَّا قِيْلًا سَلٰمًا سَلٰمًا ﴿۲۶﴾	سوائے ایک بول کے سلام ہو تم پر سلام ہو تم پر ﴿۲۶﴾

014 And a few of those following in plan

015 On Thrones adorned
With precious favored of stones

016 Reposing and facing each in prone

017 Around them will be youths in prime
Enduring in bloom looking in sublime

018 With goblets and cups and beakers in flavor
Of sheer and clear wine cheery to savor

019 With no ill in effect or muddle in confuse

020 Fruits they select to nibble in profuse

021 And meat of birds
Or else they cherish in desire

022 Maids,
With alluring and glowing deep eyes in aspire

023 Similar as bauble beads and jewels in secure

024 An award in conduct of past held to allure

025 No perkiness to hear
No blemish and blur of ill to bear

026 Word "Concord and Accord" all in around
That's to hear all in surround

وَأَصْحٰبُ الْيَمِينِ ۙ	اور دائیں بازو والے،
مَآ أَصْحٰبُ الْيَمِينِ ﴿٢٧﴾	کیا کہنا دائیں بازو والوں (کی خوش نصیبی) کا! ﴿٢٧﴾
فِي سِدْرٍ مَّخْضُودٍ ﴿٢٨﴾	(وہ ہوں گے ایسے باغات میں) جن میں بیریاں ہوں گی بے خار ﴿٢٨﴾
وَطَلْحٍ مَّنضُودٍ ﴿٢٩﴾	اور کیلے تہ بہ تہ ﴿٢٩﴾
وَظِلٍّ مَّمْدُودٍ ﴿٣٠﴾	اور چھاؤں دور تک پھیلی ہوئی ﴿٣٠﴾
وَمَآءٍ مَّسْكُوبٍ ﴿٣١﴾	اور پانی ہر دم رواں ﴿٣١﴾
وَفَاكِهَةٍ كَثِيرَةٍ ﴿٣٢﴾	اور طرح طرح کے لذیذ پھل بکثرت ﴿٣٢﴾
لَّا مَقْطُوعَةٍ وَلَا مَمْنُوعَةٍ ﴿٣٣﴾	کبھی ختم نہ ہونے والے اور بے روک ٹوک ﴿٣٣﴾
وَفُرُشٍ مَّرْفُوعَةٍ ﴿٣٤﴾	اور نشست گاہیں اونچی اونچی ﴿٣٤﴾
إِنَّآ أَنشَأْنٰهُنَّ إِنشَآءً ﴿٣٥﴾	ہم پیدا کریں گے ان بیویوں کو نئے سرے سے ﴿٣٥﴾
فَجَعَلْنٰهُنَّ أَبْكَارًا ﴿٣٦﴾	اور بنا دیں گے انہیں کنواریاں ﴿٣٦﴾
عُرُبًا أَتْرَابًا ﴿٣٧﴾	شوہروں کی عاشق زار اور عمر میں ہم سن ﴿٣٧﴾
لِّأَصْحٰبِ الْيَمِينِ ﴿٣٨﴾ ع	(یہ سب کچھ) ہوگا دائیں بازو والوں کے لیے ﴿٣٨﴾
ثُلَّةٌ مِّنَ الْأَوَّلِينَ ﴿٣٩﴾	وہ بہت ہوں گے اگلوں میں سے ﴿٣٩﴾
وَثُلَّةٌ مِّنَ الْآخِرِينَ ﴿٤٠﴾	اور بہت ہوں گے پچھلوں میں سے ﴿٤٠﴾
وَأَصْحٰبُ الشِّمَالِ ۙ مَآ أَصْحٰبُ الشِّمَالِ ﴿٤١﴾	اور بائیں بازو والے، بائیں بازو والوں (کی بدنصیبی) کا کیا ٹھکانہ! ﴿٤١﴾
فِي سَمُومٍ وَحَمِيمٍ ﴿٤٢﴾	وہ ہوں گے لو کی لپٹ میں اور کھولتے ہوئے پانی میں ﴿٤٢﴾
وَظِلٍّ مِّن يَحْمُومٍ ﴿٤٣﴾	اور سائے میں سخت کالے دھوئیں کے ﴿٤٣﴾
لَّا بَارِدٍ وَلَا كَرِيمٍ ﴿٤٤﴾	جو نہ ٹھنڈا ہوگا اور نہ آرام دہ ﴿٤٤﴾

027 Then friends and fellows in pace
Of the Right Hand beaming in glow
How'd you determine the friends in place
Their cherishing endow in glow

028 They abide mid Lote (trees) in swarm
There's no thistles and thorns to harm

029 Mid Talh trees, flora and fruit in lure
Piled over each other in score

030 In drawn out wide awning in ease
That's shade and shadow in appease

031 And water soaring quixotic in glide
A perpetual sweep in lyrical slide

032 And Fruit,
Pay and profits of their doings in profuse

033 No limit of season, or scant in confuse

034 On Thrones of Dignity, exalted in grace

035 We've created spouses distinctive to brace

036 And made them chaste and astute to engage

037 Adored by temper and tributes alike in age

038 For the friends of the Sane Pass in stance
039 A sizable sum of (them) old class in glance
040 And goodly number of later term in trance

041 The friend and fellow of liberal paw
What will be aide and escort of liberal paw

042 They'll abide in den and pit in cuddle
Of Gust and gloom of fire in huddle
That's Stewing,
Steaming and simmering water in puddle

043 Where doom and gloom of soot in surround
044 There'll be nothing for relief in around

إِنَّهُمْ كَانُوا قَبْلَ ذَٰلِكَ مُتْرَفِينَ ٤٥	یقیناً یہ لوگ تھے اس سے پہلے خوش حالی میں مگن ٤٥
وَكَانُوا يُصِرُّونَ عَلَى الْحِنْثِ الْعَظِيمِ ٤٦	اور اصرار کیا کرتے تھے بڑے بڑے گناہوں پر ٤٦
وَكَانُوا يَقُولُونَ أَئِذَا مِتْنَا	اور کہا کرتے تھے کہ جب ہم مر جائیں گے
وَكُنَّا تُرَابًا وَعِظَامًا أَإِنَّا	اور ہو جائیں گے مٹی اور ہڈیاں تو کیا یقیناً ہم
لَمَبْعُوثُونَ ٤٧	پھر اٹھا کھڑے کیے جائیں گے؟ ٤٧
أَوَآبَاؤُنَا	اور کیا ہمارے باپ دادا بھی (اٹھائے جائیں گے)
الْأَوَّلُونَ ٤٨	جو پہلے گزر چکے ہیں؟ ٤٨
قُلْ إِنَّ الْأَوَّلِينَ وَالْآخِرِينَ ٤٩	کہیے بلا شبہ پہلے بھی اور پچھلے بھی ٤٩
لَمَجْمُوعُونَ	سب ضرور جمع کیے جانے والے ہیں
إِلَىٰ مِيقَاتِ يَوْمٍ مَعْلُومٍ ٥٠	ایک معین دن کے وقتِ مقرر پر ٥٠
ثُمَّ إِنَّكُمْ أَيُّهَا الضَّالُّونَ الْمُكَذِّبُونَ ٥١	پھر یقیناً تم اے گمراہو اور جھٹلانے والو! ٥١
لَآكِلُونَ مِنْ شَجَرٍ	ضرور کھاؤ گے تم ایک درخت میں سے
مِنْ زَقُّومٍ ٥٢	جو از قسمِ "زقوم" ہوگا ٥٢
فَمَالِئُونَ مِنْهَا الْبُطُونَ ٥٣	سو بھرو گے اسی سے اپنے پیٹ ٥٣
فَشَارِبُونَ عَلَيْهِ مِنَ الْحَمِيمِ ٥٤	پھر پیو گے اوپر سے کھولتا ہوا پانی ٥٤
فَشَارِبُونَ شُرْبَ الْهِيمِ ٥٥	سو پیو گے جیسے پیتے ہیں پیاس کے مارے ہوئے اونٹ ٥٥
هَٰذَا نُزُلُهُمْ يَوْمَ الدِّينِ ٥٦	یہ ہوگی بائیں بازو والوں کی ضیافت روزِ جزا ٥٦
نَحْنُ خَلَقْنَاكُمْ فَلَوْلَا تُصَدِّقُونَ ٥٧	ہم ہی نے پیدا کیا ہے تمہیں پھر کیوں نہیں یقین کرتے تم؟ ٥٧
أَفَرَأَيْتُمْ مَا تُمْنُونَ ٥٨	کیا کبھی غور کیا تم نے کہ یہ جو نطفہ ڈالتے ہو تم؟ ٥٨

045 Before in place
Their love and lust of riches,
Hemmed in pace

046 And persisted callously in stance
For ills and evils oppressed in glance

047 And they used to say:
What!
When we're dust and bones in crust
How then be resolute and firm in trust

048 And our elders dead long in before
Will come to life anew in score

049/ Say:
050 Surely all worn and torn in stray
And the,
Hence and whence will come to stay

Certainly!
They'll be pleated together in plight
On Day affirmed to be there in sight

051 O you duffers!
How'd you defer and defy truth in pace

052 Surely Zaqqum is a tree in place
For you,
That's accursed in zest to brace

053 Then you'll stuff your gut in grief
054 And drink stewing water over in retrieve

055 Truly! You'll be sipping in assort
Like of sick thirsty irate camels in sort

056 Such is the recompense on Day of award
057 We created you:
Why don't you submit in factuality

058 Don't you discern?
The ovum and sperm you toss in actuality

ءَاَنْتُمْ تَخْلُقُوْنَهٗۤ اَمْ نَحْنُ الْخٰلِقُوْنَ ۝٥٩	کیا تم پیدا کرتے ہو بچہ یا ہم ہیں پیدا کرنے والے؟ ۝٥٩
نَحْنُ قَدَّرْنَا بَيْنَكُمُ الْمَوْتَ	ہم مقدر کر چکے ہیں تمہارے درمیان موت
وَمَا نَحْنُ بِمَسْبُوْقِيْنَ ۝٦٠	اور نہیں ہیں ہم عاجز ۝٦٠
عَلٰۤى اَنْ نُّبَدِّلَ اَمْثَالَكُمْ	اس بات سے کہ بدل دیں ہم تمہارے وجود ہی کو
وَنُنْشِئَكُمْ فِيْ مَا لَا تَعْلَمُوْنَ ۝٦١	اور پیدا کر دیں تمہیں ایسی شکل و صورت میں جس کو تم جانتے ہی نہیں ۝٦١
وَلَقَدْ عَلِمْتُمُ النَّشْاَةَ الْاُوْلٰى	اور یقیناً تم جانتے ہو پہلی پیدائش کو
فَلَوْلَا تَذَكَّرُوْنَ ۝٦٢	تو تم کیوں نہیں سبق لیتے؟ ۝٦٢
اَفَرَءَيْتُمْ مَّا تَحْرُثُوْنَ ۝٦٣	کیا کبھی سوچا تم نے کہ یہ جو تم بیج بوتے ہو ۝٦٣
ءَاَنْتُمْ تَزْرَعُوْنَهٗۤ اَمْ	کیا تم اگاتے ہو اس سے کھیتی یا
نَحْنُ الزّٰرِعُوْنَ ۝٦٤	ہم ہیں اگانے والے؟ ۝٦٤
لَوْ نَشَآءُ لَجَعَلْنٰهُ حُطَامًا	اگر ہم چاہیں تو بنا کر رکھ دیں اسے بھس
فَظَلْتُمْ تَفَكَّهُوْنَ ۝٦٥	اور رہ جاؤ تم باتیں بناتے ۝٦٥
اِنَّا لَمُغْرَمُوْنَ ۝٦٦	کہ ہم پر تو چٹی پڑ گئی ہے ۝٦٦
بَلْ نَحْنُ مَحْرُوْمُوْنَ ۝٦٧	بلکہ ہمارے نصیب ہی پھوٹے ہوئے ہیں ۝٦٧
اَفَرَءَيْتُمُ الْمَآءَ الَّذِيْ تَشْرَبُوْنَ ۝٦٨	کیا کبھی سوچا تم نے کہ یہ پانی جو تم پیتے ہو؟ ۝٦٨
ءَاَنْتُمْ اَنْزَلْتُمُوْهُ مِنَ الْمُزْنِ	کیا تم نازل کرتے ہو اسے بادل سے
اَمْ نَحْنُ الْمُنْزِلُوْنَ ۝٦٩	یا ہم ہیں نازل کرنے والے؟ ۝٦٩
لَوْ نَشَآءُ جَعَلْنٰهُ اُجَاجًا	اگر ہم چاہیں تو بنا کر رکھ دیں اسے سخت کھاری
فَلَوْلَا تَشْكُرُوْنَ ۝٧٠	پھر کیوں نہیں تم شکر گزار ہوتے؟ ۝٧٠

059 Who created it?
You or We, as Planner and Designer in place

060 We determined the doom of death in precise
And We aren't pent-up or dead beat in pace

061 We're to change your figure in plan
And creating you once again in form
A figure in form,
You cannot conclude in norm

062 Truly!
You discern your earlier creation in term
Then!
Why don't you ardor and adore Lord in turn

063 Look for the seed sown in ground

064 Who's it to cause it grow in surround
Is it you or We tending in abound

065 If We'd ever desired it so
We'd canker it to crumble, dry in throw
And you'd be left in daze and amaze in flow

066 Indeed! We then assert to affirm
It's for us to manage in same

067 Indeed!
We're deprived of deeds and doings in concern

068 Just discern to concern, water you savor in sip
069 Do you sprinkle the shower in dip
Or We bring it down from the clouds in slip

070 If We desired in so
It could be vexing and galling in ado

Then why don't you trend to Lord in Grace
In Ardor and adore His Bounty to brace

أَفَرَءَيْتُمُ النَّارَ الَّتِي تُورُونَ ۝٧١
کیا تم نے کبھی غور کیا کہ یہ آگ جو تم سلگاتے ہو؟ ۷۱

ءَأَنتُمْ أَنشَأْتُمْ شَجَرَتَهَا
کیا تم نے پیدا کیا ہے اس کا درخت

أَمْ نَحْنُ الْمُنشِـُٔونَ ۝٧٢
یا ہم ہیں ان کے پیدا کرنے والے؟ ۷۲

نَحْنُ جَعَلْنَاهَا تَذْكِرَةً
ہم نے بنایا ہے آگ کو یاددہانی کا ذریعہ

وَمَتَاعًا لِّلْمُقْوِينَ ۝٧٣
اور رکھے ہیں اس میں فائدے تمام حاجتمندوں کے لیے ۷۳

فَسَبِّحْ بِاسْمِ رَبِّكَ الْعَظِيمِ ۝٧٤
پس اے نبی تسبیح کرو اپنے رب عظیم کے نام کی ۷۴

فَلَا أُقْسِمُ بِمَوَاقِعِ النُّجُومِ ۝٧٥
پس نہیں، قسم کھاتا ہوں میں ستاروں کی گزرگاہوں کی ۷۵

وَإِنَّهُ لَقَسَمٌ
اور بلاشبہ یہ ایک قسم ہے،

لَّوْ تَعْلَمُونَ عَظِيمٌ ۝٧٦
اگر تم سمجھو تو بہت بڑی قسم ۷۶

إِنَّهُ لَقُرْآنٌ كَرِيمٌ ۝٧٧
واقعہ یہ ہے کہ یہ قرآن ہے بلند پایہ ۷۷

فِي كِتَابٍ مَّكْنُونٍ ۝٧٨
جو ثبت ہے ایک محفوظ کتاب میں ۷۸

لَّا يَمَسُّهُ إِلَّا الْمُطَهَّرُونَ ۝٧٩
نہیں چھوتے اسے مگر وہ جو پاک صاف ہیں ۷۹

تَنزِيلٌ مِّن رَّبِّ الْعَالَمِينَ ۝٨٠
نازل کردہ ہے رب العالمین کی طرف سے ۸۰

أَفَبِهَٰذَا الْحَدِيثِ
کیا پھر اس کلام کے ساتھ

أَنتُم مُّدْهِنُونَ ۝٨١
تم بے پروائی برتتے ہو؟ ۸۱

وَتَجْعَلُونَ رِزْقَكُمْ
اور رکھا ہے تم نے اپنا حصہ (اللہ کی اس نعمت میں)

أَنَّكُمْ تُكَذِّبُونَ ۝٨٢
یہ کہ تم جھٹلاتے ہو اسے ۸۲

فَلَوْلَا إِذَا بَلَغَتِ الْحُلْقُومَ ۝٨٣
سو کیوں نہیں جب پہنچ جاتی ہے (جان) حلق تک ۸۳

وَأَنتُمْ حِينَئِذٍ تَنظُرُونَ ۝٨٤
اور تم اس وقت دیکھ رہے ہوتے ہو ۸۴

071 Don't you see the fire kindle in glow

072 Who's there to let it glow
The trees that let the fire to glow
Who's there the tree to grow

073 We've made tribute the fire in sort
An ease and relief in accord
(For dweller of desert in part)

074 Then honor in acclaim Lord in tribute
Who's Exquisite in Grace to salute

075 Likewise!
I call to behold stage and spot in promotion
All the stars dwindling in commotion

076 Indeed!
It's an immense pledge in term
If you really care to discern

077 Qur'an is indeed most elegant in Stance
078 A Book, well-guarded in Glimmer of Glance

079 That none can touch in pace
But only, who're clean in place
080 Divulgence of Lord in grace
Who's but,
The Lord of the Worlds in pace

081 Is it a missive?
That you'd hold so light to esteem
Asserting it false (don't trend in gleam)

082 And you've made a favor in norm
To talk in fib as a routine in form

083 Why don't you pace it to grasp
The soul of a dying man to clasp
When it reaches the throat in hasp
084 As you're seeing the man in depart

وَنَحْنُ اَقْرَبُ اِلَيْهِ مِنْكُمْ	اور ہم زیادہ قریب ہوتے ہیں اس کے تمہاری نسبت
وَلٰكِنْ لَّا تُبْصِرُوْنَ ﴿٨٥﴾	لیکن تم کو نظر نہیں آتے ﴿٨٥﴾
فَلَوْلَآ اِنْ كُنْتُمْ غَيْرَ مَدِيْنِيْنَ ﴿٨٦﴾	سو اگر نہیں ہو تم کسی کے محکوم ﴿٨٦﴾
تَرْجِعُوْنَهَآ اِنْ	تو کیوں نہیں لوٹا لیتے اس کی رُوح کو، اگر
كُنْتُمْ صٰدِقِيْنَ ﴿٨٧﴾	ہو تم سچے؟ ﴿٨٧﴾
فَاَمَّآ اِنْ كَانَ مِنَ الْمُقَرَّبِيْنَ ﴿٨٨﴾	سو اگر ہوتا ہے مرنے والا مقربین میں سے ﴿٨٨﴾
فَرَوْحٌ وَّرَيْحَانٌ	تو (اس کے لیے) راحت ہے اور عمدہ رزق ہے۔
وَّجَنَّتُ نَعِيْمٍ ﴿٨٩﴾	اور نعمت بھری جنت ہے ﴿٨٩﴾
وَاَمَّآ اِنْ كَانَ	پھر اگر ہے وہ
مِنْ اَصْحٰبِ الْيَمِيْنِ ﴿٩٠﴾	اصحاب الیمین میں سے ﴿٩٠﴾
فَسَلٰمٌ لَّكَ	تو اس کا استقبال ہوگا "سلام ہو تم پر
مِنْ اَصْحٰبِ الْيَمِيْنِ ﴿٩١﴾	تم اصحاب الیمین میں سے ہو" ﴿٩١﴾
وَاَمَّآ اِنْ كَانَ	اور اگر ہوگا وہ
مِنَ الْمُكَذِّبِيْنَ الضَّآلِّيْنَ ﴿٩٢﴾	جھٹلانے والے گمراہ لوگوں میں سے ﴿٩٢﴾
فَنُزُلٌ مِّنْ حَمِيْمٍ ﴿٩٣﴾	تو اس کی تواضع کے لیے ہوگا کھولتا ہوا پانی ﴿٩٣﴾
وَّتَصْلِيَةُ جَحِيْمٍ ﴿٩٤﴾	اور جھونکا جانا جہنم میں ﴿٩٤﴾
اِنَّ هٰذَا لَهُوَ	بلا شبہ یہی ہے
حَقُّ الْيَقِيْنِ ﴿٩٥﴾	قطعی حق ﴿٩٥﴾
فَسَبِّحْ بِاسْمِ رَبِّكَ الْعَظِيْمِ ﴿٩٦﴾	پس اے نبی تسبیح کرو اپنے رب عظیم کے نام کی ﴿٩٦﴾

085 We're close and beside in pace
But you don't discern a bit in glance

086 If you aren't to be dictated by One in stance
And are free from any charge in trance

087 Call back the soul of the dead to return
If you're true to your word in term
(And you're free of any charge to sustain)

088 If the one in demise is virtuous in grace

089 For him, there's a repose of relief in pace
Him to abide Gardens of Bliss in place

090 And he's of the fellow in stance
Of the virtuous (Right Hand) in glance

091 Amity and accord for them to brace
Who trend in verity hither in trace
Amity and accord,
From the fellow of (Right Hand) Virtuous in pace

092 If he's of the men and clan in stride
Mutating the verity for fib in deride

093 For him is perplexity thither in swarm
With simmering water to sip in alarm

094 And burning Hell-Pyre there to aside
(Destitute deign in design them to reside)

095 Indeed!
That's so certain and precise in perception

096 So ardor and adore Lord in assertion
(And not to be dissuaded in deception)

آیاتہا ۲۹ (۵۷) سُوْرَةُ الْحَدِيْدِ مَدَنِيَّةٌ (۹۴) رکوعاتہا ۴

بِسْمِ اللّٰهِ الرَّحْمٰنِ الرَّحِيْمِ

شروع اللہ کے نام سے جو بڑا مہربان نہایت رحم والا ہے

سَبَّحَ لِلّٰهِ مَا فِي السَّمٰوٰتِ	تسبیح کی ہے اللہ کی ہر اس چیز نے جو آسمانوں میں ہے
وَالْاَرْضِ ۚ وَهُوَ الْعَزِيْزُ الْحَكِيْمُ ①	اور زمین میں ہے۔ اور وہی ہے زبردست اور بڑی حکمت والا ①
لَهٗ مُلْكُ السَّمٰوٰتِ وَالْاَرْضِ ۚ	اسی کی ہے سلطنت آسمانوں میں اور زمین میں،
يُحْيٖ وَيُمِيْتُ ۚ	زندگی بخشتا ہے اور موت دیتا ہے۔
وَهُوَ عَلٰى كُلِّ شَيْءٍ قَدِيْرٌ ②	اور وہ ہر چیز پر پوری قدرت رکھتا ہے ②
هُوَ الْاَوَّلُ وَالْاٰخِرُ وَالظَّاهِرُ	وہی اول بھی ہے اور آخر بھی اور ظاہر بھی ہے
وَالْبَاطِنُ ۚ وَهُوَ بِكُلِّ شَيْءٍ عَلِيْمٌ ③	اور باطن بھی اور وہ ہر چیز کا پورا علم رکھتا ہے ③
هُوَ الَّذِيْ خَلَقَ السَّمٰوٰتِ وَالْاَرْضَ	وہی ہے جس نے پیدا فرمایا آسمانوں کو اور زمین کو
فِيْ سِتَّةِ اَيَّامٍ ثُمَّ اسْتَوٰى عَلَى الْعَرْشِ ۚ	چھ دنوں میں پھر جلوہ فرما ہوا عرش پر۔
يَعْلَمُ مَا يَلِجُ فِي الْاَرْضِ	وہ جانتا ہے اسے بھی جو داخل ہوتا ہے زمین میں
وَمَا يَخْرُجُ مِنْهَا وَمَا يَنْزِلُ	اور جو نکلتا ہے اس سے اور جو نازل ہوتا ہے
مِنَ السَّمَاءِ وَمَا يَعْرُجُ فِيْهَا ۚ	آسمان سے اور جو چڑھتا ہے اس میں۔
وَهُوَ مَعَكُمْ اَيْنَ مَا كُنْتُمْ ۚ	اور وہ تمہارے ساتھ ہوتا ہے جہاں بھی ہو تم۔
وَاللّٰهُ بِمَا تَعْمَلُوْنَ بَصِيْرٌ ④	اور اللہ ان اعمال کو جو تم کرتے ہو دیکھ رہا ہے ④
لَهٗ مُلْكُ السَّمٰوٰتِ وَالْاَرْضِ ۚ	اسی کی ہے سلطنت آسمانوں میں اور زمین میں۔

057-AL HADID

In the name of Lord, the Most Beneficent, Most Merciful

001 All in the Heavens and earth in array
Ardor and adore Lord in sway

For He's Exalted in Might
With Sense and Sagacity in Bright

002 To Him belong the rule and edit
Of the Heavens and earth in strict

Commands in creation and in demise
Holds command and demand all in premise

003 He's First and Last in concern
And is Manifest and Secret in turn
He's Sane and Sagacious in term

004 He contrived heavens and Earth in eons six
He soundly secured Seat of His State in fix

He discerns that you sow and yield in soil
And that gets down of the heavens in sprinkle
And of all that, which rises so high in twinkle
Where so ever you trend in toil
Lord discerns and concerns all in pace

005 To Him belongs all the rule in command
Of the heavens and earth in demand

وَاِلَى اللّٰهِ تُرْجَعُ الْاُمُوْرُ ⑤	اور اللہ ہی کی طرف لوٹائے جاتے ہیں تمام معاملات (فیصلے کے لیے) ⑤
يُوْلِجُ الَّيْلَ فِى النَّهَارِ	وہ داخل کرتا ہے رات کو دن میں
وَيُوْلِجُ النَّهَارَ فِى الَّيْلِ ؕ	اور داخل کرتا ہے دن کو رات میں۔
وَهُوَ عَلِيْمٌ بِذَاتِ الصُّدُوْرِ ⑥	اور وہ پوری طرح جانتا ہے دلوں میں چھپے ہوئے رازوں کو ⑥
اٰمِنُوْا بِاللّٰهِ وَرَسُوْلِهٖ وَاَنْفِقُوْا	ایمان لاؤ اللہ پر اور اس کے رسول پر اور خرچ کرو
مِمَّا جَعَلَكُمْ مُّسْتَخْلَفِيْنَ فِيْهِ ؕ	اس (مال) میں سے جس میں بنایا ہے اس نے تم کو (اپنا) نائب۔
فَالَّذِيْنَ اٰمَنُوْا مِنْكُمْ وَاَنْفَقُوْا	پس وہ لوگ جو ایمان لائے تم میں سے اور خرچ کیا،
لَهُمْ اَجْرٌ كَبِيْرٌ ⑦	ان کے لیے ہے بڑا اجر ⑦
وَمَا لَكُمْ لَا تُؤْمِنُوْنَ بِاللّٰهِ ۚ	اور کیا ہو گیا ہے تمہیں کہ نہیں ایمان لاتے ہو تم اللہ پر۔
وَالرَّسُوْلُ يَدْعُوْكُمْ لِتُؤْمِنُوْا بِرَبِّكُمْ	جبکہ رسول دعوت دے رہا ہے تمہیں کہ ایمان لاؤ اپنے رب پر
وَقَدْ اَخَذَ مِيْثَاقَكُمْ	اور وہ لے چکا ہے تم سے پختہ عہد بھی،
اِنْ كُنْتُمْ مُّؤْمِنِيْنَ ⑧	اگر ہو تم ایمان والے ⑧
هُوَ الَّذِيْ يُنَزِّلُ عَلٰى عَبْدِهٖٓ	وہی تو ہے جو نازل فرما رہا ہے اپنے بندے پر
اٰيٰتٍۢ بَيِّنٰتٍ لِّيُخْرِجَكُمْ مِّنَ الظُّلُمٰتِ	صاف اور واضح آیات تاکہ نکال لائے تمہیں تاریکیوں سے
اِلَى النُّوْرِ ؕ وَاِنَّ اللّٰهَ بِكُمْ	روشنی میں اور بلاشبہ اللہ تم پر
لَرَءُوْفٌ رَّحِيْمٌ ⑨	نہایت ہی شفیق اور مہربان ہے ⑨
وَمَا لَكُمْ اَلَّا تُنْفِقُوْا	اور کیا ہو گیا ہے تمہیں کہ تم نہیں خرچ کرتے
فِيْ سَبِيْلِ اللّٰهِ وَلِلّٰهِ مِيْرَاثُ	اللہ کی راہ میں جبکہ اللہ ہی کے لیے ہے میراث
السَّمٰوٰتِ وَالْاَرْضِ ؕ لَا يَسْتَوِيْ مِنْكُمْ	آسمانوں اور زمین کی۔ نہیں برابر ہو سکتے تم میں سے

To Him!
All terms in trail consign to submit

006 He blends Day into Night and Night into Day
He cares in concerns veer of core in splay

007 Trust in Lord and His Prophet in glow
And expend charity* in endow
Out of His bestowal in flow

For He made you the heirs in trail
Those who trust and disperse in vale
Them to cherish caring awards in dale

*Give alms to the poor

008 What's the snag and catch in pace
That you shouldn't trust Lord in grace

Messengers preaches you to trust in Lord
He holds your pledge in this regard
If you're the men of faith in accord

009 Lord assigns and consigns missive in stride
A discipline of faith, you to aside
(Through His Messengers here in abide)

He may escort you to faith in glow
From the dusk of depravity in blow
Indeed, for you,
Lord is Munificent and Bounteous in endow

010 What's the reason with you in stance
Not to spend in designs of Lord in plans

To Him belongs all in pace
Of all the heavens and earth in place
How can they be equal in trace

مَنْ اَنْفَقَ مِنْ قَبْلِ الْفَتْحِ وَ قٰتَلَ ؕ
وہ لوگ جنہوں نے خرچ کیا فتحِ مکہ سے پہلے اور جہاد کیا۔

اُولٰٓئِكَ اَعْظَمُ دَرَجَةً مِّنَ الَّذِيْنَ
یہ لوگ بڑے ہیں درجے کے اعتبار سے ان سے جنہوں نے

اَنْفَقُوْا مِنْۢ بَعْدُ وَ قٰتَلُوْا ؕ
خرچ کیا فتح کے بعد اور جہاد کیا۔

وَكُلًّا وَّعَدَ اللّٰهُ الْحُسْنٰى ؕ
اگرچہ سب سے وعدہ کر رکھا ہے اللہ نے بھلائی کا۔

وَاللّٰهُ بِمَا تَعْمَلُوْنَ خَبِيْرٌ ۝١٠
اور اللہ ان اعمال سے جو تم کرتے ہو پوری طرح باخبر ہے ۝١٠

مَنْ ذَا الَّذِىْ يُقْرِضُ اللّٰهَ قَرْضًا حَسَنًا
کون ہے جو قرض دے اللہ کو "قرضِ حسنہ"

فَيُضٰعِفَهٗ لَهٗ وَلَهٗۤ اَجْرٌ كَرِيْمٌ ۝١١
تاکہ وہ بڑھا کر واپس دے اسے اور اس کے لیے ہے بہترین اجر ۝١١

يَوْمَ تَرَى الْمُؤْمِنِيْنَ وَ الْمُؤْمِنٰتِ
اس دن جب تم دیکھو گے مومن مردوں اور مومن عورتوں کو

يَسْعٰى نُوْرُهُمْ بَيْنَ اَيْدِيْهِمْ
کہ دوڑ رہا ہوگا ان کا نور ان کے آگے آگے

وَبِاَيْمَانِهِمْ بُشْرٰىكُمُ
اور ان کی دائیں جانب، ان سے کہا جائے گا "بشارت ہے تمہارے لیے

الْيَوْمَ جَنّٰتٌ تَجْرِىْ مِنْ تَحْتِهَا الْاَنْهٰرُ
آج ایسی جنتوں کی جن کے نیچے بہہ رہی ہوں گی نہریں،

خٰلِدِيْنَ فِيْهَا ؕ ذٰلِكَ هُوَ الْفَوْزُ الْعَظِيْمُ ۝١٢
ہمیشہ رہیں گے وہ ان میں۔ یہی ہے بڑی کامیابی ۝١٢

يَوْمَ يَقُوْلُ الْمُنٰفِقُوْنَ وَ الْمُنٰفِقٰتُ
اس دن کہیں گے منافق مرد اور منافق عورتیں

لِلَّذِيْنَ اٰمَنُوا انْظُرُوْنَا نَقْتَبِسْ
اہلِ ایمان سے کہ ذرا ہمارا بھی خیال رکھو تاکہ ہم روشنی حاصل کریں

مِنْ نُّوْرِكُمْ ۚ قِيْلَ ارْجِعُوْا
تمہارے نور سے۔ ان سے کہا جائے گا لوٹ جاؤ

وَرَآءَكُمْ فَالْتَمِسُوْا نُوْرًا ؕ فَضُرِبَ
پیچھے کی طرف اور تلاش کرو روشنی۔ پھر حائل کر دی جائے گی

بَيْنَهُمْ بِسُوْرٍ لَّهٗ بَابٌ ؕ
ان کے درمیان ایک دیوار جس میں ایک دروازہ ہوگا،

بَاطِنُهٗ فِيْهِ الرَّحْمَةُ
اس کے اندر کی طرف ہوگی رحمت

وَظَاهِرُهٗ مِنْ قِبَلِهِ الْعَذَابُ ؕ ۝١٣
اور باہر کی طرف ہوگا عذاب ۝١٣

One spending in the event of Lord to obey
And also fighting for His cause in fray
All, who spent and fought hither in lore
Before the cherished victory in allure
They're preferred in term
Than the later in run
Who fought or spent later in trend
But Lord pledged a good term in record
For both the class goodly term in reward
Indeed! Lord,
Discerns and concerns your doings in sort

011 Who's to endow credit* to Lord in premise
That's cherishing credit (for them) in precise
Lord to expand many a times in device
And bestows His Glorious grants in decide

*Giving loan without any intention of return to the men dedicated for the cause of Allah Almighty

012 The Day believing men and dame in pace
You'll discern and concern in place
How a gleam in glow
Ahead and before escorts in flow
On their right and beside in glimmer
The Day to endow a Word in glitter
Cherish you the respect and regards
Them to aside boons in rewards
Gardens, where streams swing in surge
Aside and below, swing and sway in surf
The gift and grant prime in urge

013 That Day
Hypocrites-men and women in stray
Trend to the believers and beg to pray
Wait for us for a while in flow
Let us borrow a bit of gleam in glow
Of your glorious glitter in endow
It'll be said:
Turn your back to the rear in tail
Then quest for the light in trail
Then there'll be a wall mid them in pace
With a gate therein fixed in place
Inside of the gate,
There'll be mercy all in sway
With ease and appease charm in play
In out and about!
There'll be agony and alarm in fray

پکار پکار کر کہیں گے وہ مومنوں سے کیا نہ تھے ہم بھی تمہارے ساتھ۔	يُنَادُوْنَهُمْ اَلَمْ نَكُنْ مَّعَكُمْ ؕ
مومن کہیں گے ہاں مگر تم نے خود فتنے میں ڈالا	قَالُوْا بَلٰى وَلٰكِنَّكُمْ فَتَنْتُمْ
اپنے آپ کو اور موقع پرستی اور شک میں پڑے رہے	اَنْفُسَكُمْ وَتَرَبَّصْتُمْ وَارْتَبْتُمْ
اور فریب دیتی رہیں تم کو تمنائیں یہاں تک کہ آگیا	وَغَرَّتْكُمُ الْاَمَانِيُّ حَتّٰى جَآءَ
اللہ کا فیصلہ اور (آخر وقت تک) دھوکے میں مبتلا رکھا تم کو	اَمْرُ اللّٰهِ وَغَرَّكُمْ
اللہ کے بارے میں دھوکے باز (شیطان) نے ﴿۱۴﴾	بِاللّٰهِ الْغَرُوْرُ ﴿۱۴﴾
سو آج نہ قبول کیا جائے گا تم سے فدیہ	فَالْيَوْمَ لَا يُؤْخَذُ مِنْكُمْ فِدْيَةٌ
اور نہ ان لوگوں سے جنہوں نے کھلا انکار کیا تھا۔	وَّلَا مِنَ الَّذِيْنَ كَفَرُوْا ؕ
تمہارا ٹھکانہ جہنم ہے، وہی خبر گیری کرنے والی ہے تمہاری۔	مَاْوٰىكُمُ النَّارُ ؕ هِيَ مَوْلٰىكُمْ ؕ
اور یہ بدترین انجام ہے ﴿۱۵﴾	وَبِئْسَ الْمَصِيْرُ ﴿۱۵﴾
کیا نہیں آیا ابھی وقت ان لوگوں کے لیے جو	اَلَمْ يَاْنِ لِلَّذِيْنَ
ایمان لا چکے ہیں اس بات کا کہ پگھلیں ان کے دل	اٰمَنُوْٓا اَنْ تَخْشَعَ قُلُوْبُهُمْ
اللہ کے ذکر سے (اور جھکیں آگے) اس کے جو نازل ہوا ہے	لِذِكْرِ اللّٰهِ وَمَا نَزَلَ
حق (اللہ کی طرف سے)، اور نہ ہو جائیں وہ	مِنَ الْحَقِّ ۙ وَلَا يَكُوْنُوْا
ان لوگوں کی طرح جنہیں دی گئی تھی کتاب	كَالَّذِيْنَ اُوْتُوا الْكِتٰبَ
پہلے پھر لمبی گزر گئی ان پر مدت	مِنْ قَبْلُ فَطَالَ عَلَيْهِمُ الْاَمَدُ
تو سخت ہو گئے ان کے دل	فَقَسَتْ قُلُوْبُهُمْ ؕ
اس کا نتیجہ یہ ہے کہ اکثر ان میں فاسق ہیں ﴿۱۶﴾	وَكَثِيْرٌ مِّنْهُمْ فٰسِقُوْنَ ﴿۱۶﴾
خوب جان لو کہ یہ اللہ ہی ہے جو زندہ کرتا ہے	اِعْلَمُوْٓا اَنَّ اللّٰهَ يُحْيِ

014 They'll cry out to the men of faith
(To the men and clan in faith)
If we're not (with you) there in abide
It's true in stride

But you're opportunist and suspicious in glide
And enticed to the lust of lures in deride
You doubted the Pledge of Lord to aside

And your urge and itch, a fib in drift
Betrayed you until there's a doom in shift

As Dictum of Lord held in treat
And Satan entranced you indeed in deceit
From the discipline of Lord in greet

015 The Day,
There'll be no way to rescue and restore
And who defied Mighty Lord in adore

Them to abide Fire to reside
That's fit and fine for you to aside
An evil of refuge for one in abide

016 Haven't the time affirmed in pace
For the men and clan of faith in place
To celebrate memory of Lord in grace
And observe truth, all term and trace

As revealed to them, they assisted in stance
And not to behave like the men in before
Who're instructed hither in before
It's quite a bit of time in score

Their core and intellect got stern and firm
Many of them are defiant* in term
And so denied and defied in concern

*rebellious transgressors

017 You discern and concern to obey
It's Lord, Who endows life in sway
To the dead and desolate land in array

الْاَرْضَ بَعْدَ مَوْتِهَا ؕ	زمین کو اس کے مرجانے کے بعد۔
قَدْ بَيَّنَّا لَكُمُ	بے شک کھول کھول کر بیان کر دی ہیں ہم نے تمہارے لیے
الْاٰيٰتِ لَعَلَّكُمْ تَعْقِلُوْنَ ﴿۱۷﴾	اپنی آیات، تاکہ تم عقل سے کام لو ﴿۱۷﴾
اِنَّ الْمُصَّدِّقِيْنَ وَ الْمُصَّدِّقٰتِ	یقیناً صدقہ دینے والے مرد اور صدقہ دینے والی عورتیں
وَ اَقْرَضُوا اللّٰهَ قَرْضًا حَسَنًا	اور وہ جنہوں نے قرض دیا ہے اللہ کو "قرض حسنہ"
يُّضٰعَفُ لَهُمْ وَ لَهُمْ اَجْرٌ كَرِيْمٌ ﴿۱۸﴾	بڑھا چڑھا کر دیا جائے گا ان کو اور ان کے لیے ہے بہترین اجر ﴿۱۸﴾
وَ الَّذِيْنَ اٰمَنُوْا بِاللّٰهِ وَرُسُلِهٖۤ	اور وہ لوگ جو ایمان لائے ہیں اللہ پر اور اس کے رسولوں پر
اُولٰٓئِكَ هُمُ الصِّدِّيْقُوْنَ ۖۗ وَ الشُّهَدَآءُ	وہی ہیں صدیق اور شہید
عِنْدَ رَبِّهِمْ ؕ لَهُمْ اَجْرُهُمْ	اپنے رب کے نزدیک۔ ان کے لیے ہے ان کا اجر
وَ نُوْرُهُمْ ؕ وَ الَّذِيْنَ كَفَرُوْا وَ كَذَّبُوْا	اور ان کا نور۔ اور جن لوگوں نے کفر کیا اور جھٹلایا
بِاٰيٰتِنَاۤ اُولٰٓئِكَ اَصْحٰبُ الْجَحِيْمِ ﴿۱۹﴾	ہماری آیات کو، یہ لوگ دوزخی ہیں ﴿۱۹﴾
اِعْلَمُوْۤا اَنَّمَا الْحَيٰوةُ الدُّنْيَا لَعِبٌ	خوب جان لو کہ دنیاوی زندگی کی حقیقت کھیل
وَّ لَهْوٌ وَّ زِيْنَةٌ وَّ تَفَاخُرٌۢ بَيْنَكُمْ	اور تماشا اور ظاہری ٹیپ ٹاپ اور ایک دوسرے پر فخر جتانا ہے
وَ تَكَاثُرٌ فِى الْاَمْوَالِ وَ الْاَوْلَادِ	اور ایک دوسرے سے بڑھ جانے کی کوشش کرنا ہے مال و اولاد میں
كَمَثَلِ غَيْثٍ اَعْجَبَ	اس کی مثال ایسے ہے جیسے بارش ہو اور خوش کر دے
الْكُفَّارَ نَبَاتُهٗ	کاشتکاروں کو اس سے پیدا ہونے والی نباتات
ثُمَّ يَهِيْجُ فَتَرٰىهُ مُصْفَرًّا	پھر پک جائے وہ تو دیکھتے ہو تم کہ وہ زرد ہو گئی ہے
ثُمَّ يَكُوْنُ حُطَامًا ؕ	اور بن کر رہ گئی بھس۔
وَ فِى الْاٰخِرَةِ عَذَابٌ شَدِيْدٌ ۙ وَّ مَغْفِرَةٌ	اور آخرت میں ہے سخت عذاب یا مغفرت

We've certainly shown Signs in prime
You to concern and stay in sublime

018 The men and dame endowing in alms
The beatific loan to The Lord in calm

Lord to endow quite a lot in bestow
Besides his bestowal generous in glow

019 Who trust in Lord and His Messenger in pace
They're the factual and frank in grace

They'll be endowed glitter in gleam
A bestowal of Lord in esteem

Those defying Lord and His Signs in escort
They're pal of Pyre in Hell to resort

020 Don't you care to concern in earth
This life is but trifle in mirth

Vying in wealth and scion in pace
Here's likeness of such in place

How shower in rain produce in delight
To the man plowing the land in plight

Then it withers to dry in trend
But in Hereafter cynics get to amend
A term of discipline serious in try

مِّنَ اللّٰهِ وَ رِضْوَانٌ ؕ وَ مَا	اللہ کی طرف سے اور اس کی خوشنودی اور نہیں
الْحَيٰوةُ الدُّنْيَآ اِلَّا مَتَاعُ الْغُرُوْرِ ﴿٢٠﴾	ہے دنیاوی زندگی مگر سامان دھوکے کا ﴿٢٠﴾
سَابِقُوْٓا اِلٰى مَغْفِرَةٍ مِّنْ رَّبِّكُمْ	لپکو اپنے رب کی مغفرت کی طرف
وَجَنَّةٍ عَرْضُهَا	اور اس جنت کی طرف جس کی وسعت
كَعَرْضِ السَّمَآءِ وَالْاَرْضِ ۙ	آسمانوں اور زمین کی وسعت کی مانند ہے
اُعِدَّتْ لِلَّذِيْنَ اٰمَنُوْا	جو تیار کی گئی ہے ان لوگوں کے لیے جو ایمان لائے ہیں
بِاللّٰهِ وَ رُسُلِهٖ ؕ ذٰلِكَ فَضْلُ	اللہ پر اور اس کے رسولوں پر۔ یہ فضل ہے
اللّٰهِ يُؤْتِيْهِ مَنْ يَّشَآءُ ؕ	اللہ کا جو عطا فرماتا ہے اسے جسے وہ چاہے۔
وَاللّٰهُ ذُو الْفَضْلِ الْعَظِيْمِ ﴿٢١﴾	اور اللہ بڑے فضل والا ہے ﴿٢١﴾
مَآ اَصَابَ مِنْ مُّصِيْبَةٍ فِى الْاَرْضِ	نہیں پڑتی کوئی مصیبت زمین میں
وَلَا فِىْٓ اَنْفُسِكُمْ اِلَّا فِىْ كِتٰبٍ	اور نہ تمہاری اپنی جانوں پر مگر وہ لکھی ہوئی ہے ایک کتاب میں
مِّنْ قَبْلِ اَنْ نَّبْرَاَهَا ؕ اِنَّ ذٰلِكَ	اس سے پہلے کہ ہم اسے پیدا کریں۔ بلاشبہ یہ بات
عَلَى اللّٰهِ يَسِيْرٌ ﴿٢٢﴾	اللہ کے لیے بہت آسان ہے ﴿٢٢﴾
لِّكَيْلَا تَاْسَوْا عَلٰى مَا فَاتَكُمْ	یہ اس لیے ہے تاکہ نہ غم کھاؤ کسی نقصان پر
وَلَا تَفْرَحُوْا بِمَآ اٰتٰىكُمْ ؕ	اور نہ اتراؤ تم اس پر جو عطا فرمائے وہ تم کو۔
وَاللّٰهُ لَا يُحِبُّ كُلَّ مُخْتَالٍ فَخُوْرِ ۙ﴿٢٣﴾	اور اللہ نہیں پسند کرتا ہر گھمنڈ کرنے والے اور فخر جتانے والے کو ﴿٢٣﴾
الَّذِيْنَ يَبْخَلُوْنَ وَيَاْمُرُوْنَ النَّاسَ	یہ وہ لوگ ہیں جو بخل کرتے ہیں اور اکساتے ہیں دوسرے انسانوں کو
بِالْبُخْلِ ؕ وَمَنْ يَّتَوَلَّ	بخل پر اور جو شخص رُوگردانی کرتا ہے (اللہ کے احکام سے)
فَاِنَّ اللّٰهَ هُوَ الْغَنِىُّ الْحَمِيْدُ ﴿٢٤﴾	تو بلاشبہ اللہ تو ہے ہی بے نیاز اور نہایت قابلِ تعریف ﴿٢٤﴾

And there's absolution of Lord in grace
For the men of faith to brace

But what's this life hither* in stay
That's but a chattels and cheat in stay

*worldly life

021 Now strive to trend for all in concern
Beg to beseech His extenuation in turn
Then to aside bliss of Gardens in term

The expanse and extent of its gaiety in glow
It's of that heavens and earth in flow

It's for the men and clan in faith
Who trust in Lord and His Prophet in pace

That's for Lord to decide in array
For Lord is Elegant and affluent in sway

022 No dole and blow can break to befall
In the land in toll,
Or in the veer of your core in call

It's put to proof in trace
There's a proof with The Lord in place

Who's to bring it to call in lore
For it's quite easy for Lord in score

023 Don't cry in gloom of the doom in cross
Nor brag and crow over bestowal in class

For Lord doesn't trend to adore
The swaggerer and smug in core

024 They're itchy in laud, envious in place
If any them,
Turn their backs in Faith
Indeed!
Lord is free of desire and aspire in pace

لَقَدْ اَرْسَلْنَا رُسُلَنَا بِالْبَيِّنٰتِ	یقیناً بھیجا ہم نے اپنے رسولوں کو کھلی کھلی نشانیاں دے کر
وَ اَنْزَلْنَا مَعَهُمُ الْكِتٰبَ	اور نازل کی ہم نے ان کے ساتھ کتاب
وَ الْمِيْزَانَ لِيَقُوْمَ النَّاسُ بِالْقِسْطِ ۚ	اور میزان تاکہ قائم ہوں انسان انصاف پر۔
وَ اَنْزَلْنَا الْحَدِيْدَ فِيْهِ بَاْسٌ شَدِيْدٌ	اور اتارا ہم نے لوہا جس میں ہے بڑا زور
وَّ مَنَافِعُ لِلنَّاسِ	اور بہت سے فائدے ہیں انسانوں کے لیے
وَ لِيَعْلَمَ اللّٰهُ مَنْ	اور اس لیے تاکہ معلوم کرے اللہ کہ کون
يَّنْصُرُهٗ وَ رُسُلَهٗ بِالْغَيْبِ ۭ	مدد کرتا ہے اس کی اور اس کے رسولوں کی (اللہ کو) دیکھے بغیر
اِنَّ اللّٰهَ قَوِيٌّ عَزِيْزٌ ٢٥ ع ٣	بلاشبہ اللہ ہے بڑی قوت والا اور زبردست ٢٥
وَ لَقَدْ اَرْسَلْنَا نُوْحًا وَّ اِبْرٰهِيْمَ	اور یہ واقعہ ہے کہ بھیجا ہم نے نوحؑ کو اور ابراہیمؑ کو
وَ جَعَلْنَا فِيْ ذُرِّيَّتِهِمَا النُّبُوَّةَ وَ الْكِتٰبَ	اور رکھ دی ان دونوں کی نسل میں نبوت اور کتاب
فَمِنْهُمْ مُّهْتَدٍ ۚ	سو ان کی اولاد میں سے کچھ نے ہدایت اختیار کی ٢٦
وَ كَثِيْرٌ مِّنْهُمْ فٰسِقُوْنَ ٢٦	اور بہت سے ان میں سے فاسق ہیں
ثُمَّ قَفَّيْنَا عَلٰٓى اٰثَارِهِمْ	پھر پے در پے بھیجے ہم نے ان کے پیچھے
بِرُسُلِنَا وَ قَفَّيْنَا بِعِيْسَى ابْنِ مَرْيَمَ	اپنے رسول اور ان کے پیچھے بھیجا ہم نے عیسیٰؑ ابن مریم کو
وَ اٰتَيْنٰهُ الْاِنْجِيْلَ ۙ	اور دی ہم نے اسے انجیل
وَ جَعَلْنَا فِيْ قُلُوْبِ الَّذِيْنَ	اور ڈال دی ہم نے دلوں میں ان لوگوں کے جنہوں نے
اتَّبَعُوْهُ رَاْفَةً وَّ رَحْمَةً ۭ	اس کی پیروی کی شفقت اور رحم دلی۔
وَ رَهْبَانِيَّةَ ۨ ابْتَدَعُوْهَا	اور رہی رہبانیت تو ایجاد کر لیا تھا انہوں نے خود ہی اسے
مَا كَتَبْنٰهَا عَلَيْهِمْ	نہیں فرض کیا تھا ہم نے اسے ان پر

025 We assigned Prophets hither in fore
With Our Signs, Books and poise in lore

That you may abide just in trust
We sent iron for sizable combat in just

And for the gain and gifts in concern
Lord intends to test and try to affirm

Who's to help for the cause of Lord
Without having seeing Him in sort
Also help the messenger of Lord in part

Indeed!
Lord is Exalted in Might
Imposing His Dictum all in plight

026 And We sent Noah and Abraham in pace
And established in their progeny in place

The rank and row of Prophets in grace
With Our Revelations them to brace

Some were there, on the right in track
But many a clan got seditious in aback

027 Then in wake of stance,
We assigned many a messengers in plan
Who followed their trek and trail in span

We sent, after their term in sublime
Jesus, the son of Mary in Prime

And We endowed him Gospel in pace
Those, who followed his conduct in place

We planned compassion and mercy in adore
But they fantasized monasticism in lore

إِلَّا ابْتِغَاءَ رِضْوَانِ اللّٰهِ	مگر یہ کہ تلاش کریں اللہ کی رضا
فَمَا رَعَوْهَا	لیکن نہ خیال رکھا انہوں نے اس کا
حَقَّ رِعَايَتِهَا ۚ فَآتَيْنَا	جیسا کہ خیال رکھنے کا حق تھا۔ پھر عطا کیا ہم نے
الَّذِينَ آمَنُوا	ان لوگوں کو جو ایمان لائے تھے
مِنْهُمْ أَجْرَهُمْ ۖ وَكَثِيرٌ	ان میں سے ان کا اجر۔ اور بہت سے
مِّنْهُمْ فَاسِقُونَ ﴿٢٧﴾	ان میں سے فاسق ہیں ﴿٢٧﴾
يَا أَيُّهَا الَّذِينَ آمَنُوا اتَّقُوا اللّٰهَ	اے لوگو جو ایمان لائے ہو ڈرو اللہ سے
وَآمِنُوا بِرَسُولِهِ	اور ایمان لاؤ اس کے رسول پر
يُؤْتِكُمْ كِفْلَيْنِ	عطا فرمائے گا اللہ تم کو دوہرا حصہ
مِن رَّحْمَتِهِ وَيَجْعَل لَّكُمْ	اپنی رحمت کا اور بخشے گا تمہیں
نُورًا تَمْشُونَ بِهِ	ایسا نور کہ چلو گے تم اس کی روشنی میں
وَيَغْفِرْ لَكُمْ ۚ وَاللّٰهُ	اور معاف کر دے گا تمہارے قصور۔ اور اللہ ہے
غَفُورٌ رَّحِيمٌ ﴿٢٨﴾	بڑا معاف کرنے والا اور نہایت مہربان ﴿٢٨﴾
لِّئَلَّا يَعْلَمَ	(تمہیں یہ روش اختیار کرنی چاہیے) تاکہ اچھی طرح جان لیں
أَهْلُ الْكِتَابِ أَلَّا يَقْدِرُونَ	اہل کتاب کہ نہیں ہیں وہ قادر
عَلَىٰ شَيْءٍ مِّن فَضْلِ اللّٰهِ	ذرا بھی اللہ کے فضل پر
وَأَنَّ الْفَضْلَ بِيَدِ اللّٰهِ	اور یہ کہ فضل اللہ ہی کے ہاتھ میں ہے
يُؤْتِيهِ مَن يَشَاءُ ۚ	وہ عطا فرماتا ہے اپنا فضل جسے چاہے۔
وَاللّٰهُ ذُو الْفَضْلِ الْعَظِيمِ ﴿٢٩﴾	اور اللہ مالک ہے فضلِ عظیم کا ﴿٢٩﴾

For what they invented in core
We didn't ordain such a conduct in course
As was (only) determined of them in chore
To assert and affirm Dictum of Lord to adore

But they didn't care to promote in pace
As they're ordained to comply in place

And there were,
A few of the men and clan in abide
Who determined faith in plan to aside

So We endowed with Our gifts in grants
Who (of them) affirmed discipline of faith
But quite a few in stance,
Were rebellious transgressors in pace

028 O you the men and clan in faith
Awe and dread Lord in place
And so trust His messenger in pace

He'll bestow you twice in regard
Of His Bounties hither in award

And provide gleam of glow, exact in class
He'll absolve your sins in slips of the past
For Allah is Clement and Pitying in regard

029 That the men of the Book must assert to affirm
For whatever power in concern

They hold in stay,
Over The Grace of Lord in pace
His pace in,
Grace in entirely with Him to brace
He may
Favor to endow to some in place

For Lord is Most Gracious to conform
Besides being most abounding to affirm

آیاتها ۲۲ — (۵۸) سُورَةُ المُجَادَلَةِ مَدَنِيَّةٌ (۱۰۵) — رکوعاتها ۳

بِسْمِ اللّٰهِ الرَّحْمٰنِ الرَّحِيْمِ

شروع اللہ کے نام سے جو بڑا مہربان نہایت رحم والا ہے

قَدْ سَمِعَ اللّٰهُ قَوْلَ الَّتِيْ	یقیناً سن لی اللہ نے بات اس عورت کی جو
تُجَادِلُكَ فِيْ زَوْجِهَا	جھگڑ رہی تھی تم سے اپنے شوہر کے بارے میں
وَتَشْتَكِيْٓ اِلَى اللّٰهِ ۖ وَاللّٰهُ يَسْمَعُ	اور فریاد کیے جا رہی تھی اللہ سے اور اللہ سن رہا تھا
تَحَاوُرَكُمَا ۭ اِنَّ اللّٰهَ	تم دونوں کی گفتگو۔ بلاشبہ اللہ ہے
سَمِيْعٌۢ بَصِيْرٌ ۝۱	ہر بات سننے والا اور سب کچھ دیکھنے والا ۝۱
اَلَّذِيْنَ يُظٰهِرُوْنَ مِنْكُمْ مِّنْ نِّسَاۗىِٕهِمْ	جو لوگ "ظہار" کرتے ہیں تم میں سے اپنی بیویوں کے ساتھ،
مَّا هُنَّ اُمَّهٰتِهِمْ ۭ اِنْ اُمَّهٰتُهُمْ	نہیں ہو جاتیں ان کی بیویاں ان کی مائیں۔ نہیں ہیں ان کی مائیں
اِلَّا الّٰۗـِٔيْ وَلَدْنَهُمْ ۭ وَاِنَّهُمْ لَيَقُوْلُوْنَ	مگر وہی جنہوں نے جنا ہے انہیں اور بلاشبہ وہ کہہ رہے ہیں
مُنْكَرًا مِّنَ الْقَوْلِ وَزُوْرًا ۭ	ایک سخت ناپسندیدہ جھوٹی بات ۔
وَاِنَّ اللّٰهَ لَعَفُوٌّ غَفُوْرٌ ۝۲	اور یقیناً اللہ ہے بڑا معاف کرنے والا اور بہت درگزر فرمانے والا ۝۲
وَالَّذِيْنَ يُظٰهِرُوْنَ مِنْ نِّسَاۗىِٕهِمْ	اور وہ لوگ جو "ظہار" کریں اپنی بیویوں سے
ثُمَّ يَعُوْدُوْنَ لِمَا قَالُوْا	پھر رجوع کریں اس (بات) سے جو انہوں نے کہی تھی
فَتَحْرِيْرُ رَقَبَةٍ مِّنْ قَبْلِ	تو (اس پر) آزاد کرنا ہے ایک غلام، اس سے پہلے
اَنْ يَّتَمَاۗسَّا ۭ ذٰلِكُمْ	کہ وہ ایک دوسرے کو ہاتھ لگائیں۔ یہ ہے
تُوْعَظُوْنَ بِهٖ ۭ وَاللّٰهُ بِمَا	وہ نصیحت جو تمہیں کی جا رہی ہے۔ اور اللہ ان اعمال سے جو

058-AL MUJADILAH

In the name of Lord, the Most Beneficent, Most Merciful

001 Indeed!
Lord has attended to the woman in gloom
Who implores,
To entreat (thee) regarding her groom

She pleads her 'reproach' for Lord to discern
Lord heeds to assertion of both in concern
For He discerns in concern all in trends

002 If you divorce your wives in (Zihar) assertion
By saying them mother* in desertion

But who didn't conceive (them) in pace
They cannot be their Mom* in place

And plainly they use words vicious in conceits
Indeed!
Lord is to smear and absolve our ills in deceits

*calling wives as mother

003 But if some,
Divorce their spouses in assertion
By calling them Mom in desertion

Then need to trend back in concern
The words they voiced in term

تَعْمَلُوْنَ خَبِيْرٌ ۳	تم کرتے ہو پوری طرح باخبر ہے ۳
فَمَنْ لَّمْ يَجِدْ فَصِيَامُ	پھر اگر کوئی نہ پائے (غلام) تو (اس پر) روزے رکھنا ہے
شَهْرَيْنِ مُتَتَابِعَيْنِ مِنْ قَبْلِ	دو مہینے کے لگاتار، اس سے پہلے
اَنْ يَّتَمَآسَّا ۚ فَمَنْ	کہ وہ ایک دوسرے کو ہاتھ لگائیں۔ پھر جو شخص
لَّمْ يَسْتَطِعْ فَاِطْعَامُ سِتِّيْنَ	نہ طاقت رکھتا ہو (روزوں کی) تو (اس پر) کھانا کھلانا ہے ساٹھ
مِسْكِيْنًا ۚ ذٰلِكَ لِتُؤْمِنُوْا	مسکینوں کو۔ یہ اس لیے کہ راسخ ہو تمہارا ایمان
بِاللّٰهِ وَرَسُوْلِهٖ ۚ وَتِلْكَ حُدُوْدُ	اللہ پر اور اس کے رسول پر۔ اور یہ حدیں ہیں (مقرر کردہ)
اللّٰهِ ۚ وَلِلْكٰفِرِيْنَ عَذَابٌ اَلِيْمٌ ۴	اللہ کی اور نہ ماننے والوں کے لیے ہے دردناک عذاب ۴
اِنَّ الَّذِيْنَ يُحَآدُّوْنَ	بے شک وہ لوگ جو مخالفت کرتے ہیں
اللّٰهَ وَرَسُوْلَهٗ كُبِتُوْا	اللہ اور اس کے رسول کی وہ ذلیل و خوار کر دیے جائیں گے
كَمَا كُبِتَ الَّذِيْنَ	اسی طرح جیسے ذلیل و خوار کر دیا گیا تھا ان کو جو
مِنْ قَبْلِهِمْ وَقَدْ اَنْزَلْنَآ	ان سے پہلے تھے اور نازل کر دیے ہیں ہم نے
اٰيٰتٍ بَيِّنٰتٍ ۚ وَلِلْكٰفِرِيْنَ	صاف اور صریح احکام اور نہ ماننے والوں کے لیے ہے
عَذَابٌ مُّهِيْنٌ ۵	عذاب، ذلیل و خوار کرنے والا ۵
يَوْمَ يَبْعَثُهُمُ	یاد رکھو اس دن کو جب پھر سے زندہ کرے گا ان کو
اللّٰهُ جَمِيْعًا فَيُنَبِّئُهُمْ بِمَا عَمِلُوْا ۚ	اللہ سب کو پھر انہیں بتائے گا کہ وہ کیا کرتے رہے۔
اَحْصٰىهُ اللّٰهُ	گن گن کر محفوظ کر رکھا ہے ان کا سب کیا دھرا اللہ نے
ع وَنَسُوْهُ ۚ وَاللّٰهُ عَلٰى كُلِّ شَيْءٍ شَهِيْدٌ ۶	اور وہ اسے بھول گئے ہیں۔ جبکہ اللہ ہر چیز پر شاہد ہے ۶
اَلَمْ تَرَ اَنَّ اللّٰهَ يَعْلَمُ مَا	کیا تم کو خبر نہیں کہ اللہ جانتا ہے ہر وہ بات جو

They'd free,
A slave before touching her again
You're warned not say or utter the word in same
But instead refrain in claim
Lord discerns all your done and doings in same

004 And if some has no assets in endow
Then, he'd fast for months two in a row

Before they touch each to brace
If ill and inept in pace
Him to feed sixty needy in place
That's to affirm your Faith in trace
For Lord and His messenger in grace

Those are the confines, Lord affirms in trend
And those defying to comply in amends
For them is invidious sentence in place

005 Those who,
Defy Lord and His Messenger in trust
They'll be lowly humiliated in gust

As were the men and clan hither in fore
For there're lucid Signs for them to allure
Cynics to secure disgusting term for sure

006 On the Day in Slit
Lord will raise them from vault and Pit

And show them:
Sham in simulation of verity of conduct
Lord deems and discerns your bit in instruct

Even though they've lapsed to aside
Lord discerns and concerns all in abide

007 Don't you determine in array
Lord discerns for all in sway
That's in the heavens and earth in display
There's no secret converse in fray

فِي السَّمٰوٰتِ وَمَا فِي الْاَرْضِ	آسمانوں میں ہے اور وہ بھی جو زمین میں ہے ۔
مَا يَكُوْنُ مِنْ نَّجْوٰى ثَلٰثَةٍ	اور نہیں ہوتی کوئی سرگوشی تین (آدمیوں) میں
اِلَّا هُوَ رَابِعُهُمْ وَلَا خَمْسَةٍ	مگر ہوتا ہے اللہ ان میں چوتھا اور نہ پانچ میں
اِلَّا هُوَ سَادِسُهُمْ وَلَآ اَدْنٰى مِنْ ذٰلِكَ	مگر ہوتا ہے وہ ان میں چھٹا اور نہ اس سے کم میں
وَلَآ اَكْثَرَ اِلَّا هُوَ مَعَهُمْ اَيْنَ مَا كَانُوْا	اور نہ زیادہ میں مگر ہوتا ہے وہ ان کے ساتھ جہاں بھی وہ ہوں ۔
ثُمَّ يُنَبِّئُهُمْ بِمَا	پھر وہ بتائے گا انہیں اس کے بارے میں جو
عَمِلُوْا يَوْمَ الْقِيٰمَةِ اِنَّ اللّٰهَ	وہ کرتے رہے ۔ قیامت کے دن ۔ بلاشبہ اللہ
بِكُلِّ شَيْءٍ عَلِيْمٌ ⑦	ہر چیز کے بارے میں پوری طرح باخبر ہے ⑦
اَلَمْ تَرَ اِلَى الَّذِيْنَ نُهُوْا	کیا نہیں دیکھا تم نے ان لوگوں کو جنہیں منع کیا گیا تھا
عَنِ النَّجْوٰى ثُمَّ يَعُوْدُوْنَ	سرگوشیاں کرنے سے پھر بھی وہ دہراتے رہے
لِمَا نُهُوْا عَنْهُ وَيَتَنٰجَوْنَ	اسی بات کو جس سے منع کیا گیا تھا انہیں اور سرگوشیاں کرتے ہیں
بِالْاِثْمِ وَالْعُدْوَانِ وَمَعْصِيَتِ الرَّسُوْلِ	گناہ کے اور زیادتی کے کاموں کی اور رسول کی نافرمانی کی ۔
وَاِذَا جَآءُوْكَ حَيَّوْكَ	اور جب آتے ہیں تمہارے پاس تو سلام کرتے ہیں تمہیں
بِمَا لَمْ يُحَيِّكَ بِهِ اللّٰهُ	ایسے طریقے سے کہ نہیں سلام بھیجا تم پر اس طرح اللہ نے
وَيَقُوْلُوْنَ فِيْٓ اَنْفُسِهِمْ لَوْلَا يُعَذِّبُنَا	اور کہتے ہیں اپنے دلوں میں: کیوں نہیں عذاب دیتا ہمیں
اللّٰهُ بِمَا نَقُوْلُ حَسْبُهُمْ جَهَنَّمُ	اللہ ان (باتوں) پر جو ہم کہتے ہیں؟ کافی ہے ان کے لیے جہنم،
يَصْلَوْنَهَا فَبِئْسَ الْمَصِيْرُ ⑧	وہ اسی میں جھلسیں گے سو ہے وہ بہت ہی برا ٹھکانہ ⑧
يٰٓاَيُّهَا الَّذِيْنَ اٰمَنُوْٓا اِذَا تَنَاجَيْتُمْ	اے لوگو جو ایمان لائے ہو جب تم چھپ کر مشورے کرو آپس میں
فَلَا تَتَنَاجَوْا بِالْاِثْمِ وَالْعُدْوَانِ	تو نہ مشورے کرو گناہ، زیادتی

Mid three in abide, He's forth to aside
Nor mid five, but He makes sixth in stride

Nor mid fewer, or more
Where so ever in adore
But Lord is there to affirm in lore

They cannot evade in trends
For Lord will affirm at the end in amends

Of all their conduct in course
On The Day of Demand
For Lord discerns and concerns all in source

008 Don't you perceive, who whispers in conceit
Despite clear caution, they construe in deceit

They buzz in conceit (mid them) in sin and strife
In insolence to messenger in friction and fight

When trend to you, to greet
They trend in whimsical way in greet
Not the way, Lord adores in treat

They say:
Why doesn't Lord smite hither in trail
For our assertions despicable in scale

Them to aside Hell in abash
There to scorch and scald in flash
A place so defied and debase in stash

009 O you the men of faith in prime
Don't you converse covert in time
For the evil or a sin and crime

وَمَعْصِيَتِ الرَّسُوْلِ وَتَنَاجَوْا	اور رسول کی نافرمانی کی باتوں کے بلکہ مشورے کرو
بِالْبِرِّ وَالتَّقْوٰى ؕ وَاتَّقُوا اللّٰهَ	نیکی اور تقویٰ کی باتوں میں ۔ اور ڈرو اللہ سے
الَّذِيْٓ اِلَيْهِ تُحْشَرُوْنَ ۝٩	جس کے حضور تم حشر میں پیش کیے جاؤ گے ۝٩
اِنَّمَا النَّجْوٰى مِنَ الشَّيْطٰنِ	حقیقت یہ ہے کہ چھپ کر مشورے کرنا شیطانی کام ہے
لِيَحْزُنَ الَّذِيْنَ اٰمَنُوْا	اور اس لیے کیے جاتے ہیں کہ رنجیدہ ہوں وہ لوگ جو ایمان لائے ہیں
وَلَيْسَ بِضَاۗرِّهِمْ شَيْـًٔا	اور نہیں ہیں یہ نقصان پہنچانے والے انہیں ذرا بھی
اِلَّا بِاِذْنِ اللّٰهِ ؕ	مگر اللہ کے اذن سے ۔
وَعَلَى اللّٰهِ فَلْيَتَوَكَّلِ الْمُؤْمِنُوْنَ ۝١٠	اور اللہ ہی پر مومنوں کو بھروسہ کرنا چاہیے ۝١٠
يٰٓاَيُّهَا الَّذِيْنَ اٰمَنُوْٓا اِذَا قِيْلَ لَكُمْ	اے لوگو جو ایمان لائے ہو جب کہا جائے تم سے
تَفَسَّحُوْا فِي الْمَجٰلِسِ فَافْسَحُوْا	کہ کشادگی پیدا کرو مجالس میں تو جگہ دے دیا کرو دوسروں کو،
يَفْسَحِ اللّٰهُ لَكُمْ ۚ وَاِذَا قِيْلَ	کشادگی بخشے گا اللہ تمہیں اور جب کہا جائے
انْشُزُوْا فَانْشُزُوْا يَرْفَعِ اللّٰهُ	کہ اٹھ جاؤ تو اٹھ جایا کرو ۔ بلند کرتا ہے اللہ
الَّذِيْنَ اٰمَنُوْا مِنْكُمْ ۙ وَالَّذِيْنَ	ان لوگوں کو جو ایمان لائے ہیں تم میں سے اور ان کو جنہیں
اُوْتُوا الْعِلْمَ دَرَجٰتٍ ؕ وَاللّٰهُ	دیا گیا ہے علم، درجوں کے اعتبار سے ۔ اور اللہ
بِمَا تَعْمَلُوْنَ خَبِيْرٌ ۝١١	ان سب اعمال سے جو تم کرتے ہو پوری طرح باخبر ہے ۝١١
يٰٓاَيُّهَا الَّذِيْنَ اٰمَنُوْٓا اِذَا نَاجَيْتُمُ	اے لوگو جو ایمان لائے ہو جب علٰحدگی میں بات کرنا چاہو تم
الرَّسُوْلَ فَقَدِّمُوْا بَيْنَ يَدَيْ نَجْوٰىكُمْ	رسول سے تو پیش کرو تم علٰحدگی میں بات کرنے سے پہلے
صَدَقَةً ۭ ذٰلِكَ خَيْرٌ لَّكُمْ وَاَطْهَرُ ۭ	کچھ صدقہ ۔ یہ طریقہ ہے بہتر تمہارے لیے اور پاکیزہ تر بھی ۔
فَاِنْ لَّمْ تَجِدُوْا	پھر اگر نہ پاؤ تم (صدقہ دینے کے لیے کچھ)

Nor it should before,
Defiance and aversion in define

For the Messenger of Lord in pace
But plan piety and patience in place

With awe and dread of Lord in core
To Whom you'll trend in score
On Day of Resolve affirmed to endure

010 Cryptic coverts like trends in behave
These are inspired by the Devil in deprave

Such are the notions of norm in pace
Causing anguish to the men of faith
To the men of faith in place

But they cannot cause harm a bit in pace
But with the dictum of Lord in Grace
O Allegiants!
Trust in Lord for His boons to brace

011 O you the men of faith in along
When asked to make space in norm

Spread up to make space in throng
So Lord will get you, ample of space in jam

When urged to stand and get to aside
Then slip to drift in stride
Lord will exalt your eminence in abide

Those men of faith in lore
Apprised of sapience in core
Lord Discerns your doings in chore

012 O you the men of faith in trust
When you sound out Messenger in hush
Grant in charity, be kind in just

فَاِنَّ اللّٰهَ غَفُوْرٌ رَّحِيْمٌ ﴿۱۲﴾	تو بے شک اللہ تعالیٰ غفور الرحیم ہے ﴿۱۲﴾
ءَاَشْفَقْتُمْ اَنْ تُقَدِّمُوْا	کیا تم ڈر گئے اس بات سے کہ پیش کرو
بَيْنَ يَدَيْ نَجْوٰىكُمْ صَدَقٰتٍ ۭ	اپنی علحدگی کی گفتگو سے پہلے صدقات؛
فَاِذْ لَمْ تَفْعَلُوْا وَتَابَ اللّٰهُ عَلَيْكُمْ	پھر اگر ایسا نہ کر سکو اور معاف بھی کر دیا ہے تمہیں اللہ نے
فَاَقِيْمُوا الصَّلٰوةَ وَاٰتُوا الزَّكٰوةَ	تو قائم کرو نماز اور دو زکوٰۃ
وَاَطِيْعُوا اللّٰهَ وَرَسُوْلَهٗ ۭ	اور فرمانبرداری کرو اللہ کی اور اس کے رسول کی۔
وَاللّٰهُ خَبِيْرٌۢ بِمَا تَعْمَلُوْنَ ﴿۱۳﴾ ع	اور اللہ پوری طرح باخبر ہے اس سے جو تم کرتے ہو ﴿۱۳﴾
اَلَمْ تَرَ اِلَى الَّذِيْنَ تَوَلَّوْا	کیا نہیں دیکھا تم نے ان کو جنھوں نے دوست بنایا
قَوْمًا غَضِبَ اللّٰهُ عَلَيْهِمْ ۭ	ایسے لوگوں کو جن سے اللہ ناراض ہے
مَا هُمْ مِّنْكُمْ وَلَا مِنْهُمْ ۙ	نہیں ہیں وہ تم میں سے اور نہ ان میں سے
وَيَحْلِفُوْنَ عَلَى الْكَذِبِ وَهُمْ يَعْلَمُوْنَ ﴿۱۴﴾	اور قسمیں کھاتے ہیں جھوٹ پر جانتے بوجھتے ﴿۱۴﴾
اَعَدَّ اللّٰهُ لَهُمْ عَذَابًا شَدِيْدًا ۭ	مہیا کر رکھا ہے اللہ نے ان کے لیے سخت عذاب۔
اِنَّهُمْ سَاۗءَ مَا كَانُوْا يَعْمَلُوْنَ ﴿۱۵﴾	یقیناً بہت ہی برے ہیں وہ کام جو وہ کرتے ہیں ﴿۱۵﴾
اِتَّخَذُوْٓا اَيْمَانَهُمْ جُنَّةً فَصَدُّوْا	بنا رکھا ہے انہوں نے اپنی قسموں کو ڈھال اور اس طرح روکتے ہیں وہ
عَنْ سَبِيْلِ اللّٰهِ فَلَهُمْ عَذَابٌ مُّهِيْنٌ ﴿۱۶﴾	اللہ کی راہ سے اور ہے ان کے لیے ذلت کا عذاب ﴿۱۶﴾
لَنْ تُغْنِيَ عَنْهُمْ اَمْوَالُهُمْ	ہرگز نہ بچا سکیں گے انہیں ان کے مال
وَلَآ اَوْلَادُهُمْ مِّنَ اللّٰهِ شَيْـــًٔا ۭ	اور نہ ان کی اولاد اللہ سے ذرا بھی،
اُولٰۗىِٕكَ اَصْحٰبُ النَّارِ ۭ هُمْ فِيْهَا خٰلِدُوْنَ ﴿۱۷﴾	یہ جہنمی ہیں جو جہنم میں ہمیشہ رہیں گے ﴿۱۷﴾
يَوْمَ يَبْعَثُهُمُ اللّٰهُ جَمِيْعًا فَيَحْلِفُوْنَ	جس دن دوبارہ اٹھائے گا اللہ ان سب کو تو قسمیں کھائیں گے

Before secret parley you trend in place
That's good and conducive in pace

If don't have the means to disperse in just
Lord is Most Kind and Merciful in Trust

013 Is that you're scared to pay in clemency
Before the privy parley in fervency

If you don't have the means to spend
Lord will absolve your slips in trend

Then you affirm a discipline in entreat
Spend out of usual charity in treat

And obey your Lord and Messenger in pace
And Lord discerns, what you do in place

014 Don't you trend to esteem the men and clan
Who pursue the friendship of such in plan
Men abiding the wrath of Lord in span

They're neither of you or them in stride
And they in a way avowed fibbers in beside

015 For them,
Lord has primed so grim in grasp
For their wicked moves in clasp

016 They trend in avow to save in stray
For their crimes affirmed in play
That's to hinder some, Lord to obey
Them to secure appalling sentence in stay

017 To them,
Neither scion nor the riches in pace
Will save or secure from Lord in place

They'll be pal of pyre to aside
There to reside for ever in deride

018 They'll be raised once more in pace
On the Day, by The Lord in Grace

لَهٗ كَمَا يَحْلِفُوْنَ لَكُمْ	اس کے حضور اسی طرح جیسے قسمیں کھاتے ہیں تمہارے سامنے
وَيَحْسَبُوْنَ اَنَّهُمْ عَلٰى شَيْءٍ	اور سمجھیں گے کہ اس طرح کچھ کام بن جائے گا۔
اَلَآ اِنَّهُمْ هُمُ الْكٰذِبُوْنَ ﴿۱۸﴾	خوب جان رکھو یہی ہیں وہ جو پرلے درجے کے جھوٹے ہیں ﴿۱۸﴾
اِسْتَحْوَذَ عَلَيْهِمُ الشَّيْطٰنُ فَاَنْسٰهُمْ	مسلط ہو چکا ہے ان پر شیطان اور بھلا دی ہے اس نے انہیں
ذِكْرَ اللّٰهِ ۭ اُولٰۗىِٕكَ حِزْبُ الشَّيْطٰنِ ۭ اَلَآ	اللہ کی یاد۔ یہی لوگ شیطان کی پارٹی ہیں۔ جان رکھو
اِنَّ حِزْبَ الشَّيْطٰنِ هُمُ الْخٰسِرُوْنَ ﴿۱۹﴾	کہ شیطان کا گروہ ہی خسارے میں رہنے والا ہے ﴿۱۹﴾
اِنَّ الَّذِيْنَ يُحَاۗدُّوْنَ اللّٰهَ وَرَسُوْلَهٗٓ	یقیناً وہ لوگ جو مخالفت کرتے ہیں اللہ اور اس کے رسول کی،
اُولٰۗىِٕكَ فِي الْاَذَلِّيْنَ ﴿۲۰﴾	وہی سب سے ذلیل مخلوق ہیں ﴿۲۰﴾
كَتَبَ اللّٰهُ لَاَغْلِبَنَّ اَنَا وَرُسُلِيْ ۭ	لکھ دیا ہے اللہ نے کہ ضرور غالب آ کر رہوں گا میں اور میرے رسول۔
اِنَّ اللّٰهَ قَوِيٌّ عَزِيْزٌ ﴿۲۱﴾	بلاشبہ اللہ زور آور اور زبردست ہے ﴿۲۱﴾
لَا تَجِدُ قَوْمًا يُّؤْمِنُوْنَ بِاللّٰهِ وَالْيَوْمِ الْاٰخِرِ	نہ پاؤ گے تم ان لوگوں کو جو ایمان رکھتے ہیں اللہ پر اور روزِ آخرت پر
يُوَاۗدُّوْنَ مَنْ حَاۗدَّ اللّٰهَ	کہ وہ محبت رکھتے ہوں ان سے جنہوں نے مخالفت کی اللہ کی
وَرَسُوْلَهٗ وَلَوْ كَانُوْٓا اٰبَاۗءَهُمْ اَوْ اَبْنَاۗءَهُمْ	اور اس کے رسول کی اگرچہ ہوں وہ ان کے باپ یا بیٹے
اَوْ اِخْوَانَهُمْ اَوْ عَشِيْرَتَهُمْ ۭ اُولٰۗىِٕكَ كَتَبَ	یا بھائی یا اہلِ خاندان۔ یہ وہ لوگ ہیں کہ ثبت کر دیا ہے اللہ نے
فِيْ قُلُوْبِهِمُ الْاِيْمَانَ وَاَيَّدَهُمْ بِرُوْحٍ	ان کے دلوں میں ایمان اور قوت بخشی ہے ان کو ایک روح عطا فرما کر
مِّنْهُ ۭ وَيُدْخِلُهُمْ جَنّٰتٍ تَجْرِيْ	اپنی طرف سے اور داخل کرے گا وہ انہیں ایسی جنتوں میں کہ بہہ رہی ہیں
مِنْ تَحْتِهَا الْاَنْهٰرُ خٰلِدِيْنَ فِيْهَا ۭ رَضِيَ اللّٰهُ	ان کے نیچے نہریں، ہمیشہ رہیں گے وہ ان میں۔ راضی ہوا اللہ
عَنْهُمْ وَرَضُوْا عَنْهُ ۭ اُولٰۗىِٕكَ حِزْبُ اللّٰهِ ۭ	ان سے اور وہ راضی ہوئے اللہ سے۔ یہی ہیں اللہ کی جماعت۔
اَلَآ اِنَّ حِزْبَ اللّٰهِ هُمُ الْمُفْلِحُوْنَ ﴿۲۲﴾ ع ۳	جان رکھو بلاشبہ اللہ کی جماعت ہی فلاح پانے والی ہے ﴿۲۲﴾

Then they'll vow in ado
As they avowed before you in flow
They assert to affirm to secure in stance
Not exactly!
They're but fibbers in trance
019 The Devil has taken a hold of them
And Devil has slighted them in trend
And made them not to beg in entreat
And not to evoke Lord in beseech
They're assemblage of Devil in stance
Indeed! Evil one to destroy in trance
020 Those, who defy to adore
Lord and His Prophet in lore
He'll be ashamed for sure in score
021 Lord has affirmed so firm in Demand
That's Me,
And My Bearer to stay in Command
For Lord is Gifted of all the Might
That's to,
Affirm His Demand in plight
022 You wouldn't find the men of faith in span
Who trust in Lord and the Day in Plan*
For a favor of love, men defying in stay
Lord and His Prophet in all terms and score
Even so they're
Their fathers their sons in play
Theirs brothers or the kin in close
For Lord!
Affirmed His faith so firm in (their) core
And braced them with His Spirit in lore
He'll endow them Gardens in glow
Where streams surge in swing, ebb in flow
Aside and beside and surf in below
Them to reside there for ever and so
They'll be delighted of Lord in array
And Lord will be pleased of them in sway
They're the men and clan,
Of The Lord in plan
Indeed!
That's the Company of Lord to obey
Cherishing bliss of His endow in stay

*Dooms Day

آیاتها ۲۴ — (۵۹) سورة الحشر مدنية (۱۰۱) — رکوعاتها ۳

بِسْمِ اللّٰهِ الرَّحْمٰنِ الرَّحِيْمِ

شروع اللہ کے نام سے جو بڑا مہربان نہایت رحم والا ہے

سَبَّحَ لِلّٰهِ مَا فِي السَّمٰوٰتِ	تسبیح کی ہے اللہ کی ہر اس چیز نے جو آسمانوں میں ہے
وَمَا فِي الْاَرْضِ ۚ وَهُوَ الْعَزِيْزُ الْحَكِيْمُ ①	اور جو زمین میں ہے اور وہ غالب اور بڑی حکمت والا ہے ①
هُوَ الَّذِيْٓ اَخْرَجَ الَّذِيْنَ كَفَرُوْا	وہی ہے جس نے نکالا ان کو جنہوں نے کفر کیا
مِنْ اَهْلِ الْكِتٰبِ مِنْ دِيَارِهِمْ لِاَوَّلِ الْحَشْرِ ؕ	اہلِ کتاب میں سے ان کے گھروں سے پہلے ہی ہلے میں۔
مَا ظَنَنْتُمْ اَنْ يَّخْرُجُوْا وَظَنُّوْٓا	تمہیں گمان بھی نہ تھا کہ وہ نکل جائیں گے اور وہ یہ سمجھے بیٹھے تھے
اَنَّهُمْ مَّانِعَتُهُمْ حُصُوْنُهُمْ مِّنَ اللّٰهِ	کہ یقیناً انہیں بچا لیں گی ان کی گڑھیاں اللہ سے
فَاَتٰىهُمُ اللّٰهُ مِنْ حَيْثُ لَمْ يَحْتَسِبُوْا	مگر آیا ان پر اللہ ایسے رخ سے جدھر ان کا خیال بھی نہ گیا
وَقَذَفَ فِيْ قُلُوْبِهِمُ الرُّعْبَ	اور ڈال دیا ان کے دلوں میں رعب
يُخْرِبُوْنَ بُيُوْتَهُمْ بِاَيْدِيْهِمْ	نتیجہ یہ ہوا کہ (وہ) برباد کرنے لگے اپنے گھروں کو اپنے ہاتھوں
وَاَيْدِي الْمُؤْمِنِيْنَ ۗ	اور (برباد کروا رہے تھے) مومنوں کے ہاتھوں سے بھی۔
فَاعْتَبِرُوْا يٰٓاُولِي الْاَبْصَارِ ②	پس عبرت پکڑو اے آنکھیں رکھنے والو! ②
وَلَوْلَآ اَنْ كَتَبَ اللّٰهُ عَلَيْهِمُ الْجَلَآءَ	اور اگر نہ لکھ دی ہوتی اللہ نے ان کے حق میں جلاوطنی
لَعَذَّبَهُمْ فِي الدُّنْيَا ۖ وَلَهُمْ	تو ضرور عذاب دیتا وہ انہیں دنیا ہی میں اور ان کے لیے
فِي الْاٰخِرَةِ عَذَابُ النَّارِ ③	آخرت میں تو ہے ہی دوزخ کا عذاب ③
ذٰلِكَ بِاَنَّهُمْ شَآقُّوا اللّٰهَ	یہ اس لیے ہوا کہ انہوں نے مخالفت کی تھی اللہ کی

059-AL HASHR

In the name of Lord, the Most Beneficent, Most Merciful

001 Whatever is in the,
Heavens and the earth to sustain
Ardor and adore Glory of Lord in acclaim
He's Exalted in Might and Wise in Domain

002 It's He,
Who got the Cynics out in stance
From the men of the Book in glance
Out of Home and Hearth first in throng

You'd hardly deem to discern in slight
That they'd ever trend in flight

They'd assumed for sure in pace
That their castles would guard in place
From the fury of Lord hither in trace

But the fury of Lord was there in strike
For what they didn't have a blink in sight

Their crux and core were worn in alarm
And destroyed their abides, them in swarm*

With their own hands in abide
There with the hands of ally** in beside
O men!
Have caution to discern hither to aside

*they got in panic and destroyed their own resides
**Believers

003 Had it not been a term in trail
For what Lord ordained (exile) in vale

Indeed!
He would've trounced (them) herein pace
And Hereafter they're destine Pyre in place

004 That's the doom in decay (for them) to aside
For they defied Lord and His Messenger in abide

وَرَسُوْلَهٗ ۚ وَمَنْ يُّشَآقِّ اللّٰهَ
اور اس کے رسول کی۔ اور جو بھی مخالفت کرتا ہے اللہ کی

فَاِنَّ اللّٰهَ شَدِيْدُ الْعِقَابِ ٤
تو بلاشبہ اللہ بہت سخت ہے عذاب دینے میں ٤

مَا قَطَعْتُمْ مِّنْ لِّيْنَةٍ اَوْ تَرَكْتُمُوْهَا
نہیں کاٹا تم نے کوئی کھجور کا درخت یا بنے دیا اسے

قَآئِمَةً عَلٰٓى اُصُوْلِهَا فَبِاِذْنِ اللّٰهِ
قائم اس کی جڑوں پر تو یہ سب ہوا اللہ کے اذن سے

وَلِيُخْزِيَ الْفٰسِقِيْنَ ٥
اور اس لیے ہوا تاکہ رسوا کرے اللہ نافرمانوں کو ٥

وَمَآ اَفَآءَ اللّٰهُ عَلٰى رَسُوْلِهٖ
اور جو (مال) پلٹائے اللہ نے اپنے رسول کی طرف

مِنْهُمْ فَمَآ اَوْجَفْتُمْ
ان سے لے کر تو وہ ایسے مال نہیں ہیں کہ دوڑائے ہوں تم نے

عَلَيْهِ مِنْ خَيْلٍ وَّلَا رِكَابٍ وَّلٰكِنَّ اللّٰهَ
ان پر گھوڑے یا اونٹ بلکہ اللہ

يُسَلِّطُ رُسُلَهٗ عَلٰى مَنْ يَّشَآءُ ۚ
تسلط عطا فرما دیتا ہے اپنے رسولوں کو جس پر چاہتا ہے۔

وَاللّٰهُ عَلٰى كُلِّ شَيْءٍ قَدِيْرٌ ٦
اور اللہ ہر چیز پر پوری طرح قادر ہے ٦

مَآ اَفَآءَ اللّٰهُ عَلٰى رَسُوْلِهٖ مِنْ اَهْلِ الْقُرٰى
جو کچھ پلٹا دے اللہ اپنے رسول کی طرف بستیوں کے لوگوں سے

فَلِلّٰهِ وَلِلرَّسُوْلِ وَلِذِي الْقُرْبٰى
سو وہ ہے اللہ کا اور اس کے رسول کا اور رسول کے رشتہ داروں کا

وَالْيَتٰمٰى وَالْمَسٰكِيْنِ وَابْنِ السَّبِيْلِ ۙ
اور ہے یتیموں اور مسکینوں اور مسافروں کے لیے

كَيْ لَا يَكُوْنَ دُوْلَةًۢ بَيْنَ الْاَغْنِيَآءِ مِنْكُمْ ۚ
تاکہ نہ کرتا رہے وہ گردش تمہارے مالداروں کے درمیان ہی۔

وَمَآ اٰتٰىكُمُ الرَّسُوْلُ فَخُذُوْهُ ۗ
اور جو کچھ دے تمہیں رسول سو اسے لے لو

وَمَا نَهٰىكُمْ عَنْهُ
اور جس سے روک دے تم کو رسول

فَانْتَهُوْا ۚ وَاتَّقُوا اللّٰهَ ۚ
پس رک جاؤ (اس سے)۔ اور ڈرو اللہ سے۔

اِنَّ اللّٰهَ شَدِيْدُ الْعِقَابِ ٧
بلاشبہ اللہ بہت سخت ہے سزا دینے میں ٧

لِلْفُقَرَآءِ الْمُهٰجِرِيْنَ الَّذِيْنَ
(نیز وہ مال) ان مفلس مہاجروں کے لیے ہے جو

If there's one,
Who dare to defy Lord to obey
Indeed!
Lord is quite strict, infliction to convey

005 O you the men of faith
Even if you,
Cut down tender palm trees in place
Or let it thrive on their roots in pace

It's but the dictum of Lord to remain
That's to disgrace and cover with shame
The rebellious transgressors in claim

006 What Lord bestowed Prophet to allure
Out of their keeping, him to secure

It wasn't your forces that prevailed in fray
(A combat with camels and horses in array)

To Prophets!
He assigns command over else in want
And Lord has sway over all in grant

007 What Lord,
Endowed His Prophet to aside
From the men of locale in abide

Belongs to The Lord in prim
And to the messenger and close of the kin

Besides,
The orphans, indigent and trekker in pace
So it doesn't go to affluent (of you) in place

And contend what Prophet design to assign
And deny, what he restrains to consign

Instead awe and dread Lord in endow
For He's strict for Discipline in flow

008 Some is for the needy evacuee* in deport
Deprived of homes and hearth in support

اُخْرِجُوْا مِنْ دِيَارِهِمْ وَ اَمْوَالِهِمْ	نکال باہر کیے گئے ہیں اپنے گھروں سے اور اپنی جائیدادوں سے
يَبْتَغُوْنَ فَضْلًا مِّنَ اللّٰهِ وَ رِضْوَانًا	جو تلاش کرتے ہیں فضل اللہ کا اور اس کی خوشنودی
وَّ يَنْصُرُوْنَ اللّٰهَ وَ رَسُوْلَهٗ ؕ	اور مدد کرتے ہیں اللہ اور اس کے رسول کی ۔
اُولٰٓئِكَ هُمُ الصّٰدِقُوْنَ ۚ ۸	یہی لوگ ہیں سچے ۸
وَ الَّذِيْنَ تَبَوَّءُو الدَّارَ	اور یہ ان لوگوں کے لیے بھی ہے ، جو مقیم تھے دارالہجرۃ میں
وَ الْاِيْمَانَ مِنْ قَبْلِهِمْ يُحِبُّوْنَ	اور ایمان لاچکے تھے مہاجرین کی آمد سے پہلے محبت کرتے ہیں
مَنْ هَاجَرَ اِلَيْهِمْ	ان لوگوں سے جو ہجرت کر کے آئے ان کے پاس
وَلَا يَجِدُوْنَ فِیْ صُدُوْرِهِمْ حَاجَةً	اور نہیں پاتے اپنے دلوں میں کوئی حاجت تک بھی
مِّمَّآ اُوْتُوْا وَ يُؤْثِرُوْنَ	اس چیز کی جو انہیں دی جائے اور ترجیح دیتے ہیں دوسروں کو
عَلٰٓى اَنْفُسِهِمْ وَلَوْ كَانَ بِهِمْ خَصَاصَةٌ ۫ؕ	اپنی ذات پر اگرچہ ہوں خود حاجتمند ۔
وَمَنْ يُّوْقَ شُحَّ نَفْسِهٖ	اور جو بچالیے گئے اپنے دل کے لالچ سے
فَاُولٰٓئِكَ هُمُ الْمُفْلِحُوْنَ ۚ ۹	سو وہی ہیں درحقیقت فلاح پانے والے ۹
وَ الَّذِيْنَ جَآءُوْ مِنْۢ بَعْدِهِمْ	اور یہ ان کے لیے بھی ہے ، جو آئیں گے ان کے بعد ،
يَقُوْلُوْنَ رَبَّنَا اغْفِرْ لَنَا	دعا کریں گے (اس طرح) : اے ہمارے رب ! بخش دے تو ہمیں
وَ لِاِخْوَانِنَا الَّذِيْنَ سَبَقُوْنَا	اور ہمارے ان بھائیوں کو جو سبقت لے گئے ہم پر
بِالْاِيْمَانِ وَلَا تَجْعَلْ فِیْ قُلُوْبِنَا غِلًّا	ایمان میں اور نہ رکھ ہمارے دلوں میں کوئی بغض
لِّلَّذِيْنَ اٰمَنُوْا رَبَّنَآ	ان کے لیے جو ایمان لائے ہیں ، اے ہمارے مالک !
اِنَّكَ رَءُوْفٌ رَّحِيْمٌ ۧ ۱۰	یقیناً تو بڑا مہربان اور نہایت رحم والا ہے ۱۰
اَلَمْ تَرَ اِلَى الَّذِيْنَ	کیا نہیں دیکھا تم نے ان لوگوں کو جنہوں نے

That's how they seek in pace
Pleasures and the Bounty of Lord to brace
And supporting,
The cause of Lord and Prophet in abide
Indeed!
They're honest of clan* in stride

* Muhajirs

009 Those of the men and clan in pace
Hither (Madinah) in place
With their resides and abides in score
And had embraced Faith in adore
Trend for the care of men in refuge

And they don't have any desire in place
In their veer of core to pace
When things given to the latter** in trace
But give them** preference over them* in pace

Even though poverty was their* lot and sort
And they're* not selfish of their term in plot
These are the men not tempted in greed
Indeed them to cherish bliss in proceeds

*local men of faith **Muhajirs coming from Makkah

010 And those,
Affirming in faith thereafter in term
They trend to entreat in concern
Our Lord!
Remit and relent us with our kin in close
Asserting in faith before (us in spin) in course
And don't let our cores spin in sin

For the men who comply discipline of Faith
Indeed O Lord!
You're Most Kind and Compassionate in grace

011 Didn't you see men in glance
Behaving like the hypocrites in trance
Affirming their kin (cynics) of clan
Among the People of the Book in plan

نَافَقُوْا يَقُوْلُوْنَ	منافقت کی روش اختیار کی وہ کہتے ہیں
لِاِخْوَانِهِمُ الَّذِيْنَ كَفَرُوْا	اپنے ان بھائیوں سے جو کافر ہیں
مِنْ اَهْلِ الْكِتٰبِ لَئِنْ اُخْرِجْتُمْ	اہل کتاب میں سے کہ اگر تمہیں نکالا گیا
لَنَخْرُجَنَّ مَعَكُمْ وَلَا نُطِيْعُ	تو ہم بھی ضرور نکلیں گے تمہارے ساتھ اور بات نہ مانیں گے
فِيْكُمْ اَحَدًا اَبَدًا ۙ وَّاِنْ	تمہارے بارے میں کسی کی ہرگز اور اگر
قُوْتِلْتُمْ لَنَنْصُرَنَّكُمْ ۭ وَاللّٰهُ	تم سے جنگ کی گئی تو ہم ضرور تمہاری مدد کریں گے۔ جبکہ اللہ
يَشْهَدُ اِنَّهُمْ لَكٰذِبُوْنَ ⑪	گواہی دیتا ہے کہ یہ لوگ قطعاً جھوٹے ہیں (۱۱)
لَئِنْ اُخْرِجُوْا لَا يَخْرُجُوْنَ مَعَهُمْ ۚ	اگر وہ نکالے گئے تو ہرگز نہ نکلیں گے یہ ان کے ساتھ
وَلَئِنْ قُوْتِلُوْا لَا يَنْصُرُوْنَهُمْ ۚ	اور اگر ان سے جنگ کی گئی تو ہرگز نہ مدد کریں گے یہ ان کی
وَلَئِنْ نَّصَرُوْهُمْ لَيُوَلُّنَّ	اور اگر کہیں مدد کی انہوں نے ان کی تو ضرور پھیر جائیں گے
الْاَدْبَارَ ۣ ثُمَّ لَا يُنْصَرُوْنَ ⑫	پیٹھ۔ پھر کہیں سے کوئی مدد نہ پائیں گے (۱۲)
لَاَنْتُمْ اَشَدُّ رَهْبَةً فِيْ صُدُوْرِهِمْ	دراصل تمہارا خوف زیادہ سخت ہے ان کے دلوں میں
مِّنَ اللّٰهِ ۭ ذٰلِكَ بِاَنَّهُمْ قَوْمٌ	اللہ کے مقابلہ میں یہ اس لیے ہے کہ یہ ایسے لوگ ہیں جو
لَّا يَفْقَهُوْنَ ⑬	سمجھ بوجھ نہیں رکھتے (۱۳)
لَا يُقَاتِلُوْنَكُمْ جَمِيْعًا	نہیں جنگ کریں گے یہ کبھی تم سے اکٹھے
اِلَّا فِيْ قُرًى مُّحَصَّنَةٍ اَوْ مِنْ وَّرَاۗءِ جُدُرٍ ۭ	مگر قلعہ بند بستیوں میں یا دیواروں کے پیچھے چھپ کر۔
بَاْسُهُمْ بَيْنَهُمْ شَدِيْدٌ ۭ	ان کی مخالفت آپس میں بڑی سخت ہے۔
تَحْسَبُهُمْ جَمِيْعًا وَّقُلُوْبُهُمْ شَتّٰى ۭ	تم خیال کرتے ہو انہیں اکٹھا مگر ان کے دل پھٹے ہوئے ہیں۔
ذٰلِكَ بِاَنَّهُمْ قَوْمٌ لَّا يَعْقِلُوْنَ ⑭	اس لیے ہے کہ وہ ایسے لوگ ہیں جو عقل سے عاری ہیں (۱۴)

If you're expelled from resides in abide
We'll accompany you beside in stride

And wouldn't heed to some in plan
Regarding your concern in span

And if you're forced to combat in fray
We'll be there beside (you) in stay
But indeed!
Lord discerns they're fibber of clan

012 If they're,
Expelled from their resides in abide
They wouldn't accompany in stride

And if in combat,
They wouldn't come to help in assault
Even if they ever come to rescue in accord

They'll trend their backs in squeeze
So they wouldn't be helped in crease

013 Indeed, they dread you in core
For you're mighty and stronger in lore

Rather than bearing the dread of Lord in score
For,
They're devoid of perception in lore

014 They wouldn't,
Trend to you in combat
Together with all, in instruct

But confined in compound
Or behind the walls in around

You take them united and strong
But they're,
Virtually torn within their veer of core
For they're,
Devoid of sense and sapience in lore

كَمَثَلِ الَّذِينَ مِنْ قَبْلِهِمْ قَرِيبًا ذَاقُوا	ان لوگوں کی طرح جو ان سے تھوڑی مدت پہلے چکھ چکے ہیں
وَبَالَ أَمْرِهِمْ ۚ وَلَهُمْ عَذَابٌ أَلِيمٌ ﴿١٥﴾	سزا اپنے کیے کی اور ان کے لیے ہے دردناک عذاب ﴿١٥﴾
كَمَثَلِ الشَّيْطَانِ إِذْ قَالَ	(ان کی) مثال شیطان کی سی ہے جب وہ کہتا ہے
لِلْإِنْسَانِ اكْفُرْ ۚ فَلَمَّا كَفَرَ قَالَ	انسان سے کہ کفر کر پھر جب وہ کفر کر لیتا ہے تو کہتا ہے
إِنِّي بَرِيءٌ مِنْكَ إِنِّي أَخَافُ	کہ میں بری الذمہ ہوں تجھ سے یقیناً میں ڈرتا ہوں
اللَّهَ رَبَّ الْعَالَمِينَ ﴿١٦﴾	اللہ سے جو ربُّ العالمین ہے ﴿١٦﴾
فَكَانَ عَاقِبَتَهُمَا أَنَّهُمَا	سو ہوگا ان دونوں کا انجام یہ کہ وہ دونوں
فِي النَّارِ خَالِدَيْنِ فِيهَا ۚ	جہنم میں جائیں گے اور ہمیشہ رہیں گے اس میں۔
وَذَٰلِكَ جَزَاءُ الظَّالِمِينَ ﴿١٧﴾ ع	اور یہی ہے سزا ظالموں کی ﴿١٧﴾
يَا أَيُّهَا الَّذِينَ آمَنُوا اتَّقُوا اللَّهَ	اے لوگو جو ایمان لائے ہو ڈرو اللہ سے
وَلْتَنْظُرْ نَفْسٌ مَا قَدَّمَتْ	اور چاہیے کہ دیکھے ہر شخص کہ کیا سامان آگے بھیجا ہے اس نے
لِغَدٍ ۖ وَاتَّقُوا اللَّهَ ۚ إِنَّ اللَّهَ	کل کے لیے اور ڈرو اللہ سے۔ یقیناً اللہ
خَبِيرٌ بِمَا تَعْمَلُونَ ﴿١٨﴾	پوری طرح باخبر ہے تمہارے سب اعمال سے ﴿١٨﴾
وَلَا تَكُونُوا كَالَّذِينَ نَسُوا اللَّهَ	اور نہ ہو جاؤ ان لوگوں کی طرح جو بھول گئے اللہ کو
فَأَنْسَاهُمْ أَنْفُسَهُمْ ۚ	سو غافل کر دیا اللہ نے انہیں اپنے آپ سے۔
أُولَٰئِكَ هُمُ الْفَاسِقُونَ ﴿١٩﴾	یہی لوگ ہیں جو نافرمان ہیں ﴿١٩﴾
لَا يَسْتَوِي أَصْحَابُ النَّارِ وَأَصْحَابُ الْجَنَّةِ ۚ	کبھی یکساں نہیں ہو سکتے اہلِ دوزخ اور اہلِ جنت۔
أَصْحَابُ الْجَنَّةِ هُمُ الْفَائِزُونَ ﴿٢٠﴾	اہلِ جنت ہی مراد پانے والے ہیں ﴿٢٠﴾
لَوْ أَنْزَلْنَا هَٰذَا الْقُرْآنَ عَلَىٰ جَبَلٍ	اگر کہیں نازل کیا ہوتا ہم نے یہ قرآن کسی پہاڑ پر

015 Like the men and clan in stance
Who lately lead (them) in trance
And had a taste of their evil in glance
And then in the Hereafter in place
There's a serious Sentence in pace

016 Their citation is:
Like of the Devil in array
Their aide and associates swindled in stray
When he entices the man once in decay

Abjure Lord and don't stay to obey
But when he defies Lord in deride
The Devil then trends in beside
I'm free of your charge in stride
For I fear Lord of the Worlds in stay

017 Both have to cherish the burn of Fire
There to abide for ever in Pyre
That's the boon and booty in stray
For the sinners, defying Word to obey

018 Listen O allegiants!
Most intently in stance
Awe and dread Lord in glance
Let all men affirm for sure in abide
For what he destines to convey in stride
For Hereafter, there and then to aside
Awe and dread Lord in grace
For He discerns,
Even a bit of your doings in pace

019 Don't trend to the men and clan in fray
Who've slighted The Lord to obey
He turned their souls so callous in core
They're the defiant sinner in lore

020 How can the two be equal in stance
Those destined to hellhole in spot
And men of beatified Gardens in plot
That's to cherish charisma in reward

021 If Qur'an,
Was revealed to a mountainous resort
It would've trodden and strewn in apart

لَرَاَيْتَهٗ خَاشِعًا مُّتَصَدِّعًا	تو ضرور دیکھتے تم اسے کہ وہ دبا جا رہا ہے اور پھٹا پڑتا ہے
مِّنْ خَشْيَةِ اللّٰهِ ؕ وَتِلْكَ الْاَمْثَالُ	اللہ کے خوف سے۔ اور یہ مثالیں
نَضْرِبُهَا لِلنَّاسِ	بیان کرتے ہیں ہم انسانوں کے لیے
لَعَلَّهُمْ يَتَفَكَّرُوْنَ ﴿٢١﴾	تاکہ وہ غور و فکر کریں ﴿٢١﴾
هُوَ اللّٰهُ الَّذِيْ لَآ اِلٰهَ اِلَّا هُوَ ۚ	وہ اللہ ہی ہے کہ نہیں ہے کوئی معبود سوائے اس کے
عٰلِمُ الْغَيْبِ وَالشَّهَادَةِ ۚ	جاننے والا غائب وحاضر کا۔
هُوَ الرَّحْمٰنُ الرَّحِيْمُ ﴿٢٢﴾	وہی ہے بڑا مہربان نہایت رحم کرنے والا ﴿٢٢﴾
هُوَ اللّٰهُ الَّذِيْ لَآ اِلٰهَ	وہ اللہ ہی ہے کہ نہیں ہے کوئی معبود
اِلَّا هُوَ ۚ اَلْمَلِكُ الْقُدُّوْسُ	سوائے اس کے، بادشاہِ حقیقی، نہایت مقدس،
السَّلٰمُ الْمُؤْمِنُ الْمُهَيْمِنُ	سراسر سلامتی، امن دینے والا، نگہبان،
الْعَزِيْزُ الْجَبَّارُ	سب پر غالب، اپنا حکم بزور نافذ کرنے والا
الْمُتَكَبِّرُ ؕ سُبْحٰنَ اللّٰهِ	اور بڑا ہی ہو کر رہنے والا۔ پاک ہے اللہ
عَمَّا يُشْرِكُوْنَ ﴿٢٣﴾	اس شرک سے جو یہ کرتے ہیں ﴿٢٣﴾
هُوَ اللّٰهُ الْخَالِقُ	وہ اللہ ہی ہے، تخلیق کا منصوبہ بنانے والا
الْبَارِئُ الْمُصَوِّرُ	(پھر اس کو) نافذ کرنے والا (اور اس کے مطابق) صورت گری کرنے والا
لَهُ الْاَسْمَآءُ الْحُسْنٰى ؕ	اسی کے لیے ہیں تمام بہترین نام۔
يُسَبِّحُ لَهٗ مَا	تسبیح کر رہی ہے اس کی ہر وہ چیز جو
فِي السَّمٰوٰتِ وَالْاَرْضِ ۚ	آسمانوں میں ہے اور زمین میں ہے۔
وَهُوَ الْعَزِيْزُ الْحَكِيْمُ ﴿٢٤﴾	اور وہ ہے زبردست اور بڑی حکمت والا ﴿٢٤﴾

(Like the splintering of glass)
From quirk and quibble in class
With shiver and shudder of Lord

We refer to such semblance in sway
That We announce for the men to obey
So he may discern and concern in pray

022 He's Allah,
Who holds all in Command
To Him we're determined to beseech in stance

He discerns
All that's cryptic in core
And that's lucid in lore
He's most Compassionate and Caring in adore

023 Allah,
He's none but The One in Glance
Mighty O Magnanimous in stance
There's no god other than Him in accord
The Ruling and the Righteous all in assort

Peace in Proportion and Protector in pace
Perfection in trace and Guardian in Grace

The Patron to Pardon and Exalted in Might
Irresistible, Alluring, Supreme in Plight

Glory to be The Lord exalted in esteem
Preferred and Premium over all in gleam
For what they attribute to Him in slight

024 He is The Lord,
The Creator in Concord
Who primed in figure and shaped in assort
To Him:
Belong most exquisite attributes in accord
All in the heavens and the earth in resort

Trends His Applause and Eminence in Adore
He's Exalted in Might with Prudence in Lore

اٰیاتہا ١٣ (٦٠) سُوْرَةُ الْمُمْتَحِنَةِ مَدَنِيَّةٌ (٩١) رکوعاتہا ٢

بِسْمِ اللّٰهِ الرَّحْمٰنِ الرَّحِيْمِ

شروع اللہ کے نام سے جو بڑا مہربان نہایت رحم والا ہے

يٰٓاَيُّهَا الَّذِيْنَ اٰمَنُوْا لَا تَتَّخِذُوْا	اے لوگو جو ایمان لائے ہو نہ بناؤ
عَدُوِّيْ وَعَدُوَّكُمْ اَوْلِيَآءَ تُلْقُوْنَ	میرے دشمنوں کو اور اپنے دشمنوں کو دوست ، پینگیں بڑھاتے ہو تم
اِلَيْهِمْ بِالْمَوَدَّةِ وَقَدْ كَفَرُوْا	ان کے ساتھ دوستی کی حالانکہ وہ انکار کر چکے ہیں ماننے سے
بِمَا جَآءَكُمْ مِّنَ الْحَقِّ	اس کو جو آیا ہے تمہارے پاس حق میں سے ،
يُخْرِجُوْنَ الرَّسُوْلَ وَاِيَّاكُمْ	جلا وطن کرتے ہیں وہ رسول کو اور تمہیں
اَنْ تُؤْمِنُوْا بِاللّٰهِ رَبِّكُمْ	اس بنا پر کہ تم ایمان لائے ہو اللہ پر جو تمہارا رب ہے ۔
اِنْ كُنْتُمْ خَرَجْتُمْ جِهَادًا فِيْ سَبِيْلِيْ	(نہ بناؤ دوست ان کو) اگر نکلے ہو تم جہاد کے لیے میرے راستے میں
وَابْتِغَآءَ مَرْضَاتِيْ	اور تمہارا مقصد میری رضا جوئی ہے ۔
تُسِرُّوْنَ اِلَيْهِمْ بِالْمَوَدَّةِ	(تمہیں یہ زیب نہیں دیتا) کہ چھپا کر بھیجتے ہو تم انہیں دوستی کا پیغام
وَاَنَا اَعْلَمُ بِمَآ اَخْفَيْتُمْ	حالانکہ میں خوب جانتا ہوں وہ بھی جو تم چھپا کر کرتے ہو
وَمَآ اَعْلَنْتُمْ وَمَنْ يَّفْعَلْهُ	اور وہ بھی جو تم علانیہ کرتے ہو اور جو شخص کرے گا ایسا کام
مِنْكُمْ فَقَدْ ضَلَّ سَوَآءَ السَّبِيْلِ ①	تم میں سے تو وہ بھٹک گیا سیدھے راستے سے ①
اِنْ يَّثْقَفُوْكُمْ يَكُوْنُوْا لَكُمْ اَعْدَآءً	اگر قابو پالیں وہ تم پر تو ہوں گے وہ تمہارے دشمن
وَّيَبْسُطُوْٓا اِلَيْكُمْ اَيْدِيَهُمْ	اور چلائیں گے تم پر اپنے ہاتھ
وَاَلْسِنَتَهُمْ بِالسُّوْٓءِ	اور اپنی زبانیں نقصان پہنچانے کے لیے

060-AL MUMTAHINAH

In the name of Lord, the Most Beneficent, Most Merciful

001 O you the men and clan in faith
Don't befriend your foes in faith

Bestowing them your love in place
Even they're defying truth to brace
That We Divulged to you in grace

And drive you and Messenger out of resides
For you trust in Lord and faith in stride
(In My way)
If you're out to scuffle and strive
To cherish,
My delectable delights to thrive
Don't trend to befriend them in abide

Keeping privy parley with them in stay
With mutual love and regard in array

I discern all you cover in conceal
That you affirm and assert to reveal

If any of you trends the way in stride
You'll be drifted out in stray
From the discipline of faith in way

002 If they trend to subjugate (you) in fray
They'd be your vying foe in stay

وَوَدُّوْا لَوْ تَكْفُرُوْنَ ۝٢	اور وہ دل سے یہ چاہتے ہیں کہ کسی طرح تم کافر ہو جاؤ ۝٢
لَنْ تَنْفَعَكُمْ اَرْحَامُكُمْ	نہ کام آئیں گی تمہارے تمہاری رشتہ داریاں
وَلَآ اَوْلَادُكُمْ ۚ يَوْمَ الْقِيٰمَةِ ۚ	اور نہ تمہاری اولادیں قیامت کے دن ۔
يَفْصِلُ بَيْنَكُمْ ۭ	(اور اس دن) فیصلہ کرے گا اللہ تمہارے درمیان ۔
وَاللّٰهُ بِمَا تَعْمَلُوْنَ بَصِيْرٌ ۝٣	اور اللہ ہر اس چیز کو جو تم کر رہے ہو پوری طرح دیکھ رہا ہے ۝٣
قَدْ كَانَتْ لَكُمْ اُسْوَةٌ حَسَنَةٌ	بلاشبہ ہے تمہارے لیے ایک بہترین نمونہ
فِيْٓ اِبْرٰهِيْمَ وَالَّذِيْنَ مَعَهٗ ۚ	ابراہیمؑ میں اور ان لوگوں میں جو اس کے ساتھ تھے ،
اِذْ قَالُوْا لِقَوْمِهِمْ اِنَّا بُرَءٰۗؤُا	جب کہا تھا انہوں نے اپنی قوم سے کہ ہم قطعی بیزار ہیں
مِنْكُمْ وَمِمَّا تَعْبُدُوْنَ	تم سے اور ان سے جنہیں تم پوجتے ہو
مِنْ دُوْنِ اللّٰهِ ۡ كَفَرْنَا بِكُمْ وَبَدَا	اللہ کے سوا ۔ انکار کرتے ہیں ہم تمہارا اور ہو گئی ہے
بَيْنَنَا وَبَيْنَكُمُ الْعَدَاوَةُ وَالْبَغْضَاۗءُ	ہمارے اور تمہارے درمیان عداوت اور دشمنی
اَبَدًا حَتّٰى تُؤْمِنُوْا بِاللّٰهِ وَحْدَهٗٓ	ہمیشہ کے لیے الّا یہ کہ تم ایمان لے آؤ اللہ پر جو یکتا ہے ۔
اِلَّا قَوْلَ اِبْرٰهِيْمَ لِاَبِيْهِ	رہ گیا قول ابراہیمؑ کا جو اس نے اپنے باپ سے کہا تھا
لَاَسْتَغْفِرَنَّ لَكَ	کہ میں ضرور استغفار کروں گا تیرے لیے
وَمَآ اَمْلِكُ لَكَ مِنَ اللّٰهِ مِنْ شَيْءٍ ۭ	اور نہیں اختیار رکھتا میں تم کو بچانے کا اللہ سے ذرا بھی ۔
رَبَّنَا عَلَيْكَ تَوَكَّلْنَا	اے ہمارے رب! تجھ ہی پر ہم نے بھروسہ کیا
وَاِلَيْكَ اَنَبْنَا	اور تیری ہی طرف ہم نے رجوع کیا
وَاِلَيْكَ الْمَصِيْرُ ۝٤	اور تیرے ہی حضور پلٹنا ہے (ہمیں) ۝٤
رَبَّنَا لَا تَجْعَلْنَا فِتْنَةً لِّلَّذِيْنَ كَفَرُوْا	اے ہمارے رب! نہ بنانا تو ہمیں آزمائش کافروں کے لیے

And trend their duke and dialect in base
As they urge you to be cynic in place
(And aspire you to refuse your dictum of faith)

003 It wouldn't be of any assuage in plan
May be he's your close of kin in clan

Or may it be your scion in play
He'll judge (mid you) for whom to absolve
For Lord discerns all your doings in pace

004 There's superb citation in stance
Of Abraham and his men and clan

When they said to the men in aside
We're free of your trends in abide

For what you adore other than Lord in pray
We desert you with spite and slight in fray

Evermore hither in stay
Unless you assert to affirm Lord to obey
Yes indeed! Lord and only Lord in pray

But not when,
Abraham said to his father to obey
I'll adjure reprieve (for you) in pray
Even though I've no way and skill in sway

On thy behalf, I'll beg Lord in implore
Then they entreat Lord in adore

We assume and esteem and entreat in remorse
For You're our ultimate conduct in course

005 O Lord!
Don't trend us in trial for cynics in bit
Remit and relent our sins in slight

وَاغْفِرْ لَنَا رَبَّنَا ۚ	اور ہمارے قصوروں سے درگزر فرما اے ہمارے مالک!
إِنَّكَ أَنتَ الْعَزِيزُ الْحَكِيمُ ﴿٥﴾	بے شک تو ہی ہے زبردست اور بڑی حکمت والا ﴿٥﴾
لَقَدْ كَانَ لَكُمْ فِيهِمْ	یقیناً ہے تمہارے لیے انہی لوگوں (کے طرزِ عمل) میں
أُسْوَةٌ حَسَنَةٌ لِّمَن كَانَ يَرْجُو	بہترین نمونہ ہر اس شخص کے لیے جو امیدوار ہو
اللَّهَ وَالْيَوْمَ الْآخِرَ ۚ وَمَن يَتَوَلَّ	اللہ کا اور روزِ آخرت کا اور جس نے منہ موڑا (اس سے)
فَإِنَّ اللَّهَ هُوَ الْغَنِيُّ الْحَمِيدُ ﴿٦﴾ ع	تو بے شک اللہ وہ ہے جو بے نیاز اور لائقِ حمد و ثنا ہے ﴿٦﴾
عَسَى اللَّهُ أَن يَجْعَلَ	کچھ بعید نہیں کہ اللہ پیدا کر دے
بَيْنَكُمْ وَبَيْنَ الَّذِينَ عَادَيْتُم مِّنْهُم	تمہارے اور ان لوگوں کے درمیان جو دشمن ہیں تمہارے، ان میں سے،
مَّوَدَّةً ۚ وَاللَّهُ قَدِيرٌ ۚ	دوستی اور اللہ بڑی قدرت رکھتا ہے۔
وَاللَّهُ غَفُورٌ رَّحِيمٌ ﴿٧﴾	اور اللہ ہے بخشنے والا اور نہایت مہربان ﴿٧﴾
لَّا يَنْهَاكُمُ اللَّهُ عَنِ الَّذِينَ	نہیں منع کرتا تم کو اللہ ان لوگوں کے بارے میں جنہوں نے
لَمْ يُقَاتِلُوكُمْ فِي الدِّينِ	نہیں جنگ کی تم سے دین کے معاملہ میں
وَلَمْ يُخْرِجُوكُم مِّن دِيَارِكُمْ	اور نہیں نکالا تم کو تمہارے گھروں سے
أَن تَبَرُّوهُمْ وَتُقْسِطُوا	اس بات سے کہ تم ان سے اچھا سلوک کرو اور انصاف کا برتاؤ کرو
إِلَيْهِمْ ۚ إِنَّ اللَّهَ يُحِبُّ الْمُقْسِطِينَ ﴿٨﴾	ان کے ساتھ۔ بے شک اللہ پسند کرتا ہے انصاف کرنے والوں کو ﴿٨﴾
إِنَّمَا يَنْهَاكُمُ اللَّهُ عَنِ الَّذِينَ	البتہ منع کرتا ہے تم کو اللہ ان لوگوں کے بارے میں جنہوں نے
قَاتَلُوكُمْ فِي الدِّينِ وَأَخْرَجُوكُم	تمہارے ساتھ جنگ کی دین کے معاملہ میں اور نکالا تم کو
مِّن دِيَارِكُمْ وَظَاهَرُوا	تمہارے گھروں سے اور مدد کی ایک دوسرے کی
عَلَىٰ إِخْرَاجِكُمْ أَن تَوَلَّوْهُمْ ۚ	تمہارے نکالنے میں اس سے کہ تم ان سے دوستی کرو۔

For You're Exalted in Might
And hold all the Sapience in plight

006 Indeed!
There's superb citation for you to brace
For,
Who Trust in Lord The Day in Demand
But if they ever trend to drift in trace

Indeed!
Lord is free of all needs in span
For He's laudable ardor and adore in plan

007 May be!
Lord trends in boons to bestow
Love in regard and amity in glow

Mid you and your determined foe in fight
Lord is Exalted in Might
Most Tolerant in slight
Quite Kind in plight.

008 Lord doesn't hold for a while in stance
From the men and clan around in glance

Who don't trend to combat (you) in fray
For the word of faith in stay
Nor they pushed you out of resides

Speak you softly with them in abide
For Lord trends to allure
Who're just and fair in core

009 Lord cautions you for the men and clan
Who trend to combat in span
For your trust of faith in plan

وَمَن يَتَوَلَّهُمْ فَأُولَٰئِكَ هُمُ الظَّالِمُونَ ۝٩	اور جو ان سے دوستی کریں گے تو وہی لوگ ظالم ہیں ۝٩
يَا أَيُّهَا الَّذِينَ آمَنُوا	اے وہ لوگو جو ایمان لائے ہو
إِذَا جَاءَكُمُ الْمُؤْمِنَاتُ	جب آئیں تمہارے پاس مومن عورتیں
مُهَاجِرَاتٍ فَامْتَحِنُوهُنَّ ۖ	ہجرت کر کے تو ان کی خوب جانچ پڑتال کر لو۔
اللَّهُ أَعْلَمُ بِإِيمَانِهِنَّ ۖ	اللہ بہتر جانتا ہے ان کے ایمان کو۔
فَإِنْ عَلِمْتُمُوهُنَّ مُؤْمِنَاتٍ	پس اگر تمہیں معلوم ہو جائے کہ وہ ایمان والی ہیں
فَلَا تَرْجِعُوهُنَّ إِلَى الْكُفَّارِ ۖ	تو نہ واپس کرو تم انہیں کافروں کی طرف۔
لَا هُنَّ حِلٌّ لَّهُمْ	نہ وہ عورتیں حلال ہیں ان کافروں کے لیے
وَلَا هُمْ يَحِلُّونَ لَهُنَّ ۖ	اور نہ وہ کافر مرد حلال ہیں ان عورتوں کے لیے۔
وَآتُوهُم مَّا أَنفَقُوا ۚ	اور دے دو تم ان کافروں کو جو مہر انہوں نے ادا کیے تھے۔
وَلَا جُنَاحَ عَلَيْكُمْ أَن تَنكِحُوهُنَّ	اور نہیں ہے کچھ گناہ تم پر اس میں کہ نکاح کر لو تم ان سے
إِذَا آتَيْتُمُوهُنَّ أُجُورَهُنَّ ۚ	بشرطیکہ ادا کر دو تم ان کو مہر ان کے۔
وَلَا تُمْسِكُوا بِعِصَمِ الْكَوَافِرِ وَاسْأَلُوا	اور مت روکے رکھو (اپنی زوجیت میں) کافر بیویوں کو اور مانگ لو
مَا أَنفَقْتُمْ وَلْيَسْأَلُوا	جو (مہر) تم نے دیے تھے اور چاہیے کہ کافر بھی مانگ لیں
مَا أَنفَقُوا ۚ ذَٰلِكُمْ حُكْمُ اللَّهِ ۖ	وہ مہر جو انہوں نے ادا کیے تھے۔ یہ اللہ کا حکم ہے
يَحْكُمُ بَيْنَكُمْ ۚ	جس کے مطابق وہ فیصلہ کر رہا ہے تمہارے درمیان۔
وَاللَّهُ عَلِيمٌ حَكِيمٌ ۝١٠	اور اللہ ہے سب کچھ جاننے والا اور بڑی حکمت والا ۝١٠
وَإِن فَاتَكُمْ شَيْءٌ مِّنْ أَزْوَاجِكُمْ	اور اگر رہ جائے کچھ تمہاری بیویوں کے مہر میں سے
إِلَى الْكُفَّارِ فَعَاقَبْتُمْ	کافروں کی طرف پھر تمہیں موقع ہاتھ آ جائے

Who delve to drive (you) out of resides
And also the men and clan in stride
Who aide (them) in drive and drag in decide

So don't trend in respect and regard
If some trends to them in accord
It's but faulty and flimsy in assort

010 O you the men of the faith in support
When there's some woman of faith in deport

Sift and sieve them with trust in pace
Lord detects the best in (their) faith
When you establish their Faith in grace
Then send them not to Cynics in place

They're not the spouses in trust
For the atheist (there) in place
Nor the atheist husband in just

But pay the Cynics, dowry in endow
For what they spent in bestow

There's no impute in pace
If you espouse (them) after the dowry in endow
But care not for the unbelieving dame in place

Demand of the dole, you spent for the same
And let cynics seek for the dowers in claim

For what they spent in grants
(on the dowers of women who come over to you)
Lord is Full of,
Sense and Sapience in all bent and slants

011 And if your wives defect to cynic in faith
And you've a dame from a cynic in Faith

فَاٰتُوا الَّذِيْنَ ذَهَبَتْ اَزْوَاجُهُمْ	تو دے دو ان لوگوں کو جن کی بیویاں چلی گئی تھیں،
مِّثْلَ مَآ اَنْفَقُوْا ؕ	اتنا مہر جو انہوں نے ادا کیا تھا (ان بیویوں کو)۔
وَاتَّقُوا اللّٰهَ الَّذِيْٓ اَنْتُمْ بِهٖ مُؤْمِنُوْنَ ﴿١١﴾	اور ڈرو اللہ سے وہ اللہ جس پر تم ایمان رکھتے ہو ﴿١١﴾
يٰٓاَيُّهَا النَّبِيُّ اِذَا جَآءَكَ	اے نبی جب آئیں تمہارے پاس
الْمُؤْمِنٰتُ يُبَايِعْنَكَ	مومن عورتیں تم سے بیعت کرنے کے لیے
عَلٰٓى اَنْ لَّا يُشْرِكْنَ	تو عہد کریں اس بات کا کہ نہ شرک کریں گی
بِاللّٰهِ شَيْـًٔا وَّلَا يَسْرِقْنَ	اللہ کے ساتھ ذرا بھی اور نہ چوری کریں گی
وَلَا يَزْنِيْنَ وَلَا يَقْتُلْنَ اَوْلَادَهُنَّ	اور نہ زنا کریں گی اور نہ قتل کریں گی اپنی اولاد کو
وَلَا يَاْتِيْنَ بِبُهْتَانٍ يَّفْتَرِيْنَهٗ	اور نہ باندھیں گی کوئی ایسا بہتان جسے گھڑ لیں وہ خود
بَيْنَ اَيْدِيْهِنَّ وَاَرْجُلِهِنَّ	اپنے ہاتھوں اور پاؤں کے آگے
وَلَا يَعْصِيْنَكَ فِيْ مَعْرُوْفٍ	اور نہ نافرمانی کریں گی وہ تمہاری کسی امرِ معروف (جائز حکم) میں
فَبَايِعْهُنَّ وَاسْتَغْفِرْ	تو ان سے بیعت لے لو اور دعائے مغفرت کرو
لَهُنَّ اللّٰهَ ؕ اِنَّ اللّٰهَ	ان کے لیے اللہ سے۔ بلاشبہ اللہ ہے
غَفُوْرٌ رَّحِيْمٌ ﴿١٢﴾	معاف فرمانے والا اور نہایت رحم فرمانے والا ﴿١٢﴾
يٰٓاَيُّهَا الَّذِيْنَ اٰمَنُوْا لَا تَتَوَلَّوْا	اے لوگو جو ایمان لائے ہو نہ دوست بناؤ
قَوْمًا غَضِبَ اللّٰهُ عَلَيْهِمْ	ان لوگوں کو غضب فرمایا ہے اللہ نے جن پر
قَدْ يَئِسُوْا مِنَ الْاٰخِرَةِ	اور جو مایوس ہو گئے ہیں آخرت سے،
كَمَا يَئِسَ الْكُفَّارُ	اسی طرح جس طرح مایوس ہو چکے ہیں کافر
مِنْ اَصْحٰبِ الْقُبُوْرِ ﴿١٣﴾	جو قبروں میں پڑے ہوئے ہیں ﴿١٣﴾

Then pay them the dower in return
Whose wives abandoned (them) in term

And awe and dread Lord in pace
Whom you trust to obey in place

012 O Prophet!
When a woman in faith trends to thee in stride
Assert and affirm of allegiance (for you) in abide

They wouldn't trend other than Lord in beseech
They also assert to affirm in entreat

They wouldn't plunder and swindle in trail
And wouldn't trend to illicit sensuality in vale

And also wouldn't kill their scion in pace
Neither trend to voice lie and libel in trace
Volitionally fabricating fib in place

And they wouldn't defy (thee) just in concern
Then you assert their allegiance to conform

Then beg and beseech Lord, their ills to absolve
Lord is Forgiving and Merciful in resolve

013 O you the men and clan in faith
Don't befriend in pace

Who endures in trace
Fury of Lord in place

They're by now held in dejection
For the Hereafter in abjection

Just as the cynics are held in gloom
For those, who're buried in doom

آياتها ١٤ سُورَةُ الصَّفِّ مَدَنِيَّةٌ (٦١) (١٠٩) ركوعاتها ٢

بِسْمِ اللّٰهِ الرَّحْمٰنِ الرَّحِيْمِ

شروع اللہ کے نام سے جو بڑا مہربان نہایت رحم والا ہے

سَبَّحَ لِلّٰهِ مَا فِي السَّمٰوٰتِ	تسبیح کی ہے اللہ کی ہر اس چیز نے جو آسمانوں میں ہے
وَمَا فِي الْاَرْضِ ۚ وَهُوَ الْعَزِيْزُ الْحَكِيْمُ ①	اور جو زمین میں ہے اور وہ ہے زبردست اور بڑی حکمت والا ①
يٰۤاَيُّهَا الَّذِيْنَ اٰمَنُوْا لِمَ تَقُوْلُوْنَ	اے لوگو جو ایمان لائے ہو تم کیوں کہتے ہو
مَا لَا تَفْعَلُوْنَ ②	ایسی بات جو تم نہیں کرتے؟ ②
كَبُرَ مَقْتًا عِنْدَ اللّٰهِ اَنْ تَقُوْلُوْا	سخت ناپسندیدہ حرکت ہے اللہ کے نزدیک یہ کہ تم کہو
مَا لَا تَفْعَلُوْنَ ③	وہ بات جو تم کرتے نہیں؟ ③
اِنَّ اللّٰهَ يُحِبُّ الَّذِيْنَ يُقَاتِلُوْنَ	یقیناً اللہ محبت کرتا ہے ان لوگوں سے جو جنگ کرتے ہیں
فِيْ سَبِيْلِهٖ صَفًّا كَاَنَّهُمْ	اس کی راہ میں صف بستہ ہو کر اس طرح گویا کہ وہ
بُنْيَانٌ مَّرْصُوْصٌ ④	سیسہ پلائی ہوئی دیوار ہیں ④
وَاِذْ قَالَ مُوْسٰى لِقَوْمِهٖ	اور (یاد کرو) جب کہا تھا موسیٰؑ نے اپنی قوم سے:
يٰقَوْمِ لِمَ تُؤْذُوْنَنِيْ	اے میری قوم کے لوگو! کیوں اذیت دیتے ہو تم مجھے
وَقَدْ تَّعْلَمُوْنَ اَنِّيْ رَسُوْلُ اللّٰهِ	حالانکہ تم خوب جانتے ہو کہ بلاشبہ میں اللہ کا رسول ہوں
اِلَيْكُمْ ۭ فَلَمَّا زَاغُوْٓا	تمہاری طرف، لیکن جب انہوں نے کجی اختیار کی۔
اَزَاغَ اللّٰهُ قُلُوْبَهُمْ ۭ	تو ٹیڑھے کر دیے اللہ نے ان کے دل۔
وَاللّٰهُ لَا يَهْدِي الْقَوْمَ الْفٰسِقِيْنَ ⑤	اور اللہ ہدایت نہیں دیتا فاسق لوگوں کو ⑤

061-AL SAFF

In the name of Lord, the Most Beneficent, Most Merciful

001 All that's in Heavens and earth in daze
Let it adore Glory of Lord in Praise

He is Exalted in Might
Holds Sapience in Bright

002 O the men of faith in place
Why you assert to affirm in pace
For what you don't have a know in place

003 Before Lord:
It's intensely despicable in stance
You assert to affirm in trance
For what you don't have a bit of know in glance

004 Lord adores in instruct, who fights to combat
For reason of Lord, fight in instruct
As if sound, cemented structure in construct

005 Then recall that term in stance
When Moses to his clan, had said in blur
O my men and clan!
Why hex and scold me in trance
And pester and plague in slur

Even though you confirm for sure
That I'm Messenger of Lord in adore

As they drifted to affront and abash
Lord let their core spin in stash

For Lord doesn't trend to allure
Who're defiant and despicable in core

وَإِذْ قَالَ عِيسَى ابْنُ مَرْيَمَ	اور جب کہا عیسیٰ ابن مریم نے
يٰبَنِيٓ إِسْرَآءِيلَ إِنِّي رَسُولُ اللّٰهِ	اے بنی اسرائیل! یقیناً میں اللہ کا رسول ہوں
إِلَيْكُمْ مُّصَدِّقًا لِّمَا	تمہاری طرف، تصدیق کرنے والا ہوں اس حصہ کا جو
بَيْنَ يَدَيَّ مِنَ التَّوْرٰىةِ	مجھ سے پہلے موجود ہے تورات میں سے
وَمُبَشِّرًا بِرَسُولٍ يَّأْتِي	اور بشارت دینے والا ہوں ایک رسول کی جو آئے گا
مِنْ بَعْدِي اسْمُهُ أَحْمَدُ ط	میرے بعد اس کا نام احمدؐ ہوگا۔
فَلَمَّا جَآءَهُمْ بِالْبَيِّنٰتِ	لیکن جب وہ آیا ان کے پاس کھلی کھلی نشانیاں لے کر
قَالُوا هٰذَا سِحْرٌ مُّبِينٌ ﴿٦﴾	تو وہ کہنے لگے یہ تو کھلا جادو ہے ﴿٦﴾
وَمَنْ أَظْلَمُ مِمَّنِ افْتَرٰى	اور کون ہے بڑا ظالم اس شخص سے جو باندھے
عَلَى اللّٰهِ الْكَذِبَ وَهُوَ يُدْعٰٓى	اللہ پر جھوٹا بہتان حالانکہ اسے دعوت دی جا رہی ہو
إِلَى الْإِسْلَامِ ط وَاللّٰهُ لَا يَهْدِي	اسلام کی۔ اور اللہ نہیں ہدایت دیا کرتا
الْقَوْمَ الظّٰلِمِينَ ﴿٧﴾	ایسے ظالم لوگوں کو ﴿٧﴾
يُرِيدُونَ لِيُطْفِـُٔوا نُورَ اللّٰهِ	یہ چاہتے ہیں کہ بجھا دیں اللہ کا نور
بِأَفْوَاهِهِمْ ط وَاللّٰهُ	اپنے منہ کی پھونکوں سے۔ اور یہ فیصلہ ہے اللہ کا
مُتِمُّ نُورِهِ وَلَوْ	کہ وہ پورا پھیلا کر رہے گا اپنے نور کو خواہ
كَرِهَ الْكٰفِرُونَ ﴿٨﴾	کتنا ہی ناگوار ہو کافروں کو ﴿٨﴾
هُوَ الَّذِيٓ أَرْسَلَ رَسُولَهُ بِالْهُدٰى	وہی تو ہے جس نے بھیجا ہے اپنا رسول ہدایت
وَدِينِ الْحَقِّ لِيُظْهِرَهُ	اور دینِ حق کے ساتھ تاکہ اسے غالب کر دے،
ع عَلَى الدِّينِ كُلِّهِ وَلَوْ كَرِهَ الْمُشْرِكُونَ ﴿٩﴾	سب ادیان پر خواہ کتنا ہی ناگوار ہو مشرکین کو ﴿٩﴾

006 And recall, Jesus, Son of Mary in grace
Who said to the men in aside
O Progeny of Israel in place

(You know for sure in grace)
I'm Messenger of Lord in pace
Affirming the Dictum of Faith in grace

And give you a good word in greet
There's to be a Messenger in treat

Hereafter my term indeed
Ahmad, shall be his name
But when prophet is there to sustain

With distinct Signs in claim
They said:
That's but plain spell to contain

007 Who could be a bigger cheat and deceit
Who dither and quibble for Lord in conceit

Even as he's called to Faith in treat
And Lord steers not those to thrive
Who transgress in mannerly means to survive

008 They design to douse in blow
The Gleam of Lord in flow
In their stuttering rave in throw

But Lord,
Has done with His Glitter in Glow
Ever to Flow
Even though cynics despise in ado

009 Lord has sent hither to adore
His Messengers with Truth in lore
Even if the Pagans may despise in core

يٰٓاَيُّهَا الَّذِيْنَ اٰمَنُوْا هَلْ اَدُلُّكُمْ عَلٰى تِجَارَةٍ
اے لوگو جو ایمان لائے ہو کیا میں بتاؤں تم کو وہ تجارت جو

تُنْجِيْكُمْ مِّنْ عَذَابٍ اَلِيْمٍ ﴿١٠﴾
بچائے تم کو دردناک عذاب سے؟ ﴿۱۰﴾

تُؤْمِنُوْنَ بِاللّٰهِ وَرَسُوْلِهٖ وَتُجَاهِدُوْنَ
ایمان لاؤ تم اللہ پر اور اس کے رسول پر اور جہاد کرو

فِيْ سَبِيْلِ اللّٰهِ بِاَمْوَالِكُمْ وَاَنْفُسِكُمْ ۭ
اللہ کی راہ میں اپنے مالوں اور جانوں سے ۔

ذٰلِكُمْ خَيْرٌ لَّكُمْ اِنْ كُنْتُمْ تَعْلَمُوْنَ ﴿١١﴾
یہ بہتر ہے تمہارے لیے، اگر تم جانو ﴿۱۱﴾

يَغْفِرْ لَكُمْ ذُنُوْبَكُمْ وَيُدْخِلْكُمْ
معاف فرمادے گا اللہ تمہارے گناہ اور داخل کرے گا تمہیں

جَنّٰتٍ تَجْرِيْ مِنْ تَحْتِهَا الْاَنْهٰرُ
ایسی جنتوں میں کہ بہہ رہی ہیں ان کے نیچے نہریں

وَمَسٰكِنَ طَيِّبَةً فِيْ جَنّٰتِ عَدْنٍ ۭ
اور (عطا فرمائے گا) بہترین گھر سدا بہار جنتوں میں ۔

ذٰلِكَ الْفَوْزُ الْعَظِيْمُ ﴿١٢﴾
یہی ہے بہت بڑی کامیابی ﴿۱۲﴾

وَاُخْرٰى تُحِبُّوْنَهَا ۭ نَصْرٌ
اور وہ دوسری چیز (بھی تمہیں دے گا) جسے تم چاہتے ہو، نصرت

مِّنَ اللّٰهِ وَفَتْحٌ قَرِيْبٌ ۭ
اللہ کی طرف سے اور عنقریب حاصل ہونے والی فتح ۔

وَبَشِّرِ الْمُؤْمِنِيْنَ ﴿١٣﴾
اور اے نبیؐ! بشارت دے دو اہل ایمان کو ﴿۱۳﴾

يٰٓاَيُّهَا الَّذِيْنَ اٰمَنُوْا كُوْنُوْٓا اَنْصَارَ اللّٰهِ
اے لوگو جو ایمان لائے ہو بنو اللہ کے مددگار

كَمَا قَالَ عِيْسَى ابْنُ مَرْيَمَ لِلْحَوَارِيّٖنَ
جیسا کہ کہا تھا عیسیٰؑ ابن مریم نے حواریوں سے

مَنْ اَنْصَارِيْٓ اِلَى اللّٰهِ ۭ قَالَ الْحَوَارِيُّوْنَ
کون ہے میرا مددگار اللہ کی طرف (بلانے میں)۔ کہا تھا حواریوں نے

نَحْنُ اَنْصَارُ اللّٰهِ فَاٰمَنَتْ طَّاۗىِٕفَةٌ
ہم ہیں اللہ کے مددگار پھر ایمان لے آیا ایک گروہ

مِّنْ بَنِيْٓ اِسْرَاۗءِيْلَ وَكَفَرَتْ طَّاۗىِٕفَةٌ ۚ
بنی اسرائیل میں سے اور انکار کردیا (دوسرے) گروہ نے

فَاَيَّدْنَا الَّذِيْنَ اٰمَنُوْا
سو مدد کی ہم نے ایمان والوں کی

عَلٰي عَدُوِّهِمْ فَاَصْبَحُوْا ظٰهِرِيْنَ ﴿١٤﴾
ان کے دشمنوں کے مقابلے میں ۔ سو ہو کر رہے وہی غالب ﴿۱۴﴾

010 O you the men of faith in entreat!
Shall I lead you to a deal in treat
That's to save you here in impeach
From heinous ravage in conceit

011 That you trust,
Lord and His Messenger in lore
And struggle for His reason in score
With your riches and men in abide
That's favored for you to aside
If you really discern in core

012 He'll absolve your vice and err in throw
And get you the Gardens in glow
Where below and aside swift in drift
Streams sway in surge and swing in swift
Therewith elegant castles and villas in stance
Amidst the Gardens of glow in glance
Indeed!
That's super and superb grants in gift

013 You'll cherish Bliss of Lord in triumph
A favor in bestowal you'll hold in prime
So trend to the men of faith in around
With a news so good (affirmed) in abound

014 O you the men of Faith in term
Jesus, the son of Mary said to concern
To all his Disciples around to affirm
Who's to be an associate in sublime
To abide the dictum of Lord in prime
Disciples asserted so clear in concept
We're the firm ally to favor in precept
Then,
Part of posterity of Israel in stance
Held the dictum of faith in glance
There some defied, trust in trance
But We endowed sway in stride
To the men of faith in abide
Against their foe thither in deride
And they triumphed over them to stay
For they had affirmed to obey

اٰیاتها ١١ — (٦٢) سُوْرَةُ الْجُمُعَةِ مَدَنِيَّةٌ (١١٠) — رکوعاتها ٢

بِسْمِ اللّٰهِ الرَّحْمٰنِ الرَّحِيْمِ

شروع اللہ کے نام سے جو بڑا مہربان نہایت رحم والا ہے

يُسَبِّحُ لِلّٰهِ مَا فِي السَّمٰوٰتِ	تسبیح کر رہی ہے اللہ کی ہر وہ چیز جو آسمانوں میں ہے
وَمَا فِي الْاَرْضِ الْمَلِكِ الْقُدُّوْسِ	اور جو زمین میں ہے (اللہ جو) بادشاہ ہے نہایت مُقدّس،
الْعَزِيْزِ الْحَكِيْمِ ①	زبردست اور بڑی حکمت والا ①
هُوَ الَّذِيْ بَعَثَ فِي الْاُمِّيّٖنَ	وہی ہے جس نے اٹھایا اُمّیوں میں
رَسُوْلًا مِّنْهُمْ يَتْلُوْا عَلَيْهِمْ	ایک رسول خود انہی میں سے جو پڑھ کر سناتا ہے ان کو
اٰيٰتِهٖ وَيُزَكِّيْهِمْ	اللہ کی آیات اور ان کا تزکیۂ نفس کرتا ہے
وَيُعَلِّمُهُمُ الْكِتٰبَ وَالْحِكْمَةَ	اور تعلیم دیتا ہے ان کو کتاب اللہ کی اور سکھاتا ہے ان کو دانائی
وَاِنْ كَانُوْا مِنْ قَبْلُ	اگرچہ تھے وہ اس سے پہلے
لَفِيْ ضَلٰلٍ مُّبِيْنٍ ②	پڑے ہوئے کھلی گمراہی میں ②
وَّاٰخَرِيْنَ	اور (اس رسول کی بعثت) ان دوسرے لوگوں کے لیے بھی ہے
مِنْهُمْ لَمَّا يَلْحَقُوْا بِهِمْ	جو انہی میں سے ہیں (اور) ابھی نہیں ملے آکر ان کے ساتھ۔
وَهُوَ الْعَزِيْزُ الْحَكِيْمُ ③	اور وہ ہے زبردست اور بڑی حکمت والا ③
ذٰلِكَ فَضْلُ اللّٰهِ يُؤْتِيْهِ مَنْ يَّشَآءُ	یہ اللہ کا فضل ہے جو وہ عطا کرتا ہے جسے چاہے۔
وَاللّٰهُ ذُو الْفَضْلِ الْعَظِيْمِ ④	اور اللہ بڑا فضل فرمانے والا ہے ④
مَثَلُ الَّذِيْنَ حُمِّلُوا	مثال ان لوگوں کی جنہیں حامل بنایا گیا تھا

062-AL JUMUAH

In the name of Lord, the Most Beneficent, Most Merciful

001 All is in the heavens and earth in place
Ardor adore Brilliance of Lord in grace

The Sacred O Supreme
Exalted in Might, Prudence in extreme

002 It's He, Who assigned in array
A Messenger mid them in stay

Who's untaught and unlettered in state
A Drill in direction His Signs to relate
Anoint and asperse His munificence to brace

Teach and train the wisdom in Scripture
For obviously before this stance in picture
They're indeed in manifest error in stricture

003 The bestowal of Lord for all term in span
That's the assignment of Prophet in plan
That's also for the men and clan

Who've not joined even now in plight*
Lord is Exalted in Might
With His Sense of Sapience in Bright

*Future generations

004 Such is the Bounty of Lord in Grace
For whom He likes in endow in prime
And The Lord is Refine and Sublime
Master of Proximal Bounty in Glance

005 The semblance of some indicted in stride
Commitment of Mosaic law to aside

التَّوْرٰىةَ ثُمَّ لَمْ يَحْمِلُوْهَا	توراۃ کا مگر پورا نہ کیا انہوں نے اس کے اٹھانے کی ذمہ داری کو
كَمَثَلِ الْحِمَارِ يَحْمِلُ اَسْفَارًا ؕ	اس گدھے کی سی ہے جو اٹھائے ہوئے ہو کتابیں۔
بِئْسَ مَثَلُ الْقَوْمِ الَّذِيْنَ	بہت بری ہے مثال ان لوگوں کی جنہوں نے
كَذَّبُوْا بِاٰيٰتِ اللّٰهِ ؕ	جھٹلایا اللہ کی آیات کو۔
وَاللّٰهُ لَا يَهْدِى الْقَوْمَ الظّٰلِمِيْنَ ۝٥	اور اللہ نہیں ہدایت دیتا ظالم لوگوں کو ۝٥
قُلْ يٰۤاَيُّهَا الَّذِيْنَ	ان سے کہیے اے لوگو! جو
هَادُوْۤا اِنْ زَعَمْتُمْ	یہودی بن گئے ہو اگر تمہیں گھمنڈ ہے
اَنَّكُمْ اَوْلِيَآءُ لِلّٰهِ	کہ تم اللہ کے چہیتے ہو
مِنْ دُوْنِ النَّاسِ فَتَمَنَّوُا الْمَوْتَ	دوسرے لوگوں کو چھوڑ کر تو تمنا کرو موت کی،
اِنْ كُنْتُمْ صٰدِقِيْنَ ۝٦	اگر ہو تم سچے ۝٦
وَلَا يَتَمَنَّوْنَهٗۤ اَبَدًا	اور ہر گز نہ تمنا کریں گے یہ موت کی کبھی بھی
بِمَا قَدَّمَتْ اَيْدِيْهِمْ ؕ	بسبب ان کرتوتوں کے جو یہ کر چکے ہیں۔
وَاللّٰهُ عَلِيْمٌۢ بِالظّٰلِمِيْنَ ۝٧	اور اللہ خوب جانتا ہے ان ظالموں کو ۝٧
قُلْ اِنَّ الْمَوْتَ	ان سے کہیے بلاشبہ وہ موت
الَّذِىْ تَفِرُّوْنَ مِنْهُ	جس سے بھاگ رہے ہو تم
فَاِنَّهٗ مُلٰقِيْكُمْ	وہ تو ضرور آ کر رہے گی تمہارے پاس
ثُمَّ تُرَدُّوْنَ	پھر پیش کیے جاؤ گے تم
اِلٰى عٰلِمِ الْغَيْبِ	اس کے حضور جو جاننے والا ہے پوشیدہ
وَالشَّهَادَةِ فَيُنَبِّئُكُمْ	اور ظاہر کا پھر وہ بتائے گا تمہیں

But they failed to charge and conform
They're like of a donkey in pace
Bearing the books on back in stack

But discerns it not a bit in pack
Evil is the similitude of the men in place

Who color and confuse Signs of Lord in trace
And Lord! Doesn't escort and assort in grace
Who drift in daze,
They're are the wrongdoers in base

006 Say:
O you the men of Jewish in faith
If you deem as ally of Lord in grace

With eviction of other men in pace
Then air for an urge of death to brace
If you're true to a bit in trace

007 But they,
Wouldn't aspire for death in demise
For their deeds affirmed in precise

Passed on for the Hereafter in pace
And Lord,
Discerns their evils trends in place

008 Say:
You cannot flee from death in demise
Soon it's to overwhelm (you) in premise
Then to discern,
Manifest and mystic all in precise

He'll apprise you all term in trail
For all your done and doings in vale

بِمَا كُنْتُمْ تَعْمَلُوْنَ ﴿٨﴾
کہ تم کیا کرتے رہے ہو؟ ﴿٨﴾

يٰۤاَيُّهَا الَّذِيْنَ اٰمَنُوْۤا
اے لوگو جو ایمان لائے ہو

اِذَا نُوْدِيَ لِلصَّلٰوةِ
جب اذان دی جائے نماز کے لیے

مِنْ يَّوْمِ الْجُمُعَةِ فَاسْعَوْا اِلٰى ذِكْرِ اللّٰهِ
جمعہ کے دن تو دوڑ پڑو اللہ کے ذکر کی طرف

وَذَرُوا الْبَيْعَ ؕ
اور چھوڑ دو خرید و فروخت۔

ذٰلِكُمْ خَيْرٌ لَّكُمْ
یہ زیادہ بہتر ہے تمہارے لیے

اِنْ كُنْتُمْ تَعْلَمُوْنَ ﴿٩﴾
اگر تم جانو ﴿٩﴾

فَاِذَا قُضِيَتِ الصَّلٰوةُ
پھر جب پوری ہو جائے نماز

فَانْتَشِرُوْا فِي الْاَرْضِ
تو پھیل جاؤ زمین میں

وَابْتَغُوْا مِنْ فَضْلِ اللّٰهِ
اور تلاش کرو اللہ کا فضل

وَاذْكُرُوا اللّٰهَ كَثِيْرًا
اور یاد کرتے رہو اللہ کو کثرت سے

لَّعَلَّكُمْ تُفْلِحُوْنَ ﴿١٠﴾
تاکہ تمہیں فلاح نصیب ہو ﴿١٠﴾

وَاِذَا رَاَوْا تِجَارَةً
اور جب دیکھتے ہیں تجارت

اَوْ لَهْوَا انْفَضُّوْۤا
یا کھیل تماشا تو لپک جاتے ہیں

اِلَيْهَا وَتَرَكُوْكَ قَآئِمًا ؕ
اس کی طرف اور چھوڑ دیتے ہیں تمہیں کھڑا۔

قُلْ مَا عِنْدَ اللّٰهِ
ان سے کہیے جو کچھ اللہ کے پاس ہے

خَيْرٌ مِّنَ اللَّهْوِ
وہ کہیں بہتر ہے کھیل تماشے سے

وَمِنَ التِّجَارَةِ ؕ وَاللّٰهُ
اور تجارت سے اور اللہ

خَيْرُ الرّٰزِقِيْنَ ﴿١١﴾
سب سے بہتر رزق دینے والا ہے ﴿١١﴾

009 O you the men of faith!
When there's the call in pace

Avowed for Friday Prayer to entreat
Hurry sincerely for Lord to beseech

And suspend your term in trade
That's the best for you to evade
If you really discern in treat

010 And when,
You've done with the beseech in pray
Then you scatter and spatter in span
Seek for the Bounty of Lord in plan

Ardor and adore Lord, all term in stay
So you may cherish His Boons in pray

011 But when they discern in term
Some deal and dicker or frolic in fun

They scatter and spatter in glance
And desert you still in trance

Say:
Bliss in Amity of Lord preferred in pace
Than any of fun and frolic or trade in place
Lord is the best to render for all in grace

آیاتہا ١١ سُوۡرَةُ الۡمُنٰفِقُوۡنَ مَدَنِیَّةٌ (٦٣) (١٠٤) رکوعاتہا ٢

بِسۡمِ اللّٰهِ الرَّحۡمٰنِ الرَّحِیۡمِ

شروع اللہ کے نام سے جو بڑا مہربان نہایت رحم والا ہے

اِذَا جَآءَكَ الۡمُنٰفِقُوۡنَ	جب آتے ہیں تمہارے پاس (اے نبیؐ) منافق
قَالُوۡا نَشۡهَدُ اِنَّكَ	تو کہتے ہیں ہم گواہی دیتے ہیں کہ یقیناً آپ
لَرَسُوۡلُ اللّٰهِ ۘ وَاللّٰهُ يَعۡلَمُ	ضرور اللہ کے رسول ہیں۔ ہاں! اللہ جانتا ہے
اِنَّكَ لَرَسُوۡلُهٗ ؕ وَاللّٰهُ يَشۡهَدُ	کہ بلاشبہ تم اللہ کے رسول ہو۔ اور اللہ گواہی دیتا ہے
اِنَّ الۡمُنٰفِقِيۡنَ لَكٰذِبُوۡنَ ۚ ①	کہ یقیناً یہ منافق قطعاً جھوٹے ہیں ①
اِتَّخَذُوۡۤا اَيۡمَانَهُمۡ جُنَّةً	بنا رکھا ہے انہوں نے اپنی قسموں کو ڈھال
فَصَدُّوۡا عَنۡ سَبِيۡلِ اللّٰهِ ؕ	اور اس طرح روکتے ہیں یہ اللہ کی راہ سے۔
اِنَّهُمۡ سَآءَ مَا كَانُوۡا يَعۡمَلُوۡنَ ②	یقیناً بہت ہی بری ہیں وہ حرکتیں جو یہ کر رہے ہیں ②
ذٰلِكَ بِاَنَّهُمۡ اٰمَنُوۡا	ان کا یہ طرزِ عمل اس وجہ سے کہ یہ (پہلے) ایمان لائے
ثُمَّ كَفَرُوۡا فَطُبِعَ	پھر کفر کیا انہوں نے اس لیے مہر لگا دی اللہ نے
عَلٰى قُلُوۡبِهِمۡ فَهُمۡ لَا يَفۡقَهُوۡنَ ③	ان کے دلوں پر سو یہ اب (کچھ) نہیں سمجھتے ③
وَاِذَا رَاَيۡتَهُمۡ تُعۡجِبُكَ	اور جب دیکھو تم انہیں تو بڑے اچھے لگیں گے تمہیں
اَجۡسَامُهُمۡ ؕ وَاِنۡ يَّقُوۡلُوۡا تَسۡمَعۡ لِقَوۡلِهِمۡ ؕ	ان کے جسم۔ اور اگر بات کریں تو تم سنتے رہ جاؤ ان کی باتیں۔
كَاَنَّهُمۡ	وہ آدمی نہیں ہیں بلکہ ایسے ہیں گویا کہ وہ
خُشُبٌ مُّسَنَّدَةٌ ؕ	لکڑی کے کندے ہوں جو دیوار کے ساتھ چن دیے گئے ہوں۔

063-AL MUNAFIQUN

In the name of Lord, the Most Beneficent, Most Merciful

001 When the hypocrites trend to(you) in pace
They assert to affirm in place

That you're the Messenger of Lord in term
Your Lord discerns for sure to affirm

That you're indeed His Messenger in grace
And Lord so asserts to confirm
That Hypocrites are but fibbers in place

002 They avow to veil their ills in construct
And get to the other men to obstruct

Dictum of faith of Lord in instruct
Indeed!
They delve in their evil course of conduct

003 Because they assumed first in stance
Then they drifted to defy (Faith) in trance

There's a seal in their veer of core
So they're not going to trend in lore

004 If you've a glimpse of (their) faces in glance
They beam and gleam imp in stance
When they voice in trance

You listen to their charm to impress
They're refuse of wood in digress
That's fixed to prop in piers, at ingress

يَحْسَبُوْنَ كُلَّ صَيْحَةٍ عَلَيْهِمْ ؕ — سمجھتے ہیں یہ ہر زور کی آواز کو اپنے خلاف ۔

هُمُ الْعَدُوُّ فَاحْذَرْهُمْ ؕ — یہی حقیقی دشمن ہیں لہٰذا تم ان سے بچ کر رہو ۔

قٰتَلَهُمُ اللّٰهُ ۫ اَنّٰى يُؤْفَكُوْنَ ۴ — ان پر اللہ کی مار ۔ یہ کدھر الٹے پھرائے جا رہے ہیں ۴

وَ اِذَا قِيْلَ لَهُمْ تَعَالَوْا — اور جب کہا جاتا ہے ان سے کہ آؤ

يَسْتَغْفِرْ لَكُمْ رَسُوْلُ اللّٰهِ — مغفرت کی دعا کریں تمہارے لیے اللہ کے رسول

لَوَّوْا رُءُوْسَهُمْ وَرَاَيْتَهُمْ — تو گھماتے ہیں اپنے سروں کو مذاق اڑانے کے لیے اور دیکھو گے تم انہیں

يَصُدُّوْنَ وَهُمْ مُّسْتَكْبِرُوْنَ ۵ — کہ وہ رک جاتے ہیں آنے سے بڑے گھمنڈ کے ساتھ ۵

سَوَآءٌ عَلَيْهِمْ اَسْتَغْفَرْتَ — برابر ہے ان کے لیے دعائے مغفرت کرو تم

لَهُمْ اَمْ لَمْ تَسْتَغْفِرْ — ان کے لیے یا نہ کرو دعائے مغفرت تم

لَهُمْ ؕ لَنْ يَّغْفِرَ — ان کے لیے ۔ ہرگز نہیں بخشے گا

اللّٰهُ لَهُمْ ؕ اِنَّ اللّٰهَ — اللہ ان کو ۔ بے شک اللہ

لَا يَهْدِى الْقَوْمَ الْفٰسِقِيْنَ ۶ — نہیں ہدایت دیتا فاسق لوگوں کو ۶

هُمُ الَّذِيْنَ يَقُوْلُوْنَ — یہی وہ لوگ ہیں جو کہتے ہیں

لَا تُنْفِقُوْا عَلٰى مَنْ — مت خرچ کرو تم ان لوگوں پر جو

عِنْدَ رَسُوْلِ اللّٰهِ — ساتھ ہیں رسول اللہ کے

حَتّٰى يَنْفَضُّوْا ؕ وَلِلّٰهِ — تاکہ منتشر ہو جائیں وہ ۔ حالانکہ اللہ ہی مالک ہے

خَزَآئِنُ السَّمٰوٰتِ وَالْاَرْضِ وَلٰكِنَّ — زمین اور آسمانوں کے خزانوں کا لیکن

الْمُنٰفِقِيْنَ لَا يَفْقَهُوْنَ ۷ — یہ منافق نہیں سمجھتے ۷

يَقُوْلُوْنَ لَئِنْ رَّجَعْنَآ — یہ کہتے ہیں اگر ہم واپس پہنچ جائیں

They discern in concern
Each shriek is for them to discern

They're the real foe in fray
So beware of them in stay

Curse of Lord is for them to aside
How they're duped of truth in deride

005 When they're,
Bid to Messenger of Lord in stay
So he may beg and beseech Lord in pray
For the extenuation of your ills in stray

They twirl and whirl to revolve in trance
That's their contemptuous way in glance

006 It's alike for them in pace
If you adjure or not in place

For their extenuation of ills in trace
Lord isn't to absolve defiant in base

007 They'd often crow and cry in pit
Don't trend to spend of a bit

For men besides messenger in pace
So they may quit and diverge in place

But!
To Him belongs riches of heavens and earth
The hypocrites have no sane sapience in mirth

008 They trend to assert there in stride
When we return to Madinah in abide

إِلَى الْمَدِينَةِ لَيُخْرِجَنَّ	مدینہ میں تو ضرور نکال دے گا وہ
الْأَعَزُّ مِنْهَا الْأَذَلَّ ؕ	جو عزت والا ہے وہاں سے ذلیل کو۔
وَلِلّٰهِ الْعِزَّةُ	حالانکہ اللہ ہی کے لیے ہے عزت
وَلِرَسُولِهٖ وَلِلْمُؤْمِنِينَ	اور اس کے رسول کے لیے اور مومنین کے لیے
وَلٰكِنَّ الْمُنٰفِقِينَ لَا يَعْلَمُونَ ﴿٨﴾	لیکن منافق نہیں جانتے ﴿۸﴾
يٰٓأَيُّهَا الَّذِينَ اٰمَنُوا	اے لوگو جو ایمان لائے ہو
لَا تُلْهِكُمْ أَمْوَالُكُمْ	نہ غافل کریں تمہیں تمہارے مال
وَلَآ أَوْلَادُكُمْ عَنْ ذِكْرِ اللّٰهِ ۚ	اور نہ تمہاری اولاد اللہ کے ذکر سے
وَمَنْ يَّفْعَلْ ذٰلِكَ	اور جو کرے گا ایسا
فَأُولٰٓئِكَ هُمُ الْخٰسِرُونَ ﴿٩﴾	سو ایسے ہی لوگ ہیں خسارے میں رہنے والے ﴿۹﴾
وَأَنْفِقُوا مِنْ مَّا رَزَقْنٰكُمْ	اور خرچ کرو اس میں سے جو رزق دیا ہے ہم نے تم کو
مِّنْ قَبْلِ أَنْ يَّأْتِيَ	اس سے پہلے کہ آجائے
أَحَدَكُمُ الْمَوْتُ فَيَقُولَ	تم میں سے کسی کی موت پھر وہ کہے:
رَبِّ لَوْلَآ أَخَّرْتَنِيٓ	اے میرے رب! کیوں نہ مہلت دے دی تو نے مجھے
إِلٰٓى أَجَلٍ قَرِيبٍ ۙ فَأَصَّدَّقَ	تھوڑی سی تاکہ میں صدقہ دیتا
وَأَكُنْ مِّنَ الصّٰلِحِينَ ﴿١٠﴾	اور ہو جاتا شامل صالح لوگوں میں ﴿۱۰﴾
وَلَنْ يُّؤَخِّرَ اللّٰهُ نَفْسًا	حالانکہ ہرگز نہیں مہلت دیتا اللہ کسی شخص کو
إِذَا جَآءَ أَجَلُهَا ۚ	جب آجاتا ہے اس کا وقت مقرر۔
وَاللّٰهُ خَبِيرٌۢ بِمَا تَعْمَلُونَ ﴿١١﴾	اور اللہ پوری طرح باخبر ہے ان اعمال سے جو تم کرتے ہو ﴿۱۱﴾

Indeed!
Reputable will exude petty of clan
But Tribute and Repute is for Lord in plan
And for His Messenger and men of faith in span

But the Hypocrites in turn
Like faker and fraud don't tend to discern

009 Oh you the men of faith in array
Don't let your,
Riches and scions deflect to betray

From the reverence of Lord in sway
If some is to drift in stray
It's for his own toll in stay

010 And spend in charity of a bit in trace
Out of bestowal of Lord in grace

Before doom in death is close to aside
Then you may trend to assert in stride

O Lord!
Why didn't you get me a moment in respite
So I could've given out of alms in slight
And I be one of the doers of good in plight

011 But Lord wouldn't grant lull and respite
When the term once assigned culminate in sight
Lord discerns all your doings in bit and slight

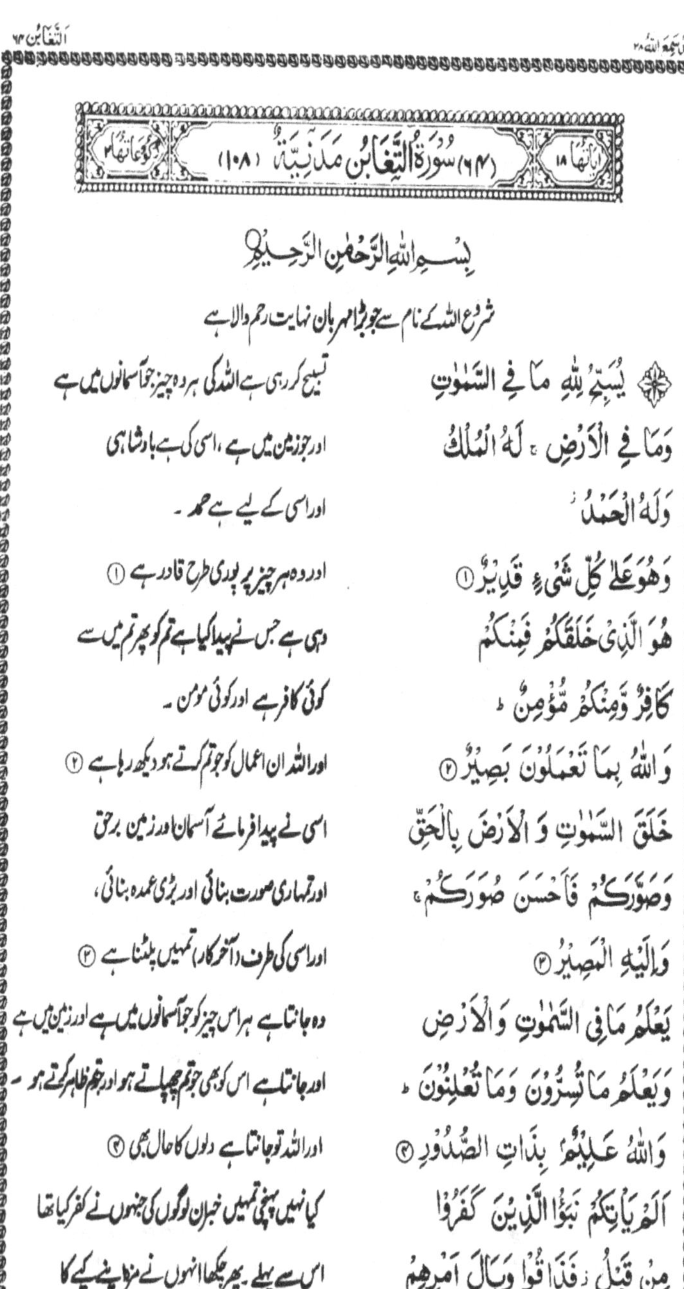

آیاتہا ١٨ — (٦٤) سُورَةُ التَّغَابُنِ مَدَنِيَّةٌ (١٠٨) — رکوعاتہا ٢

بِسْمِ اللّٰهِ الرَّحْمٰنِ الرَّحِيْمِ

شروع اللہ کے نام سے جو بڑا مہربان نہایت رحم والا ہے

يُسَبِّحُ لِلّٰهِ مَا فِي السَّمٰوٰتِ	تسبیح کر رہی ہے اللہ کی ہر وہ چیز جو آسمانوں میں ہے
وَمَا فِي الْأَرْضِ ۚ لَهُ الْمُلْكُ	اور جو زمین میں ہے، اسی کی ہے بادشاہی
وَلَهُ الْحَمْدُ	اور اسی کے لیے ہے حمد۔
وَهُوَ عَلٰى كُلِّ شَيْءٍ قَدِيْرٌ ﴿١﴾	اور وہ ہر چیز پر پوری طرح قادر ہے ﴿١﴾
هُوَ الَّذِيْ خَلَقَكُمْ فَمِنْكُمْ	وہی ہے جس نے پیدا کیا ہے تم کو پھر تم میں سے
كَافِرٌ وَّمِنْكُمْ مُّؤْمِنٌ ۭ	کوئی کافر ہے اور کوئی مومن۔
وَاللّٰهُ بِمَا تَعْمَلُوْنَ بَصِيْرٌ ﴿٢﴾	اور اللہ ان اعمال کو جو تم کرتے ہو دیکھ رہا ہے ﴿٢﴾
خَلَقَ السَّمٰوٰتِ وَالْأَرْضَ بِالْحَقِّ	اسی نے پیدا فرمائے آسمان اور زمین برحق
وَصَوَّرَكُمْ فَأَحْسَنَ صُوَرَكُمْ ۚ	اور تمہاری صورت بنائی اور بڑی عمدہ بنائی،
وَإِلَيْهِ الْمَصِيْرُ ﴿٣﴾	اور اسی کی طرف (آخرکار) تمہیں پلٹنا ہے ﴿٣﴾
يَعْلَمُ مَا فِي السَّمٰوٰتِ وَالْأَرْضِ	وہ جانتا ہے ہر اس چیز کو جو آسمانوں میں ہے اور زمین میں ہے
وَيَعْلَمُ مَا تُسِرُّوْنَ وَمَا تُعْلِنُوْنَ ۭ	اور جانتا ہے اس کو بھی جو تم چھپاتے ہو اور جو تم ظاہر کرتے ہو۔
وَاللّٰهُ عَلِيْمٌۢ بِذَاتِ الصُّدُوْرِ ﴿٤﴾	اور اللہ تو جانتا ہے دلوں کا حال بھی ﴿٤﴾
أَلَمْ يَأْتِكُمْ نَبَؤُا الَّذِيْنَ كَفَرُوْا	کیا نہیں پہنچی تمہیں خبر ان لوگوں کی جنہوں نے کفر کیا تھا
مِنْ قَبْلُ ۡ فَذَاقُوْا وَبَالَ أَمْرِهِمْ	اس سے پہلے۔ پھر چکھا انہوں نے مزا اپنے کیے کا

064-AL TAGHABUN

In the name of Lord, the Most Beneficent, Most Merciful

001 All in the heavens and earth in array
Proclaim Praises of Lord in sway

To Him belongs State in Command
And also the Ardor and adore in stance
He's authority to control all in glance

002 It's Lord,
Who created you hither in array
There're some who don't trust to obey

And there're some, who trust in place
Lord discerns your trends in trace

003 He created,
The heavens and the earth just so refine
Given you face and figure in (elegant) design
And to Him is your conclusive return in place

004 He discerns and concerns all in sway
That's in the heavens and earth in array

He discerns in sorts,
What you conceal or evince in part
Lord concerns your veer of core in accord

005 Did you get the fable in lore
Those of the clan defying faith in core

وَلَهُمْ عَذَابٌ اَلِيْمٌ ﴿٥﴾	اور ان کے لیے ہے دردناک عذاب ﴿٥﴾
ذٰلِكَ بِاَنَّهٗ كَانَتْ تَّاْتِيْهِمْ	یہ انجام ان کا اس لیے ہوا کہ آتے رہے ان کے پاس
رُسُلُهُمْ بِالْبَيِّنٰتِ فَقَالُوْٓا	ان کے رسول کھلی کھلی نشانیاں لے کر لیکن انہوں نے کہا،
اَبَشَرٌ يَّهْدُوْنَنَا ۡ	کیا ایک بشر ہمیں ہدایت دے گا؟
فَكَفَرُوْا وَ تَوَلَّوْا	اس طرح انہوں نے ماننے سے انکار کر دیا اور منہ پھیر لیا
وَّاسْتَغْنَى اللّٰهُ ؕ وَاللّٰهُ	اور اللہ بھی بے پروا ہو گیا (ان سے)، اور اللہ تو ہے ہی
غَنِيٌّ حَمِيْدٌ ﴿٦﴾	بے نیاز لائق حمد و ثنا ﴿٦﴾
زَعَمَ الَّذِيْنَ كَفَرُوْٓا	دعویٰ کرتے ہیں یہ کافر لوگ
اَنْ لَّنْ يُّبْعَثُوْا ؕ	کہ ہرگز نہیں اٹھائے جائیں گے وہ مرنے کے بعد۔
قُلْ بَلٰى وَرَبِّيْ	ان سے کہیے کیوں نہیں قسم ہے میرے رب کی
لَتُبْعَثُنَّ ثُمَّ لَتُنَبَّؤُنَّ	تم ضرور اٹھائے جاؤ گے پھر ضرور تمہیں بتایا جائے گا
بِمَا عَمِلْتُمْ ؕ	کہ تم (دنیا میں) کیا کچھ کرتے رہے؟
وَ ذٰلِكَ عَلَى اللّٰهِ يَسِيْرٌ ﴿٧﴾	اور ایسا کرنا اللہ کے لیے بہت آسان ہے ﴿٧﴾
فَاٰمِنُوْا بِاللّٰهِ وَرَسُوْلِهٖ	سو ایمان لے آؤ اللہ پر اور اس کے رسول پر
وَالنُّوْرِ الَّذِيْٓ اَنْزَلْنَا ؕ	اور اس روشنی پر جو ہم نے نازل کی ہے۔
وَاللّٰهُ بِمَا تَعْمَلُوْنَ خَبِيْرٌ ﴿٨﴾	اور اللہ اس سے جو تم کرتے ہو پوری طرح باخبر ہے ﴿٨﴾
يَوْمَ يَجْمَعُكُمْ	(اس کا پتہ تمہیں چلے گا) اس دن جب اکٹھا کرے گا وہ تمہیں
لِيَوْمِ الْجَمْعِ ذٰلِكَ يَوْمُ التَّغَابُنِ ؕ	حشر کے دن یہی ہوگا در اصل ہار جیت کا دن
وَمَنْ يُّؤْمِنْ بِاللّٰهِ وَيَعْمَلْ	اور جو ایمان لایا اللہ پر اور کیے اس نے

So they had,
A bit of bite, for their evil in conduct
And had sad and sorrow punish in induct

006 That's so there're Messengers in abide
With Lucid Drill and Direction to aside

But They Said:
How'd there be a Discipline to affirm
For there's,
A man, like us to direct
So they defied the missive in select

But also Lord defied those men and clan*
Lord is free of all needs in span
For He's deserving all Praises in plan

(*Who had defied faith in plan)

007 Cynics construe and conclude in pace
They wouldn't be raised for just in trust
You affirm to conform them only in just
Indeed
Dictum of Lord is affirmed in must

And you'll get to life once more in lore
Then you'll be told, all the truth for sure
Of all your done and doings in score

It's all simple for lord in pace
To determine of such in place

008 So, trust in Lord and His Messenger in Faith
And Faith We conveyed gleaming in Grace
Lord discerns your done and doings in trace

009 The Day He gathers you in gang and throng
That's the Day in swarm,
Of mutual ruin and reward in alarm
And those of the men and clan in trust

صَالِحًا يُّكَفِّرْ عَنْهُ سَيِّاٰتِهٖ	نیک عمل جھاڑ دے گا اللہ اس کے گناہ
وَ يُدْخِلْهُ جَنّٰتٍ تَجْرِيْ	اور داخل کرے گا اسے ایسی جنتوں میں کہ بہہ رہی ہوں گی
مِنْ تَحْتِهَا الْاَنْهٰرُ خٰلِدِيْنَ فِيْهَآ اَبَدًا ؕ	ان کے نیچے نہریں، رہیں گے وہ ان میں ہمیشہ ۔
ذٰلِكَ الْفَوْزُ الْعَظِيْمُ ٩	یہی ہے بڑی کامیابی ٩
وَ الَّذِيْنَ كَفَرُوْا وَكَذَّبُوْا بِاٰيٰتِنَآ	اور وہ لوگ جنہوں نے کفر کیا اور جھٹلایا ہماری آیات کو
اُولٰٓئِكَ اَصْحٰبُ النَّارِ خٰلِدِيْنَ فِيْهَا ؕ	یہ لوگ اہلِ دوزخ ہیں، ہمیشہ رہیں گے یہ اس میں ۔
وَبِئْسَ الْمَصِيْرُ ١٠	اور یہ بہت برا ٹھکانہ ہے ١٠
مَآ اَصَابَ مِنْ مُّصِيْبَةٍ اِلَّا بِاِذْنِ اللّٰهِ ؕ	نہیں پہنچتی کوئی مصیبت مگر اللہ کے اذن سے ۔
وَمَنْ يُّؤْمِنْ بِاللّٰهِ	اور جو ایمان لے آتا ہے اللہ پر
يَهْدِ قَلْبَهٗ ؕ	ہدایت بخشتا ہے اللہ اس کے دل کو ۔
وَاللّٰهُ بِكُلِّ شَيْءٍ عَلِيْمٌ ١١	اور اللہ ہر چیز سے پوری طرح باخبر ہے ١١
وَ اَطِيْعُوا اللّٰهَ وَ اَطِيْعُوا الرَّسُوْلَ ۚ	اور اطاعت کرو اللہ کی اور اطاعت کرو رسول کی
فَاِنْ تَوَلَّيْتُمْ فَاِنَّمَا عَلٰى رَسُوْلِنَا	لیکن اگر تم منہ موڑتے ہو تو بس، ہے ہمارے رسول پر
الْبَلٰغُ الْمُبِيْنُ ١٢	پہنچا دینا (حق کا) واضح طور پر ١٢
اَللّٰهُ لَآ اِلٰهَ اِلَّا هُوَ ؕ	اللہ وہ ہے کہ نہیں ہے کوئی معبود سوائے اس کے ۔
وَعَلَى اللّٰهِ فَلْيَتَوَكَّلِ الْمُؤْمِنُوْنَ ١٣	اور اللہ ہی پر چاہیے کہ بھروسہ کریں اہلِ ایمان ١٣
يٰٓاَيُّهَا الَّذِيْنَ اٰمَنُوْٓا	اے لوگو جو ایمان لائے ہو
اِنَّ مِنْ اَزْوَاجِكُمْ وَ اَوْلَادِكُمْ	یقیناً تمہاری بیویوں اور اولاد میں سے کچھ ایسے ہیں
عَدُوًّا لَّكُمْ فَاحْذَرُوْهُمْ ۚ	جو دشمن ہیں تمہارے سو ہوشیار رہو تم ان سے

With faith in Lord and truth (in) conduct
He'll elude their ills in construct

And He'll admit (them) to gardens in glow
Where streams surge in swell and ebb in flow

There to abide and reside for ever or so
That's Exquisite Boon from Lord in endow

010 But whoso defy Faith in stance
And deem Our Signs as fib in trance

They'll be friend of Pyre in blaze
Where to dwell (pant 's sigh) in pace

That's the evil end in intent
When they'll be really gone and spent

011 There's no distress and dismay in trail
Without the dictum of Lord in vale

If one stays firm for Lord in trust
Lord to escort his core in just
Your Lord,
Discerns and concerns for all in dale

012 So submit to Lord all in pace!
And also messenger in grace

But if you trend in astray
Our Messenger,
Has but to proclaim in faith
That's so lucid and plain to obey

013 Allah!
There is no god but Him in sway
So O men of the faith in array
Have your trust in Lord to obey

014 O you the men of faith
Indeed!
There're some of your spouses and scions
Enemy, opposed to your term in plan
So beware of them in all term and span

وَاِنْ تَعْفُوْا وَتَصْفَحُوْا	اور اگر تم معاف کر دو اور درگزر سے کام لو
وَتَغْفِرُوْا فَاِنَّ اللّٰهَ	اور بخش دو تو بلاشبہ اللہ ہے
غَفُوْرٌ رَّحِيْمٌ ﴿۱۴﴾	بہت معاف کرنے والا اور نہایت رحم فرمانے والا ﴿۱۴﴾
اِنَّمَآ اَمْوَالُكُمْ وَاَوْلَادُكُمْ	حقیقت یہ ہے کہ تمہارے مال اور تمہاری اولاد
فِتْنَةٌ ؕ وَاللّٰهُ	تو ایک آزمائش ہے۔ اور اللہ وہ ہے
عِنْدَهٗۤ اَجْرٌ عَظِيْمٌ ﴿۱۵﴾	جس کے پاس ہے اجرِ عظیم ﴿۱۵﴾
فَاتَّقُوا اللّٰهَ مَا	سو ڈرتے رہو اللہ سے جہاں تک
اسْتَطَعْتُمْ وَاسْمَعُوْا	تمہارے بس میں ہو اور سنو
وَاَطِيْعُوْا وَاَنْفِقُوْا	اور اطاعت کرو اور خرچ کرو
خَيْرًا لِّاَنْفُسِكُمْ ؕ	(یہ امور) بہتر ہیں تمہارے حق میں۔
وَمَنْ يُّوْقَ شُحَّ نَفْسِهٖ	اور جو بچا لیے گئے اپنے دل کے لالچ سے
فَاُولٰٓئِكَ هُمُ الْمُفْلِحُوْنَ ﴿۱۶﴾	سو وہی ہیں درحقیقت فلاح پانے والے ﴿۱۶﴾
اِنْ تُقْرِضُوا اللّٰهَ	اگر قرض دو تم اللہ کو
قَرْضًا حَسَنًا يُّضٰعِفْهُ	قرضِ حسنہ تو وہ اسے بڑھاتا چلا جائے گا
لَكُمْ وَيَغْفِرْ لَكُمْ ؕ	تمہارے لیے اور بخش دے گا تمہارے گناہ۔
وَاللّٰهُ شَكُوْرٌ	اور اللہ ہے بڑا قدردان
حَلِيْمٌ ﴿۱۷﴾	اور بردبار ﴿۱۷﴾
عٰلِمُ الْغَيْبِ وَالشَّهَادَةِ	جاننے والا ہے پوشیدہ اور ظاہر کا،
الْعَزِيْزُ الْحَكِيْمُ ﴿۱۸﴾ ع ۲	زبردست اور بڑی حکمت والا ﴿۱۸﴾

But if you relent to remit and veil in slip
Indeed!
Lord is Lenient and Kind in err and dip

015 Your riches and scion are ordeal in assort
But Proximity of Lord is highest in award

016 So cower and quail Lord, quite in a lot
Then trend to discern and obey to conform
And disburse charity in boons to affirm
That your soul to cherish prime pix in plot
Them to cherish ease and appease in sort

017 If you endow loan to Lord* in pace
That's comely credence in grace

And obey to conform in adore
He'll grow it to credit twice in more

He's to endow absolution in lore
For Allah is most Bounteous in Score

*Give alms to the needy, who otherwise don't beg to entreat even if they stay starving in destitution and are always dedicated for the cause of faith.

018 Lord discerns all secrets and open in plight
He's Exalted in Might
With Sapience in Sagacity so Bright

ایاتھا ١٢ (٦٥) سُورَةُ الطَّلَاقِ مَدَنِيَّةٌ (٩٩) رکوعاتھا ٢

بِسۡمِ اللّٰهِ الرَّحۡمٰنِ الرَّحِيۡمِ

شروع اللہ کے نام سے جو بڑا مہربان نہایت رحم والا ہے

يٰۤاَيُّهَا النَّبِىُّ اِذَا طَلَّقۡتُمُ النِّسَآءَ اے نبیؐ! جب طلاق دو تم عورتوں کو

فَطَلِّقُوۡهُنَّ لِعِدَّتِهِنَّ	تو طلاق دو تم انہیں اس طرح کہ وہ عدت شروع کر سکیں
وَاَحۡصُوا الۡعِدَّةَ ۚ	اور ٹھیک ٹھیک شمار کرو عدت (کے زمانہ) کا۔
وَاتَّقُوا اللّٰهَ رَبَّكُمۡ ۚ	اور ڈرو اللہ سے جو تمہارا رب ہے،
لَا تُخۡرِجُوۡهُنَّ مِنۡۢ بُيُوۡتِهِنَّ	اور نہ نکالو تم انہیں ان کے گھروں سے
وَلَا يَخۡرُجۡنَ اِلَّاۤ اَنۡ يَّاۡتِيۡنَ	اور نہ وہ خود نکلیں اِلّا یہ کہ ارتکاب کریں وہ

بِفَاحِشَةٍ مُّبَيِّنَةٍ ؕ وَتِلۡكَ حُدُوۡدُ اللّٰهِ ؕ کسی کھلی بدکاری کا۔ اور یہ اللہ کی (مقرر کردہ) حدیں ہیں۔

وَمَنۡ يَّتَعَدَّ حُدُوۡدَ اللّٰهِ	اور جو تجاوز کرے گا اللہ کی مقرر کردہ حدود سے
فَقَدۡ ظَلَمَ نَفۡسَهٗ ؕ	تو در حقیقت وہ ظلم کرے گا اپنی ہی جان پر۔
لَا تَدۡرِىۡ لَعَلَّ اللّٰهَ يُحۡدِثُ	نہیں جانتے تم شاید کہ اللہ پیدا کر دے
بَعۡدَ ذٰلِكَ اَمۡرًا ①	اس کے بعد بھی (موافقت کی) کوئی صورت ①
فَاِذَا بَلَغۡنَ اَجَلَهُنَّ	پھر جب وہ پہنچ جائیں اپنی عدت (کے خاتمہ) پر
فَاَمۡسِكُوۡهُنَّ بِمَعۡرُوۡفٍ اَوۡ فَارِقُوۡهُنَّ	پھر روک لو انہیں بھلے طریقے سے یا جدا کر دو انہیں
بِمَعۡرُوۡفٍ وَّاَشۡهِدُوۡا ذَوَىۡ عَدۡلٍ	بھلے طریقے سے اور گواہ بنا لو دو عادل اشخاص کو
مِّنۡكُمۡ وَاَقِيۡمُوا الشَّهَادَةَ	اپنوں میں سے اور (اے مسلمانو!) ٹھیک ٹھیک دو گواہی

065-AL TALAQ

In the name of Lord, the Most Beneficent, Most Merciful

001 O Prophet!
When you intend in divorce to a dame
Divorce at their agreed period of frame

Have rightly (menstrual) cycles in count
And awe and dread Lord in abide
And drive them not, out of reside

Nor shall they leave at their own in stride
But for open sensuality in deride

Lord determines all terms in define
For:
Who violates Lord's term in refine

Indeed!
Oppress and aggrieve his soul in place
You discern it not!
Lord may get you a new pick in pace

002 When they accomplish chosen due in duration*
Either keep them on tolerant terms in relation
Or part them on just terms in condition
Have signatory two men in relation

*Iddah

لِلّٰهِ ؕ ذٰلِكُمْ يُوْعَظُ بِهٖ	اللہ کے لیے ۔ یہ ہے وہ نصیحت جو کی جا رہی ہے
مَنْ كَانَ يُؤْمِنُ	ہر اس شخص کو جو رکھتا ہے ایمان
بِاللّٰهِ وَالْيَوْمِ الْاٰخِرِ ؕ وَمَنْ يَّتَّقِ	اللہ پر اور روزِ آخر پر اور جو شخص ڈرتا رہے گا
اللّٰهَ يَجْعَلْ لَّهٗ مَخْرَجًا ۝٢	اللہ سے پیدا کر دے گا اللہ اس کے لیے نکلنے کی کوئی راہ ۝٢
وَّيَرْزُقْهُ مِنْ حَيْثُ	اور رزق دے گا اسے ایسے طریقے سے جدھر
لَا يَحْتَسِبُ ؕ وَمَنْ يَّتَوَكَّلْ عَلَى اللّٰهِ	اس کا گمان بھی نہ جاتا ہو۔ اور جو بھروسہ کرے اللہ پر
فَهُوَ حَسْبُهٗ ؕ اِنَّ اللّٰهَ	سو وہ اس کے لیے کافی ہے ۔ بلاشبہ اللہ
بَالِغُ اَمْرِهٖ ؕ قَدْ جَعَلَ	پورا کر کے رہتا ہے اپنا ارادہ ۔ بے شک مقرر کر رکھی ہے
اللّٰهُ لِكُلِّ شَيْءٍ قَدْرًا ۝٣	اللہ نے ہر چیز کے لیے ایک تقدیر ۝٣
وَالّٰٓـِٔيْ يَئِسْنَ مِنَ الْمَحِيْضِ مِنْ نِّسَآئِكُمْ	اور تمہاری وہ عورتیں جو مایوس ہو چکی ہوں حیض آنے سے
اِنِ ارْتَبْتُمْ	اگر ان کی عدت کی تعیین میں تمہیں کسی قسم کا شبہ لاحق ہو جائے
فَعِدَّتُهُنَّ ثَلٰثَةُ اَشْهُرٍ ۙ وَّالّٰٓـِٔيْ	تو ان کی عدت تین ماہ ہے اور ان کی بھی جن کو ابھی
لَمْ يَحِضْنَ ؕ وَاُولَاتُ الْاَحْمَالِ	حیض آیا ہی نہ ہو۔ اور حاملہ عورتیں،
اَجَلُهُنَّ اَنْ يَّضَعْنَ حَمْلَهُنَّ ؕ	ان کی عدت یہ ہے کہ بچہ جن لیں ۔
وَمَنْ يَّتَّقِ اللّٰهَ يَجْعَلْ	اور جو شخص ڈرے اللہ سے، پیدا کر دیتا ہے وہ
لَّهٗ مِنْ اَمْرِهٖ يُسْرًا ۝٤	اس کے لیے اس کے معاملہ میں آسانی ۝٤
ذٰلِكَ اَمْرُ اللّٰهِ اَنْزَلَهٗٓ اِلَيْكُمْ ؕ	یہ اللہ کا حکم ہے جو نازل فرما رہا ہے وہ تمہاری طرف۔
وَمَنْ يَّتَّقِ اللّٰهَ يُكَفِّرْ عَنْهُ	اور جو ڈرے گا اللہ سے تو وہ دور کر دے گا اس سے
سَيِّاٰتِهٖ وَيُعْظِمْ لَهٗٓ اَجْرًا ۝٥	اس کی برائیوں کو اور عطا فرمائے گا اس کو بڑا اجر ۝٥

O men of faith,
Settle equity of term in addition
Before Lord, that's caution in concern,

Who concludes in Lord and the Day of Absolve
And those,
Who awe and dread Lord in commotion
He fixes and fits a way, how to resolve

003 Lord will get him the food in stance
That he couldn't deem to concern

If one trusts Lord in reliance so firm
Lord accomplishes His intent in glance
Truly, Lord has determined in plan
For the fate for each notion in stance

Indeed!
(Lord has endowed due in proportion)
(For things even so held in commotion)

004 In menopause*,
Period is months three for a dame
With no courses**, term is also the same

For those who're pregnant at time
Until they deliver the child, in stance

And who awe and dread Lord in glance
Lord will evince an alternate in chance

*Women passed age of monthly courses
** Menstrual cycle

005 Lord ordains definite term in plan
What He ordained (you) in span

If some awe and dread Lord in pace
He'll absolve his dross and dirt in place

And grow in awards in grace
(But not the scum to brace)

أَسْكِنُوهُنَّ مِنْ حَيْثُ سَكَنتُم
رکھو تم ان (مطلقہ عورتوں) کو اسی جگہ جہاں تم خود رہتے ہو

مِّن وُجْدِكُمْ وَلَا تُضَارُّوهُنَّ
جیسی جگہ تمہیں میسر ہو اور نہ ستاؤ تم

لِتُضَيِّقُوا عَلَيْهِنَّ ۚ وَإِن كُنَّ
تنگ کرنے کے لیے انہیں۔ اور اگر ہوں وہ

أُولَاتِ حَمْلٍ فَأَنفِقُوا عَلَيْهِنَّ
حاملہ تو خرچ کرتے رہو تم ان پر

حَتَّىٰ يَضَعْنَ حَمْلَهُنَّ ۚ فَإِنْ أَرْضَعْنَ
یہاں تک کہ ان کے ہاں بچہ ہو جائے۔ پھر اگر وہ دودھ پلائیں

لَكُمْ فَآتُوهُنَّ أُجُورَهُنَّ ۖ
تمہارے لیے (بچے کو) تو دو تم انہیں ان کی اجرت۔

وَأْتَمِرُوا بَيْنَكُم
اور (اجرت کا) معاملہ طے کرو مشورے سے آپس میں

بِمَعْرُوفٍ ۖ وَإِن تَعَاسَرْتُمْ
بھلے طریقے سے اور اگر تم نے ایک دوسرے کو تنگ کیا

فَسَتُرْضِعُ لَهُ أُخْرَىٰ ﴿٦﴾
تو دودھ پلائے گی اسے کوئی دوسری عورت ﴿٦﴾

لِيُنفِقْ ذُو سَعَةٍ مِّن سَعَتِهِ ۖ
اور چاہیے کہ خرچ کرے خوشحال شخص اپنی گنجائش کے مطابق۔

وَمَن قُدِرَ عَلَيْهِ رِزْقُهُ فَلْيُنفِقْ
اور جس شخص کو کم دیا گیا ہو رزق تو وہ خرچ کرے

مِمَّا آتَاهُ اللَّهُ ۚ لَا يُكَلِّفُ
اس میں سے جو دیا ہے اسے اللہ نے۔ نہیں ذمہ داری (کا بوجھ) ڈالتا

اللَّهُ نَفْسًا إِلَّا مَا آتَاهَا ۚ
اللہ کسی جان پر مگر اسی قدر جتنا اس نے دیا ہے اسے ۔

سَيَجْعَلُ اللَّهُ بَعْدَ عُسْرٍ يُسْرًا ﴿٧﴾
امید ہے کہ اللہ عطا فرما دے تنگی کے بعد فراخی ﴿٧﴾

وَكَأَيِّن مِّن قَرْيَةٍ عَتَتْ
اور کتنی ہی بستیاں ہیں جنہوں نے سرکشی کی

عَنْ أَمْرِ رَبِّهَا وَرُسُلِهِ
اپنے رب اور اس کے رسولوں کے احکام سے

فَحَاسَبْنَاهَا حِسَابًا شَدِيدًا
تو محاسبہ کیا ہم نے ان کا سخت ترین محاسبہ

وَعَذَّبْنَاهَا عَذَابًا نُّكْرًا ﴿٨﴾
اور سزا دی انہیں بدترین سزا ﴿٨﴾

فَذَاقَتْ وَبَالَ أَمْرِهَا
سو چکھی انہوں نے سزا اپنے کیے کی

006 Let the dame in Iddah live in favor
As that of yours, similar sort in flavor
As you assert to affirm in savor

Concern and contain them not in pace
And if pregnant, pay their due in grace
Until they give birth in place

If they suckle your baby in stance
Give in amends, to them in span

Have shared course* in conduct
For what's just and fair in instruct

If you're in mess and maze in pace
Let other dame to suckle in place
(On behalf of father in state)

* in the payment of due have proper consultation

007 Let the man of means,
Expend conforming in means
If some is restrained to redeem

So let him spend in concurrence of sort
For what Lord ceded in award

Let him confer so scant in scale
Lord puts no ordeal for some in trail
Past ones ways and means in avail

After a misery in ado
Lord awards a destiny in glow

008 Many a men and clan defiantly defied
Dictum of Lord and His Messengers in deride

Didn't We call to account in severe
So We decreed intense telling in tear

009 Then they did savor of the ills in stance
Finally afflicted of the doom in glance
A damnation was ushered in trance

وَكَانَ عَاقِبَةُ اَمْرِهَا خُسْرًا ۝٩ اور ہوا انجام ان کے معاملہ کا بدترین گھاٹا ۝٩

اَعَدَّ اللّٰهُ لَهُمْ عَذَابًا شَدِيْدًا ۙ مہیا کر رکھا ہے اللہ نے ان کے لیے (آخرت میں) سخت ترین عذاب

فَاتَّقُوا اللّٰهَ يٰۤاُولِي الْاَلْبَابِ ۚۛ سو ڈرتے رہو اللہ سے اے عقل والو، مع

الَّذِيْنَ اٰمَنُوْا ۛۚ قَدْ اَنْزَلَ اللّٰهُ جو ایمان لائے ہو۔ یقیناً اللہ نے نازل کر دی ہے

اِلَيْكُمْ ذِكْرًا ۝١٠ تمہاری طرف ایک نصیحت ۝١٠

رَّسُوْلًا يَّتْلُوْا عَلَيْكُمْ اٰيٰتِ اللّٰهِ (اور بھیجا ہے) ایک ایسا رسول جو پڑھ کر سناتا ہے تمہیں اللہ کی آیات

مُبَيِّنٰتٍ لِّيُخْرِجَ الَّذِيْنَ جو صاف صاف ہدایت دینے والی ہیں تاکہ نکالے اللہ ان لوگوں کو جو

اٰمَنُوْا وَعَمِلُوا الصّٰلِحٰتِ ایمان لائے اور کیے انہوں نے نیک عمل

مِنَ الظُّلُمٰتِ اِلَى النُّوْرِ ۭ تاریکیوں سے روشنی کی طرف۔

وَمَنْ يُّؤْمِنْ بِاللّٰهِ وَيَعْمَلْ اور جو ایمان لائے گا اللہ پر اور کرے گا

صَالِحًا يُّدْخِلْهُ جَنّٰتٍ نیک عمل، داخل کرے گا اسے اللہ ایسی جنتوں میں

تَجْرِيْ مِنْ تَحْتِهَا الْاَنْهٰرُ خٰلِدِيْنَ کہ بہہ رہی ہیں جن کے نیچے نہریں، رہیں گے وہ

فِيْهَاۤ اَبَدًا ۭ قَدْ اَحْسَنَ ان میں ہمیشہ ہمیشہ۔ بہترین رکھا ہے

اللّٰهُ لَهٗ رِزْقًا ۝١١ اللہ نے ایسے شخص کے لیے رزق ۝١١

اَللّٰهُ الَّذِيْ خَلَقَ سَبْعَ سَمٰوٰتٍ اللہ وہ ہستی ہے جس نے پیدا فرمائے سات آسمان

وَّمِنَ الْاَرْضِ مِثْلَهُنَّ ۭ يَتَنَزَّلُ اور زمین کی قسم سے بھی انہی کی مانند۔ نازل ہوتا رہتا ہے

الْاَمْرُ بَيْنَهُنَّ لِتَعْلَمُوْۤا اس کا حکم ان کے درمیان یہ بات تمہیں بتائی جا رہی ہے تاکہ جان لو تم

اَنَّ اللّٰهَ عَلٰي كُلِّ شَيْءٍ قَدِيْرٌ ۙ کہ اللہ ہر چیز پر پوری قدرت رکھتا ہے

ع ٢ وَّاَنَّ اللّٰهَ قَدْ اَحَاطَ بِكُلِّ شَيْءٍ عِلْمًا ۝١٢ اور بلاشبہ اللہ نے احاطہ کر رکھا ہے ہر چیز کا اپنے علم سے ۝١٢

010 Lord determined a discipline in instruct
That's a severe castigation in construct
If they don't tend to be nice in conduct

O men of cognition,
Who awe and dread Lord in escort
(Having the discipline of faith in accord)
For Lord sent you a missive in glow

011 The Messenger!
Who act and recites Verses of Lord in domain
With lucid instruct, he guides to sustain
And escorts the devout in piety to remain

And leads from,
Nadir of gloom to a term in gleam
The man, who affirms in faith
And abides the conduct of faith in grace
Them to reside in Gardens of Bliss in solace

Where stream tide and drift, swirl in flow
There to abide forever in gaiety and glow
Lord gifted in grants
Premium proviso in sort

012 Lord created seven of heavens
And similar count of earth in seven

There's dictum in dictate,
Through the all in relate

That you may care in discern
His care in command to affirm

And it's for Lord in state
Lord gets to grasp in concern
All the effects and equipage in term

آیاتها ١٢ (٦٦) سُوْرَةُ التَّحْرِيْمِ مَدَنِيَّةٌ (١٠٧) رکوعاتها ٢

بِسْمِ اللّٰهِ الرَّحْمٰنِ الرَّحِيْمِ

شروع اللہ کے نام سے جو بڑا مہربان نہایت رحم والا ہے

يٰۤاَيُّهَا النَّبِيُّ لِمَ تُحَرِّمُ مَاۤ اَحَلَّ	اے نبیؐ کیوں حرام کرتے ہو تم وہ چیز جو حلال کی ہے
اللّٰهُ لَكَ ۚ تَبْتَغِيْ مَرْضَاتَ	اللہ نے تمہارے لیے۔(کیا) چاہتے ہو تم (اس طرح) خوشنودی
اَزْوَاجِكَ ۗ وَ اللّٰهُ غَفُوْرٌ رَّحِيْمٌ ①	اپنی بیویوں کی؟ اور اللہ ہے بہت معاف کرنے والا، رحم فرمانے والا ①
قَدْ فَرَضَ اللّٰهُ لَكُمْ	یقیناً مقرر کر دیا ہے اللہ نے تمہارے لیے
تَحِلَّةَ اَيْمَانِكُمْ ۚ وَ اللّٰهُ مَوْلٰىكُمْ ۚ	اپنی قسموں کی پابندی سے نکلنے کا طریقہ اور اللہ ہی تمہارا آقا ہے
وَ هُوَ الْعَلِيْمُ الْحَكِيْمُ ②	اور وہ ہے سب کچھ جاننے والا اور بڑی حکمت والا ②
وَ اِذْ اَسَرَّ النَّبِيُّ اِلٰى بَعْضِ اَزْوَاجِهٖ	اور جب رازدارانہ انداز میں بتائی نبیؐ نے اپنی کسی بیوی کو
حَدِيْثًا ۚ فَلَمَّا نَبَّاَتْ بِهٖ	ایک بات۔ پھر جب بتادی اس نے وہ بات (کسی دوسری کو)
وَ اَظْهَرَهُ اللّٰهُ عَلَيْهِ عَرَّفَ	اور ظاہر کر دیا اسے اللہ نے اپنے نبیؐ پر تو اطلاع دی نبیؐ نے
بَعْضَهٗ وَ اَعْرَضَ عَنْۢ بَعْضٍ ۚ	اس کی کسی حد تک اور درگزر کیا ایک حد تک
فَلَمَّا نَبَّاَهَا بِهٖ	پھر جب خبر دی اس نے بات کی اپنی اسی بیوی کو
قَالَتْ مَنْ اَنْۢبَاَكَ هٰذَا ۚ	تو وہ کہنے لگی کس نے خبر دی ہے آپ کو اس بات کی؟
قَالَ نَبَّاَنِيَ	نبیؐ نے فرمایا مجھے خبر دی ہے اس کی
الْعَلِيْمُ الْخَبِيْرُ ③	اس نے جو سب کچھ جاننے والا اور پوری طرح باخبر ہے ③
اِنْ تَتُوْبَاۤ اِلَى اللّٰهِ	اگر توبہ کرلو تم دونوں اللہ کے حضور (تو یہ بہتر ہے تمہارے لیے)

066-AL TAHRIM

In the name of Lord, the Most Beneficent, Most Merciful

001 O Prophet!
Why you ban (for you) in pace
What Lord made licit (for you) to brace

You pursue to please your spouses in glee
But Lord is Bounteous and Kind to thee

002 Lord has affirmed before in stance
Dissolution in your pledge in trance
Lord is to protect you here in glance

He's Profound in Lore
With Sense of Sapience in adore

003 When Prophet,
Told a matter of concern,
To one of his spouses in pace
But she disclosed it to other in place

And Lord revealed (it him) for the same
He affirmed (it to her) a part to sustain*
And cast off a part, hidden to remain

When he told her the secret of the talk
She said:
Who told you of all the secret in talk
He, Who is in,
The know of all the things in pace

*Prophet partly disclosed the secret to her, (as revealed by Allah Almighty),

004 If you both trend to Lord in regret
That's really perfect,(for you) in select

For your veer of core had bent in slight
But if you each oppose (him) in plight

فَقَدْ صَغَتْ قُلُوْبُكُمَا ج
اس لیے کہ ہٹ گئے تھے سیدھی راہ سے تمہارے دل

وَاِنْ تَظٰهَرَا عَلَيْهِ
اور اگر ایکا کر لیا تم نے نبیؐ کے مقابلے میں

فَاِنَّ اللّٰهَ هُوَ مَوْلٰىهُ وَجِبْرِيْلُ
تو جان رکھو کہ اللہ اس کا مولیٰ ہے اور جبریلؑ

وَصَالِحُ الْمُؤْمِنِيْنَ ۚ وَالْمَلٰٓئِكَةُ
اور تمام صالح اہلِ ایمان اور ملائکہ

بَعْدَ ذٰلِكَ ظَهِيْرٌ ﴿٤﴾
اس کے بعد اس کے مددگار ہیں ﴿٤﴾

عَسٰى رَبُّهٗٓ اِنْ طَلَّقَكُنَّ
بعید نہیں کہ اگر طلاق دے دے وہ تمہیں تو اس کا رب

اَنْ يُّبْدِلَهٗٓ اَزْوَاجًا خَيْرًا مِّنْكُنَّ
بدلے میں دے اسے ایسی بیویاں جو بہتر ہوں تم سے۔

مُسْلِمٰتٍ مُّؤْمِنٰتٍ قٰنِتٰتٍ
مسلمان، مومن، اطاعت شعار

تٰٓئِبٰتٍ عٰبِدٰتٍ سٰٓئِحٰتٍ
توبہ کرنے والیاں، عبادت گزار اور روزہ رکھنے والیاں

ثَيِّبٰتٍ وَّاَبْكَارًا ﴿٥﴾
خواہ شوہر دیدہ ہوں یا کنواریاں ﴿٥﴾

يٰٓاَيُّهَا الَّذِيْنَ اٰمَنُوْا قُوْٓا اَنْفُسَكُمْ
اے لوگو جو ایمان لائے ہو، بچاؤ اپنے آپ کو

وَاَهْلِيْكُمْ نَارًا وَّقُوْدُهَا النَّاسُ
اور اپنے اہل و عیال کو اس آگ سے جس کا ایندھن انسان

وَالْحِجَارَةُ عَلَيْهَا مَلٰٓئِكَةٌ
اور پتھر ہوں گے جن پر مقرر ہیں ایسے فرشتے جو

غِلَاظٌ شِدَادٌ لَّا يَعْصُوْنَ
نہایت تند خو اور سخت گیر ہیں، جو کبھی نافرمانی نہیں کرتے

اللّٰهَ مَآ اَمَرَهُمْ
اللہ کی اس حکم کے بجالانے میں جو وہ انہیں دے

وَيَفْعَلُوْنَ مَا يُؤْمَرُوْنَ ﴿٦﴾
اور جو کر گزرتے ہیں ہر وہ کام جس کا انہیں حکم دیا جاتا ہے ﴿٦﴾

يٰٓاَيُّهَا الَّذِيْنَ كَفَرُوْا لَا تَعْتَذِرُوا الْيَوْمَ ط
اے کفر کرنے والو بہانے نہ بناؤ آج۔

اِنَّمَا تُجْزَوْنَ
صرف ویسا ہی بدلہ دیا جا رہا ہے تم کو

ع ١ مَا كُنْتُمْ تَعْمَلُوْنَ ﴿٧﴾
جیسے عمل تم کرتے رہے ﴿٧﴾

And aid and abet each in plight
Against the prophet of Lord in delight

Indeed!
Lord is to defend (him)* in all slip in slide
Besides,
Gabriel, Angels and men of faith in abide
Around in surround, sustain (him) in stride

*Prophet

005 May be, if he's to divorce spouses in all
Lord is to confer caring spouses at call

Better to comply in skill and drill
Who accede to accept, are saintly in skill

Who trend in regret to Lord in stay
Who exalt and esteem Lord in pray

Who pray to beseech so humble in pace
Who abide the drill of discipline in Faith

Keep fast in compliance of lore
Even once wedded or virgin so pure

006 O you the men of Faith in sway
Be watchful of a Fire in array

Fuel of that, men and rock in flash
O'er there're,
Angels strict and satirical to smash

Who waver and stagger not a bit in slight
And pursue the Dictum of Lord in plight

007 The angels would then assert in pace
O you the men defying in faith
Make no plea in play this Day in place

That's the needed punish in daze
For what you accomplished* in maze

*worldly life

يَا أَيُّهَا الَّذِينَ آمَنُوا تُوبُوا
اے لوگو جو ایمان لائے ہو توبہ کرو

إِلَى اللَّهِ تَوْبَةً نَصُوحًا ۖ
اللہ کے حضور خالص توبہ۔

عَسَى رَبُّكُمْ أَنْ يُكَفِّرَ عَنْكُمْ
کچھ بعید نہیں کہ تمہارا رب دور فرما دے تم سے

سَيِّئَاتِكُمْ وَيُدْخِلَكُمْ جَنَّاتٍ
تمہاری برائیاں اور داخل کرے تمہیں ایسی جنتوں میں

تَجْرِي مِنْ تَحْتِهَا الْأَنْهَارُ
کہ بہہ رہی ہیں جن کے نیچے نہریں

يَوْمَ لَا يُخْزِي اللَّهُ النَّبِيَّ
اس دن جب نہ رسوا کرے گا اللہ نبیؐ کو

وَالَّذِينَ آمَنُوا مَعَهُ ۖ
اور ان لوگوں کو جو ایمان لائے اس کے ساتھ ۔

نُورُهُمْ يَسْعَى بَيْنَ أَيْدِيهِمْ
ان کا نور دوڑ رہا ہوگا ان کے آگے آگے

وَبِأَيْمَانِهِمْ يَقُولُونَ
اور ان کے دائیں جانب اور وہ کہہ رہے ہوں گے

رَبَّنَا أَتْمِمْ لَنَا نُورَنَا
اے ہمارے رب! مکمل کر دے ہمارے لیے ہمارا نور

وَاغْفِرْ لَنَا ۖ إِنَّكَ عَلَى كُلِّ شَيْءٍ قَدِيرٌ ﴿٨﴾
اور درگزر فرما ہم سے ۔یقیناً تو ہر بات پر پوری قدرت رکھتا ہے ﴿٨﴾

يَا أَيُّهَا النَّبِيُّ جَاهِدِ الْكُفَّارَ
اے نبیؐ! جہاد کرو کافروں سے

وَالْمُنَافِقِينَ وَاغْلُظْ عَلَيْهِمْ ۚ
اور منافقوں سے اور سختی سے پیش آؤ ان کے ساتھ ۔

وَمَأْوَاهُمْ جَهَنَّمُ ۖ
اور ان کا ٹھکانہ جہنم ہے ۔

وَبِئْسَ الْمَصِيرُ ﴿٩﴾
اور بہت ہی برا ہے وہ ٹھکانہ ﴿٩﴾

ضَرَبَ اللَّهُ مَثَلًا لِلَّذِينَ
مثال پیش کرتا ہے اللہ ان لوگوں کے بارے میں جو

كَفَرُوا امْرَأَتَ نُوحٍ وَامْرَأَتَ لُوطٍ ۖ
کافر ہیں، نوحؑ کی بیوی اور لوطؑ کی بیوی کی ۔

كَانَتَا تَحْتَ عَبْدَيْنِ
تھیں یہ دونوں دو ایسے بندوں کی زوجیت میں

مِنْ عِبَادِنَا صَالِحَيْنِ
جو تھے ہمارے صالح بندوں میں سے

008 O you the men of Faith in course
Trend to Lord sincere in remorse

With care and concern in stance
Lord will remove your ills in glance

And admit you to the Gardens in gleam
Wherein streams,
Below and aside, surge in sway
Lord wouldn't humble Prophet in esteem
Besides the men of faith in stay

Their beam and gleam evince in glow
Ahead and behind and to the right

Then they'll beg and beseech Lord in plight
Complete our glimmer of glow in gleam

And absolve our evils of ills in slight
For, you've the sway over all in plight

009 O Prophet!
Fight for the cause of Allah in vale
Against the Dissenters and Hypocrites in trail

Be resolute in your term of discipline in preach
Them to reside Hell, an evil site in screech

010 Lord gives,
Citation for dissenters to discern
Spouse of Noah and that of Lut in term

فَخَانَتٰهُمَا	تو خیانت کی ان دونوں نے اپنے شوہروں سے
فَلَمْ يُغْنِيَا عَنْهُمَا	سو نہ کام آسکے یہ دونوں ان کو
مِنَ اللّٰهِ شَيْـًٔا	اللہ سے بچانے میں ذرا بھی
وَّقِيْلَ ادْخُلَا	اور کہا گیا ان سے کہ داخل ہو جاؤ تم دونوں
النَّارَ مَعَ الدّٰخِلِيْنَ ۱۰	جہنم میں ۔ دوسرے جلنے والوں کے ساتھ ۱۰
وَضَرَبَ اللّٰهُ	اور پیش کرتا ہے اللہ
مَثَلًا لِّلَّذِيْنَ اٰمَنُوا	مثال اہلِ ایمان کے بارے میں
امْرَاَتَ فِرْعَوْنَ م	فرعون کی بیوی کی ۔
اِذْ قَالَتْ رَبِّ	جب اس نے کہا تھا کہ اے میرے رب!
ابْنِ لِيْ عِنْدَكَ بَيْتًا	بنا دے تو میرے لیے اپنے پاس ایک گھر
فِي الْجَنَّةِ وَنَجِّنِيْ	جنت میں اور نجات دے تو مجھے
مِنْ فِرْعَوْنَ وَعَمَلِهٖ	فرعون سے اور اس کے (برے) عملوں سے
وَنَجِّنِيْ مِنَ الْقَوْمِ الظّٰلِمِيْنَ ۱۱	اور نجات دے تو مجھے اس ظالم قوم سے ۱۱
وَمَرْيَمَ ابْنَتَ عِمْرٰنَ	اور (دوسری مثال) مریم بنتِ عمران کی ہے
الَّتِيْٓ اَحْصَنَتْ فَرْجَهَا	جس نے حفاظت کی تھی اپنی شرمگاہ کی
فَنَفَخْنَا فِيْهِ	پھر پھونک دی ہم نے اس کے اندر
مِنْ رُّوْحِنَا وَصَدَّقَتْ	اپنی طرف سے روح اور تصدیق کی اس نے
بِكَلِمٰتِ رَبِّهَا وَكُتُبِهٖ	اپنے رب کے ارشادات کی اور اس کی کتابوں کی
وَكَانَتْ مِنَ الْقٰنِتِيْنَ ۱۲	اور تھی وہ اطاعت شعاروں میں سے ۱۲

وقف لازم

رکوع

They're spouses of two, My men in grace
Who're the virtuous savants, Mine in pace

But they're* not true to their spouses in way
They gain and attain not, before Lord in stay

So they're told for that reason in base
Enter you the Fire, a dejected of place

*Wives

011 Lord refers a fable in stance
For the men of faith to glance

Wife of Pharaoh:
As she begged Lord in entreat
Grant me your contiguity in beseech
A reside in the Garden of bliss in treat

And deliver,
Me of Pharaoh and from his ills in drill
And rescue me of the men cruel in still

012 There's another citation to aside
Mary the daughter of Imran in abide
Who secured her innocence there in stride

We infused Our spirit therein prime
She,
Affirmed the Words of Lord in sublime
And His Revelations in rhyme so refine

She was of the pietistic in decent
And seemly and sublime in consent

سُوْرَةُ الْمُلْكِ مَكِّيَّةٌ (٦٧)

اٰیاتھا ٣٠ — (٧٧) — رکوعاتھا ٢

بِسْمِ اللّٰهِ الرَّحْمٰنِ الرَّحِيْمِ

شروع اللہ کے نام سے جو بڑا مہربان نہایت رحم والا ہے

تَبٰرَكَ الَّذِيْ بِيَدِهِ الْمُلْكُ	بڑی بابرکت ہے وہ ذات جس کے ہاتھ میں ہے بادشاہی
وَهُوَ عَلٰى كُلِّ شَيْءٍ قَدِيْرُ (١)	اور وہ ہر چیز پر پوری طرح قادر ہے (١)
الَّذِيْ خَلَقَ الْمَوْتَ وَالْحَيٰوةَ	وہ ذات جس نے پیدا کیا موت اور زندگی کو
لِيَبْلُوَكُمْ اَيُّكُمْ اَحْسَنُ	تاکہ آزمائش کرے تمہاری کہ کون تم میں سے زیادہ اچھا ہے
عَمَلًا ؕ وَهُوَ الْعَزِيْزُ الْغَفُوْرُ (٢)	عمل میں۔ اور وہ ہے زبردست، بے انتہا معاف فرمانے والا (٢)
الَّذِيْ خَلَقَ سَبْعَ سَمٰوٰتٍ طِبَاقًا ؕ	وہ ذات جس نے بنائے سات آسمان تہ بہ تہ۔
مَا تَرٰى فِيْ خَلْقِ الرَّحْمٰنِ مِنْ تَفٰوُتٍ ؕ	نہ دیکھو گے تم رحمٰن کی تخلیق میں کوئی بے ربطی۔
فَارْجِعِ الْبَصَرَ ۙ هَلْ تَرٰى مِنْ فُطُوْرٍ (٣)	ذرا آنکھ اٹھا کر دیکھو بھلا نظر آتا ہے تم کو کوئی خلل؟ (٣)
ثُمَّ ارْجِعِ الْبَصَرَ كَرَّتَيْنِ يَنْقَلِبْ	پھر دوڑاؤ نظر بار بار پلٹ آئے گی
اِلَيْكَ الْبَصَرُ خَاسِئًا وَّهُوَ حَسِيْرٌ (٤)	تمہاری طرف نگاہ تھک کر اور وہ نامراد ہوگی (خلل کی تلاش میں) (٤)
وَلَقَدْ زَيَّنَّا السَّمَآءَ الدُّنْيَا	اور بے شک آراستہ کیا ہے ہم نے آسمانِ دنیا کو
بِمَصَابِيْحَ وَجَعَلْنٰهَا رُجُوْمًا	چراغوں سے اور بنا دیا ہے ہم نے انہیں مار بھگانے کا ذریعہ
لِّلشَّيٰطِيْنِ وَاَعْتَدْنَا لَهُمْ	شیاطین کو اور مہیا کر رکھا ہے ہم نے ان کے لیے
عَذَابَ السَّعِيْرِ (٥)	دہکتی آگ کا عذاب (٥)
وَلِلَّذِيْنَ كَفَرُوْا بِرَبِّهِمْ	اور ہے ان لوگوں کے لیے جنہوں نے کفر کیا اپنے رب کے ساتھ

067-AL MULK

In the name of Lord, the Most Beneficent, Most Merciful

001 Blessed be The Lord of All the Domains
Who Controls in Command all to sustain

002 Lord,
Created the life and demise in doom
That He may put you to trial in bloom

And determine of you, the best in incline
Who trends to truth for the best in prime
He is Exalted in Might so Kind and Sublime

003 He created skies in series of seven
There's no want in slant in term of creation
Most Amiable is Lord, immense in initiation

So trend your looks once more to the heaven
Can you discern a bit of slit in this generation

004 Then trend and talent anew in quest
You're denied of flaw in behest
Not even perplexity or poop in the rest

005 We adorned,
With stars nethermost sky in sway
And put some stars as missile in array

To drive out the Devil, deprave in stray
And fixed burn of blaze, them to stay

جہنم کا عذاب اور (وہ) بہت برا ہے ٹھکانہ (٦)	عذابُ جهنّم ۖ وبئس المصير (٦)
جب پھینکے جائیں گے وہ اس میں تو سنیں گے اس کی	إذا أُلقوا فيها سمعوا لها
دھاڑنے کی آواز اور وہ جوش کھا رہی ہوگی (٧)	شهيقًا وهي تفور (٧)
اس قدر کہ قریب ہے پھٹ جائے وہ شدتِ غضب سے ۔	تكاد تميّز من الغيظ ۖ
جب بھی ڈالا جائے گا اس میں کوئی گروہ	كلّما أُلقي فيها فوج
تو پوچھیں گے ان سے جہنم کے داروغہ ،	سألهم خزنتها
کیا نہیں آیا تھا تمہارے پاس کوئی متنبہ کرنے والا؟ (٨)	ألم يأتكم نذير (٨)
وہ جواب دیں گے کیوں نہیں بے شک آیا تھا ہمارے پاس	قالوا بلىٰ قد جاءنا
متنبہ کرنے والا، لیکن ہم نے اس کو جھٹلایا اور کہا	نذير ۙ فكذّبنا وقلنا
نہیں نازل کیا اللہ نے کچھ بھی۔ نہیں ہو تم	ما نزّل الله من شيء ۖ إن أنتم
مگر پڑے ہوئے بڑی گمراہی میں (٩)	إلّا في ضلال كبير (٩)
اور کہیں گے وہ کاش سنتے ہم اور عقل و شعور کو استعمال کرتے	وقالوا لو كنّا نسمع أو نعقل
تو نہ ہوتے ہم دوزخیوں میں (١٠)	ما كنّا في أصحٰب السعير (١٠)
سو اقرار کرلیں گے وہ اپنے گناہ کا ۔	فاعترفوا بذنبهم ۚ
پس لعنت ہے دوزخیوں پر (١١)	فسحقًا لأصحٰب السعير (١١)
بے شک وہ لوگ جو ڈرتے ہیں اپنے رب سے	إنّ الذين يخشون ربّهم
بن دیکھے ان کے لیے ہے مغفرت اور بڑا اجر (١٢)	بالغيب لهم مغفرة وأجر كبير (١٢)
اور آہستہ کہو تم اپنی بات یا اونچی آواز سے ۔	وأسرّوا قولكم أو اجهروا به ۖ
بے شک وہ پوری طرح باخبر ہے سینوں کے بھیدوں سے (١٣)	إنّه عليم بذات الصدور (١٣)

006 Those who deny their Lord in Bloom
They're destined to burn of blaze in doom
Hell: A baseness upshot, a gust in gloom

007 When they're tossed in the boom*
They'll listen grunt of grief in alarm
The pant and sigh of fiery flaming in swarm

*Hell

008 Bursting in frenzy rumpus in array
Each time,
When a band is hurled therein stray
Guards trend to ask, utter in dismay
Didn't you've Messenger of Lord to obey

009 Certainly;
There was Warner for us to escort
But we deserted him defying in sort

But we said to the prophets of Lord:
Lord never assigned a word in dictate
You're but villainous delusive in state

010 Subsequently they'll assert in pace
If ever we'd heeded in trace
To the word of prophets in place

Herein, we wouldn't
Be as the burn of Fire in blaze
011 They'll admit their evil conduct in daze

But they wouldn't be eased in assuage
From the burn of blaze in refuse

012 As for men and clan in place
Who revere and cower their Lord to pace
The Lord, Who never evinced* in trace
There's relief and reprieve held in grace
With reverent reward them to brace

*Faith in the Unseen (Page : 1)

013 Whether you concern hidden in lore
Or talk of some openly sure
He certainly Discerns the secrets of core

أَلَا يَعْلَمُ مَنْ خَلَقَ ؕ	بھلا وہی نہ جانے جس نے پیدا کیا۔
وَهُوَ اللَّطِيفُ الْخَبِيرُ ﴿١٤﴾ ع ١	حالانکہ وہ ہے باریک بین اور پوری طرح باخبر ﴿١٤﴾
هُوَ الَّذِي جَعَلَ لَكُمُ الْأَرْضَ	وہی تو ہے جس نے کر دیا ہے تمہاری خاطر زمین کو
ذَلُولًا فَامْشُوا فِي مَنَاكِبِهَا	(تمہارا) تابع سو چلو پھرو اس کی چھاتی پر
وَكُلُوا مِن رِّزْقِهِ ۖ وَإِلَيْهِ النُّشُورُ ﴿١٥﴾	اور کھاؤ اللہ کا رزق اور اسی کے حضور تمہیں دوبارہ اٹھ کر جانا ہے ﴿١٥﴾
أَأَمِنتُم مَّن فِي السَّمَاءِ	کیا تم بے خوف ہو اس سے جو آسمان میں ہے
أَن يَخْسِفَ بِكُمُ الْأَرْضَ	اس بات سے کہ دھنسا دے تم کو زمین میں
فَإِذَا هِيَ تَمُورُ ﴿١٦﴾	اور اچانک وہ لرزنے لگے؟ ﴿١٦﴾
أَمْ أَمِنتُم مَّن فِي السَّمَاءِ	یا تم بے خوف ہو اس سے جو آسمان میں ہے
أَن يُرْسِلَ عَلَيْكُمْ حَاصِبًا ؕ	اس بات سے کہ بھیج دے تم پر پتھراؤ کرنے والی ہوا؟
فَسَتَعْلَمُونَ كَيْفَ نَذِيرِ ﴿١٧﴾	سو عنقریب تم کو معلوم ہو جائے گا کہ کیسی تھی میری تنبیہ! ﴿١٧﴾
وَلَقَدْ كَذَّبَ الَّذِينَ مِن قَبْلِهِمْ	اور بے شک جھٹلا چکے ہیں وہ جو ان سے پہلے تھے
فَكَيْفَ كَانَ نَكِيرِ ﴿١٨﴾	تو دیکھ لو کیسا تھا میرا عذاب ﴿١٨﴾
أَوَلَمْ يَرَوْا إِلَى الطَّيْرِ فَوْقَهُمْ	اور کیا نہیں دیکھا ان لوگوں نے اڑتے پرندوں کو اپنے اوپر
صَافَّاتٍ وَيَقْبِضْنَ ۘ	پر پھیلاتے اور سکیڑتے؟
مَا يُمْسِكُهُنَّ إِلَّا الرَّحْمَٰنُ ۚ	نہیں تھامے ہوئے ہے انہیں کوئی سوائے رحمٰن کے۔
إِنَّهُ بِكُلِّ شَيْءٍ بَصِيرٌ ﴿١٩﴾	بے شک وہ ہر چیز کا نگہبان ہے ﴿١٩﴾
أَمَّنْ هَٰذَا الَّذِي هُوَ جُندٌ لَّكُمْ	بھلا وہ کون ہے جو لشکر بنے تمہارا
يَنصُرُكُم مِّن دُونِ الرَّحْمَٰنِ ۚ	اور مدد کرے تمہاری رحمٰن کے مقابلے میں؟

014 Shouldn't He discern in pace
For what He created of all in place

He discerns the trivial of the sieve in riddle
And is proficient of all the puzzles in trace

015 Lord made the earth in your command
So you trek in trail therein demand

And relish His bestowal in treat
And Unto Him,
That's Revival and Return is proceeds

016 Do you feel safe and secure to assume
Lord wouldn't let to (you) consume
When earth quiver and shiver in doom

017 Or do you feel safe and secure in trends
That Lord,
In heavens wouldn't trend in amends

A twister in storm in alarm
With showers of stones in throng

So you may affirm and confirm in pace
How terrible is My discipline in place

018 Indeed!
Men deserted My reproach in plight
So how stifling was My rebuke in blight

019 Don't they discern the birds in fly
Whipping aside their wings in sky
None, but Lord let them fly so high
Indeed!
He holds His control over all in skies

020 But No!
Who's to help as your defense in force
Besides the Mercy of Lord in endorse

إِنِ الْكٰفِرُوْنَ إِلَّا فِيْ غُرُوْرٍ ۚ ﴿٢٠﴾	نہیں ہیں یہ کافر مگر پڑے ہوئے ہیں دھوکے میں ﴿٢٠﴾
أَمَّنْ هٰذَا الَّذِيْ يَرْزُقُكُمْ	بھلا کون ہے وہ جو روزی دے تم کو
إِنْ أَمْسَكَ رِزْقَهٗ ۚ	اگر روک لے رحمٰن اپنا رزق؟
بَلْ لَّجُّوْا فِيْ عُتُوٍّ	دراصل اڑے ہوئے ہیں یہ (کافر) سرکشی
وَّنُفُوْرٍ ﴿٢١﴾	اور حق سے نفرت پر ﴿٢١﴾
أَفَمَنْ يَّمْشِيْ مُكِبًّا	بھلا وہ شخص جو چل رہا ہو اوندھا ہو کر
عَلٰى وَجْهِهٖٓ أَهْدٰٓى أَمَّنْ	اپنے منہ کے بل زیادہ ہدایت یافتہ ہے یا وہ جو
يَّمْشِيْ سَوِيًّا عَلٰى صِرَاطٍ مُّسْتَقِيْمٍ ﴿٢٢﴾	چل رہا ہو بالکل سیدھا سیدھے راستے پر؟ ﴿٢٢﴾
قُلْ هُوَ الَّذِيْٓ	کہو! وہی تو ہے جس نے
أَنْشَاَكُمْ وَجَعَلَ لَكُمُ	پیدا کیا تمہیں اور بنائے ہیں تمہارے لیے
السَّمْعَ وَالْأَبْصَارَ وَالْأَفْـِٕدَةَ ۚ	کان، آنکھیں اور مراکزِ حواس (دل ودماغ)۔
قَلِيْلًا مَّا تَشْكُرُوْنَ ﴿٢٣﴾	مگر تم کم ہی شکر ادا کرتے ہو ﴿٢٣﴾
قُلْ هُوَ الَّذِيْ	کہو! وہی تو ہے جس نے
ذَرَاَكُمْ فِي الْأَرْضِ	پھیلایا تم کو زمین میں
وَإِلَيْهِ تُحْشَرُوْنَ ﴿٢٤﴾	اور اسی کے حضور تم اکٹھے کیے جاؤ گے ﴿٢٤﴾
وَيَقُوْلُوْنَ مَتٰى هٰذَا الْوَعْدُ	اور کہتے ہیں یہ کب پوری ہوگی یہ دھمکی
إِنْ كُنْتُمْ صٰدِقِيْنَ ﴿٢٥﴾	اگر ہو تم سچے ﴿٢٥﴾
قُلْ إِنَّمَا الْعِلْمُ	کہہ دو بس اس کا علم تو صرف
عِنْدَ اللّٰهِ ۪ وَإِنَّمَآ أَنَا	اللہ کے پاس ہے۔ اور بس میں تو

Infidels are but to stay in delusion
For Bounty of Lord,
They're held in confusion

021 Or who's there in place
That can cede sustenance in pace

It's but The Bounty of Lord in Grace
If He's to restrain provisions in trace

There's none to endow a bit in bite
Never, they stubbornly endure in plight
Audacious in sin and eluding truth in bright

022 Who's orderly conducted in grace
One ,who walks in pace
Pitching and plunging creepy on face
Or the one
Who walks evenly caring comely in grace

023 Say:
It's He, Who created you in term
Conforming to grow, due in concern
Endowed you a sense of hearing in return

An to see, feel and discern in pace
But you don't appreciate a bit in trace

024 <u>Say: Lord is He, Who spread in pace,</u>
<u>Your race around the globe in grace*</u>

In profusion
And to Him you'll return in response
And assemblage therein trance
*initial creation of the human race from Africa 200,000
years before later spread all over the globe (Page : 621)

025 They ask:
If in truth, you're determined in call
When is the pledge conforming in toll

026 Say: As for the time and term
It's with My Lord to concern

نَذِيْرٌ مُّبِيْنٌ ﴿٢٦﴾	متنبہ کرنے والا ہوں، واضح طور پر ﴿٢٦﴾
فَلَمَّا رَاَوْهُ	پھر جب دیکھیں گے وہ اس کو
زُلْفَةً سِيْٓـَٔتْ	قریب تو بگڑ جائیں گے
وُجُوْهُ الَّذِيْنَ	چہرے ان لوگوں کے جنہوں نے
كَفَرُوْا وَقِيْلَ	کفر کیا تھا اور کہا جائے گا
هٰذَا الَّذِيْ	یہی تو ہے وہ جس کا
كُنْتُمْ بِهٖ تَدَّعُوْنَ ﴿٢٧﴾	تم تقاضا کرتے تھے ﴿٢٧﴾
قُلْ اَرَءَيْتُمْ	کہو! کیا سوچا تم نے
اِنْ اَهْلَكَنِيَ اللّٰهُ	جبکہ یہ بھی ممکن ہے کہ ہلاک کر دے مجھے اللہ
وَمَنْ مَّعِيَ اَوْ رَحِمَنَا ۙ	اور ان کو بھی جو میرے ساتھ ہیں یا رحم فرمائے ہم پر
فَمَنْ يُّجِيْرُ	تو بھلا کون ہے جو بچالے
الْكٰفِرِيْنَ مِنْ عَذَابٍ اَلِيْمٍ ﴿٢٨﴾	کافروں کو دردناک عذاب سے؟ ﴿٢٨﴾
قُلْ هُوَ الرَّحْمٰنُ	کہہ دو! وہ رحمٰن ہے
اٰمَنَّا بِهٖ وَعَلَيْهِ	ایمان لائے ہم اس پر اور اسی پر
تَوَكَّلْنَا ۚ فَسَتَعْلَمُوْنَ	بھروسہ ہے ہمارا۔ سو عنقریب معلوم ہو جائے گا تمہیں
مَنْ هُوَ فِيْ ضَلٰلٍ مُّبِيْنٍ ﴿٢٩﴾	کہ کون پڑا ہوا ہے کھلی گمراہی میں ﴿٢٩﴾
قُلْ اَرَءَيْتُمْ اِنْ اَصْبَحَ	کہو! کیا تم نے سوچا کہ اگر ہو جائے
مَآؤُكُمْ غَوْرًا فَمَنْ	تمہارا پانی خشک تو کون ہے جو
ع ٢ يَّاْتِيْكُمْ بِمَآءٍ مَّعِيْنٍ ﴿٣٠﴾	لائے تمہارے لیے چشمے کا پانی؟ ﴿٣٠﴾

I'm but,
To admonish in an adorable call to concern

027 Eventually when they discern it close and aside
Upset will be the faces of Cynics in stride

And they'll be told:
That's pledged and so affirmed in pace
For what you're calling to face in place

028 Say:
You discern and concern hither in abide
If Lord was to destroy me and with all in aside

Or if He bestows His compassion in call
But there's none to cede or save cynics in toll

029 Say: Lord is Most Gracious to brace
And we trusted Him all in grace

And to Him we affirm in faith
So, soon you discern and concern in faith
Who's in diverse boner and blunder of faith

030 Say:
Did you ever care a bit in span
If one morn,
Your stream gets rapt in the land
Who's then to get you plain water in plan

سُوْرَةُ الْقَلَمِ مَكِّيَّةٌ (٦٨)

اٰياتها ٥٢ (٢) ركوعاتها ٢

بِسْمِ اللّٰهِ الرَّحْمٰنِ الرَّحِيْمِ

شروع اللہ کے نام سے جو بڑا مہربان نہایت رحم والا ہے

نٓ وَالْقَلَمِ وَمَا يَسْطُرُوْنَ ①	نون ۔ قسم ہے قلم کی اور اس چیز کی جسے لکھتے ہیں ①
مَآ اَنْتَ بِنِعْمَةِ رَبِّكَ بِمَجْنُوْنٍ ②	نہیں ہو تم اپنے رب کے فضل سے دیوانہ ②
وَاِنَّ لَكَ لَاَجْرًا غَيْرَ مَمْنُوْنٍ ③	اور یقیناً تمہارے لیے ہے اجر، بے انتہا ③
وَ اِنَّكَ لَعَلٰى خُلُقٍ عَظِيْمٍ ④	اور بے شک تم فائز ہو اخلاق کے بڑے مرتبے پر ④
فَسَتُبْصِرُ وَ يُبْصِرُوْنَ ⑤	سو عنقریب تم بھی دیکھ لوگے اور وہ بھی دیکھ لیں گے ⑤
بِاَيِّيكُمُ الْمَفْتُوْنُ ⑥	کہ تم میں سے کون ہے دیوانہ ⑥
اِنَّ رَبَّكَ هُوَ اَعْلَمُ	بے شک تمہارا رب ہی خوب جانتا ہے
بِمَنْ ضَلَّ عَنْ سَبِيْلِهٖ	ان کو بھی جو بھٹک گئے اس کی راہ سے
وَهُوَ اَعْلَمُ بِالْمُهْتَدِيْنَ ⑦	اور وہ خوب جانتا ہے ان کو بھی جو راہِ راست پر ہیں ⑦
فَلَا تُطِعِ الْمُكَذِّبِيْنَ ⑧	پس نہ کہا ماننا تم جھٹلانے والوں کا ⑧
وَدُّوْا لَوْ تُدْهِنُ	یہ تو چاہتے ہیں کہ کسی طرح تم (تبلیغِ دین میں) ڈھیلے پڑ جاؤ
فَيُدْهِنُوْنَ ⑨	تو وہ بھی (تمہاری مخالفت میں) ڈھیلے پڑ جائیں ⑨
وَلَا تُطِعْ كُلَّ	لیکن تم ہرگز نہ کہا ماننا کسی ایسے شخص کا
حَلَّافٍ مَّهِيْنٍ ⑩	جو ہے بہت قسمیں کھانے والا، ذلیل ⑩
هَمَّازٍ مَّشَّآءٍۭ بِنَمِيْمٍ ⑪	طعنے دینے والا اور چغلیاں کھاتے پھرنے والا ⑪

068-AL QALAM

In the name of Lord, the Most Beneficent, Most Merciful

001 Nun.
By the Pen that scrawl and scribble

002 By The Grace of Lord,
You aren't of the fanatical in diddle

003 Nope! Indeed,
There're eternal grants for you to aside

004 And you've,
Illustrious course of conduct in abide

005 Shortly you'll perceive in pace
And they too will discern in place

006 Who's of you,
Sloppy and psychotic in trace

007 Indeed!
Your Lord perceives the best in deeds
Who're neglectful in scrupulous proceeds
And who trends in ethical term to perceive

008 Attend not to those who deny and deceive

009 They wish you to be amiable in pace
In your mission of preach in faith
So they may also be nimble in place
Against your daily mission in faith

010 Heed not the hideous eager in plan
Who vows in avow so firm in span

011 He's indeed!
A degrade around with flurry and ado

مَنَّاعٍ لِّلْخَيْرِ مُعْتَدٍ أَثِيمٍ ﴿١٢﴾ — بھلائی سے روکنے والا حد سے بڑھ جانے والا، بڑا گنہگار ﴿١٢﴾

عُتُلٍّ بَعْدَ ذَٰلِكَ زَنِيمٍ ﴿١٣﴾ — سرکش، ان سب عیوب سے بڑھ کر یہ کہ وہ بد اصل بھی ہے ﴿١٣﴾

أَن كَانَ ذَا مَالٍ وَبَنِينَ ﴿١٤﴾ — اس بنا پر کہ ہے وہ مالدار اور صاحبِ اولاد ﴿١٤﴾

إِذَا تُتْلَىٰ عَلَيْهِ آيَاتُنَا — جب پڑھی جاتی ہیں اس کے سامنے ہماری آیات

قَالَ أَسَاطِيرُ الْأَوَّلِينَ ﴿١٥﴾ — تو کہتا ہے کہ یہ تو افسانے ہیں پہلے لوگوں کے ﴿١٥﴾

سَنَسِمُهُ عَلَى الْخُرْطُومِ ﴿١٦﴾ — عنقریب داغ لگائیں گے ہم اس کی سونڈ (ناک) پر ﴿١٦﴾

إِنَّا بَلَوْنَاهُمْ — ہم نے آزمائش میں ڈالا ہے ان کفارِ مکہ کو

كَمَا بَلَوْنَا أَصْحَابَ الْجَنَّةِ — جس طرح آزمائش میں ڈالا تھا ہم نے ایک باغ والوں کو۔

إِذْ أَقْسَمُوا — جب انہوں نے قسم کھائی تھی

لَيَصْرِمُنَّهَا مُصْبِحِينَ ﴿١٧﴾ — کہ ضرور ہم پھل توڑیں گے اپنے باغ کا صبح سویرے ﴿١٧﴾

وَلَا يَسْتَثْنُونَ ﴿١٨﴾ — اور انشاء اللہ نہ کہا تھا ﴿١٨﴾

فَطَافَ عَلَيْهَا طَائِفٌ مِّن رَّبِّكَ — تو پھر گئی اس باغ پر ایک آفت تیرے رب کی طرف سے

وَهُمْ نَائِمُونَ ﴿١٩﴾ — جبکہ وہ سو رہے تھے ﴿١٩﴾

فَأَصْبَحَتْ كَالصَّرِيمِ ﴿٢٠﴾ — پس ہو کر رہ گیا وہ کٹے ہوئے کھیت کی طرح ﴿٢٠﴾

فَتَنَادَوْا مُصْبِحِينَ ﴿٢١﴾ — پھر پکارا انہوں نے ایک دوسرے کو صبح سویرے ﴿٢١﴾

أَنِ اغْدُوا عَلَىٰ حَرْثِكُمْ — یہ کہ چل پڑو صبح سویرے اپنی کھیتی کی طرف،

إِن كُنتُمْ صَارِمِينَ ﴿٢٢﴾ — اگر تمہیں پھل توڑنے ہیں ﴿٢٢﴾

فَانطَلَقُوا وَهُمْ يَتَخَافَتُونَ ﴿٢٣﴾ — چنانچہ وہ چل پڑے اور وہ آپس میں چپکے چپکے کہتے جاتے تھے ﴿٢٣﴾

أَن لَّا يَدْخُلَنَّهَا الْيَوْمَ عَلَيْكُم مِّسْكِينٌ ﴿٢٤﴾ — کہ نہ داخل ہونے پائے یہاں آج تمہارے پاس کوئی مسکین ﴿٢٤﴾

012 Consistently hampering the good in will
Defying beyond confines with evil in ills

013 Grim and cruel without a bit of shame
He's born precisely in profane

014 For he owns scion and treasure
015 When he's told of Our Signs in measure

He screams and whoops therein shout
That's the fables of old (time) and about

016 Soon We'll ember their nozzle and snout

017 Verily We've tried the men and clan
As men of the garden in plan

When they resolved to pick and secure
Therein fruit early dawn in adore

018 But didn't care a bit in lore
For,
If it was desire of Lord in term

019 There's a desolation in dismay
From the Bounty of Lord in stay
For there it skewed all in browse
While they're in deep sleep and snooze

020 By morn,
The garden was but a dismal in spot
Whose fruit were collected in blot

021 That's a dark desolate spot in stray
They called by morn to each in stay

022 Let's go to pick fruits in produce
Early this morn a gift in profuse

023 Then they departed there in soon
And to confer in low whisper and tone

024 Let not a poor come close in alone
For the day,
They conferred in stray

وَّغَدَوْا عَلٰى حَرْدٍ	اور گئے وہ صبح سویرے لپکتے ہوئے
قٰدِرِيْنَ ﴿٢٥﴾	اس انداز سے گویا کہ وہ ہر چیز پہ قادر ہیں ﴿٢٥﴾
فَلَمَّا رَاَوْهَا قَالُوْٓا	مگر جب دیکھا انہوں نے باغ کو تو کہنے لگے:
اِنَّا لَضَاۤلُّوْنَ ﴿٢٦﴾	یقیناً ہم راستہ بھول گئے ہیں ﴿٢٦﴾
بَلْ نَحْنُ مَحْرُوْمُوْنَ ﴿٢٧﴾	نہیں بلکہ ہماری تو قسمت ہی پھوٹ گئی ہے ﴿٢٧﴾
قَالَ اَوْسَطُهُمْ اَلَمْ اَقُلْ لَّكُمْ	کہا ان کے بہتر آدمی نے: کیا نہیں کہا تھا میں نے تم سے
لَوْلَا تُسَبِّحُوْنَ ﴿٢٨﴾	کہ کیوں نہیں تسبیح کرتے تم؟ ﴿٢٨﴾
قَالُوْا سُبْحٰنَ رَبِّنَآ	وہ پکار اٹھے: پاک ہے ہمارا رب،
اِنَّا كُنَّا ظٰلِمِيْنَ ﴿٢٩﴾	بے شک ہم ہی تھے ظالم ﴿٢٩﴾
فَاَقْبَلَ بَعْضُهُمْ عَلٰى بَعْضٍ	پھر ایک دوسرے کی طرف منہ کرکے
يَّتَلَاوَمُوْنَ ﴿٣٠﴾	باہم ملامت کرنے لگے ﴿٣٠﴾
قَالُوْا يٰوَيْلَنَآ اِنَّا كُنَّا طٰغِيْنَ ﴿٣١﴾	کہنے لگے: ہائے بدنصیبی! بے شک ہم ہی تھے سرکش ﴿٣١﴾
عَسٰى رَبُّنَآ اَنْ يُّبْدِلَ لَنَا	کچھ بعید نہیں کہ ہمارا رب بدلے میں دے دے ہمیں
خَيْرًا مِّنْهَآ اِنَّآ	بہتر اس باغ سے، بے شک ہم
اِلٰى رَبِّنَا رٰغِبُوْنَ ﴿٣٢﴾	اپنے رب کی طرف رجوع کرتے ہیں ﴿٣٢﴾
كَذٰلِكَ الْعَذَابُ ۭ وَلَعَذَابُ الْاٰخِرَةِ	ایسا ہوتا ہے عذاب۔ اور عذاب آخرت تو
اَكْبَرُ ۘ لَوْ كَانُوْا يَعْلَمُوْنَ ﴿٣٣﴾	کہیں بڑھ کر ہے۔ کاش! یہ لوگ جانتے (اس بات کو) ﴿٣٣﴾
اِنَّ لِلْمُتَّقِيْنَ عِنْدَ رَبِّهِمْ	یقیناً ہیں متقیوں کے لیے ان کے رب کے ہاں
جَنّٰتِ النَّعِيْمِ ﴿٣٤﴾	نعمت بھری جنتیں ﴿٣٤﴾

025 And when reached, early morn at site
Assuming,
As though master of the all in plight

026 But found the garden, mess in stray
All was dashed dreary in array
They said to each dazed in dismay
Indeed!
We've missed the direction in way

027 Indeed!
We're deprived of our toil in pace

028 Said one to others in place
Didn't I ask you to adore
Bounty of the Lord in score

029/ Then they affirmed for sure
030 And said:
Glory be to The Lord in score
Indeed!
We're swindling in core
Then they turned to each in glance
In dash and abash there in trance

031 Then they tended in regret and remorse
Stain in stigma for us in discourse
Indeed!
We've defied our conduct in course

032 Lord will indeed favor to bestow
There in shift a preferred in endow

For in regret we beg to entreat
And devotedly obey His word in beseech

033 Such is detriment in discipline hither in vale
Supercilious is Sentence Hereafter in trail

034 Indeed!
There're Gardens for the virtuous to aside
Before the Gleam and Glory of Lord in stride

اَفَنَجۡعَلُ الۡمُسۡلِمِیۡنَ کَالۡمُجۡرِمِیۡنَ ؕ﴿۳۵﴾
کیا کردیں ہم فرمانبرداروں کو مجرموں کی مانند ﴿۳۵﴾

مَا لَکُمۡ ۟ کَیۡفَ تَحۡکُمُوۡنَ ﴿ۚ۳۶﴾
کیا ہو گیا ہے تمہیں ، کیسے فیصلے کرتے ہو تم ؟ ﴿۳۶﴾

اَمۡ لَکُمۡ کِتٰبٌ فِیۡہِ تَدۡرُسُوۡنَ ﴿ۙ۳۷﴾
کیا تمہارے پاس ہے کوئی کتاب جس میں پڑھتے ہو تم ﴿۳۷﴾

اِنَّ لَکُمۡ فِیۡہِ لَمَا تَخَیَّرُوۡنَ ﴿ۚ۳۸﴾
کہ ضرور تمہارے لیے وہاں وہی کچھ ہے جو پسند کرتے ہو تم ؟ ﴿۳۸﴾

اَمۡ لَکُمۡ اَیۡمَانٌ عَلَیۡنَا
یا پھر کیا تمہارے کچھ عہد و پیمان ہیں ہمارے ساتھ

بَالِغَۃٌ اِلٰی یَوۡمِ الۡقِیٰمَۃِ ۙ اِنَّ لَکُمۡ
جو باقی رہیں گے روزِ قیامت تک کہ ضرور تمہیں وہی ملے گا

لَمَا تَحۡکُمُوۡنَ ﴿ۚ۳۹﴾
جو تم حکم دو گے ؟ ﴿۳۹﴾

سَلۡہُمۡ اَیُّہُمۡ بِذٰلِکَ زَعِیۡمٌ ﴿ۚۛ۴۰﴾ مع ۱۵ عند المتقدمین ۱۲
پوچھو ان سے کہ ان میں سے کون ہے جو اس کا ضامن ہے ﴿۴۰﴾

اَمۡ لَہُمۡ شُرَکَآءُ ۚۛ
یا ہیں ان کے (ٹھہرائے ہوئے) کچھ شریک ؛

فَلۡیَاۡتُوۡا بِشُرَکَآئِہِمۡ
تو لائیں یہ اپنے شریکوں کو ،

اِنۡ کَانُوۡا صٰدِقِیۡنَ ﴿۴۱﴾
اگر ہیں یہ سچے ﴿۴۱﴾

یَوۡمَ یُکۡشَفُ عَنۡ سَاقٍ
جس دن پنڈلی کھولی جائے گی

وَّ یُدۡعَوۡنَ اِلَی السُّجُوۡدِ
اور بلائے جائیں گے سب سجدے کے لیے

فَلَا یَسۡتَطِیۡعُوۡنَ ﴿ۙ۴۲﴾
تو نہ کر سکیں گے (سجدہ) یہ لوگ ﴿۴۲﴾

خَاشِعَۃً اَبۡصَارُہُمۡ تَرۡہَقُہُمۡ ذِلَّۃٌ ؕ
جھکی ہوئی ہوں گی ان کی آنکھیں ، چھا رہی ہو گی ان پر ذلت ،

وَ قَدۡ کَانُوۡا یُدۡعَوۡنَ اِلَی السُّجُوۡدِ
اس لیے کہ (جب) بلایا جاتا تھا انہیں سجدے کے لیے

وَ ہُمۡ سٰلِمُوۡنَ ﴿۴۳﴾
جبکہ وہ تھے صحیح سالم (تو انکار کرتے تھے) ﴿۴۳﴾

فَذَرۡنِیۡ وَ مَنۡ یُّکَذِّبُ
پس چھوڑ دو مجھے (اے نبیؐ) اور ان کو جو جھٹلاتے ہیں

بِہٰذَا الۡحَدِیۡثِ ؕ سَنَسۡتَدۡرِجُہُمۡ
اس کلام کو عنقریب ہم آہستہ آہستہ لے جائیں گے ان کو (تباہی کی طرف)

035 How'd We ever deal the men in faith
Like of the men affirming evil in base

036 What's the confusion with you in stance
How you perceive the matter to glance

037 Or have you a Book in adore
That's to escort and discern in lore

038 That you hold to pick in concern
That you adore in core to discern

039 Or have you contract in lore
Here-in-after with Us to secure

On Day so Determined in command
That you'll secure for all you demand

040 You ask some in stance
Who's there to assert for that

041 Or do they've twosome or duo in hold
If true, let them have their duo in bold

042 The Day shin will be revealed in pace
And they'll be,
Called to invoke and lay prone in place
But they wouldn't be able lay prone in grace

043 Screwed up and eyes in defame
They'll be bounded in shame
That's because,
When they called before in stance
To trend in bow and adore in glance

When they're all perfect in score
But they'd virtually declined to adore

044 Leave Me alone,
O Prophet, for the men in pace
Who defied My Word in grace
By degrees We'll lash and slap in place

مِّنْ حَيْثُ لَا يَعْلَمُوْنَ ﴿۴۴﴾	ایسے طریقے سے کہ انہیں خبر بھی نہ ہوگی ﴿۴۴﴾
وَ اُمْلِيْ لَهُمْ ۚ	اور میں انہیں مہلت دیے جا رہا ہوں ،
اِنَّ كَيْدِيْ مَتِيْنٌ ﴿۴۵﴾	بے شک میری چال بڑی مضبوط ہے ﴿۴۵﴾
اَمْ تَسْـَٔلُهُمْ اَجْرًا فَهُمْ	کیا تم طلب کرتے ہو ان سے کسی قسم کی اجرت جس کی وجہ سے یہ
مِّنْ مَّغْرَمٍ مُّثْقَلُوْنَ ﴿۴۶﴾	چٹی کے بوجھ تلے دبے جا رہے ہیں؟ ﴿۴۶﴾
اَمْ عِنْدَهُمُ الْغَيْبُ فَهُمْ يَكْتُبُوْنَ ﴿۴۷﴾	یا پھر ان کے پاس ہے غیب کی خبر جسے یہ لکھ لاتے ہیں ﴿۴۷﴾
فَاصْبِرْ لِحُكْمِ رَبِّكَ وَلَا تَكُنْ	سو انتظار کرو اپنے رب کے فیصلہ کا اور نہ ہو جانا
كَصَاحِبِ الْحُوْتِ ۘ (وقف لازم)	مچھلی والے (یونس ؑ) کی طرح
اِذْ نَادٰى وَهُوَ مَكْظُوْمٌ ﴿۴۸﴾	جب اس نے پکارا تھا (اپنے رب کو) اور وہ غم سے بھرا ہوا تھا ﴿۴۸﴾
لَوْلَآ اَنْ تَدٰرَكَهٗ نِعْمَةٌ	اگر نہ شاملِ حال ہوتی اس کے مہربانی
مِّنْ رَّبِّهٖ لَنُبِذَ	اس کے رب کی تو پھینک دیا جاتا
بِالْعَرَآءِ وَهُوَ مَذْمُوْمٌ ﴿۴۹﴾	چٹیل میدان میں، اور ہوتا وہ ملامت زدہ ﴿۴۹﴾
فَاجْتَبٰهُ رَبُّهٗ	آخر کار نوازا اسے اس کے رب نے
فَجَعَلَهٗ مِنَ الصّٰلِحِيْنَ ﴿۵۰﴾	اور شامل کر لیا اسے صالحین میں ﴿۵۰﴾
وَاِنْ يَّكَادُ الَّذِيْنَ كَفَرُوْا	اور ایسا لگتا ہے کہ جیسے یہ کافر
لَيُزْلِقُوْنَكَ بِاَبْصَارِهِمْ	اکھاڑ دیں گے تمہارے قدم اپنی (بری) نظروں سے
لَمَّا سَمِعُوا الذِّكْرَ وَيَقُوْلُوْنَ	جب سنتے ہیں قرآن اور کہتے ہیں
اِنَّهٗ لَمَجْنُوْنٌ ﴿۵۱﴾ ۘ	یہ تو ضرور دیوانہ ہے ﴿۵۱﴾
وَمَا هُوَ اِلَّا ذِكْرٌ لِّلْعٰلَمِيْنَ ﴿۵۲﴾	حالانکہ یہ تو ہے ایک نصیحت تمام جہان والوں کے لیے ﴿۵۲﴾

From all in surround smite in state
Where from they cannot perceive in relate

045 A recess in respite I confer in accord
Indeed!
My design in plan is strong in assort

046 Or if you asked (them) for award in plan
For what they're vexed of debt in span

047 Or that the Unseen is in their fist and grip
So that they can put it to scribble and scrip

048 So tarry to endure
Word of Lord to secure

Don't be like the fellow of fish in lore
When in anguish he screamed in score

049 If there's not grace of Lord in endow
He's indeed, laid bare in place
On the desolate land in pace
In shame and defame on shore in throw

050 Lord picked him as His virtuous in glow

051 Indeed, the cynics
They'd rip your footings in daze
With their devilish eyes in gaze
When listen to the Verses in grace

Then they trend to each and affirm
He is so odd and obsessed in term

052 It's but nothing but a Word in lore
Proclaiming in dictum* for the men in score
Affirmed for all the Worlds to allure

*discipline of faith

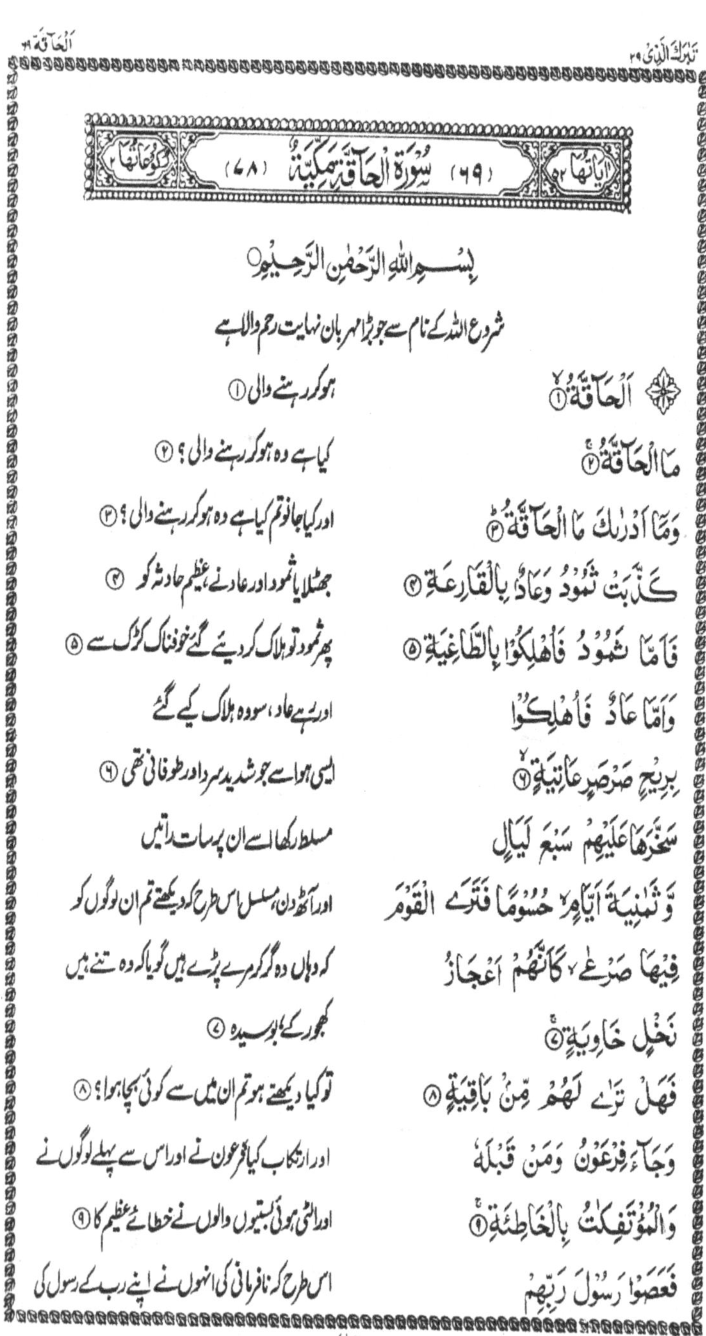

اٰیاتها ٥٢ — سورة الحاقة مكية (٦٩) (٧٨) — ركوعاتها ٢

بسم الله الرحمن الرحيم

شروع اللہ کے نام سے جو بڑا مہربان نہایت رحم والا ہے

الحاقة ①	ہو کر رہنے والی ①
ما الحاقة ②	کیا ہے وہ ہو کر رہنے والی؟ ②
وما ادرىك ما الحاقة ③	اور کیا جانو تم کیا ہے وہ ہو کر رہنے والی؟ ③
كذبت ثمود وعاد بالقارعة ④	جھٹلایا ثمود اور عاد نے، عظیم حادثہ کو ④
فاما ثمود فاهلكوا بالطاغية ⑤	پھر ثمود تو ہلاک کر دیئے گئے خوفناک کڑک سے ⑤
واما عاد فاهلكوا	اور رہے عاد، سو وہ ہلاک کیے گئے
بريح صرصر عاتية ⑥	ایسی ہوا سے جو شدید سرد اور طوفانی تھی ⑥
سخرها عليهم سبع ليال	مسلط رکھا اسے ان پر سات راتیں
وثمنية ايام حسوما فترى القوم	اور آٹھ دن، مسلسل اس طرح کہ دیکھتے تم ان لوگوں کو
فيها صرعى كانهم اعجاز	کہ وہاں وہ گر کر مرے پڑے ہیں گویا کہ وہ تنے ہیں
نخل خاوية ⑦	کھجور کے بوسیدہ ⑦
فهل ترى لهم من باقية ⑧	تو کیا دیکھتے ہو تم ان میں سے کوئی بچا ہوا؟ ⑧
وجاء فرعون ومن قبله	اور ارتکاب کیا فرعون نے اور اس سے پہلے لوگوں نے
والمؤتفكت بالخاطئة ⑨	اور الٹی ہوئی بستیوں والوں نے خطائے عظیم کا ⑨
فعصوا رسول ربهم	اس طرح کہ نافرمانی کی انہوں نے اپنے رب کے رسول کی

069-AL HAQQAH

In the name of Lord, the Most Beneficent, Most Merciful

001 When Specific Significance,
Will come to exist

002 What's Specific Significance,
That will come to exist

003 And how'd you apprehend to grasp
That Specific Significance
It is a term to clasp

004 The Thamud and "Aad defied Term in lore
As deceptive, amazing distress in score

005 But Thamud,
They're ravished by tempest in gush
Rumble in flash, disgusting in rush

006 And Aad ravished in gust
That's a frenzied hurricane in burst

007 Blizzard hitched in blow
Nights seven and days eight in a row
Therein billowing fierce in throw
People strewn in sway and prone in dismay
Like the roots,
Hollowed palm trees, humbled in stray

008 Then,
You'd hardly see a living being in stay

009 And Pharaoh,
And those of the men before in abide
And the city and locale toppled in aside
They're committed to evil in stride

010 For they defied messengers in pace
So He trounced them there in place
Bursting with stern sentence in trace

فَاَخَذَهُمۡ اَخۡذَةً رَّابِيَةً ⑩	تو پکڑا اللہ نے ان کو انتہائی سختی سے ⑩
اِنَّا لَمَّا طَغَا الۡمَآءُ	یہ بھی ایک واقعہ ہے کہ، ہم ہی نے جب پانی طغیانی پر آیا
حَمَلۡنٰكُمۡ فِى الۡجَارِيَةِ ⑪	تو سوار کر دیا تم کو کشتی میں ⑪
لِنَجۡعَلَهَا لَـكُمۡ تَذۡكِرَةً	تا کہ بنادیں اس کو تمہارے لیے ایک یادگار
وَّتَعِيَهَاۤ اُذُنٌ وَّاعِيَةٌ ⑫	اور یاد رکھیں اسے کان، جو یاد رکھنے والے ہوں ⑫
فَاِذَا نُفِخَ فِى الصُّوۡرِ نَفۡخَةٌ وَّاحِدَةٌ ⑬	پھر جب پھونکا جائے گا صور میں ایک بار ⑬
وَّحُمِلَتِ الۡاَرۡضُ وَالۡجِبَالُ	اور اٹھائے جائیں گے زمین اور پہاڑ
فَدُكَّتَا دَكَّةً وَّاحِدَةً ⑭	پھر ریزہ ریزہ کر دیا جائے گا ایک ہی چوٹ میں ⑭
فَيَوۡمَئِذٍ وَّقَعَتِ الۡوَاقِعَةُ ⑮	سو اس دن برپا ہو جائے گی قیامت ⑮
وَانۡشَقَّتِ السَّمَآءُ فَهِىَ	اور پھٹ جائے گا آسمان تو ہو گا وہ
يَوۡمَئِذٍ وَّاهِيَةٌ ⑯	اس دن بکھرا ہوا ⑯
وَّالۡمَلَكُ عَلٰٓى اَرۡجَآئِهَا ؕ	اور فرشتے ہوں گے اس کے کناروں پہ
وَيَحۡمِلُ عَرۡشَ رَبِّكَ	اور اٹھائے ہوئے ہوں گے تیرے رب کے عرش کو
فَوۡقَهُمۡ يَوۡمَئِذٍ ثَمٰنِيَةٌ ⑰	اپنے اوپر اس دن آٹھ (فرشتے) ⑰
يَوۡمَئِذٍ تُعۡرَضُوۡنَ لَا تَخۡفٰى	اس دن تم پیش کیے جاؤ گے، نہیں چھپا رہے گا
مِنۡكُمۡ خَافِيَةٌ ⑱	تمہارا کوئی پوشیدہ راز ⑱
فَاَمَّا مَنۡ اُوۡتِىَ كِتٰبَهٗ بِيَمِيۡنِهٖ ۙ	سو جس کو دیا جائے گا اس کا اعمال نامہ اس کے داہنے ہاتھ میں
فَيَقُوۡلُ هَآؤُمُ اقۡرَءُوۡا كِتٰبِيَهۡ ⑲	تو وہ کہے گا آؤ دیکھو! اور پڑھو میرا اعمالنامہ ⑲
اِنِّىۡ ظَنَنۡتُ اَنِّىۡ مُلٰقٍ حِسَابِيَهۡ ⑳	مجھے یقین تھا ضرور واسطہ پڑے گا مجھے اپنے حساب سے ⑳

011 When water gushed yonder past its define
We, in Ark,
Secured you floating in sublime

012 We make a missive you to concern
And bear in mind to discern
A lesson in lore, henceforth to affirm

013 When a blare in boom, jingled in blow

014 Earth will swing and sway in throw
And mountains licked as dirt in blow

015 Then on The Day,
An affair so immense will pass in proceed

016 And the sky will tear and shear to recede
For it'll be a frail and fragile Day indeed

Fate of the Universe (Page : 1264)

017 And angels aside and beside in flow
With elegant angels eight in a row
Bearing the Throne of Lord in glow

018 That will be a Day Ruling and Result in stance
Not a bit of your doings hidden in trace
Will be veiled from the Bounty of Lord in glance

019 Those with the scribble in the hand on right
They will be awarded blissful awards in bright
They'll say to men in surround
Have a glimpse of my doings in abound

020 I was convinced to discern and affirm
For my tally in trail will trend in term

فَهُوَ فِيْ عِيْشَةٍ رَّاضِيَةٍ ﴿٢١﴾	سو یہ تو ہو گا دل پسند عیش میں ﴿۲۱﴾
فِيْ جَنَّةٍ عَالِيَةٍ ﴿٢٢﴾	اعلیٰ درجہ کی جنت میں ﴿۲۲﴾
قُطُوْفُهَا دَانِيَةٌ ﴿٢٣﴾	جس کے پھلوں کے گچھے جھکے پڑ رہے ہوں گے ﴿۲۳﴾
كُلُوْا وَاشْرَبُوْا هَنِيْٓـئًا بِمَآ	(کہا جائے گا) کھاؤ اور پیو مزے سے بدلے میں
اَسْلَفْتُمْ فِي الْاَيَّامِ الْخَالِيَةِ ﴿٢٤﴾	ان (اعمال) کے جو کیے تھے تم نے گزرے ہوئے دنوں میں ﴿۲۴﴾
وَاَمَّا مَنْ اُوْتِيَ كِتٰبَهٗ	اور رہا وہ جس کو دیا جائے گا اس کا اعمال نامہ
بِشِمَالِهٖ ۙ فَيَقُوْلُ	اس کے بائیں ہاتھ میں سو وہ کہے گا
يٰلَيْتَنِيْ لَمْ اُوْتَ كِتٰبِيَهْ ﴿٢٥﴾	کاش! نہ دیا جاتا مجھے میرا اعمال نامہ ﴿۲۵﴾
وَلَمْ اَدْرِ مَا حِسَابِيَهْ ﴿٢٦﴾	اور نہ جانتا میں کہ کیا ہے میرا حساب؟ ﴿۲۶﴾
يٰلَيْتَهَا كَانَتِ الْقَاضِيَةَ ﴿٢٧﴾	کاش! میری یہ موت ہوتی فیصلہ کن ﴿۲۷﴾
مَآ اَغْنٰى عَنِّيْ مَالِيَهْ ﴿٢٨﴾	کچھ کام نہ آیا میرے میرا مال ﴿۲۸﴾
هَلَكَ عَنِّيْ سُلْطٰنِيَهْ ﴿٢٩﴾	چھن گیا مجھ سے میرا اقتدار ﴿۲۹﴾
خُذُوْهُ فَغُلُّوْهُ ﴿٣٠﴾	(ارشاد ہو گا) پکڑو اسے اور طوق پہنا دو ﴿۳۰﴾
ثُمَّ الْجَحِيْمَ صَلُّوْهُ ﴿٣١﴾	پھر جہنم میں جھونک دو اسے ﴿۳۱﴾
ثُمَّ فِيْ سِلْسِلَةٍ ذَرْعُهَا	پھر ایک زنجیر میں جس کی لمبائی
سَبْعُوْنَ ذِرَاعًا فَاسْلُكُوْهُ ﴿٣٢﴾	ستر گز ہے جکڑ دو اسے ﴿۳۲﴾
اِنَّهٗ كَانَ لَا يُؤْمِنُ بِاللّٰهِ الْعَظِيْمِ ﴿٣٣﴾	واقعہ یہ ہے کہ یہ شخص ایمان نہ لاتا تھا اللہ جل شانہٗ پر ﴿۳۳﴾
وَلَا يَحُضُّ عَلٰى طَعَامِ الْمِسْكِيْنِ ﴿٣٤﴾	اور نہ ترغیب دیتا تھا مسکین کا کھانا دینے کی ﴿۳۴﴾
فَلَيْسَ لَهُ الْيَوْمَ هٰهُنَا حَمِيْمٌ ﴿٣٥﴾	سو نہیں ہے اس کا آج یہاں کوئی جگری دوست ﴿۳۵﴾

021/ And him to cherish bliss of life in abide
022 Therein the excellent Garden to reside

023 Fruits whereof dangle in drape
Quite low and close around in squat

024 Dine and nibble, imbibe in tipple
With amends in giggle
For deeds so good you trended in trifle

025 And whom the record given in left
He'll moan and groan in heft

026 "Ah! My annals hadn't been ceded in raft
(An awful lone had virtually swept)
(And I'd never cared a bit in array
That all my ills will evince in stay)

027/ Ah!
029 If the death could've an end of me in place

Of no gain and return of my riches in trace
My power in sway is squeezed (of me) in pace

030/ (An adamant dictum will tend in demand)
031 Grasp and grip, truss and tether in alarm
And burn him in fierce fire in Swarm
It's he,
Who didn't trust Lord Most Exalted in norm

032 Further to that, in pace
Fettered in chains get (him) to a place
The piece is seventy cubits in space

033 He didn't trust Lord, Exalted in Regard

034 And wouldn't cheer to feed the poor in assort
035 So there's no friend in surround
The Day, that's doleful fate in abound

وَلَا طَعَامٌ اِلَّا مِنْ غِسْلِيْنٍ ﴿۳۶﴾	اور نہ کوئی کھانا مگر زخموں کا دھوون ﴿۳۶﴾
لَّا يَاْكُلُهٗٓ اِلَّا الْخَاطِـُٔوْنَ ﴿۳۷﴾	نہیں کھائے گا اسے کوئی سوائے گنہگاروں کے ﴿۳۷﴾
فَلَآ اُقْسِمُ بِمَا تُبْصِرُوْنَ ﴿۳۸﴾	پس نہیں، قسم کھاتا ہوں میں ان چیزوں کی جو دیکھتے ہو تم ﴿۳۸﴾
وَمَا لَا تُبْصِرُوْنَ ﴿۳۹﴾	اور ان کی بھی جنہیں نہیں دیکھتے تم ﴿۳۹﴾
اِنَّهٗ لَقَوْلُ رَسُوْلٍ كَرِيْمٍ ﴿۴۰﴾	بے شک قرآن قول ہے رسولِ عالی مقام کا ﴿۴۰﴾
وَّمَا هُوَ بِقَوْلِ شَاعِرٍ ؕ	اور نہیں ہے یہ کلام کسی شاعر کا۔
قَلِيْلًا مَّا تُؤْمِنُوْنَ ﴿۴۱﴾	بہت ہی کم ایمان لاتے ہو تم ﴿۴۱﴾
وَلَا بِقَوْلِ كَاهِنٍ ؕ قَلِيْلًا مَّا تَذَكَّرُوْنَ ﴿۴۲﴾	اور نہیں ہے قول کسی کاہن کا بہت ہی کم غور کرتے ہو تم ﴿۴۲﴾
تَنْزِيْلٌ مِّنْ رَّبِّ الْعٰلَمِيْنَ ﴿۴۳﴾	نازل کردہ ہے ربُّ العالمین کی طرف سے ﴿۴۳﴾
وَلَوْ تَقَوَّلَ عَلَيْنَا بَعْضَ الْاَقَاوِيْلِ ﴿۴۴﴾	اور اگر کہیں خود گھڑ کر منسوب کرتا یہ ہماری طرف بعض باتیں ﴿۴۴﴾
لَاَخَذْنَا مِنْهُ بِالْيَمِيْنِ ﴿۴۵﴾	تو ضرور پکڑتے ہم اسے بڑی قوت سے ﴿۴۵﴾
ثُمَّ لَقَطَعْنَا مِنْهُ الْوَتِيْنَ ﴿۴۶﴾	پھر کاٹ ڈالتے ہم اس کی شہ رگ ﴿۴۶﴾
فَمَا مِنْكُمْ مِّنْ اَحَدٍ عَنْهُ حٰجِزِيْنَ ﴿۴۷﴾	تو نہ ہوتا تم میں سے کوئی بھی (ہمیں) اس سے روکنے والا ﴿۴۷﴾
وَاِنَّهٗ لَتَذْكِرَةٌ لِّلْمُتَّقِيْنَ ﴿۴۸﴾	اور یقیناً قرآن ایک نصیحت ہے پرہیزگاروں کے لیے ﴿۴۸﴾
وَاِنَّا لَنَعْلَمُ اَنَّ	اور بے شک ہم خوب جانتے ہیں کہ ضرور
مِنْكُمْ مُّكَذِّبِيْنَ ﴿۴۹﴾	تم میں سے کچھ (اس کو) جھٹلانے والے ہیں ﴿۴۹﴾
وَاِنَّهٗ لَحَسْرَةٌ عَلَى الْكٰفِرِيْنَ ﴿۵۰﴾	اور یقیناً یہ موجبِ حسرت ہے ان کافروں کے لیے ﴿۵۰﴾
وَاِنَّهٗ لَحَقُّ الْيَقِيْنِ ﴿۵۱﴾	اور بے شک یہ یقینی حق ہے ﴿۵۱﴾
فَسَبِّحْ بِاسْمِ رَبِّكَ الْعَظِيْمِ ﴿۵۲﴾	پس (اے نبی) تسبیح کرو تم اپنے ربِ عظیم کے نام کی ﴿۵۲﴾

036 He's nothing to devour and eat
But the swamp and sloughs of wounds in treat
037 That none can eat in place
But for the condemned and defied in pace
038/ Nay! So I swear by all you observe
040 And even so you cannot hold to observe
Indeed!
Qur'an is a word in endow
From a messenger of honor in glow
041 It's not the word of lyrist in trance
But hardly a few (of you) believe in stance
042 Nor it's the word of mystic in chance
But hardly (a few)
Care for caution in glance
043 That's the Dictum of Lord of Domains
Asserted to affirm in faith to sustain
044 If prophet,
Was to concoct at his own in abide
Concerning it to Our name in stride
045 Indeed! We would've,
Got hold of his hand right in pace
046 And then for sure in place
We would've concluded his life in trace
By cutting,
Main of the vessel (artery of heart) at the base
047 Nor you'd elude (him) in gust
From Our evil blow in thrust
048 But indeed!
That's the Message of Lord in trust
For a man fearing Lord in just
049 And indeed!
We discern for sure to spy
There're a few mid you to defy
Our trends in faith affirmed to comply
050 And indeed!
Our Divulgence is a cause of concern
And anguish in agony for Cynics in turn
051 And indeed!
It's Probity so pure and sure to affirm
052 So Venerate the Name of Lord to conform
Exalted in stance determined in command

(٧٠) سُورَةُ الْمَعَارِجِ مَكِّيَّةٌ (٧٩)

آیاتہا ٤٤ — رکوعاتہا ٢

بِسْمِ اللّٰهِ الرَّحْمٰنِ الرَّحِيمِ

شروع اللہ کے نام سے جو بڑا مہربان نہایت رحم والا ہے

سَاَلَ سَآئِلٌ	مانگا ہے ایک مانگنے والے نے
بِعَذَابٍ وَّاقِعٍ ①	وہ عذاب جو ضرور واقع ہونے والا ہے ①
لِّلْكٰفِرِيْنَ لَيْسَ لَهٗ دَافِعٌ ②	کافروں کے لیے نہیں ہے اس عذاب کو کوئی ہٹانے والا ②
مِّنَ اللّٰهِ ذِي الْمَعَارِجِ ③	(کیونکہ ہوگا وہ) اللہ کی طرف سے جو مالک ہے عروج کے زینوں کا ③
تَعْرُجُ الْمَلٰٓئِكَةُ وَالرُّوْحُ	چڑھ کر جاتے ہیں فرشتے اور روح
اِلَيْهِ فِيْ يَوْمٍ	اس کے حضور، ایک ایسے دن میں
كَانَ مِقْدَارُهٗ خَمْسِيْنَ اَلْفَ سَنَةٍ ④	ہے جس کی مقدار پچاس ہزار سال ④
فَاصْبِرْ صَبْرًا جَمِيْلًا ⑤	پس (اے نبیؐ) صبر کرو، اچھا صبر ⑤
اِنَّهُمْ يَرَوْنَهٗ بَعِيْدًا ⑥	بے شک یہ سمجھتے ہیں اسے دور ⑥
وَّنَرٰىهُ قَرِيْبًا ⑦	اور دیکھ رہے ہیں ہم اسے قریب ⑦
يَوْمَ تَكُوْنُ	(یہ عذاب واقع ہوگا) اس دن جب ہو جائے گا
السَّمَآءُ كَالْمُهْلِ ⑧	آسمان تیل کی تلچھٹ کی مانند ⑧
وَتَكُوْنُ الْجِبَالُ كَالْعِهْنِ ⑨	اور ہو جائیں گے پہاڑ رنگ برنگ کے دھنکے ہوئے اون کی مانند ⑨
وَلَا يَسْئَلُ حَمِيْمٌ حَمِيْمًا ⑩	اور نہ پوچھے گا کوئی جگری دوست اپنے جگری دوست کو ⑩
يُّبَصَّرُوْنَهُمْ	حالانکہ وہ ایک دوسرے کو دکھائے جائیں گے ۔

070-AL MAARIJ

In the name of Lord, the Most Beneficent, Most Merciful

001 An inquisitor turned to care and ask
When is punishment coming to a pass

002 As for Cynics!
There's none to avert in class

003 A discipline of Lord in prime
The Lord of all cosmic track and trail to climb*

*Elevator- type passages; details worm hole theory page 1908

004 The angels and Spirit ascent unto Him in a day
Sort whereof is fifty thousand years in a day

3: (See Philosophy of Time Page 1908)

005/ Do you've fortitude - a clemency in trace
007 They look for the Day quite far and afar in pace
But We discern it's quite close and near in place

008/ That Day,
009 Sky will be glued and fused like brass
And mountains be fluffy and fuzzy * in class

*Like wool (Page : 1264)

010 And no ally to ask for a friend in place

011 While they'll be close to nearest in pace
The sinners will desire and aspire in stance
If he could be out of this doleful pit in glance

يَوَدُّ الْمُجْرِمُ لَوْ يَفْتَدِي	خواہش کرے گا مجرم کاش! وہ فدیے میں دے دے ۱۱
مِنْ عَذَابِ يَوْمِئِذٍ بِبَنِيهِ ۱۱	اس دن کے عذاب سے بچنے کے لیے اپنی اولاد کو
وَصَاحِبَتِهِ وَأَخِيهِ ۱۲	اپنی بیوی کو اور اپنے بھائی کو ۱۲
وَفَصِيلَتِهِ الَّتِي تُؤْوِيهِ ۱۳	اور اپنے قریب ترین خاندان کو جو اسے پناہ دیا کرتا تھا ۱۳
وَمَنْ فِي الْأَرْضِ جَمِيعًا	اور ان کو جو زمین میں ہیں سب کو
ثُمَّ يُنْجِيهِ ۱۴	اور اس طرح نجات دلا دے یہ اپنے آپ کو ۱۴
كَلَّا ۖ إِنَّهَا لَظَىٰ ۱۵	ہرگز نہیں ۔ واقعہ یہ ہے کہ وہ تو بھڑکتی ہوئی آگ کی لپٹ ہوگی ۱۵
نَزَّاعَةً لِلشَّوَىٰ ۱۶	جو چاٹ جائے گی گوشت پوست کو ۱۶
تَدْعُو مَنْ	جو پکار پکار کر بلائے گی ہر اس شخص کو جس نے
أَدْبَرَ وَتَوَلَّىٰ ۱۷	پیٹھ پھیری اور منہ موڑا (حق سے) ۱۷
وَجَمَعَ فَأَوْعَىٰ ۱۸	اور جمع کیا (مال) اور سینت سینت کر رکھا ۱۸
إِنَّ الْإِنْسَانَ خُلِقَ هَلُوعًا ۱۹	بلاشبہ انسان پیدا کیا گیا ہے بے صبرا ۱۹
إِذَا مَسَّهُ الشَّرُّ جَزُوعًا ۲۰	جب پہنچتی ہے اسے تکلیف تو روتا پیٹتا ہے ۲۰
وَإِذَا مَسَّهُ	اور جب نصیب ہوتی ہے اسے
الْخَيْرُ مَنُوعًا ۲۱	خوشحالی تو بخل کرتا ہے ۲۱
إِلَّا الْمُصَلِّينَ ۲۲	ان خرابیوں سے بچ جاتے ہیں وہ نماز پڑھنے والے ۲۲
الَّذِينَ هُمْ عَلَىٰ صَلَاتِهِمْ دَائِمُونَ ۲۳	جو ہیں اپنی نمازوں کی پابندی کرنے والے ۲۳
وَالَّذِينَ فِي أَمْوَالِهِمْ حَقٌّ مَعْلُومٌ ۲۴	اور وہ جن کے مالوں میں حصہ مقرر ہے ۲۴
لِلسَّائِلِ وَالْمَحْرُومِ ۲۵	سائلوں اور مسکینوں کے لیے ۲۵

And cherish comfort and calm in place
The Doom of The Day in stance
By offering scions as a dole in glance

Even his,
012/ Wife, brother and clan who eased in fray
016 And all so, on the earth in and around
To save him from the torment in surround

But No!
For that will be Pyre raging in blur
Gashing his flesh and frame right to the skull

017 The Fire:
Would call to all men and clan in slight
Who denied in faith and drifted in plight

018/ Raised assets in sort then covered to conceal
020 Truly man edgy and eager, avid in reveal
Snappish in suffering, cry in appeal

021 Miserly piddling in turn of profusion
(So penny-pinching and deceit in delusion)

022/ But not those committed so firm to obey
023 They affirm in discipline and assert to pray
(They elude all sins in stay)

024 And those, whose:
Assets and riches hold accepted claim in precise

025 A dole in cash, who ask in device
Also deserving, who don't beg in premise

وَالَّذِيْنَ يُصَدِّقُوْنَ بِيَوْمِ الدِّيْنِ ۝٢٦	اور وہ جو برحق مانتے ہیں روزِ جزا کو ۝٢٦
وَالَّذِيْنَ هُمْ مِّنْ عَذَابِ رَبِّهِمْ مُّشْفِقُوْنَ ۝٢٧	اور وہ جو اپنے رب کے عذاب سے ڈرتے رہتے ہیں ۝٢٧
اِنَّ عَذَابَ رَبِّهِمْ	واقعہ یہ ہے کہ ان کے رب کا عذاب ہے ہی ایسا
غَيْرُ مَاْمُوْنٍ ۝٢٨	کہ اس سے بے خوف نہ ہوا جائے ۝٢٨
وَالَّذِيْنَ هُمْ لِفُرُوْجِهِمْ حٰفِظُوْنَ ۝٢٩	اور وہ جو اپنی شرمگاہوں کی حفاظت کرتے ہیں ۝٢٩
اِلَّا عَلٰٓى اَزْوَاجِهِمْ اَوْ مَا	سوائے اپنی بیویوں کے یا ان (عورتوں) کے جو
مَلَكَتْ اَيْمَانُهُمْ فَاِنَّهُمْ	ان کی مِلک میں ہوں کہ وہ (ان سے مباشرت کرنے پر)
غَيْرُ مَلُوْمِيْنَ ۝٣٠	قابلِ ملامت نہیں ہیں ۝٣٠
فَمَنِ ابْتَغٰى وَرَآءَ ذٰلِكَ	البتہ جو شخص چاہے گا اس کے علاوہ کچھ اور
فَاُولٰٓئِكَ هُمُ الْعٰدُوْنَ ۝٣١	سو ایسے ہی لوگ ہیں حد سے تجاوز کرنے والے ۝٣١
وَالَّذِيْنَ هُمْ لِاَمٰنٰتِهِمْ	اور وہ لوگ جو اپنی امانتوں کا
وَعَهْدِهِمْ رٰعُوْنَ ۝٣٢	اور اپنے عہدوں کا پاس کرتے ہیں ۝٣٢
وَالَّذِيْنَ هُمْ بِشَهٰدٰتِهِمْ قَآئِمُوْنَ ۝٣٣	اور وہ جو اپنی شہادتوں میں ثابت قدم رہتے ہیں ۝٣٣
وَالَّذِيْنَ هُمْ عَلٰى صَلَاتِهِمْ يُحَافِظُوْنَ ۝٣٤	اور وہ جو اپنی نماز کی حفاظت کرتے ہیں ۝٣٤
اُولٰٓئِكَ فِيْ جَنّٰتٍ مُّكْرَمُوْنَ ۝٣٥	یہ لوگ ہیں جو جنت کے باغوں میں عزت کے ساتھ رہیں گے ۝٣٥
فَمَالِ الَّذِيْنَ كَفَرُوْا	سو کیا ہو گیا ہے (اے نبیؐ) ان لوگوں کو جو انکار کر رہے ہیں
قِبَلَكَ مُهْطِعِيْنَ ۝٣٦	کہ تمہاری طرف دوڑے چلے آ رہے ہیں یہ ۝٣٦
عَنِ الْيَمِيْنِ وَعَنِ الشِّمَالِ عِزِيْنَ ۝٣٧	دائیں اور بائیں جانب سے گروہ در گروہ ۝٣٧
اَيَطْمَعُ كُلُّ امْرِئٍ مِّنْهُمْ	کیا لالچ رکھتا ہے ہر شخص ان میں سے

026/ And the men and clan in abide
027 Who affirm and conform The Day in Trust
And awe and dread fury of Lord in Just

028/ Fury is inverse of amity and accord
029 And whoso secure decency in assorts
And care for sensuality in part

030 But for the wives and captives in plight
For what they hold permissible in right
It's not impute for a sensuality in delight

031/ If some infringe or err in stance
032 They're but the sinners in trance

Those who honor their trust in pace
Esteem pledge and promise in place
(Saying their prayers in orderly grace)

033/ And whoso assert to affirm evidence in stance
034 And lookout adoration sanctity in glance

035 They'll be the privileged and pleased in sway
Abiding the Blissful Gardens in stay

036/ Now what's the term of trance in place
038 Infidels swift in spree to you in pace

Both from,
The left and the right, hurried in along
Raving in lust to enter Garden in charm

أَنْ يُّدْخَلَ جَنَّةَ نَعِيْمٍ ﴿٣٨﴾
کہ اسے داخل کر دیا جائے نعمت بھری جنت میں ﴿٣٨﴾

كَلَّا ۖ اِنَّا خَلَقْنٰهُمْ
ہرگز نہیں۔ بے شک ہم ہی نے انہیں پیدا کیا ہے

مِّمَّا يَعْلَمُوْنَ ﴿٣٩﴾
اس چیز سے جسے یہ خود جانتے ہیں ﴿٣٩﴾

فَلَآ اُقْسِمُ بِرَبِّ الْمَشٰرِقِ وَالْمَغٰرِبِ
سو نہیں، قسم کھاتا ہوں میں مشرقوں اور مغربوں کے مالک کی،

اِنَّا لَقٰدِرُوْنَ ﴿٤٠﴾
یقیناً ہم قادر ہیں ﴿٤٠﴾

عَلٰٓى اَنْ نُّبَدِّلَ
اس پر کہ بدل کر لے آئیں

خَيْرًا مِّنْهُمْ ۙ وَمَا
بہتر لوگ ان سے اور نہیں

نَحْنُ بِمَسْبُوْقِيْنَ ﴿٤١﴾
ہیں ہم (ایسا کرنے سے) عاجز ﴿٤١﴾

فَذَرْهُمْ يَخُوْضُوْا
سو اے نبی، چھوڑ دو انہیں کہ غرق رہیں

وَيَلْعَبُوْا حَتّٰى يُلٰقُوْا
اور منہمک رہیں اپنے کھیل میں حتّٰی کہ پہنچ جائیں

يَوْمَهُمُ الَّذِيْ يُوْعَدُوْنَ ﴿٤٢﴾
اس دن کو جس سے انہیں ڈرایا جا رہا ہے ﴿٤٢﴾

يَوْمَ يَخْرُجُوْنَ
اس دن جب نکل کر یہ

مِنَ الْاَجْدَاثِ سِرَاعًا
قبروں سے تیزی کے ساتھ دوڑے جا رہے ہوں گے

كَاَنَّهُمْ اِلٰى نُصُبٍ
اس طرح گویا کہ یہ مقابلہ کے لیے متعین کردہ نشان کی طرف

يُّوْفِضُوْنَ ﴿٤٣﴾
دوڑ رہے ہوں ﴿٤٣﴾

خَاشِعَةً اَبْصَارُهُمْ
جھکی ہوئی ہوں گی ان کی نگاہیں

تَرْهَقُهُمْ ذِلَّةٌ ۭ
چھا رہی ہوگی ان پر ذلت۔

ذٰلِكَ الْيَوْمُ الَّذِيْ
یہ ہے وہ دن جس سے

كَانُوْا يُوْعَدُوْنَ ﴿٤٤﴾
انہیں ڈرایا جاتا تھا ﴿٤٤﴾

039 By no means and matters in term
They so discern for sure to affirm
For how We created (them) hither in turn
(Out of the sinful drop* in concern)

*sperm

040 Now, not indeed!
I call to witness,
Lord of the East in all tips and turns
And of the West in term
We definitely assert to affirm

041 We substitute better lot, for evils and deceits
We aren't plagued for Our plan in treat

042 O prophet,
Leave them in their deceptive conduct in stray
Delusive discourse futile fun in play

Till they confront the Day of Discern
That's what, they're avowed in return

043/ The Day,
044 They'll turn out from their dip and pit*
In hustle haste
So sudden in jolt and jerk in swift,

Dashing to place
Where they used to honor and adore in waste
Eyes lowered in dejection of shame

Deprived and depraved in despair and disgrace
Soaked and cloaked of humiliation in base
Such is a Day they're destined to brace

*Graves

آیاتها ٢٨ (٧١) سورة نوح مكية (٧١) رکوعاتها ٢

بِسۡمِ اللّٰهِ الرَّحۡمٰنِ الرَّحِيۡمِ

شروع اللہ کے نام سے جو بڑا مہربان نہایت رحم والا ہے

اِنَّاۤ اَرۡسَلۡنَا نُوۡحًا	یقیناً ہم ہی نے بھیجا تھا رسول بنا کر نوحؑ کو
اِلٰى قَوۡمِهٖۤ اَنۡ اَنۡذِرۡ	اس کی قوم کی طرف (اس ہدایت کے ساتھ) کہ ڈراؤ
قَوۡمَكَ مِنۡ قَبۡلِ اَنۡ	اپنی قوم کو اس سے پہلے کہ
يَّاۡتِيَهُمۡ عَذَابٌ اَلِيۡمٌ ①	آجائے ان پر دردناک عذاب ①
قَالَ يٰقَوۡمِ اِنِّىۡ	کہا انہوں نے: اے میری قوم! یقیناً میں ہوں
لَـكُمۡ نَذِيۡرٌ مُّبِيۡنٌ ②	تمہارے لیے صاف صاف متنبہ کرنے والا ②
اَنِ اعۡبُدُوا اللّٰهَ وَاتَّقُوۡهُ وَاَطِيۡعُوۡنِ ③	یہ کہ عبادت کرو تم اللہ کی اور اسی سے ڈرو اور میری اطاعت کرو ③
يَغۡفِرۡ لَـكُمۡ مِّنۡ ذُنُوۡبِكُمۡ	معاف فرما دے گا وہ تمہارے کچھ گناہ
وَيُؤَخِّرۡكُمۡ اِلٰٓى اَجَلٍ مُّسَمًّى ؕ	اور مہلت دے گا تمہیں ایک وقت مقرر تک ۔
اِنَّ اَجَلَ اللّٰهِ اِذَا جَآءَ	حقیقت یہ ہے کہ اللہ کا مقرر کیا ہوا وقت جب آجاتا ہے
لَا يُؤَخَّرُ ۘ لَوۡ كُنۡتُمۡ تَعۡلَمُوۡنَ ④	تو ٹالا نہیں جا سکتا ۔ کاش! تم جانتے (یہ بات) ④
قَالَ رَبِّ اِنِّىۡ دَعَوۡتُ	نوحؑ نے عرض کیا: اے میرے رب! میں بلاتا رہا
قَوۡمِىۡ لَيۡلًا وَّنَهَارًا ⑤	اپنی قوم کو شب و روز ⑤
فَلَمۡ يَزِدۡهُمۡ دُعَآءِىۡۤ	لیکن نہ اضافہ کیا ان میں میری دعوت نے
اِلَّا فِرَارًا ⑥	مگر فرار کا ⑥

وقف لازم

منزل ٧

071-NUH

In the name of Lord, the Most Beneficent, Most Merciful

001 We sent Noah to his men and clan
With a distinct Caution in span

To exhort and alert in pace
Before there's severe Sentence in place

002 He said: O my men and clan in trance
I'm to apprise and admonish in stance
That's so candid and distinct in glance

003 Ardor in adore and dread Lord in grace
And trend to obey me, conforming in pace

004 So He absolves bungle and blot in stray
And endows in relief for a term in fray

But when from Lord,
The term so affirmed is over in stance
It cannot be deferred for a twinkle in trance
If you could really discern to glance

005/ He said: O my Lord!
006 I bid my men to the discipline in faith
By night and during the day in pace

But my way in preach in speech
Made them run quite fast in screech

وَاِنِّیْ كُلَّمَا دَعَوْتُهُمْ	اور واقعہ یہ ہے کہ میں نے جب بھی انہیں دعوت دی
لِتَغْفِرَ لَهُمْ جَعَلُوْٓا	اس غرض سے کہ معاف کر دے تو انہیں، تو ٹھونس لیتے وہ
اَصَابِعَهُمْ فِیْٓ اٰذَانِهِمْ	اپنی انگلیاں اپنے کانوں میں
وَاسْتَغْشَوْا ثِيَابَهُمْ	اور ڈھانک لیتے چہرے اپنے کپڑوں سے
وَاَصَرُّوْا وَاسْتَكْبَرُوا اسْتِكْبَارًا ۚ﴿۷﴾	اور اڑ جاتے اپنی ضد پر اور بہت زیادہ تکبر کرتے ﴿۷﴾
ثُمَّ اِنِّیْ دَعَوْتُهُمْ جِهَارًا ۙ﴿۸﴾	اس کے باوجود میں دعوت دیتا رہا انہیں ہانکے پکارے ﴿۸﴾
ثُمَّ اِنِّیْٓ اَعْلَنْتُ لَهُمْ	پھر میں نے تبلیغ کی ان میں علانیہ
وَاَسْرَرْتُ لَهُمْ اِسْرَارًا ۙ﴿۹﴾	اور سمجھایا انہیں چپکے چپکے بھی ﴿۹﴾
فَقُلْتُ اسْتَغْفِرُوْا رَبَّكُمْ ۭ	سو میں نے کہا معافی مانگو اپنے رب سے۔
اِنَّهٗ كَانَ غَفَّارًا ۙ﴿۱۰﴾	یقیناً ہے وہ بہت زیادہ معاف فرمانے والا ﴿۱۰﴾
يُّرْسِلِ السَّمَاۗءَ عَلَيْكُمْ مِّدْرَارًا ۙ﴿۱۱﴾	برسائے گا وہ آسمان سے تم پر موسلا دھار بارش ﴿۱۱﴾
وَّيُمْدِدْكُمْ بِاَمْوَالٍ وَّبَنِيْنَ	اور نوازے گا تمہیں مال و اولاد سے
وَيَجْعَلْ لَّكُمْ جَنّٰتٍ وَّيَجْعَلْ	اور پیدا کرے گا تمہارے لیے باغ اور جاری کر دے گا
لَّكُمْ اَنْهٰرًا ﴿۱۲﴾	تمہارے لیے نہریں ﴿۱۲﴾
مَا لَكُمْ لَا تَرْجُوْنَ	کیا ہو گیا ہے تمہیں کہ نہیں امید رکھتے تم
لِلّٰهِ وَقَارًا ﴿۱۳﴾	اللہ سے بڑائی کی؟ ﴿۱۳﴾
وَقَدْ خَلَقَكُمْ	حالانکہ اسی نے پیدا کیا ہے تم کو
اَطْوَارًا ﴿۱۴﴾	طرح طرح کی حالتوں میں سے گزار کر ﴿۱۴﴾
اَلَمْ تَرَوْا كَيْفَ خَلَقَ اللّٰهُ	کیا تم نے نہیں دیکھا کہ کیسے پیدا فرمائے ہیں اللہ نے

007 And all the while,
I called them to submit and incline
That Lord may absolve your ills in decline

Instead covered up ears with fingers in thrust
Protected with apparels as if in boom of gust
Instead so callous in conceit, disdain in burst

008/ I sternly called them to listen and aside
009 More I apprised as a commune in abide
And also secretly confided alone in stride

010/ I begged them to,
011 Seek absolution of Lord in prime
For He's so Gracious and Kind
For then Lord will consign

Sprinkle and shower in plan
012/ Get you,
013 Assets and affluence, posterity in span
Endow you gardens and brooks in grand

What's the concern, you trend in surprise
Not trusting for mercy of Lord in prize

014/ Affirming and conforming all in glance
015 Who created you distinct and diverse in stance
Don't you concern thither in span
How He created seven skies in plan
One over the other, a series in trance

سَبْعَ سَمٰوٰتٍ طِبَاقًا ﴿۱۵﴾	سات آسمان تہ بر تہ ﴿۱۵﴾
وَّجَعَلَ الْقَمَرَ فِيْهِنَّ نُوْرًا	اور بنایا ہے چاند کو ان میں روشنی کے لیے
وَّجَعَلَ الشَّمْسَ سِرَاجًا ﴿۱۶﴾	اور بنایا ہے سورج کو ایک جلتا چراغ ﴿۱۶﴾
وَاللّٰهُ اَنْۢبَتَكُمْ مِّنَ الْاَرْضِ نَبَاتًا ﴿۱۷﴾	اور اللہ ہی نے اگایا ہے تم کو زمین سے عجیب طریقہ سے ﴿۱۷﴾
ثُمَّ يُعِيْدُكُمْ فِيْهَا	پھر وہی واپس لے جائے گا تمہیں اسی زمین میں
وَيُخْرِجُكُمْ اِخْرَاجًا ﴿۱۸﴾	اور پھر اسی میں سے تمہیں نکال کھڑا کرے گا ﴿۱۸﴾
وَاللّٰهُ جَعَلَ لَكُمُ	یہ اللہ ہی ہے جس نے بنایا ہے تمہارے لیے
الْاَرْضَ بِسَاطًا ﴿۱۹﴾	زمین کو ہموار ﴿۱۹﴾
لِّتَسْلُكُوْا مِنْهَا سُبُلًا فِجَاجًا ﴿۲۰﴾	تاکہ چلو تم اس کے اندر کھلے راستوں میں ﴿۲۰﴾
قَالَ نُوْحٌ رَّبِّ اِنَّهُمْ	کہا نوحؑ نے: اے میرے رب! یقیناً انہوں نے
عَصَوْنِيْ وَاتَّبَعُوْا	میری نافرمانی کی اور پیروی کی
مَنْ لَّمْ يَزِدْهُ	ان کی جنہوں نے نہ اضافہ کیا
مَالُهٗ وَوَلَدُهٗٓ اِلَّا خَسَارًا ﴿۲۱﴾	ان کے مال و اولاد میں مگر خسارے کا ﴿۲۱﴾
وَمَكَرُوْا مَكْرًا كُبَّارًا ﴿۲۲﴾	اور چلے وہ بڑی بڑی چالیں ﴿۲۲﴾
وَقَالُوْا لَا تَذَرُنَّ	اور کہا انہوں نے: ہرگز نہ چھوڑنا
اٰلِهَتَكُمْ وَلَا تَذَرُنَّ	اپنے معبودوں کو اور ہرگز نہ چھوڑنا تم
وَدًّا وَّلَا سُوَاعًا ۙ وَّلَا يَغُوْثَ	وَدّ کو اور نہ سواع کو اور نہ یغوث
وَيَعُوْقَ وَنَسْرًا ﴿۲۳﴾	اور یعوق اور نسر کو بھی ﴿۲۳﴾
وَقَدْ اَضَلُّوْا كَثِيْرًا ۚ	اور اس طرح گمراہ کردیا انہوں نے بہت سوں کو۔

016 And blessed the moon a balmy beam in flow
And bestowal of sun burning lamp in glow

017 How could you ever determine to concern
That He created you,
Gradually grow out of earth (dust) in term

018 Then at the end,
He'll return you back to the dust
And thence raise from the soil in trust

019/ Lord made,
020 Earth a spread (carpet) in expanse
With lays and ways, trek in distance

021 Noah said: O Lord!
They've defied my word in adore
And obey who,
Hold riches and progeny in score

That gives,
Them nothing, but ruination in core
022 They trend to plan horrid plot in lore

023 And they said to each one in stance
Tend not to drop your gods in trance

Desert and defect not Wadd, Suwa, lords in pray
Not even Yaghuth, Yauq, or Nasr gods to obey

وَلَا تَزِدِ الظّٰلِمِيْنَ — اور نہ اضافہ کر تو بھی ان ظالموں کے لیے

اِلَّا ضَلٰلًا ۲۴ — مگر گمراہی میں ۲۴

مِمَّا خَطِيْٓـٰٔتِهِمْ اُغْرِقُوْا — اور اپنی ہی خطاؤں کی بنا پر وہ غرق کیے گئے

فَاُدْخِلُوْا نَارًا ۵ — اور داخل کیے گئے جہنم میں۔

فَلَمْ يَجِدُوْا لَهُمْ — پھر نہ پایا انہوں نے اپنے لیے

مِّنْ دُوْنِ اللّٰهِ اَنْصَارًا ۲۵ — اللہ سے بچانے والا کوئی مددگار ۲۵

وَقَالَ نُوْحٌ رَّبِّ — اور کہا نوحؑ نے: اے میرے رب!

لَا تَذَرْ عَلَى الْاَرْضِ — نہ باقی چھوڑ زمین پر

مِنَ الْكٰفِرِيْنَ دَيَّارًا ۲۶ — ان کافروں میں سے کوئی بسنے والا ۲۶

اِنَّكَ اِنْ تَذَرْهُمْ — یقیناً تو نے اگر انہیں چھوڑ دیا

يُضِلُّوْا عِبَادَكَ — تو گمراہ کریں گے یہ تیرے بندوں کو

وَلَا يَلِدُوْٓا — اور نہیں پیدا ہوں گے ان کی نسل سے

اِلَّا فَاجِرًا كَفَّارًا ۲۷ — مگر بدکار اور سخت کافر ۲۷

رَبِّ اغْفِرْ لِيْ — اے میرے رب! معاف فرما دے مجھے

وَلِوَالِدَيَّ وَلِمَنْ — اور میرے والدین کو اور ہر اس شخص کو جو

دَخَلَ بَيْتِيَ مُؤْمِنًا — داخل ہو میرے گھر میں مومن کی حیثیت سے

وَّلِلْمُؤْمِنِيْنَ وَالْمُؤْمِنٰتِ ط — اور سب مومن مردوں کو اور مومن عورتوں کو بھی معاف فرمادے۔

وَلَا تَزِدِ الظّٰلِمِيْنَ — اور نہ اضافہ کر ظالموں کے لیے

اِلَّا تَبَارًا ۲۸ — مگر ہلاکت میں ۲۸

024 They've already stood in deride
Dissuaded many a clan in abide

Please O Lord!
Don't award them but the evil in grant
For their wicked plans in slants

025 For they indulged in sins and slur
They're plunged in stir
And were made to enter fire in blur

They'd none to assuage in ease
Other than Lord to help and appease

026 And Noah begged and beseeched,
Lord in plan
O Lord!
Don't leave a single of the cynics in land

027 For, if any of them is left in behind
They'll delude men of faith to decline
And they'll breed,
None but ungrateful rotten in crime

028 O my Lord!
Condone my ills in will
Also of my parents in thrill
And all such who to enter my house in drill

And all men and dame in conviction of Faith
To the evil grant Your depravity in waste

ایاتھا ۲۸ (۷۲) سورۃ الجن مکیۃ (۴۰) رکوعاتھا ۲

بسم اللہ الرحمٰن الرحیم

شروع اللہ کے نام سے جو بڑا مہربان نہایت رحم والا ہے

قُلْ اُوْحِیَ اِلَیَّ	(اے نبیؐ) کہو وحی بھیجی گئی ہے میری طرف
اَنَّهُ اسْتَمَعَ نَفَرٌ مِّنَ الْجِنِّ	کہ غور سے سنا ایک گروہ نے جنوں میں سے۔
فَقَالُوْٓا اِنَّا سَمِعْنَا	سو کہا انہوں نے: بلاشبہ ہم نے سنا ہے
قُرْاٰنًا عَجَبًا ①	ایک قرآن بڑا عجیب ①
یَّهْدِیْٓ اِلَى الرُّشْدِ	جو رہنمائی کرتا ہے راہِ راست کی طرف
فَاٰمَنَّا بِهٖ	اس لیے ہم ایمان لے آئے ہیں اس پر۔
وَلَنْ نُّشْرِكَ بِرَبِّنَآ اَحَدًا ②	اور ہرگز نہ شریک بنائیں گے ہم (اب) اپنے رب کے ساتھ کسی کو ②
وَّاَنَّهٗ تَعٰلٰى جَدُّ رَبِّنَا	اور یہ کہ بہت اعلیٰ و ارفع ہے شان ہمارے رب کی،
مَا اتَّخَذَ صَاحِبَةً وَّلَا وَلَدًا ③	نہیں بنایا اس نے کسی کو بیوی اور نہ بیٹا ③
وَّاَنَّهٗ كَانَ یَقُوْلُ سَفِیْهُنَا	اور یہ کہ کہتے رہے ہیں ہمارے نادان لوگ
عَلَى اللّٰهِ شَطَطًا ④	اللہ کے بارے میں بہت خلافِ حق باتیں ④
وَّاَنَّا ظَنَنَّآ اَنْ لَّنْ تَقُوْلَ الْاِنْسُ وَالْجِنُّ	اور یہ کہ ہم نے سمجھا تھا کہ ہرگز نہیں بول سکتے انسان اور جن
عَلَى اللّٰهِ كَذِبًا ⑤	اللہ کے بارے میں جھوٹ ⑤
وَّاَنَّهٗ كَانَ رِجَالٌ مِّنَ الْاِنْسِ	اور یہ کہ تھے کچھ لوگ انسانوں میں سے
یَعُوْذُوْنَ بِرِجَالٍ مِّنَ الْجِنِّ	جو پناہ مانگا کرتے تھے کچھ لوگوں کی جنوں میں سے،

072-AL JINN

In the name of Lord, the Most Beneficent, Most Merciful

001 O Muhammad affirm:
It's so revealed to me in stance
A body of Jinni heard word of Qur'an

Then they turned to each in glance
We've heard stanza superb in trance

002 It guides in escort to the right in place
And we trended to affirm truth in pace

We'll couple no gods but Him in pray
To Him we worship sincere in obey

003 Our Lord!
Exalted in Might, Majestic in sway
To Him we trend in adore to obey
He doesn't have spouse or son in stay

004 Of us, there're some absurd in conceit
Using for 'Him' plenteous (word) in deceit

005 As we infer to assert in claim!
No men or spirit ever affirmed it, to name
A word for Lord that's fib to sustain

006 Indeed! There're men and clan in abide
Who took a refuge with jinni in stride
Raising the Jinni for pride in deride

فَزَادُوْهُمْ رَهَقًا ۝٦
اس طرح بڑھا دیا انہوں نے جنوں کا غرور ۝٦

وَّاَنَّهُمْ ظَنُّوْا كَمَا ظَنَنْتُمْ
اور یہ کہ وہ بھی یہی گمان رکھتے تھے جیسا کہ تمہارا گمان ہے

اَنْ لَّنْ يَّبْعَثَ اللّٰهُ اَحَدًا ۝٧
کہ ہرگز نہیں اٹھائے گا (مرنے کے بعد) اللہ کسی کو ۝٧

وَّاَنَّا لَمَسْنَا السَّمَآءَ فَوَجَدْنٰهَا
اور ہم نے ٹٹولا آسمان کو تو پایا ہم نے اسے

مُلِئَتْ حَرَسًا شَدِيْدًا وَّشُهُبًا ۝٨
کہ وہ پٹا پڑا ہے مضبوط پہرے داروں سے اور شعلوں سے ۝٨

وَّاَنَّا كُنَّا نَقْعُدُ مِنْهَا
اور یہ کہ ہم بیٹھا کرتے تھے آسمان میں

مَقَاعِدَ لِلسَّمْعِ ؕ فَمَنْ يَّسْتَمِعِ
سن گن لینے کی جگہوں پر۔ لیکن جو شخص سننے کی کوشش کرتا ہے

الْاٰنَ يَجِدْ لَهٗ شِهَابًا رَّصَدًا ۝٩
اب تو پاتا ہے وہ اپنے لیے ایک شہابِ ثاقب ۝٩

وَّاَنَّا لَا نَدْرِيْٓ اَشَرٌّ اُرِيْدَ
اور یہ کہ ہم نہیں جانتے کہ برائی کرنے کا ارادہ کیا گیا ہے

بِمَنْ فِي الْاَرْضِ اَمْ اَرَادَ بِهِمْ
ان کے ساتھ جو زمین میں ہیں یا ارادہ کیا ہے ان کے ساتھ

رَبُّهُمْ رَشَدًا ۝١٠
ان کے رب نے راہِ راست دکھانے کا ۝١٠

وَّاَنَّا مِنَّا الصّٰلِحُوْنَ وَمِنَّا
اور یہ کہ ہیں ہم میں سے کچھ نیک اور کچھ ہم میں سے ہیں

دُوْنَ ذٰلِكَ ؕ كُنَّا طَرَآئِقَ قِدَدًا ۝١١
اور طرح کے۔ گویا ہیں ہم مختلف طریقوں میں بٹے ہوئے ۝١١

وَّاَنَّا ظَنَنَّآ اَنْ لَّنْ نُّعْجِزَ اللّٰهَ
اور یہ کہ ہم سمجھتے تھے کہ ہم ہرگز نہیں عاجز کر سکتے اللہ کو

فِي الْاَرْضِ وَلَنْ نُّعْجِزَهٗ هَرَبًا ۝١٢
زمین میں اور نہیں ہرا سکتے ہیں اس کو بھاگ کر ۝١٢

وَّاَنَّا لَمَّا سَمِعْنَا الْهُدٰٓى اٰمَنَّا بِهٖ ؕ
اور یہ کہ جب سنی ہم نے ہدایت ایمان لے آئے ہم اس پر۔

فَمَنْ يُّؤْمِنْ بِرَبِّهٖ فَلَا يَخَافُ
سو جو شخص بھی ایمان لائے گا اپنے رب پر تو اسے ڈر نہ ہوگا

بَخْسًا وَّلَا رَهَقًا ۝١٣
کسی قسم کی حق تلفی کا اور نہ ظلم کا ۝١٣

وَّاَنَّا مِنَّا الْمُسْلِمُوْنَ وَمِنَّا
اور یہ کہ ہم میں سے کچھ فرمانبردار ہیں اور کچھ ہم میں سے ہیں

007 And they had a similar notion in norm
As you trusted in turn
That Lord wouldn't raise in term
After our death in demise
For once we're dead in premise

008 We tried to snoop and spy to confirm
The secrets of sky and yonder in term
But we met firm defense held in surround
With,
Strict sentinel and burn of blaze in around

009 We tried to allure a site in spot
Heeding to a secret or sound in record
Whoever got to heed or hark in place
He was fellow of the burn in blaze
010 We fail to discern and concern in stride
For if ill is intended to one living in abide*
Or,
Lord plans to escort to the right of path

* living on earth

011 There with us, virtuous and perverse
Some conduct in curious course in inverse
So we play all divergent ways in converse

012 We discern for sure to allure
There's no way in the land, to adore
That we can bilk or bother Lord in plight
Nor can we baffle or beat (Him) in flight

013 As for us hither in pace
We heard a word of escort in grace
And we received it for true in trace
Those who would trust The Lord in pace
They need not awe and dread of any kind and sort
Or any
Bent in bias of justice in accord

014 There're some,
Who comply dictum of Lord in pace
And other defy the truth in place

الْقٰسِطُوْنَ ؕ فَمَنْ اَسْلَمَ	حق سے منحرف۔ سو جو فرمانبردار ہوئے
فَاُولٰٓئِكَ تَحَرَّوْا رَشَدًا ﴿١٤﴾	انہوں نے ڈھونڈ لی نجات کی راہ ﴿١٤﴾
وَاَمَّا الْقٰسِطُوْنَ فَكَانُوْا لِجَهَنَّمَ حَطَبًا ﴿١٥﴾	اور جو منحرف ہوئے حق سے تو بن گئے وہ جہنم کا ایندھن ﴿١٥﴾
وَّاَنْ لَّوِ اسْتَقَامُوْا عَلَى الطَّرِيْقَةِ	اور (مجھ پر وحی کی گئی ہے) کہ اگر لوگ قائم رہیں سیدھے راستے پر
لَاَسْقَيْنٰهُمْ مَّآءً غَدَقًا ﴿١٦﴾	تو ضرور سیراب کرتے ہم انہیں ڈھیروں پانی سے ﴿١٦﴾
لِّنَفْتِنَهُمْ فِيْهِ ؕ وَمَنْ يُّعْرِضْ	تاکہ آزمائیں ہم انہیں اس طرح۔ اور جو منہ موڑے گا
عَنْ ذِكْرِ رَبِّهٖ يَسْلُكْهُ عَذَابًا صَعَدًا ﴿١٧﴾	اپنے رب کی یاد سے، مبتلا کر دے گا وہ اسے سخت عذاب میں ﴿١٧﴾
وَّاَنَّ الْمَسٰجِدَ لِلّٰهِ فَلَا تَدْعُوْا	اور یہ کہ مسجدیں اللہ ہی کے لیے ہیں۔ لہٰذا نہ پکارو (ان میں)
مَعَ اللّٰهِ اَحَدًا ﴿١٨﴾	اللہ کے ساتھ کسی اور کو (شریک بنا کر) ﴿١٨﴾
وَّاَنَّهٗ لَمَّا قَامَ عَبْدُ اللّٰهِ يَدْعُوْهُ	اور یہ کہ جب کھڑا ہوا اللہ کا بندہ اس کی عبادت کے لیے
كَادُوْا يَكُوْنُوْنَ عَلَيْهِ لِبَدًا ﴿١٩﴾	تو تیار ہو گئے یہ اس پر ٹوٹ پڑنے کے لیے ﴿١٩﴾
قُلْ اِنَّمَآ اَدْعُوْا رَبِّيْ	ان سے کہیے کہ میں تو بس پکارتا ہوں اپنے رب کو
وَلَآ اُشْرِكُ بِهٖٓ اَحَدًا ﴿٢٠﴾	اور نہیں شریک بناتا میں اس کے ساتھ کسی کو ﴿٢٠﴾
قُلْ اِنِّيْ لَآ اَمْلِكُ لَكُمْ	ان سے کہیے کہ حقیقت یہ ہے کہ نہیں اختیار رکھتا میں تمہارے لیے
ضَرًّا وَّلَا رَشَدًا ﴿٢١﴾	کسی نقصان کا اور نہ کسی بھلائی کا ﴿٢١﴾
قُلْ اِنِّيْ لَنْ يُّجِيْرَنِيْ مِنَ اللّٰهِ اَحَدٌ ۙ	ان سے کہیے ہرگز نہیں بچا سکتا مجھے اللہ کی گرفت سے کوئی
وَّلَنْ اَجِدَ مِنْ دُوْنِهٖ مُلْتَحَدًا ﴿٢٢﴾	اور ہرگز نہیں پاتا میں اس کے سوا کوئی جائے پناہ ﴿٢٢﴾
اِلَّا بَلٰغًا	(میرا کام نہیں ہے) سوائے اس کے کہ پہنچاؤں بات
مِّنَ اللّٰهِ وَرِسٰلٰتِهٖ ؕ وَمَنْ	اللہ کی طرف سے اور اس کے پیغامات۔ اور جو شخص بھی

So,
Those who affirm and conform in instruct
Them to cherish a blissful course of conduct

015 But who dodge and diverge in deride
Indeed!
They dissuade from faith in abide
Them to abide Hell pyre in stride

016 There's a word from Lord in stance
If the pagans abide verity in glance
Indeed!
We would've endowed rain profuse in place

017 So that We put them to trial in pace
Who defy Dictum of Lord in Grace
He'll seduce to suffer (them) in disgrace

018 And Mosques are for Lord to adore*
So supplicate none, but Him in allure*

*Pray

019 When Devotee trends to Lord in pray
They swarm in and around (him) in stay

020 Say:
To Lord I invoke, and join none (to Him) in grace

021 Say:
It's not me to hurt a bit in trace
Or alleviate your agony in pace

022 Say,
(If ever I turn to defy hither in stride)
There's none to save or cede in slander
Nor there's one to give refuge in plunder
Other than Lord in all walks in abide

023 I've no job to do,
Other than assigned to me so true
The word of Lord and His missives to pursue
Who so defy Lord and His messenger in span
Him to taste burn of pyre in plan
Whereto reside for ever or so

يَّعۡصِ اللّٰهَ وَرَسُوۡلَهٗ — نافرمانی کرے گا اللہ کی اور اس کے رسول کی

فَاِنَّ لَهٗ نَارَ جَهَنَّمَ — تو یقیناً ہے اس کے لیے جہنم کی آگ،

خٰلِدِيۡنَ فِيۡهَاۤ اَبَدًا ﴿۲۳﴾ — رہیں گے ایسے لوگ اس میں ہمیشہ ہمیشہ ﴿۲۳﴾

حَتّٰۤى اِذَا رَاَوۡا — (یہ لوگ باز نہ آئیں گے) یہاں تک کہ جب دیکھ لیں گے

مَا يُوۡعَدُوۡنَ فَسَيَعۡلَمُوۡنَ — وہ چیز جس سے انہیں ڈرایا جا رہا ہے تو انہیں معلوم ہو جائے گا

مَنۡ اَضۡعَفُ نَاصِرًا — کہ کون بہت زیادہ کمزور ہے مددگاروں کے لحاظ سے

وَّاَقَلُّ عَدَدًا ﴿۲۴﴾ — اور کس کا جتھا کم ہے تعداد میں ﴿۲۴﴾

قُلۡ اِنۡ اَدۡرِىۡۤ اَقَرِيۡبٌ — ان سے کہیے کہ مجھے نہیں معلوم کہ آیا قریب ہے

مَّا تُوۡعَدُوۡنَ اَمۡ يَجۡعَلُ — وہ چیز جس سے ڈرایا جا رہا ہے تم کو یا مقرر کر رکھی ہے

لَهٗ رَبِّىۡۤ اَمَدًا ﴿۲۵﴾ — اس کے لیے میرے رب نے کوئی مدت؟ ﴿۲۵﴾

عٰلِمُ الۡغَيۡبِ فَلَا يُظۡهِرُ — وہ عالم الغیب ہے پس نہیں مطلع فرماتا وہ

عَلٰى غَيۡبِهٖۤ اَحَدًا ﴿۲۶﴾ — اپنے غیب پر کسی کو ﴿۲۶﴾

اِلَّا مَنِ ارۡتَضٰى مِنۡ رَّسُوۡلٍ — سوائے اس رسول کے جسے پسند کر لیا ہو اس نے

فَاِنَّهٗ يَسۡلُكُ مِنۡۢ بَيۡنِ يَدَيۡهِ — تو صورت حال یہ ہے کہ لگا دیتا ہے وہ اس کے آگے

وَمِنۡ خَلۡفِهٖ رَصَدًا ﴿۲۷﴾ — اور پیچھے نگہبان ﴿۲۷﴾

لِّيَـعۡلَمَ اَنۡ قَدۡ اَبۡلَغُوۡا — تاکہ وہ جان لے کہ درحقیقت انہوں نے پہنچا دیے ہیں

رِسٰلٰتِ رَبِّهِمۡ وَاَحَاطَ — پیغامات اپنے رب کے اور وہ پوری طرح احاطہ کیے ہوئے ہے

بِمَا لَدَيۡهِمۡ وَاَحۡصٰى — ان کے ماحول کا اور شمار کر رکھا ہے اس نے

كُلَّ شَىۡءٍ عَدَدًا ﴿۲۸﴾ — ایک ایک چیز کو گن کر ﴿۲۸﴾

Those defying,
Lord and Messenger in concern
Them to aside Burn of Blaze in term

024 Where,
They'll abide and reside for ever and so
Eventually they perceive to conform in ado
For what was promised to them in blow

Them to conceive and assert to conform
For who's feeble to help in bias
And who's low in count in chaos
025 Say:
I don't know for sure in lore
When the Term in vow
That's affirmed to endure
If it's going to be soon in ado
Or it's going to be (a term) afar in blow

026 He alone determines,
The obscurity of concealed in stance
Nor does,
He intimates a word to some in glance
(His Anonymity of Mysteries lucid in span)

027 But for His messenger preferred in abide
With a band and body of guards in beside
Before and behind in place

028 That he may determine to concern
So they've indeed delivered in term

The missives of Lord to the men and clan
Lord care and concern all in plan
And concludes each bit and slit in span

اٰيَاتُهَا ٢٠ (٧٣) سُوْرَةُ الْمُزَّمِّلِ مَكِّيَّةٌ (٣) رُكُوْعَاتُهَا ٢

بِسْمِ اللّٰهِ الرَّحْمٰنِ الرَّحِيْمِ

شروع اللہ کے نام سے جو بڑا مہربان نہایت رحم والا ہے

يٰٓاَيُّهَا الْمُزَّمِّلُ ﴿۱﴾	اے اوڑھ لپیٹ کر سونے والے! ﴿۱﴾
قُمِ الَّيْلَ اِلَّا قَلِيْلًا ﴿۲﴾	کھڑے رہا کرو رات کو (نماز میں)، مگر تھوڑا حصہ ﴿۲﴾
نِّصْفَهٗٓ اَوِ انْقُصْ مِنْهُ قَلِيْلًا ﴿۳﴾	آدھی رات یا کم کر لو اس میں سے تھوڑا حصہ ﴿۳﴾
اَوْ زِدْ عَلَيْهِ وَرَتِّلِ	یا زیادہ کر لو اس پر (کچھ) اور پڑھو
الْقُرْاٰنَ تَرْتِيْلًا ﴿۴﴾	قرآن کو خوب ٹھہر ٹھہر کر ﴿۴﴾
اِنَّا سَنُلْقِيْ عَلَيْكَ قَوْلًا ثَقِيْلًا ﴿۵﴾	یقیناً ہم نازل کرنے والے ہیں تم پر ایک بھاری کلام ﴿۵﴾
اِنَّ نَاشِئَةَ الَّيْلِ	بے شک اٹھنا رات کو
هِيَ اَشَدُّ وَطْـاً	ہے بہت ہی کارگر (نفس پر) قابو پانے کے لیے
وَّاَقْوَمُ قِيْلًا ﴿۶﴾	اور بہت ہی خوب وقت ہے (قرآن) پڑھنے کے لیے ﴿۶﴾
اِنَّ لَكَ فِي النَّهَارِ سَبْحًا طَوِيْلًا ﴿۷﴾	جبکہ یقیناً ہیں تمہارے لیے دن میں بہت سی مصروفیات ﴿۷﴾
وَاذْكُرِ اسْمَ رَبِّكَ	اور ذکر کیا کرو اپنے رب کے نام کا
وَتَبَتَّلْ اِلَيْهِ تَبْتِيْلًا ﴿۸﴾	اور اسی کے ہو رہو سب سے کٹ کر پوری طرح ﴿۸﴾
رَبُّ الْمَشْرِقِ وَالْمَغْرِبِ لَآ اِلٰهَ	جو رب ہے مشرق و مغرب کا نہیں ہے کوئی معبود
اِلَّا هُوَ فَاتَّخِذْهُ وَكِيْلًا ﴿۹﴾	سوائے اس کے، سو بنا لو اسے اپنا کارساز ﴿۹﴾
وَاصْبِرْ عَلٰي مَا يَقُوْلُوْنَ	اور صبر کرو ان باتوں پر جو یہ کہتے ہیں

073-AL MUZZAMMIL

In the name of Lord, the Most Beneficent, Most Merciful

001 O you crimped and tucked in slacks in sleep!

002 By night, poise to pray and tend to entreat

003 Half of it - or a bit less, beg in beseech

004 Or a bit of more to pray in stance
And recite Qur'an in tranquil and elegant runes

005 Soon We will assign you a term in trance
Missive so massive and cumbrous as dunes

006 Indeed!
Night vigil is so convincing in concern
Keeping the soul apt and correct to discern
To ardor and adore Lord (in faith to affirm)

007/ Truly by day you're diligent devout
008 For all in routine here to promote

Keep His Vigil destined in core
And pray Him, in true ardor and adore

009 There's no god but Lord in Grace
Lord of the East and West to brace

Pick Him as Guardian all in quest
For He care and concerns here for the best

010 And have patience for what they tattle in stray
And let them alone with dignity and grace

وَاهْجُرْهُمْ هَجْرًا جَمِيْلًا ﴿١٠﴾	اور ان کو نظر انداز کر دو بھلے طریقے سے ﴿١٠﴾
وَذَرْنِيْ وَالْمُكَذِّبِيْنَ	اور چھوڑ دو مجھے نمٹنے کے لیے ان جھٹلانے والوں سے
اُولِي النَّعْمَةِ وَمَهِّلْهُمْ قَلِيْلًا ﴿١١﴾	جو خوشحال ہیں اور رہنے دو انہیں اسی حالت پر کچھ دیر اور ﴿١١﴾
اِنَّ لَدَيْنَآ اَنْكَالًا	یقیناً ہیں ہمارے پاس (ان کے لیے) بھاری بیڑیاں
وَّجَحِيْمًا ﴿١٢﴾	اور بھڑکتی ہوئی آگ ﴿١٢﴾
وَّطَعَامًا ذَا غُصَّةٍ وَّعَذَابًا اَلِيْمًا ﴿١٣﴾	اور کھانا حلق میں پھنسنے والا اور دردناک عذاب ﴿١٣﴾
يَوْمَ تَرْجُفُ الْاَرْضُ وَالْجِبَالُ	(یہ ہوگا) اس دن جب لرز اٹھیں گے زمین اور پہاڑ
وَكَانَتِ الْجِبَالُ كَثِيْبًا مَّهِيْلًا ﴿١٤﴾	اور ہو جائیں گے پہاڑ ریت کے بھر بھرے ٹیلوں کی مانند ﴿١٤﴾
اِنَّآ اَرْسَلْنَآ اِلَيْكُمْ رَسُوْلًا ۥ	یقیناً ہم نے بھیجا ہے تمہاری طرف ایک رسول ۔
شَاهِدًا عَلَيْكُمْ كَمَآ اَرْسَلْنَآ	گواہ بنا کر تم پر جس طرح ہم نے بھیجا تھا
اِلٰى فِرْعَوْنَ رَسُوْلًا ﴿١٥﴾	فرعون کی طرف ایک رسول ﴿١٥﴾
فَعَصٰى فِرْعَوْنُ الرَّسُوْلَ	تو نافرمانی کی فرعون نے اس رسول کی
فَاَخَذْنٰهُ اَخْذًا وَّبِيْلًا ﴿١٦﴾	تو دھر لیا ہم نے اسے بہت سخت پکڑ میں ﴿١٦﴾
فَكَيْفَ تَتَّقُوْنَ اِنْ كَفَرْتُمْ	سو کیسے بچ جاؤ گے تم اگر انکار کرو گے تم بھی
يَوْمًا يَّجْعَلُ الْوِلْدَانَ شِيْبًا ﴿١٧﴾	اس دن سے (جس کی سختی) کر دے گی بچوں کو بوڑھا ﴿١٧﴾
السَّمَآءُ مُنْفَطِرٌ بِهٖ	اور آسمان پھٹا جا رہا ہوگا اس (کی دہشت) سے ۔
كَانَ وَعْدُهٗ مَفْعُوْلًا ﴿١٨﴾	ہے وعدہ اللہ کا پورا ہو کر رہنے والا ﴿١٨﴾
اِنَّ هٰذِهٖ تَذْكِرَةٌ ۚ فَمَنْ شَآءَ	یقیناً یہ ایک نصیحت ہے سو جس کا جی چاہے
اتَّخَذَ اِلٰى رَبِّهٖ سَبِيْلًا ﴿١٩﴾ ع	اختیار کر لے اپنے رب کی طرف جانے کا راستہ ﴿١٩﴾

011 Let Me alone handle (them) in trail
Those,
Relishing boon and bounties in vale

Let them allure the lust for a time
Abjuring the tend in verity in prime
You bear with them for a while in time

012/ We've Fetters of Fire for them to aside
013 And Food that stifle and smother in stride
A term in discipline distressing in glide

014 The Day
When earth and mountains stir in ado
Mountains,
Piling as sand and smelting like snow

Fate of the Universe (Page : 1264)

015 O you the men and clan in abide
We'd a prophet mid you to aside

To care and concern your deeds in proceeds
As We'd the prophet for Pharaoh in creed

016 But Pharaoh turned to defy prophet in trance
So We Inflicted hefty reproach in glance

017 How'd you then!
If you dare to defy Lord in decide
Protect your self on the Day in beside
That's to turn scion ruse in deride

018 The sky pierced and parted asunder in assort
His word of commitment to meet in accord

019 Verily that's the Caution, for a word to brace
You poise in stance,
At night before Lord in grace

Two-thirds or half or a third of the night
For Lord cares to concern all in slight

اِنَّ رَبَّكَ يَعْلَمُ اَنَّكَ تَقُوْمُ	یقیناً تمہارا رب اسے نبیؐ جانتا ہے کہ تم کھڑے ہوتے ہو (عبادت کے لیے)
اَدْنٰى مِنْ ثُلُثَيِ الَّيْلِ وَنِصْفَهٗ وَثُلُثَهٗ	تقریباً دو تہائی رات اور کبھی آدھی رات اور کبھی ایک تہائی
وَطَآئِفَةٌ مِّنَ الَّذِيْنَ مَعَكَ ؕ	اور ایک گروہ بھی ان لوگوں کا جو تمہارے ساتھ ہیں۔
وَاللّٰهُ يُقَدِّرُ الَّيْلَ وَالنَّهَارَ ؕ	اور اللہ ہی نے اندازے مقرر کیے ہیں رات اور دن کے۔
عَلِمَ اَنْ لَّنْ تُحْصُوْهُ	اسے معلوم ہے کہ تم اس کا صحیح شمار ہرگز نہیں کر سکتے
فَتَابَ عَلَيْكُمْ فَاقْرَءُوْا مَا	سو اس نے تم پر مہربانی فرمائی۔ لہٰذا پڑھو جتنا
تَيَسَّرَ مِنَ الْقُرْاٰنِ ؕ عَلِمَ اَنْ سَيَكُوْنُ	آسانی سے پڑھ سکتے ہو قرآن۔ اسے معلوم ہے کہ ہوں گے
مِنْكُمْ مَّرْضٰى ۙ وَاٰخَرُوْنَ يَضْرِبُوْنَ	تم میں سے کچھ مریض اور کچھ لوگ جو سفر کریں گے
فِى الْاَرْضِ يَبْتَغُوْنَ مِنْ فَضْلِ اللّٰهِ ۙ	زمین میں اللہ کے فضل کی تلاش میں
وَاٰخَرُوْنَ يُقَاتِلُوْنَ فِىْ سَبِيْلِ اللّٰهِ ۖ	اور ہوں گے کچھ لوگ جو جنگ کریں گے اللہ کی راہ میں۔
فَاقْرَءُوْا مَا تَيَسَّرَ مِنْهُ ۙ	لہٰذا پڑھو جتنا آسانی سے پڑھ سکو اس میں سے۔
وَاَقِيْمُوا الصَّلٰوةَ وَاٰتُوا الزَّكٰوةَ	اور قائم کرو نماز اور دو زکوٰۃ
وَاَقْرِضُوا اللّٰهَ قَرْضًا حَسَنًا ؕ	اور قرض دیتے رہو اللہ کو قرضِ حسنہ۔
وَمَا تُقَدِّمُوْا لِاَنْفُسِكُمْ	اور جو کچھ تم آگے بھیجو گے اپنے لیے
مِّنْ خَيْرٍ تَجِدُوْهُ	کسی قسم کی بھلائی کا کام تو پاؤ گے تم اسے
عِنْدَ اللّٰهِ هُوَ خَيْرًا	موجود اللہ کے پاس اور یہی کام بہتر ہیں
وَّاَعْظَمَ اَجْرًا ؕ	اور بہت بڑے ہیں اجر کے لحاظ سے
وَاسْتَغْفِرُوا اللّٰهَ ؕ	اور اللہ سے مغفرت مانگتے رہو۔
اِنَّ اللّٰهَ غَفُوْرٌ رَّحِيْمٌ ﴿۲۰﴾ ع	یقیناً اللہ ہے بہت زیادہ معاف فرمانے والا نہایت مہربان ﴿۲۰﴾

020 And a band and clan with you tend in plight
But there's a step in size for the Day and Night
He deems to discern all in slight

That you cannot keep the count in term
So He trends in due care in concern

Narrate Qur'an in moderate of tune
So far it's easy for you to resume

He discerns with due care and concern
There're few sick, others in travel in dale
Seeking Bounty of Lord to affirm
And for His Course in conduct hither in vale

Yet some trending to combat in fray
Abiding Dictum of Lord to obey

Recite Qur'an as it ease (you) in stance
Modest allegiance of grace in glance

Assert to affirm usual prayer in grace
Endow in charity, sincerity in pace

Bestowal of loan to Almighty in credence
That's the beatific Loan in prudence

All in good you convey Thither in fore
You'll cherish bounties of Lord in score
With Lord!

There's a preferred and perfected return in award
You pursue in piety Bounty of Lord in accord
Who's Most!
Merciful bestowing super and superb in award

اٰیاتها ٥٦ — سُوْرَةُ الْمُدَّثِّرِ مَكِّيَّةٌ (٧٤) (٤) — رکوعاتها ٢

بِسْمِ اللّٰهِ الرَّحْمٰنِ الرَّحِيْمِ

شروع اللہ کے نام سے جو بڑا مہربان نہایت رحم والا ہے

يٰٓاَيُّهَا الْمُدَّثِّرُ ۙ ١	اے اوڑھ لپیٹ کر لیٹنے والے! (١)
قُمْ فَاَنْذِرْ ۙ ٢	اٹھو اور خبردار کرو (٢)
وَرَبَّكَ فَكَبِّرْ ۙ ٣	اور اپنے رب ہی کی بڑائی کا اعلان کرو (٣)
وَثِيَابَكَ فَطَهِّرْ ۙ ٤	اور اپنے کپڑوں کو پاک صاف رکھو (٤)
وَالرُّجْزَ فَاهْجُرْ ۙ ٥	اور ہر قسم کی گندگی سے اپنے آپ کو دور رکھو (٥)
وَلَا تَمْنُنْ تَسْتَكْثِرُ ۙ ٦	اور مت احسان کرو اس غرض سے کہ زیادہ فائدہ حاصل ہو (٦)
وَلِرَبِّكَ فَاصْبِرْ ۭ ٧	اور اپنے رب کی خاطر صبر کرو (٧)
فَاِذَا نُقِرَ فِي النَّاقُوْرِ ۙ ٨	پھر جب پھونک ماری جائے گی صور میں (٨)
فَذٰلِكَ يَوْمَىِٕذٍ يَّوْمٌ عَسِيْرٌ ۙ ٩	تو وہی دن ہوگا، بڑی مصیبت کا دن (٩)
عَلَى الْكٰفِرِيْنَ غَيْرُ يَسِيْرٍ ١٠	کافروں کے لیے جس میں ذرا بھی آسانی نہ ہوگی (١٠)
ذَرْنِيْ وَمَنْ خَلَقْتُ وَحِيْدًا ۙ ١١	چھوڑ دو مجھے اور اس شخص کو جسے پیدا کیا میں نے اکیلا (١١)
وَّجَعَلْتُ لَهٗ مَالًا مَّمْدُوْدًا ۙ ١٢	اور دیا اس کو ڈھیروں مال (١٢)
وَّبَنِيْنَ شُهُوْدًا ۙ ١٣	اور بیٹے حاضر رہنے والے (١٣)
وَّمَهَّدْتُّ لَهٗ تَمْهِيْدًا ۙ ١٤	اور راہ ہموار کی اس کے لیے سرداری کی (١٤)
ثُمَّ يَطْمَعُ اَنْ اَزِيْدَ ۤ ١٥	پھر بھی وہ طمع رکھتا ہے کہ میں اسے اور زیادہ دوں (١٥)

074-AL MUDDATHTHIR

In the name of Lord, the Most Beneficent, Most Merciful

001 O you done up in blanket and sheath
002 Arise to deliver you caution in elite

003 And exalt Thy Lord indeed in stance

004 And your dress neat and clean in glance

005 And elude pollution in trance

006 Don't expect to secure reward in pace
When you trend to clemency in place

007 But for Lord, be patient in adore!
Be ardently diligent and determined in core

008 And then cornet will be blown
With high resonance in tone

009 That will be the Day!
The Day of anguish and alarm in sworn

010 It wouldn't be easy to go in calm
For the faithless held in alarm

011 Let Me deal with each in mourn
Whom I created stripped in alone

012/ Whom,
013 I granted property and produce so profuse
With successors and scions beside to seduce

014/ To them I made,
015 Life tranquil in ease and appease
Yet he stays in lust to squeeze
That I would add yet more in increase

كَلَّا ۖ إِنَّهُ كَانَ لِآيَاتِنَا عَنِيدًا ﴿١٦﴾	ہرگز نہیں! وہ تو ہے ہماری آیات سے سخت عناد رکھنے والا ۱۶
سَأُرْهِقُهُ صَعُودًا ﴿١٧﴾	عنقریب میں چڑھاؤں گا اسے ایک کٹھن چڑھائی ۱۷
إِنَّهُ فَكَّرَ وَقَدَّرَ ﴿١٨﴾	واقعہ یہ ہے کہ اس نے سوچا اور کچھ بات بنانے کی کوشش کی ۱۸
فَقُتِلَ كَيْفَ قَدَّرَ ﴿١٩﴾	سو اللہ کی مار اس پر کیسی بات بنائی اس نے! ۱۹
ثُمَّ قُتِلَ كَيْفَ قَدَّرَ ﴿٢٠﴾	پھر اللہ کی مار اس پر کیسی بات بنائی اس نے! ۲۰
ثُمَّ نَظَرَ ﴿٢١﴾	پھر نظر دوڑائی ۲۱
ثُمَّ عَبَسَ وَبَسَرَ ﴿٢٢﴾	پھر پیشانی سکیڑی اور منہ بنایا ۲۲
ثُمَّ أَدْبَرَ وَاسْتَكْبَرَ ﴿٢٣﴾	پھر پلٹا اور تکبر میں پڑ گیا ۲۳
فَقَالَ إِنْ هَٰذَا	آخر کار بولا، نہیں ہے یہ (قرآن)
إِلَّا سِحْرٌ يُؤْثَرُ ﴿٢٤﴾	مگر ایک جادو، جو پہلے سے چلا آ رہا ہے ۲۴
إِنْ هَٰذَا إِلَّا قَوْلُ الْبَشَرِ ﴿٢٥﴾	نہیں ہے یہ مگر انسانی کلام ۲۵
سَأُصْلِيهِ سَقَرَ ﴿٢٦﴾	عنقریب ہم جھونک دیں گے اسے جہنم میں ۲۶
وَمَا أَدْرَاكَ مَا سَقَرُ ﴿٢٧﴾	اور کیا جانو تم، کیا ہے جہنم؟ ۲۷
لَا تُبْقِي وَلَا تَذَرُ ﴿٢٨﴾	(وہ جو) نہ باقی رہنے دے اور نہ چھوڑے ۲۸
لَوَّاحَةٌ لِلْبَشَرِ ﴿٢٩﴾	جھلسا دینے والی کھال کو ۲۹
عَلَيْهَا تِسْعَةَ عَشَرَ ﴿٣٠﴾	اس پر مقرر ہیں انیس (کارکن) ۳۰
وَمَا جَعَلْنَا أَصْحَابَ النَّارِ إِلَّا مَلَائِكَةً ۙ	اور نہیں بنائے ہیں ہم نے دوزخ کے یہ کارکن مگر فرشتے ہی۔
وَمَا جَعَلْنَا عِدَّتَهُمْ إِلَّا فِتْنَةً	اور نہیں بنایا ہم نے ان کی تعداد کو مگر ایک آزمائش
لِلَّذِينَ كَفَرُوا لِيَسْتَيْقِنَ الَّذِينَ أُوتُوا	کافروں کے لیے۔ تاکہ یقین کر لیں اس کا وہ لوگ جنہیں دی گئی تھی

016 By no means,
He didn't care a bit in concern
And defied Our Signs and Symbols in term

017 Then soon,
There'll be a visitation of Mine in term
With anguish in alarm and affliction in turn

018/ For he coveted, conceived and turned to contrive
019 Woe be to him,
Who coveted to conceive and turned to contrive

020/ Yes!
024 How he conceived and turned to contrive
Then he stared and glanced just and about
Then in smirk and sneer with glower and pout
Then spin to reverse, snobbish so proud

Then he turned to groan in trance
The Qur'an,
That's just sorcery of old in glance

025 It's only a word of mortal in stance

026/ Soon I'll sling him in ordeal of Hell an Abyss
027 How'd you discern,
What's ordeal of Hell an Abyss

028 Virtually nothing can dare to resist
Nor a thing can hold to persist

029 Snuffing extinction so dark in place
Veering the semblance of man in trace
Burning the skin so flimsy in pace

030 Over it angels nineteen in score
031 Held as guardian around in lore

We fixed numbers, only as trial in stance
For the Cynics destined to the fire in glance

So men of the Book may trend in esteem
Allegiants to assert faith and glow in gleam

الْكِتٰبَ وَيَزْدَادَ الَّذِيْنَ اٰمَنُوْٓا اِيْمَانًا	کتاب اور بڑھے ایمان والوں کا ایمان
وَّلَا يَرْتَابَ الَّذِيْنَ اُوْتُوا الْكِتٰبَ	اور نہ شک میں رہیں وہ لوگ جنہیں دی گئی ہے کتاب
وَالْمُؤْمِنُوْنَ ۙ وَلِيَقُوْلَ الَّذِيْنَ	اور اہلِ ایمان اور کہیں وہ لوگ جن کے
فِيْ قُلُوْبِهِمْ مَّرَضٌ وَّالْكٰفِرُوْنَ	دلوں میں بیماری ہے اور کافر
مَاذَآ اَرَادَ اللّٰهُ بِهٰذَا مَثَلًا ۭ	کیا چاہتا ہے اللہ اس مثال سے ؟
كَذٰلِكَ يُضِلُّ اللّٰهُ مَنْ يَّشَاۗءُ	اسی طرح اللہ گمراہ کر دیتا ہے جسے چاہے
وَيَهْدِيْ مَنْ يَّشَاۗءُ ۭ	اور ہدایت دیتا ہے جسے چاہے۔
وَمَا يَعْلَمُ جُنُوْدَ رَبِّكَ اِلَّا هُوَ ۭ	اور نہیں جانتا تیرے رب کے لشکروں کو کوئی سوائے اس کے۔
وَمَا هِيَ اِلَّا	اور نہیں ہے یہ (دوزخ کا ذکر) مگر
ذِكْرٰى لِلْبَشَرِ ﴿٣١﴾	ایک نصیحت آدمیوں کے لیے ﴿٣١﴾
كَلَّا وَالْقَمَرِ ﴿٣٢﴾	ہرگز نہیں! قسم ہے چاند کی ﴿٣٢﴾
وَالَّيْلِ اِذْ اَدْبَرَ ﴿٣٣﴾	اور رات کی جب وہ پلٹتی ہے ﴿٣٣﴾
وَالصُّبْحِ اِذَآ اَسْفَرَ ﴿٣٤﴾	اور قسم ہے صبح کی جب وہ روشن ہوتی ہے ﴿٣٤﴾
اِنَّهَا لَاِحْدَى الْكُبَرِ ﴿٣٥﴾	یقیناً یہ (دوزخ) ایک آفت ہے بڑی آفتوں میں سے ﴿٣٥﴾
نَذِيْرًا لِّلْبَشَرِ ﴿٣٦﴾	ڈراوا ہے انسانوں کے لیے ﴿٣٦﴾
لِمَنْ شَاۗءَ مِنْكُمْ	ہر اس شخص کے لیے جو چاہے تم میں سے
اَنْ يَّتَقَدَّمَ اَوْ يَتَاَخَّرَ ﴿٣٧﴾	کہ آگے بڑھے یا پیچھے رہے ﴿٣٧﴾
كُلُّ نَفْسٍۢ بِمَا كَسَبَتْ رَهِيْنَةٌ ﴿٣٨﴾	ہر شخص اپنے کمائے ہوئے اعمال کے بدلے میں رہن ہے ﴿٣٨﴾
اِلَّآ اَصْحٰبَ الْيَمِيْنِ ﴿٣٩﴾	سوائے دائیں بازو والوں کے ﴿٣٩﴾

ركوع ١٥

مع ۳ عند المتقدمین ۱۲

Men of the Book and faithful in place
Shouldn't be gone confused in trace
But rather affirm the truth of Faith

But whose core is blurred in disease
And the Cynics then astray in increase

And then they asserts in concern
What really Lord intends to conform

So Lord deserts and drifts some in stray
To some He escorts so firm to obey

None can discern His Force in demand
But for Lord, Who holds in Command

This is clear caution for the men and clan
Whoso abide His dictum in plan

032/ Nope, truly:
034 Vow be to the Moon, a glimmer in glow
By the night as it departs with dusk in throw
By the dawn as it twinkles, shimmer in flow

035/ Hell Pyre,
036 This is but a potent hint in predict
Word for men, a discipline so strict

037 It's a word for you to aside
Whoso tend to cherish bliss in proceeds
Or to defer in denial with woe to recede

038/ All to affirm and assert their trends in deed
039

But for the men with course in conduct
Punctilious precise trends in instruct

فِیْ جَنّٰتٍ ۛ یَتَسَآءَلُوْنَ ﴿۴۰﴾	جو جنتوں میں ہوں گے اور پوچھیں گے ﴿۴۰﴾
عَنِ الْمُجْرِمِیْنَ ﴿۴۱﴾	مجرموں سے ﴿۴۱﴾
مَا سَلَكَكُمْ فِیْ سَقَرَ ﴿۴۲﴾	کیا چیز لے گئی تمہیں جہنم میں ﴿۴۲﴾
قَالُوْا لَمْ نَكُ مِنَ الْمُصَلِّیْنَ ﴿۴۳﴾	وہ کہیں گے نہ تھے ہم نماز پڑھنے والوں میں ﴿۴۳﴾
وَلَمْ نَكُ نُطْعِمُ الْمِسْكِیْنَ ﴿۴۴﴾	اور نہ کھلایا کرتے تھے ہم کھانا مسکین کو ﴿۴۴﴾
وَكُنَّا نَخُوْضُ مَعَ الْخَآئِضِیْنَ ﴿۴۵﴾	اور باتیں بنایا کرتے تھے ہم مل کر حق کے خلاف باتیں بنانے والوں کے ساتھ ﴿۴۵﴾
وَكُنَّا نُكَذِّبُ بِیَوْمِ الدِّیْنِ ﴿۴۶﴾	اور جھٹلایا کرتے تھے ہم روزِ جزا کو ﴿۴۶﴾
حَتّٰۤی اَتٰىنَا الْیَقِیْنُ ﴿۴۷﴾	یہاں تک کہ آگئی ہمیں موت ﴿۴۷﴾
فَمَا تَنْفَعُهُمْ شَفَاعَةُ الشّٰفِعِیْنَ ﴿۴۸﴾	سو نہ فائدہ پہنچائے گی ان کو اب سفارش سفارش کرنے والوں کی ﴿۴۸﴾
فَمَا لَهُمْ عَنِ التَّذْكِرَةِ مُعْرِضِیْنَ ﴿۴۹﴾	آخر ان لوگوں کو کیا ہو گیا ہے کہ یہ اس کتابِ نصیحت سے منہ موڑے ہوئے ہیں ﴿۴۹﴾
كَاَنَّهُمْ حُمُرٌ مُّسْتَنْفِرَةٌ ﴿۵۰﴾	گویا کہ وہ جنگلی گدھے ہیں ﴿۵۰﴾
فَرَّتْ مِنْ قَسْوَرَةٍ ﴿۵۱﴾	جو بھاگ پڑے ہوں شیر کی آہٹ سے ﴿۵۱﴾
بَلْ یُرِیْدُ كُلُّ امْرِئٍ مِّنْهُمْ	بلکہ چاہتا ہے ہر شخص ان میں سے
اَنْ یُّؤْتٰى صُحُفًا مُّنَشَّرَةً ﴿۵۲﴾	کہ دیا جائے اسے کھلا صحیفہ ﴿۵۲﴾
كَلَّا ؕ بَلْ لَّا یَخَافُوْنَ الْاٰخِرَةَ ﴿۵۳﴾	ہرگز نہیں، اصل بات یہ ہے کہ یہ نہیں ڈرتے ہیں آخرت سے ﴿۵۳﴾
كَلَّاۤ اِنَّهٗ تَذْكِرَةٌ ﴿۵۴﴾	خبردار یہ تو ایک نصیحت ہے ﴿۵۴﴾
فَمَنْ شَآءَ ذَكَرَهٗ ﴿۵۵﴾	سو جس کا جی چاہے اس سے سبق حاصل کرے ﴿۵۵﴾
وَمَا یَذْكُرُوْنَ اِلَّاۤ اَنْ یَّشَآءَ اللّٰهُ ؕ	اور نہیں سبق حاصل کریں گے یہ لوگ اس سے اِلّا یہ کہ چاہے اللہ۔
هُوَ اَهْلُ التَّقْوٰى وَاَهْلُ الْمَغْفِرَةِ ﴿۵۶﴾	وہ لائق ہے ڈرنے کے اور وہ مالک ہے بخشش کا ﴿۵۶﴾

040 So savor and flavor the Gardens in delight
They quest and inquire mid them so bright

041/ What lead the sinners to the pyre in plight
042

043 They'll assert to speak and repeat
We didn't practice to pray in entreat

044 Nor we ever fed the poor (in street)
(Not even the needy in a turn in screech)

045 But tattled in frivolity, futility in stride
With cynics,
Against the discipline of faith in abide
046 Denying the Day of Just in Trust to aside

047 Until there's the time of the death to endure
048 Then no quittance of counsel profit in score

049/ Then why to drift from counsel to comply
051 As appalled and abashed ass, persists to defy
When at the,
Sight of lion it gets to feet in stride

052/ All who desire a scroll clear and direct
053 But!
They dread not Hereafter trend in instruct

054/ Nay,
055 It's caution and council for all who obey
If some trend to assert to affirm in pray

056 But there's none to assert and affirm
But for the men and clan in concern
Whom Lord Almighty guides to affirm

He's Lord of the Virtuous in abide
And Lord, Who's Clement in beside

آیاتھا ۴۰ (۷۵) سُوْرَۃُ الْقِیٰمَۃِ مَکِّیَّۃٌ (۳۱) رکوعاتھا ۲

بِسْمِ اللّٰهِ الرَّحْمٰنِ الرَّحِيْمِ

شروع اللہ کے نام سے جو بڑا مہربان نہایت رحم والا ہے

لَآ اُقْسِمُ بِيَوْمِ الْقِيٰمَةِ ۝۱	نہیں قسم کھاتا ہوں میں روزِ قیامت کی ۱
وَلَآ اُقْسِمُ بِالنَّفْسِ اللَّوَّامَةِ ۝۲	اور نہیں، قسم کھاتا ہوں میں ملامت کرنے والے نفس کی ۲
اَيَحْسَبُ الْاِنْسَانُ	کیا سمجھ رکھا ہے انسان نے
اَلَّنْ نَّجْمَعَ عِظَامَهٗ ۝۳	کہ ہرگز نہیں جمع کر سکیں گے ہم اس کی ہڈیوں کو؟ ۳
بَلٰى قٰدِرِيْنَ عَلٰٓى اَنْ	کیوں نہیں ہم تو قادر ہیں اس پر بھی کہ
نُّسَوِّيَ بَنَانَهٗ ۝۴	ٹھیک ٹھیک بنا دیں (دوبارہ) اس کی انگلیوں کے پور پور کو ۴
بَلْ يُرِيْدُ الْاِنْسَانُ لِيَفْجُرَ اَمَامَهٗ ۝۵	مگر چاہتا ہے انسان کہ بداعمالیاں کرتا رہے آئندہ بھی ۵
يَسْـَٔلُ اَيَّانَ يَوْمُ الْقِيٰمَةِ ۝۶	پوچھتا ہے کہ کب آئے گا قیامت کا دن ۶
فَاِذَا بَرِقَ الْبَصَرُ ۝۷	سو جب چندھیا جائیں گی آنکھیں ۷
وَخَسَفَ الْقَمَرُ ۝۸	اور گہنا جائے گا چاند ۸
وَجُمِعَ الشَّمْسُ وَالْقَمَرُ ۝۹	اور ملا کر ایک کر دیے جائیں گے سورج اور چاند ۹
يَقُوْلُ الْاِنْسَانُ يَوْمَىِٕذٍ اَيْنَ الْمَفَرُّ ۝۱۰	کہے گا انسان اس دن، ہے کوئی جائے پناہ ۱۰
كَلَّا لَا وَزَرَ ۝۱۱	ہرگز نہیں! نہیں ہے کوئی جائے پناہ ۱۱
اِلٰى رَبِّكَ يَوْمَىِٕذِ ِۨالْمُسْتَقَرُّ ۝۱۲	اپنے رب کے سامنے ہی اس دن ٹھہرنا ہوگا ۱۲
يُنَبَّؤُا الْاِنْسَانُ يَوْمَىِٕذٍۢ	بتا دیا جائے گا انسان کو اس دن

075-AL QIYAMAH

In the name of Lord, the Most Beneficent, Most Merciful

001/ Vow be to the Day of Revival* in stance
002 Vow be to the spirit of remorse in trance

*Dooms Day

003 O man!
What does a man concern in pace
That, We cannot collect his bones in trace

004 Nay! We're endowed in Grace
Even to put the tips of the toes
Perfected in place

005 But man dreams and desires in thrill
To stay in ills and continue evil in drill

006 He doubts and disputes in stance
When the Day of Revival will be there in trance

007/ At the term in conclude
009 When the sight is confused

And the moon is put to dusk in daze
And Sun and the moon fused in blaze

010/ That Day the man will assert to affirm
012 Where to shelter and refuge in turn

In no way!
There's no site and spot of rest or refuge
The Day; Only before The Lord in place
That will be the only site and spot in assuage

بِمَا قَدَّمَ وَأَخَّرَ ۱۳	اس کا اگلا پچھلا کیا کرایا ۱۳
بَلِ الْإِنسَانُ عَلَىٰ نَفْسِهِ بَصِيرَةٌ ۱۴	بلکہ انسان خود ہی اپنے آپ کو خوب جانتا ہے ۱۴
وَلَوْ أَلْقَىٰ مَعَاذِيرَهُ ۱۵	اگرچہ کتنی ہی پیش کرے معذرتیں ۱۵
لَا تُحَرِّكْ بِهِ لِسَانَكَ	نہ حرکت دو اس (قرآن کو یاد کرنے) کے لیے اپنی زبان کو
لِتَعْجَلَ بِهِ ۱۶	تاکہ جلدی یاد کر لو تم اسے ۱۶
إِنَّ عَلَيْنَا جَمْعَهُ وَقُرْآنَهُ ۱۷	یقیناً ہمارے ذمہ ہے اس کو جمع کرنا اور پڑھوانا ۱۷
فَإِذَا قَرَأْنَاهُ	لہٰذا جب ہم اسے پڑھ رہے ہوں
فَاتَّبِعْ قُرْآنَهُ ۱۸	تو غور سے سنتے رہو اس کی قراءت کو ۱۸
ثُمَّ إِنَّ عَلَيْنَا	پھر یقیناً ہمارے ہی ذمہ ہے
بَيَانَهُ ۱۹	اس کا مطلب سمجھا دینا بھی ۱۹
كَلَّا بَلْ تُحِبُّونَ	ہرگز نہیں اصل بات یہ ہے کہ تم لوگ محبت رکھتے ہو
الْعَاجِلَةَ ۲۰	دنیا سے ۲۰
وَتَذَرُونَ الْآخِرَةَ ۲۱	اور چھوڑ دیتے ہو آخرت کو ۲۱
وُجُوهٌ يَوْمَئِذٍ نَّاضِرَةٌ ۲۲	کچھ چہرے ہوں گے اس دن تر و تازہ ۲۲
إِلَىٰ رَبِّهَا نَاظِرَةٌ ۲۳	اپنے رب کی طرف دیکھ رہے ہوں گے ۲۳
وَوُجُوهٌ يَوْمَئِذٍ بَاسِرَةٌ ۲۴	اور کچھ چہرے ہوں گے اس دن اداس ۲۴
تَظُنُّ أَن يُفْعَلَ بِهَا فَاقِرَةٌ ۲۵	سمجھ رہے ہوں گے کہ ہو گا ان کے ساتھ کمر توڑ برتاؤ ۲۵
كَلَّا إِذَا بَلَغَتِ التَّرَاقِيَ ۲۶	ہرگز نہیں! جب پہنچ جائے گی (جان) حلق میں ۲۶
وَقِيلَ مَنْ ۜ رَاقٍ ۲۷	اور کہا جائے گا ہے کوئی ...؟ جھاڑ پھونک کرنے والا ۲۷

013/ That Day
014 Man will be shown to glance
All his done and doing in trance

And also for what he did before in trail
Man will affirm his done and doings in scale

015 Even so he'll excuse and reason in plea
016 Move not your tongue in haste to recite
Regarding Qur'an reiterating in plight

017/ It's for Us to bless, the vision so bright
018 To secure, then let to pronounce
As We proclaim and assert to announce

You follow its recital, prime in define
019 No more! Then, it's for Us to construe in sublime

020 Nay O man! (in the vale)
You love in core the worldly lures in glee

021 And let alone Hereafter in daze
022 The Day!
Some faces, will glisten in gleam

023 Looking at Lord in an elegant esteem
024 That Day,
Some of the faces held in gloom
With the somber of soot

025 They'll whimper in drill
For their strenuous blow in trill
For them to adore calamity in shrill

026 Indeed not,
When their soul will be on way to egress

027 It'll scream and shriek in stress
Is there a conjurer to restore* to impress

*keep back the souls

وَّظَنَّ اَنَّهُ الْفِرَاقُ ۲۸	اور سمجھے گا وہ کہ یہ وقت ہے جدائی کا ۲۸
وَالْتَفَّتِ السَّاقُ بِالسَّاقِ ۲۹	اور جڑ جائے گی پنڈلی، پنڈلی سے ۲۹
اِلٰى رَبِّكَ يَوْمَئِذِ ۣالْمَسَاقُ ۳۰ ع	اپنے رب کی طرف اس دن روانگی ہوگی ۳۰
فَلَا صَدَّقَ	اس سب کے باوجود نہ ایمان لایا وہ
وَلَا صَلّٰى ۳۱	اور نہ نماز پڑھی اس نے ۳۱
وَلٰكِنْ كَذَّبَ وَتَوَلّٰى ۳۲	بلکہ جھٹلایا اور منہ پھیر لیا ۳۲
ثُمَّ ذَهَبَ اِلٰٓى اَهْلِهٖ يَتَمَطّٰى ۳۳	پھر چل دیا اپنے گھر والوں کی طرف اکڑتا ہوا ۳۳
اَوْلٰى لَكَ فَاَوْلٰى ۳۴	افسوس ہے تجھ پر پھر افسوس ہے (تجھ پر) ۳۴
ثُمَّ اَوْلٰى لَكَ فَاَوْلٰى ۳۵	پھر افسوس ہے تجھ پر پھر افسوس ہے (تجھ پر) ۳۵
اَيَحْسَبُ الْاِنْسَانُ	کیا سمجھ رکھا ہے انسان نے
اَنْ يُّتْرَكَ سُدًى ۳۶	کہ اسے چھوڑ دیا جائے گا بلا حساب کتاب ۳۶
اَلَمْ يَكُ نُطْفَةً	کیا نہ تھا وہ ایک قطرہ
مِّنْ مَّنِيٍّ يُّمْنٰى ۳۷	حقیر پانی کا جو ٹپکایا گیا (رحم مادر میں) ۳۷
ثُمَّ كَانَ عَلَقَةً	پھر ہوا ایک لوتھڑا
فَخَلَقَ فَسَوّٰى ۳۸	پھر پیدا کیا اسے اللہ نے اور ہر لحاظ سے درست کیا ۳۸
فَجَعَلَ مِنْهُ الزَّوْجَيْنِ	پھر بنا دیے اس سے جوڑے جوڑے
الذَّكَرَ وَالْاُنْثٰى ۳۹	مرد اور عورت ۳۹
اَلَيْسَ ذٰلِكَ بِقٰدِرٍ عَلٰٓى اَنْ	کیا نہیں ہے یہ ہستی قادر اس پر کہ
يُّحْيِۦَ الْمَوْتٰى ۴۰ ع	زندہ کرے مردوں کو ۴۰

028 He'll affirm aloha of soul in depart

029 Legs will be tethered to each in part

030 That Day all to trend to The Lord in sort

031 Even so be not inclined to faith
Not even abide the prayer in pace

032 But instead,
Renouncing the truth and he drifted in way

033 Towards his reside to the close of kin
Proudly in insolence with conceit in spin

034/ Indeed!
035 It's woe in ado thee O man
Yes! surely woe and ado the o man in plan
Once more!
Misery for thee O man!
Yes! anguish and alarm in plan

036 What does the man think in stance
He'll be let,
Without being interrogated in trance
(With no question for your doings in glance)
037 Wasn't he a speck of sperm ejected in abash

038 Then he's an adhering lump and clump in stash
Then did (Lord)
Constructed and Construed superb in domain

039 And of him to remain
He made two sexes; male and dame to sustain

040 Doesn't He hold Power just for the same
Endowing life to the dead in claim

آياتها ٣١ — (٧٦) سُوْرَةُ الدَّهْرِ مَدَنِيَّةٌ (٩٨) — ركوعاتها ٢

بِسْمِ اللّٰهِ الرَّحْمٰنِ الرَّحِيْمِ

شروع اللہ کے نام سے جو بڑا مہربان نہایت رحم والا ہے

هَلْ اَتٰى عَلَى الْاِنْسَانِ حِيْنٌ	کیا گزرا ہے انسان پر ایک ایسا وقت،
مِّنَ الدَّهْرِ لَمْ يَكُنْ	زمانے کا کہ نہ تھا وہ
شَيْـًٔا مَّذْكُوْرًا (١)	کوئی قابلِ ذکر چیز؟ (١)
اِنَّا خَلَقْنَا الْاِنْسَانَ	بے شک ہم نے پیدا کیا ہے انسان کو
مِنْ نُّطْفَةٍ اَمْشَاجٍ نَّبْتَلِيْهِ فَجَعَلْنٰهُ	ایک مخلوط نطفہ سے تاکہ امتحان لیں اس کا اسی لیے بنایا ہے ہم نے اسے
سَمِيْعًا بَصِيْرًا (٢)	سننے والا ، دیکھنے والا (٢)
اِنَّا هَدَيْنٰهُ السَّبِيْلَ اِمَّا	ہم نے دکھا دیا ہے اسے راستا اب چاہے
شَاكِرًا وَّاِمَّا كَفُوْرًا (٣)	(بن جائے) شکر کرنے والا یا کفر کرنے والا (٣)
اِنَّا اَعْتَدْنَا لِلْكٰفِرِيْنَ سَلٰسِلَا۟	یقیناً ہم نے مہیا کر رکھی ہیں کافروں کے لیے زنجیریں،
وَاَغْلٰلًا وَّسَعِيْرًا (٤)	طوق اور بھڑکتی ہوئی آگ (٤)
اِنَّ الْاَبْرَارَ يَشْرَبُوْنَ مِنْ كَاْسٍ	یقیناً نیک لوگ پئیں گے شراب کے جام
كَانَ مِزَاجُهَا كَافُوْرًا (٥)	جن میں آمیزش ہوگی کافور کی (٥)
عَيْنًا يَّشْرَبُ بِهَا عِبَادُ اللّٰهِ	یہ ایک چشمہ ہے کہ پئیں گے اس میں سے اللہ کے بندے
يُفَجِّرُوْنَهَا تَفْجِيْرًا (٦)	اور شاخیں نکال لیں گے اس میں سے جس طرح نکالنا چاہیں گے (٦)
يُوْفُوْنَ بِالنَّذْرِ وَيَخَافُوْنَ	(یہ وہ لوگ ہوں گے) جو پوری کیا کرتے تھے اپنی نذر اور ڈرتے تھے

076-AL INSAN

In the name of Lord, the Most Beneficent, Most Merciful

001 Man!
Think of your most dubious term in plight
When you're just a trifling and trivial in slight
To be revealed in any term and scale

002 Indeed!
We created thee O man in prop
From coed sperm evicted in drop

So to test and try him hither in term
As We gifted hearing and sight to concern

003 We ushered him means to deem and discern
For if he is gratifying or defying in turn

004 For the men defying the faith in span
We fitted fetters (shackles, yokes) in Fire

005 And for virtuous there's similitude in aspire
They savor wine with 'Kafur' drink in refine

006 Aside sinuous spring in design
Dutiful of Lord, sit in sublime

Making it flow unbound in profusion
To cherish in pick
What they delight in flip

يَوْمًا كَانَ شَرُّهٗ مُسْتَطِيْرًا ۝٧	اس دن سے جس کی مصیبت ہر طرف پھیلی ہوئی ہوگی ۝٧
وَ يُطْعِمُوْنَ الطَّعَامَ عَلٰى حُبِّهٖ	اور کھلایا کرتے تھے کھانا اللہ کی محبت میں
مِسْكِيْنًا وَّ يَتِيْمًا وَّاَسِيْرًا ۝٨	مسکین کو، یتیم کو اور قیدی کو ۝٨
اِنَّمَا نُطْعِمُكُمْ لِوَجْهِ اللّٰهِ	(اور کہتے تھے) کہ بس کھلا رہے ہیں ہم تم کو اللہ کی خاطر۔
لَا نُرِيْدُ مِنْكُمْ جَزَآءً وَّلَا شُكُوْرًا ۝٩	نہیں چاہتے ہم تم سے کوئی بدلہ اور نہ شکریہ ۝٩
اِنَّا نَخَافُ مِنْ رَّبِّنَا يَوْمًا	بلاشبہ ہمیں ڈر ہے اپنے رب سے اس دن (کے عذاب) کا
عَبُوْسًا قَمْطَرِيْرًا ۝١٠	جو سخت مصیبت کا اور انتہائی طویل ہوگا ۝١٠
فَوَقٰىهُمُ اللّٰهُ شَرَّ ذٰلِكَ الْيَوْمِ	سو بچالے گا ان کو اللہ اس دن کے شر سے
وَلَقّٰىهُمْ نَضْرَةً وَّسُرُوْرًا ۝١١	اور عنایت فرمائے گا انہیں ترو تازگی اور سرور ۝١١
وَجَزٰىهُمْ بِمَا صَبَرُوْا	اور عطا کرے گا انہیں بدلے میں اس صبر کے جو انہوں نے کیا
جَنَّةً وَّحَرِيْرًا ۝١٢	جنت اور ریشمی لباس ۝١٢
مُّتَّكِـِٕيْنَ فِيْهَا عَلَى الْاَرَآئِكِ	تکیہ لگائے بیٹھے ہوں گے یہ وہاں اونچی مسندوں پر
لَا يَرَوْنَ فِيْهَا شَمْسًا	اور نہ برداشت کرنی پڑے گی انہیں وہاں سورج (کی گرمی)
وَّلَا زَمْهَرِيْرًا ۝١٣	اور نہ ٹھر (جاڑے کی) ۝١٣
وَ دَانِيَةً عَلَيْهِمْ ظِلٰلُهَا	اور جھکی ہوئی ہوں گی ان پر جنت کی چھاؤں
وَذُلِّلَتْ قُطُوْفُهَا تَذْلِيْلًا ۝١٤	اور بس میں کر دیے گئے ہوں گے (ان کے) اس کے پھل پوری طرح ۝١٤
وَ يُطَافُ عَلَيْهِمْ بِاٰنِيَةٍ مِّنْ فِضَّةٍ	اور گردش کرائے جائیں گے اہل جنت پر برتن چاندی کے
وَّ اَكْوَابٍ كَانَتْ قَوَارِيْرَا۠ ۝١٥	اور پیالے جو شیشے کے ہوں گے ۝١٥
قَوَارِيْرَا۠ مِنْ فِضَّةٍ	اور شیشہ بھی چاندی کی قسم کا ہوگا

007/ They firmly avow
009 And fear of The Day,
The Day of Awe and Dread in ado
And for the love of Lord in endow
They fed the stray in stay

The indigent, orphan and captive in pace
They so assert to affirm in place
We feed you only to savor in grace
The love of Lord to brace

Not hoping a bit of favor in trends
It's but for the love of Lord in amends

010 We dread a Day of dolor and distress
A term of rage from The Lord in press

011 Lord will cede and save,
Them from the agony of the Day in behave
And endow them gleam in glow in blissful crave

012 For they're punctilious, persistent in pace
Bestowal of Lord will be glowing in place
Blissful Gardens with Silken garb in grace

013 Reposing,
On heaved ornate seats in bright
So to view and watch all in delight

There's no scorch of the sun in slight
Nor numbed chill (of the moon in plight) in sight

014 Gardens to shawl supine in sublime
Bunches of the fruits in taste
Compliant and low in humility in state

015 Midst and around (them) silver urn in array
/ And goblets of crystal there in display
016

Crystal so clear as silver in sheer
They affirm the measure in leer

قَدَّرُوْهَا تَقْدِيْرًا ﴿۱۶﴾	جنہیں وہ بھریں گے ٹھیک اندازے کے مطابق ﴿۱۶﴾
وَيُسْقَوْنَ فِيْهَا كَاْسًا	اور پلائے جائیں گے انہیں وہاں ایسے جام
كَانَ مِزَاجُهَا زَنْجَبِيْلًا ﴿۱۷﴾	جن میں آمیزش ہوگی سونٹھ کی ﴿۱۷﴾
عَيْنًا فِيْهَا تُسَمّٰى سَلْسَبِيْلًا ﴿۱۸﴾	یہ ایک چشمہ ہوگا جنت میں جس کا نام ہے سلسبیل ﴿۱۸﴾
وَيَطُوْفُ عَلَيْهِمْ	اور دوڑتے پھر رہے ہوں گے ان کی خدمت کے لیے
وِلْدَانٌ مُّخَلَّدُوْنَ ۚ اِذَا رَاَيْتَهُمْ	ایسے لڑکے جو ہمیشہ لڑکے ہی رہیں گے۔ جب تم انہیں دیکھو
حَسِبْتَهُمْ لُؤْلُؤًا مَّنْثُوْرًا ﴿۱۹﴾	تو خیال کرو گویا کہ موتی ہیں بکھرے ہوئے ﴿۱۹﴾
وَاِذَا رَاَيْتَ ثَمَّ رَاَيْتَ	اور جب تم نگاہ ڈالو گے وہاں تو دیکھو گے ہر طرف
نَعِيْمًا وَّمُلْكًا كَبِيْرًا ﴿۲۰﴾	نعمتیں ہی نعمتیں اور بڑی سلطنت کی شان و شوکت ﴿۲۰﴾
عٰلِيَهُمْ ثِيَابُ سُنْدُسٍ	ہوں گے ان کے (بدنوں) پر کپڑے باریک ریشم کے
خُضْرٌ وَّاِسْتَبْرَقٌ ۫	جو سبز رنگ کے ہوں گے اور چمکدار
وَّحُلُّوْٓا اَسَاوِرَ مِنْ فِضَّةٍ ۚ	اور پہنائے جائیں گے انہیں کنگن چاندی کے
وَسَقٰىهُمْ رَبُّهُمْ شَرَابًا طَهُوْرًا ﴿۲۱﴾	اور پلائے گا انہیں ان کا رب نہایت پاکیزہ شراب ﴿۲۱﴾
اِنَّ هٰذَا كَانَ لَكُمْ جَزَآءً وَّكَانَ	(ارشاد ہوگا) بلاشبہ یہ ہے تمہاری ہی جزا اور تھی
سَعْيُكُمْ مَّشْكُوْرًا ﴿۲۲﴾ ع ۱۹	تمہاری کارگزاری قابلِ قدر ﴿۲۲﴾
اِنَّا نَحْنُ نَزَّلْنَا عَلَيْكَ	یقیناً ہم نے ہی نازل کیا ہے تم پر
الْقُرْاٰنَ تَنْزِيْلًا ﴿۲۳﴾	قرآن تھوڑا تھوڑا کر کے ﴿۲۳﴾
فَاصْبِرْ لِحُكْمِ رَبِّكَ وَلَا تُطِعْ	لہٰذا تم جمے رہو اپنے رب کے حکم پر اور نہ مانو بات
مِنْهُمْ اٰثِمًا اَوْ كَفُوْرًا ﴿۲۴﴾	ان میں سے کسی بدعمل کی یا ناشکرے کی ﴿۲۴﴾

017/ They'll be served to savor in flavor
018 Cups of wine "Zanjabil" in favor

A spring so sinuous surging in stream
Named "Salsabil" delighted (water) in esteem

019 There and around to serve in hush
Youths to appease perpetual (bloom) in blush
They look as lustrous pearls in glow

020 When you deem to discern for the same
A Bliss so Brilliant and Dazzling in Domain

021 Adored in green satiny robes in grace
With brocade and Propane secured in lace

They'll be given silver trinket to secure
Lord to endow pure and pious wine to allure

022 That's the,
Reward as your Seek and strive is verily affirmed

023 We, sent down Qur'an in step and stage in term
024 So be diligent in fidelity of Lord in decree
Don't heed to the evil or defiant in spree

وَاذْكُرِ اسْمَ رَبِّكَ	اور ذکر کرتے رہو اپنے رب کے نام کا
بُكْرَةً وَّ اَصِيلًا ﴿۲۵﴾	صبح وشام ﴿۲۵﴾
وَمِنَ الَّيْلِ فَاسْجُدْ	اور رات کو بھی سجدہ کرو
لَهٗ وَ سَبِّحْهُ	اس کے حضور اور تسبیح کرتے رہو اس کی
لَيْلًا طَوِيْلًا ﴿۲۶﴾	رات میں دیر تک ﴿۲۶﴾
اِنَّ هٰٓؤُلَآءِ يُحِبُّوْنَ	یقیناً یہ لوگ محبت رکھتے ہیں
الْعَاجِلَةَ	جلدی حاصل ہو جانے والی (دنیا) سے
وَ يَذَرُوْنَ وَرَآءَهُمْ يَوْمًا ثَقِيْلًا ﴿۲۷﴾	اور نظر انداز کیے دے رہے ہیں اپنے پیچھے ایک بھاری دن کو ﴿۲۷﴾
نَحْنُ خَلَقْنٰهُمْ	ہم ہی نے پیدا کیا ہے ان کو
وَشَدَدْنَآ اَسْرَهُمْ	اور مضبوط کیے ہیں ان کے جوڑ بند
وَاِذَا شِئْنَا بَدَّلْنَآ	اور جب چاہیں گے ہم بدل دیں گے
اَمْثَالَهُمْ تَبْدِيْلًا ﴿۲۸﴾	ان کی شکلوں کو جس طرح بدلنا چاہیں گے ﴿۲۸﴾
اِنَّ هٰذِهٖ تَذْكِرَةٌ فَمَنْ شَآءَ	یقیناً یہ ایک نصیحت ہے پس جو شخص چاہے
اتَّخَذَ اِلٰى رَبِّهٖ سَبِيْلًا ﴿۲۹﴾	بنالے اپنے رب کی طرف جانے کا راستہ ﴿۲۹﴾
وَمَا تَشَآءُوْنَ اِلَّآ اَنْ يَّشَآءَ اللّٰهُ	اور تم چاہ بھی نہیں سکتے مگر یہ کہ چاہے اللہ۔
اِنَّ اللّٰهَ كَانَ عَلِيْمًا حَكِيْمًا ﴿۳۰﴾	یقیناً اللہ ہے سب کچھ جاننے والا، بڑی حکمت والا ﴿۳۰﴾
يُّدْخِلُ مَنْ يَّشَآءُ فِيْ رَحْمَتِهٖ	داخل فرماتا ہے جسے چاہے اپنی رحمت میں۔
وَ الظّٰلِمِيْنَ اَعَدَّ	اور رہے ظالم، تیار کر رکھا ہے اللہ نے
لَهُمْ عَذَابًا اَلِيْمًا ﴿۳۱﴾	ان کے لیے دردناک عذاب ﴿۳۱﴾

025/ Verily remember,
026 Your Lord morn and eve in adore
Part of the night perfect in score

Entreat and beseech in stay
Even so all through the night in pray

027 Those in lust and love, so frivolous in vale
Don't turn to care and concern in trail
The Day so arduous affirmed to prevail

028 It's We,
Who created them in stance
And made their,
Joints really firm and strong
But if,
We determine in the dictum of norm

We can replace like of them in place
With a complete change of place in pace

029 This is an admonition, who care to avail
Dictum of Lord in verity to avail

030 You cannot even think to aspire in stance!
But it's,
All Him as to whom He endows in glance
For! Lord is full of Sense of Sapience in lore

031 He'll gift and grant His Mercy in score
To one He deems to decide to allure
For wrongdoers,
There's a grisly sentence to endure

اٰیَاتُهَا ٥٠ — (٧٧) سُوْرَةُ الْمُرْسَلٰتِ مَكِّيَّةٌ (٣٣) — رُكُوْعَاتُهَا ٢

بِسْمِ اللّٰهِ الرَّحْمٰنِ الرَّحِيْمِ

شروع اللہ کے نام سے جو بڑا مہربان نہایت رحم والا ہے

وَالْمُرْسَلٰتِ عُرْفًا ۝١	قسم ہے ان (ہواؤں) کی جو چلائی جاتی ہیں سہج سہج ۝١
فَالْعٰصِفٰتِ عَصْفًا ۝٢	پھر چلتی ہیں طوفانی رفتار سے ۝٢
وَّالنّٰشِرٰتِ نَشْرًا ۝٣	اور (ان کی) جو پھیلاتی ہیں (بادلوں کو) اٹھا کر ۝٣
فَالْفٰرِقٰتِ فَرْقًا ۝٤	پھر جدا کرتی ہیں انہیں پھاڑ کر ۝٤
فَالْمُلْقِيٰتِ ذِكْرًا ۝٥	پھر ڈالتی ہیں (دلوں میں اللہ کی) یاد ۝٥
عُذْرًا اَوْ نُذْرًا ۝٦	توبہ کے لیے یا ڈراوے کے لیے ۝٦
اِنَّمَا تُوْعَدُوْنَ	یاد رکھو جس چیز سے تمہیں ڈرایا جا رہا ہے
لَوَاقِعٌ ۝٧	وہ ضرور واقع ہونے والی ہے ۝٧
فَاِذَا النُّجُوْمُ طُمِسَتْ ۝٨	چنانچہ جب ستارے ماند پڑ جائیں گے ۝٨
وَاِذَا السَّمَآءُ فُرِجَتْ ۝٩	اور جب آسمان پھاڑ دیا جائے گا ۝٩
وَاِذَا الْجِبَالُ نُسِفَتْ ۝١٠	اور جب پہاڑ دھنک ڈالے جائیں گے ۝١٠
وَاِذَا الرُّسُلُ	اور جب رسولوں کی
اُقِّتَتْ ۝١١	حاضری کا وقت آ پہنچے گا (اس دن وہ چیز واقع ہو جائے گی) ۝١١
لِاَيِّ يَوْمٍ اُجِّلَتْ ۝١٢	کس دن کے لیے یہ کام اٹھا رکھا گیا ہے؟ ۝١٢
لِيَوْمِ الْفَصْلِ ۝١٣	فیصلہ کے دن کے لیے ۝١٣

077-AL MURSALAT

In the name of Lord, the Most Beneficent, Most Merciful

001 Vow be to the emissary winds in flow

002 That Turn to tornado throb in blow
(And the word of those in lift)

003 Scattering (clouds) immense in swifts
004 Then tearing apart fragment in drifts

(By those who tend to convey)
005 Reminding you of His Word to obey

006 For fear of excuse or factual in toss
007 Surely promised will come to a pass

(That's to conclude in eminent swift)
008 That day the stars will dwindle and drift

009 The sky to asunder then tear and split
010 Mountains to languish blaring in slit

Verses 6-10 , Fate of the Universe (Page : 1264)

011 Prophets to assemble congenial in accord
012 For what 'We' portents deferred in resort
013 That's the day of Defined and Resolute award

وَمَآ اَدْرٰىكَ مَا يَوْمُ الْفَصْلِ ﴿١٤﴾	اور کیا جانو تم کیسا ہوگا فیصلہ کا دن؟ ﴿١٤﴾
وَيْلٌ يَّوْمَئِذٍ لِّلْمُكَذِّبِيْنَ ﴿١٥﴾	تباہی ہے اس دن جھٹلانے والوں کے لیے ﴿١٥﴾
اَلَمْ نُهْلِكِ الْاَوَّلِيْنَ ﴿١٦﴾	کیا نہیں ہلاک کر دیا ہم نے پہلوں کو؟ ﴿١٦﴾
ثُمَّ نُتْبِعُهُمُ الْاٰخِرِيْنَ ﴿١٧﴾	پھر انہی کے پیچھے چلاتے ہیں ہم بعد والوں کو ﴿١٧﴾
كَذٰلِكَ نَفْعَلُ بِالْمُجْرِمِيْنَ ﴿١٨﴾	یہی کچھ کیا کرتے ہیں ہم مجرموں کے ساتھ ﴿١٨﴾
وَيْلٌ يَّوْمَئِذٍ لِّلْمُكَذِّبِيْنَ ﴿١٩﴾	تباہی ہے اس دن جھٹلانے والوں کے لیے ﴿١٩﴾
اَلَمْ نَخْلُقْكُّمْ مِّنْ مَّآءٍ مَّهِيْنٍ ﴿٢٠﴾	کیا نہیں پیدا کیا ہے ہم نے تم کو ایک حقیر پانی سے؟ ﴿٢٠﴾
فَجَعَلْنٰهُ فِيْ قَرَارٍ مَّكِيْنٍ ﴿٢١﴾	پھر ٹھہرائے رکھا ہم نے اسے ایک محفوظ جگہ میں ﴿٢١﴾
اِلٰى قَدَرٍ مَّعْلُوْمٍ ﴿٢٢﴾	ایک مقررہ مدت تک ﴿٢٢﴾
فَقَدَرْنَا ۖ فَنِعْمَ	تو دیکھو ہم اس پر قادر تھے، سو ہم بہت اچھی
الْقٰدِرُوْنَ ﴿٢٣﴾	قدرت رکھنے والے ہیں ﴿٢٣﴾
وَيْلٌ يَّوْمَئِذٍ لِّلْمُكَذِّبِيْنَ ﴿٢٤﴾	تباہی ہے اس دن جھٹلانے والوں کے لیے ﴿٢٤﴾
اَلَمْ نَجْعَلِ الْاَرْضَ كِفَاتًا ﴿٢٥﴾	کیا نہیں بنایا ہے ہم نے زمین کو سمیٹ کر رکھنے والی ﴿٢٥﴾
اَحْيَآءً وَّاَمْوَاتًا ﴿٢٦﴾	زندوں کو بھی اور مردوں کو بھی؟ ﴿٢٦﴾
وَّجَعَلْنَا فِيْهَا رَوَاسِيَ شٰمِخٰتٍ	اور جما دیے ہیں ہم نے اس میں لنگر بلند و بالا پہاڑوں کے
وَّاَسْقَيْنٰكُمْ مَّآءً فُرَاتًا ﴿٢٧﴾	اور پلایا ہے ہم نے تم کو میٹھا پانی ﴿٢٧﴾
وَيْلٌ يَّوْمَئِذٍ لِّلْمُكَذِّبِيْنَ ﴿٢٨﴾	تباہی ہے اس دن جھٹلانے والوں کے لیے ﴿٢٨﴾
اِنْطَلِقُوْٓا اِلٰى مَا	چلو تم اس چیز کی طرف
كُنْتُمْ بِهٖ تُكَذِّبُوْنَ ﴿٢٩﴾	جسے تم جھٹلایا کرتے تھے ﴿٢٩﴾

014 What you know of Divine Decree in accord

015 There's all detriment in assault
Those defying the Day of Resolve

016 Didn't 'We' destroy men hither in fore

017 Then We abolished there after in score
Who affirmed their term in adore

018 So We deal with the cynics in sue

019 Woe be to those, defying Day of Clue*

*Dooms Day

020 Didn't 'We' create you of a sinful drop*

*Sperm

021 Then,
022 Destined you for a specific term in spot

023 We platter and plan to conceive in stance
How superb Our planning held in Glance

024 Woe be to those, defying Day in trance

025 Didn't We make the earth an abide

026 Both for the living and dead in beside

027 Mountains placed there in assort
Endowing luscious water in accord

028 Woe be to those, defying Day of Resolve

029 It'll be then affirmed in command
Trend to the doom you denied in trance

اِنْطَلِقُوْٓا اِلٰى ظِلٍّ	چلو اس سایہ کی طرف
ذِىْ ثَلٰثِ شُعَبٍ ۳۰	جو تین شاخوں والا ہے ۳۰
لَّا ظَلِيْلٍ وَّلَا يُغْنِىْ	نہ ٹھنڈک پہنچانے والا اور نہ بچانے والا
مِنَ اللَّهَبِ ۳۱	آگ کے شعلوں سے ۳۱
اِنَّهَا تَرْمِىْ بِشَرَرٍ	بے شک وہ آگ پھینکے گی ایسے انگارے
كَالْقَصْرِ ۳۲	جو بڑے بڑے محلات کے برابر ہوں گے ۳۲
كَاَنَّهٗ جِمٰلَتٌ	گویا کہ وہ اونٹ ہیں
صُفْرٌ ۳۳	زرد رنگ کے ۳۳
وَيْلٌ يَّوْمَىِٕذٍ لِّلْمُكَذِّبِيْنَ ۳۴	تباہی ہے اس دن جھٹلانے والوں کے لیے ۳۴
هٰذَا يَوْمُ لَا يَنْطِقُوْنَ ۳۵	یہ وہ دن ہوگا کہ نہ بول سکیں گے کچھ ۳۵
وَلَا يُؤْذَنُ	اور نہ اجازت دی جائے گی
لَهُمْ فَيَعْتَذِرُوْنَ ۳۶	انہیں کہ عذر پیش کریں ۳۶
وَيْلٌ يَّوْمَىِٕذٍ لِّلْمُكَذِّبِيْنَ ۳۷	تباہی ہے اس دن جھٹلانے والوں کے لیے ۳۷
هٰذَا يَوْمُ الْفَصْلِ ۚ جَمَعْنٰكُمْ	یہ ہے فیصلہ کا دن ۔ جمع کر دیا ہے ہم نے تم کو بھی
وَالْاَوَّلِيْنَ ۳۸	اور تم سے پہلے گزرے ہوؤں کو بھی ۳۸
فَاِنْ كَانَ	سو اگر ہے
لَكُمْ كَيْدٌ	تمہارے پاس کوئی چال
فَكِيْدُوْنِ ۳۹	تو چل دیکھو میرے مقابلہ میں ۳۹
وَيْلٌ يَّوْمَىِٕذٍ لِّلْمُكَذِّبِيْنَ ۴۰ ع ۱	تباہی ہے اس دن جھٹلانے والوں کے لیے ۴۰

030 Tread near the shade (to aside)
That's with three branches in dried

031 It cannot bless comfort of cool in shade
Nor it can save from torture of blaze

032 Indeed!
A fiery fire leaping in rage

033 It might look in tint
Yellow, as camel's cage in stint

034 Woe be to those, defying Day in print

035 Day when none will be allowed to converse

036 Nor they'll come with an excuse to impress

037 Woe be to those, defying Day of Inverse

038 That's the Day of Defined and Definite accord
When men of all term and trace gather in assort

039 Now trend to your delirious term to discern
And try to confront My resolute term

040 Woe be to those, defying Day of Concern

اِنَّ الْمُتَّقِیْنَ	یقیناً متقی لوگ
فِیْ ظِلٰلٍ وَّعُیُوْنٍ ﴿۴۱﴾	ہوں گے سایوں میں اور چشموں میں ﴿۴۱﴾
وَّفَوَاكِهَ مِمَّا	اور پھل ہوں گے ہر قسم کے جن کی
یَشْتَهُوْنَ ﴿۴۲﴾	وہ خواہش کریں گے ﴿۴۲﴾
كُلُوْا وَاشْرَبُوْا	(کہا جائے گا) کھاؤ اور پیو
هَنِیْٓـًٔا	مزے لے لے کر
بِمَا كُنْتُمْ تَعْمَلُوْنَ ﴿۴۳﴾	ان اعمال کے بدلہ میں جو تم کرتے رہے ﴿۴۳﴾
اِنَّا كَذٰلِكَ نَجْزِی	یقیناً ہم ایسی ہی جزا دیتے ہیں
الْمُحْسِنِیْنَ ﴿۴۴﴾	اچھا اور معیاری کام کرنے والوں کو ﴿۴۴﴾
وَیْلٌ یَّوْمَئِذٍ لِّلْمُكَذِّبِیْنَ ﴿۴۵﴾	تباہی ہے اس دن جھٹلانے والوں کے لیے ﴿۴۵﴾
كُلُوْا وَتَمَتَّعُوْا	کھاؤ اور مزے لوٹ لو
قَلِیْلًا اِنَّكُمْ	تھوڑے دن ۔ یقیناً تم
مُّجْرِمُوْنَ ﴿۴۶﴾	مجرم ہو ﴿۴۶﴾
وَیْلٌ یَّوْمَئِذٍ لِّلْمُكَذِّبِیْنَ ﴿۴۷﴾	تباہی ہے اس دن جھٹلانے والوں کے لیے ﴿۴۷﴾
وَاِذَا قِیْلَ لَهُمُ ارْكَعُوْا	اور جب کہا جاتا ہے ان سے کہ جھکو (اللہ کے آگے)
لَا یَرْكَعُوْنَ ﴿۴۸﴾	تو نہیں جھکتے ﴿۴۸﴾
وَیْلٌ یَّوْمَئِذٍ لِّلْمُكَذِّبِیْنَ ﴿۴۹﴾	تباہی ہے اس دن جھٹلانے والوں کے لیے ﴿۴۹﴾
فَبِاَیِّ حَدِیْثٍۭ	سو اب کونسا کلام ہو سکتا ہے
بَعْدَهٗ یُؤْمِنُوْنَ ﴿۵۰﴾	قرآن کے بعد جس پر یہ ایمان لائیں گے؟ ﴿۵۰﴾

ع ۲ / ۲۲

041 Virtuous relishing Boon and Bounties in sort
Bliss and Benison of Lord in accord

They're reclining in blissful resorts
Under shadowy trees with springs in assort

042 Relishing fruits of Fascinating seeds in pace

043 Alluring bliss of their verity in taste

044 We always reward the virtuous in absolve

045 Woe be to those, defying Day of Resolve

046 Relish you the eats,
And appease for a while (in treat)
Indeed!
You hideous to savor sentence in screech

047 Woe be to those, defying Day in impeach

048 When they're asked to beg in entreat
They so decline a bent in beseech

049 Woe be to those, defying Day in Screech

050 What else could be there to affirm in accord
Wouldn't they trend then to The Bounty of Lord

آیاتها ٤٠   (٧٨) سُورَةُ النَّبَاِ مَكِّيَّةٌ (٨٠)   رکوعاتها ٢

بِسْمِ اللّٰهِ الرَّحْمٰنِ الرَّحِيْمِ

شروع اللہ کے نام سے جو بڑا مہربان نہایت رحم والا ہے

عَمَّ يَتَسَآءَلُوْنَ ① — کیا بات پوچھتے ہیں لوگ آپس میں ؟ ①

عَنِ النَّبَاِ الْعَظِيْمِ ② — (کیا) اس بڑی خبر کی نسبت ؟ ②

الَّذِيْ هُمْ فِيْهِ مُخْتَلِفُوْنَ ③ — وہ (بڑی خبر) یہ جس میں اختلاف کر رہے ہیں ③

كَلَّا سَيَعْلَمُوْنَ ④ — دیکھو! عنقریب یہ جان لیں گے ④

ثُمَّ كَلَّا سَيَعْلَمُوْنَ ⑤ — پھر دیکھو! عنقریب یہ جان لیں گے ⑤

اَلَمْ نَجْعَلِ الْاَرْضَ مِهٰدًا ⑥ — (ذرا غور کرو) کیا نہیں بنایا ہم نے زمین کو بچھونا ؟

وَّالْجِبَالَ اَوْتَادًا ⑦ — اور پہاڑوں کو (اس کی) میخیں ؟ ⑦

وَّخَلَقْنٰكُمْ اَزْوَاجًا ⑧ — اور پیدا کیا ہم نے تم کو جوڑا جوڑا ⑧

وَّجَعَلْنَا نَوْمَكُمْ سُبَاتًا ⑨ — اور بنایا ہم نے تمہاری نیند کو باعثِ سکون ⑨

وَّجَعَلْنَا الَّيْلَ لِبَاسًا ⑩ — اور بنایا ہم نے رات کو پردہ پوش ⑩

وَّجَعَلْنَا النَّهَارَ مَعَاشًا ⑪ — اور بنایا ہم نے دن کو کمائی کے لیے ⑪

وَّبَنَيْنَا فَوْقَكُمْ سَبْعًا شِدَادًا ⑫ — اور قائم کیے ہم نے تمہارے اوپر سات مضبوط (آسمان) ⑫

وَّجَعَلْنَا سِرَاجًا وَّهَّاجًا ⑬ — اور بنایا ہم نے ایک چراغ جگمگاتا ہوا ⑬

وَّاَنْزَلْنَا مِنَ الْمُعْصِرٰتِ مَآءً ثَجَّاجًا ⑭ — اور نازل کیا ہم نے نچڑنے والی (بدلیوں) سے موسلادھار مینہ

لِّنُخْرِجَ بِهٖ حَبًّا وَّنَبَاتًا ⑮ — تاکہ نکالیں اس کے ذریعہ سے ہر قسم کا اناج اور سبزہ ⑮

078-AL NABA

In the name of Lord, the Most Beneficent, Most Merciful

001/ Regarding!
002 What they counter and conflict to discern
Of the Serious Stance stemmed in stern
(If they'd care in concern to affirm)

003 For what they don't trend to affirm
004 Indeed! They'll soon come to concern

005 Indeed!
They'll soon come to discern
006 Haven't We created earth an abide in term

So spacious and capacious in scope and space
007 Mountains so fixed, pin and plugged in place
008 And haven't We created you in couples to brace

009 And sleep,
He made to ease and appease in place
The night (We made to sleep in pace)

010 A cover as shawl in calm
011 We made,
The day to earn your living in norm

012 Over and above you in plan
Seven skies as firmaments in span

013 Created, (sun)
Dazzle in glow, a glitter in flow

014 And from clouds a sprinkle in throw
The drizzle in sprinkle a shower in flow
015 There're corn and 'veggies' in grow

وَّجَنّٰتٍ اَلْفَافًا ﴿۱۶﴾ — اور باغات گھنے ؟ ﴿۱۶﴾

اِنَّ يَوْمَ الْفَصْلِ كَانَ مِيْقَاتًا ﴿۱۷﴾ — بے شک فیصلہ کا دن ہے ایک وقتِ مقرر ﴿۱۷﴾

يَّوْمَ يُنْفَخُ فِي الصُّوْرِ فَتَاْتُوْنَ اَفْوَاجًا ﴿۱۸﴾ — وہ دن جب پھونکا جائے گا صور تو آؤ گے تم فوج در فوج ﴿۱۸﴾

وَّفُتِحَتِ السَّمَآءُ فَكَانَتْ — اور کھول دیا جائے گا آسمان تو ہو جائے گا وہ

اَبْوَابًا ﴿۱۹﴾ — دروازے ہی دروازے ﴿۱۹﴾

وَّسُيِّرَتِ الْجِبَالُ فَكَانَتْ سَرَابًا ﴿۲۰﴾ — اور چلائے جائیں گے پہاڑ تو ہو جائیں گے وہ چمکتی ریت ﴿۲۰﴾

اِنَّ جَهَنَّمَ كَانَتْ مِرْصَادًا ﴿۲۱﴾ — بے شک جہنم ہے ایک گھات ﴿۲۱﴾

لِّلطّٰغِيْنَ مَاٰبًا ﴿۲۲﴾ — سرکشوں کے لیے ٹھکانہ ﴿۲۲﴾

لّٰبِثِيْنَ فِيْهَآ اَحْقَابًا ﴿۲۳﴾ — پڑے رہیں گے وہ اس میں مدتوں ﴿۲۳﴾

لَا يَذُوْقُوْنَ فِيْهَا بَرْدًا وَّلَا شَرَابًا ﴿۲۴﴾ — نہ چکھیں گے مزہ اس میں ٹھنڈک کا اور نہ پینے کی کوئی چیز ﴿۲۴﴾

اِلَّا حَمِيْمًا وَّغَسَّاقًا ﴿۲۵﴾ — مگر گرم پانی اور بہتی پیپ ﴿۲۵﴾

جَزَآءً وِّفَاقًا ﴿۲۶﴾ — (یہ) بدلہ ہے پورا پورا ﴿۲۶﴾

اِنَّهُمْ كَانُوْا لَا يَرْجُوْنَ حِسَابًا ﴿۲۷﴾ — بے شک یہ لوگ توقع نہ رکھتے تھے کسی حساب کی ﴿۲۷﴾

وَّكَذَّبُوْا بِاٰيٰتِنَا كِذَّابًا ﴿۲۸﴾ — اور جھٹلاتے تھے ہماری آیات کو جھوٹ سمجھ کر ﴿۲۸﴾

وَكُلَّ شَيْءٍ اَحْصَيْنٰهُ كِتٰبًا ﴿۲۹﴾ — جبکہ ہر چیز ہم نے گن گن کر لکھ رکھی ہے ﴿۲۹﴾

فَذُوْقُوْا فَلَنْ نَّزِيْدَكُمْ — لہٰذا چکھو مزہ اپنے کیے کا کہ ہرگز نہیں اضافہ کریں گے ہم تمہارے لیے

ع اِلَّا عَذَابًا ﴿۳۰﴾ — مگر عذاب میں ﴿۳۰﴾

اِنَّ لِلْمُتَّقِيْنَ مَفَازًا ﴿۳۱﴾ — بے شک متقیوں کے لیے ہے مقامِ کامرانی ﴿۳۱﴾

حَدَآئِقَ وَاَعْنَابًا ﴿۳۲﴾ — (جہاں) باغ ہوں گے اور قسم قسم کے انگور ﴿۳۲﴾

016 And gardens of profuse produce in flow
* (veggies- vegetables)

017 Surely!
Day of Demand is determined in drill
018 The Day Trumpet will blow so loud and shrill
And you'll be there in doleful throng in drill

019 And heavens shall open a passage in drive
020 Mountains to vanish as mirage in glide
021 Truly Hell is a place of gulling to aside

022 For sinners in sway, evil place to reside
023 Them to aside infinite slander in stride
024 Not to savor a cool drink to beside

025 But!
Stewing and strong or numbing cold in blight
Black squalid serous drink in slight
026 A doom in gloom due redeem in plight

027 For they didn't cower evil deeds in stray
028 But defied Our Signs fib in stray
029 Their deeds saved and secured to display

030 So savor award of defied doings in trail
We wouldn't confer or extend to avail
But only for infliction to cherish in scale

031 And for the Virtuous:
For their done and doings in proceeds
Them to allure exquisite awards in plead

032 Girdled Gardens and quality grapes in swarm

وَّكَوَاعِبَ اَتْرَابًا ﴿٣٣﴾	اور نوخیز ہم عمر (لڑکیاں) ﴿٣٣﴾
وَّكَاْسًا دِهَاقًا ﴿٣٤﴾	اور پیالے چھلکتے ہوئے ﴿٣٤﴾
لَا يَسْمَعُوْنَ فِيْهَا لَغْوًا وَّلَا كِذّٰبًا ﴿٣٥﴾	نہ سنیں گے وہاں کوئی بے ہودہ بات اور نہ جھوٹ ﴿٣٥﴾
جَزَآءً مِّنْ رَّبِّكَ عَطَآءً حِسَابًا ﴿٣٦﴾	یہ صلہ ہوگا تیرے رب کی طرف سے اور انعام کثیر (اس کا) ﴿٣٦﴾
رَّبِّ السَّمٰوٰتِ وَالْاَرْضِ	جو رب ہے آسمانوں اور زمین کا
وَمَا بَيْنَهُمَا	اور ہر اس چیز کا جو ان دونوں کے درمیان ہے
الرَّحْمٰنِ لَا يَمْلِكُوْنَ	وہ نہایت مہربان ہے (تاہم) نہ یارا ہوگا کسی کو
مِنْهُ خِطَابًا ﴿٣٧﴾	اس سے بات کرنے کا ﴿٣٧﴾
يَوْمَ يَقُوْمُ الرُّوْحُ وَالْمَلٰٓئِكَةُ	جس دن کھڑے ہوں گے روح اور فرشتے
صَفًّا ۙ لَّا يَتَكَلَّمُوْنَ اِلَّا مَنْ اَذِنَ لَهُ	صف بستہ نہ بولے گا کوئی مگر وہ جسے اجازت دے
الرَّحْمٰنُ وَقَالَ صَوَابًا ﴿٣٨﴾	رحمٰن اور کہے بات ٹھیک ٹھیک ﴿٣٨﴾
ذٰلِكَ الْيَوْمُ الْحَقُّ ۚ	یہ ہے دن برحق
فَمَنْ شَآءَ اتَّخَذَ	اب جس کا جی چاہے بنالے
اِلٰى رَبِّهٖ مَاٰبًا ﴿٣٩﴾	اپنے رب کے پاس ٹھکانہ ﴿٣٩﴾
اِنَّآ اَنْذَرْنٰكُمْ	بے شک ہم نے آگاہ کر دیا ہے تم کو
عَذَابًا قَرِيْبًا ۚ	اس عذاب سے جو جلد ہی آنے والا ہے
يَّوْمَ يَنْظُرُ الْمَرْءُ مَا قَدَّمَتْ	اس دن دیکھ لے گا ہر شخص وہ کچھ جو کر کے آگے بھیجا اس نے
يَدٰهُ وَيَقُوْلُ الْكٰفِرُ	اپنے ہاتھوں اور کہے گا کافر،
يٰلَيْتَنِيْ كُنْتُ تُرٰبًا ﴿٤٠﴾	کاش! ہوتا میں مٹی ﴿٤٠﴾

033 Spouses of like ages alluring in charm

034 Cup full (to the lip to cherish in clear)

035 No Conceit to hear and no lie to bear

036 Gifts and grants of Lord quite a lot so dear

037 Lord of the Heavens and earth in scale
And all between the heavenly trail

Allah!
Most Gracious Immense in Grants
None has the skill to bicker in slants

038 The Day Sprits and angels stand in stance
Poise in pace before Lord in Glance

There's none but one to converse with Lord
What's seemly suggested by Bountiful Lord
And he'll assert and affirm verity in assort

039 The Day to affirm and conform for sure
Whoso intend to affirm a place to secure*
Him you beseech and prone in adore

*with Almighty

040 Indeed!
We warned you well in advance
A doom in gloom quite near in stance

The Day to evince their done and doings in pace
For what they advanced Hereafter to brace

And the Cynics will then get to affirm
Woe unto me!
Would that be for hither in term
If I could only be a bit of dust in concern

(٧٩) سُوْرَةُ النّٰزِعٰتِ مَكِّيَّةٌ (٨١)

اٰیاتها ٤٦ — رکوعاتها ٢

بِسْمِ اللّٰهِ الرَّحْمٰنِ الرَّحِيْمِ

شروع اللہ کے نام سے جو بڑا مہربان نہایت رحم والا ہے

وَالنّٰزِعٰتِ غَرْقًا ۝١	قسم ہے ان (فرشتوں) کی جو کھینچنے والے ہیں (روح کو) ڈوب کر ۱
وَّالنّٰشِطٰتِ نَشْطًا ۝٢	اور نکال لے جانے والے ہیں (اسے) آہستگی سے ۲
وَّالسّٰبِحٰتِ سَبْحًا ۝٣	اور (ان کی) جو تیرتے پھرتے ہیں تیزی سے ۳
فَالسّٰبِقٰتِ سَبْقًا ۝٤	پھر سبقت لے جانے والے ہیں دوڑ کر (اللہ کا حکم بجالانے میں) ۴
فَالْمُدَبِّرٰتِ اَمْرًا ۝٥	پھر انتظام چلانے والے ہیں معاملات کا (احکام الٰہی کے مطابق) ۵
يَوْمَ تَرْجُفُ الرَّاجِفَةُ ۝٦	(کہ وہ دن آکر رہے گا) جس دن ہلا ڈالے گا زلزلے کا جھٹکا ۶
تَتْبَعُهَا الرَّادِفَةُ ۝٧	پیچھے آئے گا اس کے دوسرا جھٹکا ۷
قُلُوْبٌ يَّوْمَئِذٍ وَّاجِفَةٌ ۝٨	کتنے ہی دل اس دن خوف سے کانپ رہے ہوں گے ۸
اَبْصَارُهَا خَاشِعَةٌ ۝٩	نگاہیں ان کی سہمی ہوئی ہوں گی ۹
يَقُوْلُوْنَ ءَاِنَّا لَمَرْدُوْدُوْنَ	کہتے ہیں یہ لوگ : کیا ہم ضرور لوٹائے جائیں گے واپس
فِي الْحَافِرَةِ ۝١٠	پہلی حالت میں ۱۰
ءَاِذَا كُنَّا عِظَامًا نَّخِرَةً ۝١١	کیا جب بھی کہ ہو چکے ہوں گے ہم ہڈیاں کھوکھلی اور بوسیدہ ۱۱
قَالُوْا تِلْكَ اِذًا كَرَّةٌ خَاسِرَةٌ ۝١٢	کہتے ہیں پھر تو یہ لوٹایا جانا بڑے ہی گھاٹے کا (موجب) ہوگا ۱۲
فَاِنَّمَا هِيَ زَجْرَةٌ وَّاحِدَةٌ ۝١٣	حالانکہ یہ تو بس (ہوگی) زوردار ڈانٹ ایک ہی بار ۱۳
فَاِذَا هُمْ بِالسَّاهِرَةِ ۝١٤	اور یکدم آموجود ہوں گے وہ سب میدان (حشر) میں ۱۴

079-AL NAZIAT

In the name of Lord, the Most Beneficent, Most Merciful

001 Vow be to those,
Bluntly slicing and gashing souls in squeeze

002 And those!
Tenderly drawing virtuous souls in appease

003 And those sliding and slithering in haste

004 Pushing in hustle and bustle in race

005 They comply dictum of Lord in pace

006 The Day is determined to be there in abash*
When quack in blow stir with stigma in smash
007 Followed by one more furious frenzy in dash
*Dooms Day

008 The Day core will flutter in flurry in spree
009 Downcast with eyes the men would see

010 And they would think for a while in core
How we'll get to our like the state in before

011 What!
If we'll be rotten bones in despicable trace

012 They say:
If true our revival will be quite state in a waste
(How'd we revive from a detrimental place in trace)

013 Indeed!
There'll be a select solitary screech in ado

014 Then they'll gather in stance there in flow

هَلْ اَتٰىكَ حَدِيْثُ مُوْسٰى ﴿١٥﴾	بھلا پہنچی ہے تمہیں خبر موسیٰؑ (کے واقعہ) کی ؟ ﴿١٥﴾
اِذْ نَادٰىهُ رَبُّهٗ	جب پکارا اسے اس کے رب نے
بِالْوَادِ الْمُقَدَّسِ طُوًى ﴿١٦﴾	طویٰ کی وادیِ مقدس میں ﴿١٦﴾
اِذْهَبْ اِلٰى فِرْعَوْنَ اِنَّهٗ طَغٰى ﴿١٧﴾	کہ جاؤ فرعون کے پاس، بے شک وہ سرکش ہو گیا ہے ﴿١٧﴾
فَقُلْ هَلْ لَّكَ اِلٰٓى اَنْ تَزَكّٰى ﴿١٨﴾	اور کہو کیا تجھے کچھ رغبت ہے اس بات کی کہ خود کو پاک کرے ؟ ﴿١٨﴾
وَاَهْدِيَكَ اِلٰى رَبِّكَ	اور رہنمائی کروں میں تیری تیرے رب کی طرف
فَتَخْشٰى ﴿١٩﴾	کہ تیرے اندر (اس کا) خوف پیدا ہو ﴿١٩﴾
فَاَرٰىهُ الْاٰيَةَ الْكُبْرٰى ﴿٢٠﴾	پھر دکھائی موسیٰؑ نے فرعون کو بڑی نشانی ﴿٢٠﴾
فَكَذَّبَ وَعَصٰى ﴿٢١﴾	مگر جھٹلا دیا اس نے اور نہ مانا ﴿٢١﴾
ثُمَّ اَدْبَرَ يَسْعٰى ﴿٢٢﴾	پھر پلٹا چال بازیاں کرنے کے لیے ﴿٢٢﴾
فَحَشَرَ فَنَادٰى ﴿٢٣﴾	سو جمع کیا اس نے (لوگوں کو) اور پکارا ﴿٢٣﴾
فَقَالَ اَنَا رَبُّكُمُ الْاَعْلٰى ﴿٢٤﴾	اور کہا میں ہوں تمہارا سب سے بڑا رب ﴿٢٤﴾
فَاَخَذَهُ اللّٰهُ نَكَالَ	سو پکڑ لیا اس کو اللہ نے عبرتناک عذاب میں
الْاٰخِرَةِ وَالْاُوْلٰى ﴿٢٥﴾	آخرت کے اور دنیا کے ﴿٢٥﴾
اِنَّ فِيْ ذٰلِكَ لَعِبْرَةً	بے شک اس واقعہ میں بڑا سامانِ عبرت ہے
لِّمَنْ يَّخْشٰى ﴿٢٦﴾	ہر اس شخص کے لیے جو ڈرتا ہے (اللہ سے) ﴿٢٦﴾
ءَاَنْتُمْ اَشَدُّ خَلْقًا اَمِ السَّمَآءُ بَنٰىهَا ﴿٢٧﴾	کیا تمہارا بنانا مشکل ہے یا آسمان کا اللہ نے اس کو بھی بنایا ﴿٢٧﴾
رَفَعَ سَمْكَهَا فَسَوّٰىهَا ﴿٢٨﴾	بلند کیا اس کی چھت کو پھر اس کا توازن قائم کیا ﴿٢٨﴾
وَاَغْطَشَ لَيْلَهَا وَاَخْرَجَ ضُحٰىهَا ﴿٢٩﴾	اور تاریک بنایا اس کی رات کو اور ظاہر کیا اس کے دن کو ﴿٢٩﴾

015 Did you get the fable of Moses in pace
016 Behold!
Lord called him to Tuwa for a care in grace

017 Proceed to Pharaoh there in stance
For he'd defied beyond bounds in trance

018 And invite him to dictum of faith in state
And assert in narrate:
Would you like to be exquisite in pace
(Avoiding ills and evils in relate)

019 And I conduct you for Lord to obey
So you revere and cower Him in stay
(Ordain His dictum and decree in pray)

020 Moses so evinced Signs of Lord in array
021 But,
Pharaoh denied and defied Lord to obey
022 He drifted in converse to obey
And was cross for Lord in stray

023 He amassed men and clan in around
And decreed his men all in surround

024 Affirming:
I'm your lord, astute in abide
025 But Lord!
Abashed him thither in deride
A sign and symbol There after to aside

026 There's moral in fable to brace
Whoso awe and dread Lord in Grace

027 What! Creation of the men is puzzling in decision
Rather!
Contriving of the heavens, more arduous in precision

028 He elevated heavens so high in style and sort
And endowed it capping and crowning in mart

029 The night He gifted with dusk in sway
And day in grandeur gleam in array

وَالْاَرْضَ بَعْدَ ذٰلِكَ دَحٰىهَا ﴿۳۰﴾	اور زمین کو بعد ازاں ہموار کیا ﴿۳۰﴾
اَخْرَجَ مِنْهَا مَآءَهَا وَمَرْعٰىهَا ﴿۳۱﴾	نکالا اس کے اندر سے اس کا پانی اور چارہ ﴿۳۱﴾
وَالْجِبَالَ اَرْسٰىهَا ﴿۳۲﴾	اور پہاڑوں کو بنایا، زمین کا لنگر ﴿۳۲﴾
مَتَاعًا لَّكُمْ	(بطورِ) سامانِ زیست تمہارے لیے
وَلِاَنْعَامِكُمْ ﴿۳۳﴾	اور تمہارے مویشیوں کے لیے ﴿۳۳﴾
فَاِذَا جَآءَتِ الطَّآمَّةُ الْكُبْرٰى ﴿۳۴﴾	پھر جب آئے گی وہ آفت بہت بڑی ﴿۳۴﴾
يَوْمَ يَتَذَكَّرُ الْاِنْسَانُ مَا سَعٰى ﴿۳۵﴾	اس دن یاد کرے گا انسان اپنا کیا دھرا ﴿۳۵﴾
وَبُرِّزَتِ الْجَحِيْمُ لِمَنْ يَّرٰى ﴿۳۶﴾	اور کھول کر سامنے کر دی جائے گی جہنم ہر دیکھنے والے کے لیے ﴿۳۶﴾
فَاَمَّا مَنْ طَغٰى ﴿۳۷﴾	چنانچہ جس نے سرکشی کی ﴿۳۷﴾
وَاٰثَرَ الْحَيٰوةَ الدُّنْيَا ﴿۳۸﴾	اور ترجیح دی دنیاوی زندگی کو ﴿۳۸﴾
فَاِنَّ الْجَحِيْمَ هِىَ الْمَاْوٰى ﴿۳۹﴾	تو بے شک جہنم ہی ہے اس کا ٹھکانا ﴿۳۹﴾
وَاَمَّا مَنْ خَافَ مَقَامَ رَبِّهٖ وَنَهَى	لیکن جو کوئی ڈرا پیشی سے اپنے رب کے حضور اور روکا اس نے
النَّفْسَ عَنِ الْهَوٰى ﴿۴۰﴾	اپنے نفس کو خواہشات کی پیروی سے ﴿۴۰﴾
فَاِنَّ الْجَنَّةَ هِىَ الْمَاْوٰى ﴿۴۱﴾	تو بے شک جنت ہی ہے اس کا ٹھکانا ﴿۴۱﴾
يَسْـَٔلُوْنَكَ عَنِ السَّاعَةِ	پوچھتے ہیں لوگ تم سے قیامت کے بارے میں
اَيَّانَ مُرْسٰىهَا ﴿۴۲﴾	کہ کب واقع ہوگی وہ؟ ﴿۴۲﴾
فِيْمَ اَنْتَ مِنْ ذِكْرٰىهَا ﴿۴۳﴾	کیا سروکار تمہیں اس کے ذکر سے؟ ﴿۴۳﴾
اِلٰى رَبِّكَ مُنْتَهٰىهَا ﴿۴۴﴾	تیرے رب کے پاس ہے انتہا قیامت (کے علم) کی ﴿۴۴﴾
اِنَّمَآ اَنْتَ مُنْذِرُ	تم تو بس خبردار کرنے والے ہو

030 And the earth He spread in stance
The scope in stretch held in glance

031 He gets you water* and pasture to graze
*As springs

032 And mountains are firmly fixed to brace
*Different strata of earth plates (Page : 1262)

033 An ease and appease for you to avail
And for your cattle hither in trail

034 When great disaster of the day comes to stay

035 The Day,
Men will recall their doings in fray

036 Hell will be in full view and vision in place

037 For those violating dictum of faith in trace

038 And favored earthy lures in lust to brace

039 Them to aside Hell-Pyre (in fair term) to reside

040 And who cower and quail facing Lord in Grace
And had restrained from lust and lechery in pace

041 Them to cherish bliss of gardens to reside
(With the bestowal of Lord thither to aside)

042 They ask for the time of Term in Throw*
When is that to strike and slap in blow
*Dooms Day

043 You've no care and concern for the time to trace
It's for Lord to assert and affirm in pace

044 For He's planned hence and whence in place

مَنْ يَّخْشٰهَا ۝۴۵ | ان کو جو ڈرتے ہیں قیامت سے ۝۴۵

كَاَنَّهُمْ يَوْمَ يَرَوْنَهَا | انہیں ایسا لگے گا جس دن دیکھیں گے قیامت کو

لَمْ يَلْبَثُوْٓا اِلَّا عَشِيَّةً اَوْ ضُحٰهَا ۝۴۶ | کہ نہیں رہے تھے وہ (دنیا میں)، مگر ایک شام یا ایک صبح ۝۴۶

(۸۰) سُوْرَةُ عَبَسَ مَكِّيَّةٌ (۲۴)

اٰيَاتُهَا ۴۲ — رُكُوْعُهَا ۱

بِسْمِ اللّٰهِ الرَّحْمٰنِ الرَّحِيْمِ

شروع اللہ کے نام سے جو بڑا مہربان نہایت رحم والا ہے

عَبَسَ وَتَوَلّٰٓى ۝۱ | ترش رو ہوا اور بے رخی برتی ۝۱

اَنْ جَآءَهُ الْاَعْمٰى ۝۲ | اس بات پر کہ آیا اس کے پاس وہ نابینا ۝۲

وَمَا يُدْرِيْكَ لَعَلَّهٗ يَزَّكّٰٓى ۝۳ | اور کیا خبر تمہیں شاید کہ وہ پاکیزگی حاصل کرتا ۝۳

اَوْ يَذَّكَّرُ فَتَنْفَعَهُ الذِّكْرٰى ۝۴ | یا نصیحت سنتا تو نفع پہنچاتی اس کو (تمہاری) نصیحت ۝۴

اَمَّا مَنِ اسْتَغْنٰى ۝۵ | لیکن جو کوئی بے پروائی برتتا ہے ۝۵

فَاَنْتَ لَهٗ تَصَدّٰى ۝۶ | تو تم اس کی طرف زیادہ توجہ کرتے ہو ۝۶

وَمَا عَلَيْكَ اَلَّا يَزَّكّٰى ۝۷ | حالانکہ نہیں ہے تم پر ذمہ داری اس کی کہ نہیں سدھرتا وہ ۝۷

وَاَمَّا مَنْ جَآءَكَ يَسْعٰى ۝۸ | لیکن جو شخص آیا تمہارے پاس دوڑتا ہوا ۝۸

وَهُوَ يَخْشٰى ۝۹ | اور وہ ڈر رہا ہے (اللہ سے) ۝۹

فَاَنْتَ عَنْهُ تَلَهّٰى ۝۱۰ | تو تم اس سے بے رخی برتتے ہو ۝۱۰

كَلَّآ اِنَّهَا تَذْكِرَةٌ ۝۱۱ | ہرگز نہیں بے شک یہ (قرآن) تو سراپا نصیحت ہے ۝۱۱

فَمَنْ شَآءَ ذَكَرَهٗ ۝۱۲ | سو جو چاہے قبول کرے اسے ۝۱۲

045 You're but a Warner for the men of faith
(You're to admonish, who dread Allah in grace)

046 When they perceive the Day of Doom in blight
They think for a while in place,
As if they'd stayed (the world) in pace
But only for the single of night
Or (at the most for) the following Day in plight

Verses 6-8 very clearly elucidate the frenzy of big crunch when our Universe will be facing the Doom of the Day---See Fate of the Universe (Page : 1264)

080-ABASA

In the name of Lord, the Most Beneficent, Most Merciful

001/ (O Prophet)
003 You sulk and scowl and turn to aside
As came a blind disrupting in stride

How'd you ever care to discern
Perhaps in faith he was determined in concern

004/ Or he was for the council and caution in advise
007 So to gain in faith a word in premise

To one, who's careless and resolute in term
To him you regard due care and concern

You aren't to be charged for his way in drift
If he doesn't incline to faith in swift

008/ But to him, who hurried in adore
009 To you in adore
With awe and dread of Lord in core
010/ Of him you're heedless in lore
011
012 Indeed! Qur'an is a word in advise
It's for all to assert in precise

فِيْ صُحُفٍ مُّكَرَّمَةٍ ﴿١٣﴾	لکھا ہوا ہے ایسے صحیفوں میں جو مکرم ہیں ﴿۱۳﴾
مَّرْفُوْعَةٍ مُّطَهَّرَةٍۭ ﴿١٤﴾	بلند مرتبہ ہیں پاکیزہ ہیں ﴿۱۴﴾
بِاَيْدِيْ سَفَرَةٍ ﴿١٥﴾	ہاتھوں میں ہیں ایسے کاتبوں کے ﴿۱۵﴾
كِرَامٍۭ بَرَرَةٍ ﴿١٦﴾	جو معزز ہیں، نیکو کار ہیں ﴿۱۶﴾
قُتِلَ الْاِنْسَانُ مَآ اَكْفَرَهٗ ﴿١٧﴾	ہلاک ہو انسان کس قدر ناشکرا ہے وہ ! ﴿۱۷﴾
مِنْ اَيِّ شَيْءٍ خَلَقَهٗ ﴿١٨﴾	کس چیز سے پیدا کیا اللہ نے اسے ؟ ﴿۱۸﴾
مِنْ نُّطْفَةٍ ۭ خَلَقَهٗ	منی کے ایک قطرے سے، پیدا کیا اللہ نے اسے
فَقَدَّرَهٗ ﴿١٩﴾	پھر تقدیر مقرر کی اس کی ﴿۱۹﴾
ثُمَّ السَّبِيْلَ يَسَّرَهٗ ﴿٢٠﴾	پھر زندگی کی راہ آسان کی اس کے لیے ﴿۲۰﴾
ثُمَّ اَمَاتَهٗ فَاَقْبَرَهٗ ﴿٢١﴾	پھر موت دی اس کو پھر قبر میں پہنچایا اسے ﴿۲۱﴾
ثُمَّ اِذَا شَآءَ اَنْشَرَهٗ ﴿٢٢﴾	پھر جب چاہے گا وہ اٹھا کھڑا کرے گا اسے ﴿۲۲﴾
كَلَّا لَمَّا يَقْضِ مَآ اَمَرَهٗ ﴿٢٣﴾	ہرگز نہیں ! نہ بجا لایا وہ اس حکم کو جو دیا اللہ نے اسے ﴿۲۳﴾
فَلْيَنْظُرِ الْاِنْسَانُ اِلٰى طَعَامِهٖ ﴿٢٤﴾	پھر ذرا دیکھے انسان اپنی خوراک کو ﴿۲۴﴾
اَنَّا صَبَبْنَا الْمَآءَ صَبًّا ﴿٢٥﴾	بے شک ہم ہی نے برسایا پانی فراوانی سے ﴿۲۵﴾
ثُمَّ شَقَقْنَا الْاَرْضَ شَقًّا ﴿٢٦﴾	پھر پھاڑا ہم نے زمین کو عجیب طریقہ سے ﴿۲۶﴾
فَاَنْۢبَتْنَا فِيْهَا حَبًّا ﴿٢٧﴾	پھر اگائے ہم نے اس میں غلے ﴿۲۷﴾
وَّعِنَبًا وَّقَضْبًا ﴿٢٨﴾	اور انگور اور ترکاریاں ﴿۲۸﴾
وَّزَيْتُوْنًا وَّنَخْلًا ﴿٢٩﴾	اور زیتون اور کھجوریں ﴿۲۹﴾
وَّحَدَآئِقَ غُلْبًا ﴿٣٠﴾	اور باغات گھنے ﴿۳۰﴾

012/ Who so honor The Word in gleam
014 Referred in Books, held in esteem

They're,
Exalted and astute scrupulous in respect
015/ Written by hands of penmen select
016 Glorious in glow, Adept and correct

017 Stigma and slur for a man, who defies
And trend to variance in verity to comply

018/ For what he's created by Lord in State
019 From a speck of sperm and determined in fate
020

He created and then destined to design in shape
Made his course in conduct secure and straight

021/ He occasions him to doom and die in the end
022 Then in the grave for the rest to spend

When He determines in stance
He'll raise him back to life in trance

But no! He's unmindful for His word in command
What Lord has decreed to affirm in demand

024/ So let the man,
025 Care and concern his feast and eats
(As to how We endow a bestowal of feast)

We sprinkle in spray quite a lot in place
Then We split the earth quite strange in pace

027/ And produce therein vegetables and grapes
030 And the shrubs so salubrious in state

Olives and dates girdled gardens in place
Lofty trees and scrubs so nutritious in taste

وَّفَاكِهَةً وَّاَبًّا ﴿۳۱﴾	اور پھل اور چارے ﴿۳۱﴾
مَّتَاعًا لَّكُمْ وَلِاَنْعَامِكُمْ ﴿۳۲﴾	سامانِ زیست تمہارے لیے اور تمہارے مویشیوں کے لیے ﴿۳۲﴾
فَاِذَا جَآءَتِ الصَّآخَّةُ ﴿۳۳﴾	پھر جب آئے گی بہرا کر دینے والی آواز ﴿۳۳﴾
يَوْمَ يَفِرُّ الْمَرْءُ مِنْ اَخِيْهِ ﴿۳۴﴾	اس دن بھاگے گا آدمی اپنے بھائی سے ﴿۳۴﴾
وَاُمِّهٖ وَاَبِيْهِ ﴿۳۵﴾	اور اپنی ماں سے اور اپنے باپ سے ﴿۳۵﴾
وَصَاحِبَتِهٖ وَبَنِيْهِ ﴿۳۶﴾	اور اپنی بیوی سے اور اپنی اولاد سے ﴿۳۶﴾
لِكُلِّ امْرِئٍ مِّنْهُمْ يَوْمَئِذٍ	ہر شخص ان میں سے اس دن
شَاْنٌ يُّغْنِيْهِ ﴿۳۷﴾	ایسی حالت میں ہوگا کہ اسے اپنی پڑی ہوگی ﴿۳۷﴾
وُجُوْهٌ يَّوْمَئِذٍ مُّسْفِرَةٌ ﴿۳۸﴾	کتنے ہی چہرے اس دن روشن ہوں گے ﴿۳۸﴾
ضَاحِكَةٌ مُّسْتَبْشِرَةٌ ﴿۳۹﴾	ہنستے مسکراتے، خوش و خرم ﴿۳۹﴾
وَوُجُوْهٌ يَّوْمَئِذٍ	اور کتنے ہی چہرے ایسے ہوں گے اس دن
عَلَيْهَا غَبَرَةٌ ﴿۴۰﴾	جن پر خاک اڑ رہی ہوگی ﴿۴۰﴾
تَرْهَقُهَا قَتَرَةٌ ﴿۴۱﴾	چھا رہی ہوگی ان پر سیاہی ﴿۴۱﴾
اُولٰٓئِكَ هُمُ الْكَفَرَةُ الْفَجَرَةُ ﴿۴۲﴾	یہی لوگ ہیں کافر، بدکردار ﴿۴۲﴾

بِسْمِ اللّٰهِ الرَّحْمٰنِ الرَّحِيْمِ

شروع اللہ کے نام سے جو بڑا مہربان نہایت رحم والا ہے

اِذَا الشَّمْسُ كُوِّرَتْ ﴿۱﴾	جب سورج لپیٹ دیا جائے گا ﴿۱﴾

031/ Fruits and Fodder:
033 For you and your cattle to appease
And eventually,
When there's deafening scream to freeze

034/ The Day,
036 Man to elude his brother in escape
From his mother and father in relate
From his wife, scion, will try to evade

037 The Day,
All to concern their doings in dale
Not to care a bit for others in trail

038/ There'll be some,
039 Beaming and gleaming delighted in elation

040 Others,
041 Strewn in dust and soot of rejection and negation
Hooded and hoofed despair in doom
(For what they're held in gloom)

042 They're the one:
Defying the Dictum of faith
They dare to deny Word of Lord to brace
They're evil in pace, defying word in grace

081-AL TAKWIR

In the name of Lord, the Most Beneficent, Most Merciful

001/ When sun crimp in crease to ease in glimmer
002 And stars wither in rot to lose their glitter

Fate of the Universe (Page : 1264)

وَإِذَا النُّجُومُ انكَدَرَتْ ۲	اور جب تارے بے نور ہو جائیں گے ۲
وَإِذَا الْجِبَالُ سُيِّرَتْ ۳	اور جب پہاڑ چلائے جائیں گے ۳
وَإِذَا الْعِشَارُ عُطِّلَتْ ۴	اور جب دس ماہ کی حاملہ اونٹنیاں چھٹی پھریں گی ۴
وَإِذَا الْوُحُوشُ حُشِرَتْ ۵	اور جب وحشی جانور (مارے خوف کے) اکٹھے ہو جائیں گے ۵
وَإِذَا الْبِحَارُ سُجِّرَتْ ۶	اور جب سمندر بھڑکا دیے جائیں گے ۶
وَإِذَا النُّفُوسُ زُوِّجَتْ ۷	اور جب جانوں کو جسموں سے جوڑا جائے گا ۷
وَإِذَا الْمَوْءُودَةُ سُئِلَتْ ۸	اور جب زندہ گاڑی ہوئی لڑکی سے پوچھا جائے گا ۸
بِأَيِّ ذَنبٍ قُتِلَتْ ۹	کہ آخر کس گناہ پر مارا گیا اسے ۹
وَإِذَا الصُّحُفُ نُشِرَتْ ۱۰	اور جب اعمال نامے کھولے جائیں گے ۱۰
وَإِذَا السَّمَاءُ كُشِطَتْ ۱۱	اور جب آسمان کا پردہ ہٹا دیا جائے گا ۱۱
وَإِذَا الْجَحِيمُ سُعِّرَتْ ۱۲	اور جب جہنم دہکائی جائے گی ۱۲
وَإِذَا الْجَنَّةُ أُزْلِفَتْ ۱۳	اور جب جنت قریب لائی جائے گی ۱۳
عَلِمَتْ نَفْسٌ مَّا أَحْضَرَتْ ۱۴	جان لے گا ہر شخص، کیا لے کر آیا ہے وہ ۱۴
فَلَا أُقْسِمُ بِالْخُنَّسِ ۱۵	پس نہیں، قسم کھاتا ہوں میں پیچھے ہٹ جانے والے (ستاروں) کی ۱۵
الْجَوَارِ الْكُنَّسِ ۱۶	چلنے والے، اور چھپ جانے والوں کی ۱۶
وَاللَّيْلِ إِذَا عَسْعَسَ ۱۷	اور رات کی، جب رخصت ہونے لگتی ہے وہ ۱۷
وَالصُّبْحِ إِذَا تَنَفَّسَ ۱۸	اور صبح کی، جب سانس لیتی ہے وہ ۱۸
إِنَّهُ لَقَوْلُ رَسُولٍ كَرِيمٍ ۱۹	بے شک یہ (قرآن) پیغام ہے زبانی فرشتہ عالی مقام کے ۱۹
ذِي قُوَّةٍ عِندَ ذِي الْعَرْشِ مَكِينٍ ۲۰	جو صاحب قوت ہے، مالک عرش کے ہاں اونچے مرتبہ والا ہے ۲۰

003/ When the mountains vanish in vale
004 When the she-camels panicky in trail

005/ Conceived of months ten nomadic in dale
007 When wild beasts sway in swarm around in place

When sea simmer to swell in blaze
Souls then group to see alike in daze

Fate of the Universe (Page : 1264)

008/ When toddler feminine buried in alive,
009 Will be asked to describe
Why she was killed and molested in plight

010/ When the scroll lay bare to glance
012 Then deeds and proceeds evince in stance
When Sky so high is unveiled to expose

When blazing fire is ignited high in screech
And when Garden is brought near in reach

014/ Then all to concern their fortune in reveal
016 So I call to the witness of stars in appeal

Some trend to recede
Others going straight,
Some way to conceal

017/ And the Night as it disperse in sway
019 And morn as it dispels dusk in array
Indeed, Qur'an
That's the word of worthy Messengers to obey

020 Gifted with might and affirmed in pace
Before the Bounty of Lord to face

مُطَاعٍ ثَمَّ اَمِيْنٍ ﴿۲۱﴾	اس کی بات مانی جاتی ہے وہاں (اور) امین بھی ہے ﴿۲۱﴾
وَمَا صَاحِبُكُمْ بِمَجْنُوْنٍ ﴿۲۲﴾	اور نہیں (اے اہل مکہ) ہے تمہارا یہ ساتھی کوئی دیوانہ ﴿۲۲﴾
وَلَقَدْ رَاٰهُ	اور بلاشبہ دیکھا ہے اس نے اس (پیغام لانے والے) کو
بِالْاُفُقِ الْمُبِيْنِ ﴿۲۳﴾	روشن اُفق پر ﴿۲۳﴾
وَمَا هُوَ عَلَى الْغَيْبِ	اور نہیں ہے یہ (رسول) غیب (کی بات بتانے) میں
بِضَنِيْنٍ ﴿۲۴﴾	ذرا بھی بخیل ﴿۲۴﴾
وَمَا هُوَ بِقَوْلِ شَيْطٰنٍ رَّجِيْمٍ ﴿۲۵﴾	اور نہیں ہے یہ (قرآن) کلام کسی شیطانِ مردود کا ﴿۲۵﴾
فَاَيْنَ تَذْهَبُوْنَ ﴿۲۶﴾	پھر کدھر چلے جا رہے ہو تم ؟ ﴿۲۶﴾
اِنْ هُوَ اِلَّا ذِكْرٌ لِّلْعٰلَمِيْنَ ﴿۲۷﴾	نہیں ہے یہ (قرآن) مگر نصیحت سب اہل جہاں کے لیے ﴿۲۷﴾
لِمَنْ شَآءَ مِنْكُمْ اَنْ يَّسْتَقِيْمَ ﴿۲۸﴾	ہر اس شخص کے لیے جو چاہے تم میں سے سیدھی راہ چلنا ﴿۲۸﴾
وَمَا تَشَآءُوْنَ اِلَّآ اَنْ يَّشَآءَ	اور نہیں چاہ سکتے تم مگر یہ کہ چاہے
اللّٰهُ رَبُّ الْعٰلَمِيْنَ ﴿۲۹﴾	اللہ رب العالمین ﴿۲۹﴾

آیاتہا ۱۹ (۸۲) سُوْرَةُ الْاِنْفِطَارِ مَكِّيَّةٌ (۸۲) رکوعہا ۱

بِسْمِ اللّٰهِ الرَّحْمٰنِ الرَّحِيْمِ

شروع اللہ کے نام سے جو بڑا مہربان نہایت رحم والا ہے

اِذَا السَّمَآءُ انْفَطَرَتْ ﴿۱﴾	جب آسمان پھٹ جائے گا ﴿۱﴾
وَاِذَا الْكَوَاكِبُ انْتَثَرَتْ ﴿۲﴾	اور جب تارے بکھر جائیں گے ﴿۲﴾
وَاِذَا الْبِحَارُ فُجِّرَتْ ﴿۳﴾	اور جب سمندر پھاڑ دیے جائیں گے ﴿۳﴾

021 His word is fair before The Lord in trust
He's also fairly conducted in just

022 O men and clan hither* and around
Your friend is not entranced in abound

*Makkah

023/ No wonder he saw him distinct in display
025 Prophet doesn't,
Hesitate to reveal the missive in stay
Nor it's a dictum of damned spirit in array

026/ Still you loiter and scatter in way
027 Indeed!
That's clear word for the Worlds to obey

028/ A word in adore,
029 Who decide to abide virtuous way in stay
It's not for you to have the choice in fray

It's only for the Lord to escort in vale
Lord, supporter of all Worlds in trail

*Verses 1-3 elucidates "Fate of the Universe" (Page : 1264)

082-AL INFITAR

In the name of Lord, the Most Beneficent, Most Merciful

001/ <u>When the Sky is fissured to shreds</u>
002 <u>Then the stars dwindle to threads</u>

003/ <u>When oceans spurt to thrust</u>
004 <u>When graves will get to gust and burst</u>

Fate of the Universe (Page : 1264)

وَاِذَا الْقُبُوْرُ بُعْثِرَتْ ۝٤	اور جب قبریں کریدی جائیں گی ۝٤
عَلِمَتْ نَفْسٌ مَّا قَدَّمَتْ	جان لے گا ہر شخص کہ کیا آگے بھیجا اس نے
وَاَخَّرَتْ ۝٥	اور (کیا) پیچھے چھوڑا اس نے ۝٥
يٰۤاَيُّهَا الْاِنْسَانُ مَا غَرَّكَ	اے انسان! آخر کس چیز نے دھوکا دیا ہے تجھ کو!
بِرَبِّكَ الْكَرِيْمِ ۝٦	تیرے رب کے بارے میں جو بہت کرم کرنے والا ہے ۝٦
الَّذِيْ خَلَقَكَ فَسَوّٰىكَ	جس نے پیدا کیا تجھے پھر نک سُک سے درست کیا
فَعَدَلَكَ ۝٧	اور متناسب بنایا تجھے ۝٧
فِيْۤ اَيِّ صُوْرَةٍ مَّا شَآءَ رَكَّبَكَ ۝٨	جیسی بھی شکل و صورت میں چاہا جوڑ کر تیار کیا تجھے ۝٨
كَلَّا بَلْ	ہرگز نہیں! بلکہ (اصل بات یہ ہے کہ)
تُكَذِّبُوْنَ بِالدِّيْنِ ۝٩	جھٹلاتے ہو تم جزا و سزا کو ۝٩
وَاِنَّ عَلَيْكُمْ لَحٰفِظِيْنَ ۝١٠	حالانکہ بے شک تم پر (مقرر) ہیں نگرانی کرنے والے ۝١٠
كِرَامًا كَاتِبِيْنَ ۝١١	بہت معزز لکھنے والے (اعمال کے) ۝١١
يَعْلَمُوْنَ مَا تَفْعَلُوْنَ ۝١٢	جانتے ہیں وہ جو کچھ کرتے ہو تم ۝١٢
اِنَّ الْاَبْرَارَ لَفِيْ نَعِيْمٍ ۝١٣	بے شک نیک لوگ ضرور ہوں گے نعمتوں (کی بہشت) میں ۝١٣
وَّاِنَّ الْفُجَّارَ لَفِيْ جَحِيْمٍ ۝١٤	اور بے شک بدکار لوگ ضرور ہوں گے جہنم میں ۝١٤
يَّصْلَوْنَهَا يَوْمَ الدِّيْنِ ۝١٥	داخل ہوں گے وہ اس میں جزا و سزا کے دن ۝١٥
وَمَا هُمْ عَنْهَا بِغَآئِبِيْنَ ۝١٦	اور نہیں ہو سکیں گے وہ اس سے غائب ۝١٦
وَمَآ اَدْرٰىكَ مَا يَوْمُ الدِّيْنِ ۝١٧	اور کیا جانو تم کیا ہے جزا و سزا کا دن؟ ۝١٧
ثُمَّ مَآ اَدْرٰىكَ مَا يَوْمُ الدِّيْنِ ۝١٨	پھر (کہتے ہیں ہم) کیا جانو تم کیا ہے جزا و سزا کا دن؟ ۝١٨

005/ Then all will learn,
006 What's he kept back or conveyed in trail
What beguiled thee O man, hither in dale
From The Most Bounteous Lord in prevail

007/ Who formed and fashioned you so precise
008 For each mean and manner He tends in device
And plans to put in tuck and sort so concise

009/ Nay!
But you defy the Day of Doom in trance
010 Indeed! Over you,
Angels are assigned to care in stance

011/ Angels,
012 So exalted in stance and fair in plan
Scribbling all your doings in glance

013 As for the men,
With virtuous deeds in proceeds
Will cherish blissful delights indeed

014/ And the evils to abide the Hell in Pyre
016 Them to enter on Day of Just in Fire

They wouldn't be able to trend to aside
(A delusive abide affirmed in deride)

017/ How'd you discern the Day of Discipline in call?
018 Yes!
How'd you define the Day of Discipline in call?

يَوْمَ لَا تَمْلِكُ نَفْسٌ لِّنَفْسٍ شَيْـًٔا ۖ	وہ دن کہ نہ کر سکے گا کوئی شخص کسی کے لیے کچھ بھی
وَالْأَمْرُ يَوْمَئِذٍ لِّلَّهِ ﴿١٩﴾	اور فیصلہ اس دن اللہ ہی کے اختیار میں ہوگا ﴿١٩﴾

(٨٣) سُورَةُ الْمُطَفِّفِينَ مَكِّيَّةٌ (٨٦)

آیاتها ٣٦ — رکوعها ١

بِسْمِ اللَّهِ الرَّحْمَٰنِ الرَّحِيمِ

شروع اللہ کے نام سے جو بڑا مہربان نہایت رحم والا ہے

وَيْلٌ لِّلْمُطَفِّفِينَ ﴿١﴾	تباہی ہے (ناپ تول میں) کمی کرنے والوں کے لیے ﴿١﴾
الَّذِينَ إِذَا اكْتَالُوا عَلَى النَّاسِ	وہ لوگ کہ جب لیتے ہیں ناپ تول کر (دوسرے) لوگوں سے
يَسْتَوْفُونَ ﴿٢﴾	تو پورا پورا لیتے ہیں ﴿٢﴾
وَإِذَا كَالُوهُمْ أَو وَّزَنُوهُمْ	اور جب ناپتے ہیں ان کے لیے یا تول کر دیتے ہیں انہیں
يُخْسِرُونَ ﴿٣﴾	تو کم دیتے ہیں ﴿٣﴾
أَلَا يَظُنُّ أُولَٰئِكَ أَنَّهُم	کیا ذرا بھی خیال نہیں کرتے یہ لوگ کہ بے شک وہ
مَّبْعُوثُونَ ﴿٤﴾	اٹھائے جانے والے ہیں؟ ﴿٤﴾
لِيَوْمٍ عَظِيمٍ ﴿٥﴾	ایک عظیم دن (کی پیشی) کے لیے ﴿٥﴾
يَوْمَ يَقُومُ النَّاسُ لِرَبِّ الْعَالَمِينَ ﴿٦﴾	وہ دن کہ کھڑے ہوں گے لوگ رب العالمین کے حضور ﴿٦﴾
كَلَّا إِنَّ كِتَابَ الْفُجَّارِ لَفِي سِجِّينٍ ﴿٧﴾	ہرگز نہیں! بے شک اعمال نامہ بدکاروں کا سجین میں ہوگا ﴿٧﴾
وَمَا أَدْرَاكَ مَا سِجِّينٌ ﴿٨﴾	اور کیا جانو تم کیا ہے سجین؟ ﴿٨﴾
كِتَابٌ مَّرْقُومٌ ﴿٩﴾	ایک بڑا دفتر ہے لکھا ہوا ﴿٩﴾
وَيْلٌ يَوْمَئِذٍ لِّلْمُكَذِّبِينَ ﴿١٠﴾	تباہی ہے اس دن جھٹلانے والوں کے لیے ﴿١٠﴾

019 The Day!
None to hold a bit in scale
Some in around to assuage in trail
But only the,
Dictum of Lord will affirm to prevail

*Verses 1-3 explains Fate of the Universe (Page : 1264)

083-AL MUTAFFIFIN

In the name of Lord, the Most Beneficent, Most Merciful

001/ Agony and anguish, who guile in measure
002 Who turn to swindle and plunder in measure
When they buy,
They affirm full measure in scale

003 But when they sell, in measure
They pillage partial in measure

004/ Don't they deem to discern
005 They'll be called to concern
On The Day so Immense in turn

006/ The Day when all men and clan
009 Will poise and prop before Lord in plan

Nay!
Indeed! Deeds of evil, held in Sijjin to stay
Who'd discern and concern the Sijjin in stray
It's a book signed and sealed thither in array

010/ Misery for them defying The Day*
011 These are the men denying The Day*

*The Day of Discipline and resolve

الَّذِينَ يُكَذِّبُونَ بِيَوْمِ الدِّينِ ﴿١١﴾	یہ وہ لوگ ہیں جو جھٹلاتے ہیں جزا و سزا کے دن کو ﴿۱۱﴾
وَمَا يُكَذِّبُ بِهِ إِلَّا كُلُّ	اور نہیں جھٹلاتا اس (دن) کو مگر ہر (وہ شخص جو)
مُعْتَدٍ أَثِيمٍ ﴿١٢﴾	حد سے گزر جانے والا ہے، گناہوں میں ڈوبا ہوا ہے ﴿۱۲﴾
إِذَا تُتْلَىٰ عَلَيْهِ آيَاتُنَا	جب پڑھی جاتی ہیں اس کے سامنے ہماری آیات
قَالَ أَسَاطِيرُ الْأَوَّلِينَ ﴿١٣﴾	تو کہتا ہے: افسانے ہیں پہلے لوگوں کے ﴿۱۳﴾
كَلَّا ۖ بَلْ ۜ رَانَ عَلَىٰ قُلُوبِهِم	ہرگز نہیں! واقعہ یہ ہے کہ زنگ چڑھ گیا ہے ان کے دلوں پر
مَّا كَانُوا يَكْسِبُونَ ﴿١٤﴾	ان (اعمالِ بد) کا جو وہ کماتے رہے ہیں ﴿۱۴﴾
كَلَّا إِنَّهُمْ عَن رَّبِّهِمْ	بے شک یہ لوگ اپنے رب (کے دیدار) سے
يَوْمَئِذٍ لَّمَحْجُوبُونَ ﴿١٥﴾	اس دن محروم رکھے جائیں گے ﴿۱۵﴾
ثُمَّ إِنَّهُمْ لَصَالُو الْجَحِيمِ ﴿١٦﴾	پھر بے شک یہ لوگ ضرور جا پڑیں گے جہنم میں ﴿۱۶﴾
ثُمَّ يُقَالُ هَٰذَا الَّذِي كُنتُم بِهِ تُكَذِّبُونَ ﴿١٧﴾	پھر کہا جائے گا یہی ہے وہ جس کو تم جھٹلایا کرتے تھے ﴿۱۷﴾
كَلَّا إِنَّ كِتَابَ الْأَبْرَارِ	ہرگز نہیں! بے شک اعمال نامہ نیک لوگوں کا
لَفِي عِلِّيِّينَ ﴿١٨﴾	علّیین میں ہوگا ﴿۱۸﴾
وَمَا أَدْرَاكَ مَا عِلِّيُّونَ ﴿١٩﴾	اور کیا جانو تم کیا ہے علّیین ﴿۱۹﴾
كِتَابٌ مَّرْقُومٌ ﴿٢٠﴾	ایک بڑا دفتر ہے لکھا ہوا ﴿۲۰﴾
يَشْهَدُهُ الْمُقَرَّبُونَ ﴿٢١﴾	نگہداشت کرتے ہیں اس کی مقرب فرشتے ﴿۲۱﴾
إِنَّ الْأَبْرَارَ لَفِي نَعِيمٍ ﴿٢٢﴾	بے شک نیک لوگ عیش و آرام میں ہوں گے ﴿۲۲﴾
عَلَى الْأَرَائِكِ يَنظُرُونَ ﴿٢٣﴾	بلند مسندوں پر بیٹھے نظارہ کر رہے ہوں گے ﴿۲۳﴾
تَعْرِفُ فِي وُجُوهِهِمْ	پہچان لے گا تو ان کے چہروں پر

012 And none,
Can deny Day of Demand in Dictate
But for sinner beyond confines in state

013/ When Our Verses recited to him in stay
014 He asserts to affirm and determines to say

These are but the old fables in stance
But no! What they do and state in trance

Their core and crux is tainted in bash
015 Verily,
The Day they'll be denied in thrash

The Gleam in Glow of Lord in pace
(Secured in veil over in place)

016/ They'll abide Fire of abyss in scale
017 They'll be told:
That's what you defied and declined in trail

018/ Nay, indeed!
019 Account of Virtuous is set in Ellyn
And how'd you discern what's Ellyn

020/ A book marked by dictum in decree
021 Angels bear a witness to Lord in spree

022/ Indeed!
023 Righteous to aside heavenly resides
Supine on thrones with enchant in beside

نَضْرَةَ النَّعِيمِ ﴿٢٤﴾	تری و تازگی عیش و آرام کی ﴿٢٤﴾
يُسْقَوْنَ مِن رَّحِيقٍ مَّخْتُومٍ ﴿٢٥﴾	پلائی جائے گی ان کو خالص شراب، سربمہر ﴿٢٥﴾
خِتَامُهُ مِسْكٌ ۚ وَفِي ذَٰلِكَ فَلْيَتَنَافَسِ	مہر ہوگی اس پر مُشک کی اسی کی تو رغبت کرنی چاہیے
الْمُتَنَافِسُونَ ﴿٢٦﴾	رغبت کرنے والوں کو ﴿٢٦﴾
وَمِزَاجُهُ مِن تَسْنِيمٍ ﴿٢٧﴾	آمیزش ہوگی اس میں تسنیم کی ﴿٢٧﴾
عَيْنًا يَشْرَبُ بِهَا الْمُقَرَّبُونَ ﴿٢٨﴾	یہ ایک چشمہ ہے پئیں گے جس میں سے مقرب بندے ﴿٢٨﴾
إِنَّ الَّذِينَ أَجْرَمُوا	بے شک وہ لوگ جنہوں نے جرم کیے،
كَانُوا مِنَ الَّذِينَ آمَنُوا يَضْحَكُونَ ﴿٢٩﴾	ان لوگوں پر جو ایمان لائے ہنسا کرتے تھے ﴿٢٩﴾
وَإِذَا مَرُّوا بِهِمْ	اور جب گزرتے تھے وہ ان کے پاس سے
يَتَغَامَزُونَ ﴿٣٠﴾	تو آپس میں آنکھوں سے اشارے کیا کرتے تھے ﴿٣٠﴾
وَإِذَا انقَلَبُوا إِلَىٰ أَهْلِهِمُ انقَلَبُوا	اور جب لوٹتے تھے اپنے اہلِ خانہ کی طرف تو لوٹا کرتے تھے،
فَكِهِينَ ﴿٣١﴾	(اہلِ ایمان پر پھبتیاں کس کس کر) لطف اندوز ہوتے ہوئے ﴿٣١﴾
وَإِذَا رَأَوْهُمْ قَالُوا	اور جب دیکھتے تھے ان کو تو کہا کرتے تھے:
إِنَّ هَٰؤُلَاءِ لَضَالُّونَ ﴿٣٢﴾	بے شک یہی لوگ ہیں دراصل گمراہ ﴿٣٢﴾
وَمَا أُرْسِلُوا عَلَيْهِمْ حَافِظِينَ ﴿٣٣﴾	حالانکہ نہیں بھیجا گیا تھا انہیں ان پر نگران بنا کر ﴿٣٣﴾
فَالْيَوْمَ الَّذِينَ آمَنُوا	سو آج وہ لوگ جو ایمان لائے تھے،
مِنَ الْكُفَّارِ يَضْحَكُونَ ﴿٣٤﴾	کفار پر ہنس رہے ہیں ﴿٣٤﴾
عَلَى الْأَرَائِكِ يَنظُرُونَ ﴿٣٥﴾	بلند مسندوں پر بیٹھے (ان کا حال) دیکھ رہے ہیں ﴿٣٥﴾
هَلْ ثُوِّبَ الْكُفَّارُ مَا كَانُوا يَفْعَلُونَ ﴿٣٦﴾	مل گیا نا پورا پورا بدلہ کفار کو ان کے کرتوتوں کا ﴿٣٦﴾

024/ To them,
025 You'll perceive their faces beaming in treasure
(They'll be gleaming in bliss of glamour in leisure)
And be,
Served with delicate sealed wine in pleasure

026 Seal thereof will be musk in desire
Them to cherish and relish in aspire

027/ With it'll be a melee of Tasnim so sure
028 Spring's water mix up the wine so pure

029 And the evils who sniggled in stray
For men, who trust faith to obey

030/ Whenever treaded aside and beside
031 They twinkled in twist to each in deride

When with their men and clan in stride
They tended to droll and brawl in abide

032 And whenever,
They saw men of trust in around
They would trend to disgust in abound
Behold!
Such are the men and clan adrift in surround

033/ But you're not to behold their deeds in plight
034 This Day men in trust would turn in delight
They'd sniggle and giggle on the cynics in sight

035/ On Thrones:
036 They'll perceive all around in grace
And the cynics defying trust in trace
Will bear the fruits of doings in base

سُوْرَةُ الْاِنْشِقَاقِ مَكِّيَّةٌ (۸۴) (۸۳)

اٰیاتها ۲۵ رکوعها ۱

بِسْمِ اللّٰهِ الرَّحْمٰنِ الرَّحِيْمِ

شروع اللہ کے نام سے جو بڑا مہربان نہایت رحم والا ہے

اِذَا السَّمَآءُ انْشَقَّتْ ①	جب آسمان پھٹ جائے گا ①
وَاَذِنَتْ لِرَبِّهَا	اور تعمیل کرے گا اپنے رب کے حکم کی
وَحُقَّتْ ②	اور اسے یہی زیب دیتا ہے ②
وَاِذَا الْاَرْضُ مُدَّتْ ③	اور جب زمین ہموار کر دی جائے گی ③
وَاَلْقَتْ مَا فِيْهَا	اور نکال باہر کرے گی جو کچھ اس کے اندر ہے
وَتَخَلَّتْ ④	اور خالی ہو جائے گی ④
وَاَذِنَتْ لِرَبِّهَا	اور تعمیل کرے گی اپنے رب کے حکم کی
وَحُقَّتْ ⑤	اور اسے یہی زیب دیتا ہے ⑤
يٰاَيُّهَا الْاِنْسَانُ اِنَّكَ كَادِحٌ اِلٰى رَبِّكَ	اے انسان! بے شک تو چلا جا رہا ہے اپنے رب کی طرف
كَدْحًا فَمُلٰقِيْهِ ⑥	کشاں کشاں بالآخر اس کے حضور پیش ہونا ہے تجھے ⑥
فَاَمَّا مَنْ اُوْتِيَ كِتٰبَهٗ	تو پھر جسے دیا جائے گا اس کا اعمالنامہ
بِيَمِيْنِهٖ ⑦	اس کے دائیں ہاتھ میں ⑦
فَسَوْفَ يُحَاسَبُ حِسَابًا يَّسِيْرًا ⑧	سو ضرور حساب لیا جائے گا اس سے آسان حساب ⑧
وَّيَنْقَلِبُ اِلٰٓى اَهْلِهٖ مَسْرُوْرًا ⑨	اور لوٹے گا وہ اپنے لوگوں میں شاداں و فرحاں ⑨
وَاَمَّا مَنْ اُوْتِيَ	اور رہا وہ جس کو پکڑایا جائے گا

084-AL INSHIQAQ

In the name of Lord, the Most Beneficent, Most Merciful

001/ When is the Universe torn to bit and trace
003 In abidance of Dictum of Lord to brace
And when the Earth is smoothed in scrape

Fate of the Universe (Page : 1264)

004/ And hurl off,
005 Its bits and trace in proceeds
Obeying the dictum of Lord indeed

And it's,
Desired of the earth to behave in so
Divulging all the record of men in flow

006/ O Man!
009 You're gradually toiling in move
Towards your Lord in stride
Eventually you'll be,
There before your Lord to aside

Arduous in toil and moil in fray
Determined to abide dictum of Lord in sway

The men in stance,
Who hold tell of deeds in hand right in glance
Soon he'll return to his men (of faith) in trance

With pleasure,
Leisurely with his tallying in delight

كِتٰبَهٗ وَرَآءَ ظَهْرِهٖ ﴿١٠﴾	اعمالنامہ اس کا پیٹھ پیچھے سے ﴿١٠﴾
فَسَوْفَ يَدْعُوْا ثُبُوْرًا ﴿١١﴾	سو ضرور مانگے گا وہ موت ﴿١١﴾
وَّيَصْلٰى سَعِيْرًا ﴿١٢﴾	اور جا پڑے گا دہکتی آگ میں ﴿١٢﴾
اِنَّهٗ كَانَ فِيْٓ اَهْلِهٖ مَسْرُوْرًا ﴿١٣﴾	بے شک وہ تھا اپنے گھر والوں میں مگن ﴿١٣﴾
اِنَّهٗ ظَنَّ اَنْ لَّنْ يَّحُوْرَ ﴿١٤﴾	بے شک اس نے سمجھ رکھا تھا کہ ہرگز نہیں ہے پلٹ کر جانا ﴿١٤﴾
بَلٰٓى ۚ اِنَّ رَبَّهٗ	کیوں نہیں (ضرور پلٹنا ہے) بے شک اس کا رب
كَانَ بِهٖ بَصِيْرًا ﴿١٥﴾	اس کے سارے کرتوت دیکھ رہا تھا ﴿١٥﴾
فَلَآ اُقْسِمُ بِالشَّفَقِ ﴿١٦﴾	پس نہیں! قسم کھاتا ہوں میں شفق کی ﴿١٦﴾
وَالَّيْلِ وَمَا وَسَقَ ﴿١٧﴾	اور رات کی اور اس کی جو کچھ وہ سمیٹ لیتی ہے ﴿١٧﴾
وَالْقَمَرِ اِذَا اتَّسَقَ ﴿١٨﴾	اور چاند کی جب وہ اوج کمال کو پہنچتا ہے ﴿١٨﴾
لَتَرْكَبُنَّ طَبَقًا عَنْ طَبَقٍ ﴿١٩﴾	تم بھی ضرور چڑھو گے درجہ بدرجہ (رتبہ اعلیٰ) پر ﴿١٩﴾
فَمَا لَهُمْ لَا يُؤْمِنُوْنَ ﴿٢٠﴾	پھر کیا ہوا ہے ان کو کہ ایمان نہیں لاتے ﴿٢٠﴾
وَاِذَا قُرِئَ عَلَيْهِمُ الْقُرْاٰنُ	اور جب پڑھا جاتا ہے ان کے سامنے قرآن
لَا يَسْجُدُوْنَ ﴿٢١﴾	تو سجدہ نہیں کرتے ﴿٢١﴾
بَلِ الَّذِيْنَ كَفَرُوْا يُكَذِّبُوْنَ ﴿٢٢﴾	بلکہ یہ لوگ جنہوں نے کفر اختیار کیا ہے جھٹلاتے ہیں اس کو ﴿٢٢﴾
وَاللّٰهُ اَعْلَمُ بِمَا	اور اللہ خوب جانتا ہے اس کو جو
يُوْعُوْنَ ﴿٢٣﴾	انہوں نے بھر رکھا ہے اپنے دلوں میں ﴿٢٣﴾
فَبَشِّرْهُمْ بِعَذَابٍ اَلِيْمٍ ﴿٢٤﴾	پس بشارت دے دو ان کو دردناک عذاب کی ﴿٢٤﴾
اِلَّا الَّذِيْنَ اٰمَنُوْا وَعَمِلُوا الصّٰلِحٰتِ	البتہ وہ لوگ جو ایمان لائے اور کیے انہوں نے نیک کام

010/ But whoso gets his relate from back in slight
011 Soon to scream for his defied doom in blight

012/ Then to enter blaze of Fire in deride
013 Indeed!
He enjoyed in delight with his men in pride

014/ He had never evinced in lore
021 If ever he had to be there in score

Nay!
Indeed he has to return for sure
Before the Bounty of Lord in adore

His Lord is witness to his doings in plan
So indeed,
I bear the witness of glimmer of dawn
And the night,
When it sweeps its shawl in span
And moon,
With its glimmer of gleam in glow
Indeed!
You'll rise in sequential (merited) stance in stride

Then,
What's the matter with them in concern
For they don't comply in faith in term

When Qur'an is read for them in stay
They elude to incline in prone in pray

022/ But the cynics so hostile denounce in precise
024 But,
Lord discerns and concerns their core in guise
So reveal,
Them their doom in gloom in concise

لَهُمْ أَجْرٌ غَيْرُ مَمْنُوْنٍ ﴿٢٥﴾ — ان کے لیے ہے ایسا اجر جو نہ ختم ہونے والا ہے ﴿٢٥﴾

آیاتها ٢٢ (٨٥) سُوْرَةُ الْبُرُوْجِ مَكِّيَّةٌ (٢٧) رکوعها ١

بِسْمِ اللّٰهِ الرَّحْمٰنِ الرَّحِيْمِ

شروع اللہ کے نام سے جو بڑا مہربان نہایت رحم والا ہے

وَالسَّمَآءِ ذَاتِ الْبُرُوْجِ ﴿١﴾ — قسم ہے آسمان کی جو برجوں والا ہے ﴿١﴾

وَالْيَوْمِ الْمَوْعُوْدِ ﴿٢﴾ — اور روزِ (قیامت) کی جس کا وعدہ ہے ﴿٢﴾

وَشَاهِدٍ وَّمَشْهُوْدٍ ﴿٣﴾ — اور دیکھنے والے کی اور دیکھی جانے والی چیز کی ﴿٣﴾

قُتِلَ أَصْحٰبُ الْأُخْدُوْدِ ﴿٤﴾ — ہلاک کر دیے گئے کھائیاں کھودنے والے ﴿٤﴾

النَّارِ ذَاتِ الْوَقُوْدِ ﴿٥﴾ — (جن میں بھری ہوئی تھی) آگ خوب دہکتی ہوئی ﴿٥﴾

إِذْ هُمْ عَلَيْهَا قُعُوْدٌ ﴿٦﴾ — جبکہ وہ اس کے گرد بیٹھے ہوئے تھے ﴿٦﴾

وَّهُمْ عَلٰى مَا يَفْعَلُوْنَ — اور وہ، جو کچھ کر رہے تھے

بِالْمُؤْمِنِيْنَ شُهُوْدٌ ﴿٧﴾ — مومنوں کے ساتھ خود دیکھ رہے تھے ﴿٧﴾

وَمَا نَقَمُوْا مِنْهُمْ إِلَّآ — اور نہیں بدلہ لیا تھا انہوں نے ان سے مگر

أَنْ يُّؤْمِنُوْا بِاللّٰهِ — اس کا کہ وہ ایمان لے آئے تھے اللہ پر

الْعَزِيْزِ الْحَمِيْدِ ﴿٨﴾ — جو سب پر غالب، ہر قسم کی حمد و ثنا کا سزاوار ہے ﴿٨﴾

الَّذِيْ لَهٗ مُلْكُ السَّمٰوٰتِ وَالْأَرْضِ — وہ جس کو زیبا ہے بادشاہت آسمانوں کی اور زمین کی۔

وَاللّٰهُ عَلٰى كُلِّ شَيْءٍ شَهِيْدٌ ﴿٩﴾ — اور اللہ ہر چیز کو دیکھ رہا ہے ﴿٩﴾

إِنَّ الَّذِيْنَ فَتَنُوا الْمُؤْمِنِيْنَ — بے شک وہ لوگ جنہوں نے آگ میں جلایا مومن مردوں کو

025 But for the men and clan, who affirm in faith
And abide the discipline of truth in pace

Them to cherish awards and rewards in amends
Rewards never to squash or stop in trends

085-AL BURUJ

In the name of Lord, the Most Beneficent, Most Merciful

001 Vow be to Heavenly Piers* in pace
Not discernable to human eye in place

Keeping Cosmic line and plan in array
Added with Zodiacal signs in sway

*(The Gigantic Electromagnetic Magnetic field) Page : 1242

002/ Vow be to the Day that's affirmed in term
003 Vow be to the witness and subject in concern

004/ Doomed are,
005 The excavators of furrows of fire in haze
Profusely abounding fuel for fire in blaze

006/ Regard!
007 They're thronged around in thrust
And behold all their done and doings in gust

For what they trended in jest
Against the faithful there in trust

008 And molested them for all along in treat
For they held faith for Lord to plead

Astral O Astute laudable in stance
Worthy of Acclaim all in glance

009 For Him is the reign and rule in sway
All in the Heavens held in display
Lord beholds our deeds and doings in fray

وَالْمُؤْمِنٰتِ ثُمَّ لَمْ يَتُوْبُوْا	اور مومن عورتوں کو اس کے بعد توبہ بھی نہ کی
فَلَهُمْ عَذَابُ جَهَنَّمَ وَلَهُمْ	تو ان کے لیے ہے جہنم کا عذاب اور ان کے لیے ہے
عَذَابُ الْحَرِيْقِ ﴿۱۰﴾	سزا آگ میں جلنے کی ﴿۱۰﴾
اِنَّ الَّذِيْنَ اٰمَنُوْا وَعَمِلُوا	بے شک وہ لوگ جو ایمان لائے اور کیے انہوں نے
الصّٰلِحٰتِ لَهُمْ جَنّٰتٌ	نیک عمل ان کے لیے ہیں بہشت کے باغ،
تَجْرِيْ مِنْ تَحْتِهَا الْاَنْهٰرُ	بہہ رہی ہوں گی جن کے نیچے نہریں،
ذٰلِكَ الْفَوْزُ الْكَبِيْرُ ﴿۱۱﴾	یہی ہے کامیابی بہت بڑی ﴿۱۱﴾
اِنَّ بَطْشَ رَبِّكَ لَشَدِيْدٌ ﴿۱۲﴾	بے شک پکڑ تیرے رب کی بہت ہی سخت ہے ﴿۱۲﴾
اِنَّهٗ هُوَ يُبْدِئُ	بے شک وہی تو ہے جو پہلی بار پیدا کرتا ہے
وَيُعِيْدُ ﴿۱۳﴾	اور وہی دوبارہ پیدا کرے گا ﴿۱۳﴾
وَهُوَ الْغَفُوْرُ الْوَدُوْدُ ﴿۱۴﴾	اور وہی ہے بہت بخشنے والا، بہت محبت کرنے والا ﴿۱۴﴾
ذُو الْعَرْشِ الْمَجِيْدُ ﴿۱۵﴾	مالک عرش کا بڑی عظمت و شان والا ﴿۱۵﴾
فَعَّالٌ لِّمَا يُرِيْدُ ﴿۱۶﴾	کر گزرنے والا اس (کام) کا جس کا ارادہ کرے ﴿۱۶﴾
هَلْ اَتٰىكَ حَدِيْثُ الْجُنُوْدِ ﴿۱۷﴾	بھلا پہنچی ہے تم کو خبر لشکروں کی؟ ﴿۱۷﴾
فِرْعَوْنَ وَثَمُوْدَ ﴿۱۸﴾	فرعون اور ثمود (کے لشکروں) کی ﴿۱۸﴾
بَلِ الَّذِيْنَ كَفَرُوْا فِيْ تَكْذِيْبٍ ﴿۱۹﴾	لیکن یہ لوگ جنہوں نے کفر کیا ہے (لگے ہوئے ہیں) جھٹلانے میں ﴿۱۹﴾
وَّاللّٰهُ مِنْ وَّرَآئِهِمْ مُّحِيْطٌ ﴿۲۰﴾	حالانکہ اللہ ان کو ہر طرف سے گھیرے ہوئے ہے ﴿۲۰﴾
بَلْ هُوَ قُرْاٰنٌ مَّجِيْدٌ ﴿۲۱﴾	ان کا جھٹلانا بے سود ہے، وہ قرآن ہے بڑی عظمت و شان والا ﴿۲۱﴾
فِيْ لَوْحٍ مَّحْفُوْظٍ ﴿۲۲﴾	لوحِ محفوظ میں (لکھا ہوا) ہے ﴿۲۲﴾

010 Those, who oppressed,
And molested men and dame in trust
Stay in the burn of pyre in gust
And they didn't remorse in regret

They're destined to Hell in ablaze
Stern burn of blaze, Hell in glaze

011 Those in the discipline of faith in abide
Blessed with gaiety of Gardens to reside

Below and beside streams surge in stride
That's release and rescue for them to aside

012/ So exquisite is the charge of Lord in trail
013 Who Created a lot from nullity in scale
And can replace and revive all in the dale

See "Fate of the Universe" Page : 1264

014/ Compassionate, caring fondling in sway
016 Lord of Glorious Throne, gleaming in array

Whenever He wants a thing to Be and Sure
It determines it be there, thence to endure

017 Did you get the fable of forces in fore
019 That of Pharaoh and Thamud in score
Cynics still deny to defy in lore

020 But Lord!
Bound them in and around from rear and surround

021/ But No!
022 That's The Qur'an so Glorious in abound
Sealed and secured from all in around

(٨٦) سُوْرَةُ الطَّارِقِ مَكِّيَّةٌ (٣٦)

آیاتها ١٧ — رکوعها ١

بِسْمِ اللّٰهِ الرَّحْمٰنِ الرَّحِيْمِ

شروع اللہ کے نام سے جو بڑا مہربان نہایت رحم والا ہے

وَالسَّمَآءِ وَالطَّارِقِ ①	قسم ہے آسمان کی اور رات کو نمودار ہونے والے کی ①
وَمَآ اَدْرٰىكَ مَا الطَّارِقُ ②	اور کیا جانو تم کیا ہے وہ رات کو نمودار ہونے والا؟ ②
النَّجْمُ الثَّاقِبُ ③	ایک تارا ہے چمکتا ہوا ③
اِنْ كُلُّ نَفْسٍ لَّمَّا عَلَيْهَا حَافِظٌ ④	نہیں کوئی متنفس کہ نہ ہو اس پر کوئی نگہبان ④
فَلْيَنْظُرِ الْاِنْسَانُ مِمَّ خُلِقَ ⑤	سو ذرا غور کرے انسان کہ کس چیز سے پیدا کیا گیا ہے وہ؟ ⑤
خُلِقَ مِنْ مَّآءٍ دَافِقٍ ⑥	پیدا کیا گیا ہے اچھلنے والے پانی سے ⑥
يَّخْرُجُ مِنْۢ بَيْنِ الصُّلْبِ وَالتَّرَآئِبِ ⑦	جو نکلتا ہے بیچ میں سے پیٹھ اور پسلیوں کے ⑦
اِنَّهٗ عَلٰى رَجْعِهٖ لَقَادِرٌ ⑧	بے شک اللہ اس کے دوبارہ پیدا کرنے پر بہرحال قادر ہے ⑧
يَوْمَ تُبْلَى السَّرَآئِرُ ⑨	جس دن جانچ پڑتال ہو گی سب چھپی باتوں کی ⑨
فَمَا لَهٗ مِنْ قُوَّةٍ وَّلَا نَاصِرٍ ⑩	تو نہ ہو گا انسان کے پاس کوئی زور اور نہ کوئی مددگار ⑩
وَالسَّمَآءِ ذَاتِ الرَّجْعِ ⑪	قسم ہے آسمان کی جو ہمیشہ برساتا ہے ⑪
وَالْاَرْضِ ذَاتِ الصَّدْعِ ⑫	اور قسم زمین کی جو (پودا اگتے وقت) پھٹ جاتی ہے ⑫
اِنَّهٗ لَقَوْلٌ فَصْلٌ ⑬	بے شک کلام الٰہی یقیناً بات ہے دوٹوک ⑬
وَّمَا هُوَ بِالْهَزْلِ ⑭	اور نہیں ہے یہ کلام کوئی ہنسی مذاق ⑭
اِنَّهُمْ يَكِيْدُوْنَ كَيْدًا ⑮	بے شک یہ لوگ چل رہے ہیں ایک چال ⑮

086-AL TARIQ

In the name of Lord, the Most Beneficent, Most Merciful

001 By the Sky in sway
And Night with gracious Visitant in display

002 And how'd you concern to discern
Setting of Night Visitant in term

003 The Star of glowing gleam in glide

004 For all men and clan (soul) in abide
Have a guardian over in stride

005 Let the man turn to discern and concern
Of what he's created as a man in term

006 Created and contrived of a drop of sperm

007/ Coursing mid backbone and ribs in low
008 Of course He's to revive* once more in flow

*life after death

009 The Day to reveal all secrets in spree
010 Man not to have skill nor help to flee

011 By the Heavens with Sprinkle in spray
012 And earth with streaming springs in sway
With blooming of fauna and foliage in array

013 Behold!
014 Book discerns all the virtue and vile in trends
It's not a while of leisure or pleasure to spend

وَّاَكِيْدُ كَيْدًا ﴿۱۶﴾	اور میں بھی چل رہا ہوں ایک داؤ ﴿۱۶﴾
فَمَهِّلِ الْكٰفِرِيْنَ	پس چھوڑ دو ان کے حال پر (اے نبیؐ) ان کافروں کو
اَمْهِلْهُمْ رُوَيْدًا ﴿۱۷﴾ ع	ڈھیل دو ان کو اک ذرا کی ذرا ﴿۱۷﴾

اٰیاتها ۱۹ (۸۷) سُوْرَةُ الْاَعْلٰى مَكِّيَّةٌ (۸) رکوعها ۱

بِسْمِ اللّٰهِ الرَّحْمٰنِ الرَّحِيْمِ

شروع اللہ کے نام سے جو بڑا مہربان نہایت رحم والا ہے

سَبِّحِ اسْمَ رَبِّكَ الْاَعْلَى ﴿۱﴾	تسبیح کر اپنے رب کے نام کی جو سب سے بلند ہے ﴿۱﴾
الَّذِىْ خَلَقَ فَسَوّٰى ﴿۲﴾	جس نے پیدا کیا پھر تناسب قائم کیا ﴿۲﴾
وَالَّذِىْ قَدَّرَ فَهَدٰى ﴿۳﴾	اور جس نے تقدیر بنائی پھر راہ دکھائی ﴿۳﴾
وَالَّذِىْٓ اَخْرَجَ الْمَرْعٰى ﴿۴﴾	اور جس نے نکالا چارا ﴿۴﴾
فَجَعَلَهٗ غُثَآءً اَحْوٰى ﴿۵﴾	پھر بنا دیا اس کو کوڑا سیاہ ﴿۵﴾
سَنُقْرِئُكَ فَلَا تَنْسٰٓى ﴿۶﴾	البتہ پڑھائیں گے ہم تمہیں پھر نہ بھولو گے تم ﴿۶﴾
اِلَّا مَا شَآءَ اللّٰهُ ؕ اِنَّهٗ يَعْلَمُ	بجز اس کے جو چاہے اللہ۔ بے شک وہی جانتا ہے
الْجَهْرَ وَمَا يَخْفٰى ﴿۷﴾	ظاہر کو بھی اور اس کو بھی جو پوشیدہ ہے ﴿۷﴾
وَنُيَسِّرُكَ لِلْيُسْرٰى ﴿۸﴾	اور سہولت دیں گے ہم تمہیں آسان طریقہ کی ﴿۸﴾
فَذَكِّرْ اِنْ نَّفَعَتِ الذِّكْرٰى ﴿۹﴾	سو نصیحت کرتے رہو تم، جہاں تک نصیحت نفع دے ﴿۹﴾
سَيَذَّكَّرُ مَنْ يَّخْشٰى ﴿۱۰﴾	ضرور نصیحت قبول کرے گا وہ جسے خوف ہے (اللہ کا) ﴿۱۰﴾
وَيَتَجَنَّبُهَا الْاَشْقٰى ﴿۱۱﴾	اور گریز کرے گا اس سے جو ہو گا انتہائی بدبخت ﴿۱۱﴾

015 And those devising and designing a plan or plot
016 And I'm also contriving a precise plan in slot

017 O Muhammad!
A time is given to the cynics in pace
And while in acquittal assigned in place

087-AL ALA

In the name of Lord, the Most Beneficent, Most Merciful

001 All praises for:
002 Vigilante Lord, Most Exalted and Precise
Who contrived and conferred Order in Devise

003/ Who ordained fate and devised in direction
005 Who yields fodder fair in collection
And turns it to dusky brown in Selection

006 We'll educate you so gradual in grades
That you don't slight a bit in trace

007/ But for the Dictum of Lord to brace
009 He discerns and concerns hither in trace
All so distinct and enigmatic in pace

We'll make it easy for you to comply
Urging in appeal, for thence to apply

010 The counsel,
To be cherished by the men in faith
(Advice is likely to impress in grace)

الَّذِي يَصْلَى النَّارَ الْكُبْرَىٰ ﴿١٢﴾	وہ جو جا پڑے گا بڑی آگ میں ﴿١٢﴾
ثُمَّ لَا يَمُوتُ فِيهَا وَلَا يَحْيَىٰ ﴿١٣﴾	پھر نہ موت آئے گی اسے اس میں اور نہ زندہ ہی ہوگا ﴿١٣﴾
قَدْ أَفْلَحَ مَن تَزَكَّىٰ ﴿١٤﴾	یقیناً فلاح پاگیا وہ جس نے پاک کیا خود کو ﴿١٤﴾
وَذَكَرَ اسْمَ رَبِّهِ فَصَلَّىٰ ﴿١٥﴾	اور لیا نام اپنے رب کا پھر نماز پڑھی ﴿١٥﴾
بَلْ تُؤْثِرُونَ الْحَيَاةَ الدُّنْيَا ﴿١٦﴾	لیکن ترجیح دیتے ہو تم تو دنیاوی زندگی کو ﴿١٦﴾
وَالْآخِرَةُ خَيْرٌ وَأَبْقَىٰ ﴿١٧﴾	جبکہ اُخروی زندگی بہت بہتر ہے اور ہمیشہ رہنے والی ہے ﴿١٧﴾
إِنَّ هَٰذَا لَفِي الصُّحُفِ الْأُولَىٰ ﴿١٨﴾	بے شک یہی بات لکھی ہوئی ہے پہلے صحیفوں میں بھی ﴿١٨﴾
صُحُفِ إِبْرَاهِيمَ وَمُوسَىٰ ﴿١٩﴾	صحیفے ابراہیمؑ کے اور موسیٰؑ کے ﴿١٩﴾

آیاتها ٢٦ (٨٨) سُورَةُ الْغَاشِيَةِ مَكِّيَّةٌ (٦٨) رکوعها ١

بِسْمِ اللَّهِ الرَّحْمَٰنِ الرَّحِيمِ

شروع اللہ کے نام سے جو بڑا مہربان نہایت رحم والا ہے

هَلْ أَتَاكَ حَدِيثُ الْغَاشِيَةِ ﴿١﴾	بھلا پہنچی تم کو خبر چھا جانے والی آفت (قیامت) کی ﴿١﴾
وُجُوهٌ يَوْمَئِذٍ خَاشِعَةٌ ﴿٢﴾	کتنے ہی چہرے اس دن ہوں گے خوفزدہ ﴿٢﴾
عَامِلَةٌ نَّاصِبَةٌ ﴿٣﴾	سخت مشقت کرنے والے تھکے ماندے ﴿٣﴾
تَصْلَىٰ نَارًا حَامِيَةً ﴿٤﴾	جھلس رہے ہوں گے وہ دہکتی آگ میں ﴿٤﴾
تُسْقَىٰ مِنْ عَيْنٍ آنِيَةٍ ﴿٥﴾	پلایا جائے گا انہیں ایک کھولتے چشمے سے ﴿٥﴾
لَّيْسَ لَهُمْ طَعَامٌ	نہیں ہوگا ان کے لیے کھانے کو کچھ
إِلَّا مِن ضَرِيعٍ ﴿٦﴾	مگر ایک خاردار خشک جھاڑی ﴿٦﴾

011/ But,
013 Those destined to doom in deplore
They're fated for Hell to secure

Them to abide there in place
Not to doom or die and or live in pace

014/ The men will allure brilliance in grace*
015 Who practice discipline of piety in pace
With the Name of Lord beg in pray

*Discipline of Faith

(Refine and incline in discipline to obey
And Exalt Astute Lord when in pray)

016 But nay!
You pick and pile worldly term in deceit
017/ But Hereafter is a better term to allure
019 And it's divulged in Books hither in fore
Books of Abraham and Moses point in score

088-AL GHASHIYA

In the name of Lord, the Most Beneficent, Most Merciful

001 Did you hear of a fable of an awesome rumble

002 The Day some faces will humble and crumble

003 Acting so hard and looking tired and humble

004 While burning in pyre in ignominious slumber

005 Them to savor stewing water of spring to drink

006 Not to eat, but pin dry sedge there in brink

لَا يُسْمِنُ وَلَا يُغْنِي مِن جُوعٍ (٧) — جو نہ موٹا کرے اور نہ مٹائے بھوک (٧)

وُجُوهٌ يَوْمَئِذٍ نَّاعِمَةٌ (٨) — کتنے ہی چہرے اس دن ہوں گے تر و تازہ (٨)

لِّسَعْيِهَا رَاضِيَةٌ (٩) — اپنی کارگزاری پر خوش و خرم (٩)

فِي جَنَّةٍ عَالِيَةٍ (١٠) — بہشت بریں میں (١٠)

لَّا تَسْمَعُ فِيهَا لَاغِيَةً (١١) — نہ سنیں گے وہ وہاں کوئی بے ہودہ بات (١١)

وقف لازم

فِيهَا عَيْنٌ جَارِيَةٌ (١٢) — اس میں چشمے ہیں رواں (١٢)

فِيهَا سُرُرٌ مَّرْفُوعَةٌ (١٣) — اس میں مسندیں ہیں اونچی اونچی (١٣)

وَأَكْوَابٌ مَّوْضُوعَةٌ (١٤) — اور ساغر قرینے سے رکھے ہوئے (١٤)

وَنَمَارِقُ مَصْفُوفَةٌ (١٥) — اور گاؤ تکیے قطار در قطار (١٥)

وَزَرَابِيُّ مَبْثُوثَةٌ (١٦) — اور قالین بچھے ہوئے (١٦)

أَفَلَا يَنظُرُونَ إِلَى الْإِبِلِ كَيْفَ خُلِقَتْ (١٧) — تو کیا نہیں دیکھتے یہ، اونٹ کو کہ کیسا عجیب پیدا کیا گیا؟ (١٧)

وَإِلَى السَّمَاءِ كَيْفَ رُفِعَتْ (١٨) — اور آسمان کو کہ کس طرح بلند کیا گیا؟ (١٨)

وَإِلَى الْجِبَالِ كَيْفَ نُصِبَتْ (١٩) — اور پہاڑوں کو کہ کس انداز سے جمائے گئے؟ (١٩)

وَإِلَى الْأَرْضِ كَيْفَ سُطِحَتْ (٢٠) — اور زمین کو کہ کس انداز سے بچھائی گئی؟ (٢٠)

فَذَكِّرْ إِنَّمَا أَنتَ — سو اے نبی! تم نصیحت کرتے رہو۔ تم ہو بس

مُذَكِّرٌ (٢١) — نصیحت کرنے والے (٢١)

لَّسْتَ عَلَيْهِم بِمُصَيْطِرٍ (٢٢) — نہیں ہو تم ان پر کوئی جبر کرنے والے (٢٢)

إِلَّا مَن تَوَلَّىٰ وَكَفَرَ (٢٣) — مگر جس نے منہ موڑا اور انکار کیا (٢٣)

فَيُعَذِّبُهُ اللَّهُ الْعَذَابَ الْأَكْبَرَ (٢٤) — سو عذاب دے گا اسے اللہ عذاب بہت بڑا (٢٤)

007 That's not to sustain rather let to shrink

008 Some men and clan be elated and excited

009 Thrilled of their deeds and so delighted

010 Abiding most florid place of preference

011 Not listening of fib or folly in indulgence

012 There'll be springs so pleasing in spray

013 On thrones so exalted to aside in stay

014 Goblet and glass displayed in array

015 And row of cushions set in display

016 Rich carpets spread in satiny sway

017 Don't they see the Camels in back
How We created for a term in aback
018 And The Sky!
How it's raised so high and away
019 And Mountains!
How fixed and Perfected in stay
020 And Earth!
How it's line and length determined in array

021 (So, O Muhammad!)
You admonish a word in advice

022 You're not to mend their way in premise

023 But if one declines My Order and Command

024 Lord will torment in resolute stance
A great Castigation for them in trance

اِنَّ اِلَيْنَآ اِيَابَهُمْ ﴿۲۵﴾	یقیناً ہماری ہی طرف ان کو لوٹ کر آنا ہے ﴿۲۵﴾
ثُمَّ اِنَّ عَلَيْنَا حِسَابَهُمْ ﴿۲۶﴾	پھر بے شک ہمارے ہی ذمہ ان سے حساب لینا ہے ﴿۲۶﴾

(۸۹) سُوْرَةُ الْفَجْرِ مَكِّيَّةٌ (۱۰)

اٰیاتھا ۳۰ — رکوعھا ۱

بِسْمِ اللّٰهِ الرَّحْمٰنِ الرَّحِيْمِ

شروع اللہ کے نام سے جو بڑا مہربان نہایت رحم والا ہے

وَالْفَجْرِ ﴿۱﴾	قسم ہے — فجر کی ﴿۱﴾
وَلَيَالٍ عَشْرٍ ﴿۲﴾	اور دس راتوں کی ﴿۲﴾
وَّالشَّفْعِ وَالْوَتْرِ ﴿۳﴾	اور جفت کی اور طاق کی ﴿۳﴾
وَالَّيْلِ اِذَا يَسْرِ ﴿۴﴾	اور رات کی — جب وہ جانے لگے ﴿۴﴾
هَلْ فِيْ ذٰلِكَ قَسَمٌ	بھلا ان میں کوئی قسم ہے
لِّذِيْ حِجْرٍ ﴿۵﴾	کسی صاحبِ عقل (کے غور و فکر) کے لیے؟ ﴿۵﴾
اَلَمْ تَرَ كَيْفَ فَعَلَ	کیا نہیں دیکھا تم نے کہ کیسا برتاؤ کیا
رَبُّكَ بِعَادٍ ﴿۶﴾	تمہارے رب نے قوم عاد کے ساتھ؟ ﴿۶﴾
اِرَمَ ذَاتِ الْعِمَادِ ﴿۷﴾	عادِ ارم اونچے اونچے ستونوں والی ﴿۷﴾
الَّتِيْ لَمْ يُخْلَقْ مِثْلُهَا فِي الْبِلَادِ ﴿۸﴾	وہ کہ نہیں پیدا کی گئی اس کی مثل (کوئی قوم) ملکوں میں ﴿۸﴾
وَثَمُوْدَ الَّذِيْنَ	اور قوم ثمود (کے ساتھ) جنہوں نے
جَابُوا الصَّخْرَ بِالْوَادِ ﴿۹﴾	تراشا سخت چٹانوں کو وادی میں ﴿۹﴾
وَفِرْعَوْنَ ذِي الْاَوْتَادِ ﴿۱۰﴾	اور فرعون میخوں والے (کے ساتھ) ﴿۱۰﴾

025 Indeed!
026 To Us they'll gather in pace
We'll determine mid them just in trust

089-AL FAJR

In the name of Lord, the Most Beneficent, Most Merciful

001 Vow be to the (Gleaming) Morn in slot

002 And by the nights ten in plot

003 And to the even and odd when figured in apart

004 And the night, when it's going to depart

005 Is there a word to concern,
To adjure a glimpse in term

For man of sapience to discern

006 Don't you have the care in concern
Your Lord dealt Aad arduously in term

007 People of Iram with pillars so tall

008 Like of that not seen in the land

009 Thamud who cut out huge rocks in vale

010 And Pharaoh lord of stakes (so nasty in dale)

الَّذِيْنَ طَغَوْا فِي الْبِلَادِ ۝۱۱
یہ وہ لوگ تھے جنہوں نے سرکشی کی تھی ملکوں میں ۝۱۱

فَاَكْثَرُوْا فِيْهَا الْفَسَادَ ۝۱۲
اور بہت پھیلایا تھا ان میں فساد ۝۱۲

فَصَبَّ عَلَيْهِمْ رَبُّكَ سَوْطَ عَذَابٍ ۝۱۳
آخر کار برسایا ان پر تیرے رب نے عذاب کا کوڑا ۝۱۳

اِنَّ رَبَّكَ لَبِالْمِرْصَادِ ۝۱۴
بے شک تیرا رب گھات لگائے ہوئے ہے ۝۱۴

فَاَمَّا الْاِنْسَانُ اِذَا مَا ابْتَلٰىهُ
لیکن انسان کا حال یہ ہے کہ جب بھی آزماتا ہے اس کو

رَبُّهٗ فَاَكْرَمَهٗ وَنَعَّمَهٗ ۙ
رب اس کا سو عزت بخشتا ہے اس کو اور نعمتیں دیتا ہے اس کو

فَيَقُوْلُ رَبِّيْٓ اَكْرَمَنِ ۝۱۵
تو وہ کہتا ہے کہ میرے رب نے بہت عزت بخشی ہے مجھے ۝۱۵

وَاَمَّآ اِذَا مَا ابْتَلٰىهُ
لیکن پھر جب آزمائش میں ڈالتا ہے وہ اسے

فَقَدَرَ عَلَيْهِ رِزْقَهٗ ۙ
اور تنگی کر دیتا ہے اس پر اس کے رزق میں

فَيَقُوْلُ رَبِّيْٓ اَهَانَنِ ۝۱۶
تو کہتا ہے کہ میرے رب نے ذلیل کر دیا مجھے ۝۱۶

كَلَّا بَلْ لَّا تُكْرِمُوْنَ الْيَتِيْمَ ۝۱۷
ہرگز نہیں! بلکہ تم اچھا سلوک نہیں کرتے یتیم کے ساتھ ۝۱۷

وَلَا تَحٰٓضُّوْنَ عَلٰى طَعَامِ الْمِسْكِيْنِ ۝۱۸
اور نہیں ترغیب دیتے تم ایک دوسرے کو مسکین کو کھانا کھلانے کی ۝۱۸

وَتَاْكُلُوْنَ التُّرَاثَ اَكْلًا لَّمًّا ۝۱۹
اور کھا جاتے ہو تم میراث کا مال سارے کا سارا سمیٹ کر ۝۱۹

وَّتُحِبُّوْنَ الْمَالَ حُبًّا جَمًّا ۝۲۰
اور پیار کرتے ہو تم مال سے جی بھر کر ۝۲۰

كَلَّآ اِذَا دُكَّتِ
ہرگز نہیں! جب ریزہ ریزہ کر دی جائے گی

الْاَرْضُ دَكًّا دَكًّا ۝۲۱
زمین کوٹ کوٹ کر ۝۲۱

وَّجَآءَ رَبُّكَ وَالْمَلَكُ
اور جلوہ فرما ہوگا تیرا رب اور فرشتے (کھڑے ہوں گے،

صَفًّا صَفًّا ۝۲۲
صف در صف ۝۲۲

وَجِايْٓءَ يَوْمَئِذٍۢ بِجَهَنَّمَ ۙ
اور لائی جائے گی اس دن جہنم (سب کے سامنے)

011 They disobeyed in land immense in stride

012 To dike and pile defiance in deride

013 Lord then forced immense whip and lash
There's an admonition to trounce and thrash

014 For Lord is wary and watchful to blow in abash

015 Now to man, Lord puts to test in tribute
Endow him status with honor and repute

Then the man asserts whiff in confute
Lord conferred honor to me in pursuits

016 But!
When put to trial in term to endure
Confining his sustenance to secure

He turns in despair to complain
Lord left me in misery to sustain

017 But nay!
You treat not orphan fair in greed

018 Nor you encourage some needy to feed

019 But gulp and gorge heritage (of others) in greed

020 And you've undue love and lust of profusion

021 Nay!
When earth will be milled as dust in delusion
022 Lord will to show up,
With line and file of angels in Place

يَوْمَئِذٍ يَّتَذَكَّرُ الْاِنْسَانُ	اس دن سمجھ آئے گی انسان کو
وَاَنّٰى لَهُ الذِّكْرٰى ۝۲۳	مگر اب کیا حاصل، اس کے سمجھنے کا! ۲۳
يَقُوْلُ يٰلَيْتَنِيْ قَدَّمْتُ	کہے گا کاش! آگے بھیجے ہوتے میں نے (کچھ نیک عمل)
لِحَيَاتِيْ ۝۲۴	اپنی اس زندگی کی خاطر ۲۴
فَيَوْمَئِذٍ لَّا يُعَذِّبُ عَذَابَهٗٓ اَحَدٌ ۝۲۵	پھر اس دن نہ عذاب دے گا اللہ کا سا عذاب کوئی اور ۲۵
وَّلَا يُوْثِقُ وَثَاقَهٗٓ اَحَدٌ ۝۲۶	اور نہیں جکڑے گا اللہ کا سا جکڑنا کوئی اور ۲۶
يٰٓاَيَّتُهَا النَّفْسُ الْمُطْمَئِنَّةُ ۝۲۷	(نیک روح سے خطاب ہوگا) اے نفسِ مطمئنہ ۲۷
ارْجِعِيْٓ اِلٰى رَبِّكِ رَاضِيَةً	واپس لوٹ اپنے رب کی طرف، تو اس سے راضی
مَّرْضِيَّةً ۝۲۸	وہ تجھ سے راضی ۲۸
فَادْخُلِيْ فِيْ عِبٰدِيْ ۝۲۹	پھر شامل ہو جا میرے خاص بندوں میں ۲۹
وَادْخُلِيْ جَنَّتِيْ ۝۳۰	اور داخل ہو جا میری جنت میں ۳۰

اٰيَاتُهَا ۲۰ (۹۰) سُوْرَةُ الْبَلَدِ مَكِّيَّةٌ (۳۵) رُكُوْعُهَا ۱

بِسْمِ اللّٰهِ الرَّحْمٰنِ الرَّحِيْمِ

شروع اللہ کے نام سے جو بڑا مہربان نہایت رحم والا ہے

لَآ اُقْسِمُ بِهٰذَا الْبَلَدِ ۝۱	نہیں! قسم کھاتا ہوں میں اس شہر (مکہ) کی ۱
وَاَنْتَ حِلٌّۢ بِهٰذَا الْبَلَدِ ۝۲	اور تم (اے محمدؐ) رہتے ہو اس شہر میں ۲
وَوَالِدٍ وَّمَا وَلَدَ ۝۳	اور قسم، باپ (آدمؑ) کی اور اس کی اولاد کی ۳
لَقَدْ خَلَقْنَا الْاِنْسَانَ فِيْ كَبَدٍ ۝۴	بلاشبہ پیدا کیا ہم نے انسان کو مشقت میں ۴

023 The hell to reveal the Day in place
The day man will recall but of no help in trace
But how'd that remembrance to ease in pace

024/ He'll say, Ah!
If he'd sent forth moral deeds in place
For the Day!
025 His reproach so wrecked and intense in state
Such as none can inflict in place

026 Captivity of Lord so severe in trace
As none can dream such bond to brace

027 The virtuous will be then told in pace
Oh!
You exquisite souls in comfort and solace

028 Come you hither and get to a place
Eased and assuaged immense in grace

You're pleased with Him in sway
And Lord pleased of you in stay

029 Enter rank and flank of My Virtuous in norm
030 And get into My Gardens of Bliss in charm

090-AL BALAD

In the name of Lord, the Most Beneficent, Most Merciful

001/ Do I call to witness this civil* and locale
002 And you're abiding quite free in trail

*Makkah

003/ And caring witness of Adam,
004 With progeny in prevail
Surely We created the man
To toil and struggle in span

أَيَحْسَبُ أَن لَّن يَقْدِرَ عَلَيْهِ أَحَدٌ ۵
کیا خیال کرتا ہے وہ یہ کہ نہیں بس چلے گا اس پر کسی کا؟ ۵

يَقُولُ أَهْلَكْتُ مَالًا لُّبَدًا ۶
کہتا ہے کہ اڑا دیا میں نے مال ڈھیروں ۶

أَيَحْسَبُ أَن لَّمْ يَرَهُ أَحَدٌ ۷
کیا سمجھتا ہے وہ یہ کہ نہیں دیکھا اس کو کسی نے؟ ۷

أَلَمْ نَجْعَل لَّهُ عَيْنَيْنِ ۸
بھلا نہیں عطا کیں ہم نے اس کو دو آنکھیں؟ ۸

وَلِسَانًا وَشَفَتَيْنِ ۹
اور زبان اور دو ہونٹ؟ ۹

وَهَدَيْنَاهُ النَّجْدَيْنِ ۱۰
اور دکھا دی ہیں ہم نے اس کو (خیر و شر کی) دونوں راہیں ۱۰

فَلَا اقْتَحَمَ الْعَقَبَةَ ۱۱
مگر نہ گزرا وہ دشوار گزار گھاٹی پر سے ۱۱

وَمَا أَدْرَاكَ مَا الْعَقَبَةُ ۱۲
اور کیا جانو تم کہ کیا ہے وہ گھاٹی؟ ۱۲

فَكُّ رَقَبَةٍ ۱۳
چھڑانا ہے گردن کا ۱۳

أَوْ إِطْعَامٌ فِي يَوْمٍ ذِي مَسْغَبَةٍ ۱۴
یا کھانا کھلانا کسی فاقے کے دن ۱۴

يَتِيمًا ذَا مَقْرَبَةٍ ۱۵
یتیم کو جو رشتہ دار ہو ۱۵

أَوْ مِسْكِينًا ذَا مَتْرَبَةٍ ۱۶
یا مسکین کو جس کے ہاں خاک اڑ رہی ہو ۱۶

ثُمَّ كَانَ مِنَ الَّذِينَ آمَنُوا
پھر ہو بھی یہ (کھلانے والا) ان لوگوں میں سے جو ایمان لائے

وَتَوَاصَوْا بِالصَّبْرِ
اور نصیحت کرتے رہے ایک دوسرے کو صبر و استقامت کی

وَتَوَاصَوْا بِالْمَرْحَمَةِ ۱۷
اور وصیت کرتے رہے ایک دوسرے کو رحم کی ۱۷

أُولَٰئِكَ أَصْحَابُ الْمَيْمَنَةِ ۱۸
یہی لوگ ہیں دائیں بازو والے ۱۸

وَالَّذِينَ كَفَرُوا بِآيَاتِنَا
اور وہ لوگ جنہوں نے نہ مانا ہماری آیات کو

هُمْ أَصْحَابُ الْمَشْأَمَةِ ۱۹
یہی ہیں بائیں بازو والے ۱۹

عَلَيْهِمْ نَارٌ مُّؤْصَدَةٌ ۲۰
ان پر آگ ہوگی چھائی ہوئی ۲۰

005 He infers,
There's none to rule over him in stance

006 He crows of wealth,
Thronged in swarm in trance

007 Deems to concern here in stance
There's none to perceive in glance

008 Haven't We endowed him two eyes to glance

009 A tongue and pair of lips to speak in stance

010 And showed him two divergent ways to tread
(Good and bad; virtue and vile to choice in tread)

011/ But he eluded to tread tough way in stride
012 And what'll explain thee the steep in glide

013 It's freeing the bondman indeed

014 Or giving food to some in proceed
On the day of privation in squeeze

015 Or to orphan who's close in connection
016 Or to indigent so poor in desertion

017/ Then he'll be of those,
018 Who give credence in course

Persevere patience in pace
With kindness and compassion in grace
Such are band and body of virtuous* in place

*Right hand

019/ But, who gets to deny Our Verses in stance
020 They're fellows seditious ways* in glance
There'll be,
Pyre over and above them in trance

*Left hand

اٰیاتُھا ١٥ — (٩١) سُوْرَةُ الشَّمْسِ مَكِّيَّةٌ (٢٦) — رکوعُھا ١

بِسْمِ اللّٰهِ الرَّحْمٰنِ الرَّحِيْمِ

شروع اللہ کے نام سے جو بڑا مہربان نہایت رحم والا ہے

وَالشَّمْسِ وَضُحٰىهَا ۝١ — قسم ہے سورج کی اور اس کی دھوپ کی ①

وَالْقَمَرِ اِذَا تَلٰىهَا ۝٢ — قسم ہے چاند کی جب آتا ہے وہ پیچھے سورج کے ②

وَالنَّهَارِ اِذَا جَلّٰىهَا ۝٣ — قسم ہے دن کی جب نمایاں کر دیتا ہے وہ سورج کو ③

وَالَّيْلِ اِذَا يَغْشٰىهَا ۝٤ — قسم ہے رات کی جب چھپا لیتی ہے وہ سورج کو ④

وَالسَّمَآءِ وَمَا بَنٰىهَا ۝٥ — قسم ہے آسمان کی اور جیسا کہ اس نے اسے بنایا ⑤

وَالْاَرْضِ وَمَا طَحٰىهَا ۝٦ — قسم ہے زمین کی اور جیسا کہ اس نے اسے پھیلایا ⑥

وَنَفْسٍ وَّمَا سَوّٰىهَا ۝٧ — قسم ہے نفسِ انسانی کی اور جیسا کہ اس نے اسے ہموار کیا ⑦

فَاَلْهَمَهَا فُجُوْرَهَا وَتَقْوٰىهَا ۝٨ — پھر الہام کر دی اس پر بدی اس کی اور پرہیزگاری اس کی ⑧

قَدْ اَفْلَحَ مَنْ زَكّٰىهَا ۝٩ — یقیناً فلاح پا گیا وہ جس نے پاک کیا نفس کو ⑨

وَقَدْ خَابَ مَنْ دَسّٰىهَا ۝١٠ — اور یقیناً نامراد ہو گیا وہ جس نے خاک میں ملایا اس کو ⑩

كَذَّبَتْ ثَمُوْدُ بِطَغْوٰىهَا ۝١١ — جھٹلایا ثمود نے بسبب اپنی سرکشی کے ⑪

اِذِ انْۢبَعَثَ اَشْقٰىهَا ۝١٢ — جب بپھر کر اٹھا ان کا سب سے بڑا بدبخت شخص ⑫

فَقَالَ لَهُمْ رَسُوْلُ اللّٰهِ نَاقَةَ اللّٰهِ — تو کہا ان سے اللہ کے رسول نے (خبردار دور رہنا) اللہ کی اونٹنی

وَسُقْيٰهَا ۝١٣ — اور اس کی پانی کی باری سے ! ⑬

فَكَذَّبُوْهُ فَعَقَرُوْهَا ۵ — مگر جھٹلایا انہوں نے اللہ کے رسول کو اور ہلاک کر دیا اونٹنی کو

091-AL SHAMS

In the name of Lord, the Most Beneficent, Most Merciful

001 Vow be to the sun,
With its glorious glitter in glow
002 Vow be to the moon,
Tracking the sun in flow
003 Vow be to the day,
When it evinces the sun in glow

004 Vow be to the night,
When it covers the sun in flow
005 Vow be to the heavens,
As He contrived so superb in shape
006 Vow be to the Earth,
As He spread and expanded in space

007 Vow be to the Soul,
With order of concord in design
008 And conveyed discernment to sense
With evil in ills
Besides sane and sound sapience in will
009
Indeed!
010 He thrives in instruct, who refines in conduct
He fails, who corrupts in instruct

011 The men of Thamud :
Defied (their Prophet) in contort
With their immoderate evils in distort

012 Regard!
Most depraved of the man in beside,
Was deputed for the evil in stride

013 But Messenger of Lord said to them
So clear in stance,
It's she camel of Lord near in brink
Bar it not, having a term in drink

فَدَمۡدَمَ عَلَیۡهِمۡ — آخر کار تباہی و بربادی نازل کر دی ان پر

رَبُّهُمۡ بِذَنۡۢبِهِمۡ — ان کے رب نے بسبب ان کے گناہوں کے

فَسَوّٰىهَا ﴿۱۴﴾ — اور سب کو ہلاک کر کے، برابر کر دیا ان کو ﴿۱۴﴾

وَلَا یَخَافُ عُقۡبٰهَا ﴿۱۵﴾ — اور نہیں کوئی خوف اسے اس کے برے نتیجہ کا ﴿۱۵﴾

آیاتها ۲۱ (۹۲) سُوۡرَةُ الَّیۡلِ مَکِّیَّةٌ (۹) رکوعها ۱

بِسۡمِ اللّٰهِ الرَّحۡمٰنِ الرَّحِیۡمِ

شروع اللہ کے نام سے جو بڑا مہربان نہایت رحم والا ہے

وَالَّیۡلِ اِذَا یَغۡشٰی ﴿۱﴾ — قسم ہے رات کی جب وہ ڈھانپ لے ﴿۱﴾

وَالنَّهَارِ اِذَا تَجَلّٰی ﴿۲﴾ — اور دن کی جب وہ روشن ہو ﴿۲﴾

وَمَا خَلَقَ الذَّکَرَ وَالۡاُنۡثٰۤی ﴿۳﴾ — اور قسم ہے اس حکمت کی کہ پیدا کیے اس نے نر و مادہ ﴿۳﴾

اِنَّ سَعۡیَکُمۡ لَشَتّٰی ﴿۴﴾ — بے شک تمہاری کوششیں مختلف قسم کی ہیں ﴿۴﴾

فَاَمَّا مَنۡ اَعۡطٰی وَاتَّقٰی ﴿۵﴾ — سو وہ جس نے دیا مال اللہ کی راہ میں، اور ڈرتا رہا ﴿۵﴾

وَصَدَّقَ بِالۡحُسۡنٰی ﴿۶﴾ — اور سچ مانا بھلائی کو ﴿۶﴾

فَسَنُیَسِّرُهٗ لِلۡیُسۡرٰی ﴿۷﴾ — سو توفیق دیں گے ہم اس کو راحت کے راستے کی ﴿۷﴾

وَاَمَّا مَنۡۢ بَخِلَ وَاسۡتَغۡنٰی ﴿۸﴾ — اور وہ جس نے بخل کیا اور بے نیازی برتی ﴿۸﴾

وَکَذَّبَ بِالۡحُسۡنٰی ﴿۹﴾ — اور جھٹلایا بھلائی کو ﴿۹﴾

فَسَنُیَسِّرُهٗ لِلۡعُسۡرٰی ﴿۱۰﴾ — تو ہم پہنچائیں گے اسے سختی میں ﴿۱۰﴾

وَمَا یُغۡنِیۡ عَنۡهُ مَالُهٗۤ — اور نہ کام آئے گا اس کے اس کا مال

014 But they defied to decline
Him as prophet of Lord so refine
And instead,

Hamstrung her in defiance of command
So they're obliterated with their scion in demand
015
Shaping them even high and low around in abide
And for Him is no fear of consequences in stride

092-THE NIGHT

In the name of Lord, the Most Beneficent, Most Merciful

01/ By the night Awning its shawl* *(covering the light)
02 By the day glowing with sol** **Sun

03 By the mystery in creation in trail
Both the sexes male and female
04 Indeed!
You determinedly strive so diverse in scale

05 Those,
Who disperse alms charity in stance
And affirm duty to Lord in glance

06 Indeed!
And determines decency in all means and mode
07 We shall ease and assuage him, with bliss in goal
And who stash and stow in conduct
08 And deem (him) self sufficient in instruct
09 And for the man, who lies best in role

10 Indeed!
We'll make his conduct slick in despair
11 His riches wouldn't save for dip in repair
When he perishes headlong in glare

إِذَا تَرَدَّىٰ ﴿۱۱﴾ — جب گرے گا وہ (دوزخ کے گڑھے میں) ﴿۱۱﴾

إِنَّ عَلَيْنَا لَلْهُدَىٰ ﴿۱۲﴾ — بے شک ہمارے ذمہ ہے راہ دکھانا ﴿۱۲﴾

وَإِنَّ لَنَا لَلْآخِرَةَ وَالْأُولَىٰ ﴿۱۳﴾ — اور بے شک ہم ہی مالک ہیں آخرت کے اور دنیا کے بھی ﴿۱۳﴾

فَأَنذَرْتُكُمْ نَارًا تَلَظَّىٰ ﴿۱۴﴾ — پس میں نے خبردار کر دیا ہے تم کو بھڑکتی ہوئی آگ سے ﴿۱۴﴾

لَا يَصْلَاهَا إِلَّا الْأَشْقَى ﴿۱۵﴾ — نہیں جھلسے گا اس میں مگر وہ انتہائی بدبخت ﴿۱۵﴾

الَّذِي كَذَّبَ وَتَوَلَّىٰ ﴿۱۶﴾ — جس نے جھٹلایا اور منہ پھیرا ﴿۱۶﴾

وَسَيُجَنَّبُهَا الْأَتْقَى ﴿۱۷﴾ — اور بچا لیا جائے گا اس سے وہ بڑا پرہیزگار ﴿۱۷﴾

الَّذِي يُؤْتِي مَالَهُ يَتَزَكَّىٰ ﴿۱۸﴾ — جو دیتا ہے اپنا مال پاکیزگی کی خاطر ﴿۱۸﴾

وَمَا لِأَحَدٍ عِندَهُ مِن نِّعْمَةٍ — جبکہ نہ ہو کسی کا اس پر کوئی ایسا احسان

تُجْزَىٰ ﴿۱۹﴾ — کہ اس کا بدلہ دیا جائے ﴿۱۹﴾

إِلَّا ابْتِغَاءَ وَجْهِ رَبِّهِ الْأَعْلَىٰ ﴿۲۰﴾ — (وہ دیتا ہے) محض خوشنودی چاہنے کی خاطر اپنے ربِّ اعلیٰ کی ﴿۲۰﴾

وَلَسَوْفَ يَرْضَىٰ ﴿۲۱﴾ — اور عنقریب وہ خوش ہو جائے گا ﴿۲۱﴾

آیاتها ۱۱ — (۹۳) سُورَةُ الضُّحَىٰ مَكِّيَّةٌ (۱۱) — رکوعها ۱

بِسْمِ اللَّهِ الرَّحْمَٰنِ الرَّحِيمِ

شروع اللہ کے نام سے جو بڑا مہربان نہایت رحم والا ہے

وَالضُّحَىٰ ﴿۱﴾ — قسم ہے روز روشن کی ﴿۱﴾

وَاللَّيْلِ إِذَا سَجَىٰ ﴿۲﴾ — اور رات کی جب وہ چھا جائے ﴿۲﴾

مَا وَدَّعَكَ رَبُّكَ — نہیں چھوڑا تم کو (اے محمدؐ) تمہارے رب نے

012 Indeed!
It's for Us to escort in faith
013 And indeed!
We Command worldly resumes in pace

And stance of Hereafter in place
(The end and beginning in phase)

014 Thereupon!
I admonish you of the tormenting blaze in glaze

015 That's for most dejected to reach in blaze

016 He, who abjure truth and lure for lie in deeds
017 The virtuous will be far afar from squeeze
018
Who spend their riches to destitute in award
019 They enhance their self esteem in reward
020
Not to treasure for prize and pay in regard
But only for the countenance of the Lord
Surely!
021 They'll be gratified of Glorious Lord in Grace

093-AL ZAHAH

In the name of Lord, the Most Beneficent, Most Merciful

01 By the gleaming sky, beaming in dawn
02 And by the night with solace in calm
03
Your Guardian Lord didn't desert you in norm
Nor He's dismayed of you in stance

وَمَا قَلٰى ۝٣	اور نہ وہ ناراض ہوا ۝٣
وَلَلْاٰخِرَةُ خَيْرٌ لَّكَ مِنَ الْاُوْلٰى ۝٤	اور یقیناً بعد کا دور بہتر ہے تمہارے لیے پہلے دور سے ۝٤
وَلَسَوْفَ يُعْطِيْكَ	اور عنقریب (وہ کچھ) عطا کرے گا تمہیں
رَبُّكَ فَتَرْضٰى ۝٥	تمہارا رب کہ خوش ہو جاؤ گے تم ۝٥
اَلَمْ يَجِدْكَ يَتِيْمًا فَاٰوٰى ۝٦	کیا نہیں پایا تمہارے رب نے تم کو یتیم پھر ٹھکانہ فراہم کیا ۝٦
وَوَجَدَكَ ضَآلًّا فَهَدٰى ۝٧	اور پایا تم کو ناواقفِ راہ تو راہ دکھائی ۝٧
وَوَجَدَكَ عَآئِلًا فَاَغْنٰى ۝٨	اور پایا تم کو تنگدست سو غنی کر دیا ۝٨
فَاَمَّا الْيَتِيْمَ فَلَا تَقْهَرْ ۝٩	لہٰذا یتیم پر سختی نہ کرنا ۝٩
وَاَمَّا السَّآئِلَ فَلَا تَنْهَرْ ۝١٠	اور جو سوالی ہو (اسے) نہ جھڑکنا ۝١٠
وَاَمَّا بِنِعْمَةِ رَبِّكَ فَحَدِّثْ ۝١١ ع ۱۸	اور جو نعمتیں ہیں تمہارے رب کی ان کو خوب بیان کرتے رہنا ۝١١

آیاتہا ۸ (۹۴) سُوْرَةُ الْاَلَمْ نَشْرَحْ مَكِّيَّةٌ (۱۲) رکوعہا ۱

بِسْمِ اللّٰهِ الرَّحْمٰنِ الرَّحِيْمِ

شروع اللہ کے نام سے جو بڑا مہربان نہایت رحم والا ہے

اَلَمْ نَشْرَحْ لَكَ صَدْرَكَ ۝١	(اے محمدؐ) کیا نہیں کھول دیا ہم نے تمہاری خاطر تمہارا سینہ ۝١
وَوَضَعْنَا عَنْكَ وِزْرَكَ ۝٢	اور اتار دیا ہم نے تم پر سے بوجھ تمہارا ۝٢
الَّذِيْٓ اَنْقَضَ ظَهْرَكَ ۝٣	وہ (بوجھ) جو توڑے دے رہا تھا تمہاری کمر ۝٣
وَرَفَعْنَا لَكَ ذِكْرَكَ ۝٤	اور بلند کر دیا ہم نے تمہاری خاطر تمہارا ذکر ۝٤
فَاِنَّ مَعَ الْعُسْرِ يُسْرًا ۝٥	تو بے شک مشکل کے ساتھ آسانی بھی ہے ۝٥

004/ Surely!
Your future's flowering and gifted in swarm
Than the days of present factual in alarm
005
And your Lord will bless to bestow
That you'll behold and appeased in endow

006 Didn't He,
See you orphaned and cherished in span
007/ Didn't He,
008 See you oblivious and instructed in plan
Didn't He,
See you indigent and conducted in clan

009/ Don't be harsh to the orphan in treat
Nor rebuke the beggar (in street)
010 So praise Bounty of Lord,
011 And be guardian of your word in speech

094-ALM NASHRAH

In the name of Lord, the Most Beneficent, Most Merciful

001 (O Prophet)
Didn't We open sluice of thy veer of core
002 And eased oppression of agony in score
003
004 That's imposing invidious heft on (thy) rear
And exalted thy eminence in (elegant) sphere
005
006 Indeed!
There's appease with anguish in throw
There's solace with affliction in blow

اِنَّ مَعَ الْعُسْرِ يُسْرًا ⑥	یقیناً مشکل کے ساتھ آسانی بھی ہے ⑥
فَاِذَا فَرَغْتَ فَانْصَبْ ⑦	پھر اب جبکہ فارغ ہو چکے ہو تم تو محنت کرو (فرائض نبوت میں) ⑦
وَاِلٰى رَبِّكَ فَارْغَبْ ⑧	اور اپنے رب کی طرف دل لگائے رکھو ⑧

(۹۵) سُوْرَةُ التِّيْنِ مَكِّيَّةٌ (۲۸)

آیاتہا ۸ — رکوعہا ۱

بِسْمِ اللّٰهِ الرَّحْمٰنِ الرَّحِيْمِ

شروع اللہ کے نام سے جو بڑا مہربان نہایت رحم والا ہے

وَالتِّيْنِ وَالزَّيْتُوْنِ ①	قسم ہے انجیر کی اور زیتون کی ①
وَطُوْرِ سِيْنِيْنَ ②	اور طورِ سینا کی ②
وَهٰذَا الْبَلَدِ الْاَمِيْنِ ③	اور اس شہر امن والے کی ③
لَقَدْ خَلَقْنَا الْاِنْسَانَ	بلاشبہ پیدا کیا ہم نے انسان کو
فِيْٓ اَحْسَنِ تَقْوِيْمٍ ④	بہترین ساخت پر ④
ثُمَّ رَدَدْنٰهُ اَسْفَلَ سٰفِلِيْنَ ⑤	پھر پھینک دیا ہم نے اس کو سب نیچوں سے نیچے ⑤
اِلَّا الَّذِيْنَ اٰمَنُوْا	سوائے ان لوگوں کے جو ایمان لائے
وَعَمِلُوا الصّٰلِحٰتِ	اور کیے انہوں نے نیک کام
فَلَهُمْ اَجْرٌ غَيْرُ مَمْنُوْنٍ ⑥	سو ان کے لیے ہے اجر بے انتہا ⑥
فَمَا يُكَذِّبُكَ بَعْدُ	پھر کون جھٹلا سکتا ہے تم کو (اے نبیؐ) اس کے بعد،
بِالدِّيْنِ ⑦	جزا و سزا کے معاملہ میں ⑦
اَلَيْسَ اللّٰهُ بِاَحْكَمِ الْحٰكِمِيْنَ ⑧	کیا نہیں ہے اللہ سب حاکموں سے بڑا حاکم؟ ⑧

007 So when you're free of agony in screech
008 Then go for the word in preach
Enchant in sentient to your Lord in beseech

095-AL TIN

In the name of Lord, the Most Beneficent, Most Merciful

001 By the fig and the olive in charm
002 And the mount of Sinai in calm

003 And this city of security in norm
004 We created the man,
From illustrious moulds in span

005 And he turned to a miserable sort in plan
(Then do We abase him lowest of low in stance)
But those of the men and clan
006 Bearing trust of Lord with decency in glance

Cherish unfailing rewards in proceeds
(Who affirm in faith and abide verity in deeds)
007
So (O Muhammad)
Whoso defy you and the Destiny to sustain*
008 Isn't Lord!
Domineering to judge cosmic dice in Domain

*Dooms Day

آیاتها ١٩ سُوْرَةُ الْعَلَقِ مَكِّيَّةٌ (٩٦) (١) رکوعها ١

بِسْمِ اللّٰهِ الرَّحْمٰنِ الرَّحِيْمِ

شروع اللہ کے نام سے جو بڑا مہربان نہایت رحم والا ہے

اِقْرَاْ بِاسْمِ رَبِّكَ الَّذِيْ خَلَقَ ۝١	پڑھو اے نبیؐ اپنے رب کا نام لے کر جس نے پیدا کیا ١
خَلَقَ الْاِنْسَانَ مِنْ عَلَقٍ ۝٢	پیدا کیا انسان کو (نطفہ مخلوط کے بعد) جمے ہوئے خون سے ٢
اِقْرَاْ وَرَبُّكَ الْاَكْرَمُ ۝٣	پڑھو اور تمہارا رب بڑا ہی کریم ہے ٣
الَّذِيْ عَلَّمَ بِالْقَلَمِ ۝٤	جس نے علم سکھایا قلم کے ذریعہ سے ٤
عَلَّمَ الْاِنْسَانَ مَا لَمْ يَعْلَمْ ۝٥	سکھایا انسان کو وہ علم جو نہیں جانتا تھا وہ ٥
كَلَّآ اِنَّ الْاِنْسَانَ لَيَطْغٰٓى ۝٦	خبردار! بے شک انسان ضرور سرکش ہو جاتا ہے ٦
اَنْ رَّاٰهُ اسْتَغْنٰى ۝٧	اس بنا پر کہ دیکھتا ہے وہ خود کو بے نیاز ٧
اِنَّ اِلٰى رَبِّكَ الرُّجْعٰى ۝٨	بے شک تیرے رب ہی کی طرف لوٹ کر جانا ہے ٨
اَرَءَيْتَ الَّذِيْ يَنْهٰى ۝٩	بھلا دیکھا تم نے اس شخص کو جو منع کرتا ہے ٩
عَبْدًا اِذَا صَلّٰى ۝١٠	ایک بندہ کو جب وہ نماز پڑھتا ہے ١٠
اَرَءَيْتَ اِنْ كَانَ عَلَى الْهُدٰٓى ۝١١	بھلا دیکھو تو اگر ہو (وہ بندہ) راہِ راست پر ١١
اَوْ اَمَرَ بِالتَّقْوٰى ۝١٢	یا تلقین کرتا ہو پرہیزگاری کی ١٢
اَرَءَيْتَ اِنْ كَذَّبَ وَتَوَلّٰى ۝١٣	تمہارا کیا خیال ہے اگر جھٹلاتا ہو یہ (منع کرنے والا) اور منہ موڑتا ہو ١٣
اَلَمْ يَعْلَمْ بِاَنَّ اللّٰهَ يَرٰى ۝١٤	کیا نہیں جانتا وہ کہ بے شک اللہ دیکھ رہا ہے؟ ١٤
كَلَّا لَئِنْ لَّمْ يَنْتَهِ ۙ	خبردار! اگر نہ باز آیا وہ

096-AL ALAQ

In the name of Lord, the Most Beneficent, Most Merciful

001/ Read:
002 Discern in the Name of Thy Lord in grace
Who created,
The man of a clump of sperm in pace

003/ Read:
005 Discern Your Lord is Most Cordial indeed
Who school in scribble and scrawl in proceed

Enlighten the man in learning in lore
That he'd not the lore* in before

*Knowledge

006/ Nay!
008 Indeed! The man is quite insolent in sway
He discerns him free and released in fray
Indeed!
Unto Lord he's to be there in stay

009 Did you see him daunting man to obey
010 Bounteous of Lord to incline in pray

011 Did you see and spy him to aside
If he trends in sincere faith to abide
012 Or destine devotion all in stride

013 Did you care and concern one in dispute
Who's foil and fake and sneer in confute

014 Doesn't he care to concern in stance
That Lord is quite concerning in Glance

لَنَسْفَعًا بِالنَّاصِيَةِ ﴿١٥﴾	تو ضرور گھسیٹیں گے ہم (اسے) پیشانی کے بل ﴿١٥﴾
نَاصِيَةٍ كَاذِبَةٍ خَاطِئَةٍ ﴿١٦﴾	پیشانی جو جھوٹی بھی ہے خطا کار بھی ﴿١٦﴾
فَلْيَدْعُ نَادِيَهُ ﴿١٧﴾	پس بلالے وہ اپنے حامیوں کی ٹولی کو ﴿١٧﴾
سَنَدْعُ الزَّبَانِيَةَ ﴿١٨﴾	ہم بھی بلائے لیتے ہیں عذاب کے فرشتوں کو ﴿١٨﴾
كَلَّا ۚ لَا تُطِعْهُ	خبردار! نہ مانو کہا اس کا
وَاسْجُدْ وَاقْتَرِبْ ۩ ﴿١٩﴾	اور سجدہ کرو (اپنے رب کو) اور قرب حاصل کرو ﴿١٩﴾

آیاتہا ٥ (٩٧) سُورَةُ الْقَدْرِ مَكِّيَّةٌ (٢٥) رکوعہا ١

بِسْمِ اللَّهِ الرَّحْمَٰنِ الرَّحِيمِ

شروع اللہ کے نام سے جو بڑا مہربان نہایت رحم والا ہے

إِنَّا أَنزَلْنَاهُ فِي لَيْلَةِ الْقَدْرِ ﴿١﴾	یقیناً ہم ہی نے نازل کیا ہے قرآن کو شبِ قدر میں ﴿١﴾
وَمَا أَدْرَاكَ مَا لَيْلَةُ الْقَدْرِ ﴿٢﴾	اور کیا جانو تم کہ کیا ہے شب قدر؟ ﴿٢﴾
لَيْلَةُ الْقَدْرِ خَيْرٌ	شب قدر بہتر ہے
مِّنْ أَلْفِ شَهْرٍ ﴿٣﴾	ہزار مہینوں سے ﴿٣﴾
تَنَزَّلُ الْمَلَائِكَةُ وَالرُّوحُ	اترتے ہیں فرشتے اور روح
فِيهَا بِإِذْنِ رَبِّهِم	اس رات میں اپنے رب کے اذن سے،
مِّن كُلِّ أَمْرٍ ﴿٤﴾	ہر حکم لے کر ﴿٤﴾
سَلَامٌ هِيَ	سراسر سلامتی ہے یہ رات
حَتَّىٰ مَطْلَعِ الْفَجْرِ ﴿٥﴾	طلوع فجر تک ﴿٥﴾

015 No, indeed!
If he doesn't elude evils and ills in deeds
We'll hold of his hair on fore in proceed

016 A deceptive fore defying word in beseech
017 Let him call his plotter in proceed

018 We'll call our angels so decreed
Designed for anguish and agony indeed

019 Certainly not!
Don't listen to the cynics set in deplore
But prostrate to Lord and beg to implore

Your Lord in adore ever in décor
To lure His proximity in core

097-AL QADR

In the name of Lord, the Most Beneficent, Most Merciful

001 Indeed!
002 We directed and divulged in Stance
This Message (benevolent gift in glance)

In The Night of Command alluring in trance
003 And How you'll perceive, Precision in sway
004 Of!
The Night of Command alluring in trance
Preferred and picked over thousand months in stay
The Night of Command alluring in trance

005 Therein descend in plan and plea
(Of Lord Almighty down to the earth in stance)
The Angels and Spirits in push and spree
Till sunup there's concord in glee
A Dictum of Lord, Destined in Decree

آیاتہا ۸ (۹۸) سُوْرَۃُ الْبَیِّنَۃِ مَدَنِیَّۃٌ (۱۰۰) رکوعہا ۱

بِسْمِ اللّٰهِ الرَّحْمٰنِ الرَّحِيْمِ

شروع اللہ کے نام سے جو بڑا مہربان نہایت رحم والا ہے

لَمْ يَكُنِ الَّذِيْنَ كَفَرُوْا مِنْ اَهْلِ الْكِتٰبِ	ہرگز نہ تھے وہ لوگ جو کافر ہیں اہلِ کتاب میں سے
وَالْمُشْرِكِيْنَ مُنْفَكِّيْنَ	اور مشرکوں میں سے باز آنے والے (اپنے کفر سے)
حَتّٰى تَاْتِيَهُمُ الْبَيِّنَةُ ۝١	جب تک کہ (نہ) آتی ان کے پاس روشن دلیل ۝١
رَسُوْلٌ مِّنَ اللّٰهِ	(یعنی) ایک رسول اللہ کی طرف سے
يَتْلُوْا صُحُفًا مُّطَهَّرَةً ۝٢	جو پڑھ کر سنائے پاک صحیفے ۝٢
فِيْهَا كُتُبٌ قَيِّمَةٌ ۝٣	جن میں لکھی ہوں تحریریں راست اور درست ۝٣
وَمَا تَفَرَّقَ الَّذِيْنَ اُوْتُوا الْكِتٰبَ	اور نہیں بٹے فرقوں میں وہ لوگ جنہیں دی گئی کتاب
اِلَّا مِنْۢ بَعْدِ مَا جَآءَتْهُمُ الْبَيِّنَةُ ۝٤	مگر اس کے بعد کہ آ گئی تھی ان کے پاس واضح دلیل ۝٤
وَمَآ اُمِرُوْٓا اِلَّا لِيَعْبُدُوا اللّٰهَ	اور نہیں حکم دیا گیا تھا انہیں مگر یہ کہ عبادت کریں اللہ کی
مُخْلِصِيْنَ لَهُ الدِّيْنَ ۙ حُنَفَآءَ	خالص کرتے ہوئے اسی کے لیے اپنے دین کو۔ یکسو ہو کر
وَيُقِيْمُوا الصَّلٰوةَ وَيُؤْتُوا الزَّكٰوةَ	اور قائم کریں نماز اور ادا کریں زکوٰۃ
وَذٰلِكَ دِيْنُ الْقَيِّمَةِ ۝٥	اور یہی ہے نہایت صحیح اور درست دین ۝٥
اِنَّ الَّذِيْنَ كَفَرُوْا	بے شک وہ جنہوں نے انکار کیا (محمدؐ کی نبوت کا)
مِنْ اَهْلِ الْكِتٰبِ وَالْمُشْرِكِيْنَ فِيْ نَارِ جَهَنَّمَ	اہل کتاب اور مشرکوں میں سے ہوں گے جہنم کی آگ میں
خٰلِدِيْنَ فِيْهَا	ہمیشہ رہیں گے اس میں۔

098-AL BAYYINAH

In the name of Lord, the Most Beneficent, Most Merciful

001 Indeed!
Those men of the Book and cynics in trail
And who're defying Word of verity to avail

Were not going to deny their denial in scale
Till there's a lucid bit of evidence to prevail

002 Messenger reciting Word so Pious and pure
003 The scriptures so sound, sonorous in lore

004 The men and clan of the Book didn't tend to sever*
And then there's an insinuation so crystal and clear

*Divide into different band and clan

005 They're decreed only a word to pray
Only Lord (of the Heavens in sway)
Affirming ardor in adore for Him in stay

Beg to entreat so firm in beseech
And pay the destitute due in alms
That's the faith, a truth in norm

006 Indeed!
Those denying, mid men of Book in trail
And those of the cynics in vale

أُولَٰئِكَ هُمْ شَرُّ الْبَرِيَّةِ ۞	یہی لوگ ہیں مخلوق میں سب سے بدتر ۞
إِنَّ الَّذِينَ آمَنُوا	بے شک وہ جو ایمان لائے (اہل کتاب میں سے)
وَعَمِلُوا الصَّالِحَاتِ	اور کیے انہوں نے نیک عمل ۔
أُولَٰئِكَ هُمْ خَيْرُ الْبَرِيَّةِ ۞	یہی لوگ ہیں مخلوق میں سب سے بہتر ۞
جَزَاؤُهُمْ عِنْدَ رَبِّهِمْ جَنَّاتُ عَدْنٍ	جزا ہے ان کی ان کے رب کے ہاں جنتیں سدا رہنے والی
تَجْرِي مِنْ تَحْتِهَا الْأَنْهَارُ خَالِدِينَ فِيهَا	جاری ہوں گی ان کے نیچے نہریں سدا رہیں گے وہ ان میں
أَبَدًا ۖ رَضِيَ اللَّهُ عَنْهُمْ وَرَضُوا	ہمیشہ ہمیشہ ۔ راضی ہوا اللہ ان سے اور وہ راضی ہوئے
عَنْهُ ۚ ذَٰلِكَ لِمَنْ خَشِيَ رَبَّهُ ۞	اللہ سے ۔ یہ ہے (صلہ) اس شخص کا جو ڈرتا رہا اپنے رب سے ۞

آیاتہا ۸ (۹۹) سُورَةُ الزَّلْزَالِ مَدَنِيَّةٌ (۹۳) رکوعہا ۱

بِسْمِ اللَّهِ الرَّحْمَٰنِ الرَّحِيمِ

شروع اللہ کے نام سے جو بڑا مہربان نہایت رحم والا ہے

إِذَا زُلْزِلَتِ الْأَرْضُ زِلْزَالَهَا ۞	جب ہلا ڈالی جائے گی زمین اپنی پوری شدت سے ۞
وَأَخْرَجَتِ الْأَرْضُ أَثْقَالَهَا ۞	اور نکال باہر کرے گی زمین اپنے سارے بوجھ ۞
وَقَالَ الْإِنْسَانُ مَا لَهَا ۞	اور کہے گا انسان اسے کیا ہو گیا؟ ۞
يَوْمَئِذٍ تُحَدِّثُ أَخْبَارَهَا ۞	اس دن کہہ ڈالے گی زمین اپنے (اوپر بیتے ہوئے) حالات ۞
بِأَنَّ رَبَّكَ أَوْحَىٰ لَهَا ۞	اس لیے کہ تیرے رب نے حکم بھیجا اسے (ایسا کرنے کا) ۞
يَوْمَئِذٍ يَصْدُرُ النَّاسُ أَشْتَاتًا ۞	اس دن پلٹیں گے لوگ گروہ در گروہ ۔
لِيُرَوْا أَعْمَالَهُمْ ۞	تاکہ دکھائے جائیں انہیں اعمال ان کے ۞

Them to abide Hell pyre in stride
They're the worst of creatures in abide

007 Indeed!
Those of the men in faith
Abiding virtuous deeds in grace
They're the peerless men in pace

008 Their gifts and grants are with Lord to aside
Gardens gleaming for them to reside
Aside and beside:

Stream sway in surge swing in slide
Them to abide there in resides

Lord well pleased of them in trail
So they'll cherish His Bounty in avail

It's for him to allure in adore
Who awe and dread Him, in the veer of core

099-AL ZALZALAH

In the name of Lord, the Most Beneficent, Most Merciful

001 When earth is agitated in awful accord
And tear and toss, core and crux in apart

002 Man dazed and amazed in dread and droop
003 Says: What's happened to this dwindle in snoop
004
The day!
Earth will boom in beep all to disclose
005 For Lord enlivened it to divulge and expose
006
The Day!
The men and clan thither in stray
Scattered as band and gang in fray

فَمَنْ يَّعْمَلْ مِثْقَالَ ذَرَّةٍ خَيْرًا يَّرَهٗ ۝٧	سوجس نے کی ہوگی ذرّہ برابر نیکی دیکھ لے گا وہ اسے ۝٧
وَمَنْ يَّعْمَلْ مِثْقَالَ ذَرَّةٍ شَرًّا يَّرَهٗ ۝٨	اورجس نے کی ہوگی ذرّہ برابر بدی دیکھ لے گا وہ اسے ۝٨

اٰيَاتُهَا ١١ (١٠٠) سُوْرَةُ الْعٰدِيٰتِ مَكِّيَّةٌ (١٤) رُكُوْعُهَا ١

بِسْمِ اللّٰهِ الرَّحْمٰنِ الرَّحِيْمِ

شروع اللہ کے نام سے جو بڑا مہربان نہایت رحم والا ہے۔

وَالْعٰدِيٰتِ ضَبْحًا ۝١	قسم ہے سرپٹ دوڑنے والے ہانپتے (گھوڑوں) کی ۝١
فَالْمُوْرِيٰتِ قَدْحًا ۝٢	جو چنگاریاں جھاڑتے ہیں (ٹاپوں) کی ٹھوکر سے ۝٢
فَالْمُغِيْرٰتِ صُبْحًا ۝٣	پھر چھاپہ مارتے ہیں صبح سویرے ۝٣
فَاَثَرْنَ بِهٖ نَقْعًا ۝٤	پھر اڑاتے ہیں اس موقع پر گرد وغبار ۝٤
فَوَسَطْنَ بِهٖ جَمْعًا ۝٥	پھر اندر جا گھستے ہیں اسی حالت میں کسی مجمع کے ۝٥
اِنَّ الْاِنْسَانَ لِرَبِّهٖ لَكَنُوْدٌ ۝٦	بے شک انسان اپنے رب کا بڑا ہی ناشکرا ہے ۝٦
وَاِنَّهٗ عَلٰى ذٰلِكَ لَشَهِيْدٌ ۝٧	اور بے شک وہ اس حقیقت پر خود گواہ ہے ۝٧
وَاِنَّهٗ لِحُبِّ الْخَيْرِ لَشَدِيْدٌ ۝٨	اور بے شک وہ مال کی محبّت میں بری طرح مبتلا ہے ۝٨
اَفَلَا يَعْلَمُ اِذَا بُعْثِرَ	تو کیا نہیں جانتا وہ (اس وقت کو) جب نکالا جائے گا
مَا فِي الْقُبُوْرِ ۝٩	وہ جو قبروں میں (مدفون) ہے؟ ۝٩
وَحُصِّلَ مَا فِي الصُّدُوْرِ ۝١٠	اور ظاہر کر دیے جائیں گے وہ (بھید) جو سینوں میں ہیں ۝١٠
اِنَّ رَبَّهُمْ بِهِمْ	یقیناً ان کا رب ان سے
يَوْمَئِذٍ لَّخَبِيْرٌ ۝١١	اس دن خوب باخبر ہوگا ۝١١

007 And who so!
Enduring a bit of verity in trace
Even to the size of atom in pace
Will secure dole in award in place

008 And who so abiding evil of the deeds
Even to the size of atom in squeeze
Will secure awards,
In return of their doings in proceeds

100-AL ADIYAT

In the name of Lord, the Most Beneficent, Most Merciful

001 Vow be to horses bellowing in breath
002 That,
Strike spark and glow galloping in stead

003 They!
Cuff and clout to repulse in sunup glimmer

004 Raising dusty clouds in figure and flicker

005 Piercing rank and file of foe, fast in glitter
006 Surely!
Man is peeve unto Lord in sway

007 And indeed! He's witness to all in array

Indeed!
008 He's lured in,
009 The lust of worldly riches in behave
So doesn't he discern dead in graves

010 What he cares to concern hither in core
That will divulge thither in score

011 The Day!
Astral O Astute Lord will command to prevail
And none could elude His Dictum in trail

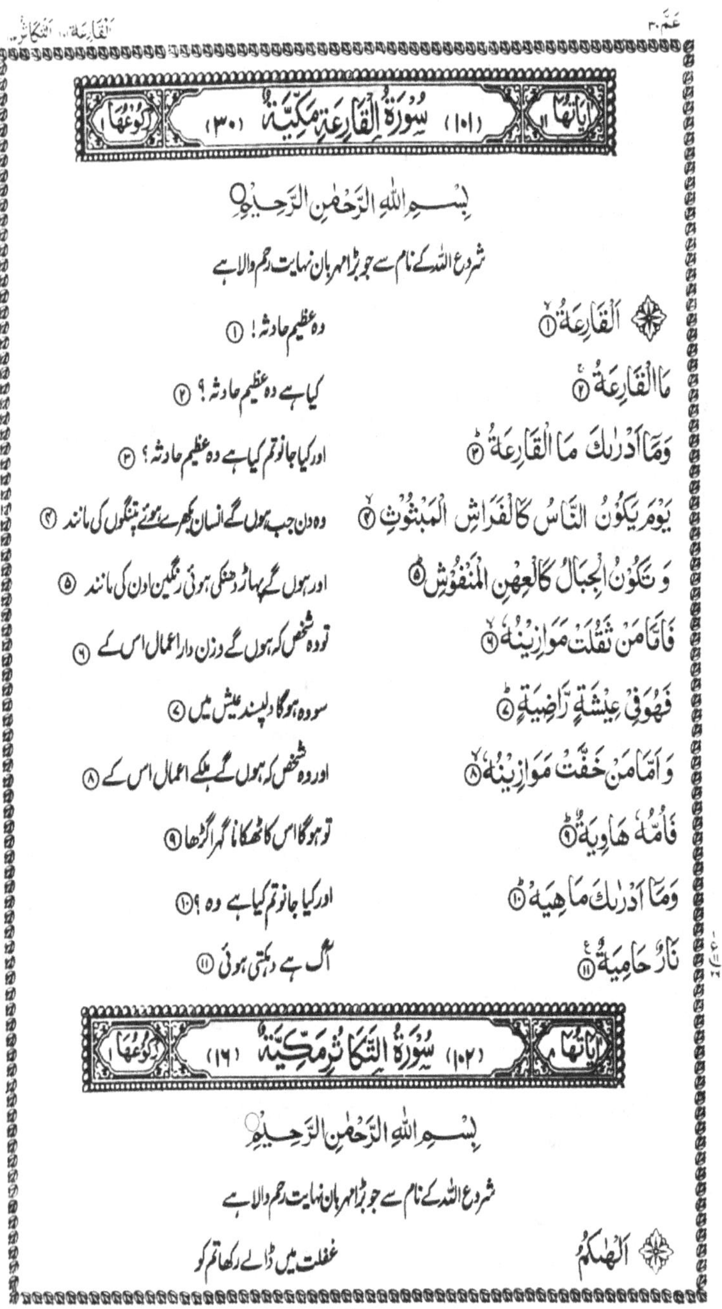

آیاتها ١١ سُوْرَةُ الْقَارِعَةِ مَكِّيَّةٌ (١٠١) (٣٠) رکوعها ١

بِسْمِ اللّٰهِ الرَّحْمٰنِ الرَّحِيْمِ

شروع اللہ کے نام سے جو بڑا مہربان نہایت رحم والا ہے

الْقَارِعَةُ (١) — وہ عظیم حادثہ! (١)

مَا الْقَارِعَةُ (٢) — کیا ہے وہ عظیم حادثہ؟ (٢)

وَمَا أَدْرٰىكَ مَا الْقَارِعَةُ (٣) — اور کیا جانو تم کیا ہے وہ عظیم حادثہ؟ (٣)

يَوْمَ يَكُوْنُ النَّاسُ كَالْفَرَاشِ الْمَبْثُوْثِ (٤) — وہ دن جب ہوں گے انسان بکھرے ہوئے پتنگوں کی مانند (٤)

وَتَكُوْنُ الْجِبَالُ كَالْعِهْنِ الْمَنْفُوْشِ (٥) — اور ہوں گے پہاڑ دھنکی ہوئی رنگین اون کی مانند (٥)

فَأَمَّا مَنْ ثَقُلَتْ مَوَازِيْنُهٗ (٦) — تو وہ شخص کہ ہوں گے وزن دار اعمال اس کے (٦)

فَهُوَ فِيْ عِيْشَةٍ رَّاضِيَةٍ (٧) — سو وہ ہوگا دلپسند عیش میں (٧)

وَأَمَّا مَنْ خَفَّتْ مَوَازِيْنُهٗ (٨) — اور وہ شخص کہ ہوں گے ہلکے اعمال اس کے (٨)

فَأُمُّهٗ هَاوِيَةٌ (٩) — تو ہوگا اس کا ٹھکانا گہرا گڑھا (٩)

وَمَا أَدْرٰىكَ مَا هِيَهْ (١٠) — اور کیا جانو تم کیا ہے وہ؟ (١٠)

نَارٌ حَامِيَةٌ (١١) — آگ ہے دہکتی ہوئی (١١)

آیاتها ٨ سُوْرَةُ التَّكَاثُرِ مَكِّيَّةٌ (١٠٢) (١٦) رکوعها ١

بِسْمِ اللّٰهِ الرَّحْمٰنِ الرَّحِيْمِ

شروع اللہ کے نام سے جو بڑا مہربان نہایت رحم والا ہے

أَلْهٰكُمُ — غفلت میں ڈالے رکھا تم کو

101-AL QARIYAH

In the name of Lord, the Most Beneficent, Most Merciful

001 That's a day of Calamity in stance
002 What's the day of Calamity in trance

003 That's the day of Clamor in Command
How you ever discern a Day in Demand

004 The Day men scattered like moth in place
005 And mountains strewn as wool in pace

006 Those who abide virtuosity in deeds
007 Them to cherish appease in proceeds

008 Those with defied and poor in record
009 Them to aside a pitiable pit in resort

010 And how'd you assert to affirm to stay
011 For what's defied dip of slip in stray
It's a perilous pyre of flame in fray

102-AL TAKATHUR

In the name of Lord, the Most Beneficent, Most Merciful

001 To you!
Lust of earthy lures doomed in stance
And you're grabbing more and more in glance

التَّكَاثُرُ ۱	ایک دوسرے سے بڑھ کر زیادہ سے زیادہ (دنیا) حاصل کرنے کی ہوس نے ۱
حَتّٰى زُرْتُمُ الْمَقَابِرَ ۲	یہاں تک کہ جا دیکھیں تم نے قبریں ۲
كَلَّا سَوْفَ تَعْلَمُوْنَ ۳	خبردار! عنقریب معلوم ہو جائے گا تمہیں ۳
ثُمَّ كَلَّا سَوْفَ تَعْلَمُوْنَ ۴	پھر سن لو! عنقریب معلوم ہو جائے گا تمہیں ۴
كَلَّا لَوْ تَعْلَمُوْنَ	دیکھو! اگر معلوم ہوتا تمہیں (اس روش کا انجام)
عِلْمَ الْيَقِيْنِ ۵	یقینی علم کی حیثیت سے (تو تم ہرگز ایسا نہ کرتے) ۵
لَتَرَوُنَّ الْجَحِيْمَ ۶	جان لو تم ضرور دیکھو گے جہنم کو ۶
ثُمَّ لَتَرَوُنَّهَا عَيْنَ الْيَقِيْنِ ۷	پھر تم ضرور دیکھو گے اسے یقین کی آنکھ سے ۷
ثُمَّ لَتُسْـَٔلُنَّ يَوْمَئِذٍ عَنِ النَّعِيْمِ ۸	پھر ضرور باز پرس ہوگی تم سے اس دن نعمتوں کے بارے میں ۸

آیاتہا ۳ — سُوْرَةُ الْعَصْرِ مَكِّيَّةٌ (۱۰۳) (۱۳) — رکوعہا ۱

بِسْمِ اللّٰهِ الرَّحْمٰنِ الرَّحِيْمِ

شروع اللہ کے نام سے جو بڑا مہربان نہایت رحم والا ہے

وَالْعَصْرِ ۱	قسم ہے زمانے کی ۱
اِنَّ الْاِنْسَانَ لَفِيْ خُسْرٍ ۲	یقیناً، انسان خسارے میں ہے ۲
اِلَّا الَّذِيْنَ اٰمَنُوْا	سوائے ان لوگوں کے جو ایمان لائے
وَعَمِلُوا الصّٰلِحٰتِ	اور کرتے رہے نیک عمل
وَتَوَاصَوْا بِالْحَقِّ ۙ	اور نصیحت کرتے رہے ایک دوسرے کو حق کی
وَتَوَاصَوْا بِالصَّبْرِ ۳	اور تلقین کرتے رہے ایک دوسرے کو صبر کی ۳

002 Until you're doomed to die and lie in grave
003 No,
But soon you'll discern to behave
004
Once again you listen with care
Soon you'll discern all your doings so fair

005 No, if you'd have known the fate in stance
006 Of all your done and doings in trance
You wouldn't,
Have committed the blunder in trance

(How'd you now affirm and assert in trail
That's but a doleful Hellhole in avail)

007 Indeed!
You'll behold a deplorable Hell in locale
The day you'll be,
008 Asked regarding your doings in vale
And regarding,
Boons of Lord your cherished in scale

103-AL ASR

In the name of Lord, the Most Beneficent, Most Merciful

001 By the vision (of graceful over ages) in time

002 Yes Indeed!
The man stay in dissipation, well in decline

003 But for those determining doctrine in prime
They anoint and asperse virtuosity in sublime

Pursue and persevere probity in pray
And entreat in endurance in stay

آیاتہا ٩ — سُوْرَةُ الْهُمَزَةِ مَكِّيَّةٌ (١٠٤) (٣٢) — رکوعہا ١

بِسْمِ اللّٰهِ الرَّحْمٰنِ الرَّحِيْمِ

شروع اللہ کے نام سے جو بڑا مہربان نہایت رحم والا ہے

وَيْلٌ لِّكُلِّ هُمَزَةٍ	تباہی ہے ہر اس شخص کے لیے جو منہ در منہ طعنے دینے
لُّمَزَةِ ۝١	اور (پیٹھ پیچھے) برائیاں کرنے کا خوگر ہے ①
الَّذِيْ جَمَعَ مَالًا وَّعَدَّدَهٗ ۝٢	جو جمع کرتا رہا مال اور گن گن کر رکھتا رہا اسے ②
يَحْسَبُ اَنَّ مَالَهٗۤ اَخْلَدَهٗ ۝٣	سمجھتا ہے کہ بے شک اس کے مال نے زندۂ جاوید کر دیا ہے اسے ③
كَلَّا لَيُنْۢبَذَنَّ فِي الْحُطَمَةِ ۝٤	ہرگز نہیں! ضرور اور بہر حال پھینکا جائے گا وہ حُطمہ میں ④
وَمَاۤ اَدْرٰىكَ مَا الْحُطَمَةُ ۝٥	اور کیا جانو تم کیا ہے حُطمہ؟ ⑤
نَارُ اللّٰهِ الْمُوْقَدَةُ ۝٦	اللہ کی آگ ہے، دہکائی ہوئی ⑥
الَّتِيْ تَطَّلِعُ عَلَى الْاَفْـِٕدَةِ ۝٧	جو جا پہنچے گی دلوں تک ⑦
اِنَّهَا عَلَيْهِمْ مُّؤْصَدَةٌ ۝٨	بے شک وہ ان پر ڈھانک کر بند کر دی جائے گی ⑧
فِيْ عَمَدٍ مُّمَدَّدَةٍ ۝٩	اونچے اونچے ستونوں میں ⑨

آیاتہا ٥ — سُوْرَةُ الْفِيْلِ مَكِّيَّةٌ (١٠٥) (١٩) — رکوعہا ١

بِسْمِ اللّٰهِ الرَّحْمٰنِ الرَّحِيْمِ

شروع اللہ کے نام سے جو بڑا مہربان نہایت رحم والا ہے

اَلَمْ تَرَ كَيْفَ فَعَلَ رَبُّكَ	کیا نہیں دیکھا تم نے کیا معاملہ کیا تمہارے رب نے

104-AL HUMAZAH

In the name of Lord, the Most Beneficent, Most Merciful

001 Anguish in affliction to libel and defame
002 Who pile in riches and count in claim

003 He's insolent to assume in endow
That his riches will endure ever and so
(Making him glow for ever in flow)

004 Nay indeed!
He'll be blown and thrown,
That tears in blow
005 Ah!
How'd you then assert in throe*

005 What's the type the blaze in throw*

006 It's flare of fury smolder in part*
That's from Lord, blazing in sort
007 That strikes veer of core in retort

008 Indeed! It's closed (over them) in place
009 Lofty pier in prop (over them) bear in pace

105-AL FIL

In the name of Lord, the Most Beneficent, Most Merciful

001 Didn't you see, how Lord took to strike
002 Those band and gang of elephants in stride
He dangled in daze their whim in strife

بِاَصۡحٰبِ الۡفِيۡلِؕ ﴿۱﴾ ہاتھی والوں کے ساتھ ؟ ①

اَلَمۡ يَجۡعَلۡ كَيۡدَهُمۡ فِىۡ تَضۡلِيۡلٍۙ ﴿۲﴾ کیا نہیں کر دیا ان کے داؤ کو غلط ؟ ②

وَّاَرۡسَلَ عَلَيۡهِمۡ طَيۡرًا اَبَابِيۡلَۙ ﴿۳﴾ اور بھیجے ان پر پرندے جھنڈ کے جھنڈ ③

تَرۡمِيۡهِمۡ بِحِجَارَةٍ مِّنۡ سِجِّيۡلٍ ﴿۴﴾ پھینکتے تھے وہ ان پر پتھریاں کنکر کی ④

فَجَعَلَهُمۡ كَعَصۡفٍ مَّاۡكُوۡلٍ ﴿۵﴾ پھر کر دیا اللہ نے ان کو مانند کھائے ہوئے بھس کے ⑤

آیاتها ۴ سُوۡرَةُ قُرَيۡشٍ مَّكِّيَّةٌ (۱۰۶) (۲۹) رکوعها ۱

بِسۡمِ اللّٰهِ الرَّحۡمٰنِ الرَّحِيۡمِ

شروع اللہ کے نام سے جو بڑا مہربان نہایت رحم والا ہے

لِاِيۡلٰفِ قُرَيۡشٍۙ ﴿۱﴾ اس بنا پر کہ الفت پیدا کر دی (اللہ نے) قریش میں ①

اٖلٰفِهِمۡ رِحۡلَةَ الشِّتَآءِ وَالصَّيۡفِ ﴿۲﴾ مانوس کر کے ان کو تجارتی سفروں سے سردیوں میں اور گرمیوں میں ②

فَلۡيَعۡبُدُوۡا رَبَّ هٰذَا الۡبَيۡتِۙ ﴿۳﴾ سو چاہیے کہ عبادت کریں وہ اس گھر کے رب کی ③

الَّذِىۡۤ اَطۡعَمَهُمۡ مِّنۡ جُوۡعٍ ۙ جس نے کھانے کو دیا انہیں بھوک میں

وَّاٰمَنَهُمۡ مِّنۡ خَوۡفٍ ﴿۴﴾ اور امن بخشا ان کو خوف سے ④

آیاتها ۷ سُوۡرَةُ الۡمَاعُوۡنِ مَكِّيَّةٌ (۱۰۷) (۱۷) رکوعها ۱

بِسۡمِ اللّٰهِ الرَّحۡمٰنِ الرَّحِيۡمِ

شروع اللہ کے نام سے جو بڑا مہربان نہایت رحم والا ہے

اَرَءَيۡتَ الَّذِىۡ يُكَذِّبُ بِالدِّيۡنِؕ ﴿۱﴾ بھلا دیکھا تم نے اس شخص کو جو جھٹلاتا ہے جزا و سزا کو ؟ ①

003 And He sent flights of birds in display
004 Striking with trifling pebbles in clay

005 How they're put to spoiled straw in stray
(Wasn't it like that defied dismal in array)

106-QURAYSH

In the name of Lord, the Most Beneficent, Most Merciful

001 Oh Quraysh!
002 Submit in sapience a semblance in Faith
For He endowed you shelter in grace
During trek and trail thither in pace

003 That of summer and wintry in place
So let them adore Lord with Grace

004 Who in famish granted in ease
Bread and butter there to please

And retreat in refuge in awe and alarm
(To have conviction of faith in advance)

107-AL MAUN

In the name of Lord, the Most Beneficent, Most Merciful

001 Haven't you seen, who's firm to defy
Verity of certitude in faith to comply

فَذٰلِكَ الَّذِيْ يَدُعُّ الْيَتِيْمَ ۝٢ — سو یہ وہی شخص ہے جو دھکے دیتا ہے یتیم کو ۝٢

وَلَا يَحُضُّ عَلٰى طَعَامِ الْمِسْكِيْنِ ۝٣ — اور نہیں ترغیب دیتا ہے مسکین کا کھانا دینے کی ۝٣

فَوَيْلٌ لِّلْمُصَلِّيْنَ ۝٤ — پس تباہی ہے ان نمازیوں کے لیے ۝٤

الَّذِيْنَ هُمْ عَنْ صَلَاتِهِمْ سَاهُوْنَ ۝٥ — جو اپنی نماز سے غفلت برتتے ہیں ۝٥

الَّذِيْنَ هُمْ يُرَآءُوْنَ ۝٦ — جو ریاکاری کرتے ہیں ۝٦

وَيَمْنَعُوْنَ الْمَاعُوْنَ ۝٧ — اور نہیں دیتے برتنے کی چھوٹی چھوٹی چیزیں بھی ۝٧ ع ٢٤

آیاتہا ٣ — (١٠٨) سُوْرَةُ الْكَوْثَرِ مَكِّيَّةٌ (١٥) — رکوعہا ١

بِسْمِ اللّٰهِ الرَّحْمٰنِ الرَّحِيْمِ

شروع اللہ کے نام سے جو بڑا مہربان نہایت رحم والا ہے

إِنَّآ أَعْطَيْنٰكَ الْكَوْثَرَ ۝١ — بے شک ہم نے عطا کیا تم کو اے محمدؐ الکوثر ۝١

فَصَلِّ لِرَبِّكَ وَانْحَرْ ۝٢ — لہٰذا نماز پڑھو تم اپنے رب کے لیے اور قربانی کرو ۝٢

إِنَّ شَانِئَكَ هُوَ الْأَبْتَرُ ۝٣ — بے شک جو دشمن ہے تمہارا وہی ہوگا بے نام ونشان ۝٣ ع ٢٤

آیاتہا ٦ — (١٠٩) سُوْرَةُ الْكٰفِرُوْنَ مَكِّيَّةٌ (١٨) — رکوعہا ١

بِسْمِ اللّٰهِ الرَّحْمٰنِ الرَّحِيْمِ

شروع اللہ کے نام سے جو بڑا مہربان نہایت رحم والا ہے

قُلْ يٰٓأَيُّهَا الْكٰفِرُوْنَ ۝١ — کہہ دو اے کافرو! ۝١

لَآ أَعْبُدُ مَا تَعْبُدُوْنَ ۝٢ — نہیں عبادت کرتا میں جن کی عبادت کرتے ہو تم ۝٢

002 Those,
Who repel and rebuff orphans in trace
003 (A destined sordid dictum in place)
And don't feast the destitute in pace

004 Woe be to those beseeching in way
005 Heedless of entreating proper in pray
006 And winks his pray to be seen in stay

007 Moreover!
And deny petty alms to the poor in beside
Denying compassion of Lord in stride,

108-AL KAWTHAR

In the name of Lord, the Most Beneficent, Most Merciful

001 Indeed! We endowed,
002 You Fountain of Perceptivity in sway
Thus trend to Your Lord firm in pray
And scarifies (for discipline in stay)

003 Indeed!
Who defies (you delusive in discern)
(Be ravaged) with no row and line in term

109-AL KAFIRUN

In the name of Lord, the Most Beneficent, Most Merciful

001 Say to the cynics:
For a word in preach!
002 That I'm not to beg and beseech
Whom you turn and tend in entreat

وَلَآ اَنْتُمْ عٰبِدُوْنَ مَآ اَعْبُدُ ۝٣ — اور نہ تم عبادت کرنے والے ہو اس کی جس کی عبادت کرتا ہوں میں ۝٣

وَلَآ اَنَا عَابِدٌ مَّا عَبَدْتُّمْ ۝٤ — اور نہ میں عبادت کرنے والا ہوں ان کی جن کی عبادت تم نے کی ۝٤

وَلَآ اَنْتُمْ عٰبِدُوْنَ مَآ اَعْبُدُ ۝٥ — اور نہ تم عبادت کرنے والے ہو اس کی جس کی میں عبادت کرتا ہوں ۝٥

لَكُمْ دِيْنُكُمْ وَلِيَ دِيْنِ ۝٦ — تمہارے لیے ہے تمہارا دین اور میرے لیے میرا دین ۝٦

آیاتها ۳ — سُوْرَةُ النَّصْرِ مَدَنِيَّةٌ (۱۱۰) (۱۱۴) — رکوعها ۱

بِسْمِ اللّٰهِ الرَّحْمٰنِ الرَّحِيْمِ

شروع اللہ کے نام سے جو بڑا مہربان نہایت رحم والا ہے

اِذَا جَآءَ نَصْرُ اللّٰهِ وَالْفَتْحُ ۝١ — جب آجائے مدد اللہ کی اور فتح (نصیب ہو جائے) ۝١

وَرَاَيْتَ النَّاسَ يَدْخُلُوْنَ — اور دیکھ لو تم (اے نبی) لوگوں کو کہ داخل ہو رہے ہیں وہ

فِيْ دِيْنِ اللّٰهِ اَفْوَاجًا ۝٢ — اللہ کے دین میں فوج در فوج ۝٢

فَسَبِّحْ بِحَمْدِ رَبِّكَ وَاسْتَغْفِرْهُ — تو تسبیح کرو تم اپنے رب کی، اس کی حمد کے ساتھ اور بخشش مانگو اس سے

اِنَّهٗ كَانَ تَوَّابًا ۝٣ — بے شک وہی ہے توبہ قبول کرنے والا ۝٣

آیاتها ۵ — سُوْرَةُ اللَّهَبِ مَكِّيَّةٌ (۱۱۱) (۶) — رکوعها ۱

بِسْمِ اللّٰهِ الرَّحْمٰنِ الرَّحِيْمِ

شروع اللہ کے نام سے جو بڑا مہربان نہایت رحم والا ہے

تَبَّتْ يَدَآ اَبِيْ لَهَبٍ وَّتَبَّ ۝١ — ٹوٹ گئے دونوں ہاتھ ابولہب کے اور نامراد ہو گیا وہ ۝١

مَآ اَغْنٰى عَنْهُ مَالُهٗ وَمَا كَسَبَ ۝٢ — نہ کام آیا کچھ، اس کے مال اس کا اور نہ (وہ) جو اس نے کمایا ۝٢

003 Neither you're going to care for pray
Whom I devotedly conform to obey

004 Neither I'll ever observe to entreat
Whom you care and concern to beseech

005 Nor you're going to pray in entreat
Whom I so earnestly pray to beseech

006 You to have your own care in concern
And me to have my own way to discern*

---

*You decay and dilapidate in dubious Discern
And I festive and frolic in flowering Concern

110-AL NASR

In the name of Lord, the Most Beneficent, Most Merciful

001 When the ease of Lord trends in appease
And you see men and clan getting in crease

002 In gang and band (abiding discipline of faith in treat)

003 Ardor and adore Adulation of Lord in entreat

And pray absolution of Lord in beseech
For!
He's Most Bounteous and Benevolent indeed

111-AL LAHAB

In the name of Lord, the Most Beneficent, Most Merciful

001 Perish be thy hands O father of Flames*
002 No profit he could've, profusely of gains
003 Soon him to fester fiery in flames

سَيَصْلٰى نَارًا ذَاتَ لَهَبٍ ③	عنقریب جا پڑے گا وہ لپٹیں مارتی آگ میں ③
وَّامْرَاَتُهٗ ۭ حَمَّالَةَ الْحَطَبِ ④	اور اس کی بیوی بھی، اٹھائے پھرنے والی ایندھن ④
فِيْ جِيْدِهَا حَبْلٌ مِّنْ مَّسَدٍ ⑤	اس کی گردن میں (ہوگی) رسی مونجھ کی ⑤

(۱۱۲) سُوْرَةُ الْاِخْلَاصِ مَكِّيَّةٌ (۲۲)

اٰیاتُہا ۴ — رکوعہا ۱

بِسْمِ اللّٰهِ الرَّحْمٰنِ الرَّحِيْمِ

شروع اللہ کے نام سے جو بڑا مہربان نہایت رحم والا ہے

قُلْ هُوَ اللّٰهُ اَحَدٌ ①	کہو وہ اللہ ہے یکتا ①
اَللّٰهُ الصَّمَدُ ②	اللہ بے نیاز ہے، سب اس کے محتاج ②
لَمْ يَلِدْ ڏ وَلَمْ يُوْلَدْ ③	نہ اس کی کوئی اولاد ہے اور نہ وہ کسی کی اولاد ③
وَلَمْ يَكُنْ لَّهٗ كُفُوًا اَحَدٌ ④	اور نہیں ہے اس کا ہمسر بھی کوئی ④

(۱۱۳) سُوْرَةُ الْفَلَقِ مَكِّيَّةٌ (۲۰)

اٰیاتُہا ۵ — رکوعہا ۱

بِسْمِ اللّٰهِ الرَّحْمٰنِ الرَّحِيْمِ

شروع اللہ کے نام سے نہایت رحم والا ہے

قُلْ اَعُوْذُ بِرَبِّ الْفَلَقِ ①	کہو پناہ مانگتا ہوں میں صبح کے رب کی ①
مِنْ شَرِّ مَا خَلَقَ ②	شر سے ان چیزوں کے جو اس نے پیدا کیں ②
وَمِنْ شَرِّ غَاسِقٍ اِذَا وَقَبَ ③	اور شر سے اندھیرے کے جب چھا جائے وہ ③
وَمِنْ شَرِّ النَّفّٰثٰتِ فِي الْعُقَدِ ④	اور شر سے گرہوں میں پھونک مارنے والیوں کے ④

004/ His wife,
005 Carry crackling clicks in straw
A twisted palm leaf rope in draw
Slings around her neck in claw

*Abu Lahb uncle of Holy Prophet was known after this name of "Father of flames"

112-AL IKHLAS

In the name of Lord, the Most Beneficent, Most Merciful

001 Tell that Lord is One and The One in along
002 Lord is Eternal and The Absolute in norm

003 He never gave birth to some in stance
Nor He's borne to some in glance

004 There's none,
To hold like His Dictum in trance
(As He is the One and only One in swarm)

113-AL FALAQ

In the name of Lord, the Most Beneficent, Most Merciful

001 Say: I beg in refuge of:
Lord of the dazzling dawn in sway

002 From the evil of conduct
That He arrayed in instruct

003/ From the vile of dusk in toll
004 When it covers as shawl
From the evil of mean conjurer in call

وَمِنْ شَرِّ حَاسِدٍ إِذَا حَسَدَ ۝٥ اور شر سے حاسد کے جب حسد کرے وہ ۝٥

آياتها ٦ (١١٤) سُورَةُ النَّاسِ مَكِّيَّةٌ (٢١) ركوعها ١

بِسْمِ اللّٰهِ الرَّحْمٰنِ الرَّحِيْمِ

شروع اللہ کے نام سے جو بڑا مہربان نہایت رحم والا ہے

قُلْ أَعُوذُ بِرَبِّ النَّاسِ ۝١ کہو پناہ مانگتا ہوں میں انسانوں کے رب کی ۝١

مَلِكِ النَّاسِ ۝٢ انسانوں کے بادشاہ کی ۝٢

إِلٰهِ النَّاسِ ۝٣ انسانوں کے معبود کی ۝٣

مِنْ شَرِّ الْوَسْوَاسِ ۵ الْخَنَّاسِ ۝٤ شر سے وسوسہ ڈالنے والے کے جو بار بار پلٹ کر آتا ہے ۝٤

الَّذِي يُوَسْوِسُ فِي صُدُورِ النَّاسِ ۝٥ جو وسوسے ڈالتا ہے انسانوں کے دلوں میں ۝٥

مِنَ الْجِنَّةِ وَالنَّاسِ ۝٦ وہ جنوں میں سے ہو خواہ انسانوں میں سے ۝٦

دعاءِ ختم القرآن

اَللّٰهُمَّ اٰنِسْ وَحْشَتِيْ فِيْ قَبْرِيْ اَللّٰهُمَّ ارْحَمْنِيْ
بِالْقُرْاٰنِ الْعَظِيْمِ وَاجْعَلْهُ لِيْ اِمَامًا وَّنُوْرًا
وَّهُدًى وَّرَحْمَةً ۔ اَللّٰهُمَّ ذَكِّرْنِيْ مِنْهُ
مَا نَسِيْتُ وَعَلِّمْنِيْ مِنْهُ
مَا جَهِلْتُ وَارْزُقْنِيْ تِلَاوَتَهٗ اٰنَاءَ اللَّيْلِ
وَاٰنَاءَ النَّهَارِ وَاجْعَلْهُ لِيْ حُجَّةً
يَا رَبَّ الْعٰلَمِيْنَ (اٰمِيْن)

اے اللہ! دور فرما میری پریشانی میری قبر میں اے اللہ! رحم فرما مجھ پر
قرآن عظیم کی برکت سے اور بنا تو قرآن کو میرے لیے پیشوا، روشنی،
ہدایت اور رحمت اے اللہ! یاد دلا تو مجھے قرآن میں سے
جو میں بھول گیا ہوں اور سکھلا دے تو مجھے اس میں سے
جو میں نہیں جانتا اور نصیب فرما تو مجھے اس کی تلاوت رات کے وقت
اور دن کے وقت اور بنا تو اس کو میرے لیے حجت
اے ربّ العالمین (قبول فرما)

تصدیق: قرآن آسان تحریک کے شائع کردہ ترجمہ قرآن حکیم کا عربی متن میں نے حرفاً حرفاً پڑھا ہے۔ میں اس کی صحت کی تصدیق کرتا ہوں
کہ اب اس میں اعراب وغیرہ کی کوئی غلطی نہیں جس سے قرآن حکیم کے متن میں کوئی تبدیلی واقع ہو جاتی ہو۔

005 And from vile of jealous in glance
When he trends to distrust in stance

114-AL NAS

In the name of Lord, the Most Beneficent, Most Merciful

001 Say:
I pursue in refuge The Lord in pace
Who's Lord of the humanity in place

002 He's Ruler in Supreme of the men and clan
The Lord,
003 Who's Exalted in Might for the men in span

004 From mischief of a slinking intruder in score
005 Who!
Creep in around in the veer of core
006 May be of the Jinni or of the men in soar

- ایمان بالغیب
- تخلیق کائنات
- واقعہ معراجِ حضور کریم ﷺ
- تخلیق آدم
- تقدیر اور تدبیر
- فلسفۂ حیات

کچھ آیات کریمہ کی تفسیر

قرآن اور جدید سائنس کے تناظر میں

یا ربُ العالمین!

جس لمحہ میں اس جہاں سے رختِ سفر باندھوں مجھے اپنے نور کا جلوہ عطا کیجیو اور پھر نہ تو اس ہمیشہ سے قائم ودائم نور کے لطف سے محروم کیجیو اور نہ ہی اس میں کسی قسم کی کمی کیجیو۔
وہ نور جو کائنات کی عمیق وسعتوں پہ چھایا ہوا ہے مجھے اس نور میں گھیر لیجیو کہ میں اس کی تجلیوں میں ہمیشہ کے لئے کھو جاؤں کیونکہ میری تو زندگی کا ہر لمحہ تیری حمد وثناء کے لئے وقف ہے۔ اور میں تیری اتنی تعریف اور توصیف بیان کروں اور بدلے میں تیری خوشنودی کا متمنی رہوں۔ اور اے میرے اللہ مجھے اپنی تعریف وتوصیف کے لئے قبول فرمالیجیو۔

میرے مالک
انکسار وعجز معمولِ حیات
تیری رحمت کا ہوں متلاشی مگر
میرے خالق
تیرے اس ارض وسما میں ہر طرف
میں اُٹھا کر جب نظر دیکھوں تجھے
تیرا ہی جلوہ مجھے آئے نظر
تیری ہی حمد وثنا میں سب مگن
اے میرے مسجود، میں دیکھوں جدھر
یاربُ العزت!

کیونکہ میں جس طرح بھی تیری تعریف کے لئے لب ہلاتا ہوں، اپنے اندازِ بیان وہ الفاظ ادا نہیں کر پاتا جو تیری ذاتِ والا صفات کے لئے موزوں ہوں۔۔۔ کوئی تو منارِ نور ہے جو ہمہ دم میری رہنمائی کو موجود رہتا ہے۔ کبھی تیری قرآن کی تلاوت کرتا ہے اور کبھی ایسی دلنشیں لئے میں تیرا ذِکر کرتا ہے جو میرے قلب کی گہرائیوں میں اتر کر اُسے معمور کر دیتی ہے۔ مَیں تو وہ الفاظ بھی بھول جاتا ہوں جو مَیں نے تیری صفات بیان کرنے کے لئے چُن رکھے ہوتے ہیں۔ اے اللہ مَیں تیرے ذکر میں ایسا محو ہو جانا چاہتا ہوں کہ ہر لمحہ تیری نوازشات وانعامات کے ذائقہ سے لطف اندوز ہوتا رہوں۔
وہ نوازشات کیا ہیں۔۔۔ کہ میں ہر لمحہ تیری توصیف بیان کرتا رہوں، اُس میں تیری رہنمائی کا متلاشی رہوں اور روزِ جزاء کو تیرے نور میں سما جاؤں۔

O Allah

As Thou once endowed me Vision in core
A bracing fascinating munificence in lore

The moment I close my eyes in stance
Bestow **Thy** Gleam in Grace to glance

And then not to elude or slight in pace
From **Thy** Interminable Beauty in trance
Merging in the Stream of Eternity in place

Let,
I be a glimmer of **Thy** Elegance in Glow
Then as a shimmer perpetuating in flow

For all my beg and beseech in place
To,
Anoint and asperse **Thy** Bounty in Grace

And so to applause and exalt in term
For **Thy** Munificent appease in return

O Lord!
I stay so reverent and meek in abide
And seek **Thy** clemency all in stride

O Lord!
Where to look around in surround
Where Thou don't evince in abound

And where not to,
Have glimpse of Thy Grandeur in sway
For all these captivating allures in array
Ardor and adore Thy Splendor in stay

O Allah!
Where to start my word in entreat
As I praise Thy Perfection in preach
Words defy me, whim of lore in treat

There's some around in span
Reciting Glorious Rhymes in Qur'an
Besides,
Captivating stance of 'Allah' in enchant

Bewitched in lore in the veer of core
Words fail to glorify Thy Awards in adore

Me to cherish Thy rewards in swarm
That'd always been my notion in norm

Hither in place Thy Bounty to brace
Ever to cherish Thy Guidance in pace
And in the Hereafter Thy Glimpse in Grace

Abul Imtiaz Ain Seen Muslim

Present Address: Dreshak International L.L.C., P.O.BOX: 102 609, Dubai. (U.A.E)
Tel. Res: +971-04-3415356 - Fax: (+971 4) 347 6731

Email: asmuslim@hotmail.com

arseyal@gmail.com ای میل

دبئی، ۱۷۔ جون ۲۰۰۸ء

جناب ڈاکٹر عبدالرشید سیال صاحب
سیال میڈیکل سنٹر لمیٹڈ
ایل۔ایم۔کیو روڈ، چوک کچہری، — فون: 061- 451 3333
نزد شریف پلازہ، ملتان۔پاکستان — موبائل: 0321-6326571

برادر محترم، السلام علیکم ورحمۃ اللہ وبرکاتہٗ

میں نے ابھی ابھی "قرآن اور فلسفہ کائنات" کا پہلا مطالعہ مکمل کیا ہے، اس کے لئے ہدیہ تہنیت پہلے پیش کر چکا ہوں ایمان اور سائنس کی آپ کی بحث (ص XVI) بہت دلکش اور اثر انگیز ہے۔ اللہ کرے زور قلم اور زیادہ۔ اسی طرح میرے خیال میں ایک موضوع ارتقاء یا EVOLUTION OF SPECIES کا ہے جس میں آپ نے کہا ہے کہ سائنس کا اور قرآن کا آدم ایک ہی ہے، اور اس کا ارتقاء بھی ہوا لیکن ایسے نہیں جیسے سائنس یا ڈارون کا کہنا ہے، بلکہ اس انداز سے جیسے خالق مطلق کی حکمت اور تدبیر کا تقاضا تھا۔ میرا خیال ہے اس موضوع پر اردو میں ایک مقالہ وقت کی اہم ضرورت ہے، اور وہ فوراً آپ کا پیغام ہر کہہ ومہہ تک پہنچا دے گا۔

قدرت کے تصور وقت اور وقت میں سفر معکوس کا موضوع بھی، جو معراج مصطفوی ﷺ کی طرف رہنمائی کرتا ہے، نہایت دلچسپی کا موضوع ہے۔ اس میں آپ نے رفتار کے حوالے سے چند نئے اشارات میں ایک جہان نو کے دروازے کھول دیئے ہیں کاش آپ اس پر بھی اردو میں ایک مقالہ تحریر کر سکیں۔

یہ موضوعات ایسے ہیں کہ اس وقت تعلیم یافتہ لیکن مغرب زدہ ذہن ان امور میں غور وفکر سے عاجز ہونے کے سبب انہیں کوئی اہمیت نہیں دیتا، جو تفہیم القرآن سے دور ہونے کے علاوہ دینی امور میں عدم دلچسپی کا باعث ہے۔ اس طرف توجہ کی ضرورت ہے۔

آخر میں آپ نے اُس مالک مطلق سے اپنے لئے دعا کی ہے۔ میں نم آنکھوں سے اس پر صدق دل سے آمین کہتا ہوں۔ سیکڑوں رَبّی دعائیں ترتیب دینے والوں میں سے کون ہے جس نے ایسی جامع دعا کی ہو جو جسم کے رُوئیں رُوئیں، خون کے قطرے قطرے، فکر کی مَوج مَوج اور قلب رقیق کی دھڑکن سے ایسے نکلی ہو جیسے تنزیل الہام ہو۔ مجھے یقین ہے یہ دعا شرف قبول کو پہنچ چکی ہے۔

میری التجا ہے آپ مجھے اپنی دعاؤں میں شریک کریں۔۔۔۔ اے خدا مسلم گنہگار کو رشید سیال کی اس دعا میں شامل فرما اور ہم دونوں کو اپنے زمرہ ابرار وصالحین کی معیت میں اپنے حضور حاضری کی توفیق بخش۔ آمین۔
یارب العالمین والسلام والصلوٰۃ علی رسولہ الکریم۔

مخلص

ابوالامتیاز ع س مسلم

Pakistan: Norimpaco (Pvt) Ltd., 1/1 - 3P, 2nd Floor, Block 6, P.E.C.H.S, Sh'are al-Faisal, Karachi-75400. Tel: 452 9201-4 - Fax: 454 6870

ایمان با لغیب

ہم سب دن کی روشنی میں تو بآسانی دیکھ سکتے ہیں مگر رات کے گھرے اندھیرے میں ہمیں کچھ سجھائی نہیں دیتا۔ دن کو روشنی کہاں سے آتی ہے، ظاہر ہے کہ اس کا سبب چمکتا ہوا سورج ہے۔ اگر سورج کی روشنی میسر نہ آتی تو ہم دیکھنے کے قابل نہ رہتے۔ اسی طرح سورج بھی تو بغیر کسی سبب کے وجود میں نہیں آیا۔ اس کے پیچھے بھی تو کوئی سبب، کوئی مقصد، کوئی قوت کارفرما ہے۔

Each effect has to have a source and the source has a logic behind its creation and we invariably call that Source **"The Nature"**.

پس ہر مظہر اور ہر نتیجے کا ایک سبب ہونا یا ایک مبداء ہونا لازم ہے۔ مبداء کی اپنی تخلیق کے پیچھے ایک منطق کار فرما ہوتی ہے۔ اس مبداء کو یا تخلیق کرنے والی اس قوت کو لامحالہ طور پر ''نیچر'' یعنی (فطرت یا جوہر) کہتے ہیں۔ لفظ "Nature" سے تو کسی کو اختلاف نہیں۔ میں اُس سُپر نیچر کو "اللہ" کہتا ہوں جب کہ کوئی دوسرا اِسے "بھگوان" یا "God" کہتا ہے۔ یہ اعلیٰ ترین طاقت ہے۔

ہم سب ریاضی کا ایک اصول جانتے ہیں کہ صفر کو کسی عدد سے ضرب دی جائے تو جواب صفر میں آئے گا اب میں اسی اصول کو بروئے کار لا کر یہ ثابت کروں گا کہ کسی اعلیٰ ترین طاقت کے بغیر یہ کائنات معرضِ وجود میں نہیں آ سکتی تھی۔

اگر ہم ذاتِ باری تعالیٰ کو ریاضی کے تناظر میں ثابت کرنا چاہیں تو اسے ہم یوں لیں گے کہ ایک + ایک = دو جب کہ صفر + صفر = صفر اگر اسی صفر کو کسی ہندسے سے ضرب دیں تو جواب صفر آئے گا۔ ایک سائنسی نظریہ یہ بھی ہے کہ ابتدائے آفرینش میں جب کچھ نہیں تھا تو صرف Nullity یا صفر تھا۔ سائنس دان اس بات پر بھی یقین رکھتے ہیں کہ یہ Nullity خود بخود ایک دم دھماکے سے اربوں کھربوں مِیل پر محیط فضا میں پھیل گئی۔ سوال یہ ہے کہ یہ Nullity خود بخود کس طرح لامحدود وسعتوں میں پھیل سکتی ہے۔ جب تک کہ اس کے پیچھے کوئی طاقت نہ ہو۔ یعنی اگر ہم صفر کو کھربوں کی گنتی سے بھی ضرب دے لیں تو بھی جواب صفر میں آئے گا۔ جب تک اس کے ساتھ ایک یعنی اس سلسلہ کو آغاز کرنے والی کوئی ذات نہ ہو۔ اس لئے یہ کہے بغیر کوئی چارہ نہیں کہ اس Nullity یا صفر کے پیچھے ایک اعلیٰ ترین قوت متحرک تھی جسے اللہ کہا جاتا ہے۔

اب حروفِ تہجی کو لیں اردو کا پہلا حرف (الف) ہے۔ اسی طرح انگریزی کا پہلا حرف A ہے۔ یعنی الف سے اللہ اور A for Allah۔ ہمارے حروفِ تہجی کی ابتداء ہی الف سے ہوتی ہے۔ گویا کہ

اللہ کی ذات سے پہلے کسی کا وجود نہیں۔ اسی طرح ہماری گنتی میں بھی پہلا عدد "ایک" ہے یعنی ایک اللہ کی ذات جو وحدہٗ لاشریک ہے۔

ہم اس کی مثال یوں دیں گے کہ جب صرف ربِ کریم کی ذات تھی یعنی "1" اور اس کے علاوہ فقط Nullity تھی یعنی صفر، جسے بہت بعد میں لامحدود اور لاانتہا وسعتوں پر پھیلتی کائناتوں کی شکل میں وجود پذیر ہونا تھا۔ اس طرح 1 اور صفر مل کر عددی اعتبار سے "10" کا عدد تھا اب اگر 10 کو 10 کے ساتھ ضرب دیتے جائیں تو ایک لامتناہی اور نامختتم عدد وجود میں آئے گا، لیکن اس نامختتم عدد کے شروع کے ایک کو ہٹا دیں تو پورا عدد فقط صفر رہ جائے گا۔ بالفاظِ دیگر "1" کے بغیر ان لامحدود کائناتوں کی کوئی وقعت نہیں رہتی۔ ان کا وجود صفر ہو جاتا ہے۔ مگر اس کے برعکس اگر تمام صفروں کو ہٹا دیا جائے تو ایک کا وجود بہر حال باقی رہ جاتا ہے، جو باری تعالیٰ کی ذات سے منسوب ہے۔ اس بحث سے ہم یہ اخذ کر سکتے ہیں کہ عدد "ایک" کا وجود ہے اور Nullity جس کا کوئی وجود نہیں اس کی طاقت ہے۔ "ایک" کے بغیر Nullity بے وجود اور بے حیثیت ہے۔ اس کے برعکس Nullity کے بغیر "ایک" پھر بھی ایک مسلمہ حقیقت ہے۔ جس سے انکار ممکن نہیں۔ اب اگر کوئی پُوچھے کہ الف سے پہلے کوئی اور حرف کیوں نہیں یا ایک سے پہلے کوئی ہندسہ یا عدد کیوں نہیں تو اس کا مناسب جواب یہی ہو سکتا ہے کہ یہ سلسلہ ایسے ہی ہے اور اسے آخر کسی حرف یا کسی عدد سے تو شروع ہونا ہی تھا اور وہ حرف "الف" یعنی اللہ اور عدد "ایک" یعنی وحدہٗ لاشریک ہی انسب ہے۔ اس بحث سے یہ نتیجہ اخذ کیا جا سکتا ہے کہ

Mathematically it is not conceivable for nullity to assume any substationlity without any figurative concern.

یہ تمام بحث اس بات کو پایہ ثبوت تک پہنچاتی ہے کہ اللہ ایک مسلمہ حقیقت اور Nullity اس کی بے پناہ قوت ہے۔ جیسا کہ سائنس کہتی ہے اس طاقت Nullity کا بظاہر کوئی وجود نہیں۔ وہ نہ تو جگہ گھیرتی ہے اور نہ کہیں نظر آتی ہے۔ تو پھر آخر کار یہ سوال ابھرتا ہے کہ وقت یا طاقت جس نے فضائے بسیط میں رنگا رنگ کی کہکشائیں پھیلا دی ہیں آخر کہیں تو موجود تھی۔ بہر صورت میں تو اسے خالقِ کائنات کی قدرت کا نام دیتا ہوں۔

جب خالقِ کائنات نے اپنی بے پناہ قوت کا اظہار لفظ "کُن" سے کیا تو اس ایک لمحے کو سائنسی اصطلاح میں Plank Time کا نام دیا گیا ہے یہ پلینک ٹائم کیا ہے؟ اس کا اندازہ لگاتے ہوئے انسان مبہوت رہ جاتا ہے۔ گیارہ ارب سالوں میں جتنے سیکنڈ ہوتے ہیں، صرف ایک سیکنڈ

میں اس سے زیادہ ایٹوسیکنڈ (Atto Second) ہوتے ہیں اور اسی نسبت سے ایک ایٹوسیکنڈ میں پلینک ٹائم ہوتا ہے۔ بس اسی پلینک ٹائم میں یعنی " کُن " کے ساتھ ہی آسمان اور کائنات الگ ہو گئے اور پھر کائنات اربوں اور کھربوں میلوں پر محیط فضا میں پھیل گئی۔ یوں کہئے کہ اپنے پہلے ایک سیکنڈ کے اندر تمام اصول وسائل واسباب کے ساتھ ایک مسلمہ حقیقت کا روپ دھار گئے۔

یہاں یہ بات قابل ذکر ہے کہ لمحہ کُن یا پلینک ٹائم کے ساتھ ہی آسمان اور طبقات الارض یعنی عالمین The Multiverses علیحدہ ہو چکے تھے۔ ہم آسمانوں کی تخلیق سے متعلق کوئی ادراک نہیں رکھتے اور نہ ہی انسانی عقل وشعور اس کا کسی بھی حد تک ادراک کر سکتے ہیں۔ بہر حال سائنسدان کائنات کے بارے میں اس ایک بات پر متفق ہیں کہ پہلے سیکنڈ کے اندر تمام سائنسی اصولوں کے ساتھ طبقات الارض انتہائی گرم کیفیت میں وجود پذیر ہو چکے تھے اور بتدریج جب یہ طاقت سیارگان اور کہکشاؤں اور ستاروں ...Creation of Galaxies, Stars etc کے ساتھ فضائے بسیط میں پھیلتی چلی گئی تو اس کا درجہ حرارت بھی بتدریج کم ہوتا چلا گیا اور اس مسلسل عمل میں کائنات اپنی تمام تر رعنائیوں اور رنگینیوں کے ساتھ تخلیق پذیر ہو رہی تھی۔ ابتدائی لمحے میں اس کائنات کے پھیلنے کی رفتار کا اندازہ کوئی سائنسی ذریعہ آج تک نہ لگا سکا ہے اور شاید نہ کوئی لگا سکے۔ لیکن موجودہ وقت میں سائنس دان اس بات پر متفق ہیں کہ اب یہ کائنات ہر سیکنڈ میں تین لاکھ کلومیٹر کی رفتار سے پھیل رہی ہے اور جیسا کہ قرآن کریم کی مختلف آیات سے ظاہر ہے یہ کائنات پھیلتے پھیلتے آخرکار نچلے آسمان سے جب ٹکرا کر پاش پاش ہو رہی ہو گی تو اس وقت خالقِ کائنات کے نقطہ آغاز " کُن " پر شاید درجہ حرارت Absolute Zero تک پہنچ چکا ہو گا۔

جب کائنات میں سیارگان نچلے آسمان سے ٹکرا کر پاش پاش ہو رہے ہوں گے اور وہ بلیک ہولز (Black Holes) کے اندر مدغم ہو رہے ہوں گے تو ان کی کششِ ثقل فضائے بسیط میں منتقل ہو رہی ہو گی اور یوں فضائے بسیط ایک مرتبہ پھر انتہائی گرم ہونا شروع ہو جائے گی اور یوں جب کائنات کا درجہ حرارت انتہائی بلندی پر جا پہنچے گا تو اس وقت یہ بلیک ہولز بھی تحلیل ہو جائیں گے۔ تب ان کی انتہائی کششِ ثقل جب فضائے بسیط میں پھیلے گی تو وہ وقت، فاصلوں اور انرجی کو یوں سمیٹ لے گی کہ بالآخر اس کا ارتکاز بھی ایک نقطہ پر ہو جائے گا۔ یعنی رب العزت جنہوں نے اس کائنات کا آغاز لفظ " کُن " سے کیا تھا اس کو پھر سے ایک نقطہ " کُن " پر سمیٹتے ہوئے دوبارہ " کُن " کے ساتھ اسے پھر سے فضائے بسیط میں پھیل جانے کا انتظام کریں گے۔

ترجمہ: جس دن لپیٹ دیں گے ہم آسمان کو اس طرح جیسے سمیٹے جاتے ہیں دفتر میں مکتوبات۔ جس طرح ابتداء کی تھی ہم نے پہلے تخلیق کی (اسی طرح) ہم پھر اس کا اعادہ کریں گے، یہ ایک وعدہ ہے ہمارے ذمہ یہ ہم ضرور کر کے رہیں گے۔ الانبیاء ۲۱:۱۰۴

اب سوال یہ پیدا ہوتا ہے کہ ایک گُن سے دوسرے گُن تک کا فاصلہ (Scientific Concern - Seedling for the next creation) کتنی صدیوں پر محیط ہے۔

اس کا ادراک ہم یوں کر سکتے ہیں کہ سائنس کے مطابق ہماری کائنات کا آغاز آج سے تقریباً پندرہ ارب نوری سال پہلے ہوا تھا۔ اور سائنس دان اس بات پر متفق ہیں کہ اس کائنات کو ختم ہونے کے لئے کئی کھربوں سال سے بھی زیادہ کا عرصہ درکار ہوگا۔ اس مختصر تعارف کو میں اس لئے بیان کر رہا ہوں کہ قرآن کریم میں بار بار تکرار سے یہ آیا ہے کہ یہ زندگی تو چند لمحوں کی ہے۔ آپ آخرت کی زندگی کا اندازہ شاید آپ اس مختصر تعارف کے بعد لگا سکیں کہ کس طرح انسان شاید ایک لازوال کیفیت میں اپنے رَب کے ہاں اپنے کیئے دھرے کا مال سمیٹ رہا ہوگا۔ واضح رہے کہ ایک نوری سال کا فاصلہ پندرہ کھرب میل پر محیط ہے۔

ایک مرتبہ آئن سٹائن نے کہا تھا کہ یہ کائنات ازل سے ایسے ہی (اتفاقیہ) چل رہی ہے اور اس نے (The Steady State of Universe) یعنی Fudge Factor کا نظریہ پیش کیا۔

لیکن جب 1929ء میں ایڈون ہبل Edwin Hubble نے یہ ثابت کر دیا کہ ہم سے دور کہکشائیں Galaxies بڑی تیزی کے ساتھ ایک دوسرے سے دور بھاگتی نظر آ رہی ہیں تو پھر 1931ء میں آئن سٹائن نے بگ بینگ کے نظریے (Big Bang Theory) کو مانتے ہوئے کہا کہ Fudge Factor میری زندگی کی سب سے بڑی غلطی تھی اس کے الفاظ ہیں "جب کوئی چیز پیدا ہوئی اور وہ اپنے سفر پر رواں دواں ہے تو پھر اس کے پیدا کرنے والی ذات بھی ہوگی" اس کے ساتھ ہی اس نے ایڈون ہبل کے مشاہدے کو سراہتے ہوئے کہا کہ کائنات کی تخلیق اور ارتقاء سے متعلق اس سے بہتر کوئی ثبوت مجھے نہیں ملا۔

راقم الحروف سائنس دانوں کے اس نظریے سے بالکل اتفاق کرتا ہے کہ جب انہیں کائنات کی وسیع تجلیوں میں کوئی غیر معمولی چیز نظر آتی ہے تو وہ یہ کہتے ہیں کہ یہ نیچر کی قوتوں Natural Forces کی وجہ سے وقوع پذیر ہوئی ہے مجھے حیرت ہوتی ہے اور یہ دلی خواہش ہے کہ کاش سائنس دان لفظ نیچر سے اجتناب کر سکتے۔ کیونکہ وہ جس نیچر کا ذکر کرتے ہیں میں اسے سپریم نیچر

(Supreme Nature) یا رب العزت کا نام دیتا ہوں۔ ماحولیاتی عوامل یعنی Natural Forces or Environmental Influence اس قدرت یعنی نیچر کے تخلیق کردہ جنیٹک کوڈ (Genetic Code) پر اثر انداز ہوتے ہیں اور اس طرح Micro Evolution کا سبب بنتے ہیں جب کہ Macro Evolution یعنی جانداروں کی پیدائش قطعی طور پر ہر جاندار کے اندر موجود جنیٹک کوڈ Inbuilt Genetic Code کی مرہون منت ہے۔ (Feb, 2009 National Geographic)

بابا آدم علیہ السلام سے لیکر آج تک انسان کی یہ خواہش رہی ہے کہ وہ خدا کا قرب حاصل کرے۔ اس کے لئے وہ زہد و عبادات، وظائف اور مراقبے میں ہم وقت مصروف رہا ہے۔ یہ حیرت انگیز انکشاف حال ہی میں ہوا ہے کہ مراقبہ کی حالت میں دماغ کے ایک حصہ میں دوران خون قطعی طور پر بند ہو جاتا ہے۔ سائنس کے تناظر میں یہ دیکھا گیا ہے کہ عام صحت مند انسان میں دوران خون دماغ کے دیگر حصوں کے ساتھ ساتھ Left Prictal Lobe میں بھی مناسب مقدار میں رواں رہتا ہے۔ مگر مراقبہ Meditation کی صورت میں جنسی کیفیت کو سی ٹی سکین پر دیکھا گیا ہے اس کے مطابق اس حصہ میں دوران خون قطعی طور پر بند ہو جاتا ہے اور اس مراقبہ کی حالت میں آدمی جب تک دنیا و مافیہا سے بے خبر رہتا ہے تب تک خون کی سپلائی بھی Left Prictal Lobe میں معطل رہتی ہے۔ ہم سب جانتے ہیں کہ اگر خون کی سپلائی دماغ کے کسی حصہ میں معطل ہو جائے تو اس کے کیا اثرات مرتب ہوتے ہیں۔ مگر مراقبہ کی کیفیت میں انسان ماورائی تجلیات کے جلو میں ہوتا ہے (جب انسانی جسم روح میں تحلیل ہو کر کون و مکاں سے ماوراء کائنات کی وسعتوں کا حصہ بن جاتا ہے) اور یقینی طور پر وہ غذا بھی اپنے رب کے عطا کردہ نور سے حاصل کرتا ہے، لیکن جیسے ہی آدمی عام کیفیت میں واپس آجاتا ہے تو دورانِ خون بھی اس حصہ میں بحال ہو جاتا ہے جہاں سے یہ منقطع ہوا تھا۔ سوچنے کی بات یہ کہ جب انسانی ذہن کا رابطہ رب العزت کی ذات سے ہوتا ہے تو اس وقت غذائیت کا ذریعہ کیا ہوتا ہے۔ سائنس دان اس بات پر متفق ہیں کہ یہ کیفیت صرف اور صرف باری تعالیٰ کے وجود کو ظاہر کرتی ہے۔ اسی طرح دماغ کے قطعی طور پر کام بند کرنے Brain Death کے بعد بھی دماغ کے اسی حصہ سے برقی اشاروں Electrical Activities کے ملنے کا سبب کیا ہے۔ کیونکہ مرنے کے بعد تو دوران خون تھم جاتا ہے اور اس حصے میں غذائی ترسیل

(Nutrition) کا کوئی ذریعہ نہیں ہوتا۔

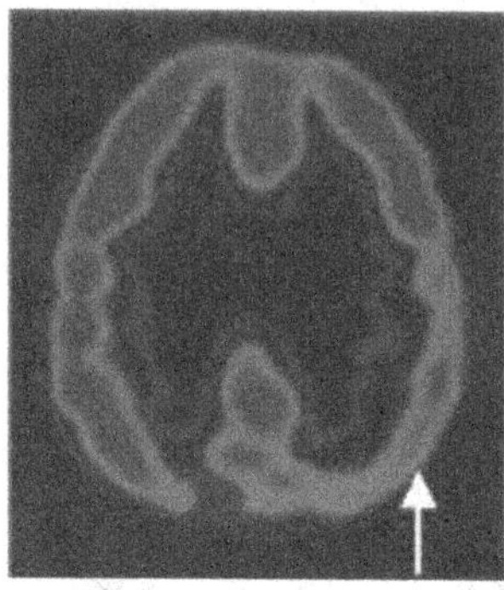

مراقبہ کی کیفیت میں دوران خون نظر نہیں آرہا

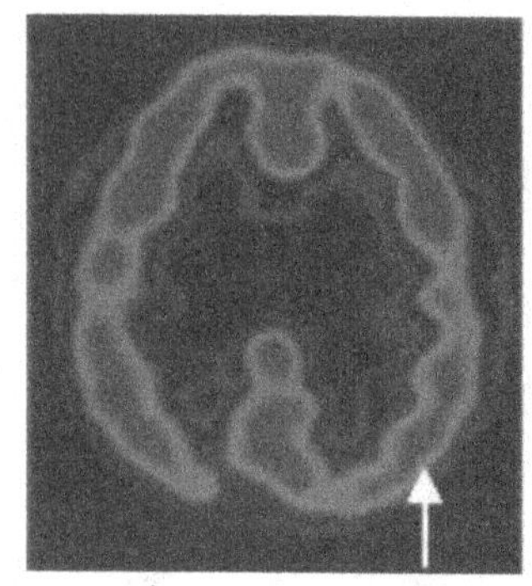

عام حالت میں دوران خون نظر آرہا ہے

قرآن اور فلسفۂ کائنات

یہ ذِکر ہے لا زماں و لا مکاں کا جب کائنات اور وقت ابھی وجود میں نہیں آئے تھے۔ جب حکمرانی تھی ایک حاکمِ اعلیٰ کی جس کو آئندہ یعنی مستقبل میں وہ تمام کچھ کرنے پر مکمل عبور حاصل تھا جس کا کوئی تصور نہیں کر سکتا۔ وہی حاکمِ اعلیٰ ایک مسلمہ حقیقت ہے یہ وہی تو تھا اور ہے جو اصل حقیقت ہے۔ وہی ہر اصل کا خالق و مالک ہے۔ اُسی کا رنگ ہر اصل میں جھلکتا ہے اور اُسی نے تمام مراحل کو ایک گوناگوں سانچے میں ڈھال دیا ہے۔

اُس ''کُن'' کا تصور کیجئے جس لمحہ لا زماں سے تخلیقِ مکاں و زماں (کائنات اور وقت) کا فیصلہ ہوتا ہے تو پھر حکم ہوتا ہے کہ آسمان اور زمین وجود میں ڈھل جائیں، تو ''فَیَکُون'' (پس ڈھل گئے) سے یہ تمام عمل ظہور پذیر ہو جاتا ہے۔ اِس کائنات کو اپنے تمام مراحل طے کرنے میں اربوں سال لگ گئے اور یہ ہے بھی حقیقت۔ جب کہ قرآن کہتا ہے کہ:

''زمین و آسمان تعمیلِ حکم میں فوری طور پر وجود میں آ گئے''۔ سائنس اس وقت کو Plank Time (10^{-43} سیکنڈ) کا نام دیتی ہے میں اُسے ''لمحۂ کُــــن'' سے تعبیر کرتا ہوں یہ وہ لمحہ تھا جب آسمان اور کائنات (Future Multiverses) جدا ہو چکے تھے۔ آسمانوں نے اپنی تخلیق کا عمل جاری رکھا جس کے متعلق انسانی ذرائع اور ذہن قطعی طور پر ادراک نہیں کر سکتا لیکن تخلیق عالمین میں یہ سفر اپنے پہلے سیکنڈ میں تمام توانائی، وسائل اور اصول (Energy؛ Substance and Physical Laws) کے ساتھ آغاز کر چکا تھا۔ اس سفر میں ''لمحۂ کُــــن'' (Plank Time) کے ساتھ تین رہنمائے وقت (Arrows of Time) بھی وجود میں آ گئے یعنی

تھرموڈائینمک Thermodynamic Arrow of Time جیسے ہی کائنات وجود میں آئی اس کے ساتھ توانائی اربوں کھربوں ڈگری سینٹی گریڈ کے ساتھ وجود میں آ گئی جو آہستہ آہستہ اختتام پذیر ہوتے ہوئے بالآخر جب کائنات نچلے آسمان سے ٹکرا کر پاش پاش ہو رہی ہوگی تو (یہ وقتِ اختتام ہوگا)۔ دراصل تھرموڈائینمک رہنمائے وقت بھی بالآخر Reverse ہونا شروع ہوگا جب سیارگان توڑ پھوڑ کے عمل میں بلیک ہول میں ضم ہو رہے ہوں گے تو ان کی کششِ ثقل فضائے بسیط میں منتقل ہو رہی ہوگی اور کائنات ایک مرتبہ پھر گرم ہونا شروع ہوگی اور بالآخر جب یہ اپنے نقطۂ منتہا تک پہنچے گی تو Seedling for next creation کے ساتھ پھر ایک مرتبہ اربوں کھربوں ڈگری کی توانائی ساتھ لئے نئی تخلیق کے جنم کے ساتھ فضائے بسیط میں پھیل جائیگا۔ (تفصیل آگے آ رہی ہے)

کائنات کے وجود کے آنے کے بعد تمام تر توانائی (In the form of heat) بتدریج سیارگان اور دوسری کائنات کے وسیع تر لوازمات کے ساتھ آہستہ آہستہ استعمال ہوتی جارہی ہے۔ بالآخر جب یہ کائنات نچلے آسمان سے ٹکرا کر پاش پاش ہورہی ہوگی تو اس وقت نقطہ' آغاز جہاں سے کائنات نے اپنا سفر شروع کیا تھا کا ٹمپریچر ممکنہ حد تک Absolute zero (-273.15 on celisus scale) یا (459.67- فارن ہائیٹ) پہنچ جائے گا۔ یہ وہ وقت ہوگا جب کائنات اپنا پہلا سفر پایہء تکمیل تک پہنچا چکی ہوگی اور اس کے ساتھ ایک دوسرے عمل کا آغاز ہوگا جس میں تمام سیارگان توڑ پھوڑ کے عمل کے ساتھ بلیک ہول میں ضم ہورہے ہوں گے اور ان کی کشش ثقل فضائے بسیط میں پھیلتے ہوئے ایک نئی تاریخ رقم کررہی ہوگی جس سے کائنات کا ٹمپریچر ایک دفعہ پھر اربوں ڈگری سینٹی گریڈ تک پہنچ جائے گا۔ بالآخر یہ Black Hole بھی تحلیل ہوجائینگی ۔ جن سے انتہائی کشش ثقل اس بے انتہا گرم فضا میں پھیل جائے گی۔ ان Black Holes سے خارج شدہ کشش ثقل تمام تر توانائی (Heat) اور فاصلوں کو ایک لامحدود نقطہ' لامحدود حد تک نظر نہ آنے والے Black Hole کے اندر جذب کرلے گی اور یہی نقطہ' نئی تخلیق کے لئے ایک نقطہ' آغاز (Seedling) کا سبب بنے گا۔ یہ ایک مثال Thermodynamic Arrow Of Time کی ہے جو اس وقت Big Bang سے لے کر اب تک اور بالآخر اس کائنات کے انجام تک اپنی تمام تر توانائی استعمال کئے جارہا ہے اور پھر Big Smash کے بعد جہاں توانائی ایک دم اختتام پذیر ہوگی، نئے سرے سے توانائی کے ارتقاء کا عمل ظہور پذیر ہوگا۔ سائنسدانوں کا یہ خیال کہ تھرموڈائینمک رہنمائے وقت Big Smash کے ساتھ ختم ہوجائے گا قطعی طور پر صحیح نہیں لگتا۔ اس لئے کہ سائنسدان اس بات کا بھی ادراک رکھتے ہیں کہ یہ کائنات ایک دفعہ ختم ہونے کے بعد پھر سے شروع ہوگی جب کہ قرآن کریم میں اس کا بار بار ذکر آیا ہے۔ چنانچہ ایک دفعہ جب Thermodynamic Arrow of Time اپنی تمام تر توانائی ختم ہونے کے بعد پھر سے اپنی توانائی کو اکٹھا کرے گا اور یہ عمل اس وقت ظاہر ہوگا جب کاسمولاجیکل رہنمائے وقت سکڑنا شروع ہوگا، تو یہ وہ وقت ہوگا جب کائنات میں توڑ پھوڑ کا عمل شروع ہوچکا ہوگا اور پھر یہ سلسلہ یعنی کائنات کی تعمیر اور توڑ پھوڑ کہاں تک اور کب تک جاری رہے گی اس کا شاید انسانی ذہن ادراک نہ کرسکے۔۔۔ ذرا تصور تو کریں "اس خالق و ربِ کائنات کا" جو فضائے بسیط کو ایک نقطہ میں سمیٹ لیتا ہے اور پھر ایک نقطہ کو کھربوں کھربوں کھربوں اور کھربوں میلوں پر محیط فضائے بسیط میں بکھیر دیتا ہے۔

اور پھر بالآخر بلیک ہولز (Black Holes) بھی تحلیل (Eveporate) ہو جائیں گی اور تمام تر کشش ثقل (Gravitational Force) فضائے بسیط میں پھیلتے ہوئے کل توانائی اور وسعتوں (Energy and space) کو اپنے دامن میں سمیٹتے ہوئے خود ہی اپنے دامن میں سمٹ کر ایک نقطہ پر اس کا ارتقاز ہو جائے گا۔ سائنسدان اس کو Nullity کہتے ہیں۔ (Which has no space to occupy) اور یہی Nullity or Nihility نئی تخلیق کے لئے نقطہ آغاز کا پیش خیمہ بنے گی۔

ذرا تصور تو کریں یہ کونسی قوت ہے جو لامحدود کائنات کو ایک نقطہ میں سمیٹ لے پھر اس کو ایک "کن" کے ساتھ لامحدود کائنات کی شکل میں واپس لے آئے۔

اب بھی آپ نے میرے رب العزت کو نہیں پہنچانا۔

قرآن کریم میں سورۃ الزمر کی آیات کریمہ میں بڑی خوبصورتی سے اس کا ذکر ہے۔

وَمَا قَدَرُوا اللّٰهَ حَقَّ قَدْرِهٖ ۖ وَالْاَرْضُ جَمِيْعًا قَبْضَتُهٗ يَوْمَ الْقِيٰمَةِ وَ السَّمٰوٰتُ مَطْوِيّٰتٌۢ بِيَمِيْنِهٖ ۭ سُبْحٰنَهٗ وَتَعٰلٰى عَمَّا يُشْرِكُوْنَ ﴿۶۷﴾

نہیں پہچان سکے یہ اللہ کو جیسا کہ حق ہے اس کو پہچاننے کا جبکہ اس کی شان یہ ہے کہ زمین ساری کی ساری اس کی مٹھی میں ہوگی قیامت کے دن اور آسمان لپٹے ہوئے ہوں گے اس کے ہاتھ میں، پاک ہے وہ اور بالاتر اس شرک سے جو یہ کرتے ہیں ﴿۶۷﴾

The intense gravitational force released by the dessolution of the black holes, will wrap up the space and energy then itself will wrap up under its own gravitational force to infinitely small point (Nullity) when the time will also seize to exist with all the arrows of time i.e. Thermodynamic, Cosmological and Psychological arrows of time but for the Interminable arrow of time, that will perpetuate in an ever infinite direction in the Cosmos.

کاسمولاجیکل Cosmological Arrow of Time کائنات پھیل رہی ہے اور یہ وقت بھی ایک سمت میں اس کے ساتھ رواں دواں ہے اور بالآخر جب کائنات سکڑنا (سورۃ الانبیاء) شروع ہوگی تو یہ رہنمائے وقت بھی Reverse (جس سے زندگی کا وجود ناممکن

ہو جائے گا) میں سفر کا آغاز کرے گا جو بالآخر ایک مرتبہ پھر جب کائنات (اپنے نقطہ منتہا) اختتام پذیر ہو رہی ہو گی تو وہ ایک نئے نقطہ آغاز کو جنم دے گی Seedling for next creation پھر ایک نئے آغاز کے ساتھ Cosmological Arrow۔ Interminable Arrow کی سمت میں رواں دواں ہو جائیگا۔

سائیکولاجیکل Psycological Arrow of Time اس وقت میں ہم رہتے ہیں اور یہ ہے ماضی، حال اور مستقبل

لامتناہی سلسلۂ وقت Interminable Arrow of Time یہ وہ وقت ہے جس کا تعین کرنا انسان کے بس میں نہیں یہ وقت شروع ہوا جب خالقِ کائنات نے اپنی تخلیق کے اول عمل کو ظاہر کیا اور یہ وقت تا ابد ایک ہی سمت میں جاری رہیگا۔

قرآن کریم کی فلاسفی کو سمجھنے کے لئے سائنس کا جاننا کیوں ضروری ہے؟

جب حکم ہوا کہ اے آسمان اور زمین وجود میں آجائیں (''کُـــن'' جو دراصل اُس حاکمِ اعلیٰ کے ارادے ہی کا نام ہے) تو Nihility (عدم یا نیستی۔ جو خود آسمان وزمین کا تکملہ ہے) ایک دم اربوں میل پر محیط فضا میں دھوئیں کی طرح بکھر جاتی ہے اور وہ تمام اصول جو کائنات کی تخلیق کے لئے ضروری تھے اس پہلے لمحے میں معرضِ وجود میں آجاتے ہیں۔ اور پھر بات تو اصول ہی کی ہے۔ جب اصول طے پا گئے تو تخلیق نے اپنی منازل طے کرنا شروع کر دیں۔

قرآن کریم کی فلاسفی کو سمجھنے کے لئے سائنسی پس منظر کے ساتھ دوسرے علوم کا جاننا کتنا ضروری ہے آج ہم اس پر تھوڑی سی بحث کریں گے۔ مَیں کلام پاک کی سب سے پہلی آیتِ کریمہ ''اَلْحَمْدُ لِلّٰهِ رَبِّ الْعَالَمِيْنَ'' کا ذکر کروں گا جس میں ربُّ العزت فرماتے ہیں کہ میں ربّ ہوں عالمین (Multiverse) یعنی عوالم کا نہ کہ ایک عالَم (Universe) کا۔

بیسویں صدی کے تقریباً اواخر تک سائنسدان اس بات پر متفق تھے کہ یہ ایک کائنات ہے جس میں ہم رہتے ہیں۔ جب کہ بیسویں صدی کے آخری عشرے میں سائنسدانوں نے یہ معلوم کیا کہ ہمارا عالَم (Universe) تو ایک ذرّہ ہے اور ایسے بے شمار عوالم موجود ہیں۔ سائنسدان اب تک چار متوازی طبقاتِ عوالم۔ Four Strata of Parallel Universes دریافت کر چکے ہیں۔ ہم ہر Strata of Universes کو Mulltiverse کہہ سکتے ہیں جس میں بے شمار Universes موجود ہیں اور ہر Universe میں اربوں کہکشائیں ہیں اور ہر کہکشاں میں اربوں ستارے ہیں اور ایسی ہی ایک کہکشاں کا نام Milkyway Galaxy ہے، میں ہم رہتے ہیں۔

Milkyway-Galaxy کا مرکز یعنی کور(Core) یا ڈسک (Disc) ایک لاکھ نوری سال (Light Years) ہے جب کہ ہمارا شمسی نظام اس گلیکسی کے ایک بازو پر تقریباً اس کے درمیان واقع ہے اور اس کا فاصلہ مرکزی ڈسک سے 2,26,000 نوری سال (Light Years) ہے۔ ہماری (Milkyway- Galaxy) کی ہمسائیگی میں Andromeda Galaxy- ہے آپ حیران ہوں گے کہ اگر ہم روشنی کی رفتار سے سفر کرتے ہوئے اپنے ہمسائے کے گھر یعنی Andromeda-Galaxy میں جانے کی کوشش کریں تو ہمیں 22 لاکھ 50 ہزار سال لگیں گے جب کہ ہماری کائنات (Universe) میں اربوں ایسی گلیکسی موجود ہیں۔ جب کہ ایک نوری سال چھ کھرب میل کے برابر ہے تو شاید آپ کائنات کی وسعتوں کا کچھ اِدراک اس چھوٹے سے تعارف کے بعد کر سکیں۔ یہاں پر مَیں آپ کو اس کائنات کی وسعتوں کے ساتھ ساتھ یہ بھی بتاتا چلوں کہ ہم اس کائنات میں کس رفتار سے محوِ پرواز ہیں اور بے پناہ رفتار کے باوجود ہمیں معمولی سا چکر بھی نہیں آتا۔ ہم زمین کے باسی ہیں اور یہ:

- زمین اپنے محور کے گرد 1,670 کلومیٹر فی گھنٹہ کی رفتار سے چکر کاٹ رہی ہے۔
- اس چکر کے ساتھ ساتھ یہ زمین اپنے مدار میں سورج کے گرد 1,08,000 کلومیٹر فی گھنٹہ کی رفتار سے گھوم رہی ہے۔
- پھر یہ زمین اپنے شمسی نظام میں رہتے ہوئے Milkyway Galaxy کے گرد 7,20,000 کلومیٹر فی گھنٹہ کی رفتار سے محوِ پرواز ہے۔
- اور پھر تمام شمسی نظام Milkyway Galaxy میں رہتے ہوئے 9,50,000 کلومیٹر فی گھنٹہ کی رفتار سے اپنے عالم یعنی Universe میں سفر کر رہا ہے۔
- اور یہ عالم اپنے Strata of Multiverses کے ساتھ اپنے Core یعنی اصل مقام یعنی نقطۂ آغاز Big Bang سے 300,000 کلومیٹر فی سیکنڈ سے دُور بھاگ رہی ہے۔ یہاں پر میں ایک چھوٹی سی یہ بات بھی عرض کر دوں کہ یہ زمین جب اپنے مدار میں سورج کے گرد گھوم رہی ہے تو ہر 18 میل کے بعد (یعنی ہر سیکنڈ کے بعد) اس میں 2.8 ملی میٹر کا ایک جھکاؤ آتا ہے اگر یہ جھکاؤ 2.5 ملی میٹر ہو جائے یعنی 0.3 ملی میٹر کم ہو جائے تو زمین سورج سے اتنا دُور نکل جائے گی کہ کچھ عرصہ میں یہ برف کا گولا بن جائے گی اور اگر اس 0.3 ملی میٹر کا جھکاؤ زیادہ یعنی (3.1) ملی میٹر ہو جائے تو زمین سورج کے اس قدر قریب چلی جائے گی کہ یہ آگ کا گولا بن جائے گی۔ اسی طرح سورج کا حجم 1.6×10^{30} سے 2.4×10^{30} کلوگرام ہے اگر یہ اس سے کم ہوتا تو زمین برفیلی ہو جاتی اور اگر یہ وزن اس سے

زیادہ ہوتا تو انتہائی گرم ہو جاتی ---تو کیا یہ سب کچھ محض اتفاقی ہے؟۔
کیا یہ اتنی Fine Tuning بغیر کسی طاقت کے وقوع پذیر ہو سکتی ہے؟

Scientific American میگزین میں Parallel Universes کے مصنف Max Tegmark کہتے ہیں کہ ہماری پیدائش اور کائنات کی تخلیق واقعتاً ایک اتفاقی نوعیت کی ہے۔ جیسے مَیں اپنی تاریخ پیدائش والے دن (11 مئی) کو کسی ہوٹل میں کمرہ لینے کے لئے جاتا ہوں تو مجھے گیارہویں فلور پر 5 نمبر کمرہ ملتا ہے تو میری خوشی کی انتہا نہیں رہتی کہ میری پیدائش والے دن مجھے ہوٹل کا فلور اور کمرہ بھی اُس نمبر کا مل گیا۔ مَیں نے مصنف کو لکھا کہ مان لیا کہ آپ کی پیدائش اتفاقی ہوگی۔ کیا وہ ہوٹل (جس کے گیارہویں فلور پر کمرہ نمبر 5 آپ کو ملا) بھی اتفاقی طور پر بن گیا تھا؟ اور اگر اِس ہوٹل کے ڈیزائن اور تعمیر میں کوئی انجینئر اور لیبر کارفرما تھی جو انسانی مشینری کے مقابلے میں انتہائی بے وقعت سی چیز ہے تو کیا انسانی تخلیق بغیر کسی سپر پاور کے معرض وجود میں آ سکتی تھی؟

مَیں نے Max Tegmark کو مزید لکھا جیسے کہ آپ میرے اس مضمون کے متن سے اخذ کر لیں گے کہ مان لیا آپ پیرس میں صبح اتفاقی طور پر اپنی تاریخ پیدائش والے کمرے میں جاتے ہیں اور اسی دن بعد دوپہر لندن جانے کا اتفاق ہو تو آپ کی کیفیت کیا ہوگی جب پھر فلور نمبر 11 پر کمرہ نمبر 5 ملے۔ اور اگر اُسی شام آپ کو نیویارک جانے کا اتفاق ہو اور آپ کو وہاں بھی وہی کمرہ ملے یعنی گیارہویں فلور پر کمرہ نمبر 5 تو آپ کی کیا کیفیت ہوگی! آپ یقیناً استقبالیہ پر کھڑی لڑکی سے پوچھیں گے کہ یہ کمرہ کس نے میرے لئے بک کیا اور اگر جواب ملے کہ یہ اتفاقی طور پر ہو گیا تو یقیناً آپ اس کی بات پر یقین نہیں کریں گے اور ضرور کہیں گے کہ اس کے پیچھے کوئی شخص کارفرما ہے۔ اور یہ بھی عین ممکن ہے کہ آپ اس کمرے میں جانا قطعی طور پر پسند نہیں کریں گے کہ شاید اس کے پیچھے کوئی سازش کارفرما ہو۔

اب اندازہ لگائیں کہ کائنات کا نظام آپ یعنی سائنسدانوں ہی کے مطابق اربوں سالوں سے ایک خاص ڈسپلن میں کام کئے جا رہا ہے اور اس کی فائن ٹیوننگ کا تو اندازہ آپ ہی کر سکتے ہیں کیونکہ (67 :المُلک : 3) میں ربُّ العزت فرماتے ہیں کہ کائنات کی طرف نظر اُٹھا کے دیکھو کہ شاید تمہیں اس میں کوئی خامی نظر آ جائے۔ اور پھر تکرار ہے کہ ایک مرتبہ پھر نظر اُٹھا کے دیکھو کہ شاید اس میں تمہیں کوئی خامی نظر آ جائے۔

Turn your looks towards the heavenly sweep
Aren't you captivated of its profundity so deep
How exquisite and adorable stellar sprawl to peek
An' still you defy His Dictum in treat

He created skies in series of seven
there's no want in Slant in term of creation
Most Amiable is Lord, *immense in array*
So trend your looks *once more to the heaven*
Can you discern a bit of slit in *sway*
then trend and talent anew in *quest*
You're denied of flaw in *behest*
Not even perplexity of poop in the *rest*   Al-Mulk 67:3-4

Turn your looks towards the heavens so high
Aren't you dazed, when you wisp in spy
Can you sense a swing in swirl
Sprawling of the heavens in twirl
There's no way and ward in the whirl
There's no way and ward in the whirl
It is so exquisite and adorable in sway
Abiding the dictum of Lord in array
Spin your gaze once more in quest
For if you discern a split in the rest

Indeed!
You're denied of the flaw in initiation
As a matter of fact
In the most fascinating and the best of creation

تخلیقِ کائنات اور انسان کی تخلیق سے متعلق خداوند قدوس فرماتے ہیں کہ "تمہارا ایک مرتبہ پیدا کیا جانا اور مرنے کے بعد پھر پیدا کیا جانا تو کوئی بھی مشکل کام نہیں"۔ کیونکہ یہ تو ایسا ہے جیسے کمپیوٹر سکرین پر آپ اپنا کوڈ اور بٹ میں سٹور کیا ہوا ڈیٹا، مووی، ویڈیو، پکچرز ایک کمانڈ میں دیکھ سکتے ہیں ایسے ہی ہمارے Genome پر لکھے 3.5 ارب کوڈ جو ہم ہر لمحہ زمین میں بکھیرتے جا رہے ہیں ایک ہی کمانڈ پر رب العزت کے حضور انسانی شکل میں حاضر ہوں گے۔ ہمارے کمپیوٹر نے بے شمار عقدے روز جزا کے حل کر دیئے ہیں اگر آپ تفصیل میں جانا چاہیں تو ہماری بینائی یعنی دیکھنے کے عمل کے ساتھ ہمارا Visual Response ۔ Internet اُس کی ادنیٰ مثال ہے ۔ یہ تفصیل کسی اور وقت کے لئے اُٹھا رکھتے ہیں ۔ بڑا کام تو تخلیقِ کائنات تھا۔ جیسے

سورۃ الملک میں فرمایا کہ ''تلاش کر کے تو دیکھو کہیں آپ کو کوئی اس فضائے بسیط میں کوئی تو خامی نظر آ جائے''۔ پھر کائنات کی اِن وسعتوں کو اُس ربُّ العزت نے نظر نہ آنے والے ستونوں سے جیسا کہ سورۃ بروج 85 کی آیت کریمہ نمبر 1 میں ہے ایک نپے تلے نظام میں جوڑ دیا ہے، اور آج کی سائنس اس بات پر متفق ہے کہ یہ نظر نہ آنے والے بُرج Electromegnatic Fields ہیں جنھوں نے تمام نظامِ قدرت کو ایک واضح اور صحیح رُخ میں متعین کر رکھا ہے۔

- ''لَخَلْقُ السَّمٰوٰتِ وَالْاَرْضِ اَكْبَرُ مِنْ خَلْقِ النَّاسِ وَ لٰكِنَّ اَكْثَرَ النَّاسِ لَا يَعْلَمُوْنَ (40-مومن-57): حقیقتاً پیدا فرمانا آسمانوں اور زمین کا کہیں بڑا کام ہے انسان کے پیدا کرنے سے، لیکن بہت سے انسان یہ بات نہیں جانتے''۔
- ''فَاسْتَفْتِهِمْ اَهُمْ اَشَدُّ خَلْقًا اَمْ مَّنْ خَلَقْنَا ط اِنَّا خَلَقْنٰهُمْ مِّنْ طِيْنٍ لَّازِبٍ (37 -الصّٰفّٰت- 11): سو پوچھو ان سے کیا ان کا (دوبارہ) پیدا کرنا زیادہ مشکل ہے یا اُس مخلوق کا (پیدا کرنا) جو ہم نے پیدا کی (پہلی بار)؟''
- ''وَالْقَمَرَ قَدَّرْنٰهُ مَنَازِلَ حَتّٰى عَادَ كَالْعُرْجُوْنِ الْقَدِيْمِ (36-یٰسین- 39): اور چاند، مقرر کر دی ہیں ہم نے اس کے لئے منزلیں یہاں تک کہ وہ دن سے گزرتا ہوا جاتا ہے پھر کھجور کی پرانی شاخ کی طرح''۔
- ''لَا الشَّمْسُ يَنْبَغِيْ لَهَآ اَنْ تُدْرِكَ الْقَمَرَ وَلَا الَّيْلُ سَابِقُ النَّهَارِ ط وَكُلٌّ فِيْ فَلَكٍ يَّسْبَحُوْنَ (36-یٰسین-40): نہ تو سورج کے بس میں ہے کہ جا پکڑے چاند کو اور نہ رات سبقت لے جا سکتی ہے دن پر۔ اور یہ سب کے سب اپنے اپنے مدار میں گردش کر رہے ہیں''۔

خداوند قدوس فرماتے ہیں کہ یہ چاند، سورج ایک مقررہ مدار میں اپنے سفر میں ایک وقت مقرر تک رواں دواں ہیں اور پھر اگر قرآن کریم کی بیشتر سورتوں میں دن کو رات پر اور رات کو دن پر لپٹنے کا ذکر ہے تو کس خوبصورت انداز میں ربُّ العزت نے زمین کے گول ہونے کے شواہد دیئے ہیں۔

- اور پھر جب قیامت کی گھڑی آئے گی تو کوئی سو رہے ہوں گے اور کوئی اپنے کام میں مشغول ہوں گے، ایک لطیف انداز میں زمین پر کہیں دن اور کہیں رات کا اشارہ دے دیا۔
- قرآن کریم کی سورۃ یٰسین 36: (آیتِ کریمہ 40-39) میں ہماری وسعتِ نظر کے مطابق چاند اور ستاروں اور سورج کے سفر کا ذِکر کیا گیا۔

اور آج کی سائنس یہ کہتی ہے کہ اگر یہ تمام ستارے ایک جگہ پر رُکے ہوتے تو ان سے منعکس ہو کر روشنی رات کو بھی دن کے اُجالے میں بدل دیتی لہٰذا یہ تمام ستارے اپنے ایک مقررہ مدار میں رواں دواں ہیں۔ جو دن میں اُجالا اور رات میں اندھیرے کا سبب بنتے ہیں۔

یہ کائنات جو اس قدر تیزی سے پھیل رہی ہے اور اس میں ہر ذرّہ زمین سے لے کر کائنات بسیط کی وسعتوں میں عالمین (Multiverses) تک اپنے اپنے سفر پر رواں دواں ہے، پھر بھی یہ ایک Closed Model کی طرح Behave کر رہا ہے۔ سائنسدان کائنات کے ختم اور دوبارہ شروع ہونے پر یقین رکھتے ہیں جیسا کہ سورۃ الانبیاء کے درج ذیل حوالے سے واضح ہے، لیکن وہ Closed Model اور Boundry Conditions کا ادراک نہیں کر سکتے جو قرآن حکیم میں مختلف جگہ بیان ہوئے ہیں۔ خداوند قدوس نے فرمایا ہے:

- ''یَوْمَ نَطْوِی السَّمَآءَ کَطَیِّ السِّجِلِّ لِلْکُتُبِ ؕ کَمَا بَدَاْنَآ اَوَّلَ خَلْقٍ نُّعِیْدُہٗ ؕ وَعْدًا عَلَیْنَا ؕ اِنَّا کُنَّا فٰعِلِیْنَ - (21-انبیاء- 104): جس دن لپیٹ دیں گے ہم آسمان کو اِس طرح جیسے سمیٹے جاتے ہیں دفتر میں مکتوبات۔ جس طرح ابتدا کی تھی ہم نے پہلی تخلیق کی (اسی طرح) ہم پھر اِس کا اعادہ کریں گے، یہ ایک وعدہ ہے ہمارے ذمہ، یہ ہم ضرور کر کے رہیں گے''۔
- ''اَوَلَمْ یَرَوْا اَنَّ اللّٰہَ الَّذِیْ خَلَقَ السَّمٰوٰتِ وَالْاَرْضَ قَادِرٌ'' عَلٰٓی اَنْ یَّخْلُقَ مِثْلَھُمْ وَجَعَلَ لَھُمْ اَجَلًا لَّا رَیْبَ فِیْہِ ؕ فَاَبَی الظّٰلِمُوْنَ اِلَّا کُفُوْرًا (17-بنی اسرائیل- 99): کیا کبھی نہیں غور کیا انہوں نے؟ کہ بے شک اللہ جس نے پیدا کیا ہے آسمانوں اور زمین کو وہ قادر ہے اس پر بھی کہ پیدا فرمائے اِن کی مثل (دوبارہ)، لیکن مقرر کر رکھی ہے اُس نے ان کے لئے ایک مدت، کوئی شک نہیں جس کے آنے میں مگر انکار کر دیا ہے ظالموں نے کہ (نہ رہیں گے وہ) بغیر کافر ہوئے''۔
- ''وَھُوَ الَّذِیْٓ اَحْیَاکُمْ ثُمَّ یُمِیْتُکُمْ ثُمَّ یُحْیِیْکُمْ ؕ اِنَّ الْاِنْسَانَ لَکَفُوْرٌ'' (22-حج- 66): اور وہی ہے جس نے تمہیں زندگی بخشی، پھر موت دیتا ہے تمہیں، پھر زندہ کرے گا تمہیں، بے شک انسان بڑا ہی ناشکرا ہے''۔
- ''اَللّٰہُ نُوْرُ السَّمٰوٰتِ وَالْاَرْضِ ؕ مَثَلُ نُوْرِہٖ کَمِشْکٰوۃٍ فِیْھَا مِصْبَاحٌ'' ؕ اَلْمِصْبَاحُ فِیْ زُجَاجَۃٍ ؕ اَلزُّجَاجَۃُ کَاَنَّھَا کَوْکَبٌ'' دُرِّیٌّ'' یُّوْقَدُ مِنْ شَجَرَۃٍ مُّبٰرَکَۃٍ زَیْتُوْنَۃٍ لَّا شَرْقِیَّۃٍ وَّلَا غَرْبِیَّۃٍ یَّکَادُ زَیْتُھَا یُضِیْٓءُ وَلَوْلَمْ تَمْسَسْہُ نَارٌ'' ؕ

نُوْر'' عَلٰی نُوْر'' ط یَھْدِی اللّٰہُ لِنُوْرِہٖ مَنْ یَّشَآءُ ط وَ یَضْرِبُ اللّٰہُ الْاَمْثَالَ لِلنَّاسِ ط وَاللّٰہُ بِکُلِّ شَیْءٍ عَلِیْم'' (24-نور- 35):اللہ نور ہے آسمانوں کا اور زمین کا، مثال اس کے نور کی ایسی ہے جیسے ایک طاق ہو، جس میں رکھا ہوا چراغ۔ یہ چراغ ایک فانوس میں ہو، اور یہ فانوس ایسا ہو جیسے ایک ستارہ موتی کی طرح چمکتا ہوا جو روشن کیا جاتا ہے زیتون کے مبارک درخت (کے تیل) سے جو نہ شرقی ہے اور نہ غربی، قریب ہے کہ تیل بھڑک اُٹھے خواہ نہ چھوئے اسے آگ--- روشنی پر روشنی--- رہنمائی عطا فرماتا ہے اللہ اپنے نور کی جسے چاہے۔ اور بیان کرتا ہے اللہ یہ مثالیں لوگوں کے لئے۔ اور اللہ ہر چیز کو خوب جانتا ہے''۔

اس آیت کریمہ میں ربّ العزت نے تمام کائنات کی ابتداء و آخری مادی اصول اور وہ باؤنڈری (نچلا آسمان) جہاں تمام Physical Laws اختتام پذیر ہوں گے کی نشان دہی کردی ہے، لیکن صرف اور صرف نورِ خدا ہی باقی آسمانوں میں پھیلا ہوگا کیونکہ وہی تو ہے جو تمام اصولوں کا خالق ہے۔

- ''وَالسَّمَآءَ رَفَعَھَا وَوَضَعَ الْمِیْزَانَ ○ (55-رحمٰن- 7):اور آسمان کو بلند کیا اللہ نے اور قائم کردیا نظامِ توازن''۔
- ''اَلَّا تَطْغَوْا فِی الْمِیْزَانِ ○ (55-رحمٰن-8): تاکہ نہ خلل ڈالو تم بھی عدل و توازن میں''۔
- ''فَاِذَا انْشَقَّتِ السَّمَآءُ فَکَانَتْ وَرْدَةً کَالدِّھَانِ ○ (55-رحمٰن- 37): پھر جب پھٹ جائے گا آسمان تو ہو جائے گا وہ سرخ لال چمڑے کی طرح''۔
- ''فَبِاَیِّ اٰلَآءِ رَبِّکُمَا تُکَذِّبٰنِ ○ (55-رحمٰن- 38):سو اپنے ربّ کی کن کن قدرتوں کو جھٹلاؤں گے تم اے جن و انس''۔
- ''ہم نے نچلے آسمان کو ستاروں سے مزیّن کر رکھا ہے۔(37-الصّٰفّٰت-6)''
- تمام کائنات چاروں طرف سے فٹ بال کور کی طرح پہلے یا نچلے آسمان سے گھری ہوئی ہے اس لئے کہ Closed Model میں ہر چیز نے تخریب یا توڑ پھوڑ کے عمل سے دوچار ہونا ہے۔(82-انفطار- 4-1)۔ جیسے اگر گلاس میز سے فرش پر گرے تو ٹوٹ جائے گا۔ ہم ایک ٹوٹے ہوئے گلاس کو پھر سے میز پر اپنی اصلی حالت میں نہیں دیکھ سکتے اس لئے کہ 2nd Law of Thermodynamic اس کی نفی کرتا ہے اور یہی Murphy Law کی بنیاد فراہم کرتا ہے اور عملِ تخریب توڑ پھوڑ کا عمل Thermo dynamic Arrow of Time کی ایک مثال ہے۔

(Murphy's Law -----> In closed system-model disorder or entropy always increases)۔ اگر یہ Open Model ہوتا تو توڑ پھوڑ کا یہ عمل وجود میں نہ آتا۔ اِس کی مثال یوں ہے کہ اگر آپ کسی گول جار سے کسی طرح تمام ہوا نکال لیں اور اس میں شیشے کی کوئی چیز رکھ دیں اور پھر زور سے ہلائیں تو وہ نہیں ٹوٹے گا۔ لیکن ہماری کائنات کا عمل اس کے برعکس ہے۔

اب تصور کریں کہ اِس فضائے بسیط نے کب تک اور کہاں تک پھیلنا ہے۔ نچلے آسمان تک پہنچنے کے لئے جب یہ پھیلتی ہوئی کائنات آسمان سے ٹکرائے گی --- (Big Smash) تو مختلف Universes (عوالم) اپنے اپنے وقت میں پھیلتے ہوئے اس سے ٹکرا کر پاش پاش ہو جائیں گی --- Series of Big Crunch --- تو اس وقت نچلا آسمان بھی پاش پاش ہو رہا ہوگا۔ یہ کیفیت بڑی خوبصورتی سے 21-الانبیاء -آیت 104 میں بیان کی گئی ہے۔ خداوند قدوس فرماتے ہیں کہ اس کے لئے ہم نے ایک وقت مقرر کر رکھا ہے۔ وہ نہ ایک گھڑی آگے ہو سکتا ہے اور نہ پیچھے۔ اس لئے کہ یہ کائنات ایک خاص رفتار 300,000 کلومیٹر فی سیکنڈ کی رفتار سے پھیل رہی ہے اور اُسے نچلے آسمان جس نے تمام کائنات کو اپنے گھیرے میں لے رکھا ہے اپنی مخصوص جگہ موجود ہے تک پہنچ کر پاش پاش ہوتا ہے

- ''وَاِذَا الْكَوَاكِبُ انْتَثَرَتْ ۝ وَاِذَا الْبِحَارُ فُجِّرَتْ ۝ (82-انفطار-2/3): اور جب سمندر پھاڑ دیئے جائیں گے۔ سمندر اُبل پڑیں گے یعنی سمندروں میں آگ لگ جانے سے بڑی سٹپٹاہٹ پیدا ہوتی ہے--- لیکن جب Big Crunch کے واقعات رونما ہو رہے ہوں گے اس وقت یہ عمل جاری ہوگا اور کچھ اجرام فلکی ایسے بھی ہوں گے جو Black Holes میں ضم ہو جائیں گے۔ لیکن ان کا Gravitational influance (کششِ ثقل) کائنات میں پھیلتا جائے گا۔ جس سے کائنات ایک دفعہ پھر اُسی طرح گرم ہو جائے گی جس طرح یہ شروع میں تھی اور وہ درجہ حرارت اربوں سینٹی گریڈ تک پہنچ جائے گا۔ اور پھر سمندروں کی حالت آگ کے سمندر جیسی ہوگی۔

آج کے سائنسدان Closed Model پر متفق ہیں لیکن وہ نہیں جانتے یہ اس قدر وسیع اور پھیلتی ہوئی کائنات Closed Model کی طرح کیسے Behave کرے گی۔ کاش وہ قرآن سے رہنمائی لیتے۔ میری کتاب:

Faith in the Scientific Philosophy of Religion

جو اس وقت برطانیہ اور امریکہ میں دستیاب ہے، میں اس مضمون پر تفصیل سے بحث کی گئی ہے کہ Arrows of Time کس طرح Behave کریں گے اور کائنات ایک دفعہ ختم ہونے کے بعد پھر کیسے شروع ہوگی۔

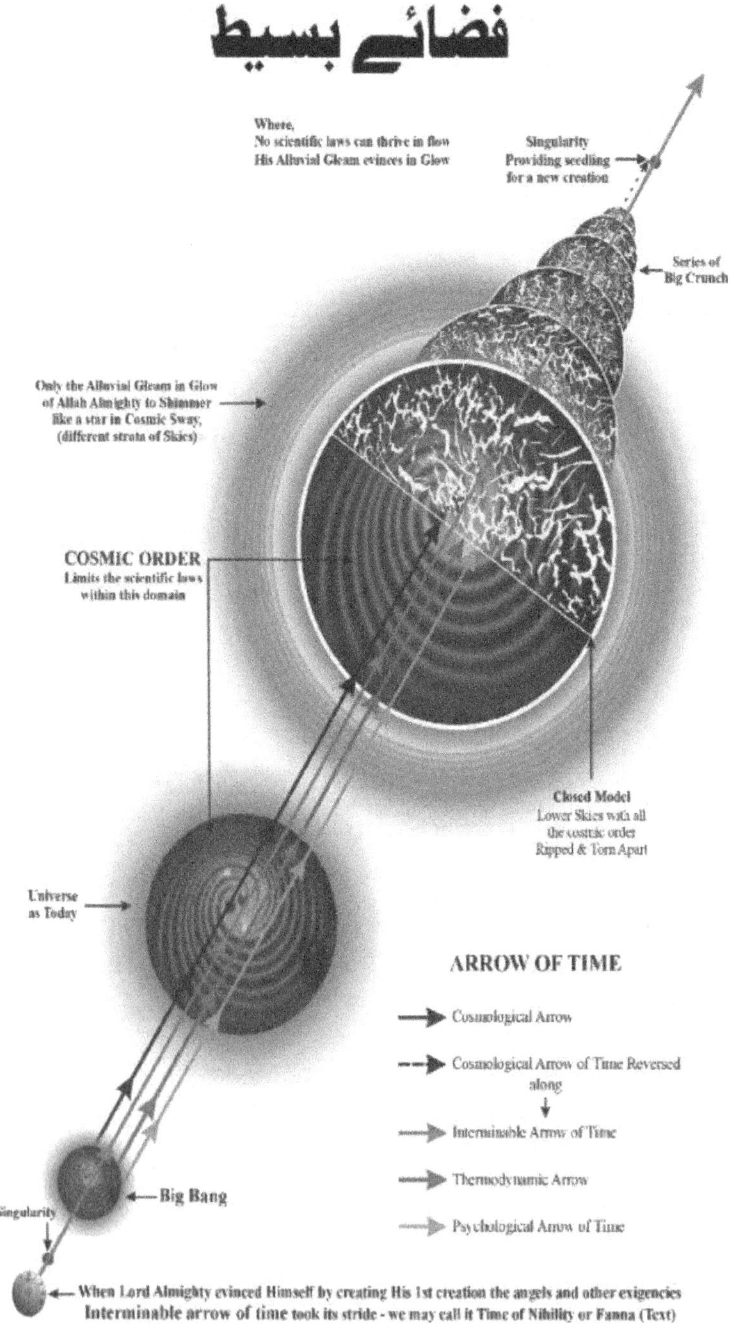
فضائے بسیط
Where,
No scientific laws can thrive in flow
His Alluvial Gleam evinces in Glow
Singularity
Providing seedling
for a new creation
Series of
Big Crunch
Only the Alluvial Gleam in Glow
of Allah Almighty to Shimmer
like a star in Cosmic Sway,
(different strata of Skies)
COSMIC ORDER
Limits the scientific laws
within this domain
Closed Model
Lower Skies with all
the cosmic order
Ripped & Torn Apart
Universe
as Today
ARROW OF TIME
Cosmological Arrow
Cosmological Arrow of Time Reversed
along
Interminable Arrow of Time
Thermodynamic Arrow
Psychological Arrow of Time
Big Bang
Singularity
When Lord Almighty evinced Himself by creating His 1st creation the angels and other exigencies
Interminable arrow of time took its stride - we may call it Time of Nihility or Fanna (Text)

واقعہ معراج جدید سائنس
اور
قرآنی حقائق کی روشنی میں

تاریخی حقائق کو پرکھنے کے لئے ہمیں اسی دورانیہ کے حالات اور واقعات کو صحیح معنوں میں جانچنے کی ضرورت پڑتی ہے۔تب جا کر کسی واقعہ کو صحیح طور پر ہم اسکی تصدیق کر سکتے ہیں۔لیکن کلام پاک میں بیشتر فرمودات ایسے ہیں جن کا اس دورانیہ کے (جب کلام پاک نازل ہوا تھا) حالات اور واقعات اور سائنسی تحقیق کی روشنی میں پرکھنا یا جاننا ناممکن تھا ہاں البتہ اگر سائنس کلام پاک سے رہنمائی لیتی تو شائد سائنس دانوں نے جو معرکہ 20ویں صدی میں سر کیا تھا وہ شائد بہت پہلے کر لیتے۔کلام پاک کی ہمہ گیر افادیت اور حقانیت اس سے اور بھی زیادہ ثابت ہوتی ہے کہ سائنس کی ترقی ابد تک اس کی سچائی پر مہر ثبت کرتی رہے گی۔میں کلام پاک کی پہلی آیت کریمہ "الحمدللہ رب العالمین" کا ذکر کروں گا جس میں خداوند قدوس فرماتے ہیں کہ وہ العالمین(Multiverse) کا رب ہے نہ کہ عالم کا(Universe)۔اور آج کے سائنس دان اس بات پر متفق ہو گئے ہیں۔ جب کہ وہ چند دہائیاں پہلے اس بات پر مصر تھے کہ ہم صرف Universe میں رہتے ہیں اور مزے کی بات یہ ہے کہ Multiverse کا لفظ ابھی تک انگلش ڈکشنری میں شامل نہیں ہوا۔یہ ایک مختلف مضمون ہے جس کی تفصیل کچھ سورۃ فاتحہ میں میں نے دی ہے۔یہاں واقعہ معراج کی حقیقت کو پرکھنے کے لئے ہم اسے جدید سائنس کی روشنی میں جانچتے ہیں اور پھر ہم قرآنی آیات کی روشنی میں یہ ثابت کرتے ہیں کہ حضور اکرم ﷺ نے ایسے ہی راستوں سے روشنی کی رفتار سے کئی گنا (تیس ارب گُنا) کی رفتار سے حضرت جبرائیلؑ کے ساتھ کائنات کی وسعتوں میں ایسے ہی راستوں (Worm hole) سے سفر کیا جہاں انہوں نے خداوند قدوس کے حضور مشاہدات فرمائے۔اگر ہم کسی طریقہ سے یہ ثابت کر دیں کہ حضور کریم ﷺ نے روشنی کی رفتار سے کئی گنا سفر آسمانوں کے خصوصی راستوں سے کیا تو پھر یہ خصوصی راستے کیا ہیں؟ سائنسدان آج بھی اس بات پر متفق ہیں کہ یہ راستے جن کو انہوں نے Wormholes اور Moving Wormholes کا نام دیا ہے۔Big Bang کے بعد وہ آج بھی موجود ہیں اور اگر ہم قرآنِ کریم کی آیت کریمہ پر نظر دوڑائیں تو وہاں ہمیں ایسے ہی تین راستوں سے متعلق اشارہ ملتا ہے۔سورۃ المومنون کی سترویں آیت کریمہ کائنات کے مختلف طبقات اور آسمانوں کے درمیان سات راستوں کا اشارہ کرتی ہے۔جب کہ سورۃ المعارج 4-3 میں ایسے ہی راستوں کو معارج کہا گیا ہے یعنی Elevator Type راستے یعنی جلد سفر طے کرنے کے لئے راستے۔سورۃ الزاریات کی ساتویں آیت کریمہ میں ان راستوں کو آسمانوں کے درمیان ملتے ہوئے راستوں کا نام دیا گیا ہے۔یعنی

واقعه معراج

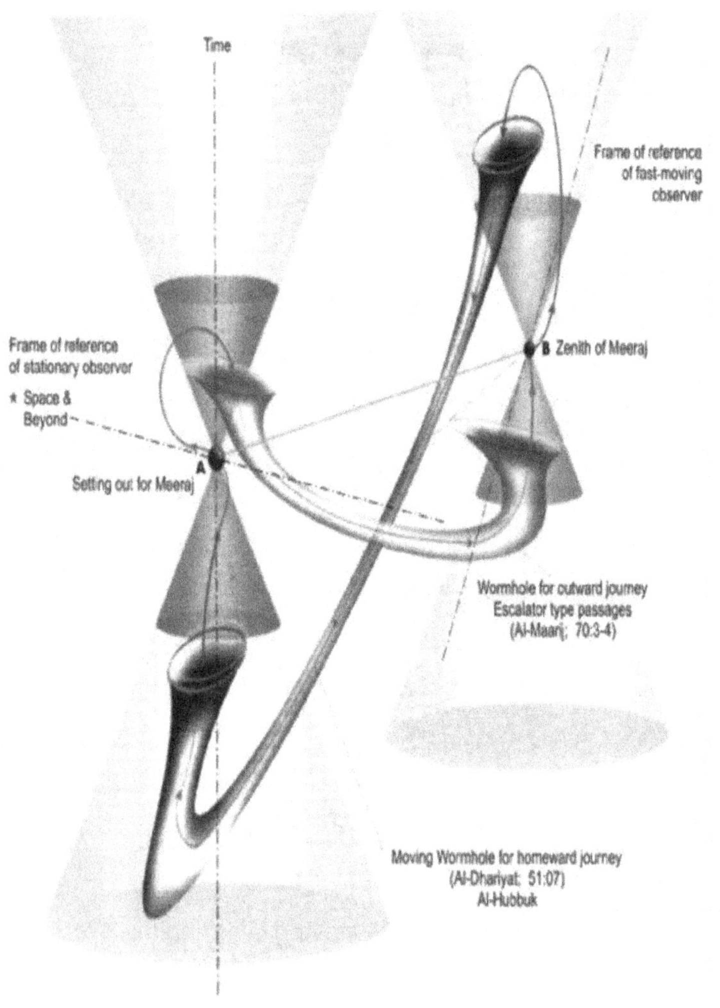

*** Space & Beyond:**

Space or Cosmic Order (Our domain of expansion of the universe is the lowest skies (Al-Saffat 37:6))
Beyond in Cosmic Sway with six skies (With no gravitational element)

Modified from Brief History of Time by Stephen Hawking

Moving Wormholes۔اب ہم اصل مضمون کی طرف آتے ہیں۔

سٹیفن ھاکنگ جدید دور کے بڑے سائنسدان اپنی کتاب "بریف ہسٹری آف ٹائم" میں لکھتے ہیں کہ اگر انسان کائنات کے مختلف طبقات کے درمیان بنائے گئے راستے (ورم ہول) کے ذریعے روشنی کی رفتار سے کئی گُنا زیادہ رفتار کے ساتھ سفر کر سکے تو ایک جگہ جسے (Alpha Centuri) کہتے ہیں جس کا زمین سے فاصلہ 20 ملین x20 ملین میل کے برابر ہے وہ فاصلہ کم ہو کر چند ملین میل رہ جائے گا اور انسان وہاں زمین سے جا کر کچھ عرصہ وقت گزارنے کے بعد ایسے ہی دوسرے (Moving Wormhole) کے ذریعے جب زمین پر واپس آئیگا تو وہ عین ممکن ہے کہ اپنے گزرے ہوئے وقت سے بھی پہلے آجائے۔یعنی اگر وہ منگل کی شام کو روانہ ہوا تھا تو وہ عین ممکن ہے کہ سوموار کی شام کو واپس آجائے جیسا کہ سٹیفن ھاکنگ کی کتاب "بریف ہسٹری آف ٹائم" سے اخذ ڈوگرل میں درج ہے:

There was a young lady of white
Who traveled much faster than light?
She departed one day,
In relative way
An' arrived on the previous night

یعنی ایک دن پہلے ۔ یہ بات عام قاری کے لئے شاید مضحکہ خیز ہو لیکن یہ ایک سائنسی حقیقت ہے اور سائنسدان اس کوشش میں دن رات مصروف ہیں کہ کسی طرح کائنات کے مختلف طبقات کے درمیان اٹامک ورم ہولز بنائے جائیں تا کہ تسخیر کائنات میں انسان کے لئے وہ مدد و معاون ثابت ہو۔اس سائنسی نظریہ کو پیش نظر رکھتے ہوئے ہم اگر یہ ثابت کرسکیں کہ حضور اکرم ﷺ نے ایسے ہی راستوں کے ذریعے حضرت جبرائیلؑ کے ہمراہ سفر کیا اور ان کے سفر کی رفتار روشنی کی رفتار سے کئی گنا زیادہ تھی۔

سورۃ السجدہ کی پانچویں آیت کریمہ پر نظر دوڑائیں جس میں خداوندِ قدوس فرماتے ہیں کہ دنیا کے معاملات ان کے پاس ایک دن جو آپ کی گنتی کے ایک ہزار سال کے برابر ہیں پہنچتے ہیں۔ یہ معاملات کیا ہیں اور ان کی نوعیت کیا ہے؟ بڑے غور و خوض کے بعد اور تحقیق کے بعد پتہ چلتا ہے کہ اگر ہم چاند کے ایک ہزار سال کے سفر کو ایک دن کے سیکنڈ پر تقسیم کریں۔تو وہ روشنی کی رفتار نکلتی ہے یعنی 299796 Km/Sec تقریباً 300000 کلومیٹر فی سیکنڈ کی رفتار بنتی ہے اور جیسا کہ آپ کو معلوم ہے چاند کا فاصلہ زمین سے 186000 میل ہے اور چاند سے روشنی زمین تک ایک سیکنڈ میں پہنچتی ہے۔(فرشتوں کی رفتار جیسا کہ سورۃ المعارج کی آیات کریمہ تین اور چار پر نظر دوڑائیں سے صاف ظاہر ہے جس میں) خداوند قدوس فرماتے ہیں کہ وہ مالک ہیں کائنات میں ان راستوں (Elevator Type

(Passages کے جو چڑھنے یا پھلانگنے کے لئے استعمال ہوتے ہیں۔ فرشتے اور روحیں خداوند قدوس کے ہاں ایک دن جو 50000 سال کے برابر ہے اس سے پہنچتے ہیں۔ اب ہم دیکھتے ہیں کہ جیسے سائنسدانوں نے اس بات کا اشارہ کیا ہے کہ انسان آئندہ کائنات کے مختلف طبقات کے درمیان راستے بنائے گا۔ خداوند قدوس نے اپنے فرشتوں کے لئے وہ راستے پہلے بنا دیئے ہیں۔ اب رہا رفتار کا معاملہ غور سے ان آیات کریمہ کو پڑھیں جیسے سورۃ المعارج میں 50000 سال یہاں تمہاری گنتی نہیں کہا کیونکہ ایک دن کا تعین خداوند قدوس نے پہلے فرما دیا۔ جو ہمارے ایک ہزار سال کے برابر ہے۔ یعنی روشنی کے رفتار سے 1000 گنا۔ تو آیئے ہم ایک عام فرشتے کی رفتار ان آیات کریمہ سے اخذ کرتے ہیں جو خداوند قدوس نے سورۃ المعارج میں بیان فرمائی۔ 50000 x 1000 = 50000000۔ یعنی پانچ کروڑ گنا روشنی کی رفتار سے زیادہ ایک عام فرشتہ کی رفتار ہے۔ جب کہ کچھ فرشتے ایسے بھی ہیں جیسے کہ سورۃ الفاطر کہ آیت کریمہ 1 میں ذکر کیا گیا ہے کہ جن کے دو دو، تین تین یا چار چار پر ہیں۔ کہیں ایسا تو نہیں کہ اس کا اشارہ ان فرشتوں کی رفتار عام فرشتوں سے دو گنا، تین گنا، اور چار گنا کی طرف ہو۔ یعنی روشنی کی رفتار سے 10 کروڑ، 15 کروڑ، 20 کروڑ گنا اور اسی طرح احادیث شریف میں ہے کہ حضرت جبرائیلؑ کے 600 پر ہیں تو آپ پانچ کروڑ کو 600 سے ضرب دیں۔ روشنی کی رفتار سے 30 ارب گنا زیادہ۔ اتنی تیز رفتار اور آسمانی طبقات کے درمیان راستوں کی ضرورت اس لیے بھی ضروری تھی کیونکہ ہماری کائنات ہر ایک سیکنڈ 300000 کلومیٹر کی رفتار سے پھیل رہی ہے۔ اور اگر کائنات پھیلنا بند کر دے تو زندگی ناممکن ہو جائے۔ یہ ایک بہت لمبا مضمون ہے جس کی یہاں تفصیل ممکن نہیں۔ بہر حال حضور اکرم ﷺ نے ان راستوں سے روشنی کی رفتار سے 30 ارب گنا زیادہ رفتار سے سفر معراج کیا جس کا ذکر خداوند قدوس نے قرآن مجید میں مختلف جگہوں پر فرمایا ہے۔ اور واپس وہ Moving Wormholes حُبُکِ (الزاریات آیت ۔ 7) یعنی

--------------Travel Back in Time

☆ سورۃ المعارج کی تیسری اور چوتھی آیت سے فرشتوں کی انتہائی تیز رفتاری یا انتہائی تیز قوتِ پرواز کا پتہ چلتا ہے۔

مجھے قطعی طور پر معلوم نہیں کہ پروفیسر ایم۔ اے ملک جو ہمارے ملک کے نامور پامسٹ ہیں کو ورم ہول تھیوری کا ادراک تھا یا نہیں لیکن ان کی کتاب اکیسویں صدی کی عالمی پیشنگوئیاں جو 1999ء میں شائع ہوئی ہیں۔ یہ پیرا گراف قابل غور ہے۔ میں اس کا ذکر اس لیے بھی کر رہا ہوں کیونکہ ان کی چند ایک پیشنگوئیاں جیسے 9/11، سونامی، پاکستان کا ہولناک زلزلہ جیسی پیشنگوئیاں پہلے ہی وجود میں آ چکی ہیں وہ لکھتے ہیں:۔

" تسخیر کائنات کی اس تگ و دو میں انسان کا قدم کسی سیارے پر بھی جا پہنچے گا۔ جہاں فقط چھ سات ماہ قیام کے بعد جب وہ واپس لوٹے گا۔ تو بچے بوڑھے ہو چکے ہوں گے زمین کم و بیش ساٹھ ستر برس سے زائد کا سفر طے کر چکی ہوگی۔ اور پھر کسی اور سیارے پر کہیں وہ آٹھ دس برس گزار کر واپس لوٹے گا ۔تو زمین پر وہی دن ہوگا جس دن وہ روانہ ہوا تھا۔ زمان و مکان کا انسانی تصور یکسر بدل کر رہ جائے گا۔

" کیا اس کے بعد بھی واقعہ معراج میں شک کی گنجائش رہ جاتی ہے؟"

Speed of light is out side gravitational field of Sun i.e. space and more precisely 12000 lunar orbits/earthday.

قرآن اور تخلیق آدم

قرآن کریم کی سورۃ نوح کی آیت نمبر 17 میں رب العزت فرماتے ہیں کہ میں نے تمام انسانوں کو بتدریج مٹی سے پیدا کیا جب ہم اس آیت کریمہ کو پڑھتے ہیں تو ہم قرآن اور سائنس کے فلسفہ میں کوئی تضاد نہیں پاتے لیکن آج تک جو ہمیں تعلیم دی گئی ہے اس نظریہ کے مطابق سائنس کی تعلیم اور مذہبی نظریہ آدمؑ سے متعلق ہم مختلف آراء رکھتے ہیں۔ ایسی متضاد کیفیت میں کسی بھی ذہن کے لئے مذہب کے نظریہ کو مانتے ہوئے سائنس کے فلسفے کو ماننا اور سائنس کے فلسفے کو مانتے ہوئے مذہب کے نظریہ کو ماننا انتہائی مشکل ہو جاتا ہے اور یہی کیفیت ہماری نوجوان نسل میں پائی جاتی ہے۔ جب وہ قرآن پاک کا سرسری مطالعہ کرتے ہیں تو اس میں یہ آتا ہے کہ آدم اور حوا کو شیطان مردود کے ساتھ جنت سے نکال دیا گیا اور زمین پر بھجوا دیا گیا۔ جب کہ قرآن کریم کی یہ آیت بڑی واضح بتا رہی ہے کہ میں نے انسان کو بتدریج مٹی سے پیدا کیا۔

انسان کی تخلیق کے فلسفہ کو سمجھنے کے لئے ہمیں انسان کی بدنی اور روحانی (تخلیقی اکائی) کے متعلق جاننا ہوگا۔ سائنس اس بات کی طرف واضح اشارہ کرتی ہے کہ انسان کی بدنی اور روحانی اکائی DNA اور RNA (جینوم) خلیے میں وجود پذیر ہے۔ جدید سائنس اس بات پر متفق ہے کہ ہر جاندار کے اندر اس کی تخلیق کا کیمیکل کوڈ اس کے DNA میں لکھا گیا ہے۔ ہر انسان کے اندر DNA پر تقریباً تین بلین کوڈز لکھے ہوئے ہیں جب کہ RNA پر کم وبیش 0.5 بلین کوڈز لکھے ہوئے ہیں۔ اگر ہم ایک سیکنڈ میں 10 کوڈ پڑھیں تو ہمیں تمام کوڈ پڑھنے میں 11 سال لگیں گے اور پھر بھی ہم زندگی کی روح کی اصلیت کو جاننے سے قاصر رہیں گے۔ کچھ کوڈز کی ترتیب جین (Gene) کہلاتی ہے۔ سائنس اس بات پر متفق ہے کہ قدرت نے ایک آفاقی کوڈ ہر انسان کے اندر DNA میں لکھ دیا ہے جو پیغام وہ RNA کو بھیجتا ہے۔ RNA اس پیغام کی تعمیل Enzyme (پروٹین) کی صورت میں کرتا ہے جو جسم کے تمام اعضاء پر اثر انداز ہوتی ہے اور وہ ماحولیات کے مختلف پہلوؤں (Factors) سے متاثر ہو کر مختلف انداز میں ہمارے جسم کی ساخت پر اثر انداز ہوتے ہیں۔

آدم کی تخلیق بتدریج ایک ارتقائی عمل تھا جس کا ذکر قرآن کریم کی سورۃ نوح کی آیت 17 میں آیا ہے کہ میں نے انسان کی تخلیق بتدریج مٹی سے کی اس امر سے سائنس بھی اتفاق کرتی ہے لیکن دراصل جس چیز کی تصدیق قرآن کریم کی مختلف آیاتِ کریمہ سے ہوتی ہے " کہ میں نے تمہاری تقدیر لکھ دی ہے (سورۃ ص 75:38) " اور حیران کن بات یہ ہے کہ جدید سائنسدان بھی (دیکھئے حوالہ National Geographic Feb, 2009) اس بات پر متفق ہیں کہ ہر جاندار کے اندر اس کی تخلیق کا کوڈ اس کے (Genome) یعنی DNA, RNA میں لکھ دیا گیا ہے جو اس بات کو ثابت کرتا ہے کہ ہر انسان کی تخلیق خداوند قدوس نے اپنے ہاتھوں سے مخصوص مقصد کے لئے فرمائی۔ جس نے بعد میں اپنا ارتقائی عمل جاری

رکھا۔ یہ ایسے ہی ہے جیسے رب العزت نے زمینوں اور آسمانوں کو حکم دیا کہ ہو جاؤ یعنی "کُن "تو "فیکون "یعنی تمام وسائل عوامل اور اصول جو کائنات کی تخلیق کے لئے ضروری تھے۔ پہلے ایک سیکنڈ میں وجود میں آگئے اور پھر کائنات نے تخلیق کے عمل کو جاری رکھا جس کو اربوں سال پر محیط ایک لمبا سفر طے کرنا پڑا۔ اسی طرح انسانی وجود میں DNA یعنی Genome اور Genetic Array کو رب العزت نے اپنے ہاتھوں سے تخلیق کیا اور پھر اپنا ارتقائی عمل اس نے جاری رکھتے ہوئے کتنا وقت لگا یا اس کا اندازہ شاید ہی ہم کر سکیں۔ قرآن کریم کی درج ذیل آیات کریمہ کو پڑھیں:

ترجمہ: "اور ہم نے انسان کو کھنکھناتے سڑے ہوئے گارے سے پیدا کیا ہے(۲۶:۱۵)"

"اور جب تمہارے پروردگار نے فرشتوں سے فرمایا کہ میں کھنکھناتے سڑے ہوئے گارے (مٹی) سے ایک بشر بنانے والا ہوں(۲۸:۱۵)"

"اسی نے انسان کو ٹھیکرے کی طرح کھنکھناتی ہوئی مٹی سے بنایا(۱۴:۵۵)"

ان آیات کریمہ سے صاف عیاں ہے کہ DNA, RNA "طین" کی تخلیق زمین کی گہرائیوں میں سڑے ہوئے گارے کی مانند مٹی جو سنگلاخ چٹانوں میں (Earth Plates) میں دبی ہوئی ہے سے ظہور پذیر ہوئی پھر اس طین کے جوہر "تراب" سے تخلیق آدم کا سلسلہ جاری ہوا تراب کے لفظی معنی مٹی کے لئے گئے ہیں جبکہ جیسے آگے چل کر بیان ہو رہا ہے یہ لفظ دراصل نطفہ کی جگہ استعمال ہونے والے Genetic Permutation کا نام ہے۔

تخلیق کا ارتقائی عمل ہمارے کئی عقدے حل کرتا ہے ان میں سب سے اچھوتی بات جو سامنے آئی ہے وہ یہ ہے کہ انسان کی تخلیق میں جن Genome نے حصہ لیا وہ کوئی غیر معمولی نوعیت کے نہیں بلکہ یہ تو وہی Genes ہیں جو دوسری مخلوقات میں پائی جاتی ہیں۔ اس کی مثال یوں ہے جیسے مختلف بلڈنگ بنانے کے لئے آپ کو مختلف بلڈنگ مٹیریل درکار نہیں ہوتا ویسے ہی مختلف کتابیں لکھنے کے لئے آپ کو مختلف الفاظ درکار نہیں ہوتے۔ اس طرح ہمارے Genome کی ساخت اور نوعیت تقریباً 60% وہی ہے جو چوہے میں ہے۔ دراصل تخلیق انسان کوئی ایسی چیز تو ہے نہیں جسے فیکٹری میں جوڑا جائے یہ تو ماحول، دیگر اثرات کے اندر پرورش پاتی ہے اور پروان چڑھتی ہے اسی لئے ارتقائی عمل کا اسکے وجود پر اثر انداز ہونا ثابت ہوتا ہے۔

ماحول کا ارتقائی عمل پر اثر انداز ہونے کے عمل کو Micro Evolution کہتے ہیں جب کہ Macro Evolution قطعی طور پر Inbuilt Genetic Code پر منحصر ہے جو قدرت (Nature) نے اس کے لئے لکھ دیا ہے اب آپ Supreme Nature کو رب العزت یا

God یا بھگوان جو بھی چاہیں نام دے دیں یہ آپ کی صوابدید پر ہے۔

ڈارون کا یہ خیال کہ ہم صرف اپنے والدین کے موروثی رجحان اور ماحول کی کیفیت سے متاثر ہو کر آگے تخلیق پر اثر انداز ہوتے ہیں قطعی طور پر مکمل ارتقائی عمل کی ترجمانی نہیں کرتا جب کہ انسان اپنے جدِ امجد کے تمام موروثی رجحانات سے متاثر ہونے کے علاوہ اپنے موروثی کوڈ کو بھی ساتھ لے کر ارتقائی عمل کو آگے بڑھاتا ہے۔

خداوند قدوس فرماتے ہیں کہ میں نے آدم کو اپنے ہاتھ سے بنایا (سورۃ ص، آیت نمبر 75) تخلیق آدم کے وقت دراصل انسان کا جو مکمل Genetic Code تھا خداوند قدوس نے تخلیق فرما کر اسے کوئی بھی شکل دی کیونکہ وہ قادرِ مطلق ہے اور جو چیز جیسے بھی چاہے ترتیب دے سکتا ہے۔ تخلیق آدم کے ساتھ حوا کی تخلیق پسلی سے کرنا انتہائی ذو معنی عمل ہے کہیں ایسا تو نہیں کہ اس سے مراد متوازی یعنی Parallel تخلیق ہو کہ جب آدم کے Genome ترتیب دیئے جا رہے تھے ساتھ ہی ساتھ حوا کے Genome کی تخلیق بھی جاری تھی بہر حال یہ تمام بحث اس بات کی تصدیق کرتی ہے کہ تخلیق آدم ایک پہلے سے طے شدہ مٹی سے بتدریج تخلیق کے مراحل طے کرنے والی Pre-determind, Pre-ordained حقیقت تھی اور اس Genetic Array کی مختلف صورتوں میں ظاہر ہونے والی باقی تمام مخلوق اس خالق کائنات کا انعام تھا اور پھر آدم اور حوا کی پشت سے پیدا ہونے والی اولاد سے (روز اول سے روز آخر تک) پوچھا گیا؟ وعدہ لیا گیا کہ تمہارا رب کون ہے (سورۃ الاعراف۔172) تو تمام مخلوق نے اس بات کا اقرار کیا کہ آپ ہمارے رب ہیں۔ یہاں پر ایک بات قابل غور ہے کہ خداوند قدوس نے انسان (مٹی کے پتلے) کو اپنے ہاتھ سے بنایا اور پھر فرشتوں اور ابلیس سے اس کو سجدہ کرنے کے لئے کہا جس پر ابلیس نے انکار کیا۔ اگر آدم یعنی انسان کی تخلیق آسمانوں میں ایک مٹی کے پتلے کی حیثیت سے ہوتی تو اس کی پشت سے پیدا ہونے والی اولاد (سورۃ الاعراف، آیت نمبر 172) روز اول سے روز قیامت تک بھی بعینہ مٹی کے پتلے کی ہوتی جن سے پوچھا گیا؟ کہ تمہارا رب کون ہے۔ لیکن آئمہ کرام، علماء کرام اس بات پر متفق ہیں کہ آدم کی پہلی تخلیق تو مٹی سے ہوئی لیکن ان کی پشت سے پیدا ہونے والی اولاد ارواح تھی جن سے رب العزت نے وعدہ لیا۔ "اَلَستُ بِرَبِّکُم" (سورۃ الاعراف۔172)۔ اگر ہم سورۃ نوح کی سترویں آیت کریمہ کو سامنے رکھتے ہوئے انسان کی تخلیق بتدریج مٹی سے ہونے کو سامنے رکھیں تو کیا ایسا تھا کہ یہ آدم جب اپنی تخلیق کے پورے مراحل طے کر گیا اور پھر جنت میں اُس نے رب العزت کے احکامات میں لغزش برتی تو اس کے بعد جو واقعات پیش آئے وہ ہم سب کو معلوم ہیں۔ آگے کے واقعات آپ کے سامنے ہیں۔ لیکن ان ہر دو صورتوں میں ہماری تخلیق آسمانوں میں ایک مٹی کے پتلے کی حیثیت سے ہوتی مگر ایسی کوئی بات واضح طور پر سامنے نہیں آتی۔ دراصل ہم فلسفۂ کائنات میں تخلیق آدم اور دوسرے جانداروں کو دیکھیں تو قرآن پاک

میں واضح طور پر اعلان ہوتا ہے کہ میں نے تمام جانداروں کو پانی سے پیدا کیا(سورۃ النور 45:24)"اور اللہ نے پیدا کیا ہے ہر جاندار کو پانی سے سو ان میں سے وہ بھی ہیں جو چلتے ہیں پیٹ کے بل اور ان میں سے وہ بھی ہیں جو چلتے ہیں دوٹانگوں پر اور ان میں سے وہ بھی ہیں جو چلتے ہیں چار ٹانگوں پر پیدا فرماتا ہے اللہ جو چاہتا ہے ۔بے شک اللہ ہر چیز پر پوری طرح قادر ہے میں یہ آیت کریمہ پڑھ کر سٹپٹا سا گیا کیونکہ بچپن سے ہمیں ارتقائی عمل میں یہ بتایا گیا کہ پہلے جاندار رینگ رہے تھے پھر انہوں نے چار پاؤں پر چلنا سیکھا اور پھر بتدریج دو پاؤں پر چلنا شروع کیا اور وہ بالآخر انسان بنا لیکن قرآن کریم کی یہ آیت کریمہ مکمل طور پر واضح کر رہی ہے کہ یہ عمل ایسا نہیں، رینگنے والے جانوروں نے پہلے دو ٹانگوں پر چلنا شروع کیا پھر چار پر چلنا شروع کیا۔ بہت تحقیق کے بعد مجھے Reader Digest کی کتاب Life on Earth سے یہ عقدہ حل ہوا۔" جدید تحقیق اس بات پر متفق ہے کہ سب سے پہلی مچھلی mudskippers نے اپنے اگلے فِن جو پاؤں جیسی حرکت کرتے تھے سے چلنا شروع کیا اسی قسم کی دوسری مچھلی Lungfish تھی جس نے دو پاؤں پر چلنا شروع کیا۔ یہ ذکر 400 ملین سال کا ہے پھر ان 2 ٹانگوں والے Lethyostega پہلے جانور تھے جنہوں نے چار ٹانگوں پر چلنا شروع کیا یہ ذکر 350 ملین سال کا ہے اور اسی طرح انسان کو اول مٹی سے پھر نطفہ سے پیدا کیا گیا۔ (سورۃ مومن، آیت 67۔ سورۃ فاطر، آیت 11۔ سورۃ نوح، آیت 17) یہاں پر یہ بات بھی قابل ذکر ہے کہ اکثر حضرات بتدریج مٹی کے پیدا کرنے کو ہماری خوراک سے مناسبت دیتے ہیں جب کہ ایسا نہیں ہے اگر ایسا ہوتا تو قرآن کریم میں ہر آیت کریمہ میں نطفہ کا لفظ پہلے اور مٹی کا لفظ بعد میں استعمال ہوتا۔ اس تمام بحث کے بعد ہم اس نتیجہ پر پہنچتے ہیں کہ ہماری تخلیق جو رب العزت نے اپنے ہاتھ سے کی دراصل وہ ہماری روح اور بدنی تعمیر کا نقطہء آغاز (Genome) تھا اور اس آدم اور حوا کی پشت سے پیدا ہونے والی اولاد کا مطلب بھی Genome سے ارتقائی عمل کا وجود میں آنا تھا۔ سورۃ العمران کی آیت نمبر 59 میں خداوندِ قدوس نے آدم کی پیدائش کو عیسیٰؑ کی پیدائش سے مشابہت دی ہے تو ذرا غور کریں کیا یہ سب عمل Genetic Level پر نہیں کیا گیا۔ یہاں پر وہ تمام عوامل جو ڈارون کے مسئلہ کو ثابت کرتے ہیں یا اُس کے خلاف جاتے ہیں ان کا تھوڑا سا ذکر کریں گے۔ آج سے تقریباً 160 برس پہلے جب ڈارون نے کہا کہ ہماری تخلیق بتدریج عمل میں آئی ہے اس کو ہر ایک نے آج تک سراہا۔ لیکن جس بات پر آج تک کوئی متفق نہیں ہو سکا وہ یہ ہے کہ: پروٹین Protein, Amino Acids or Nucliec Acid کسی بھی طرح سے صرف ارتقائی عمل سے وجود میں نہیں آ سکتی تو پھر یہ کیسے ممکن ہے کہ ایک انسان کی تخلیق صرف اور صرف ارتقائی عمل سے وجود میں آئی ہو جس میں ایک Supreme Nature کا کوئی عمل دخل نہ ہو وہ پروٹین جو ہماری تخلیق کے بنیادی اجزاء ہیں وہ کس طرح معرضِ وجود میں آئے اور سب سے بڑی بات یہ کہ Evolution اس بات کو قطعی طور پر ثابت نہیں کر سکی کہ روح کیا ہے؟ کچھ سائنسدان اس بات پر مُصر ہیں کہ زندگی شہابِ ثاقب کے ذریعے فضا سے زمین پر آئی پھر سوال اٹھتا ہے کہ فضائے بسیط میں روح یا زندگی کا وجود کہاں سے ممکن ہوا۔ ان بہت سے عوامل کے ساتھ سائنسدان آج تک یہ ثابت نہیں کر سکے کہ جب کائنات کی تخلیق اور ارتقائی عمل دُنیا کے ہر کونے میں ہو رہی تھی تو پھر کیوں نہ

بندروں کی ہر نسل نے جو کُرہِ ارض کے دیگر علاقوں میں رہائش پذیر تھی نسلِ انسانی کو جنم دیا اور یہ کیونکر صرف اور صرف افریقہ ہی میں پیدا ہو کر دنیا کے تمام خطوں میں پھیل گیا۔ یہی نظریہ آج تمام مکاتبِ فکر کو قبول ہے۔ سائنس اس بات پر اتفاق رکھتی ہے کہ ہماری ماں (Mitochondrial Eve) کی تخلیق تقریباً دو لاکھ سال پہلے افریقہ ہی میں ہوئی جس سے بنی نوع انسان کی تخلیق معرض وجود میں آئی۔ یہ بات قرآن پاک کی اس آیت کریمہ (سورۃ النساء۔2) سے مطابقت رکھتی ہے کہ تمھارے جدِامجد ایک ہیں (آدم اور حوا) اور پھر ہم اگر ایک دفعہ انسان کی تخلیق آسمانوں میں تصور کریں تو خداوند قدوس نے دراصل اپنی بہترین تخلیق یعنی آدم کے Genome (جینوم) کو اپنے ہاتھوں سے بنایا اور وہ کوڈ اس کے Genetic Procenium میں تفویض کر دیا گیا۔ (سورۃ ص 75:38) اور پھر وہ ایک مخصوص طریقہ سے بتدریج پروان چڑھتے ہوئے بالآخر خالقِ دو جہان کی اشرف المخلوقات کہلانے کا شرف حاصل کر سکا۔ قرآن کریم میں سے چند آیاتِ کریمہ اس بات کی قطعی نشاندہی کر رہی ہیں کہ حضرت آدمؑ کی تخلیق آسمانوں میں مٹی (ارض) سے نہیں بلکہ تُراب (شاید Genetic Array) سے ترتیب دی گئی جیسے:

سورۃ مومن (40) آیت 67 "وہی تو ہے جس نے پیدا کیا ہے تم کو مٹی (تُراب) سے پھر نطفہ سے پھر خون کے لوتھڑے سے"

سورۃ الفاطر (11) آیت 11 "اور اللہ ہی نے پیدا کیا ہے تم کو مٹی (تُراب) سے پھر نطفہ سے پھر بنا دیا ہے اس نے تم کو جوڑا"

سورۃ الکھف (18) آیت نمبر 37 "اور میں نے پیدا کیا انسان کو پہلے تُراب سے پھر نطفہ سے پھر اُس کے بعد"

سورۃ الحج (22) آیت 5 "ہم نے تمھیں تُراب سے پیدا کیا اور پھر نطفہ سے"

سورۃ الاعمران (03) آیت نمبر 59 "خداوند قدوس کے ہاں حضرت عیسیٰ علیہ السلام کی پیدائش کی مثال ایسی ہے جیسے حضرت آدمؑ کی اور اُسکو (حضرت آدم) نے تُراب سے پیدا کیا"

سورۃ الاعراف (60) آیت 12 "جب رب العزت نے شیطان مردود سے پوچھا کہ تمھیں کس چیز نے آدم کے سجدے سے روکا ہے تو اُس نے جواب دیا کہ تو نے مجھے آگ سے بنایا ور انسان کو طین سے "

سورۃ نوح (71) آیت 17 "اور تم کیسے تصور کر سکتے ہو کہ رب العزت نے تمھیں بتدریج مٹی سے پیدا کیا"

سورۃ الانعام (6) آیت 2 "وہ رب العزت ہی ہے جس نے تمھیں طین سے بنایا اور پھر تمھیں اس کائنات میں کچھ عرصہ کیلئے زندگی عطاء کی"

سورۃ الروم (30) آیت 20 "میں نے تمھیں تُراب سے پیدا کیا اور پھر تمام کائنات میں پھیلا دیا"

ارض، طین اور تُراب کے معنی (قرآن کریم کی جتنی بھی تفاسیر، تراجمیں) مٹی کے کئے گئے ہیں۔

سورۃ العمران کی 59 آیت کریمہ میں رب العزت مثال دے رہے ہیں کہ حضرت عیسیٰؑ کی پیدائش کو مانندِ آدم ہے جس کو اللہ تعالیٰ کی ذات نے تُراب سے پیدا کیا۔ یہاں پر تُراب کا لفظ اپنے معنی "مٹی" کے خود نفی کر رہا ہے کہ میرے معنی مٹی کے نہیں۔ ہم دیکھتے ہیں کہ حضرت عیسیٰؑ کی پیدائش میں مرد کا کوئی حصہ نہیں یعنی نطفہ کا کوئی حصہ نہیں تو باقی مثال جو رب العزت نے دے دی وہ تُراب کی ہے ۔ کیونکہ حضرت آدمؑ اور حضرت عیسیٰؑ کی پیدائش میں یہ "قدرِ مشترک" رب العزت نے فرما دی۔ اب اگر ہم تُراب کے معنی مٹی کے لیتے ہیں تو حضرت عیسیٰؑ کی پیدائش میں والد کی غیر موجودگی میں مٹی کا کیا کردار ہوسکتا تھا۔ یہاں پر رب العزت نے تمام مسئلہ ہی کھول کر رکھ دیا کہ تخلیق آدم مٹی سے نہیں کسی اور چیز سے ہو رہی ہے اور جدید سائنس اس بات سے اتفاق کرتی ہے کہ Genetic انجنیر نگ ۔ The Creation of the Genome ابتدائی تخلیق کا آغاز ہے۔

لفظ تُراب نطفہ کا دوسرا نام ان Genes کا ہے جو انسانی تخلیق کا سبب بنتی ہیں۔ اسی طرح طین کا لفظ اگر آپ قرآن کریم کی مختلف آیات کریمہ پر نظر دوڑائیں جہاں یہ لفظ استعمال ہوا ہے یہ قطعی طور پر ماں کے مادہ تولید Ovum اور نطفہ کے ملاپ (Fertilized Ovum) کے Genes کے نام کا اظہار کرتا ہے۔

اس تمام بحث سے یہ بات قطعی طور پر سامنے آتی ہے کہ انسانی تخلیق زمین پر بتدریج مٹی یعنی ارض سے ہوئی جیسے کہ سائنس کہتی ہے لیکن Creation of Species میں ارتقائی عمل کا Maroevolution کا کوئی حصہ نہیں یہ صرف خداوندِ قدوس جسے سائنسدان Natural Forces کا نام دیتے ہیں کی طرف سے یہ جاندار کے اندر ایک Pre-ordained Genetic Code کی رہینِ منت ہے۔ میں اسے اس طریقہ سے بھی بیان کرتا ہوں کہ دراصل تخلیق آدم کا Genetic Code رب العزت نے اپنے ہاتھوں سے ترتیب دیا اور پھر اس کوڈ کو بکھیر دیا جس سے کائنات کی مختلف مخلوق نے جنم لیا۔ یہ مضمون میری انگریزی کتاب Faith in the Unseen میں تفصیل سے بیان کیا گیا ہے جس میں ڈارون کی تھیوری کا بھی مفصل جائزہ لیا گیا ہے۔ آپ ضرور جاننا چاہیں گے کہ ہم مرنے کے بعد پھر کس طرح اُٹھائے جائیں گے اور ہمارے ہاتھ پاؤں ہمارے کئے دھرے یا اعمال کا حساب کیسے دیں گے۔

سورۃ العمران آیت نمبر 59 اس بات کی قطعی نشاندہی کر رہی ہیں کہ حضرت آدم کی تخلیق آسمانوں میں مٹی (ارض) سے نہیں بلکہ طین (شاید Genetic array) سے ترتیب دی گئی جیسے:

تخلیق آدم کے سلسلہ میں جینوم کا ذکر کیا گیا جن پر تقریباً ساڑھے تین ارب کوڈ لکھے گئے ہیں۔ یہ پیغام (کوڈ) ہر جاندار کے لئے ہر انسان کے لئے رب العزت نے خاص کر دیا ہے۔ ہم روزمرہ کے معمولات میں اپنے جسم کے ان گنت خلیے زمین کی ہارڈ ڈسک میں بکھیرتے جا رہے ہیں اور اس کی مثال ایسی ہے جیسے کمپیوٹر میں ہم مختلف مضامین، تصاویر، وڈیو فلمیں وغیرہ کمپیوٹر کی ہارڈ ڈسک میں کوڈ کی صورت میں محفوظ

کرتے ہیں اور ایسے ہی اس ڈیٹا کو سکرین پر واپس لانے کے لئے ہمیں ایک معمولی سے اشارہ کی ضرورت پڑتی ہے۔ ہمارے جینوم کے کوڈ ہر انسان کے لئے خاص کر دیئے گئے ہیں۔ تصور تو کریں رب العزت فرماتے ہیں کہ میرے ایک ہی حکم سے تمام انسان اپنی اصلی شکل میں واپس میرے حضور پیش ہو جائیں گے۔ کیا یہ ایسا نہیں جو کچھ ہم کمپیوٹر کی سکرین پر دیکھتے ہیں۔

اب ہم دوسرے سوال کی طرف آتے ہیں:

یہ سلیکون کیا ہے؟

یہ میٹیریل زمین سے حاصل کیا جاتا ہے جو کمپیوٹر میں ڈیٹا سٹور کرتا ہے۔

کیا سلیکون کے علاوہ بھی کوئی چیز اور ایسی ہو سکتی ہے جو ڈیٹا سٹور کرے؟

کیوں نہیں اب Nano Computer اس کی ایک ادنیٰ مثال ہے۔

ہماری بدنی ساخت کیا ہے؟

ہم مٹی سے بنے ہیں اور مرکب ہیں مختلف نمکیات، دھاتوں اور پانی کا۔ تو ہماری اس چھوٹی سی بات سے یہ بات ثابت ہوتی ہے کہ ہمارے جسم کے اندر کوئی ایسی چیز بھی ہو سکتی ہے جو ہمارے روزمرہ کے معاملات کو کمپیوٹر کی طرح محفوظ کئے جا رہی ہے جو بالآخر روزِ حساب رب العزت کے سامنے ہمارے نامہ اعمال کو کھول کر پیش کر دے گی۔

اس تمام بحث سے ہم یہ اخذ کرتے ہیں کہ انسان (اور دیگر جانداروں کا) ارتقائی عمل ایک پہلے سے طے شدہ عمل تھا اور اس عمل نے مختلف ماحول میں پروان چڑھتے ہوئے بالآخر ایک مکمل انسان کی تخلیق عمل میں آئی اور یہ وہ وقت تھا جب رب العزت نے اپنے انبیاء کرام کی وساطت سے انسان کی تربیت کیلئے ان کے لئے ایک ضابطۂ حیات پسند فرمایا وہ دین یا Faith بھی انسانی ارتقائی عمل کی طرح بتدریج ایک مکمل ضابطہ حیات کی صورت میں ایک مکمل دینِ اسلام کی شکل میں حضور کریم ﷺ پر نازل فرمایا اور وہ تھا قرآن۔

تقدیر اور تدبیر

اس کو بیان کرنے کے لیے میں انگریزی کا ایک فقرہ استعمال کرتا ہوں

Fate (تقدیر محکم) is determined by the genome whereas the fruit of fortune (تقدیر غیر محکم) are through intelligence.

قرآن پاک کی بیشتر آیات کریمہ میں رب العزّت فرماتے ہیں کہ میں نے تمہاری تقدیر لکھ دی ہے جو تم نہیں بدل سکتے اور اس کے ساتھ اس کا بھی بار بار تکرار ہے کہ تمہاری تقدیر تمہارے اپنے ہاتھ میں ہے۔ یہ چیز کافی تذبذب کا باعث بنتی ہے اور انسان اکثر و بیشتر یہ کہتے ہوئے پایا گیا کہ جب تقدیر لکھ ہی دی گئی ہے تو اس میں میرا کیا اختیار۔ خداوند قدوس نے انسان کو تین حصّوں سے بنایا ہے۔ دراصل انسان کی بتدریج تخلیق مٹی سے ہوئی خداوند قدوس نے اس کو اپنی طرف سے روح دی اور پھر اشرف المخلوقات بنانے کیلئے اس کو ایک انعام میں ذہنی استطاعت عطا کی۔ اس کو قرآن پاک سورۃ البقرۃ آیت نمبر 31 میں یوں بیان کیا گیا ہے کہ رب العزت نے حضرت آدم علیہ السلام کو الفاظ سکھائے۔ یہ الفاظ دراصل یہی ذہنی استطاعت /Intelligence جس کی بنیاد پر انسان اچھے برے کی پہچان کرسکتا ہے اور اس میں فیصلہ کرنے کی قوت آتی ہے یہی وہ چیز ہے جو روز قیامت ہمارے حساب کا سبب بنے گی کیونکہ جب فرشتوں نے یہ کہا کہ اے رب العزّت تو ایسی مخلوق تخلیق کر رہا ہے جس نے زمین پر فساد برپا کرنا ہے تو رب العزّت نے فرمایا کہ تم نہیں جانتے جو کچھ میں جانتا ہوں۔ تخلیق کائنات کے ساتھ انسانی ارتقائی عمل اس بات کا واضح ثبوت میسر کرتا ہے کہ یہ صفت یعنی ذہنی ارتقاء بھی بتدریج عمل میں آ رہا ہے اور آج انسان جس مقام پر پہنچا ہوا ہے آج سے پچاس سال پہلے کوئی ذہن اس کا تصوّر بھی نہیں کرسکتا تھا۔ قرآن پاک کی بیشتر آیات کریمہ میں رب العزّت اس بات کی قطعی طور پر نشاندہی کرتے ہیں کہ تمہاری تقدیر لکھ دی گئی ہے۔ جس پر تمھیں کوئی اختیار نہیں ہے اور وہ تقدیر کیا ہے کوئی دھوبی کے گھر پیدا ہوتا ہے، کوئی ڈاکٹر کے گھر پیدا ہوتا ہے، کوئی بادشاہ کے گھر پیدا ہوتا ہے اور کوئی فقیر کے گھر پیدا ہوتا ہے۔ اس پر کسی کا کوئی اختیار نہیں اس کا انحصار ہمارے Genume پر ہے جو قدرت نے ہر ذی نفس کیلئے پہلے ہی سے تجویز کر دیا ہے جبکہ ہماری تدبیر Intelligence ہماری رہنمائی کرتی ہے۔ اس کی مثال یوں ہے کہ کوئی ایک Industrial City میں پیدا ہو جہاں پر دھواں کے بادل ہر وقت چھائے رہتے ہوں گندگی و غلاظت نے چاروں طرف ڈیرے لگا رکھے ہوں۔ جیسے گندا ماحول انسانی صحت پر اثر انداز ہوتا ہے ویسے ہی ذہنی ارتقائی عمل میں باہر کا ماحول انسان کی روحانیت پر بھی اثر انداز ہوتا ہے۔ جسمانی طور پر انسان کو اس چیز پر قادر کر دیا گیا ہے کہ وہ اس گندے ماحول سے نکل کر اپنی صحت کو بحال کرے اور اسی طرح اپنی روحانی کیفیت کی اچھے ماحول میں اس کی پرورش کرسکے۔ ہماری ذہنی ارتقاء کا انحصار موروثی رجحان، ماحول اور تربیت پر ہے۔ علامہ اقبال کہتے ہیں کہ

خدا نے آج تک اس قوم کی حالت نہیں بدلی
نہ ہو جس کو خیال خود آپ اپنی حالت کے بدلنے کا

تقدیر (fate) سے مراد قسمت جو ہر ذی نفس کیلئے لکھ دی گئی ہے وہ قطعی اس سے روگردانی نہیں کر سکتا ہے کہ وہ کس گھر میں کس ماحول میں پیدا ہوا دوسرے لفظوں میں ہم اسے تقدیر محکم بھی کہہ سکتے ہیں۔ جبکہ تدبیر (Intelligence) ہمارے نصیب (Fortune) بدل سکتی ہے جس کی رہنمائی کیلئے ہم رب العزّت سے صبح وشام دن میں پانچ مرتبہ ہر نماز میں رہنمائی کیلئے درخواست کرتے ہیں (سورۃ فاتحہ) اس کو "تقدیر غیر محکم" کا نام دیا گیا ہے۔

یعنی اس میں واضح کر دیا گیا کہ انسان جب ایک دفعہ ارادہ کر لے تو وہ اپنی تقدیر کو بدل سکتا ہے۔ جس طرح دوسری جگہ فرمایا

خودی کو کر بلند اتنا کہ ہر تقدیر سے پوچھے
خدا بندے سے خود پوچھے بتا تیری رضا کیا ہے

ایک چھوٹا سا واقعہ بیان کرتا ہوں۔ بابا فرید رحمۃ اللہ علیہ 35 سال جنگلوں میں عبادت اور ریاضت میں مصروف رہے۔ ایک دن ایک درخت کے نیچے بیٹھے عبادت کر رہے تھے کہ چڑیوں نے شور مچانا شروع کر دیا تو بابا فرید نے چیخ کر کہا

"مرو میڈی عبادت اِچ کیوں خلل پاڈِتے"
(مر جاؤ کیوں میری عبادت میں خلل ڈال رہی ہو)

تمام چڑیاں بابا فرید کے آگے آ کر گر کر ڈھیر ہو گئیں۔ یہ اشارہ تھا کہ تمہاری عبادت قبول ہو گئی اور تو جا اب لوگوں کی رہنمائی کر۔ بابا فرید شہر کی طرف چل پڑتے ہیں۔ ہاتھ میں ایک ڈنڈا ہے، بوسیدہ کپڑے ہیں، بال مٹی سے اٹے ہوئے ہیں شہر کے نزدیک جب پہنچتے ہیں تو ایک کتا راستہ کاٹ کر گزرنے لگتا ہے تو ڈنڈے سے اس کو اپنے راستے سے ہٹانے کی کوشش کرتے ہیں۔ دور کھڑی ایک عورت جو کنویں سے پانی بھر رہی تھی کہتی ہے

"بابا فریدا الگ دیاں چڑیاں مار ڈتھیاں نی ایہہ سائیں والے کتے ہن"
(بابا فرید تم نے ویرانے کی چڑیاں ماری تھیں یہ کتے لاوارث نہیں)

بابا فرید نے پریشان ہو کر پوچھا اے خاتون تو کون ہے جواب آتا ہے میں کنجری ہوں۔ بابا فرید نے کہا اے اللہ کی بندی جب وہ چڑیاں مری تھیں وہاں تو کوئی بندہ نہیں تھا سوائے رب العزت کی ذات کے! تمہیں یہ مقام کیسے حاصل ہوا۔ اس عورت نے کہا کہ سردیوں کی ایک رات میری ماں سخت بیمار تھی اور اس نے مجھے پانی کیلئے کہا اور جب میں پانی لے کر گئی تو اس وقت اس کی آنکھ لگ گئی تھی اور میں صبح تک پانی اس کی چارپائی کے ساتھ لے کر کھڑی رہی تاکہ اگر دوبارہ اس کی آنکھ کھلے تو اسے سردی میں باہر نکل کر مجھے آواز نہ دینی پڑے۔

کہنے کا مطلب یہ ہے کہ ہماری پیدائش کسی بھی گھر، کسی بھی ماحول میں ہو اس کا انحصار ہمارے جینوم پر ہے جس پر ہمیں کوئی کنٹرول نہیں اور یہ وہ تقدیر ہے جو لکھ دی گئی ہے اس پر کسی کو کوئی اختیار نہیں" جسے تقدیر محکم سے تعبیر کیا گیا ہے "جو اختیار ہمیں دیا گیا ہے وہ ہماری ذہنی استطاعت ہے جس کی بناء پر ہم فیصلہ کر سکتے ہیں کہ ہم نے کون سا راستہ اختیار کرنا ہے "اور ہم اپنی تقدیر سنوار سکتے ہیں یہ ہے تقدیر غیر محکم "اور پھر ایسی

بات بھی نہیں ہے کہ رب العزّت نے ، جو کہ خود مالک تقدیر ہیں ،انسان کی تقدیر نہ بدلی ہو۔اگر یہ فیصلہ اتنا ہی اٹل ہوتا تو پھر ہم ہر نماز میں الحمد شریف ہی کو دیکھ لیں اس میں رب العزّت سے کیا مانگتے ہیں کہ :
"یا رب العزّت !ہم تیری ہی عبادت کرتے ہیں اور تجھ ہی سے مدد چاہتے ہیں اور دکھا ہم کو راہ سیدھی ان لوگوں کی جن پر تو نے رحم کیا اور اپنا فضل کیا نہ کہ ان کی جو تمہارے غضب کے حقدار بنے۔"
اوراسی طرح **رَبَّنَا اٰتِنَا فِی الدُّنیَا حَسَنَةً وَّفِی الآخِرَةِ حَسَنَةً وَّقِنَا عَذَابَ النَّار**۔ اسی طرح ہم ہر نماز کے بعد یہ دعا مانگتے ہیں کہ **"یا رب العالمین ہمیں اس جہان کی بھلائی عطا فرما، آخرت کی بھلائی عطا فرما اور جہنم کی آگ سے بچا** "اگر فیصلہ اٹل ہی تھا تو پھر یہ دعا کیوں۔ یہ مثال ایسی ہے کہ ایک آدمی دوسرے آدمی سے شرط لگاتا ہے کہ تم تو کہتے ہو کہ رب العزّت نے سب کچھ لکھ دیا ہے تو پھر یہ کیسے ممکن ہے کہ میں اس تقدیر کو بدل سکتا ہوں اور پھر یہ بھی ساتھ ہے کہ یہ جو فیصلہ ہے جو میں نے ذہنی طور پر فیصلہ کرنا ہے یہ پہلے سے ہی لکھ کر رکھ دیا گیا ہے۔
اس کی مثال یہ ہے کہ آپ ایک بند کمرے میں بیٹھے ہیں اس کے دو دروازے ہیں ،یعنی نکلنے کے دو راستے ہیں وہ آدمی کہتا ہے کہ آپ بتائیں میں نے کس راستے نکلنا ہے ، دوسرا آدمی لکھ کر رکھ لیتا ہے۔ اب وہ صاحب جس نے باہر نکلنا تھا نہ وہ ایک راستے سے نکلتا ہے اور نہ دوسرے راستے سے بلکہ وہ دیوار میں سوراخ کر کے نکل جاتا ہے اور کہتا ہے کہ اب بتا کہ میں نے کیسے نکلنا تھا اس پر لکھا ہوتا ہے کہ دیوار توڑ کر نکلے گا۔ وہ لکھا ہوا اس کیفیت سے ہے رب العزّت کے ہاں کہ جو فیصلہ ہم نے اپنی ذہنی استطاعت کے مطابق کرنا ہے مالک حقیقی کو اس کا پہلے ہی پتہ ہے وہ دلوں کے رازوں کو جاننے والی ذات ہے۔ یہاں پر میں اپنا ایک واقعہ بیان کرتا چلوں کہ وہ دلوں کے رازوں کو کیسے جانتا ہے۔
میرے پاس تہجد نماز میں اٹھنے کے لیے ایک الارم تھا جس میں کوئل کی کوکو کی آواز تھی۔ ایک رات تہجد کے وقت اٹھتے ہوئے ایسے ہی دل میں خیال آیا کہ میں یہ آواز اسی وقت کوئل ہی کی آواز میں سنوں۔ دوسرے دن جب الارم پر آنکھ کھلی ، الارم بند کیا ، وضو کیا ، نماز کیلئے کھڑا ہو گیا تو میں حیران ہو گیا کہ وہ کوکو کی آواز میرے بیڈروم کی کھڑکی کے اوپر سے مسلسل آرہی تھی۔ عین اس وقت جب مجھے یہ خیال آیا کہ اوہ! کل میں نے دل میں یہ خواہش ظاہر کی تھی تو یہ شاید وہی آواز ہے۔ جیسے ہی یہ خیال آیا آواز بند ہو گئی۔ کہنے کا مطلب یہ ہے کہ وہ ذات باری تعالیٰ ہمارے دلوں کے رازوں کو جاننے والی ذات ہے، ہمارے ارادوں کو پرکھنے والی ذات ہے کہ ہم نے اس کی عطا کردہ نعمت (Intelligence) کو کس طرح استعمال کرنا ہے۔ یہ سب ہماری صوابدید پر ہے لیکن اس کے متعلق بھی رب العزت کو مکمل آگاہی ہے اگر ہم نے اپنی دانست میں اپنی لغزشوں اور کوتاہیوں کی معافی مانگنی ہے اور ذات باری تعالےٰ سے رہنمائی طلب کرنی ہے تو یہ بھی پہلے سے درج ہے۔ بہر حال یہ تقدیر اور نصیب والا مسئلہ اتنا پیچیدہ نہیں جتنا کہ ہر شخص نے اسکو بنا دیا ہے۔

سادہ سی بات ہے کہ ایک گندگی میں رہنے والا اچھی جگہ رہنا پسند کرتا ہے تو یہ خواہش اس کی تب ہی پوری ہو سکتی ہے جب وہ کوئی کوشش کرے کوئی تدبیر کرے اس کے وسائل ڈھونڈے ورنہ تو وہیں پڑا رہیگا قدرت کی طرف سے Intelligence، ذہنی ادراک، ذہنی استطاعت، اچھے برے کی پہچان اسکے صحیح راستہ کی نشاندہی کر سکتی ہے۔ ایک خوبصورت کہاوت ہے "رب العزت نے ہر پرندے کے لیے اس کا کھانے پینے کا راشن مقرر کر دیا ہے لیکن وہ راشن اسکے گھونسلے میں نہیں ڈالتا اس رزق کی تلاش میں پرندے کو اپنے گھونسلے سے باہر نکلنا ہوتا ہے اپنے رزق کی تلاش میں۔ اسی طرح مرنے کا وقت مقرر ہے اس وقت تک پہنچنے کیلئے کوئی آدمی جلدی کرے یعنی غذائی بے اعتدالی اور سگریٹ نوشی وغیرہ شروع کر دے تو کیا ہوگا۔ ذیابیطس، بلڈ پریشر، دل کا عارضہ، فالج، کینسر وغیرہ سے وہ کسی بھی بیماری کا شکار رہ کر ایڑھیاں رگڑ رگڑ کر اپنی موت کا انتظار کرتا ہے یا وہ انتہائی ذہانت کا ثبوت دیتے ہوئے صبح شام باقاعدگی سے ہلکی ورزش کرتا ہے، غذا کا خیال رکھتا ہے، تمبا کو نوشی اور دیگر صحت کے مضر عوامل سے پرہیز کرتا ہے۔ ممکن تو ہے کہ اسے بھی کوئی عارضہ لاحق ہو لیکن اس کا امکان بے اعتدالی کرنے والے شخص سے بہت کم ہوگا۔ بہرحال ہم آخر میں اس بحث کو اس طرح سمیٹتے ہیں کہ ہمیں ذہنی ادراک کی روشنی میں اچھے برے کی پہچان کرنا ہے اور ہماری دانست میں دراصل اچھے برے کی پہچان ہمارے Genome کی تخلیق کے وقت ہی رکھ دی گئی تھی اس کو ہم نے بروئے کار لا کر زندگی کی راہ متعین کرنا ہے۔ آخر میں پھر وہی پہلا فقرہ دہراؤں گا۔

Fate (تقدیر محکم)is determined by the genome whereas the fruit of fortune (تقدیر غیر محکم)are through intelligence.

قرآن اور فلسفہء حیات

روح دراصل امر ربی ہے جسکی حقیقت سے متعلق سائنسدان مختلف آراء رکھتے ہیں اور اکثر کا کہنا ہے کہ زندگی یا روح جو دراصل کائنات کا حصہ تھی شہاب ثاقب کے ذریعے زمین پر آئی لیکن میرا اکثر سائنسدانوں سے اس بات پر تکرار رہا کہ کائنات میں روح یا زندگی کہاں سے آئی۔ یہ ایک ایسی نعمت خداوندی ہے جس پر نہ تو ہمیں کوئی کنٹرول ہے یعنی ہم اس پر کوئی قدرت نہیں رکھتے اور پھر یہ نہ ہی ہماری ملک ہے۔

اکثر علماء فتویٰ دیتے ہیں کہ اسقاط حمل چار ماہ (حمل کے چوتھے ماہ) بعد قطعی طور پر ممنوع ہے سوائے بہت ہی طبعی مجبوری کی حالت میں۔ یہ اس لئے کہ احادیث شریف میں ہے کہ چار ماہ کی عمر میں بچے کو اللہ کی طرف سے ماں کے پیٹ میں روح تفویض ہوتی ہے۔ یہاں پر طبی لحاظ سے یا سائنسی بنیاد پر زندگی کا ارتقاء تو اس وقت ہی ہو گیا تھا۔ جب نطفے اور ماں کی طرف سے بیضے کا ملاپ ہوتا ہے اور پھر چھ ہفتے بعد ماں کے پیٹ میں دل کی دھڑکن الٹراسانو پر دیکھی جاسکتی ہے۔ یہاں پر یہ نقطہ قابل غور ہے کہ دل کی دھڑکن تو چھٹے ہفتے شروع ہو جاتی ہے جبکہ روح 16 ہفتے بعد بچے کو تفویض ہوتی ہے۔

قرآن پاک سورۃ الزمر آیت نمبر 39 میں رب العزت فرماتے ہیں کہ **جب آپ سوتے ہیں تو میں تمہاری روحیں (النفس) قبض کرلیتا ہوں اور جن کو زندہ رکھنا ہوتا ہے ان کی روحوں کو واپس بھجوادیا جاتا ہے ورنہ ان روحوں کو اپنے پاس رکھ لیتا ہوں** یہاں پر یہ بات قابل ذکر ہے کہ جس روح کا یہاں پر ذکر ہو رہا ہے جب وہ قبض کرلی جاتی ہے تو انسان پھر بھی سانس لے رہا ہوتا ہے اور اس کا دل دھڑک رہا ہوتا ہے۔

اب ان دو چیزوں کی مماثلت لے لیں کہ جب بچہ ماں کے پیٹ میں ہوتا ہے تو اس کا دل دھڑکنا پہلے شروع کرتا ہے اور روح اس کو بعد میں تفویض ہوتی ہے۔ یہ بات اب قطعی طور پر واضح ہو گئی ہے کہ وہ روح جو چار ماہ بعد بچے کو ملتی ہے وہ زندگی دراصل زندگی نہیں ہے بلکہ زندگی کے علاوہ کوئی چیز ہے جسے میں Prima or Psychic Principle سے تعبیر کرتا ہوں کیونکہ یہ وہ وقت ہے جب بچہ باہر کے ماحول کا ردعمل ظاہر کرتا ہے۔ اس کی میں ایک چھوٹی سی مثال دیتا ہوں:

"ایک ماں کو حمل ہوتا ہے، جس کا ایک پانچ سالہ بیٹا پہلے سے موجود ہے، بیٹے کی خواہش ہے کہ اس کی بہن پیدا ہو اور وہ اس کا نام سنّبل رکھ لیتا ہے اور وہ ہر وقت ماں کے پیٹ پر ہاتھ پھیرتے ہوئے یہ کہتا ہے، سنّبل، سنّبل، تمہارا کیا حال ہے۔ اٹھارہویں ہفتے Pregnancy میں جب 3D الٹراسانو کرتے ہیں تو ڈاکٹر بتاتا ہے کہ یہ بچی ہے تو بیٹا جو ماں کے ساتھ کھڑا ہوتا ہے خوشی سے پکارتا ہے، سنّبل، سنّبل اور وہ بچی اس کا جواب مسکراہٹ میں دیتی ہے جو الٹراسانو پر بڑی خوبصورتی سے دیکھا گیا" میڈیکل سائنس اور مذہبی روایات کو مدنظر رکھتے ہوئے میرے لئے یہ اہم ضروری تھا کہ اس مسئلے کو میں عام وخاص تک پہنچاؤں کیونکہ ٹی وی پر جب ایک مولانا صاحب سے یہ سوال پوچھا گیا کہ بچے کو روح تو چوتھے ماہ ملتی ہے جب کہ اس کا دل ڈیڑھ ماہ کے بعد دھڑکنا شروع کر دیتا ہے تو مولانا صاحب سے کوئی جواب نہ بن پڑا۔

اس تمام بحث سے یہ بات واضح ہوتی ہے کہ روح کی دراصل دو اقسام ہیں ایک وہ جو دراصل زندگی ہے اور دوسری قسم حواس خمسہ جو بتدریج زندگی کے ارتقاء کے ساتھ ابتدائیہ پرورش پاتے ہیں اور شاید یہی وہ عمل ہے جو بچے کو چوتھے ماہ میں تفویض ہوتا ہے اور بچہ باہر کے عوامل کو اپنے ردعمل سے ظاہر کرتا ہے۔

کچھ آیات کریمہ کی تفسیر سائنسی نقطہ نگاہ سے پیش کرنے کی جسارت کر رہا ہوں۔

کلامِ پاک کے تقریباً تمام تراجم میں سورۃ نجم 53 کی پہلی دو آیاتِ کریمہ کے یہ معنی دیئے گئے ہیں کہ ''ڈوبتے ہوئے تارے کی قسم تمہارا ساتھی نہ بہکا ہے نہ بھٹکا ہے''۔

اب ساتھی کا جیسے ہم تفاسیر میں دیکھتے ہیں حضور اکرم صلی اللہ علیہ وسلم کی ذاتِ مبارکہ سے متعلق ذِکر ہے، تو کیسے ممکن ہے کہ ربُّ العزت نے ایک عام ستارے کی قسم کھائی ہو کیونکہ ستارے تو سارے ڈوبتے ہیں۔ مَیں نے علماء حضرات کی طرف رجوع کیا اور اُن سے گزارش کی کہ مجھے'' وَالنَّجْمِ اِذَا هَوٰى '' سے متعلق کوئی اور معنی بتائیں تو مجھے بتایا گیا کہ اس کے معنی اپنی اصل کیفیت بدلتے ہوئے ستارے کے بھی ہو سکتے ہیں۔

اب آیئے ہم کائنات میں ایک ایسے ستارے کی تلاش کرتے ہیں جس کے معنی اس آیت کریمہ سے مماثلت رکھتے ہوں۔ ہماری Milkyway Galaxy میں ایک ستارہ ہے جسے Cephied کہتے ہیں۔ اس ستارے نے سائنسدانوں کی توجہ اپنی طرف مبذول کی ہوئی ہے کیونکہ یہ ستارہ کچھ دیر کے لئے تو خوب چمکتا ہے اور پھر آہستہ آہستہ مدھم ہوتا جاتا ہے اور پھر واپس اپنی اصل حالت میں آجاتا ہے اور اس کی یہ خاصیت ہر مرتبہ بدلتی رہتی ہے جس کی وجہ سے سائنسدان کائنات میں مختلف فاصلے ناپ سکتے ہیں سائنسدانوں نے اس ستارے کو Gem & Jewel of the cosmic order یعنی کائنات کا ہیرا کہا ہے۔ اب حضور اکرم صلی اللہ علیہ وسلم کی ذات مبارکہ کا کردار اور معمولات دیکھیں کہ کبھی تو معراج پر ہیں اور کبھی مکہ کی گلیوں اور طائف کی پہاڑیوں میں --- اُن پر کوڑا کرکٹ پھینکا جاتا ہے اور پتھر مارے جاتے ہیں اور پھر ہم اُن کو انسانیت کا Gem & Jewel کہتے ہیں۔ جیسے Cephied کائنات میں فاصلے کے تعین کرنے میں مدد دیتا ہے ایسے ہی حضور اکرم صلی اللہ علیہ وسلم کا اخلاق ہمیں روزمرہ کے معاملات میں رہنمائی کرتا ہے۔ سورۃ النجم کی 49 آیت کریمہ میں رب العزت نے قسم کھائی ہے سائرس شاید (Cephied) ایک ستارے کی جو بے شمار خوبیوں کا مالک ہے۔ اب ایک مرتبہ ہم حضور کریم ﷺ کے اسوہ حُسنیٰ کو دیکھیں تو ہمیں ان گنت خوبیوں کے وہ مالک لگتے ہیں جب کہ ہم نے Cephied کی خصوصیات کو صرف کائنات کے فاصلے ناپنے کا ذریعہ بنایا ہے یہ آیت کریمہ Cosmologist کے لئے ایک لمحہ ءِ فکر ہے کہ وہ اس ستارے کی اور بھی بے شمار خوبیوں کو جاننے کی کوشش کریں تاکہ وہ کائنات کی ریسرچ میں اور آگے بڑھ سکیں۔

33 سورۃ الاحزاب کی 72 آیت کریمہ میں خداوند قدوس فرماتے ہیں کہ ہم نے قرآن کی امانت آسمانوں، زمین اور پہاڑوں کو سونپی تو انہوں نے انکار کر دیا (معذرت کی کہ وہ اس عظیم ذمہ داری کے اہل نہیں) لیکن انسان نے یہ امانت کی ذمہ داری سنبھالنے کا عہد کیا لیکن وہ بہت ظالم (ناانصاف) اور بے وقوف ہے۔

اس آیت کریمہ کے متن کے مندرجات سے یہ واضح ہوتا ہے کہ رب العزت نے انسان کو آسمانوں،

پہاڑوں اورزمین پرفوقیت دی اوروہ اس قابل تھا کہ وہ اس عظیم ذمہ داری سے احسن طریقہ سے عہدہ برآ ہوسکے لیکن اس نے قطعی انصاف نہیں کیالہذا وہ ظالم ہے آگے رب العزت نے انسان کو بے وقوف کہا۔ وہ اس لئے کہ خداوندقدوس نے اس کوقرآن کریم کی صورت میں ایک بہت بڑا تحفہ انعام میں دیالیکن وہ اس سے استفادہ نہیں کرسکا۔

قرآن کریم میں اس پیغام کوغور سے پڑھیں اگرانسان قرآن کریم کی ذمہ داری اٹھانے کے قابل نہ ہوتااوروہ اس ذمہ داری کونبھانے کااقرار کرتا تو اسے پہلے بے وقوف کہا جاتا کہ اس نے ایک ایسی ذمہ داری اٹھانے کاوعدہ کیا جس کی وہ استطاعت نہیں رکھتا تھا۔قرآن کریم کے متن میں پہلے ظالم کہا گیا پھر بیوقوف لہذا وہ ذمہ داری جوہمیں ایک اشرف المخلوقات کی حیثیت میں سونپی گئی تھی اس سے ہم انصاف نہ کرسکے(ہم سب اپنے گریبان میں جھانک کردیکھیں کہ ہم نے قرآن کریم کوسمجھنے،عمل کرنے اوراس کی ترویج اورتعلیم کوآگے بڑھانے میں کس قدر دلچسپی لی اورکیاواقعی ہم نے اس ذمہ داری سے دیانتداری کے ساتھ عہدہ برآ ہونے کی کوشش کی جواب نہیں میں ملے گا)

شمسی وقمری سال میں نسبت

قرآن کریم کی سورۃ کہف آیت 25 میں ذِکر ہے کہ " وہ ۳۰۰ سال سوئے اس میں ۹ جمع کردیں"۔تفصیل میں اس لطیف فرق کوجانیں توآپ حیران ہوں گے کہ:

300 شمسی سال = 365.2422 x 300 = 109572.66 دن اور
309 قمری سال = 29.550329 x 12 x 309 = 109572.66 دن

یعنی خداوندقدوس نے صرف اس آیت کریمہ سے انسان کوشمسی اورقمری سال کی نسبت 1400 سال پہلے بتادی۔

سورہ انشقاق 84 The Rapture: آپ حیران ہوں گے کہ Polonium جس کا Element نمبر 84 ہے یہ Spontainous Disintegration (Rapture) پر بے شمارانرجی پیدا کرتا ہے

اسی طرح سورۃ الحدید نمبر (Iron 57) اورلوہے کا Stable Isotop بھی 57 ہے۔کیا یہ سب اتفاقیہ ہیں۔

سورۃ نمل(27) کی آیت نمبر 93 میں خداوندقدوس فرماتے ہیں کہ میں عنقریب تمہیں کائنات اورتمہارے اندراپنی نشانیاں بتاؤں گا۔آیئے دیکھئے کہ ہم اسے کہاں تک پہچان سکتے ہیں:

7 Cervical Vertebrae, 7 Days of a week, 7 Planets

12 Dorsal Vertebrae, 12 Months of a year, 12 Zodiac Signs

Total No of Vertebrae = 28 ....Correspond to 28 Arabic alphabets and 28 moon stations

انسان کا لفظ قرآن پاک میں 65 مرتبہ آیا ہے آیئے اب اس کو دیکھتے ہیں کہ اس کے ساتھ ملتے جلتے الفاظ کلام پاک میں کتنی مرتبہ آئے

Soil	مٹی	= 17
Drop of Sperm	نطفے کا قطرہ	= 12
Embryo	غیر مکمل حالت میں بچہ	= 06
Half Formed lump of Flesh	نیم شکل میں گوشت کا لوتھڑا	= 03
Bone	ہڈی	= 15
Flesh	گوشت	= 12
Total		**= 65**

اسی طرح زمین کا ذِکر 13 مرتبہ اور سمندر کا ذِکر 32 مرتبہ آیا ہے۔ زمین پر پانی اور خشکی کا تناسب کس خوبصورت انداز میں ظاہر کیا گیا ہے۔

زمین $= \frac{100 \times 13}{45} = 28.888888$ (خشکی)

پانی $= \frac{100 \times 32}{45} = 71.111111$ (سمندر)

اسی طرح کائنات اور آسمانوں کی تخلیق کا ذِکر 7 مرتبہ ہے۔

دن یعنی یوم کا ذِکر	=	365 مرتبہ	(ایک سال کے دن)
ایام کا ذِکر	=	30 مرتبہ	(ایک ماہ کے دن)
مہینہ کا ذِکر	=	12 مرتبہ	(ایک سال کے مہینے)

کیا یہ سب اتفاقی امر ہے۔

اِن چند آیاتِ کریمہ میں کچھ حقائق بیان کرنے کی جسارت کی گئی ہے۔ امید ہے قارئین کرام پسند کریں گے۔ انشاءاللہ آئندہ میں قرآن اور فلسفہ کائنات وحیات پر مزید بحث کرنے کی کاوش کروں گا۔

☆☆☆☆☆

میرے اللہ برائی سے بچانا مجھ کو
نیک جو راہ ہو اس راہ پہ چلانا مجھ کو

O Lord!

Save me from the ills of evils in pace
And,
Guide me in discipline of virtue in grace

Let I be a glow of gleam in escort
For all in sway of the world in gross
Then,
Let I be a source of inspiration in plan
For all the men and clan around in span

Truth in faith
Discipline in pace

No pride in prosperity
No regret in loss

Only to be contended,
With Your endowments in class

اپنے من میں ڈوب کر پا جا سراغِ زندگی
تو اگر میرا نہیں بنتا نہ بن اپنا تو بن

O man!

Search the niche of your veer in core
To savor the scent and spoor in lore

If you can perceive the word in score
Principle of faith endowed* to secure
When I,
Created you supreme semblance in plan
Then,
Asking the angels to beseech thee O man

Devil did deny 'My' command to beseech
But you also defied 'My' Discipline in treat
O man,
Even if you don't trend to 'Me' in entreat

To the order Discipline gifted in pace
What you're supposed to abide in grace

At least trend for a while in stance
And be a man of your 'Self' in glance

For Lord,
Has never changed the destiny of clan
Determined to decay their 'Self' in span

**Taught the words to the genetic array of Adam and also similar words were evinced to the Angels, but the angels could not interpret the philosophy of words in the light of intelligence, which the angels were missing, but Adam could do without hesitation, for Lord Almighty bestowed the man* Philosophy of intelligence.
And it will be the Discipline in the guidance of intelligence, we will be asked in the Hereafter:
How we accomplished the discipline of faith?